American Women Writers

A Critical Reference Guide
from Colonial Times to the Present

A Critical Reference Guide from Colonial Times to the Present

IN FIVE VOLUMES

VOLUME 5: SUPPLEMENT

AMERICAN WOMEN WRITERS

Edited by Carol Hurd Green
and Mary Grimley Mason

A Frederick Ungar Book
CONTINUUM • NEW YORK

1994

The Continuum Publishing Company
370 Lexington Avenue
New York, NY 10017

Library of Congress Cataloging in Publication Data

(Revised for vol. 5)

American women writers.

    Includes bibliographical references and index.
    1. American literature—Women authors—History and
criticism.   2. Women and literature—United States.
3. American literature—Women authors—Bibliography.
4. Women and literature—United States—Bibliography.
I. Mainiero, Lina.
PS147.A4   810'.9'9287   78-20945
ISBN 0-8044-3151-5 (v. 1)
ISBN 0-8264-0603-3 (v. 5 : alk. paper)

Prefatory Note

The editors of the Supplement to *American Women Writers* faced three major tasks when compiling this volume. First, we had to update entries from the original *American Women Writers* of those women who have continued to write extensively since its publication. Next, we reevaluated the earlier volumes to discover and review writers who had not been included. Many were minority voices; some were recently discovered diarists and autobiographical writers of earlier centuries; others were contemporary writers who had not, by 1980, sufficient oeuvre to warrant inclusion. Finally, we reviewed literature by and about women that has appeared since the original work in order to determine the new entries for the supplement. The current volume is the result of a decision-making process that included an advisory board and consultants who offered invaluable suggestions about updating and inclusion, and recommended contributors. The final decisions, however, are the editors' responsibility.

In preparing the volume, we have retained the style of the earlier four-volume work with some minor changes. We have added the names and (when available) birth dates of subjects' children to the biographical information. We have also eliminated the repetition of titles of books referred to in the body of an article and list only the subject's "other works" in the bibliographical section. When articles refer to writers who are included either in the original volumes or in the supplement, those names appear in boldface. Bibliographies in this volume represent individual contributors' decisions about useful sources for seeking further information about authors. Because of the easy access today to electronic bibliographies, and because of space considerations, the editors have not tried to provide exhaustive bibliographies.

Readers may look in vain for some of their favorite writers: space constraints forced the editors to make difficult and often painful decisions about the final shape of the volume. Although we cast our definitions of women's writing rather widely to include some representative journalists, food writers, and in one case a cartoonist, the

vi   □   PREFATORY NOTE

majority of the entries discuss novelists, poets, and dramatists. We made a particular effort to represent the new work of American women who have been marginalized and silenced in the past, particularly African American, Asian American, Latina, and lesbian writers. In compiling this volume, we imagine our audience to be primarily teachers and their students; we have tried to select the writers about whom they would be seeking information and to make that information as accessible as possible.

Unfortunately, women scholars are largely absent. The decision to impose this limitation was made solely on the basis of space: the list of women scholars was long enough to demand a volume of its own. Finally, although the supplement represents the greatest possible range of women writers that space would allow, many young writers also await another volume.

Acknowledgments

We are very grateful to the many scholars and friends who offered us their wisdom, help, and good will through the process of compiling this volume. Our advisers and consultants provided invaluable assistance, guiding us in the difficult process of making choices and directing us to contributors. We want especially to thank our Advisory Board—Margo Culley, Daria Donnelly, Mary Anne Ferguson, Marcia McClintock Folsom, Mary A. McCay, Alicia Ostriker, Gail Pool, Jennifer Tebbe, Cheryl A. Wall, Yvonne Yarbro-Bejarano, and Bonnie Zimmerman—the record of whose fine critical judgment is evident throughout this book.

Our thanks also go to Sue Craycraft for her efficiency and dedication to the arduous work of typing the manuscript and to our research assistants whose care and patience made all the difference. Linda Marsh, Gina Biancarosa, and Jerome Chou worked with us at the early stages of the project. Beth Grierson has brought her academic and research skills, her concern for detail, and her enthusiasm for the work of women writers to the project over the last two years: our debt to her is vast. We also want to thank the Office of the Dean, College of Arts and Sciences, Boston College, for its assistance. Throughout, Evander Lomke has been both wise and patient, an exemplary editor.

CAROL HURD GREEN
MARY GRIMLEY MASON

Introduction
American Women Writers
Volume 5: Supplement

The appearance of the four volumes of *American Women Writers* between 1979 and 1982 marked a new direction for reference works on literary women. Gathering together a record of many women writers who had been lost and/or forgotten, the volumes opened "new vistas," as the editor noted, for readers to appreciate the contributions of women writers. The publisher also promised that the volumes would be supplemented in the future with articles on contemporary writers—many of them minority women—who were starting to publish in the seventies but were not included in the volumes. This supplement to *American Women Writers* fulfills that promise to continue to record and acknowledge the outpouring of writings by women. Some groups of authors, such as African American women or lesbian writers, who were just beginning to be noted in the original volumes, are more fully represented in this supplement. They are joined by the many other women who have been publishing recently; Asian American, Native American, and Latina writers, for instance, who have added their voices to the many other diverse voices of American women writers.

In compiling a volume of American women writers most of whose work has been published since the 1970s, we have become aware not only of the growing diversity of the authors but also of the remarkable changes in the way writing by women has been approached and evaluated over the past two decades. The responsibility for these changes has come from the development of feminist criticism that not only has flowered but also has had a great impact on the whole enterprise of literary study. In "Feminist Literary Criticism: How Feminist? How Literary? How Critical?" Susan Lanser notes that in one generation many feminist critics have left the "Outsiders' Society," as Virginia Woolf called it, and joined the mainstream of the once exclusively male domain of criticism.* In the 1990s women writers cannot be dismissed as a subtopic in the literary canon despite the continuing attempts to marginalize Women's Studies in the academy. In the area of literary discourse, feminist criticism has a central role.

As feminist criticism has come of age it has developed a sense of its own history—the stages it has gone through and the conflicting tendencies and ideologies that characterize it as an intellectual enterprise. Some knowledge of this history and of the variety and richness of the study of women's lives and writing since the women's movement began in the 1970s helps to illuminate the achievement of contemporary women writers. There is an inevitable interaction between the critical, theoretical, and political work and the creative work. Whether or not individual women writers acknowledge the work of their feminist sisters, the reception of their work and the creative work itself is affected. Many of the pioneer feminist critics, such as Adrienne Rich and Alice Walker, are themselves authors of great significance. Their work and their criticism are all of one piece. Often the stages in the history of feminist criticism are paralleled in the individual consciousness of writers such as Marge Piercy or Audre Lorde; similarly the stages often parallel the collective changes in the literary history of marginalized groups, such as African American writers or lesbian writers. On the other hand, in "Feminism on the Border: From Gender Politics to Geopolitics," Sonia Saldivar-Hull argues that much of the history of feminist literary criticism and the formation of its stages has been too Eurocentric and does not adequately represent the diversity of women's voices, particularly Chicana women's voices.† Nevertheless, a look at one of the major theorists will help to establish some of the issues that enliven that discourse.

In her essay, "Women's Time, Women's Space: Writing the History of Feminist Criticism," Elaine Showalter identifies two major "waves" of feminist criticism.‡ The first wave, which came before 1975, derived its impulse from the women's movement and women's studies and concentrated on the specificity of women's writing: the task of finding lost texts,

---

*Susan S. Lanser, "Feminist Literary Criticism: How Feminist? How Literary? How Critical?" in *NWSA Journal* 3: 1 (Winter 1991): 3–19.

†Sonia Saldivar-Hull, "Feminism on the Border: From Gender Politics to Geopolitics," in *Criticism in the Borderlands*, ed. Hector Calderon and Jose David Saldivar (Duke University Press, 1991), 203–20.

‡Elaine Showalter, "Women's Time, Women's Space: Writing the History of Feminist Criticism," in *Feminist Issues in Literary Scholarship*, ed. Shari Benstock (Indiana University Press, 1987), 30–44.

rediscovering texts, codifying, and describing. Here pioneer scholars such as Patricia Spacks in *The Female Imagination* or Showalter in *A Tradition of Their Own* looked for and acknowledged unique women's traditions. Others, like Gubar and Gilbert in *The Madwoman in the Attic,* examined the way women's literature reacted to the dominant male tradition. Also in this period the idea of a female aesthetic was proposed by such writers as Adrienne Rich, Marge Piercy, Alice Walker, and Alicia Ostriker. Showalter names these feminist critics *gynocritics.* Postmodernist critics have identified them as part of "essentialist" feminist theory.

The second wave of feminist literary criticism, placed after 1975, derives, according to Showalter, more from theory—psychoanalytic, poststructuralist, and deconstructionist—and comes from the Continent and theorists such as Derrida, Althusser, and Lacan, and their French feminist followers. This kind of criticism has been named *gynesis* by Alice Jardine. Showalter describes it as the task of exploring the textual consequences of "the feminine" and how "the feminine has been defined and represented in symbolic systems of language, metaphysics, psychoanalysis and art." This wave or "school" has used deconstructionist theory to challenge the idea of women's categories of culture or traditions and has emphasized differentiation and multiplicity rather than unity. African American and lesbian theorists have challenged white mainstream feminist theory as myopic and exclusionary. Critics in the French/Continental school question the validity of claiming a female aesthetics or culture (or, for that matter, black culture or black aesthetics). In *Feminist Issues of Literary Scholarship* these two contrasting definitions of the work of feminist literary criticism are represented in essays by critics such as Nina Baym, Lillian Robinson, and Shari Benstock.

When we look at the literary history of contemporary women writers, particularly ethnic or minority writers, we can see parallels with the development of feminist theory as described above. African American literary criticism, for instance, has moved from retrieval and discovery of lost women writers by pioneers such as Mary Helen Washington, Alice Walker, and Barbara Christian, who have attempted to identify and define common African American women's traditions, to an emphasis on the differences among writers and finally, in poststructuralist critics such as Deborah MacDowell, to questioning the validity of categories and traditions. Moreover, parallels sometimes exist between the different stages of feminist theory and the development and formation of literary movements. For instance, in *The Safe Sea of Women: Lesbian Fiction 1969–1989*, Bonnie Zimmerman traces the stages of the lesbian-feminist literary movement, stages that seem to correspond closely to changes in feminist literary theory.* Fiction about questions of identity and definition ("Coming out novels") is succeeded, according to Zimmerman, by fiction celebrating a lesbian/feminist utopia, a "women-only world," parallel to the essentialist focus of early feminist theory. This kind of fiction gives way to novels that question and challenge notions of a lesbian identity or are more skeptical and detached from the ideology, more willing to "deconstruct" the world of lesbian identity. It would be impossible to disentangle the exact anatomy of these interactions of practice and theory and, indeed, there is a danger of fitting any individual author into a group whether it be defined by gender, race, ethnicity, or sexual preference. An author as complex, for instance, as Toni Morrison† not only reflects the energies of the political and intellectual discourse of feminism as well as of African American literary theory but also has undoubtedly helped to formulate that discourse and, beyond that, to "re-vision," as Adrienne Rich predicted, the notion of what *is* fiction.

Whether or not the theorists and critics can agree on a new feminist literary criticism is not a primary concern of this volume, but the ferment and energy and controversy that the past two decades of feminist scholarship have generated has certainly had an impact on our consideration of women's writing. Whether as directly relevant, or at times, irrelevant, there now exists a set of aesthetic, linguistic, cultural, and political considerations that firmly place women's writing in the mainstream of intellectual and aesthetic discourse.

CAROL HURD GREEN
MARY GRIMLEY MASON

---

*Bonnie Zimmerman, *The Safe Sea of Women: Lesbian Fiction 1969–1989* (Beacon Press, 1990).

†As this book went to press, Toni Morrison was awarded the 1993 Nobel Prize for Literature, the first African American woman to become a Nobel laureate. The prize both honors the richness of her work and acknowledges the power of the new body of writing created by American women, particularly by women of color, in the late twentieth century.

Advisers and Consultants, Volume Five

Sarah Appleton-Weber
poet
Syracuse, New York

Clarissa Atkinson
Divinity School,
Harvard University

Susan Bloom
Simmons College

Alanna Brown
Montana State University

Fahamisha Patricia Brown
Boston College

Leonard Casper
Boston College

Margo Culley
University of Massachusetts,
Amherst*

Daria Donnelly
Boston University*

Josephine Donovan
University of Maine

Mary Anne Ferguson
University of Massachusetts,
Boston, *emerita**

Anne Fleche
Boston College

Marcia McClintock Folsom
Wheelock College*

Antoinette Frederick
freelance writer
Newton, Massachusetts

K. C. Frederick
University of Massachusetts,
Boston

Barbara Haber
Schlesinger Library,
Radcliffe College

Anne Halley, poet
poetry editor, *Massachusetts
Review*

James Harvey
State University of New York,
Stony Brook

Ruth Hsiao
Tufts University

Eugenia Kaledin
independent scholar
Lexington, Massachusetts

Felicia Hardison Londré
University of Missouri

Mary A. McCay
Loyola University,
New Orleans*

Suzanne Matson
Boston College

Catherine Mercier
Simmons College

Writers Included, Volume 5: Supplement

Entries are given under the names listed below. Pen names, pseudonyms, etc., are also noted here with cross references to the main listing.

Adrienne Kennedy
Jamaica Kincaid
Barbara Kingsolver
Maxine Hong Kingston
Carolyn Kizer
Elisabeth Kübler-Ross
Maxine Kumin
Ursula K. Le Guin
Madeleine L'Engle
Gerda Lerner
Meridel Le Sueur
Denise Levertov
Bette Bao Lord
Audre Lorde
Lois Lowry
Alison Lurie
Mary Therese McCarthy
Alice McDermott
Shirley MacLaine
Terry McMillan
Sandra McPherson
Nancy Mairs
Paule Marshall
Valerie Martin
Bobbie Ann Mason
Eve Merriam
June Meyer. *See June M. Jordan*
Josephine Miles
Isabel Miller. *See Alma Routsong*
Kate Millett
Valerie Miner
Janice Mirikitani
Jessica Mitford
Nicholosa Mohr
A. G. Mojtabai
Cherríe Moraga
Robin Morgan
Hilda Morley
Toni Morrison
Mourning Dove

Gloria Naylor
Lorine Niedecker
Marsha Norman
Naomi Shihab Nye
Joyce Carol Oates
Sharon Olds
Mary Oliver
Tillie Olsen
Judith Ortiz Cofer
Brenda Marie Osbey
Martha Ostenso
Alicia Ostriker
Rochelle Owens
Cynthia Ozick
Grace Paley
Mary Frances Parrish. *See Mary Frances Kennedy Fisher*
Linda Pastan
Katherine Paterson
Jayne Ann Phillips
Marge Piercy
Dawn Powell
Nancy Gardner Prince
Christal Quintasket. *See Mourning Dove*
Margaret Randall
Kit Reed
Anne Rampling. *See Anne Rice*
Anne Rice
Adrienne Cecile Rich
Alfrida Rivers. *See Marion Zimmer Bradley*
Carolyn M. Rodgers
A. N. Roquelare. *See Anne Rice*
Judith Rossner
Alma Routsong
Rosemary Radford Ruether
Joanna Russ
Sonia Sanchez
May Sarton

Susan Fromberg Schaeffer
Lynne Sharon Schwartz
Ruth Seid
Mary Lee Settle
Ntozake Shange
Gail Sheehy
Alix Kates Shulman
Carolyn Sidlosky. *See Carolyn Forché*
Leslie Marmon Silko
Kate Simon
Jo Sinclair. *See Ruth Seid*
Lee Smith
Rosamond Smith. *See Joyce Carol Oates*
Mara Solwoska. *See Marilyn French*
Cathy Song
Susan Sontag
Elizabeth Spencer
Gloria Steinem
Ruth Stone
Sui Sin Far. *See Edith Maud Eaton*
May Swenson
Amy Tan
Mildred Delois Taylor
Megan Terry
Barbara Tuchman
Linda Ty-Casper

Anne Tyler
Yoshiko Uchida
Jean Valentine
Mona Van Duyn
Helen Hennessy Vendler
Helena Maria Viramontes
Cynthia Voigt
Ellen Bryant Voigt
Diane Wakoski
Alice Walker
Margaret Walker
Michele Wallace
Mildred Pitts Walter
Wendy Wasserstein
Gloria Jean Watkins. *See bell hooks*
Sarah Appleton Weber. *See Sarah Appleton-Weber*
John J. Wells. *See Marion Zimmer Bradley*
Eudora Welty
Ruth Whitman
Kate Wilhelm
Nancy Willard
Sherley Anne Williams
Harriet E. Adams Wilson
Jade Snow Wong
Mitsuye Yamada
Hisaye Yamamoto
Helen Yglesias

Abbreviations

Most periodical abbreviations are self-explanatory. Generic abbreviations are *J.* (Journal); *Mag.* (Magazine) *Q.* (Quarterly); *Rev.* (Review). Listed below are abbreviations for reference books, newspapers, and those periodicals that appear frequently enough to be listed in shortened form.

APR	*American Poetry Review*
CA	*Contemporary Authors*
CAAS	*Contemporary Authors Autobiography Series*
CANR	*Contemporary Authors New Revision Series*
CB	*Current Biography*
CBY	*Current Biography Yearbook*
CLA J.	*College Literary Association Journal*
CLC	*Contemporary Literary Criticism*
CLHUS	*Cambridge Literary History of the United States*
CLR	*Children's Literature Review*
DAB	*Dictionary of American Biography*
DLB	*Dictionary of Literary Biography*
DLBY	*Dictionary of Literary Biography Yearbook*
DAI	*Dissertation Abstracts International*
FC	*Feminist Companion*
LATBR	*Los Angeles Times Book Review*
LJ	*Library Journal*
NAW:MP	*Notable American Women: The Modern Period*
NBAW	*Notable Black American Women*
NYRB	*New York Review of Books*
NYT	*New York Times*
NYTBR	*New York Times Book Review*
PMLA	*Publication of the Modern Language Association*
PW	*Publishers Weekly*
SATA	*Something about the Author*

TLS	*[London] Times Literary Supplement*
VV	*Village Voice*
WRB	*Women's Review of Books*
WWAW	*Who's Who of American Women*

American Women Writers

*A Critical Reference Guide
from Colonial Times to the Present*

Volume 5: Supplement

Kathy Acker

B. 18 April 1947, New York City
D. of Claire (Weill) and Donald Lehman; m. Robert Acker, 1966, div.; m. Peter
  Gordon, 1976, div.

Often referred to as a punk and, later, postmodern writer, A. is actively involved in the construction of new myths by which to live. Like many of the artists and writers who have influenced her work, she does not draw easy distinctions between life and art, sometimes consciously making up contradicting stories about her past. In this way, "Kathy Acker" becomes as much of a construction as any of her characters.

The daughter of wealthy Jewish parents who disowned her, A. grew up in Manhattan where she wrote poetry from an early age and read voraciously. She was so attached to her books that she sometimes performed ceremonies in which she married them. She received a B.A. from the University of California, San Diego, in 1968, having transferred there from Brandeis two years earlier. She also completed two years of graduate work at New York University and City University of New York, studying English, classics, and philosophy. After *Blood and Guts in High School* (1984) sold well in England, she moved to London for several years, finding it more supportive of writers than New York. Subsequently, she moved to San Francisco, where she teaches at the San Francisco Art Institute.

A.'s influences are many and include photographers, filmmakers, and artists. Having grown up in New York's post-Beat art world, it is those writers and poets who had the strongest influence on the early shaping of her sensibility. The explorations of memory and the "madeness" of language through formal styles such as repetition, used in the work of Black Mountain poets like Charles Olson, Jerry Rothenberg, and David Antin, and Beats like Jack Kerouac and William Burroughs, appear in much of A.'s writing.

Her first privately published book, *Politics* (1972), came out of her experience working in sex shows on Forty-Second Street—something of a "test" of the sexual revolution of the 1960s. Since then A.'s work has always had an important political edge. Because labels tend to diffuse that edge, she rejects words like *experimental* to describe her work. Even so, A. is an experimental writer, in what has become the conventional understanding of that term. She is perhaps best known, and least understood, for her extensive formal use of plagiarism.

To call attention to the already appropriated status of their images and to her refusal or inability to partake in similar, patriarchally determined productions, A. literally copies from a number of mostly Western, classic literary texts (Freud, Genet, de Sade, Cervantes, Twain). Not a response to a Barthian understanding of the diminished possibilities of literature in its postmodern state of exhaustion, instead A.'s "plagiarism" critiques and rewrites Western cultural myths in ways that consciously disclaim any pretension to originality or mastery. As such it can also be recognized as a survival strategy in a world where master narratives of freedom and truth have been exposed as such, leaving these appropriated acts the only ones available.

Although often criticized by feminists for the violent and pornographic elements of her novels, A. is clearly involved in a project that explores the conditions of living in a society that depends on the economic and sexual dependence of some of its members, including women. Her main characters, who are often on some sort of quest, are always outside of the mainstream; they are would-be pirates, or cyborgs, or sex-show workers. In this sense, A.'s feminist sensibility is in evidence in most of her writing. Her most explicitly feminist novel is probably *Don Quixote* (1986) in which A. refigures the title character as a contemporary woman on a search for love. The obstacles she encounters are historical, mythical, and literary patriarchal figures (Christ, Machiavelli, Richard Nixon).

A. carries out the examinations of power structures and relations on both the thematic and formal levels. Her writing occasionally resembles that of **Gertrude Stein** in its careful and consistent attention to the material qualities of language and the possibilities they provide. Like Stein too, A. connects these with the materiality of the body, going a step further and as Ellen G. Friedman notes, locating the body itself as a potential "site of revolution." In *Empire of the Senseless* (1988) she looks to tattoos, a material writing on the body, as a possibility of controlling the means of sign production and self-representation.

OTHER WORKS: I Don't Expect You'll Do the Same, by Clay Fear (1974). *I Dreamt I Became a Nymphomaniac! Imagining* (1974). *The Adult Life of Toulouse Lautrec by Henri Toulouse Lautrec* (1975). *The Childlike Life of the Black Tarantula by the Black Tarantula* (1975). *Persian Poems* (1978). *New York City in 1979* (1981). *Great Expectations* (1982). *Hello, I'm Erica Jong* (1982). *Algeria: A Series of Invocations because Nothing Else Works* (1984). *Literal Madness: Kathy Goes to Haiti; My Death My Life by Pier Paolo Pasolini; Florida* (1988). *In Memoriam to Identity* (1990). *Hannibal Lecter, My Father* (1991). *Portrait of the Eye: Three Novels* (reprints, 1992). *My Mother: Demonology* (1993).

BIBLIOGRAPHY: Dick Leslie, "Feminism, Writing, Postmodernism," in *From My Guy to Sci-fi: Genre and Women's Writing in the Postmodern World*, Helen Carr, ed. (1989). Hulley, Kathleen, "Transgressing Genre: Kathy Acker's Intertext," in *Intertextuality and Contemporary American Fiction*, Patrick O'Donnell and Robert Davis, eds. (1989). McCaffery, Larry, "The Artists of Hell: Kathy Acker and 'Punk' Aesthetics," in *Breaking the Sequence: Women's Experimental Fiction*, Ellen G. Friedman and Miriam Fuchs, eds. (1989).
Other references: *Rev of Contemp. Fiction* 9 (Fall 1989).

MONICA DORENKAMP

Alice Adams

B. 14 Aug. 1926, Fredericksburg, Virginia
D. of Agatha Erskine (Boyd) and Nicholson Barney Adams; m. Mark Linenthal, Jr., 1946, div. 1958; c.: Peter Adams Linenthal, b. 1951

The only child of Nicholson, a Spanish professor, and Agatha Adams, a "failed" writer, A. wrote poetry as a child hoping that if she were a writer, her mother would "like" her. Raised in a "semi-intellectual atmosphere" that was "materially comfortable but emotionally unsatisfying," A. graduated from high school at the age of fifteen and from Radcliffe College in 1946. Her recurring themes of change, economic independence, and survival, which can often be paralleled to events in her life, earn her both praise and criticism.

At the end of a writing course at Radcliffe, A.'s professor advised her to "get married and forget" writing. Following his prescription, she married within a year, spending the next twelve years in the expected 1950s' domestic role. For the first year, she lived in Paris where her husband studied at the Sorbonne (the setting of her first published story, "Winter Rain," 1959). In 1948, the couple moved to California. After the birth of her son, she found little time for writing.

A.'s first novel, *Careless Love,* appeared in 1966. It satirizes the 1960s San Francisco dating scene in a remotely autobiographical tale about a newly divorced woman. Often widowed or divorced, A.'s characters not only survive changes but transcend them, ultimately gaining economic independence and experiencing growth. This gain becomes an integral part of A.'s plots. Having been disinherited by her father when he left their family home to her stepmother, and having spent the years following her divorce in constant struggle with "part-time secretarial job[s]," A. has firsthand knowledge of the importance of economic independence.

In the six novels following *Careless Love,* A.'s maturity and focus as a writer become increasingly evident in the complexity of her female protagonists. Usually well-educated, upper-middle-class female visual artists who are enacting a journey to womanhood, the characters are often developed through the use of parenthetical comments by an omniscient narrator. In A.'s second novel, *Families and Survivors* (1975), Louisa Calloway undergoes many changes before finding happiness in a second marriage and realizing her talent as a painter. In *Listening to Billie* (1978) Eliza Quarles attains a sense of freedom as a poet; in *Rich Rewards* (1980) Daphne Matthiesen earns respect as a self-supporting interior decorator; in *Superior Women* (1985) Megan Greene, a financially successful publisher, cosponsors a temporary haven for Atlanta's homeless women. *Second Chances* (1988) again explores A.'s "trademark themes," and also examines "people's changing expectations of aging." In *Caroline's Daughters* (1991) the vicissitudes of the five daughters' lives "intrude" into Caroline's long-awaited contented space, but Caroline endures and survives.

A.'s stories have appeared in numerous periodicals, including *The New Yorker, Atlantic,* and the *Paris Review,* and she has published four short-story collections. *Beautiful Girl* (1979) contains her first O. Henry Award winning story "A Gift of Grass." The women in the stories in *To See You Again* (1982) abide by an Adams's "code": "She behaves well, even under emotional stress. She does not make scenes, does not cry in public, rarely cries alone." In *Return Trips* (1985) as women recall or revisit people who "shaped their lives" they recognize the irreversible and continuing effects of past events. The stories in *After You've Gone* (1989) are about loss: some characters are devastated by it; most recover from it, and some are even freed by it.

Seeing marriage as "primarily concerned with property," A. has lived in San Francisco with interior designer Robert McNie since 1964. She has taught at the University of California at Davis and at Berkeley and at Stanford University. The 1982 recipient of the O. Henry Special Award for Continuing Achievement, A. has been anthologized in *The Best American Short Stories* as well as in all but one edition of *Prize Stories: The O. Henry Awards* from 1971 to 1989.

OTHER WORKS: *Mexico: Some Travels and Some Travelers There* (1990). *Almost Perfect* (1993).

BIBLIOGRAPHY: *CA 81–84* (1979). *CBY* (1989). *CLC* 46 (1988). *DLBY* (1986). *CANR* 26 (1989). *Maj Twent Cent Writers* (1991). *NYTBR* (May 1988; April 1991).

PHYLLIS S. GLEASON

Ai

B. 21 Oct. 1947, Albany, Texas; m. Lawrence Kearney, c. 1975, div.

A. is a narrative poet. Her work is intense, her writing efficient and vivid. Her poems reveal an intimacy between emotions and values that traditionally have been viewed as oppositional: love and hate are enmeshed, tenderness and violence interconnected. The characters who speak through A.'s poetry are as varied as the American, multiracial, multicultural society from which they, and she, emerged. All voices—of men, women, teenagers, children; of black, white, red, yellow, brown; famous and anonymous, infamous and obscure—are heard at equal volume. Each speaks of the effort and desire to assert one's will, to make an impact, to understand pain. Their voices are clear and even-toned, yet their messages are wrenching and sometimes shocking.

A. grew up in the Southwest and in San Francisco. She earned a B.A. in English/Oriental Studies from the University of Arizona in 1969. While an undergraduate, she met the poet Galway Kinnell, who became a mentor for her, the "most important literary relationship of my life." Through Kinnell, she went to the University of California at Irvine, where she completed an M.F.A. in 1971. A. taught subsequently at SUNY-Binghamton, the University of Massachusetts-Amherst, and Wayne State University. She received a Guggenheim Foundation fellowship in 1975.

Her first book of poems, *Cruelty* (1973), established her as a new, strong voice in contemporary poetry. *Cruelty* projects rugged images of sexuality, death, sensuality, and blood, and challenges the stereotype of "women's poetry." "If you want nice poems to 'like,'" wrote **Alice Walker,** "this [*Cruelty*] is not your book."

Killing Floor (1979) won the 1978 Lamont Poetry Selection Award for the best second book by an American poet. The poems in this collection intensify the themes of sexuality and violence introduced in *Cruelty* and expand A.'s cast of characters to include public figures from history and popular culture. After winning the Lamont Prize, A. moved to New York to "actually . . . enter the world of poetry." Since her move, she has published two more books of poetry, *Sin* (1986) and *Fate* (1991). The settings of the later poems also moved from the rural, small-town world of her first two books into the urban arena.

In *Sin*, which won an American Book Award from the Before Columbus Foundation, and *Fate* A. creates the voices, the "secret souls," of public figures such as Robert and John F. Kennedy *(Sin)* and Mary Jo Kopechne *(Fate)*. Still, the voices of anonymous Americans are also heard. The persona poems in *Sin* and *Fate* are longer, detailed portraits rather than the snapshots found in her earlier volumes.

In "On Being ½ Japanese, ⅛ Choctaw, ¼ Black and 1/16 Irish" (1978) and "Arrival" (1991), A. discusses her multiracial heritage and her struggle to forge an identity, the importance of her "true" name (Ai means "love" in Japanese), and her development as a narrative poet. (Given the name Florence Anthony at birth, she has also used the names Florence Haynes and Pelorhanke Ai Ogawa; she learned from her mother in 1973 that her father's surname was Ogawa.)

A.'s passion for poetry pervades her autobiographical works. She explains, "I wanted to write poetry with a capital P." She continues to do so.

OTHER WORKS: *Audiocassettes*: "The Poetry of Jane Kenyon, Ai, Lawrence Kearney, and Kathleen Spivak" (1978). "Nothing but Color" (1981). "Ai" (1988). *Greed* (1993).

BIBLIOGRAPHY: *Reference works*: *CA* 85–88 (1980). *CLC* 4 (1975), 14 (1980). Other references: *Belles Lettres* (Spring 1991). *Chicago Rev.* 30:4 (Spring 1979). *Ms.* (June 1974). *NYTBR* (17 Feb. 1974; 8 July 1979; 8 June 1986). *Poetry* (Jan. 1987; Nov. 1991). *Virginia Q. Rev.* (Summer 1991).

DALE A. DOOLEY

Paula Gunn Allen

B. Paula Marie Francis, 24 Oct. 1939, Cubero, New Mexico

An American Indian of Laguna Pueblo and Sioux heritage, A. was raised in Cubero, New Mexico, a Spanish land-grant town fifty miles west of Albuquerque, abutting the Laguna Reservation. A.'s mother is of Laguna Pueblo and Sioux heritage and her father was Lebanese-American. The writings of her mother's uncle, John Gunn, an anthropologist and researcher of Native American cultures, was a major source of information for A.'s writings. A.'s sister is poet Carol Lee Sanchez and her cousin is writer **Leslie Marmon Silko,** both of whom were reared in her community.

After attending mission schools in rural Cubero, San Fidel, and a convent school in Albuquerque, A. went on to receive her B.A. in English from the University of Oregon (1966). After college, she married, had two children, and subsequently divorced. She returned to school and in 1968 received an M.F.A. in Creative Writing, also from the University of Oregon. A. returned to New Mexico and in 1975 received a Ph.D. in American Studies and American Indian Studies from the University of New Mexico. She was a postdoctoral fellow in American Indian

Studies at UCLA in 1981–82. Between 1986 and 1990 she was professor of Ethnic Studies and Native American Studies at the University of California at Berkeley. Subsequently, A. has been a professor of English at the University of California, Los Angeles.

Three components central to Native American culture are the individual, the land, and the spiritual world; the way in which they are woven together forms the fabric of life for the community and the basis for A.'s work. A. encourages her reader to see the multiplicity present in all things. Nature is welcomed and accepted in all forms. Spirits are continually present and the individual aware of the power present in the world and prepared to "walk in balance" can move down a path toward spiritual exploration and knowledge.

A. has written numerous books of poetry, many of which explore the issue of the relationship between the individual and a "mythic space" or the spiritual realm. Even as she continues to explore these issues through her poems, they also permeate her work as a novelist exploring the depths of the individual; as an essayist and editor looking at feminist and historical perspectives; and as an anthologist of Native American tales and myths looking at the works from an anthropological feminist standpoint.

A.'s novel, *The Woman Who Owned the Shadows* (1983), introduces a recurrent theme, depicting a Native American woman struggling both to discover her own place in a world bent on judging her behavior and restricting her options and to integrate her sense of herself as a modern woman with the power of ancient spiritual beliefs. The vital healing process and reeducation that emerge at the end of the novel reappear in the form of theoretical, feminist historical essays in the nonfiction collection *The Sacred Hoop* (1986). Here A. strikingly reconstructs the gynocratic and gynocentric visions of the world as captured in the stories and religions of Native Americans, examining the traditional and sacred teachings centered within the sacred hoop of life in which everything has a place and role. Asserting that many of the orally transmitted tales have been influenced by the encroaching Anglo-American patriarchal system of politics and religion, A. presents the tales in their original gynocentric forms.

A.'s strong commitment to textual restoration also appears in essays that explore the incompatibilities between female-centered traditions and those espoused by individuals raised in patriarchal societies; the differences between the European monotheistic and individualist model of society and the community-based, multitheistic Native American model; and the impact of writing and thinking from a position of "tribal-feminism" and "feminist-tribalism" that respects the separate natures of men and women while stressing the need for both sexes to work in balance with each other.

Spider Woman's Granddaughters (1989) explores one hundred years of the strong and vital tradition of Native American women in a collection that includes traditional tales, biographical writings, and short stories. A. feels these are the stories of "women at war" who have become captives in their own lands. The major figures include "Sacred Woman," "Grandmother Spider," and "Yellow Corn Woman" who appear repeatedly, under various names, throughout Native American traditional songs and writings. The stories capture the resistance and continuing hope that endures in Native American cultures and that continues to be spoken and written about by the women of the culture.

Grandmothers of the Light: A Medicine Woman's Sourcebook (1991) continues the discussion of mythic stories that incorporate a polytheistic female-based belief structure with its concepts of duty to the larger group, balance in all things, and connections to the earth. Substantiating her assertions with extensive research in the belief structures of many Native American cultures, A. stresses the applicability of these stories to the present day, and the necessity of these beliefs in a modern world that has not only become estranged from the earth, the source of all things, but destroys it as well.

As a writer, A. believes it is her responsibility to bring forth the visions that exist within herself as poet, essayist, novelist, activist, teacher, woman, lesbian, and Laguna Pueblo-Sioux. Her work makes a major contribution to the female strength, and the tribal and native female resistance and hope of Native American cultures. As A. re-remembers the past of Native American cultures and history, she embodies her hope that her readers and the Native communities will "walk in balance" with the surrounding world.

OTHER WORKS: *The Blind Lion* (1974). *Coyote's Daylight Trip* (1978). *A Cannon between My Knees* (1981). *Shadow Country* (1981). *Star Child* (1981). *Studies in American Indian Literature: Critical Essays and Course Designs* (editor, 1983). *Wyrds* (1987). *Skins and Bones* (1988). *Women's Friendship: A Collection of Short Stories* (1991).

BIBLIOGRAPHY: Balassi, William, *This Is about Vision: Interviews with Southwestern Writers* (1990). Bruchac, Joseph, *Survival This Way: Interviews with American Indian Poets* (1987). Jahner, Elaine, "A Laddered, Rain-Bearing Rug:

Paula Gunn Allen's Poetry," in *Women and Western American Literature*, Helen W. Stauffer and Susan Rosowski, eds. (1982). Reference works: *Benet's* (1991). *FC* (1990). *Tw. Cent. West. Wr.* (1991).

Other references: *Amer. Indian Q.* (Spring 1983). *NDQ* (interview, Spring 1989). *MELUS* (interview, Summer 1983).

DACIA GENTILELLA

Lisa Alther

B. Elisabeth Greene Reed, 23 July 1944, Kingsport, Tennessee
D. of Alice Margaret (Greene) and John Shelton Reed; m. Richard Philip Alther,
1966, div.; c.: Sara Halsey, b. 1968

Though she was born and grew up in the South, A. has spent all of her adult life in the North. She graduated from Wellesley College, married in 1966, and has lived for many years on the edge of a small town in Vermont. She identifies herself as a Southern writer, however, because of the influence of storytelling in her home and her early exposure by her English-teacher mother to the works of **Eudora Welty, Flannery O'Connor, Katherine Anne Porter,** and **Carson McCullers.** From her father, a surgeon, she acquired an interest in science, which was reflected in her earliest publications about the environment and her continuing use of scientific metaphors. Her first two novels are set in her native South; the second two in New England. All of them reflect small-town life and deal with problems of community.

A. has said that she had over two hundred rejection slips before her first fiction publication, *Kinflicks* (1976). That novel was so financially successful that she has been able since to write in her preferred manner, taking several months between multiple drafts and a year between books. Though widely admired for her comic tone, A. is a serious writer who has focused on the ironies involved in the search for meaning by characters trying to avoid stereotypical, inherited responses to the hostile forces of twentieth-century life.

Kinflicks deals with the sixties generation's agonized conflicts over sex, religion, education, and the war in Vietnam. In half the chapters, Ginny Babcock recapitulates her youthful rebellion against her parents' life pattern and goals and savagely rejects religious rationalizations of their greed, racism, and class prejudices. Adolescent sexual initiation rites furnish ironic views of the older generation's hypocrisy about sex, and Ginny's search for alternatives includes experiments with backseat petting, heterosexual and homosexual monogamy, and lesbian communes. In alternate chapters, A. uses a third-person narrator to show Ginny's return home at twenty-seven to the bedside of her dying mother and their reconciliation when Ginny realizes that her mother had deliberately played the stereotypical mother role in order to meet her children's need for meaning. Mrs. Babcock's self-awareness frees Ginny from guilt and the necessity of role playing.

Kinflicks has been very popular; in July 1990 it was in its twenty-ninth paperback reprint. As with all of A.'s books, it was highly praised and also strongly condemned. Most critics praised it for its verbal wit and for the irony with which the sexual escapades target stereotypes, male sexual conquest, and adult sanctimoniousness; many recognized it as serious social criticism. Very few mentioned the serious mother-daughter plot or perceived the female bildungsroman structure of the book.

In *Original Sins* (1981) A. juggles the stories of five protagonists who find their small-town Southern environment pernicious. Whereas *Kinflicks* is picaresque in its emphasis on the journey away, *Original Sins* focuses on home and its limitations. But as "the Five" mature, their self-awareness, like that of Mrs. Babcock, offers more hope for them than for their parents. Critics agreed that the two female characters' sexual experiences are the most vivid aspects of this book. In *Other Women* (1984) A. again juxtaposes the lives of two women, a confused nurse who has experimented sexually as had Ginny Babcock in her search for meaning, and an older woman psychotherapist, whose counsel stems from her own tragic experiences. The book is unusual in focusing equally on patient and therapist and offers their relationship as a model of feminist therapy, nonhierarchical and eventuating in friendship. Though friendship between two women that blossoms into love is central to *Bedrock* (1990), the focus really is on a town in Vermont to which one of them flees in her search for meaning. We see all the hypocrisy and self-delusion of less than admirable characters, but the tone—sometimes almost farcical—is accepting and hopeful. Clea Shawn loses her romantic illusions about a small town, remodels a decaying house, and finds happiness when she recognizes that her long friendship with Elka is the basis of a lesbian relationship.

A.'s works trace the experiences of her generation and continue to be popular. Though critical acceptance of *Bedrock* was somewhat grudging, her work is now being seriously considered by critics and scholars.

OTHER WORKS: "Encounter," *McCall's* (Aug. 1976). "Will the South Rise Again?" *NYT* (16 Dec. 1979). "Termites," in *Homewords*, Douglas Paschall and Alice Swanson, eds. (1986). "The Politics of Paradise," in *Louder than Words*, William Shore, ed. (1990).

BIBLIOGRAPHY: Braendlin, Bonnie H., "New Directions in the Contemporary Bildungsroman: Lisa Alther's *Kinflicks*," in *Gender and Literary Voice*, Janet Todd, ed. (1980). Ferguson, Mary Anne, "Lisa Alther: The Irony of Return?" reptd. in *Women Writers of the Contemporary South*, Peggy Prenshaw, ed. (1984), and "The Female Novel of Development and the Myth of Psyche," in *The Voyage In: Fictions of Female Development*, Elizabeth Abel et al., eds. (1983). Reference works: *CA* 65–68 (1977). *CLC* 7 (1987), 41 (1977). *CANR* 12 (1984), 30 (1990). *FC* (1990). *Maj Twent Cent Writers* (1991).

Other references: *Arizona Q* 38 (Winter 1982). *Appalachia/America* (1980). *DIA* 49 (1988). *Frontiers* 4 (1979).

MARY ANNE FERGUSON

Joseph Maree Andrew. *See Marita Bonner*

Maya Angelou

See AWW *1*, 53–55

A.'s career as poet, writer of autobiographical narratives, dramatist, and teacher continued in the 1980s and 1990s in much the same energetic vein as her earlier career. Appointed to a lifetime chair as Z. Smith Reynolds Professor of American Studies at Wake Forest University in 1981, A. has since published two autobiographical narratives, three volumes of poetry, and a book-length poem for children entitled *Life Doesn't Frighten Me* (1993). She has also authored the screenplay for a television drama and hosted and written a series of documentaries, *Maya Angelou: A Journey of the Heart.* During the 1993 inaugural ceremony of President Clinton, A. read her celebratory poem.

The Heart of a Woman (1981), A.'s fourth autobiographical narrative, describes her beginnings as a serious writer and her involvement with the Harlem Writers Guild. It also traces her career as a performer during the period of the Civil Rights and Black Power movements of the 1950s and 1960s and her move to Egypt with her husband, a South African revolutionary. Becoming increasingly active politically, she shifted away from the pacifist politics of Martin Luther King towards the nationalist philosophy of Malcolm X. Much of the book is concerned with the question of gender roles in her relationships to her son, Guy Johnson (b. 1944), and to her husband. The book ends with the breakup of her marriage and her decision to take a job at the University of Ghana.

A.'s fourth collection of poetry, *Shaker, Why Don't You Sing?* (1983), consists primarily of short lyrics marking personal and broader social losses. The poems often strike a muted "blues" tone, describing the effects of racism and disappointed, betrayed, or faded love. A number of poems as well as the title—taken from the song "John Henry"—invoke the culture and history of African Americans in the South.

All God's Children Need Traveling Shoes (1986) continues the story of A.'s life in Ghana, describing her search for and encounters with an African heritage as well as with the patriarchal aspects of postcolonial African society and her difficulties in raising her son. Concluding the book with a description of African oral memory of the slave trade and its losses, A. reaffirms her African inheritance as she returns to the United States.

Now Sheba Sings the Song (1987), a single long poem illustrated by Tom Feeling, is an answer to the biblical Song of Solomon, praising the beauty of all women from the woman's point of view. The moods of A.'s fifth collection of poetry, *I Shall Not Be Moved* (1990), vary considerably from poem to poem. Some are celebratory, chronicling personal and general African American survival in the face of racism and the decay of urban America; others are elegiac. A number reflect the legacy of colonialism and the international slave trade and what she sees as continuing American neocolonialism. As elsewhere, A. seeks to establish the continuity of African American culture and the struggles for freedom on the part of black women from slavery to the present, most notably in "Our Grandmothers."

While A.'s poetry and prose writings are arguably uneven, her autobiographical narrative, viewed in its entirety, forms a moving chronicle of a black woman's very personal engagement with the great movements and moments of African American history since the 1940s. It is also perhaps the most important modern extension of the tradition of African American autobiography that reaches back to the eighteenth century.

OTHER WORKS: Lessons in Living (1993).

BIBLIOGRAPHY: Cudjoe, Selwyn, "Maya Angelou and the Autobiographical Statement" in *Black Women Writers (1950–1980): A Critical Evaluation*, Mari Evans, ed. (1984); "Maya Angelou: The Autobiographical Statement Updated," in *Reading Black, Reading Feminist*, Henry Louis Gates, Jr., ed. (1990). Kinnamon, Kenneth, "Call and Response: Intertexuality in Two Autobiographical Works by Richard Wright and Maya Angelou," in *Belief vs. Theory in Black American Literary Criticism*, Joe Weixlmann, ed. (1986). McPherson, Dolly, *Order Out of Chaos: The Autobiographical Works of Maya Angelou* (1990). *Black Women Writers at Work*, Claudia Tate, ed. (1983). Reference works: *CANR* 19 (1987). *FC* (1990). *Mod. Amer. Women Writers* (1991).

Other references: *Black Amer. Lit. Forum* 22:2 (1988). *Mass. Rev.* 28:2 (1989).

JAMES SMETHURST

Gloria Anzaldúa

B. 26 Sept. 1942, Jesus Maria of the Valley, Texas
D. of Amalia García and Urbano Anzaldúa

A., a seventh-generation American, grew up in the Rio Grande Valley of South Texas. In the hardship of fieldwork, A. found a love and respect for the land and the people who work it. She received her B.A. from Pan American University (1969) and an M.A. in English and Education from the University of Texas at Austin (1972). She has done further study at the University of California at Santa Cruz, and has taught creative writing, Chicano Studies, and Feminist Studies at the University of Texas, San Francisco State University, Vermont College of Norwich University, and the University of California at Santa Cruz. A. has been a contributing editor of the journal *Sinister Wisdom* since 1984.

As a working-class Chicana lesbian, A. experiences multiple sources of oppression; her writing traces the complex interrelations among them in texts that blend poetry and theory, analysis and visceral engagement, Spanish and English. Besides her collection of essay and poems, *Borderlands/La Frontera: The New Mestiza* (1987), A. has edited two anthologies of writing by United States women of color, both of which commonly appear as required reading on Women's Studies' syllabi.

This Bridge Called My Back: Writings by Radical Women of Color (1981), is coedited with **Cherríe Moraga.** The book grew out of the experiences of women of color active in the women's movement who were politicized by the need to develop a feminist analysis of all structures of domination, including race, class, culture, and sexual practice as well as gender. Besides calling attention to the absence of gender and sexuality in Ethnic Studies research paradigms, *Bridge* has also played a crucial role in the shift of white feminist theory from an exclusive focus on gender oppression and "sexual difference" to differences among and within women. In "Speaking in Tongues: A Letter to Third World Women Writers," A. writes of the need for women of color to legitimate the voice that emerges from their specific experiences, rather than imitating dominant literary models. "La Prieta" (the dark girl or woman) foreshadows *Borderlands* in its focus on her relationship to the dark, Indian part of her self and the place of the indigenous in her culture and her sexuality.

In 1990, A. edited *Making Face, Making Soul/Haciendo Caras: Creative and Critical Perspectives by Women of Color*, intended "to continue where *This Bridge Called My Back* left off." The first section, "Still Trembles Our Rage in the Face of Racism," contains several earlier pieces, an unfortunate indicator that the problems identified in *Bridge* persist. More recent essays focus on new forms of racism and the appropriation of the discourse on difference. A.'s introduction addresses the continuing marginalization of women of color and the silencing of their voices, and her essay "En rapport, in Opposition: Cobrando cuentas a las nuestras" contributes to the significant debate on colorism and cross-racial hostility.

The first six essays of *Borderlands/La Frontera* introduce the concept of mestizaje, or hybridity, and inscribe a serpentine movement through different kinds of mestizaje—of races, genders, languages, and the mind/body dichotomy. These mestizajes break down dualisms in the production of a third thing that is neither the one nor the other but something else: the mestiza, Chicano language, the lesbian and gay, the animal soul, the writing that "makes face."

"Homeland" relates the history of the border between the United States and Mexico. Problematizing the concept of "home" in the second essay, A. records her rebellion against her culture's betrayal of women and rejection of the Indian side of Mexican cultural identity. To remain within the safe boundaries of "home" required the repression of her gender, her dark-skinned self, and her lesbian identity. Paradoxically, she must leave home to find home.

In the next two essays, A. formulates her project as self-writing subject: to create a new home, a new mythology, a new mestiza culture, to "fashion my own gods out of my entrails." "How to Tame a Wild Tongue" recounts both A.'s refusal to remain silent and the ways in which her language is not "appropriate" according to dominant norms. The language of the border transgresses the boundaries between Spanish and English, high and low decorum, insider and outsider speech, forming another kind of homeland. Using the Nahuatl notion of writing as creating face, heart, and soul, A. elaborates the notion that it is only through the body that the soul can be transformed.

In the last essay, A. defines "mestiza" or "border" consciousness: not relativism or pluralism, not a repositioning of the subject as Other or Different in binary relationship to the Same or Dominant, but rather the "tolerance for contradictions." The new mestiza is the site or point of confluence of conflicting subject positions.

Images in A.'s poetry in *Borderlands* show the mestiza consciousness "in the flesh." In "Letting Go," the female subject—part fish, part woman—is produced through the transgression of the body's borders. The mestiza survivors of the nuclear holocaust have newly evolved double eyelids that give them the power to "look at the sun with naked eyes" in "No se raje, Chicanita," and the border crossing between the "alien" and the "human" occurs in "Interface."

Anchoring the sense of fragmented identity in the specific historical experience of the borderlands, A.'s writing makes a crucial contribution to the development of theories of diversity and subjectivity.

OTHER WORKS: Friends from the Other Side (1993).

BIBLIOGRAPHY: Andrist, Debra D., "La semiótica de la chicana: La escritura de Gloria Anzaldúa," *Mujer y literatura mexicana y chicana: Culturas en contacto*, Aralia López González et al, eds. (1990). Fishkin, Shelley, "Borderlands of Culture: Writing by W. E. B. DuBois, James Agee, and Gloria Anzaldúa," *Literary Journalism in the Twentieth Century*, Norman Sims, ed. (1990). Saldivar-Hull, Sonia, "Feminism on the Border: From Gender Politics to Geopolitics," in *Criticism in the Borderlands. Studies in Chicano Literature, Culture, and Ideology*, Héctor Calderón and José David Saldivar, eds. (1991). Torres, Hector A., "Experience, Writing, Theory: The Dialectics of *Mestizaje* in Gloria Anzaldúa's *Borderlands/La frontera*," in *Understanding Others: Cultural and Cross-Cultural Studies and the Teaching of Literature*, J. Trimmer and T. Warnock eds. (1992). Yarbro-Bejarano, Yvonne, "Gloria Anzaldúa's *Borderlands/La frontera*: Cultural Studies, 'Difference,' and the Non-Unitary Subject," in *Rearticulations: The Practice of Chicano Cultural Studies*, Mario Garcia and Ellen McCracken, eds. (forthcoming). Other references: *Matrix* (May 1988, interview). *Third Woman* 4 (1989, article by Cherríe Moraga). *Trivia* 14 (Spring 1989). *Women and Language* 12:1 (Spring 1989).

YVONNE YARBRO-BEJARANO

Sarah Appleton. *See Sarah Appleton-Weber*

Sarah Appleton-Weber

B. 14 April 1930, New York City
Writes under: Sarah Appleton
D. of Ellen S. (Merriman) and William C. Appleton; m. Joseph G. Weber, 1965;
  c.: Elizabeth, b. 1968; David, b. 1970

A.-W. is a poet, scholar, and translator whose work is unified by a trans-forming movement into poetry, plant and animal life, and evolutionary forms. Preparation for this work has involved the study of poetry and sacred history, analogy and symbolism, and the natural sciences, as well as training in cosmic forms through making a new edition and translation of Teilhard de Chardin's *Le Phénomène humain*.

A.-W.'s poetry (published under the name Sarah Appleton) is marked by the "utter attentiveness, heart delicacy" with which we need to listen to and read the "book of the Earth." Her first sequence of poems, *A Plenitude We Cry For* (1972), written in the rhetoric of a small horse chestnut tree outside her window in Northampton, Massachusetts, re-cords the transformations of the tree and her own life through a season's growth. *Ladder of the World's Joy* (1977) was born from the energy and joy of reading Teilhard de Chardin's *Le Phénomène humain*, recording the stages, as she read, of human cosmic birth and transformation.

After completing *Ladder of the World's Joy*, A.-W. returned to Teilhard's book, translating it word by word, to discover the secret of its energy. Out of this came a third sequence of poems, *Book of My Hunger, Book of the Earth* (unpublished; many portions have appeared in poetry journals). This is an autobiographical sequence reflecting the work of the poet and the voice of the earth, the precariousness of ever bringing a work together, the continuity of the call and the grace to do so. In her writing, A.-W. explores the transforming correspondence between herself as a woman and poet—barren, fecund, nurturing, evolving—and the earth.

A.-W. was raised in a small hunting lodge in rural Rhode Island, where her life was nurtured by the pond, woods, and living things around her. She was educated at the Old Field School and received her B.A. from Vassar College (1952). She studied fiction writing at Vassar and spent a semester at the Iowa Writer's Workshop, leaving to join **Dorothy Day** at the Catholic Worker's Maryfarm in Newburgh, New York. At the same time she began her growth as a poet under the guidance of **Elizabeth Sewell**. In 1953 she was received into the Roman Catholic church. She studied analogy and symbolism at Fordham University with William Lynch, S.J. (1955–56) and worked at a children's shelter, then at the magazines *Thought* and *Jubilee*.

A.-W. received her M.A. (1957) and Ph.D. (1961) from Ohio State University and wrote her dissertation on medieval liturgy and the relationship between sacred history and poetic form, as a way of integrating Christianity and her work of poetry. This study was published as *Theology and Poetry in the Middle English Lyric* (1969). She taught for three years at Smith College. From 1965–68 she was poetry editor of *Literature East and West*. Along with poetry readings and workshops at colleges and universities, A.-W. has read poetry on tree walks sponsored by the Academy of American Poets in the New York area.

A.-W. has received grants and fellowships from Smith College (1964), the John Anson Kitteredge Educational Fund (1968–70), and the Creative Arts Public Service Program (1975–76). She was a Bunting Institute Fellow at Radcliffe College (1970–72) and has had residencies at Yaddo and Blue Mountain Center.

In France from 1981–83 A.-W. studied Chardin's essays, correspondence, journal, and earlier texts of *Le Phénoméne humain*. On her return to the United States she began a new edition and translation of the work for an American publisher, to make the coherence and synthesis of the book available to readers, and also as a deeper training and tuning to the movements of cosmic evolutionary forms.

OTHER WORKS: "Avatara in the West," *Literature and the West* (with Joseph Weber, June 1966). "Movement into Plantlife," *Hand Book* (1978). "The Breath of Blessing that Brings Us to Speech," *studia mystica* (Fall 1979). Articles in *Teilhard Perspective:* "Reading Teilhard in China" (Dec. 1985); "The Chantilly Conference" (Dec. 1987); *"Le Christ universel et l'evolution selon Teilhard de Chardin"* (Dec. 1990); "Teilhard's Transforming Thought" (Dec. 1991).

BIBLIOGRAPHY: Commonweal (24 June 1977). *Modern Philology* (May 1971). *NYTBR* (11 Nov. 1973). *North American Rev.* (Spring 1977). *Rev. of English Studies* (Aug. 1971).

DARIA DONNELLY

Natalie Babbitt

B. 28 July 1932, Dayton, Ohio
D. of Genevieve (Converse) and Ralph Zane Moore; m. Samuel Fisher Babbitt,
1954; c.: Christopher Converse, b. 1956; Thomas Collier II, b. 1958; Lucy
Cullyford, b. 1960

Despite its intimacy, all B.'s work for young readers has a dramatic scope and is celebratory in nature. Her verbal pageantry, often accompanied by prologues and epilogues, imparts a sense of theatricality. The roots of theater go back to her earlier history. In high school, B. coauthored a musical comedy; at Smith College, she began her studies as a theater major, although she soon changed her major to art claiming she was a "wooden actress."

A proud grandmother, B. has been crafting a picture book that names her grandson the crown prince, her golden retriever the court jester; members of her family and friends assume the roles of the other characters. That she should venture into drawing as well as writing is consistent with her life history. Her mother, an amateur artist, encouraged B.'s early painterly efforts. Even when her books provide no visuals, her imagistic language creates the landscape and brings substance and believability to the characters. Her settings have the majesty and sweep of the air, the sea, the forest, the woods; her characters have the dignity of individuals and the power of archetypes. The ritualistic quality inherent in place and person pervades her work; a mythic lyricism serves both to quiet and excite the reader.

With her mastery of tone and mood, B.'s stories resonate beyond their particulars to embrace the universal and to speak of broad truths. In her well-loved *Tuck Everlasting* (1975) the highly credible eleven-year-old Winnie faces ultimate questions about the meaning of life and death and the novel speaks poignantly about the place of death in the life cycle. The book's gentle and poetic wisdom places it among the classics in children's literature.

Despite the importance of her themes, B. infuses her work with genuine levity and her wry, humorous perspective attracts younger readers. Her early *Search for Delicious* (1969), *Kneeknock Rise* (1970), a Newbery honor book, and *The Something* (1970) are the stages for her homey tales with levels of meaning beyond their apparent lightheartedness. Twice, in *The Devil's Storybook* (1976) and *The Devil's Other Storybook* (1987), B. claims the devil as her protagonist. He is a comic earthbound fellow victimized by his mischievous pranks as he plots against others. B.'s restrained satire renders him an endearing character. B. enjoys providing her readers with characters outside the mainstream of children's literature. In *Eyes of the Amaryllis* (1977) Jenny's Gran, an irascible woman who has not made loving her easy, must grow in ways more expected of her young granddaughter. Reality and illusion crash up against one another along the stormy shoreline of the novel to challenge the readers' belief in things they cannot explain. Her quirky *Herbert Rowbarge* (1982), B.'s personal favorite, does not have an appealing character with whom young readers can identify. Even as a child, Herbert is distant and inaccessible. The novel's philosophic truth about sense and self and loss of self remains more ambiguous, less tangible, though no less wise than her other writings. Although B.'s canon has wide appeal to adults as well as children, the characters and theme of *Herbert Rowbarge* presume adult experience.

Nellie: A Cat on Her Own (1989), a full-color picture book, relates the tale of the beguiling, highly spirited, yet wooden cat, intent on her freedom and independence. Even in books for the youngest child, B. crafts original stories of fantasy, enlivened with charm and whimsy, inviting provocative and challenging reflection.

OTHER WORKS: *Dick Foote and the Shark* (1967). *Phoebe's Revolt* (1968). *Goody Hall* (1971). *Innocence and Experience: Essays and Conversations on Children's Literature*, Barbara Harrison and Gregory Maguire, eds. (1987). *Children and Literature*, Virginia Haviland, ed. (1973). *Bub—or the Very Best Thing* (1994). As illustrator: *The Forty-ninth Magician* (1966). *Small Poems* (1972). *More Small Poems* (1976). *Still More Small Poems* (1978). *Curlicues* (1980). *Small Poems Again* (1986). *All the Small Poems* (1987). Articles: *The Horn Book Mag.* (March/April 1986; Sept./Oct. 1988; Nov./Dec. 1989; Nov./Dec. 1990).

BIBLIOGRAPHY: *Horn Book Mag.* (Nov./Dec.1984). Reference works: *CA* 49–52 (1975). *CANR* 19 (1987). *CLR* 2 (1976). *DLB* 52 (1986). *SATA, Autobiog. Series*, 5 (1987). *Tw Cent. Children's Writers*, 3rd ed. (1989).

SUSAN P. BLOOM

Toni Cade Bambara

B. 25 March 1939, New York City
Wrote under: Toni Cade (prior to 1971)
D. of Helen Brent (Henderson) Cade; c.: Karma Bambara

For B., writing is one means of celebrating movements toward personal and political change. "The issue," she explains, "is salvation. I write to save our lives." In her work as a writer of stories, a novel, essays, and film scripts, as well as a teacher and community organizer, B. transmits an African American cultural heritage, records the strong communities and characters who struggle with the effects of racism, and envisions new and more humane conditions for our lives.

B. began writing as a child, encouraged by her mother and inspired by visits to the Apollo Theater with her father. Listening to impassioned trade unionists, Pan-Africans, Father Divinists, Muslims, and Ida B. Wells supporters at Speakers Corner in Harlem, she learned the power of words to shape and share visions. B. earned a B.A. at Queens College and an M.A. at the City College of New York. She has done further graduate work in American Studies and has studied commedia dell'arte, mime, linguistics, dance, and filmmaking at various institutions in Europe and the United States.

B.'s early writing and editing redefined African American identities, particularly black women's complex and varied selves, beyond the confines of racist and sexist stereotypes. *The Black Woman* (1970, as Toni Cade) is a groundbreaking anthology of essays, poems, and fiction that grapples with the intersections of race and gender in women's lives. *Tales and Stories for Black Folks* (1971) offers children contemporary African American stories and black renditions of fairy tales reset in twentieth-century America.

The stories in B.'s first collection, *Gorilla, My Love*, (1977), are primarily first-person vignettes of urban life narrated by an array of black girls and women in rhythmic, pointed, poetic, black-inflected language. Critics praised the depth and range of B.'s characters, and her nonpolemical emphasis on the strength of African American community in the face of racist patriarchal conditions. They also acclaimed B.'s language as sounding the musical improvisations of bop and the raptures of gospel throughout her stories.

The collection *Sea Birds Are Still Alive* (1977) moves outward in scope to address other cultures, and focuses upon characters committed to more directly political struggles such as revolutions in Southeast Asia and the civil rights and Black Power movements. B.'s novel, *The Salt Eaters* (1980), which won the American Book Award from the Before Columbus Foundation, expands this vision of cultural and social transformation, portraying the intertwined lives of culture workers, political activists, and healers within a Southern community. The novel develops the interconnections between personal well-being, spiritual growth, and political commitment. *The Salt Eaters* was highly praised by critics, particularly for its lyric and dreamlike experimental narration, which created complex webs of communal connections. "Yeah, but Not under Capitalism," a collection of stories in progress, pursues similar concerns. A novel in progress is based upon the Atlanta child murders of the early 1980s.

B.'s interest in experimental narration has led her into film work. She has written historical scripts on figures such as **Zora Neale Hurston,** W. E. B. Du Bois, and activist Cecil B. Moore, as well as renditions of her own and others' fictions.

B. is an active teacher and organizer. She has taught and served as a consultant in a range of settings, from colleges and universities such as City College, Rutgers, Emory, and Spelman, to community centers, prisons, libraries, and museums. She conducts workshops on writing and community organizing and is an instructor at Scribe Video Center in Philadelphia, a media access facility, training community groups in the use of video as a tool for social change.

OTHER WORKS: *Black Utterances Today* (editor, 1975). FILM SCRIPTS: *Zora* (1971). *The Johnson Girls* (1972). *Transactions* (1979). *The Long Night* (1981). *Epitaph for Willie* (1982). *Tar Baby* (1984). *Raymond's Run* (1985). *The Bombing of Osage* (1986). *Cecil B. Moore: Master Tactician of Direct Action* (1987).

BIBLIOGRAPHY: *Black Women Writers (1950–1980): A Critical Evaluation,* Mari Evans, ed. (1984). *Black Women Writers at Work,* Claudia Tate, ed. (1983). Reference works: *Black Writers* (1989). *CA 29–32* (1978). *CANR* 24 (1988). *CLC* 19 (1981). *DLB* 38 (1985). *FC* (1990). *Maj Twent Cent Writers* (1991).

RACHEL STEIN

Ann Beattie

B. 8 Sept. 1947, Washington, DC
D. of Charlotte (Crosby) and James A. Beattie; m. David Gates, 1973, div.;
m. Lincoln Perry, 1988

Novelist and short-story writer B. has earned her critical reputation as a storyteller of the sixties' generation. While her work includes both a children's book, *Spectacles* (1985), and a collection of essays in art criticism, *Alex Katz* (1987), her primary preoccupation is with fictional characters who came of age during the turbulent sixties and are struggling with that legacy. B.'s spare and direct prose style, which has been linked to the social realism tradition of Hemingway and John Updike, is marked by pop culture references, quotidian details, spiritually lost characters, and deliberately open endings. Although generally praised as a skillful writer, she has been faulted for the apparent lack of purpose in her characters' lives. B. notes that "If I knew what it was that was missing [in her characters' lives], I'd certainly write about it. I'd write for Hallmark cards."

A self-described "artsy little thing" and only child of a housewife and a federal government administrator, B. grew up in suburban Washington, DC. In 1968, while a student at American University (B.A. 1969), she was invited to serve as one of several student guest editors for *Mademoiselle* magazine. B. completed an M.A. in English at the University of Connecticut at Storrs (1970) and remained there until 1972 to do further study in English literature. She married musician and fellow graduate student David Gates in 1973. From 1975–77 B. was visiting writer and lecturer at the University of Virginia, and in 1977–78 she was the Briggs-Copeland Lecturer at Harvard University.

While still a graduate student, B. began submitting her short stories for publication. In April 1974 *The New Yorker* accepted "A Platonic Relationship," her twentieth submission. Her first collection of nineteen stories, *Distortions*, and her first novel, *Chilly Scenes of Winter*, both appeared in 1976. The novel, which she claims to have written in three weeks, is perhaps her best-known work. Its main characters float through the book, incapable of decisive action that would change their unrewarding lives.

Charles, mired in a dull job, longs to reestablish his broken relationship with Laura who left him to marry someone else. He is surrounded by his mentally unbalanced mother and by Sam, his best friend and Phi Beta Kappa graduate who cannot afford law school and so must settle for selling men's jackets, and Pete, his well-meaning but tactless stepfather. The novel became a film entitled *Head over Heels* (1979), with B. playing a minor role as a waitress. The recipient of a Guggenheim fellowship in 1977, B. moved to Redding, Connecticut, and became a full-time writer. She published *Secrets and Surprises*, a collection of fifteen stories in 1979. The idea for her next novel, *Falling in Place* (1980), came to her while she was contemplating a peach tree outside her Redding home. It chronicles a disconnected and disintegrating suburban Connecticut family. At the end of the novel, the family faces a crisis when John Joel, their ten-year-old son, accidentally shoots his sister with a gun belonging to his only friend. The novel received a literature award from the American Academy and Institute of Arts and Letters in 1980.

B.'s marriage to Gates ended in May 1982. She later told Kim Hubbard of *People* magazine, that "Getting divorced affected everything, my writing included. It affected the way I walked the dog. I did not recover from it quickly." *The Burning House*, sixteen short stories published in 1982, was seen as evidence of B.'s growing artistic maturity and confirmation of the fact that the short story seemed the form that best suited her talents. After her divorce, B. lived in New York City until 1984 when she moved to Vermont for the summer and wrote her second novel, *Love Always* (1985), which chronicles the life of Lucy Spenser, editor of the humorous magazine *Country Daze*. It was followed in 1986 by *Where You'll Find Me and Other Stories*.

B. met her second husband, painter Lincoln Perry, in Charlottesville, Virginia, where she had moved following her brief sojourn in Vermont. He provided her with the title to her fourth novel, *Picturing Will* (1989), the story of five-year-old Will and his mother who moves him from Charlottesville to New York City to pursue her photography career, her boyfriend Mel, and Will's ne'er-do-well father. Unlike many of her previous works, this novel took B. three years to complete and was "the single hardest thing I've ever worked on." *What Was Mine*, another collection of short stories, appeared in 1991. It received praise for its "honest introspection" and "greater sympathy and tenderness." While she continues to remain reticent about offering answers in her fiction to life's most puzzling questions, in these stories B. again demonstrates her remarkable ability to re-create the anxiety and angst inherent in white, middle-class twentieth-century America.

BIBLIOGRAPHY: Murphy, Christina, *Ann Beattie* (1986). Reference works: *CA* 81–84 (1979). *CLC* 8 (1978), 13 (1980), 18 (1981), 40 (1986), 63 (1991). *DLBY* (1982). *CBY* (1985). *FC* (1990).
Other references: *NYTBR* (26 May 1991). *People* 33 (5 Feb. 1990).

LISA STEPANSKI

Anne Bernays

See AWW *1, 147–48*

Working in 1991 on her ninth novel, B. has explored in her fiction the culture of social privilege in America. From New York City's high society (*The New York Ride*, 1965; *Growing Up Rich*, 1975) to the cloistered environment of an exclusive Cambridge boarding school (*The School Book*, 1980), B. has exposed with humor and poignancy these often-hermetic institutions of privilege.

In two novels in the 1980s, B. turned her attention to issues that concern professional women. *The Address Book* (1983) features a successful, middle-aged editor at a Boston publishing house who is offered a new job with a top New York firm. As Alicia Baer—wife, mother, professional woman—struggles with the decision to move on in her career or to remain with her family, she is confronted by her own fears of loneliness and death, as well as by her repressed ambition and sexuality. Submerged elements of her inner life become personified as mysterious old acquaintances who make claims upon her. *The Address Book* successfully portrays the conflict between Alicia's genuine love of and attachment to her family and her longings to escape the personal restrictions it imposes upon her.

Professor Romeo (1989) deals with sexual harassment on the college cam-

pus. Assuming a male voice, B. tells the story of compulsive sexual exploitation from the point of view of the perpetrator, psychology professor
Jake Barker, and reveals the profound emptiness looming behind Barker's
accomplished facade. Finally called to account for his unethical behavior,
Barker faces his dismissal from Harvard, and the professional demise
it represents, with bewildered incomprehension. A shallow man from
beginning to end, he shows no sign of reform or redemption.

In 1990, B. published with Pamela Painter a manual for students of
creative writing. Composed of eighty-three lessons in twelve sections,
each addressing a facet of fiction writing, *What If? Writing Exercises for
Fiction Writers* avoids theoretical and technical jargon, focusing instead
on practical exercises, revision, and the study of great authors.

In addition to pursuing her own writing career, B. is busy on behalf
of other writers. She is a founding and active member of PEN New
England, a regional offshoot of the national anticensorship and writer
advocacy organization. She is chair of the Fine Arts Work Center, which
funds writers and visual artists for a year's stay in Provincetown; she also
serves on the board of the National Writers Union.

In 1991 B. joined the faculty at Holy Cross College in Worcester,
Massachusetts. With her husband, critic and biographer Justin Kaplan,
she jointly holds the Jenks Chair in Contemporary Letters.

BIBLIOGRAPHY: *College Comp. and Communic.* (Feb. 1992). *Hudson Rev.* (Autumn 1984). *NYT* (19 July 1989). *NYTBR* (13 Nov. 1983; 23 July 1989).
Reference works: *CA* 1–4 (1967). *CANR* 5 (1982). *SATA* 32 (1983).

MELISSA BURNS

Victoria Berne. *See Mary Frances Kennedy Fisher*

Doris Betts

See AWW *1, 151–52*

Between 1954 and 1973 B. produced three volumes of short stories and three novels, all focused on her native North Carolina. She has always been well received in her region: each novel won the Sir Walter Raleigh Award for the best fiction of its year by a North Carolinian. Her third volume of short stories, *Beasts of the Southern Wild and Other Stories* (1973), broadened her reputation; it was widely reviewed and one of the stories, "The Ugliest Pilgrim," was filmed for the Public Broadcasting System.

In B.'s fourth novel, *Heading West* (1981), a Book-of-the-Month selection, the author's wider scope is paralleled by that of her female epic hero, Nancy Finch, an unmarried librarian in a small North Carolina town desperate to escape her dull life. Maintaining the comic voice evident in many of her short stories, B. makes her story of Nancy's journey to the Grand Canyon a mock epic. The Grand Canyon parallels Melville's white whale as a symbol of the American quest for meaning, which B. locates, finally, in the American dream of family. Instead of Melville's mad hero, B.'s protagonist is the victim of a mad kidnapper who introduces himself with the words "Call me Dwight," echoing Melville's "Call me Ishmael." Nancy's vocation as librarian gives B. ample opportunity for other literary parallels and allusions; the Bible, *Pilgrim's Progress*, *Paradise Lost*, proverbs, fairy tales, and popular songs furnish opportunities for irony and also deepen the universality of Nancy's predicament and ambivalence. B. subverts the myth of the "imperial hero," a loner who ruthlessly prevails over all obstacles. Like Odysseus, Nancy returns home to complete her spiritual journey before heading west for good.

Through irony and the witty inner voice of her protagonist, B. makes Nancy's adventures credible and the characters convincing. Using the form of a suspenseful mystery story in which the good guys win, B. has solved the dilemma of writers in a democracy of how to make a serious work accessible to many levels of readers. A published excerpt from a novel in progress, *Souls Raised from the Dead*, makes it clear that B. has mastered the novel form as well as she had already mastered that of the short story. Her status as an important American writer is assured.

B. has been a long time between books and has published few stories in recent years. Instead she has been fully occupied in her academic career. Though she never graduated from college, B. has received two honorary doctorates and is Alumni Distinguished Professor of English at the University of North Carolina, Chapel Hill. She was elected to a three-year term as chair of the Faculty Senate (1982–85) and has won several awards for excellence in teaching, including the designation "Master Teacher" from the Modern Language Association. B. has published many articles on writing and teaching, as well as many book reviews, especially of fellow Southerners, and has lectured widely. In 1989 she received three major literary awards, including the Medal of Merit in the Short Story from the American Academy of Arts and Letters.

OTHER WORKS: *Halfway Home and a Long Way to Go: The Report of the 1986 Commission on the Future of the South* (1986).

BIBLIOGRAPHY: Scura, Dorothy M., "Doris Betts's Nancy Finch: A Heroine for the 1980s," reptd. in *Women Writers of the Contemporary South*, Peggy W. Prenshaw, ed. (1984). *The Home Truths of Doris Betts*, Sue Laslie Kimball and Lynn Veach Sandler, eds., (1991).
Other references: *Southern Q.* 21:2 (Winter 1983), 3 (Summer 1983). B.'s papers are in Special Collections, Boston University Libraries.

MARY ANNE FERGUSON

Judy Blume

B. 12 Feb. 1938, Elizabeth, New Jersey
D. of Esther (Rosenfeld) and Rudolph Sussman; m. John Blume, 1959, div.;
m. Thomas Kitchens, 1976, div.; m. George Cooper, 1987; c.: Randy Lee,
b. 1961; Lawrence Andrew, b. 1963

Best known for her realistic fiction for adolescents, B. is one of the most popular authors in the contemporary history of children's books. She creates frank, straightforward stories that focus characteristically on the immediate social and emotional concerns of her mainly female characters. Her taboo-breaking books address topics like menstruation, wet dreams, and premarital sex, but B. also writes of friendship, divorce, peer group approval, religion, and death. B.'s books accurately, honestly, and with great earnestness capture the speech, emotions, and private thoughts of adolescents.

B. received a B.A. from New York University (1960). Her earliest books were the result of her participation in a graduate writing course. *The One in the Middle Is the Green Kangaroo* (1969), a picture book, involves a second grader who feels neglected by his family until he lands a part in his school play. *Iggie's House* (1970) deals with the impact of a black family moving into an all-white neighborhood. When both books met a cool reception from reviewers, B. decided to write a book about adolescence based on her vivid memories of her own sixth-grade experience. The resulting book, *Are You There God? It's Me, Margaret* (1970), explores a young girl's private thoughts about the onset of menstruation, her acceptance by a new peer group, and her struggle to find a religion. B.'s almost complete recall of how it felt to be young spoke directly to readers and the book was immediately successful. Although it stirred some controversy among parents, librarians, and teachers for its unflinchingly honest treatment of a topic like menstruation, the book made B.'s reputation: hundreds of letters from preteen girls attested to the fact that they identified with Margaret.

B.'s books address subjects that children's books tend to disregard, leading critics to label her an issue-oriented author, an author of "problem novels." Despite her critics, B. believes there is nothing one should not or cannot tell a child. "I don't care about rules and regulations of writing for children," B. comments. "My responsibility to be honest with my readers is my strongest motivation." Many of B.'s books are about coping with difficult situations. Told in the first person, they foster a strong sense of intimacy and immediacy, convincing the reader B. writes the truth about what kids think and feel. *Then Again, Maybe I Won't* (1971) deals with a twelve-year-old's budding sexual identity. *It's Not the End of the World* (1972) documents the effects of divorce on a preteen girl. In *Deenie* (1973) a seventh grader copes with scoliosis. *Blubber* (1974) is the story of a fat girl who becomes the target of ridicule in her class. *Forever* (1975), a book consistently placed on censored lists, explicitly details the joy and frustration of a first sexual relationship. A young girl in *Tiger Eyes* (1981) struggles to overcome grief after her father's violent death.

Just as Long as We're Together (1987) depicts teenage girls grappling with friendship and other issues.

B. leavens the seriousness of her often heavy-handed "problem" books with humorous dialogue and wit, while her books for younger readers include humor in the broad, sometimes slapstick manner that children find so appealing. *Tales of A Fourth Grade Nothing* (1972) and *Superfudge* (1980) relate the hilarious stories of ten-year-old Peter and the antics of his mischievous little brother Fudge. *Otherwise Known as Sheila the Great* (1972), a story of overcoming fears, delights with its funny verbal sparring and the outrageous lies children tell to impress each other. *Fudge-a-Mania* (1990) features Peter and Fudge, as well as Sheila Tubman, otherwise known as Sheila the Great. While their families share a summer vacation house, Peter and Sheila have great fun being enemies.

In her career as an author of children's books, B. has achieved both unprecedented popularity and fierce criticism, primarily for the content of her books rather than their execution. Reviewers have commended her for her close observation of childhood, for the honesty and lack of condescension with which she writes, for her warm sense of humor, and for her courage in breaking taboo and convention. Her critics cite flawed character development, permissive attitudes, the use of issues as starting points for creative writing, uninhibited language, thin narrative, and a lack of social consciousness. Most agree, however, that she has made reading easy and agreeable for many children. Her ability to communicate with her audience has endeared her to a loyal readership, and she receives thousands of letters a month from them. The most moving of these are collected in *Letters to Judy* (1986).

OTHER WORKS: *Freckle Juice* (1971). *Starring Sally J. Freedman as Herself* (1982). *The Pain and the Great One* (1984).

BIBLIOGRAPHY: *The Marble in the Water*, David Rees, ed. (1980). Reference works: *CA* 29–32 (1978). *CANR* 13 (1984). *CLC* 12 (1980), 30 (1984). *DLB* 52 (1986). *Maj Tw Cent Writers* (1991). *Tw Cent Children's Writers*, 3rd ed. (1989). Other references: *Elemen. English* (Sept. 1974). *Horn Book Mag.* (Jan./Feb. 1985). *School Librarian* (May 1987).

CAROLYN SHUTE

Erma Louise Bombeck

B. 21 Feb. 1927, Dayton, Ohio
D. of Erma and Edwin Cassius Fiste; m. William Bombeck, 1949; c.: Betsy,
Andrew, Matthew

"Mostly I worry about surviving," B. wrote in the introduction to one of her books. "Keeping up with the times in a world that changes daily. Knowing what to keep and what to discard. What to accept and what to protest. That is what this book is about. Surviving." B. has taught her readers, mostly housewives, to survive boredom, frustration, and alienation through laughter, exaggeration, truth, parody, and sarcasm.

The product of a secure, middle-class family, B. found her life changed in 1936 when her father died suddenly. Her young mother and nine-year-old Erma moved into one bedroom of her grandmother's home. As a growing child, B. interpreted her mother's preoccupation with work and her later remarriage as desertion. She reconsidered as an adult, and the cruel self-centeredness of children recurs as a theme in her writing. Because she was a shy child, her mother enlisted her in tap-dancing lessons. B. developed a stage presence and remained a local radio performer, singing and tapping, for almost eight years.

B.'s writing career began with a humor column for the junior high school newspaper. During high school she contributed to the newsletter at the department store where she worked. She started secretarial courses after high school and worked at the Dayton Herald as a copy girl. She studied at Ohio University in Athens until her money ran out, went back to work, and entered the University of Dayton, where William Bombeck was also a student. Upon graduation (1949) the Dayton Herald hired her as a reporter.

Her marriage in 1949 and the subsequent plunge into suburban tract housing became the building blocks of her writing. Leaving her job to stay home with her children, B. became aware of the people around her. In the 1950s a child-filled home in a suburban tract was advertised as the family dream. B. knew the isolation that came with the mortgage and subsequently wrote about it. For many years her syndicated columns targeted child rearing, marriage, friends, cups of coffee, car pools, pets, holidays, and common worry. The house-bound housewives read and realized they were not alone. Although other female writers wrote humorously about being a housewife, B. was the first to focus on those middle-class women living in the new suburbs.

In 1963, B. started a weekly column for the *Kettering-Oakwood Times.* In 1965, she was offered two columns a week at the Dayton paper. Three weeks later her column was acquired by the Newsday syndicate. Books and financial success followed.

By the 1990s B. was writing two columns and filling three television slots each week from the family's Paradise Valley, Arizona, home. As William Bombeck retired from his job as school teacher and administrator and her children became adults, the focus of her columns changed. She writes of the working woman, grown children, retirement, and aging. Her commentaries astutely combine humor and poignancy.

A convert to Roman Catholicism when she was twenty-two, B. has strong religious and political beliefs, but does not use her columns as a vehicle to promote them. She campaigned for two years for passage of the Equal Rights Amendment, and expresses some impatience with women who do not realize the precariousness of equality. B. has been named to the list of twenty-five most influential women in America by the World Almanac since 1979, was grand marshal of the 1986 Rose Bowl Parade, holds fifteen honorary doctorates, is a member of the Society of Professional Journalists, and was the first woman named to the American Academy of Humor Columnists. She was appointed to the President's Advisory Committee for Women in 1978. B. also served as a commentator on ABC's "Good Morning America" for eleven years from 1975. Her book of interviews with children surviving cancer, *I Want to Grow Hair, I Want to Grow Up, I Want to Go to Boise,* received the American Cancer Society's 1990 Medal of Honor.

OTHER WORKS: *At Wit's End* (1967). *"Just Wait till You Have Children of Your Own!"* (1971). *I Lost Everything in the Post-Natal Depression* (1973). *The Grass Is Always Greener over the Septic Tank* (1976). *If Life Is a Bowl of Cherries, What Am I Doing in the Pits?* (1978). *Aunt Erma's Cope Book* (1979). *Motherhood: The Second Oldest Profession* (1984). *Family Ties That Bind . . . and Gag!* (1987). *When You Look Like Your Passport Photo It's Time to Go Home* (1991). *A Marriage Made in Heaven—or, Too Tired for an Affair* (1993).

BIBLIOGRAPHY: Dressner, Zita, "Domestic Comic Writers," in *Women's Comic Visions,* June Sochen, ed. (1991). Walker, Nancy, and Zita Dressner, *Redressing the Balance* (1989). Reference works: *CA* 21–24 (1977). *CANR* 12

(1984), 39 (1992). *Celebrity Register* (1990). *Maj Twent Cent Writers* (1991). *WWAW* (1991).

JANET M. BEYER

Marita Bonner

B. 16 June 1898, Brookline, Massachusetts; d. 6 Dec. 1971, Chicago, Illinois
Wrote under: Joseph Maree Andrew
D. of Mary Anne (Nowell) and Joseph Bonner; m. William Almy Occomy, 1930;
* c.: William Almy, Jr.; Warwick Gale; Marita Joyce*

B. was among the foremost artists, educators, and intellectuals of the Harlem Renaissance. She began her writing career as a student at Brookline High School where her contributions to the student magazine drew the attention of a faculty member who encouraged her to enroll at Radcliffe. There she majored in English and comparative literature and studied creative writing with the celebrated Professor Charles "Copey" Copeland. A lifelong student of music and German language and literature, B. received a B.A. from Radcliffe in 1922. She went on to publish a host of plays, essays, reviews, and short fiction, some of which received long-overdue publication in the prize-winning collection, *Frye Street and Environs* (1987), edited by B.'s daughter with Joyce Flynn.

While residing in Boston, Washington, DC, and then Chicago, B. taught English, participated in a theater company, and was actively involved in an eminent literary "salon." A regular contributor to the major journals of the Harlem Renaissance, *Crisis* and *Opportunity* magazines, B. won the 1925 *Crisis* Award for her essay, "On Being Young—a Woman—and Colored" and the 1927 *Crisis* Contest Award for four other works in three genres. She received honorable mention in the 1925 *Opportunity* Awards for her short story, "The Hands."

B.'s heightened awareness of her role as a black woman artist surfaces in "On Being Young." She boldly articulates the unenviable and taxing position of a relatively privileged black woman who is deeply concerned with the spiritual and political welfare of her "people," particularly those who are socially and economically impoverished, less fortunate than herself.

B.'s drama and short stories are marked by a diverse range of literary devices and strategies. Experimentally and thematically expansive, her fiction explores on one level the psychological states of black American women enduring the yoke of racial, sexual, and class oppression. On another level, her short fiction—commonly set in Chicago in the 1920s and 1930s—treats the experiences of the historically disenfranchised black community engaged with the racist American society at large. Her best-known play, *The Purple Flower* (1928), is a vexing allegorical portrayal of racism in America. In several of her stories, B. meticulously examines the problematics of class and complexion within the black community; here, she is a thematic associate of **Jessie Fauset** and **Nella Larsen.** Also evident in B.'s work is her penetrating vision of the human condition, manifested through her symbolic thoroughfare, Frye Street.

The quilt, by now a familiar icon of black women's writing, most faithfully symbolizes the colorful and complex body of B.'s works. The quilt epitomizes as well B.'s snugly interwoven place in the black women's writing tradition.

OTHER WORKS: Exit, an Illusion (1923). *The Pot Maker: A Play to Be Read* (1927). Short fiction in *Opportunity* (Aug. 1925; Dec. 1927; July 1933; Aug. 1933; Sept. 1933; July 1934; March 1936; July 1938; Jan. 1939) and in *Crisis* (Sept. 1926; May 1928; June 1939; Dec. 1939; March 1940; Feb. 1941). Marita Bonner's papers are in the Radcliffe College Archives.

BIBLIOGRAPHY: Roses, Lorraine Elena, and Ruth Elizabeth Randolph. *Harlem Renaissance and Beyond: Literary Biographies of 100 Black Women Writers 1900–1945* (1987). Reference works: *DLB* 51 (1987). *Dict. of the Harlem Renaissance* (1984). *Early Black American Playwrights and Dramatic Writers* (1990).

Other references: *Black Amer. Lit. Forum 1/2* (Spring/Summer 1987). *Saga* 2:1 (1985).

SHARON A. LEWIS

Kay Boyle

See AWW *1, 207–9*
D. 27 Dec. 1992, Mill Valley, California

B., whose first book appeared in 1929, continued until her death to write with the same enthusiasm and dedication. Her publications after 1980 included two collections of stories, a volume of essays, a book of poems and a collected edition of her poems, and a translation. She also continued her work on books about Irish and German women, projects that she had saved for her " *very* old age." An excerpt from the first book, the story of an Englishman's insensitivity on Dublin's "St. Stephen's Green," appeared in the *Atlantic* (June 1980).

A retrospective of B.'s work is emerging as her writing is introduced to a new generation. Several novels have been reprinted in Modern Classics editions. Both *Fifty Stories* (1980) and *Life Being the Best* (1988) offer representative short fiction from five previous collections, stories both personal and political, shaped by her years in pre- and postwar Europe, blazing with anger and compassion.

Most of the essays in *Words That Must Somehow Be Said* (1985) first appeared in magazines, from early book reviews in *transition* to the sharper political essays of the postwar and Vietnam era. In contrast, the poems in *This Is Not a Letter* (1985) represent her writing from the late 1960s to the 1980s. The mellowing in these poems ("Dwell . . . on the courage of the dead") reflects a new acceptance of age, but never a surrender.

In a sense B.'s emphasis shifted from her initial concern with the word to a concern with the world, though both were always of great importance to her. She believed that "writers . . . must bear the full weight of moral responsibility." Biographer Sandra Whipple Spanier argues that B.'s "reputation as a serious writer has suffered precisely because she has taken her writing so seriously," often leading her to choose unpopular positions, although her passionate defense of human dignity seems better understood now in the light of history.

B. finally achieved the recognition she should have received long ago. In the 1980s she was honored for her lifetime of writing, with grants and fellowships from the Before Columbus Foundation, the National Endowment for the Arts, the Fund for Poetry, and in 1989, its first year of awards to "writers who have made significant contributions to English-language literature," a special award for outstanding literary achievement from the Lannan Foundation.

B. says, "Camus demanded that the voices of all those who could speak must ring out above the clamor of a world, ring out in the doomed silence of the persecuted, and in this way make the destiny of other men less lonely than before." Her life and writing were a testament to this ideal.

OTHER WORKS: Being Geniuses Together by Robert McAlmon (revised, with supplementary chapters by B., 1984). *Babylon* by René Crevel (trans. with afterword, 1985). *A Woman on Paper: Georgia O'Keeffe* by Anita Pollitzer (introduction, 1988). *Collected Poems of Kay Boyle* (1991). *Winter Night* (1993). Most of B.'s manuscripts and other papers are at the Morris Library, Southern Illinois University, Carbondale.

BIBLIOGRAPHY: Ford, H., *Four Lives in Paris* (1985). Spanier, S. W., *Kay Boyle: Artist and Activist* (1986). *Women Writers of the West Coast: Speaking of Their Lives and Careers*, M. Yalom, ed. (1983). Kay Boyle Special Issue, *Twentieth Cent. Lit.* (Fall 1988). Reference works: *CAAS* 1 (1984). *CANR* 29 (1990). *CLC* 58 (1990). *DLB* 4 (1980), 9 (1981), 48 (1986). *FC* (1990). *Maj Twent Cent Writers* (1991).

Corrections and Additions to AWW 1: Biographical. B. 19 Feb. 1902. M. Joseph Von Franckenstein, 1943 (d. 1963). Six children: Sharon (1st marriage); Apple-Joan, Kathe, Clover (2nd marriage); Faith, Ian Savin (3rd marriage). *Bibliographical:* Additional Works: *Relations and Complications: Being the Recollections of H. H. the Dayang Muda of Sarawak* by Gladys Palmer Brooke (ghostwriter, 1929). *Short Stories* (1929). *Wedding Day, and Other Stories* (1930). *Landscape for Wyn Henderson* (1931). *Don Juan* by Joseph Deltail (trans. 1931). *Mr. Knife, Miss Fork* by René Crevel (trans. 1931). *A Statement* (1932). *The Devil in the Flesh* by Raymond Radiguet (trans. 1932). *Poems and Sonnets* by Ernest Walsh (ed. anonymously, 1934). *Death of a Man* (1936, rept. 1989). *365 Days* (ed. with contributions by B., with Laurence Vail and Nina Conarain, 1936). *Yellow Dusk* by Bettina Bedwell (ghostwriter, 1937). *American Citizen Naturalized in Leadville, Colorado* (1944). *The Smoking Mountain: Stories of Postwar Germany* (1951; reissued as *The Smoking Mountain: Stories of Germany during the Occupation*, 1963). *The Youngest Camel Reconsidered and Rewritten* (1959). *At Large* (with Herbert Kubly, 1963). *The Lost Dogs of Phnom Penh* (1968). *Enough of Dying! Voices for Peace* (ed. with J. Van Gundy, with introduction and three selections by B., 1972). *A Poem for February*

First 1975 (1975). *Four Visions of America* (with E. Jong, T. Sanchez, and H. Miller, 1977).

JOANNE MCCARTHY

Marion Zimmer Bradley

B. 3 July 1930, near Albany, New York
Writes under: Lee Chapman, John Dexter, Mariam Gardner, Valerie Graves,
*   Morgan Ives, Alfrida Rivers, John J. Wells*
D. of Evelyn (Conklin) and Leslie Raymond Zimmer; m. Robert Alden Bradley
*   1949, div. 1964; m. Walter Breen 1964, div. 1990; c.: David, Patrick, Moira*

B. grew up on a farm in upper New York state, where she very early developed a love for reading and writing. Having won a National Merit Scholarship, she attended New York State College for Teachers (1946–48), but left to marry a fellow science fiction fan, Robert Bradley, many years her senior, and moved to Texas. She had begun writing as a teenager, and after her marriage and the birth of David began a prolific output, mostly romances, gothics, and fantasies, to help support her family and pay for her return to college. Beginning in 1952 she published under a number of pseudonyms.

B. graduated from Hardin-Simmons College in Abilene in 1964 and went on to do graduate work at Berkeley (1966–67). Divorced from Robert Bradley, she married Walter Breen, had two more children, and continued her writing career. She has continued to live in California, and, despite several strokes, she acts as the doyenne of a productive group of younger fans and writers, continues to produce novels, and edits two series of anthologies and *Marion Zimmer Bradley's Fantasy Magazine*.

B.'s most popular series of novels, beginning with *Planet of Exile* and *Sword of Aldones* in 1962, are set on Darkover, a snowy and forbidding planet originally settled by colonists from Earth. In the centuries following, the "lost" settlers have developed a patriarchal feudal society ruled by an aristocracy that holds power partly through hereditary psychic abilities. The planet's rediscovery leads to interesting conflicts between Earth's modern technology and Darkover conservatism.

The nineteen Darkovan novels are almost ideal illustrations of the ways in which attitudes toward women as writers and subjects of science fiction have changed. The earliest, designed to appeal to a young and almost entirely male audience, are essentially exotic adventure stories centered on white male heroes, with few female characters. But beginning with *The Heritage of Hastur* (1975), B. began to write more complex novels focused on personal relationships and politics rather than action, and gradually to shift from male to female protagonists. Acknowledging her own lesbianism, she began to explore sexual roles and show both male and female homosexuals in a positive light. Particularly influential has been her invention of the Free Amazons (or Renunciates) in *The Shattered Chain* (1976). These are women who in a male-centered world have freed themselves from a dependence on men. Their lives are not easy or trouble-free, but their community offers an alternative to Darkover's oppressed women.

B. has written and edited at least forty other novels and anthologies. Of particular interest to women are *The Ruins of Isis* (1979), an ambiguous depiction of a society in which women dominate men, and two historical novels: *The Mists of Avalon* (1983), a retelling of the Arthurian Legend from the point of view of Morgan Le Fay, and *The Firebrand* (1987), Cassandra's version of the Trojan War.

SELECTED OTHER WORKS: "Darkover" Novels: *The Forbidden Tower* (1977). *Stormqueen* (1978). *Sharra's Exile* (1981). *Hawkmistress* (1982). *Thendara House* (1983). *City of Sorcery* (1984). *The Heirs of Hammerfell* (1989). *Rediscovery* (1993, with Mercedes Lackey). Other Fiction: *The Endless Voyage* (1979). *House between the Worlds* (1981). *Lythande* (1986). *The Best of Marion Zimmer Bradley* (1988). *Black Trillium* (1990, with Andre Norton and Julian May). *Sword and Sorceress: An Anthology of Heroic Fiction* (ed., 1992). Nonfiction: "Responsibilities and Temptations of Women Science Fiction Writers," *Women Worldwalkers: New Dimensions of Science Fiction and Fantasy*, Jane B. Weedman, ed. (1985). "One Women's Experience in Science Fiction," *Women of Vision: Essays by Women Writing Science Fiction*, Denise DuPont, ed. (1988).

BIBLIOGRAPHY: Arbor, Rosemarie, *Leigh Brackett; Marion Zimmer Bradley; Anne McCaffrey: A Primary and Secondary Bibliography* (1982); also, *Marion Zimmer Bradley* (1986). Hornum, Barbara, "Wife/Mother, Sorceress/Keeper, Amazon/Renunciate: Status Ambivalence and Conflicting Roles on the

Planet Darkover," in *Women Worldwalkers: New Dimensions of Science Fiction and Fantasy*, Jane B. Weedman, ed. (1985). Schwartz, Susan M., "Marion Zimmer Bradley's Ethic of Freedom," in *The Feminine Eye: Science Fiction and the Women Who Write It*, Tom Staicar, ed. (1982). Spivack, Charlotte, "Marion Zimmer Bradley," in *Merlin's Daughters* (1987). Wood, Diane S., "Gender Roles in the Darkover Novels," in *Women Worldwalkers*. Reference works: *CANR* 31 (1990). *FC* (1990). *Tw Cent Sci Fi Writers*, Noelle Watson and Paul Schellinger, eds. (1991; bio-bibliography current to 1991).
    Other references: *Science Fic. Studies* 20 (March 1980).

LYNN F. WILLIAMS

Germaine Brée

See AWW 1, 223–25

With more than ten books published between 1940 and 1978 and more than eighteen honorary degrees, B. had established a firm position for herself in the field of French literature by the beginning of the 1980s. Her brilliant and varied career has included teaching positions in the United States and Algiers, a stint as an ambulance driver and member of the liaison staff of the French Intelligence Corps in Algiers, for which she was made a Chevalier de la Legion d'Honneur in 1953. She holds membership in more than ten academic and writing associations, including the Writer's Guild and PEN, and received a National Book Award nomination for *Camus and Sartre: Crisis and Commitment* (1972). B. also served as the president of the Modern Language Association in 1975.
    As an author B. is noted mostly for her academic works in French literature. Although retired from her position as the Kenan Professor of Humanities at Wake Forest University, she has continued to make important contributions to this field. In 1983, she updated and revised her 1978 work, *Literature Française, 1920–1970*, published in English as

Twentieth Century French Literature. This "nimble, if promiscuous, study of literary history," as one critic called it, covers a vast amount of territory. B. is at her strongest when speaking of the writers she knows well, such as Jean-Paul Sartre and Marguerite Duras.

In 1990, at the age of eighty-three, B. published *Le Monde Fabuleux de J. M. G. Le Clézio,* a study of the French author and his works. Bettina Knapp commented: "Clarity and cogency, two of Germaine Brée's many remarkable characteristics as a critic, serve her well in her latest volume. . . . The novels . . . are all explored by Brée in her typically scrupulous manner, underscoring their thematic significance, artistic value, and fascination for young and old."

B. has edited more than fifteen additional books and is a frequent contributor of forewords and introductions to scholarly volumes. As a critic whose reviews and critical essays remain in demand, B. is in little danger of falling into obscurity. Her early contributions to the field, such as her works on Proust and Gide, are still considered among the most comprehensive and clearly written books on these much-discussed authors. Truly a grande dame of French literary study, B. has continued to provide the academic world with fresh work and to tackle new problems, for which the scholars in her field can be truly grateful.

BIBLIOGRAPHY: Knapp, Bettina, *"Le Monde Fabuleux de J. M. G. Le Clézio,"* *World Lit. Today* 65:4 (Autumn 1991). Reference works: *CA* 16 (1981).

Other references: *NYT* (31 July 1983; 9 Dec. 1984). *Virginia Q. Rev.* (Winter 1984).

LISI SCHOENBACH

Linda Brent. *See Harriet Jacobs*

E. M. Broner

See AWW 1, 239–40

As a novelist, playwright, and teacher, B. is concerned with establishing spiritual and artistic traditions for women. In the late 1970s and 1980s her interest in tradition led to explorations of women and Judaism. A feminist, she maintains that male authority in both the literary and the religious traditions has excluded women from positions of equality.

In 1980, B. and Cathy Davidson jointly edited *The Lost Tradition: Mothers and Daughters in Literature,* a large and diverse selection of essays by female scholars. In the introduction, the editors assert that the patriarchal tradition in literature has separated mothers from daughters. The essays discuss the depiction of women in literature from the ancient Near East and ancient Greece, the Old Testament, the Middle Ages, and the Renaissance through to the twentieth century.

In recent years B. has worked to reconcile her feminism with her religious faith. After her father's death in 1986, she participated in an Orthodox prayer ceremony to mourn his passing. She recounts her experience at the Orthodox synagogue in "Mornings and Mourning: A Kaddish Journal" (1989). Prohibited because of her gender from participating fully in the ceremony, B. resisted the sexist precepts of the Orthodox ritual, even as she became a part of the small group of men who participated in the Kaddish. With a straightforward style and a good deal of humor, the story chronicles her attempt to bring women into the religious community as full partners. B. treats the same experience in her play, *Half-a-Man* (1989), which was performed in both Los Angeles and Detroit. Two other plays, *Letters to My Television Past* (1985) and *The Olympics* (1986), have been performed in New York City.

B.'s interest in Judaism and feminism continues in her novel-in-progress, *The Repair Shop,* which features a female rabbi; she received support for her work on this novel from the National Endowment for the Arts (1987) and a MacDowell Fellowship (1989–90). *The Telling* (1993) charts the spiritual journey of a group of Jewish women, which includes B. herself, **Gloria Steinem,** Bella Abzug, and other prominent feminists.

It includes B.'s feminist Women's Haggadah, originally published in *Ms.* in 1977.

B. is an active teacher and lecturer as well as a writer. She is professor emeritus at Wayne State University, where she taught English and creative writing from 1964 to 1987. During the eighties she was a guest writer at Sarah Lawrence, Columbia, Ohio State, Tulane, and City College of New York. B. is a contributing editor of *Tikkun* and *Lilith*, and a regular book reviewer for *Women's Review of Books.*

OTHER WORKS: "Ghost Stories," *Tikkun* 5:6 (Nov./Dec. 1990). "Ghost Writing," *WRB* (Aug. 1991). *Her Mothers* (1975) and *A Weave of Women* (1978) both reissued (1985).

BIBLIOGRAPHY: Barkowski, Fran. *Feminist Utopias* (1989). *On Being a Jewish Feminist*, Susannah Heschel, ed. (1983). *Women in Search of Utopia*, Ruby Roreck and Elaine Hoffman-Baruch, eds. (1984). Reference works: *CA* 17–20 (1976). *CANR* 8 (1983), 25 (1989). *CLC* 19 (1981). *DLB* 28 (1984). *Contemp. Novelists* (1986). *FC* (1990).

Other references: *Dispatch* 7:1 (Fall 1988). *Kalliope: J. of Women's Art* 7:1–2 (1985). *MELUS* 9:3 (Winter 1982). *Studies in Amer. Jewish Lit.* 10:1 (Spring 1991).

MELISSA BURNS

Gwendolyn Brooks

See AWW *1, 241–43*

B.'s seventieth birthday in 1987 occasioned an outpouring of public affection and gestures of critical respect for this still-vital and productive poet. 1987 also saw the publication of *Blacks*, an anthology that collects B.'s writing of four decades. The volume's succinct title expresses a unity in B.'s canon to which critics, readers, and perhaps B. herself had been blind. Bearing the imprint of the David Company, founded by B., the volume testifies to her commitment to build alternative publishing institutions. Paradoxically, B.'s principled stance resulted in her work's being less accessible to the reading public at the moment when it might have been in greatest demand. Generated by the burgeoning interest in black women's writing, demand was enhanced by B.'s enormous success as a lecturer. Visiting scores of colleges and universities annually, she has brought to enthusiastic audiences her message that "poetry was life distilled."

Her later work has distilled the most urgent and fundamental issues of contemporary life. Whether in the struggle against apartheid in South Africa or racism in the United States, B. extracted for her poetry profiles of both heroic action and wary resistance. Among the public figures she has reimagined in verse are freedom fighter Winnie Mandela, poet Haki Madhubuti, social reformer Jane Addams, and child-abuse victim Elizabeth Steinberg. Sensitive as ever to the extraordinary dimensions of ordinary lives, B. has written poems narrating experiences of "the near-Johannesburg boy" fighting the "Fist-and-the-Fury" and of Lincoln West, the black American child who is liberated from self-hatred when he learns his African features make him the "real thing." Although she rued the decline of activism in the 1980s—in her coinage, "a giantless time"—she has continued to etch vivid portraits of those who "take today and jerk it out of joint."

In *Report from Part One* (1972) B. had promised not to imitate the voices of the young black poets of the sixties, but to extend and adapt her own voice. Determined to address a black audience that did not normally read poetry, she abandoned the sonnet and rhyme generally for free verse and sparer diction. The results were uneven, as B.'s repeated revision of several poems seemed to concede, and the output was slender. Yet the best work fused formal eloquence and colloquial speech into a poetic language that was inimitably "Brooksian."

The first monograph analyzing B.'s writing appeared in 1980; subsequently, in two critical biographies, a collection of essays, and numerous journal articles and chapters in books, critics and scholars began to give B.'s work its due. She was inducted into the National Women's Hall of Fame in 1988 and received a Lifetime Achievement Award from the National Endowment for the Arts in 1989.

Perhaps the critics' most striking discovery was that B.'s aesthetic had always been "black." Devoted from the start to representing the lives of the black urban poor, B. had drawn them as complex, spiritual, and contradictory human beings. Revisiting her early work, feminist critics noted that B. had pioneered in portraying multidimensional black female characters. Most important, her words almost always retain the capacity to surprise, delight, and instruct. B.'s is among the major voices in twentieth-century American poetry.

OTHER WORKS: *Primer for Blacks* (1980). *Young Poet's Primer* (1980). *To Disembark* (1981). *Mayor Harold Washington and Chicago, the I Will City* (1983). *Very Young Poets* (1983). *The Near-Johannesburg Boy* (1986). *Gottschalk and the Grande Tarantelle* (1988). *Winnie* (1988). "Keziah," *TriQuarterly* 75 (Spring/Summer 1989). *Children Coming Home* (1991).

BIBLIOGRAPHY: Kent, George. *A Life of Gwendolyn Brooks* (1990). *Say That the River Turns*, Haki Madhubuti, ed. (1987). Melhem, D. H., *Gwendolyn Brooks: Poetry and the Heroic Voice* (1987). Miller, R. Baxter, *Langston Hughes and Gwendolyn Brooks: A Reference Guide* (1978). *A Life Distilled: Gwendolyn Brooks, Her Poetry and Fiction*, Marie K. Mootry, and Gary Smith, eds. (1987). Shaw, Harry B., *Gwendolyn Brooks* (1980). Reference works: *Black Writers* (1991). *CANR* 27 (1989). *CLC* 15 (1980), 49 (1988). DLB 76 (1988). *FC* (1990). *Maj Tw Cent Writers* (1991). *Modern AmerWomen Writers* (1991).

CHERYL A. WALL

Olga Broumas

See AWW 1, 245–47

B's poems are voluptuous, exuberant, lyrical, rooted in history, and charged with political meaning. Poetry is for her both socially meaningful and a source of deep personal pleasure. Even when the poems concern pain and suffering, they take pleasure in their own sounds, shapes, and rhythms. Because of this play in language, there is more joy in B.'s poetic world than sorrow.

Born in Greece in 1949, B. lived briefly in the United States as a child, and returned in 1967 to attend college. She earned her B.A. in architecture from the University of Pennsylvania (1970) and an M.F.A. in creative writing from the University of Oregon (1973). She has won fellowships from the Guggenheim Foundation and the National Endowment for the Arts and has taught widely—at the University of Oregon, the University of Idaho, Goddard College, Boston University, and Brandeis University. In 1982, she helped found Freehand, a learning community of women artists and writers, in Provincetown, Massachusetts.

In "Demeter" B. honors her poetic maternity—**Anne Sexton, Sylvia Plath,** Virginia Woolf, and **Adrienne Rich**—but she has forged her own feminist, poetic idiom that is neither despairing nor homiletic. Rejecting the poetry of the crazy lady, the "Classic, almost Plathian stance that I'd been taught," she seeks instead to affirm women's power and health. In pursuit of the "adequate myth" to accomplish this affirmation, she reinscribes Greek myths in terms of ordinary women's lives in the opening sequence, "Twelve Aspects of God," of *Beginning with O* (1977) and reclaims *god* as a feminine principle.

B. is a bodywork therapist, and her aesthetic is intertwined with this work; the human body has a mythic, immediate presence in her poems. In "The Moon of Mind against the Wooden Louver" she writes to and honors a dying friend: "the pluck and humor of the song / your bones thrum while the blood still leaves / their broadside and their flank. / I kiss your bones." The female body is powerfully and vitally erotic. In *Caritas* she regrets the lack of language for female sexuality: "A woman-made language would / have as many synonyms for pink / light-filled / holy as / the Eskimo does / for snow." She seeks free and joyful language and imagery for lesbian love poems, in which the woman is both beloved and lover, giver and recipient.

B.'s approach to poetry is expansive and syncretic. Her formal considerations derive from architecture and music, as well as from literary sources: she conceives of stanzas as spatial forms, words on the page "as notation for the voice." Since *Beginning with O* she has published three volumes of poetry, *Soie Sauvage* (1979), *Pastoral Jazz* (1983), and *Perpetua* (1989), and collaborated with Jane Miller to produce a book of prose poems, *Black Holes, Black Stockings* (1985). She has also translated two books of Odysseas Elytis's poetry from the Greek and has been working on a translation of his essays, *Open Pages*. To create her art B. draws on the many parts of her life: her Greek and European background; her experiences as a woman; her feminist and liberation politics; her massage work. Her poems take daring leaps, almost greedily appropriating and juxtaposing disparate images, words, and experiences.

OTHER WORKS: Restlessness (in Greek, 1967). *Lyricism: Some Notes on Pleasure* (1978). *Namaste* (1978). *What I Love: Selected Poems of Odysseas Elytis, 1943–1978* (translation, 1986). *The Little Mariner,* poems by Odysseas Elytis (translation, 1988).

BIBLIOGRAPHY: Casto, Estella Kathryn, *Reading Feminist Poetry: A Study of the Work of Anne Sexton, Adrienne Rich, Audre Lorde, and Olga Broumas.* Unpublished diss., Ohio State Univ. (1990). Duncan, Erika, *Unless Soul Clap Its Hands: Portraits and Passages* (1984). Rose, Ellen Cronan, "Through the Looking Glass: When Women Tell Fairy Tales," *The Voyage In: Fictions of Female Development*, Elizabeth Abel et al., eds. (1983). Reference works: *CA* 85–88 (1980). *CANR* 20 (1987). *CLC* 10 (1979). *FC* (1990).

Other references: *Amer. Poetry Rev.* 8:1 (Jan.–Feb. 1979). *Northwest Rev.* 18:3 (1980). *Hudson Rev.* 36:2 (Summer 1980).

NORA MITCHELL

Rita Mae Brown

See AWW 1, 257–59

B. published nine works between 1979 and 1993, in addition to a number of screenplays. She has succeeded in reaching a wider, more mainstream audience than she had with *Rubyfruit Jungle* (1973), the autobiographical novel that made her America's best known "lesbian author." B. consciously and vociferously rejects this categorization, saying in a 1978 interview that "classifying fiction by race, sex, or sex preference of the author is a discreet form of censorship" that ghettoizes fiction and insults its authors. While moving towards a mainstream readership, however, her literary reputation has suffered.

B.'s loss of literary stature is largely the result of the publication of two flawed novels—*Sudden Death* (1983) and *Venus Envy* (1993)—and of a style of wit that many critics insist on reading as a lack of seriousness. Developments in the field of lesbian literature in the 1980s and 1990s also played a part. The emergence of a larger body of works emboldened lesbian and feminist reviewers to feel more comfortable delivering harsh criticism, yet this collection of works was still small enough to burden individual works with higher expectations. Further, mainstream reviewers remained more critical of work they perceived as noncanonical.

The most persistent criticism of B.'s oeuvre has been that she is over-present and obvious as a narrator and that she resolves crucial issues too simplistically or avoids resolution altogether. From Nickle Smith of *Six of One* (1978) and *Bingo* (1988), to Frazier Armstrong of *Venus Envy* (1993), B. is more likely to tell, or have her protagonists tell, who her characters are and what is going on than to let readers discover for themselves.

Although B.'s conclusions are sometimes rushed, critics often overstate the problem. In her review of *Southern Discomfort* (1983), a historical novel set in 1918 and 1928 Alabama, Charlotte Meyer makes a common complaint: "the private and social costs involved in" the affair between the aristocratic protagonist and a young black man "are not worked out . . . because Hercules is accidentally—and conveniently—killed." Yet this apparent solution complicates in some ways rather than simplifies. Hercules's death may save Hortensia from a public reckoning, but the circumstances of his death must bring a more painful personal reckoning. She has refused to run away with him to the North; the very social structure that gives her the power and position she is unable to relinquish for him is directly responsible for his death. A "whites only" ambulance refuses to take him to the hospital and leaves him bleeding to death on the ground. Tragedy here, as elsewhere in B.'s works, is relieved by comedy in most other sections of the novel; slapstick humor and witty dialogue abound.

B.'s strength is in her sense of humor and her ability as a storyteller. Her characters are vividly drawn and the situations she places them in usually outrageous and entertaining. With access to a wider audience than most so-called lesbian writers, B. tries to use her wit as a weapon, to present that audience with strong lesbian and gay characters, with issues of race, class and gender with which they may be uncomfortable. She also assails social conventions that she sees as being at odds with human nature, all in a generally humorous and therefore less threatening format. If the risk is that those issues then become easier to dismiss, and that critics will find B. herself easier to dismiss, it seems a risk that she is willing to take.

In addition to *Venus Envy*, B. has recently published two mystery novels, *Wish You Were Here* (1990) and *Rest in Pieces* (1992), "co-authored" with her cat, Sneakie Pie.

OTHER WORKS: Screenplays: *Slumber Party Massacre* (1982); *I Love Liberty* (co-author, 1982); *The Long Hot Summer, Part One* (1985) and *Part Two* (with Dennis Turner, 1985); *My Two Loves* (1986); *Rich Men, Single Women* (1989). *High Hearts* (1986). *Poems* (1987). *Starting from Scratch: A Different Kind of Writers' Manual* (1988).

BIBLIOGRAPHY: Ward, Carol M., *Rita Mae Brown* (1993). Reference works: *CANR* 35 (1992). *CLC* 43 (1987). *CBY* (1986). Other references: *Amer. Book Rev.* 5:10 (Jan./Feb. 1983, rev. by Charlotte Meyer). *Lambda Rising Book Report* (Dec. 1988/Jan. 1989). *NYTBR* (21 Mar. 1982; 19 June 1983; 20 Apr. 1986; 16 Dec. 1990). *PW* (2 Oct. 1978, interview). *Signs* (Summer 1984). Additional biog. information: d. of Ralph and Julia (Buckingham) Brown.

BETH GRIERSON

Rosellen Brown

B. 12 May 1939, Philadelphia, Pennsylvania
D. of Blossom (Lieberman) and David H. Brown; m. Marvin Hoffman, 1963; c.:
Elana; Adina

In "A Fragment of Autobiography," B. recounts her first memories of writing while her older brother was at school. It was during World War II and her memories include air raids, ration books, and "terrifying thunder." Even before she learned to write, B. practiced letters imagining a story to suit her mood. She also remembers early reading, and her grade-school librarian's policy of having children "sell" books they enjoyed to other classmates. Reading and writing focused much of her childhood, and B. has said that she felt, even as a child, the need to "replenish, just a little bit, the pool of words I'm drinking from, to give back a book or two."

Both her parents respected learning. Her mother, who mastered English in a few months after arriving from the Ukraine, became a teacher for other immigrants, and B. says that she was a "natural poet" even though she never wrote a word. Her father supplemented his eighth-grade education by voracious reading and writing. He sold many of his poems to New York newspapers and wrote articulate and sensible letters to the editor. His reading journals, B. says, were monuments to a writing talent he could not pursue while supporting his family.

Despite the seeming security in the family, B. felt keenly her rootless childhood, moving from town to town for her father's job. When she was nine, they moved to Los Angeles, where B. was frightened, lonely, and depressed. To compensate, she turned to writing. B. remembers herself as obnoxious in her self-advertisement, but she wrote and imagined, even at age nine and with no women's movement, that she could combine marriage and family with writing.

During her years at Barnard (B.A. 1960) B. wrote and worked with Robert Pack and George P. Elliot who encouraged her talent, and Pack obtained a place for her in the Cummington Writers' workshop. She published her first poem, a sestina, in *Poetry* magazine when she was a senior in college.

B.'s marriage in 1963 initiated a return to the rootless life she had known as a child. She and her husband lived first in California, then in Mississippi, the setting for *Civil Wars* (1984), and subsequently in Boston, in Brooklyn, the neighborhood of her book of short stories, *Street Games* (1974), in New Hampshire, and finally in Houston, where since 1982 she has taught creative writing at the University of Houston. Of her constant relocation, both as a child and as an adult, she comments that it has given the theme of exile to her writing. She says that exile "can be just as deep an obsession as devotion to (or aversion to) home": the theme is seen in almost all of her work—poetry, short stories, and novels.

B.'s first novel, *Autobiography of My Mother* (1976), pits two women against one another. The mother, Gerda Stein, is a successful civil rights lawyer; her daughter, Renata, has become a flower child and has a baby out of wedlock. The two women not only represent poles of the political spectrum, but they also show readers how far apart and how hurtful mothers and daughters can be to each other.

Tender Mercies (1978), the story of a young woman paralyzed in a boating accident caused by her husband, again rubs raw the nerve that connects people. The marriage of Dan Courser and Laura tests the strength of both and illustrates how people survive after they have committed monumental acts of carelessness.

Civil Wars (1984), perhaps B.'s most ambitious novel, combines political and personal themes and explores the public and private histories of a group of civil rights workers in Mississippi. Jessie and Teddy Carll are two 1960s liberals trying to survive and to keep their marriage together when the raison d'etre of their lives, The Movement, seems no longer to exist. The book is about families and about the politics that bring them together and drive them apart.

Before and After (1992) again makes use of a sixties liberal couple: Ben, who has dropped out, makes casseroles and does sculpture; Carolyn, his wife, practices medicine in a small New Hampshire town. Both are trying to live without losing the aura that the sixties brought to their lives. When their teenaged son Jacob murders his girlfriend, the family must begin the long journey to reconstitute itself with this enormous burden. Like *Tender Mercies*, *Before and After* tears people's lives apart and examines how the characters mend themselves.

In her two books of poetry, *Some Deaths in the Delta* (1970) and *Cora Fry* (1977), B. again combines public politics and private dreams. *Some Deaths* is a series of trenchantly critical poems about the new South, and the tone often foreshadows *Civil Wars*. *Cora Fry*, a series of narrative poems about marriage and family, reveals the ways in which personal relationships recapitulate larger social forces. Cora, wanting only freedom, runs away with her children, but returns to her marriage and the risk that her husband may well destroy them all.

B. also collaborated on the *Whole World Catalogue*, a compendium of creative writing ideas for elementary and secondary schools. Here, as in her fiction, she replenishes the pool of words.

OTHER WORKS: Men Portray Women, Women Portray Men (editor, 1978).

BIBLIOGRAPHY: LeClair, T., and L. McCaffery, *Interviews with Contemporary American Novelists* (1983). Porter, N., "Women's Interracial Friendships and Visions of Community in *Meridian, The Salt Eaters, Civil Wars,* and *Dessa Rose,*" in *Tradition and the Talents of Women,* F. Howe, ed. (1991). Seligman,

D., "Jewish Mothers' Stories: Rosellen Brown's *The Autobiography of My Mother*," in *Mother Puzzles*, M. Pearlman, ed. (1989). Reference books: *CA* 77–80 (1979). *CAAS* 10 (1989). *CANR* 14 (1985). *CLC* 32 (1985). *FC* (1990).

Other references: *American Imago* 45:2 (Summer 1988). *Chicago Rev.* 33:3 (Winter 1983, interview). *Contemporary Lit.* 27:2 (Summer 1986, interview). *So. Atl. Q.* 90:3 (Summer 1991).

MARY A. MCCAY

Octavia Estelle Butler

B. 22 June 1947, Pasadena, California
D. of Octavia Margaret and Laurice Butler

Hailed as the first African American woman science fiction writer, B. began writing at age twelve after "watching a bad science fiction movie and [deciding] I could write a better story than that." She admits, however, that she kept on writing science fiction because she needed "fantasies to shield her from the world." B. grew up in a strong matriarchal family with strict Baptist morals. Her mother and grandmother were the primary influences in her life; her father, a shoeshine man, died when she was an infant. B.'s mother, who has worked as a maid, was born on a sugar plantation in Louisiana. At age ten, she was taken out of school so that she could work. It was perhaps this hard family life and history that made B.'s family worry that a writing career would not be reliable employment for her. One of her aunts, the first in the family to earn a college degree, agreed, but encouraged her niece to do what she wanted.

After earning an associates degree at Pasadena City College in 1968, B. went on to California State College (CSC) at Los Angeles. She left CSC when she could not major in creative writing and began taking evening writing classes at UCLA. While at CSC, B. met Harlan Ellison, a prominent science fiction writer, who encouraged her to attend the summer 1970 Clarion Science Fiction Writer's Workshop. Her first two stories were written during this intensive Pennsylvania workshop. In 1980, B. won the YWCA Achievement Award for Creative Arts; in 1984, at the 42nd World Science Fiction Convention, fans voted her the winner of the Hugo Award for Best Short Story; and in 1985, at the 43rd World Science Fiction Convention, B.'s peers, other science fiction writers, voted her the winner of the Nebula Award for Best Novelette.

B.'s first five novels are part of her Patternist saga, based on imposing generations of Patternists, the telepathic humans who wrestle for control of the earth. Her novel *Kindred* (1979), though set apart from the serial stories, continues the Patternist tradition of independent women of color who challenge the power structures of their societies and are embroiled in intense social relationships, and for whom self-expression and leadership roles are vital. B. probes female experiences in terms of women's survival, sexual objectification, threats to their autonomy, and full expression of their psychic and healing talents, as well as their strong, abiding kinship ties. Her female characters represent a dazzling array of experience and origins—both futuristic and historically grounded. Anyanwu of *Wild Seed* (1980) is a three-hundred-year-old woman that B. fashioned after a mythological Onitsha Ibo woman named Atagbusi; Mary of *Mind of My Mind* (1977), a twentieth-century woman and descendant of Anyanwu, is a gifted telepath who has survived physical abuse and become the mother of a new race of beings. Both Alanna, the Afro-Asian heroine of *Survivor* (1978), and Lilith, the matriarch of a small dislocated group of humans, forge bonds between different ethnic groups and species within their futuristic societies. Dana, the modern African American heroine of *Kindred*, is repeatedly dragged back into her family's slavery past and becomes an elusive, but nevertheless affected accomplice, victim, and link between her enslaved and free ancestors and her own, less-peopled, postslavery American future.

One of the signs that B. has posted above her desk reminds her that "tension and conflict can be achieved through uncompromising characters in a death struggle." Indeed, the societies and communities of B.'s fiction are inundated by a host of unpredictable, unrelenting individuals. The human, mutant, or hybrid life forms in B.'s works are often engaged in violent struggles for power and mental freedom. B.'s central female characters are not always protectors or mediators in these intense, high-stake struggles; women such as Mary in *Mind of My Mind* rely heavily on their warlike, competitive natures to reach positions of formidable power. Yet, in places so diverse as the Patternist domains and the floating Oankali nations of *Dawn* (1987), *Adulthood Rights* (1988), and *Imago* (1989),

B. also suggests that there are nurturing environments that can be culled from besieged nations and embattled histories.

B. capitalizes on the science fiction genre most dynamically in her representations of history as a layered entity—one that can be traversed, reentered, and never separated. *Kindred* and the works that form B.'s Xenogenesis trilogy, *Dawn*, *Adulthood Rites*, and *Imago*, are especially gripping because of the ways in which B. constructs versions of historical reality. Of B.'s central characters, the women are especially imposing figures whose identities as women, consorts, and child bearers are under siege by the social, racial, or genetic chaos of their communities. For the individuals—remnants of nations, and newly forming societies—drawn into such timeless and time-laden environments, tortured contemplation and mourning are inevitable. Yet, the historical burdens and traditions of which they are so conscious also propel them to achieve increasingly symbolic victories against their oppressors. In her treatment and revisions of history, and her consistent development of evolving multiracial women, B. puts a most distinctive mark upon the science fiction genre. She grounds her work in African American history and complements her fictional plots with realistic debates on such contemporary issues as race, bigotry, sexism, and expansionism.

The ways in which B.'s characters have to resolve their "otherness" with their essential membership within groups may be seen as a telling metaphor for her own place within the realm of science fiction. B. and writer Samuel Delany are the only well-known African American science fiction writers and B. is perhaps the only African American woman science fiction writer. Although she believes that science fiction is "potentially the freest genre in existence," she acknowledges the confines and preferred foci that have been encouraged for writers of the genre. Describing science fiction as having begun "in this country as a genre for young boys," she argues that it is this fact that explains the traditional exclusion of issues of race or sex from science fiction texts of the past. B. uses powerful historical fact, African American experience, and facets of the science fiction genre itself to challenge these narrow parameters. Her compelling stories masterfully blend traditional aspects of the genre and innovative futuristic designs with sobering contemplations of the realities of the world's racial and historical present and past.

OTHER WORKS: Patternmaster (1976). *Clay's Ark* (1984). *The Evening and the Morning and the Night* (1991). *Parable of the Sower* (1993).

BIBLIOGRAPHY: Reference works: *Black Writers* (1989). *CANR* 24 (1988). *CLC* 38 (1986). *DLB* 33 (1984). *FC* (1990). *Maj Twent Cent Writers* (1991). *NBAW* (1992). *Tw Cent Sci Fi Writers* (1991).

Other references: *Black Amer. Lit. Forum* 18 (Summer 1984). *Black Scholar* 17:2 (March–April 1986). *Callaloo* 14:2 (1991). *Equal Opportunity Forum Mag.* 8 (1980). *Essence* 9 (April 1979). *Extrapolation* 23 (Spring 1982). *MELUS* 13:1–2 (Spring–Summer 1986). *Salaga* (1981). *Sanus* 4 (Winter 1978–79). *Thrust: SF in Review* (Summer 1979).

LOIS BROWN

Toni Cade. *See Toni Cade Bambara*

Hortense Calisher

See AWW *1, 185–87*

In her work in the 1980s C. expanded the range of her fictional forms and subjects. *Mysteries of Motion* (1983) imagines the first civilian space travel. In what C. claims is the first novel of "character" rather than science fiction set in space, six lives are revealed on a space journey. In 1985 she published five short works under the title *Saratoga, Hot,* including "Gargantua Real Impudence," "The Library," "The Sound Track," "The Passenger," "The Tenth Child," "Survival Techniques," and the title story.

The strict roles assigned both sexes and the complexities of gender and sexuality are recurrent themes in C.'s work, as are loneliness and individuality. *The Bobby Soxer* (1986) takes these themes to the limit, narrating, through the eyes of a teenage girl, her discovery that Aunt Leo, a maiden aunt, had male and female organs. Although Leona is the pivotal character, she has little to do with the story that unfolds; that of the girl, her town, her extended family, her genteel Southern mother, her father, and his business ventures. The book won the Kafka Prize in 1987.

An aging couple, Gemma and Rupert, agree (*Age,* 1987) that each should keep a diary for the other to read after the partner's death. Their awareness that they are facing the end of life is reinforced through the suicide of two friends and the death of Rupert's first wife. They abandon the diaries when they realize one will have to read alone.

The deepening sense of loss that comes with advancing age continues as a theme in *Kissing Cousins* (1988), a memoir in which C. pays tribute to both her Southern and Northern heritages, as she has done in other novels, and to the value of memory. Nurse Katie Pyle is a relative only through the connection of their Southern families and their Southern Jewish heritage; she and C. remain emotionally close throughout lives. The independent Pyle went to war as an army nurse and later continued a nursing career. As they reminisce, Southern expressions color New York memories and the extended family appears loving and eccentric. Pyle dies, C. has her memories.

C.'s work is sorrowful, rich in language, loving in tone. Her language is powerful, her dialogue accurate, her memories vivid. The people in her stories are not terrible, eccentric, or bizarre, but believable in their faults and virtues.

From 1986–87 C. was president of PEN; she was president of the American Academy of Arts and Letters from 1987 to 1990.

OTHER WORKS: *In the Palace of the Movie King* (1993).

BIBLIOGRAPHY: Reference works: *CANR* 22 (1986). *Contemp. Novelists* (1986). *FC* (1990).
Other references: *NYT* (18 Dec. 1988). *NYTBR* (6 Nov. 1983; 20 May 1984; 30 March 1986). *Saturday Rev.* (interview, July/August 1985). *Southwest Rev.* 71 (Spring 1986). *Texas Studies in Lit.* 31 (Winter 1989).

JANET M. BEYER

Ana Castillo

B. 15 June 1953, Chicago, Illinois
D. of Raquel (Rocha) and Ramón (Ray) Castillo; c.: Marcel Herrera

C. grew up in Chicago, where she received a B.A. from Northwestern University (1975) and an M.A. from the University of Chicago. In 1991 she completed a Ph.D. in American Studies at the University of Bremen, Germany. The voices that populate C.'s texts speak from a multiplicity of positions that at times complement and at times contradict one another. Their subjectivity is a weave of differences, complex and potentially transformative.

The epistolary novel *The Mixquiahuala Letters* (1988) explores the geographic and psychic borderlands between the United States and Mexico as internalized by Chicanas. It also maps the borderlands between women and women and women and men. Much of the bonding, both positive and negative, between Teresa and Alicia is established through their relationships with men, while they struggle with the differences between them. Teresa begins Letter 13, "Alicia, why i hated white women and sometimes didn't like you," and ends balancing Alicia's class- and skin-privilege against her inferior physical attractiveness. While Teresa feels betrayed by Alicia's ignorance of Mexican culture, she in turn hides from Alicia her perception that men are more attracted to her because she has internalized femininity as submissive.

The text's structure insists on polyvalence, presenting four possible combinations of the letters. As published, the ending foregrounds the bonding between the two women through failed relationships with men. The other endings represent the triumph of maternal and cultural dictates, the confirmation of women's betrayal of women, and the quixotic preparations for yet another trip to Mexico.

C.'s second novel *Sapogonia* (1990) positions women readers not to identify with the male subject Maximo, yet Pastora's contradictory subjectivity is both revealed and concealed by the narrative. Maximo's subjectivity is constructed in opposition to woman as inaccessible enigma and *vagina dentata*. He both desires the primordial unity he projects onto Pastora, and is terrified of being absorbed by her. Although various alternative narratives are available to her, Pastora is complicit in her own objectification as enigma and object of desire. Her opacity also functions as a shield from intimacy; she is both contemptuously independent of men and dependent on them. *Sapogonia* explores male fantasy, its potential violence to women and the female subject's struggle to interpret herself both within and outside of this discourse on femininity.

My Father Was a Toltec (1988), monolingual poems in English and Spanish, explores a subjectivity of marginalization: what it means to be poor, to be hated because of skin color and culture, to be the daughter of a Mexican woman and a Mexican man. The first section, "The Toltec," focuses on what was received and rejected from father and mother; "La Heredera" on the ways heterosexual relationships have been culturally defined; "Ixtacihuatl Died in Vain" presents female bonding as a nonutopian possibility.

The last section privileges the collective struggle against domination. "A Christmas Gift . . ." exposes literary authority as male, white, and privileged: "so these are not poems, i readily admit, / as i grapple with non-existence, / making scratches with stolen pen." The book ends with "In My Country," a utopian vision of a world that has put an end to multiple oppressions: "In my world the poet sang loud / and clear and everyone heard / without recoiling. It was sweet / as harvest, sharp as tin, strong / as the western wind, and all had / a coat warm enough to bear it."

Chicana writers question the authority of dominant discourses that "forget" race and class oppression. C.'s struggle to claim the "I" of literary discourse is inseparable from her struggle for empowerment in the economic, social, and political spheres.

OTHER WORKS: *The Invitation* (1979). *Women Are Not Roses* (1984). *Esta puente, mi espalda. Voces de mujeres tercermundistas en los Estados Unidos* (coeditor, 1988). *Third Woman 4: The Sexuality of Latinas* (coeditor, 1989). *So Far from God* (1993).

BIBLIOGRAPHY: Alarcón, Norma, "Ana Castillo's *The Mixquiahuala Letters:* The Sardonic Powers of the Erotic," in *Breaking Boundaries. Latina Writing and Critical Readings*, Asunción Horno-Delgado et al, eds. (1989). Yarbro-Bejarano, Yvonne, "The Multiple Subject in the Writing of Ana Castillo," *Critical Approaches to Hispanic Women's Literature*, Norma Alarcón, ed. (forthcoming). Reference works: *CA* (1991). *Hispanic Writers* (1990). *WW Hispanic Americans* (1991, 1992).

Other references: *Americas Rev.* 20:1 (1992). *Discurso Literario: Revista de Estudios Iberoamericanos* 7:1 (1990).

YVONNE YARBRO-BEJARANO

Lorna Dee Cervantes

B. 6 Aug. 1954, San Francisco, California

C. was born in the Mission District of San Francisco. She traces her ancestry to the Chumash Indians of the Santa Barbara coast on her mother's side, and to the Tarascan Indians of Michoacán, Mexico, on her father's. After her parents separated when she was five years old, her mother resettled with C.'s grandmother in San Jose, California. C. has written poetry since she was eight, her love of language fed by the books that she found in the houses her mother cleaned. In 1974 she founded Mango Publications, editing *Mango*, a literary review, and also publishing poetry chapbooks. In 1978 she received a National Endowment for the Arts grant, and subsequently spent nine months at the Fine Arts Work Center in Provincetown. After completing her B.A. at California State University, San Jose, C. studied in the Ph.D. program in the History of Consciousness at the University of California, Santa Cruz. She joined the Creative Writing Department of the University of Colorado at Boulder in 1989; she also coedits the cross-cultural poetry magazine *Red Dirt*.

The title of C.'s first book of poetry, *Emplumada* (1981), combines connotations of "feathered" (*emplumado/a*) and "flourish with the pen" (*plumada*); bird imagery abounds, resonant in both Mexican and United States cultures. The poems of this collection explore what it means to be connected to nature and to the urban wasteland, to be female and brown, in a voice remarkable for its clarity, depth of passion, and striking imagery. In "Visions of Mexico while at a Writing Symposium in Port Townsend, Washington," the poetic voice expresses the urgent need to speak for those who have been silenced, to rewrite history from the point of view of the oppressed, and to challenge racist stereotypes of Mexican and Chicano people: "I come from a long line of eloquent illiterates / whose history reveals what words don't say. / Our anger is our way of speaking, / the gesture is an utterance more pure than word." Other poems explore the multiple facets of Chicana identity, for example the clash between her mirror image ("bronzed skin, black hair") and the loss of the mother tongue ("My name hangs about me like a loose tooth"). In the process of self-naming, the poetic voice juxtaposes her experience with that of other Chicanas. In "To Virginia Chavez" class differences are momentarily balanced by gender solidarity: "ignoring what / the years had brought between us: / my diploma and the bare bulb / that always lit your bookless room." In "Beneath the Shadow of the Freeway" the granddaughter prefers her grandmother's ways to her mother's hard pragmatism: "I tie up my hair into loose braids, / and trust only what I have built / with my own hands."

After a prolonged period of introspection following a family tragedy in 1982, C. began producing the poems that form her second collection, *From the Cables of Genocide* (1991). The subtitle cues the book's thematic concerns: *Poems of Love and Hunger.* In some ways very like her first collection thematically, *Cables* is at the same time more personal and less readily accessible. "Pleiades from the Cables of Genocide" exemplifies the poems' layered fusion of the personal and the political, referring simultaneously to the heritage of the Chumash, who believed they descended from the Pleiades, and to the "Seven Sisters" constituted by the seven major oil companies: "The power / peace / Of worthless sky that unfolds me—now—in its greedy / Reading: Weeder of Wreckage, Historian of the Native / Who says: *It happened. That's all. It just happened. /* And runs on."

BIBLIOGRAPHY: Sanchez, Martha E., "The Chicana as Scribe: Harmonizing Gender and Culture in Lorna Dee Cervantes' 'Beneath the Shadow of the Freeway,'" *Contemporary Chicana Poetry* (1985). Reference books: *CA* 131 (1991). *DLB* 82 (1990).

Other references: *Tecolote* 3 (Dec. 1982). *MELUS* 11 (Summer 1984).

YVONNE YARBRO-BEJARANO

Lee Chapman. *See Marion Zimmer Bradley*

Kim Chernin

B. 7 May 1940, The Bronx, New York
D. of Rose (Chernin) and Paul Kusnitz; m. David Netboy, 1958, div.; m. Robert
Cantor, 1971, div; c.: Larissa Nicole, b. 1963

C., daughter of Russian-Jewish immigrants, spent the first five years of her life in New York City, moving with her father (an engineer) and her mother (a radical organizer) to Los Angeles after an older sister died. Her early life was profoundly influenced by the loss of her sister, her mother's political activism, and the jailings and trials of the McCarthy years. C.'s writings reflect this heritage, joining the poetic intuition of the child's memory to a political voice, and presenting a mother/daughter conflict embedded in the modern woman's search for self and the immigrant's search for home. While a student at the University of California at Berkeley, she met and married David Netboy. They traveled to England and Ireland where C. studied at Oxford and at Trinity College in Dublin. Returning to the United States, she received her B.A. from the University of California in 1965 and an M.A. in psychology from New College of California in 1990.

C.'s dual career as writer and therapist and the tension of her political and poetic sensibilities are evident in her publications, which include poetry, fiction, fictional autobiography, and meditative studies on women's psychological issues. Work as a consultant on writing projects and on women's eating disorders led her to focus initially on a series of books about contemporary problems of female development: *The Obsession: Reflections on the Tyranny of Slenderness* (1981), *The Hungry Self: Women, Eating, and Identity* (1985), and *Reinventing Eve: Modern Woman in Search of Herself* (1987). In this trio of autobiographically framed works, C. addresses first the middle-class ideal of slenderness as a problem with women's power, and then the mother/daughter bonds and patriarchal culture as influences on female development. Through these books she evolves a visionary yet theorizing form to describe the essential psychological challenge, coming in *Reinventing Eve*, with its formulation of modern woman as the "Woman Who Is Not Yet," to insist that theory be developed out of experience, particularly of the body. Her thesis leads her to challenge traditional psychoanalytic interpretation with the voices of the women who have come to her for consultation, and to confront Judeo-Christian mythologies with the narrative of her own identity crisis, attempting to find the form that will successfully realize the female self and unite its conflicting voices.

C. both uses and revises traditional psychology in her volume of poetry, *The Hunger Song* (1982), presenting childhood memory as a tool for the reimagination and recovery of a female goddess. C.'s use of story to present psychological ideas is pronounced in her fiction and fictionalized autobiographies, which develop the themes of ethnic identity and modern intergenerational conflict. *In My Mother's House* (1983) begins when Rose Chernin asks her to write about her Communist party activities. C. uses this request to make a point about identity and interconnection, as she weaves a narrative that is as much a story of mother-daughter encounters as a transcription of the tales she and her mother tell. Different voices allow the author both to reclaim her heritage, beginning with life in the Russian shtetl, and proclaim her difference from it. Furthermore, as the two women's stories of themselves as daughters and mothers come into counterpoint, the presumed narrative of Rose Chernin's life becomes C.'s own tale, the story of four generations of immigrant Jewish women and their intimate connection.

The Flame-Bearers (1986) and *Sex and Other Sacred Games* (1989) also reflect the themes of C.'s psychological writings. *The Flame-Bearers* tells the story of Rae (Israel) Shadmi, the rebellious inheritor of leadership in a mystical Jewish women's sect. Once again exploring the relationships between several generations of Russian-Jewish immigrant women, and tracing their heritage back to the Old World, C. both claims for her heroine the wisdom of a matriarchal spiritual tradition and identifies the reasons why this tradition must be reformulated. *Sex and Other Sacred Games* connects this spiritual drama directly to the social world. C. and coauthor Renate Stendahl tell a story of relationship by tracing conversations on women's sexuality. Using two voices, plus written letters and journals, to reinvent the Platonic dialogue on eros and beauty, they participate in a project that both utilizes tradition and creates a new and uniquely feminine narrative.

One very powerful contribution to C.'s work is its demonstration of the way women's narratives are reinventing form and in so doing are beginning to integrate the conflicting voice of personal and political, psychological, and literary consciousness. *The Border: A Memoir* (1993), set in an Israeli kibbutz on the Lebanese border and dealing with cultural conflict, and a work in progress on her own experience of psychoanalysis in which the psychological and literary traditions of narrative come together, continue this significant project.

BIBLIOGRAPHY: Reference works: *CA* 107 (1983).

Other references: *Feminist Studies* 17 (Spring 1991). *PW* 228:1 (5 July 1985, interview). *WRB* 7:6 (March 1990). *Women's Studies* 14:1 (1987). Telephone interview with Chernin (18 May 1992).

KAREN E. WALDRON

Phyllis Chesler

See AWW 1, 348–50

Author of five books and coauthor of a sixth, C. is a politically active feminist, psychotherapist, editor, and psychology professor whose theories have had a large impact on modern-day feminist thought. Her first book, *Women and Madness* (1972), suggests that women, in a male-defined society, may be seen as insane simply because they are not like men. *Women, Money, and Power* (1976), cowritten with Emily Jane Goodman, is an exploration of women's economic powerlessness. C.'s third book, *About Men* (1978), consists of her reflections on the male experience.

In 1977 C. became pregnant with her first child, son Ariel. *With Child: A Diary of Motherhood* (1979) is a journal of her experiences during pregnancy, childbirth, and her first year as a mother. In this work, punctuated with insights as well as unresolved questions, C. gives voice to rarely expressed ambivalences of motherhood, the intensity with which a mother both loves and hates her child.

This book marks a turn in C.'s career, and the beginning of a series of books concerned with mothering. While *With Child* explores the personal aspects of mothering, her next two works examine the legal side of motherhood. In *Mothers on Trial: The Battle for Children and Custody* (1986), C. exposes gender biases in the child-custody decision process. Refuting the popular belief that mothers are given preference in custody cases, C. shows that in the contested custody cases she studied, fathers were awarded custody more often than were mothers, even when the father was abusive.

C.'s concerns and arguments about motherhood and custody were crystallized in a single case. *Sacred Bond: The Legacy of Baby M.* (1988) discusses the Baby M. surrogate-mother case of the 1980s as it reflected wider societal patterns of paternal rights and maternal obligations, the abuse of women by the legal system, and of women and children through the practice of adoption. C. also describes her own involvement in the case, which extended beyond the role of author to that of supporter and advocate for the biological mother, Mary Beth Whitehead.

C. is a provocative and controversial writer whose work has been both hailed and dismissed by critics. Reviewers have criticized her books as messy, biased, and inconclusive, while others have found the same books to be groundbreaking, courageous, and convincing.

BIBLIOGRAPHY: J. of Marriage and the Family 42 (Aug. 1980). *NYTBR* (5 Jan. 1986; 26 June 1988). *Psychology Today* 20:72 (Feb. 1986). *PW* (13 May 1988).

EILEEN M. ANDERSON

Julia Child

B. 15 Aug. 1912, Pasadena, California
D. of Carolyn (Weston) and John McWilliams; m. Paul Child, 1946

Author and television's French Chef, C. coauthored the influential and best-selling *Mastering the Art of French Cooking*, volumes 1 and 2 in 1961 and 1970 respectively. She thereby translated French culinary techniques into an American idiom and established the standards for authoritative culinary writing in what has become known as America's gastronomical coming of age.

Enrolled in Smith College by her mother when she was born, C. majored in history (B.A., 1934). Although she aspired to become either a basketball star or a novelist, she accepted a copywriting position at the W. & J. Sloane department store and lived in New York for three years before returning to the leisurely life of Pasadena and its Junior League in 1937. When World War II began, C. went to Washington to work as a typist in a government information agency. After six months, she joined the Office of Strategic Services (O.S.S.), opted for duty in the Far East, and was in charge of document centers in Ceylon and later in China.

While in Ceylon, she met Paul Child, a former painter and language teacher, who designed war rooms for the O.S.S. in the Far East. After the war they married and lived in Washington, DC, until her husband was assigned to the American Embassy in Paris in 1948 as the exhibits officer for the U.S. Information Agency.

During the next four years in Paris, C. took French lessons at Berlitz, studied with Max Bugnard, Claude Thillmont, and Pierre Mangelette at the Cordon Bleu, and at the suggestion of Simone Beck became a member of an exclusive society of women known as Le Cercle des Gourmettes. "From the beginning, I fell in love with everything I saw," C. said. Her life was irrevocably changed by the experience of living in France.

C.'s culinary career began when a group of American friends asked her to give cooking lessons in her Left Bank apartment. Assisted by Simone Beck, Louise Bertholle, and chefs from the Cordon Bleu, the classes developed into L'Ecole des Trois Gourmandes. When C.'s husband was reassigned to the American embassies in Marseille, Bonn, and

Oslo, classes were taught whenever and wherever they could be arranged. The school was so successful that the two Frenchwomen invited C. to collaborate in the writing of a cookbook adapting French culinary techniques to American ingredients and kitchens. Eight years in preparation, the first volume of *Mastering the Art of French Cooking* was published by Knopf in 1961, one year after C.'s husband had retired and the Childs were established in their home in Cambridge, Massachusetts.

The book was hailed by the *New York Times* as "the finest volume on French cooking ever published in English," and widely praised by the culinary establishment. Invited to appear on a book-review program at WGBH, Boston's educational television station, C. demonstrated beating egg whites with a balloon whisk as she talked about her book. Letters requesting more of the same led to "The French Chef" series that premiered on 11 Feb. 1963. More than two-hundred shows were added to the original series of twenty-six black-and-white programs during the next nine years. C. had invented the theater of cooking; "Julia" had become a household name.

After the publication of *The French Chef Cookbook* in 1968, three subsequent television series were the basis for *From Julia Child's Kitchen* (1975), *Julia Child and Company* (1978), and *Julia Child and More Company* (1979). Recipes and techniques from four years of monthly *Parade* magazine articles, six one-hour videocassettes called *The Way to Cook*, segments from the television program "Good Morning America," and the "Dinner at Julia's" television series contributed to the comprehensive cookbook *The Way to Cook* (1989). Over more than forty years C. has developed the techniques to master fine cooking and fulfilled the joint possibilities of television and culinary instruction.

Recognition as a television celebrity tends to deflect attention from C.'s writing. Her seven books, however, force their readers to reexamine the canon, to look at culinary writing as a genre with its own potential for excellence. She has insisted that each book be a "teaching" book rather than a collection of recipes. In the later books, however, her Olympian tone about utensils has given way to an informal and personalized discussion of options.

C.'s favorite book is *From Julia Child's Kitchen*. "It is entirely my own, written the way I wanted to do it." Indeed, the book resonates with the truest authorial voice and tells the most compelling stories of all of her books. The reader comes to know the narrator intimately, her voice inspires confidence, and every recipe becomes the beginning of a plot in whose denouement the reader participates.

The book that represents the culmination of C.'s career, however, is *The Way to Cook*. She breaks with conventional organization by structuring the chapters around master recipes, provides over six hundred colored photographs to illustrate the methods employed, and blends classic techniques with freestyle American cooking. The award-winning book is her magnum opus, and the distinction it has achieved ranks with the Peabody (1965) and Emmy (1966) Awards and the Careme Medal (1974) that have also celebrated her culinary career.

OTHER WORKS: Julia Child's Menu Cookbook (rept., 1991). *Cooking at Home with the Master Chefs* (1993).

Julia Child's papers (professional and personal correspondence, scripts and proofs, fan letters, research notes, and various newspaper and magazine articles) are at the Schlesinger Library, Radcliffe College, Cambridge, Massachusetts.

BIBLIOGRAPHY: Chase, Chris, *The Great American Waistline* (1981). Fussell, Betty, *Masters of American Cookery* (1983). Tomkins, Calvin, "Profiles: Good Cooking," *New Yorker* (23 Dec. 1974). Over two hundred magazine and newspaper articles from 1963 to 1991. Reference works: *CA* 41–44 (1979). *CB* (1967). *WWAW* (1974–75). *One Hundred Greatest Women, No. 1. Who's Who in Television and Cable. The Women's Book of World Records and Achievements* (1983).

JOAN REARDON

Alice Childress

B. 12 Oct. 1920, Charleston, South Carolina
Granddaughter of Eliza Campbell; m. (second) Nathan Woodard, 1957; c.: Jean

C. moved north to Harlem at the age of five to be raised by her dynamic grandmother, Eliza Campbell. She deems her grandmother's influence immeasurable for exposing her at an early age to New York's cultural and artistic offerings. Under her tutelage and with only two years of high school education, C. struck out on her own to become an actress. By 1941 she had joined the American Negro Theatre in Harlem and was on her way to becoming not only an accomplished actress but in time a playwright, screenwriter, novelist, director, and a crusader for striving artists. C. was married briefly in the 1940s and had one daughter. While struggling to support herself and her daughter on an actress's wages, she also worked as a domestic and in other low-paying jobs. Her experiences during this period shaped her career-long interest in portraying working-class African American women caught in oppressive situations yet maintaining their dignity. A 1956 book, *Like One of the Family: Conversations from a Domestic's Life*, selects from her newspaper column "Here's Mildred," which appeared in the *Baltimore Afro-American* and *Freedom*. C. successfully used satire to underscore the realities of the black domestic worker's life.

Although C. has written plays, novels, young adult fiction, television scripts, and a screenplay, she is best known as a dramatist. Her first play, *Florence* (1949), draws on her early acting years. Like most of her subsequent plays, it revolves around black female protagonists who are battling against a contradictory and often racist environment. (The play is set at a segregated train station). In a 1967 essay C. describes her characteristic and memorable heroines as "created and constructed on what hurts and what heals, slowly built and put in order out of the conflict which comes from the daily search for bread, love, and a place in the sun." Consistently, C.'s black women characters possess a depth and sensitivity that had not been granted to black subjects in American theater.

C.'s second play, *Just a Little Simple* (1950), was based on stories by Langston Hughes. *Gold through Trees* (1952) was the first play by an African American woman to have a professional production. C.'s 1955 play, *Trouble in Mind*, ran for ninety-one performances and won an Obie Award, the first presented to a woman playwright. The play also draws on C.'s acting career, showing black actors resisting stereotypical portrayals of black characters.

In the 1960s, C. challenged convention with *Wedding Band: A Love/Hate Story in Black and White*, focusing on an interracial relationship between a black man and a white woman in South Carolina in 1918. Initial attempts to mount a production met with resistance; the first production took place at the University of Michigan in 1966. The play was adapted for television in 1973. Her comedy-drama, *Wine in the Wilderness* (1969), contradicts image and role stereotypes of black women. It also appeared on television as part of a series, "On Being Black."

Aware of the tradition of African American drama that had long produced plays in schools, churches, and in community centers across the country, C. has sought to bring this tradition to the forefront of the American theater. In addition to her work as a playwright, she has also been an active supporter of her fellow artists. During the 1950s, her crusades in the Dramatists Guild led to union contracts for black performers and stagehands.

Since the 1970s C. has written and produced works specifically for young adults. Her most popular children's novel, *A Hero Ain't Nothin' but a Sandwich* (1973), propelled C. into the role of screenwriter for the 1977 film featuring Cicely Tyson and Paul Winfield. C.'s later works include two other novels for young adults, *Rainbow Jordan* (1981) and *Those Other People* (1989).

With her husband, composer Nathan Woodward, C. has written two plays focusing on the Gullah-speaking people who live off the coast of South Carolina and Georgia, *Sea Island Song* (produced 1979) and *Gullah* (produced 1984). *Moms*, based on the life of blues singer and humorist Moms Mabley, appeared in 1986. C. has received various acknowledgments of her contributions to American theater. In 1965 she appeared with James Baldwin, Leroi Jones (Imiri Baraka), and Langston Hughes on a British Broadcasting Corporation panel discussion on "The Negro in the American Theatre." She received a Rockefeller Foundation fellowship in 1967 and from 1966–68 was a fellow at the Radcliffe (College) Institute for Independent Study.

OTHER WORKS: *String* (1969). *The Freedom Drum* (1970). *Mojo: A Black Love Story* (1970). *Mojo and String: Two Plays* (1971). *Black Scenes* (editor, 1973). "For a Negro Theater," *Masses and Mainstream* (1951). "The Negro Woman in American Literature," *Freedomways* 6:1 (Winter 1966).

BIBLIOGRAPHY: Keyssar, Helene, *Feminist Theater* (1984). Reference works: *Black American Writers Past and Present* (1975). *Black American Playwrights* (1976). *Black Playwrights* (1978). *Black Writers* (1989). *CA* 45–48 (1974). *CANR* 3 (1981), 27 (1989). *CLC* 12 (1980), 15 (1980). *FC* (1990). *Maj Twent Cent Writers* (1991). *More Black Playwrights* (1978). *Notable Women in Amer. Theater* (1989). *SATA* 7 (1975).
Other references: *Sage* 4:1 (Spring 1987).

CAROL ALLEN

Carolyn Chute

B. *14 June 1947, Portland, Maine*
D. *of Annie Prindall and Joseph R. Penny; m. James Hawkes, 1963, div. 1971;*
   m. Michael Chute, 1978; c.: Joannah; Reuben (died in infancy)

The oldest of three children, C. grew up in a military housing develop-ment in Cape Elizabeth, Maine. At sixteen, she married a factory worker, James Hawkes, who was as disenchanted with school as she. Divorced at twenty-four, C. picked potatoes, scrubbed floors, cleaned chickens, and did low-paying jobs to supplement the meager child support that Hawkes could provide for their daughter Joannah. In 1978 C. married a some-times-employed woodsman eight years her junior, Michael Chute—a man slow with words because of illiteracy and a mild speech impediment. Though C. completed high school by evening classes and took several courses at the University of Southern Maine, she is a slow reader and probably had read no more than thirty books by the time her first novel was published.

Her two novels and her stories are authentic, powerful regional fiction about what it means to be poor in backwoods Maine. Some critics have denounced the novels for wallowing in deprivation, while others com-mend C.'s humor, sensitivity, and compassion for those who do not take part in the American dream. Clearly it is not the social implications of her characters' lives that interest her, for she writes, "Ever since the beginning of time, and until the world ends, there will be some people who will get everything and others that don't." It is rather the struggle, and the human dignity of those, like C. herself, who have lived in hunger, shame, and deprivation that she wants to make known. Despite their enraged, violent, incestuous, tacky, frustrated, and ignorant ways, the characters in *The Beans of Egypt, Maine* (1985) and *Letourneau's Used Auto Parts* (1989) exact from the reader not only attention but also respect.

Poverty and human connectedness are central themes in C.'s fiction, as in the author's life. The first novel is dedicated to her son Reuben Chute, who died in infancy from the negligent medical attention available to the poor. C. began writing it as self-help. She gave her son's name to the worst Bean character, whose rage is bred by poverty. Often the violence is against women. Reuben used to beat his ex-wife; his cousin, Beal, rapes Earlene Pomerleau. Earlene drifts into marriage with Beal but ends up Reuben's woman, after Beal is killed before her eyes and Reuben has come home from prison for nearly beating a game warden to death. In contrast to Reuben and his rage is green-thumbed Roberta Bean, earth mother to a brood of adoring children, some of them Beal's. And just down the road from Egypt is Miracle City, the setting of C.'s second novel, whose name reflects the heart of gold of Big Lucien Letourneau, who fills his home with stray individuals along with all the children he sires. He operates a trailer park free of charge for the down-and-outs in his battle against the book's only real villain, the housing code man.

C. started writing, the only activity for which she feels qualified, when she was eight. As a part-time correspondent for the *Portland Evening Express*, she learned to edit and to detach herself emotionally from what she was writing. Her widely disparate narrative styles, as in Earlene's rural first person next to articulate narration in *Beans*, together with the anecdotal prose of *Auto Parts*, belie a meticulous writing process. C. considers herself a perfectionist who edits her work painstakingly, particularly at its inception. In C., who has taught creative writing at the University of Southern Maine, the state has a powerful native voice.

OTHER WORKS: Stories have appeared in *Ploughshares, Ohio Review, Shenandoah, Agni Review,* and been anthologized in *Best American Short Stories,* 1983, and *Inside Vacationland: New Fiction from the Real Maine* (1985).

BIBLIOGRAPHY: Reference works: *CA* 123 (1988). *CLC* 39 (1986).
Other references: *Ms.* (April 1986). *New England Rev. and Bread Loaf Q.* 8:2 (Winter 1985, interview). *People Weekly* (25 March 1985).

ELISABETH SANDBERG

Sandra Cisneros

B. 1954, Chicago, Illinois
D. of Elvira Cordero Anguiano and Alfredo Cisneros del Moral

The daughter of a Mexican father and a Mexican-American mother, and sister to six brothers, C. has worked as a teacher to high school dropouts, a poet-in-the-schools, a college recruiter, and an arts administrator. She has also taught as a visiting writer at a number of universities around the country. C. is a graduate of the University of Iowa's Writers Workshop and recipient of three writing fellowships for poetry and fiction, two from the National Endowment for the Arts and one from the Lannan Foundation (1991). She is the first Chicana writer to be published by a mainstream press (Random House).

Told through the point of view of a young girl, C.'s first book of fiction, *The House on Mango Street* (1984), is characterized by a deceptively simple, accessible style and structure. The novel's short sections are marvels of poetic language that capture a girl's vision of the world she inhabits. Esperanza is already painfully aware of the racial and economic oppression her community suffers, but it is the fate of the women in her barrio that has the most profound impact on her, especially as she begins to develop sexually and learns that the same fate might be hers. The parade of women victimized by their culture's rigid gender roles begins with her great-grandmother, "a wild horse of a woman, so wild she wouldn't marry until my great-grandfather threw a sack over her head and carried her off. And the story goes she never forgave him. She looked out the window all her life, the way so many women sit their sadness on an elbow. . . . I have inherited her name, but I don't want to inherit her place by the window." Esperanza bears witness to the hard lessons taught Chicanas about being women and belonging to men: Rafaela whose husband locks her up because she is too beautiful, Minerva who takes her husband back every time he leaves her, Sally whose father beats her. Sally gets married before the eighth grade to escape her father's domination, only to fall under the control of her husband: "She is happy except sometimes her husband gets angry and once he broke the door when his foot went through, though on most days he is okay. Except he won't let her talk on the telephone. And he doesn't let her look out the window."

By the end of the book, Esperanza's journey toward independence merges two central themes, that of writing and a house of her own. Her rejection of woman's place in the culture involves not only writing but also leaving the barrio, raising problematic issues of changing class and cultural identity. But Esperanza concludes the book with the promise to return, understood metaphorically, through her writing: "They will not know I have gone away to come back. For the ones I left behind. For the ones who cannot get out."

Mango Street captures the dialectic between self and community in Chicana writing. Esperanza finds her literary voice through her own cultural experience and that of other Chicanas. She seeks self-empowerment through writing, while recognizing her commitment to Chicanas. Her promise to pass down to other women the power she has gained from writing is fulfilled by the text itself.

In C.'s 1984 collection of poetry, *My Wicked Wicked Ways*, the young voice of *Mango Street* coexists with that of the grown woman/poet struggling with her contradictory desires, a combination carried through in *Woman Hollering Creek* (1991), a collection of stories. Set on both sides of the border, the stories of *Woman* capture the "in-between" of Chicano identity, as in "Mericans," when *gringo* tourists are disappointed to learn that the picturesque children they have photographed are Americans visiting their grandmother. The stories mine the rich vein of popular culture, as in "Little Miracles, Kept Promises," and continue C.'s thematic concern with male/female relationships, whether spiraling in old patterns ("Never Marry a Mexican") or telling the story of a woman's escape from a battering husband through the legend of La Llorona in the title story "Woman Hollering Creek."

Woman represents the full maturing of C.'s unique voice and vision, her often breathtakingly insightful and wickedly witty musings on men's and women's experience with love in a culture besieged from within and without.

OTHER WORKS: Bad Boys (1980).

BIBLIOGRAPHY: McCracken, Ellen, "Sandra Cisneros' *The House on Mango Street:* Community-Oriented Introspection and the Demystification of Patriarchal Violence," in *Breaking Boundaries: Latina Writing and Critical Reading,* Asuncion Horno-Delgado et al., eds. (1989). Martin-Rodriguez, Manuel M.,

"The Book on Mango Street: Escritura y liberacion en la obra de Sandra Cisneros," *Mujer y literatura mexicana y chicana: Culturas en contacts*, A. Lopez-Gonzalez et al, eds. (1990). Rosaldo, Renato, "Fables of the Fallen Guy," in *Criticism in the Borderlands: Studies in Chicano Literature, Culture, and Ideology*, Hector Calderon and Jose David Saldivar, eds. (1991). Saldivar-Hull, Sonia, "'Ya soy mujer': Crossing the Border, Changing the Subject in Chicana/ Mexicana Discourse," in *Rearticulations: The Practice of Chicano Cultural Studies*, Mario Garcia and Ellen McCracken, eds. (forthcoming).

Reference works: *CA* 131 (1991). *Hispanic Writers* (1991).

Other references: *The Americas Review* 15 (Fall-Winter), 18 (Spring 1990, interview). *Critica* 1 (1986). *Revista Chicano-Riquena* 13 (1985).

YVONNE YARBRO-BEJARANO

Amy Kathleen Clampitt

B. 15 June 1920, New Providence, Iowa
D. of Lutie Pauline (Felt) and Roy Justice Clampitt

Raised in an Iowa farming community, C. graduated with honors in English from Grinnell College in 1941. Going to Columbia University on a graduate fellowship, she left within a year to work for Oxford University Press in New York as a secretary and promotion director. She remained there for nine years. In 1951, she left to travel in Europe for five months, returning in 1952 to become a reference librarian for the National Audubon Society. From 1960–77, C. worked in New York as a freelance editor and researcher; during this time, she also resumed the writing of poetry. From 1977–82, she worked as an editor for E. P. Dutton Publishers, but since 1982 she has supported herself primarily with her poetry. She served as a writer in residence at the College of William and Mary in 1984–85 and at Amherst College in 1986–87; in 1988 she was Hurst Professor at Washington University.

C.'s honors and awards include a 1982 Guggenheim Fellowship; the Academy of American Poets Fellowship Award (1984); American Academy and Institute of Arts and Letters Award (1984); a D.H.L. from Grinnell College (1984); and a three-year Lila Acheson Wallace Reader's Digest Fellowship (1991).

Both narrative and lyric, C.'s poetry conveys a strong sense of place. Many of her poems celebrate her native Midwest; the coast of Maine, where she summers; and the various locations to which she has traveled in Europe and Greece. Her work also focuses on social justice issues, perhaps a legacy from her father's Quaker activism. At times meditative, her work often merges concerns of the intellect with concerns of the spirit.

Published when she was sixty-three years old, *The Kingfisher* (1983), her first major collection, presents poems on a range of issues, from the life sciences to classical Greece. Included is the widely praised "Beach Glass," illustrating the poet's interest in the environment and her eye for detail. Although not exclusively a nature poet, C. draws from, and examines closely, the workings of the natural world, while at the same time going beyond the merely descriptive.

What the Light Was Like (1985) is strongly elegiac. Particularly notable is the suite of poems on the life of John Keats, "Voyages: A Homage to John Keats," based on the well-known biography of the poet by Walter Jackson Bate. Continuing to merge themes from nature, the ancient world, and personal memory, the collection emphasizes the importance of place. *Archaic Figures* (1987) best exemplifies C.'s concern with women's lives. Invoking Virginia Woolf in the epigraph, the book is a commentary on the experiences of women. C. draws from mythical and literary figures such as Medusa, Athena, George Eliot, **Margaret Fuller,** and Dorothy Wordsworth to tell the collective and individual stories of women throughout history. Central to the book is an exploration of consciousness, a recurring theme in all her work.

Westward (1990) presents trajectory from childhood to old age. It is a book of memory, of returnings and moving forward, of the delicate balance between past and present. The book concludes with a long sequence on "The Prairie," which returns the poet to her past. As with all her major collections, C. includes notes that explain her more esoteric references.

In 1991 C. published a collection of essays called *Predecessors, Et Cetera,* as part of the "Poets on Poetry" series published by the University of Michigan. Included is an interview with C., in which she talks about her own work. C. has also written a play called *The Three of Us,* based on the diaries and letters of Dorothy Wordsworth. She continues to live and write in New York City.

OTHER WORKS: Multitudes, Multitudes (limited edition, 1973). *The Isthmus* (limited edition, 1981). *The Summer Solstice* (limited edition, 1983). *A Homage to John Keats* (limited edition, 1984).

BIBLIOGRAPHY: McGuiness, D. M., "Some Measures of Contemporary Poetry." Unpublished Ph.D. diss., Univ. of Iowa, 1986; *DIA* (Jan. 1987). Reference works: *CA* 110 (1984). *CANR* 29 (1990). *CLC* 32 (1985). *Contemp. Poets* (1991). *DLB* 105 (1991). *FC* (1990).

Other references: *Brno Studies in English* 18 (1989). *Chicago Tribune* (26 May 1987). *Georgia Rev.* 37:2 (Summer 1983). *Hudson Rev.* 43 (Winter 1991). *Keats-Shelley Rev.* 3 (Autumn 1988). *NYRB* (3 March 1983). *NYTBR* (7 Aug. 1983; 19 May 1985; 20 Dec. 1987; 23 Dec. 1990). *Parnassus* (Spring/Summer 1983). *Partisan Rev.* (Summer 1991). *Ploughshares* 11:4 (1985). *Raritan* 10:3 (Winter 1991). *Sunday Times* [London] (21 Feb. 1988). *Wash. Post Book World* (3 April 1983).

LOLLY OCKERSTROM

Beverly Cleary

See AWW *1, 376–77*

Author of more than thirty books for young people, C. has established herself as a humorist of enduring appeal who has amply fulfilled her often-reiterated desire to capture on her pages the humor in the everyday lives of children. She is able to blend a healing laughter into even the more serious moments in her fiction. C.'s 1984 Newbery Medal winner *Dear Mr. Henshaw* (the letter-and-diary account of young Leigh Bott's struggle to come to terms with his parents' separation) is, as **Natalie Babbitt** says, a "first-rate poignant story" in which C. "never allows Leigh's writing to slide a millimeter away from the natural humor and unconscious pathos that make it work so honestly." *Dear Mr. Henshaw* also won the 1984 Christopher Award and made many best books lists. Throughout her career C. has won numerous awards from both juvenile readers and professional critics, including the American Library Association's Laura Ingalls Wilder Award (1975) and the Everychild Award from the Children's Book Council (1985) for her thirty-five-year contribution to children's literature.

C.'s later books both present new protagonists and add further sequels. A new character appears in *Lucky Chuck* (1984), in which Chuck, unable to learn from that adolescent primer, the traffic regulations manual, must learn through on-the-road experience that motorcycles and laws deserve respect. *Muggie Maggie* (1990), a book with another new character, deals humorously with that bane of school children's lives, cursive writing. C. adds herself as a child character in her warmly praised memoir of her own growing-up years, *A Girl from Yamhill* (1988).

New sequels feature her one fantasy character, Ralph the motorcycle mouse, the twins Janet and Jimmy, and the unquenchable Ramona. In *Ralph S. Mouse* (1982), Ralph serves as a peacemaker at school. The twins return in *The Growing-up Feet* (1987), a book whose emphasis on the virtues of red boots will recall an incident in *Ramona the Pest* (1968). In *Janet's Thingamagigs* (1987), Janet learns to share with her twin brother.

C. has added three books to the six in which Ramona Quimby, C.'s most memorable character, either appears or is featured. *Ramona and Her Mother* (1979) deals sympathetically with the family conflicts engendered when Mrs. Quimby retains her job even after Mr. Quimby finds an interim job and then decides to return to college. In *Ramona Quimby, Age Eight* (1981) Ramona shows a maturing attitude about her parents' problems and about four-year-old Willa Jean, a minor-league pest with whom Ramona must contend after school each day. *Ramona Forever* (1984) takes the Quimby family saga through the wedding of Aunt Bea, the birth of a third girl, and an acceptable if not ideal resolution of the father's job situation. Observing all that her baby sister has to learn, Ramona speculates, "It is hard work to be a baby," and her father pronounces, "Growing up is hard work." This respect for the difficulties of childhood runs through all of C.'s books, keeping the humor sound and strong.

The Ramona stories became a television series, an experience C. recounts in *Ramona Quimby: The Making of a Television Film* (1988). A Ramona paper-doll book and two children's diaries also appeared in the

1980s. Ramona seems well on her way to joining the pantheon of humorous characters in American literature.

OTHER WORKS: *Cutting Up with Ramona* (paper dolls, 1983). *The Ramona Quimby Diary* (1984). *The Beezus and Ramona Diary* (1986). *Strider* (1991). *Petey's Bedtime Story* (1993).

BIBLIOGRAPHY: *Children's Lit. Assoc. Q.* (Fall 1988). *Horn Book Mag.* (Aug. 1984). *Language Arts* 56 (Jan. 1979). *NYTBR* (23 Oct. 1983).

CELIA CATLETT ANDERSON

Michelle Cliff

B. 2 Nov. 1946, Kingston, Jamaica

C. spent her early years in Jamaica and in New York City where her parents emigrated when she was a child. Although legally an American born abroad, C. claims a Jamaican identity. She calls herself "Jamaican by birth, heritage and indoctrination," an indoctrination that she sees as separating Jamaicans into a hierarchy based on the gamut of skin tones from white to red to dark. C. went to a girls' private school on the island conducted by English women. Her experience there confirmed her sense of the divisive effects of color.

C. received a B.A. in European history at Wagner College in New York City (1969). Subsequently, at the Warburg Institute in London she earned a master's in philosophy (1974) for her work in languages and comparative historical studies. Between 1969 and 1979 she held a variety of positions in publishing in New York City.

Very light skinned, one of the fairest in her family, C. uses this relationship to society as a "white" woman of color as a central theme in her writing. C.'s characters are frequently based on herself and members of her family who are challenged by the dualities of colonialism and revolution, white and black, America and the third world.

C.'s first publication, *The Winner Names the Age* (1978), is an edition of antiracist writings by the Southern American writer **Lillian Smith.** Raised in the South, Smith was acutely aware of its racial divisions and uneasy with the privileges that came with whiteness.

Claiming an Identity They Taught Me to Despise (1980) brings together poetry and prose, autobiography and history, to evoke the colors of Jamaica and memories of her family and to "conjure a knowledge" and vivid portrayal of her past. *The Land of Look Behind* (1985) demonstrates her strengthening feminist voice against colonialism.

In her first novel, *Abeng* (1984), C. writes of a light-skinned Jamaican girl, Clare Savage, and her relation to the dark-skinned Zoe. The story focuses on the status and the damages with which Clare's lightness is associated. Within the power that her skin color gives her, she sees the true history of colonialism, racism, and privilege. At the novel's end Clare is left unsure of herself and her place in society. C. describes the book as "emotionally an autobiography."

No Telephone to Heaven (1987), the sequel to *Abeng*, follows the Savage family's decision to leave Jamaica and migrate to America, leaving a predestined life in a racist and classist society for a place where so much more could belong to them. Tracing the adjustment of each family member to a new life, she focuses again on Clare who, like C., moves through America, Europe, and back to Jamaica. On the island she is brought through an old friend into a group of revolutionaries; embracing their beliefs, Clare rejects the privilege of her skin color and turns to her community to find wholeness. C.'s sense of history and its effects on the present recurs in a collection of reflective short stories, *Bodies of Water* (1990).

C.'s understanding of the destructiveness of racism informs her feminist voice. As editor (1981–83) with her longtime companion **Adrienne Rich** of *Sinister Wisdom*, she enabled the publication of significant lesbian feminist writing. She has also written of the influence on her of Simone Weil and of the work of black women visual artists, and provided the introduction to **Audre Lorde** and **Adrienne Rich**'s book on black feminism in Germany, *Macht und Sinnlichkeit* (1983).

C.'s work has been recognized by fellowships from the MacDowell Colony (1982), the National Endowment of the Arts (1982), and the Massachusetts Artists Foundation (1984); she was Eli Kantor Fellow at Yaddo in 1984. She has taught at the New School for Social Research

(1974–76), Hampshire College (1980 and 1981), the University of Massa-chuetts-Amherst (1980), Norwich University (1983–84), Vista College (1985), and at Trinity College in Connecticut (1991–92). In addition to teaching, C. has been an invited participant at workshops and sympo-siums around the world and a member of the editorial board at *Signs: A Journal of Women in Culture and Society* (1981–89). Her stories and essays have appeared in *Chrysalis, Conditions, Sojourner, Heresies, Feminist Review, Black Scholar*, and other journals.

OTHER WORKS: *Free Enterprise* (1993). "I Found God in Myself and I Loved Her / I Loved Her Fiercely: More Thought on the Work of Black Women Artists," in *Between Women*, Carol Ascher et al, eds. (1984). See also: *Extended Outlooks*, Jane Cooper, ed. (1982). *Home Girls*, Barbara Smith, ed. (1983). *The Graywolf Annual Five: Multi-Cultural Literacy*, Rick Simonson and Scott Walker, eds. (1988). *Caribbean Women Writers: Essays from the First International Conference*, Selwyn R. Cudjoe, ed. (1990).

BIBLIOGRAPHY: Reference works: *Black Writers* (1989). *CA* 116 (1986). *FC* (1990).
Other references: *Conditions* 13 (1986). *NYTBR* (15 July 1987). *WRB* 5:2 (Nov. 1987).

SUZANNE GIRONDA

Lucille Clifton

B. *Thelma Lucille Sayles, 27 June 1936, DePew, New York*
D. *of Thelma (Moore) and Samuel Louis Sayles; m. Fred James Clifton, 1958 (d. 1984); c.: Sidney; Fredrica; Channing; Gillian; Graham; Alexis*

Born in a small town in upstate New York, C. grew up in an extended family of grandparents, uncles, and aunts, two sisters (each with a differ-ent mother), and a brother (same mother). That family would become a part of the subject matter of her writing. The last chapter of her memoir, *Generations* (1976), concludes with a genealogy, but the entire work retraces C.'s ancestry from her paternal great-great-grandmother, Mammy Caroline, born in Dahomey in 1822. C. details her life and background, her concerns, and her beliefs as much in her poetry as she does in her memoir. In fact, her poetry can be said to constitute an extended memoir. Her subjects are the people and communities of her immediate and historical experience.

The first of her family to go away to school, C. attended Howard University (1953–55), where she majored in drama, and Fredonia State Teachers College (1955). Married in 1958, she gave birth to five children. She published her first book of poems, *Good Times*, in 1969.

Although C.'s work has been well received, its quiet tones are often overshadowed by the brasher militancy of such contemporaries as **Sonia Sanchez** or of younger artists such as **Nikki Giovanni.** However, wider recognition continued to develop, including a nomination for the Pulitzer Prize in poetry in 1980 for *Two-Headed Woman.*

Equally as important as her poetry and comprising a significant body of work on their own are C.'s writings for children. She has authored some twenty books for young readers ranging from several tales of young Everett Anderson to the folkloric generational tales of *The Lucky Stone* (1979).

In her children's books as in her poetry, C.'s ear for the rhythms, vocabulary, and metaphors of African American vernacular speech enable her to transform the language into art. At different times she employs the voice of the storyteller, the witness, and the seer. The past is contained in the present, enabling her to discern and posit a possible future. Her subject matter ranges from the personal and autobiographical turns of her immediate experience (the lives and deaths of her parents, the death of her husband) to the overtly political and social (poems about contemporary public figures from **Angela Y. Davis** and Bobby Seale to Winnie Mandela, and about Palestinian women and children and the Native American experience).

In addition, the sounds of her work move easily into the realm of song. Snatches of traditional and popular songs may head a particular poem or be alluded to in a given line. This musicality coupled with a simplicity of word choice makes her work accessible to a wide range of readers.

C. received poetry fellowships from the National Endowment for the Arts in 1970 and 1972 and was appointed poet laureate for the state of Maryland from 1969 to 1972. She also served as poet in residence at

Coppin State College (1971–74) and was the Jenny Moore Visiting Writer at George Washington University from 1982 to 1983. In 1985, she was appointed professor of literature and creative writing at the University of California, Santa Cruz, where she continues to teach and write.

OTHER WORKS: *Good News about the Earth: New Poems* (1972). *An Ordinary Woman* (1974). *Next: New Poems* (1987). *Good Woman: Poems and a Memoir, 1969–1980* (1987). *Quilting: Poems 1987–1990* (1991). *Three Wishes* (1992). *The Book of Light* (1993). Children's books: *The Black BC's* (1970). *Some of the Days of Everett Anderson* (1970). *Good, Says Jerome* (1973). *All Us Come Cross the Water* (1973). *Don't You Remember* (1973). *The Boy Who Didn't Believe in Spring* (1973). *Everett Anderson's Year* (1974). *The Times They Used to Be* (1974). *My Brother Fine with Me* (1975). *Everett Anderson's Friend* (1976). *Three Wishes* (1976). *Amifika* (1977). *Everett Anderson's 1 2 3* (1977). *Everett Anderson's Nine Month Long* (1978). *My Friend Jacob* (1980). *Sonora Beautiful* (1981). *Everett Anderson's Good-bye* (1983). *Everett Anderson's Christmas Coming* (1991). *The Book of Light* (1993).

BIBLIOGRAPHY: Beckles, Frances W., *Twenty Black Women* (1978). *Black Women Writers (1950–1980): A Critical Evaluation*, Mari Evans, ed. (1983). *Coming to Light: American Women Poets in the Twentieth Century*, D. Middlebrook and M. Yalow, eds. (1985). Davenport, D. "Four Contemporary Black Women Poets." Unpublished Ph.D. diss., Univ. of Southern Calif., 1987. Reference works: *CLC* 19 (1981). *CLR* 5 (1983). *DLB* 5, 41 (1980, 1985). *CA* 49–52 (1975). *CANR* 24 (1988). *Maj Twent Cent Writers* (1991). *SATA* (1982).

Other references: *Children's Lit Assn. Q.* (Winter 1989). *Pacific Coast Phil.* (Nov. 1983). *Southern Rev.* (Summer 1989). *Sage* (Spring 1985).

FAHAMISHA PATRICIA BROWN

Jane Cooper

B. 9 Oct. 1924, Atlantic City, New Jersey
D. of Martha (Marvel) and John C. Cooper

Although C. worked "strenuously and perfectly seriously on a book of poems" between the ages of twenty-two and twenty-six, she did not publish her first book until she was in her midforties. Since then she has published three books of poems and a long poem, *Threads: Rosa Luxemburg from Prison* (1979).

C. lived until she was ten in Jacksonville, Florida, and spent summers in the North Carolina mountains. In 1934 C. and her family moved north to Princeton, New Jersey, where she attended Miss Fine's School (1934–42). She studied at Vassar College from 1942–44 and received a B.A. in comparative literature from the University of Wisconsin in 1946, completing an honors thesis on García Lorca's "vocabulary of images." The following year C. attended the first Oxford (England) Summer School where she began to think about writing "a book of war poems from a woman's point of view." Some of these poems appeared in a section of *Maps and Windows* (1974) called "Mercator's World (Poems 1947–1951)." After a stint of freelance editing, C. began teaching literature and creative writing at Sarah Lawrence College in 1950 and remained a faculty member there until 1987. She spent a year at the University of Iowa (M.A. 1954) where she worked on her poems and did a creative thesis with Robert Lowell and John Berryman.

The structure of C.'s books is architectural, like a house she has built to which she keeps adding rooms and wings. Her own "vocabulary of images" includes many doors, windows, roofs, and walls. C. has always seen her poems as parts of a larger whole and all of her books have included earlier poems reprinted from previous books as well as new ones. Her poems often use architecture as metaphor, and two of her books use the language of building as title, *Maps and Windows* and *Scaffolding* (1984). As in Emily Dickinson's poems, the house in C.'s work is also the body. People often appear in the protective shells of their houses: "Houses, houses, we lodge in such husks" ("Souvenirs," 1971) and in the context of their "fragile human settlement" ("The Blue Anchor," 1978).

The language of house construction serves for both private and public spaces—both our mortal bodies and the imperiled world.

C.'s first book of poems, *The Weather of Six Mornings* (1969), won the Lamont Poetry Award of the Academy of American Poets (then a first-book prize) in 1968. The award gave C.'s work the approval of some of the leading male poets of the 1960s (the judges included Hayden Carruth, Donald Hall, and James Wright) and brought her critical attention. C. was also at this time part of a vigorous and supportive group of women writers whose companionship and guidance she has continued to acknowledge in all of her works. They included **Sarah Appleton, Grace Paley, Adrienne Rich, Muriel Rukeyser,** and **Jean Valentine.**

The poems of *The Weather of Six Mornings* show the tension of a generous political vision struggling with anger and of an imagination struggling to work freely despite the press of the diurnal. In the title poem C. addresses the courage it takes for a woman writer simply to come to speech at all: "I try to speak / of what is so hard for me."

Maps and Windows includes poems from 1947–51, new poems, and the first printing of C.'s essay, "Nothing Has Been Used in the Manufacture of This Poetry That Could Have Been Used in the Manufacture of Bread." Here, she writes of "the sort of upper-middle-class education that encourages writing, painting, music, theater so long as they aren't taken too seriously," and poses a central question about her early work: "Why, then, didn't I publish? And why, even more, did I give up writing poems." In this essay, C. traces her "poetry of development," which the poems themselves demonstrate, and confronts honestly women's need to be modest or generous at the expense of full creative exploration.

Scaffolding, published in England in 1984, includes most of the poems from her two earlier books as well as five "Reclaimed Poems" from 1954–1969 and new poems from 1970–1983, including her long poem "Threads: Rosa Luxemburg from Prison." C. does here the feminist work of retrieval on herself by resurrecting poems she had earlier discounted as unfinished or unimportant. Welcoming the "opportunity to see my work arranged chronologically," C. writes that "*Scaffolding* gives a sense of the continuous journey the work has been for me all along." A fourth collection, *Green Notebook, Winter Road*, is forthcoming.

C.'s many awards include grants from the Guggenheim Foundation (1960), the Ingram Merrill Foundation (1971), the National Endowment for the Arts (1981), and a Bunting Fellowship from Radcliffe College in 1988. In 1978 she was the corecipient of the Poetry Society of America's Shelley Award. She has frequently been a fellow at the MacDowell Colony, Yaddo, and the Blue Mountain Center. She received the Maurice English Poetry Award for a book of poems by a writer in her sixth decade or older for *Scaffolding*.

C.'s poems document a journey in search of "necessary truths." In his juror's statement for the English award, poet Galway Kinnell wrote, "Looking at the whole body of Jane Cooper's work, one sees an artist who changes: who confronts unsettling experience and learns to see the world and herself in new ways." Never afraid to take the next surprising turn, C. has written, "If my poems have always been about survival— and I believe they have been—then survival too keeps revealing itself as an art of the unexpected."

BIBLIOGRAPHY: Reference works: *CA* 25–28 (1977). *CANR* 17 (1986). *Contemp. Poets* (1985, 1991).

Other references: *Belles Lettres* (1985). *Parnassus: Poetry in Review* 15:1 (1989). *WRB* (1986).

MAGGIE ANDERSON

Jayne Cortez

B. 19 May 1936, Arizona
c.: Denardo Coleman, b. 1956

C., a poet of extraordinary musicality, was born in Arizona but reared in the Watts section of Los Angeles. A participant in writers' workshops in Watts during the sixties, she published her first volume of poems, *Pissstained Stairs and the Monkey Man's Wares* in 1969. Since then, she has published six volumes of poetry, made three recordings of readings of her work, and has had her poems included in numerous anthologies, magazines, and journals. In 1979 she received a National Endowment for the Arts Fellowship in Poetry. A performing poet, C. has lectured and read widely in the United States, Latin America, and Africa, often reading to musical accompaniment.

C. has been described as a "surrealist" poet because of her startling use of symbol and imagery. In her poems, colors have tastes, sounds have texture and shape, odors are visible and audible. C. yokes opposites and contradictories, such as "signifying stones" and "tattooed holes." She juxtaposes the beautiful and the ugly, the sublime and the disgusting, often in the same line or phrase.

C.'s images combine with her use of language and sound. Often the poems have a sense of incantation achieved through a judicious use of repetition. In addition, she is a student of black musical traditions, ancient and modern, grounding poems in African rhythms, blues lines, and *avant-garde* jazz structures. Orality is central to C.'s art. The sounds of the words reinforce their sense. In C.'s performances, the English language also becomes tonal as she varies pitch and duration of syllables to enhance the musicality of her lines. Vocalized breaths provide rhythmic punctuation for other lines in the mode of the traditional African American preacher.

A high priestess for the human race, C. has, nonetheless, a black woman's vision. She is seer and healer, singer and chastiser. She self-consciously assumes a "griot" stance, singing praise of such cultural figures as Billie Holiday and Duke Ellington, Cuban drummer Chano Pozo, Martinican poet Leon Damas, South African freedom fighter Solomon Mahlangu. Praises for the works of people such as these who have joined the ancestors commingle with exhortations to the living. C. orates from a pulpit of Pan-African cultural identity, environmental concerns, and human rights advocacy. "Push Back the Catastrophes," she urges in her poem of the same name. Her poems see as catastrophic all ideas and actions that prevent the actualization of human potential, dignity, and creativity.

Beginning her career as a writer during a period when poets often took to the public platform, C. has become known as a highly polished performer. In 1975, she recorded her first album, *Celebrations and Solitudes: The Poetry of Jayne Cortez*, with bassist Richard Davis. Subsequent recordings have featured other noted jazz musicians, including her son Denardo Coleman.

OTHER WORKS: *Festivals and Funerals* (1971). *Scarifications* (1973). *Mouth on Paper* (1977). *Firespitter* (1982). *Coagulations: New and Selected Poems* (1984).

Poetic Magnetic (1991). Recordings: *Unsubmissive Blues* (1980). *There It Is* (1982).

BIBLIOGRAPHY: Heroism in the New Black Poetry: Introductions and Interviews, D. H. Melhem, ed. (1990). Reference works: *CA* 73–76 (1978). *CANR* 13 (1984). *DLB* 41 (1985). *FC* (1990).

FAHAMISHA PATRICIA BROWN

Kit Craig. *See Kit Reed*

Mary Daly

See AWW 1, 451–52
B. 16 Oct. 1928, Schenectady, New York
D. of Catherine (Morse) and Frank X. Daly

Radical feminist theorist D., who holds doctoral degrees in philosophy (1965) and theology (1963) from the University of Fribourg, and a doctorate in theology from St. Mary's College, Indiana (1954), is an associate professor in the Department of Theology at Boston College. The corpus of her writing is central in shaping the questions and debates of feminist theology/religious studies and theory.

The Church and the Second Sex (1968) was reissued with a "Feminist Postchristian Introduction" (1975), including a chapter-by-chapter review from D.'s transformed post-Christian vantage point. Her "New Archaic Afterwords" to a 1985 reissue, greatly influenced by her later development of "New Words" to describe women's experience, offers a further reflection on her departure from Christianity. Here, D. views "the earlier Daly as a foresister whose work is an essential source."

In her 1985 "Original Reintroduction" to *Beyond God the Father* (1973, 1985) D. maintains most of the views expressed in her second book, but rejects traditional theological vocabulary. In her later work, language becomes paramount. While always passionate, her words become increasingly lyrical, alliterative, and specialized. Irregular capitalization in her works and in this article are used to delineate words she has revitalized and reclaimed.

D.'s 1975 article, "The Qualitative Leap beyond Patriarchal Religion," provides the trajectory of a new constructive phase. In the "New Intergalactic Introduction (1990)" of *Gyn/Ecology* D. reiterates a plan for a three-volume work based on the identification of eight Deadly Sins of the Fathers. *Gyn/Ecology* (1978) deals with "Processions," "Professions," and "Possessions" (deception, pride, and avarice). *Pure Lust* (1984) deals with "Aggression" and "Obsession" (anger and lust). The third volume, *Outercourse: The Be-Dazzling Voyage* (1993) addresses "Assimilation," "Elimination," and "Fragmentation" (gluttony, envy, and sloth), also tacitly dealt with in the 1987 *Wickedary of the English Language*.

In *Gyn/Ecology* (1978, 1990) D. criss-crosses cultures and continents painstakingly exposing Indian *suttee*, Chinese foot binding, African genital mutilation, European witch burning, and the development of American gynecology to show that gynocidal practices are universal. She begins here her journey of creating women-identified Time/Space. D. differentiates between Background, "the divine depth within the Self," and Foreground, "surface consciousness," analytical distinctions upon which she draws in her later work.

In *Pure Lust*, D. journeys into the Background through three realms: (1) archespheres, uncovering "the Archimage—the Original Witch—within our Selves," (2) pyrospheres, the space of Elemental E-motions and ontological Passions, and (3) metamorphospheres, the center of Be-longing and Be-friending. The discussion of each realm ensues with the exposure of the foreground that patriarchy has created to mask the spheres: sadospirituality, potted passions and plastic virtues, and patriarchal, inauthentic belonging and befriending. D. retrieves "lust" from a phallocentric lechery and renews it with its other meanings of eagerness, craving, and intense longing.

Websters' First New Intergalactic Wickedary of the English Language brings together a collection of D.'s New Words and their various meanings. The volume has preliminary articles on spelling, grammar, pronunciation, and guides that mirror the image of a dictionary but are actually theoretical pieces. The presentation of words and meanings, woven "in cahoots with Jane Caputi," appears in the second phase of the book. Readers unfamiliar with D.'s work will be impeded from using *Wickedary* as a reference tool because the words are divided into three different word-webs that depend upon a basic understanding of her thought. A third phase, "Appendicular Webs," contains four further essays by D.

In *Outercourse: The Be-Dazzling Voyage* (1992) D. intertwines both auto-biographical and philosophical material to portray her intellectual voyage in four interconnected spiral galaxies. These spirals roughly correspond to the writing of each of her books, although the first spiral includes many memories from preexistence through the writing of *The Church and the Second Sex*. The volume focuses on the power that recollections of a woman who has journeyed through the spirals and understands their interrelatedness can have to energize women and D. herself for further voyaging.

In 1979 **Audre Lorde** penned the most well-known criticism of D., citing D.'s failure to include the writings and experiences of women of color except as victims. D. publicly acknowledged the criticism in *Gyn/Ecology*'s second edition and in *Outercourse*. In *Pure Lust* and *Wickedary* D. does try to address diversity. The 1990 edition of *Gyn/Ecology* also includes an afterword by Bonnie Mann portraying the usefulness of D.'s analysis in Mann's work with battered women, an effort to show the accessibility of the work to different classes. Writers of feminist criticism and texts on theory generally label D. as cultural feminist, an appellation D. does not espouse in her own self-descriptions. She prefers Positively Revolting Hag, i.e., "a stunning, beauteous Crone, one who inspires positive revulsion from phallic institutions and morality, inciting Others to Act of Pure Lust."

OTHER WORKS: *Natural Knowledge of God in the Philosophy of Jacques Maritain: A Critical Study* (1966).

BIBLIOGRAPHY: Lorde, Audre, "An Open Letter to Mary Daly," in *This Bridge Called My Back: Writings by Radical Women of Color*, Cherríe Moraga and Gloria Anzaldúa, eds. (1981). Raymond, Janice G., "Mary Daly: A Decade of Academic Harrassment and Feminist Survival," in *Handbook for Women Scholars: Strategies for Success*, Mary L. Spencer, Monika Kehoe, and Karen Speece, eds. (1982). Reference works: *CANR* 30 (1990). *FC* (1990). *Maj Twent Cent Wr* (1991).

BARBARA ANNE RADTKE

Angela Yvonne Davis

B. 26 Jan. 1944, Birmingham, Alabama
D. of Sallye (Bell) and Benjamin Frank Davis

Born to a middle-class African American family whose social circle included Communist Party members, D. became one of the most prominent political activists of the 1960s and 1970s. An American Friends Service Committee scholarship allowed her to leave Birmingham to attend the progressive Elizabeth Irwin High School in New York City where she became active in a Marxist-Leninist youth group and supported the antinuclear and civil rights movements. Later, at Brandeis University she became a student of Marxist philosopher Herbert Marcuse. D. spent her junior year in Paris at the Sorbonne and returned to Europe after graduation from Brandeis (B.A. 1965) to continue her education at the University of Frankfurt (1965–67). D. received a master's degree in philosophy from the University of California, San Diego, in 1968, working again with Marcuse.

By the late 1960s, the civil rights movement was in full swing. D. joined several activist groups, including the Student Non-Violent Coordinating Committee, the Communist Party of the United States, and the Black Panthers. While working on her doctoral dissertation, she was hired to teach philosophy at UCLA. Then Governor Ronald Reagan, citing a law that banned Communist Party members from teaching at state universities, protested her appointment and D. was dismissed. The law was ultimately declared unconstitutional while the ensuing controversy propelled D. into the political spotlight.

As a champion of the work of the Black Panthers, D. became involved with the plight of black prison inmates. She was an especially strong advocate of a group called the Soledad Brothers and of their leader, George Jackson. In August 1970, Jackson's younger brother, Jonathan, sought to force his release by taking hostages at gunpoint in a California courthouse. During the shootout that followed, the judge and several others were killed. Police accused D. of purchasing the guns used in the shooting and charged her with conspiracy, kidnapping, and murder. Fleeing underground, D. was on the FBI's Ten Most Wanted List for several months until her capture. With the rallying cry, "Free Angela," the civil rights movement and the activist left rallied to her defense through her imprisonment and a lengthy court trial. *If They Come in the Morning: Voices of Resistance* (1971) collects D.'s prison writings and those of other black activists, including Erika Huggins, Black Panther leader Bobby Seale, and George Jackson. It is a firsthand account of political, racial, class, and economic oppression focusing primarily on the plight of African Americans in the United States prison system in the 1960s.

D. was acquitted of all charges in 1972. *Angela Davis, an Autobiography* (1974; reptd. as *Angela Davis: With My Mind on Freedom*, 1974), written in the wake of her exoneration, is a compelling book that chronicles her life as it intersected with the emergence of the civil rights movement. The book also details the rise of the Black Panther party and D.'s involvement with the group.

D. continued her activist work on behalf of black prisoners and against racism. Remaining in the Communist Party, she ran for vice president on the party ticket in 1980. She has held faculty positions in a number of universities in the United States and abroad.

D.'s groundbreaking feminist analysis of the intersecting oppressions of race, class, and gender in American culture, *Women, Race, and Class*, appeared in 1982. The book provides an overview of oppression as it is constructed, conducted, and institutionalized by the dominant majority. *Women, Culture, and Politics* (1988) is a collection of D.'s lectures, essays, and commentary on the changing social order in the 1980s. Her topics include violence against women, nuclear disarmament, apartheid in South Africa, health care, and the role of black artists.

D. is a passionate social and cultural critic whose writing is consistently informed by a black, radical, and feminist consciousness. In addition to her writing and teaching, D. lectures widely in the United States and abroad on numerous progressive issues ranging from antiapartheid efforts to reproductive rights.

OTHER WORKS: Important shorter works include "Violence against Women and the Ongoing Challenge to Racism," published by Kitchen Table Press (1987), and "Radical Perspectives on the Empowerment of African-American Women," *Harvard Educational Rev.* (Aug. 1988).

BIBLIOGRAPHY: Aptheker, Bettina, *The Morning Breaks: the Trial of Angela Davis* (1975). Lanker, Brian, *I Dream a World: Portraits of Black Women Who Changed America* (1989). Reference works: *Afro-American Encyc.* 3 (1974). *Be-*

net's (1991). *CA* 57–60 (1976). *CANR* 10 (1983). *Encyc. of the Amer. Left* (1990). *FC* (1990). *NBAW* (1992).

Other references: *Feminist Rev.* 31 (Spring 1989). *New Statesman* 114 (14 Aug. 1987).

EVELYN C. WHITE

Julia de Burgos

B. 17 Feb. 1914, Carolina, Puerto Rico; d. 6 July 1953, New York City
D. of Paula Garcia de Burgos and Francisco Burgos Hans; m. Rubén Rodriguez
Beauchamp, 1934, div. 1937; m. Armando Marín, 1943 (?)

B. revealed herself in her poetry and her life as a woman ahead of her times. In both she challenged the social conventions that ruled over the Puerto Rican women of her epoch.

B.'s humble origins in the rural barrio of Santa Cruz in Carolina, Puerto Rico, where she grew up as the eldest of a large family, gave her the strong unity with nature that appears constantly in her poetry. When her family moved to Rio Piedras in 1928, B. enrolled at the University of Puerto Rico High School where her studiousness won her recognition. In 1931 she entered the University of Puerto Rico, earning a teaching certificate in 1933. Financial difficulties prevented her from continuing her studies. In 1934, the year of her first marriage, she started working for the Puerto Rico Economic Reconstruction Administration in a day-care center. The following year (1935), she taught in another rural area in Naranjito and took courses during the summer at the university.

Although poets like Luis Palés Matos, Evaristo Ribera Chevremont, and Luis Llorens Torres would influence her work, it was the revolutionary patriotism of the president of the Nationalist party, Pedro Albizu Campos, that inspired her early poems, which called for social and political reform. B.'s first collection, *Poemas exactos a mí misma* (Exact poems to myself), was published in 1937 in a private edition. Apparently dissatisfied with this work, she tried to suppress it. *Poema en veinte surcos* (Poem in twenty furrows), containing her famous poem "Río Grande de Loíza," appeared in 1938. The river of her childhood is a powerful image throughout her work; it is in the river that the poet seems to search for her essence. Her recurrent themes of the eternal search for her true self, love, social reform, and art as a means of liberation first appear in this collection.

Canción de la verdad sencilla (Song of the simple truth, 1939), which received an award from the Institute of Puerto Rican Literature, presents love as its central theme. The river is present in various poems, now also as a rival of her lover. In "Confesión del Sí y del No" B. repeats her resistance to the imposition of social values, earlier seen in "Á Julia de Burgos." In an attempt to free herself from social constraint, in 1940 B. moved first to New York and then to Cuba with the man who had inspired her love poems. In Havana she met the Chilean poet Pablo Neruda, the writer who most deeply influenced her work.

In 1942, a love disillusionment that marked her for the rest of her life occasioned her return to New York. While living there, she actively collaborated in the publication of *Pueblos Hispánicos*, founded and directed by the Puerto Rican poet Juan Antonio Correjer. Although she continued to write, in her last years alcoholism weakened both her spirit and health. She spent most of this time in various hospitals. B. collapsed on a Harlem street in 1953. Her body was taken to Puerto Rico for burial near the river she had made famous.

A posthumous volume *El mar y tú, y otros poemas* (1954) pays tribute again to her one great love and reflects her disillusionment and final disintegration. The sea, symbol of the infinite and witness of the cosmic union of the lovers, becomes the deathbed that called her. A compilation of her works, *Obra Poética*, appeared in 1961.

Critics have seen influences of modernism in B.'s work. José Emilio González, pointing out imperfections in her poetry, contrasts her lack of interest in the discussion of aesthetics with her deep concern with social problems. The importance she placed on truth and justice, and her understanding of poetry as an instrument for social and political change, gave priority to the message rather than to the form. The result was the revelation of the essence of the poet herself, making her poetry so strikingly unique.

BIBLIOGRAPHY: González, Jose E., *La Poesía Contemporánea de Puerto Rico, 1930–1960* (1972). Jiménez de Baez, Lvette, *Julia de Burgos: Vida y Poesía*

(1966). Manrique Cabrera, Francisco, *Historia de la Literatura Puertoriquena* (1971). Reference works: *NAW: MP* (1980). *Puerto Rican Authors: A Biobibliographic Handbook* (1974).

Other references: *La Torre* 13 (Sept.–Dec. 1965). *Sin Nombre* 7:6 (Oct.–Dec. 1976).

AMIRIS PEREZ-GUNTIN

Margaret Randall de Mondragon. *See Margaret Randall*

Ella Cara Deloria (Anpetu Waśte)

B. 31 Jan. 1889, at White Swan on the Yankton Sioux Reservation, South
    Dakota;
d. 12 Feb. 1971, Vermillion, South Dakota
D. of Mary Sulley (Bordeaux) and Philip Deloria

Anpetu Waśte (which means Beautiful Day) was D.'s Dakota name. Her father was a deacon in the Episcopal church and D. was greatly influenced by the church as well as by her Sioux heritage. Dakota was the primary language spoken in her home, and Sioux culture was practiced there alongside Christianity. D. grew up on the Standing Rock Reservation, and graduated from the All Saints boarding school in Sioux Falls, South Dakota. Following her graduation in 1910, she attended Oberlin College in Ohio, and then transferred in 1913 to Columbia Teacher's College, receiving a B.S. in 1915.

About 1927, D. began a long collaboration with Franz Boas, the distinguished anthropologist, with whom she had worked and studied while at Teacher's College. She produced for him an immense body of research notes on Plains Indian language and culture. *Speaking of Indians* (1944) is D.'s analytical description of Sioux culture. *Waterlily* (1988), first published seventeen years after her death, is based on her ethnographic work, but written in the form of a novel in order to convey the details of her culture to a wide range of readers. Those who wish to know more about Native American women, as well as about Sioux culture, change, and more important continuity, will find the novel richly rewarding.

D. was bilingual as well as bicultural. Her work reveals the value of an insider's perspective, providing a bridge of understanding about Sioux society for those outside her tradition, as witnessed through the eyes of a Sioux woman. The paucity of books written by Native American women also makes her work an important contribution to Native American studies as well as to American literature. The major part of D.'s work is focused on the period just prior to white settlement on the western plains of North America in the mid–nineteenth century. Much of it challenges the still commonly held stereotypes of Native American peoples and especially the images of Indian women.

Waterlily offers answers to questions about the role of women by providing a platform on which they speak for themselves. D. also provides perspectives on tribal history as well as the social and religious ideas centered on the obligations of reciprocity to one's kin that are evident in Sioux tradition to the present day. Unlike her extensive ethnographic and linguistic work, *Waterlily* explores a series of important concepts in an intriguing fictional narrative. Engaging anecdotes alternate with serious commentary on issues that arise while contemplating life in the mid-nineteenth-century Teton (Tiyospaye) extended family camp circle. Enriched with her own experiences and views, and the insights of a writer who combines previous research on her own culture with the skills of the trained insider, the author creates excellent fiction. No one was better qualified than D. to draw a series of Sioux female characters such as the ones central to this novel.

Against the exaggerated representation of the Sioux Nation as fabricated by contemporary media image makers, D.'s work stands firmly and honestly, portraying Sioux tradition and especially Sioux women in the visibly important roles they held and continue to hold within their culture.

OTHER WORKS: Dakota Grammar (1941, with Franz Boas). *Speaking of Indians* (1944). *Some Notes on the Santee* (1967). *Deer Women and Elk Men: The Lakota Narratives of Ella Deloria,* Julian Rice, ed. (1992). "The Sun Dance," *Jour. of Amer. Folklore* (1929).

BIBLIOGRAPHY: Mead, Margaret, *Cooperation and Competition among Primitive Peoples* (1937, chapter by Jeannette Mirsky based on D.'s research). Murray, Janette K., "Ella Deloria: A Biographical Sketch and Literary Analysis." Unpublished Ph.D. diss., Univ. of North Dakota, 1974. Rice, Julian, *Deer Women and Elk Men* (1992). Reference works: *NAW:MP* (1980). The unpublished MSS of D., including her voluminous correspondence with Franz Boas, are in the Library of the American Philosophical Society, Philadelphia. MS of *Waterlily* is at the Dakota Indian Foundation, Chamberlain, South Dakota.

                                                          INÉS TALAMANTEZ

Agnes de Mille

See AWW 1, 487–89
D. 7 Oct. 1993, New York City

Author of thirteen books, D. maintained her visibility in the dance world as well as her general arts activism despite the 1975 cerebral hemorrhage that left her permanently paralyzed on the right side. In 1980 she received the Kennedy Center award for lifetime achievement in the performing arts. A 1987 PBS television documentary, "Agnes, the Indomitable de Mille," reviewed her life and work. Among the accomplishments highlighted there were the Aaron Copland ballet *Rodeo* (1942) and the Rodgers and Hammerstein musical comedy *Oklahoma!* (1943), which together revolutionized American dance. Both thematically and stylistically, she introduced Americana into the ballet. Among her contributions to the Broadway musical was an unprecedented integration of dance and story line.

    The stroke that crippled D. two hours before curtain time on the opening night of her Heritage Dance Theatre production of *Conversations about the Dance* on 15 May 1975 is described in *Reprieve: A Memoir* (1981). Interspersed with notes by Fred Plum, M.D., neurologist-in-chief at the New York Hospital, the text also chronicles her remarkable recovery, followed by a heart attack, and culminates in the resounding success of the production when she finally premiered it in November 1978, wearing the same red dress and narrating the program onstage just as she had set out to do two and a half years earlier. *Reprieve* is also a meditation on the important things in life as perceived by the hairbreadth survivor, and it offers a feisty, often humorously self-mocking commentary on the problems of the invalid and the handicapped within a family and in society at large. Richard Philp's assessment typifies the book's favorable reception: "Had de Mille never set foot on stage as either dancer or choreographer, she would still be known to us . . . as a critic, keen observer of human nature, biographer, humorist, and historian. *Reprieve*, she insists these days, has nothing to do with dance. And yet, I contend, it has *everything* to do with dance, with everybody who has ever felt the keen surge of life in movement, in being able to move."

America Dances (1980) was a work in progress at the time of D.'s stroke. The lavishly illustrated volume traces the development of the dance in North America, beginning with the original inhabitants: "Their feet . . . felt the earth, caressed it, made love to it—the whole foot, like the palm of the hand. The Indian foot and the earth are like two voices in a duet. The white man who wears hard leather soles cannot approximate this manner of moving and stepping. The Indian foot talks." The book's coverage includes ballet and popular forms, and extends to dance in films and dance for television and videotape. A final section treats the twin problems of inadequate state subsidization for the arts and the role of labor unions in driving up the costs of production. D. admits to personal bias in her treatment of American dance history. Nor does she neglect her own pivotal role in shaping its course. In *Portrait Gallery* (1990) D. blends memoir with vivid, sometimes sharp portraits of such prominent dance figures as Isadora Duncan, Alicia Markova, and her admired teacher, Carmelita Maracci.

Commenting on D.'s "bracing" prose, reviewer Mindy Aloff notes, "There is little on Earth as fearsome as a sentence by Agnes de Mille that is going to set a misapprehension straight." D.'s thirteenth book, a biography of dancer Martha Graham, appeared in 1991.

OTHER WORKS: Martha: The Life and Work of Martha Graham (1991).

BIBLIOGRAPHY: For articles in reference works, see: *CB* (Jan. 1985). *Notable Women in the Amer. Theater* (1989).

Other references: *American Artist* (Jan. 1982). *Architectural Digest* (Dec. 1984). *Boston Globe* (12 Aug. 1990, rev. by Mindy Aloff). *Dancemagazine* (Feb. 1980; Nov. 1981; Jan. 1982, rev. by Richard Philp, May 1986, June 1987, Sept. 1987). *Horizon* (Sept. 1980; Oct. 1980). *NYT* (31 May 1992; 8 Oct. 1993, obituary). *Opera News* (17 Jan. 1981). *People Weekly* (21 Sept. 1981).

FELICIA HARDISON LONDRÉ

Barbara Deming

B. 23 July 1917, New York City; d. 2 Aug. 1984, Sugarloaf Key, Florida
D. of Katherine (Burritt) and Harold S. Deming

D.'s fiction, essays, and poetry were all grounded in her personal experiences. From the age of sixteen when she realized she was a lesbian and began to write, D.'s life and writing were joined in a Gandhian struggle to "cling to the truth" *(satyagraha)*. This struggle later led D. to perceive herself as a lifelong activist, even though she did not enter public politics until 1960. Writing, D. felt, "could itself be named activism" because it was a process through which she discovered and "affirmed" what she knew about herself and the world around her. Living her life as a lesbian—defying the homophobic society that tried to define her—was another aspect of her activism.

Although literary periodicals published some of her poems, short stories, and reviews in the 1940s and 1950s, it was not until D. began writing news articles about the peace and civil rights movements that her work steadily reached a large audience. These pieces, initially published in left-wing journals, detailed her own and others' participation in social movements and offered her reflections on nonviolence and other issues. Whether because of the reputation she had gained or because changes in American society made personal narratives and social analysis more acceptable, both her earlier and new work reached print after the late

1960s. D.'s powerful feminist critiques, veiled in her early work and central after the early 1970s, gained her a devoted audience among women. Her almost spiritual theorizing about the connections among people and political movements continues to challenge readers to claim their lives as their own while respecting the same right of others.

D. and her three brothers grew up in New York and New City, New York. Her father was an admiralty lawyer, her mother a former singer. When D. was sixteen, she fell in love with an older woman and began writing poetry. Their relationship probably lasted until D. went to Bennington College where she majored in drama (B.A. 1938) and learned that a "woman's sensibility" was incongruent with good writing. She earned an M.A. from Cleveland's Western Reserve University (1941) and became an analyst for the Library of Congress film project at New York's Museum of Modern Art (1942–44). In 1945 she decided to become a full-time freelance writer. Her theater essays, film reviews, and some poetry were published in *New Directions, Chimera, The New Yorker,* and other periodicals, and in 1950 she finished a book analyzing the dreams and heroes portrayed in American films of the 1940s. A work of sociocultural criticism, *Running Away from Myself: A Dream Portrait of America Drawn from the Films of the Forties* was not published until 1969. D. notes that this "psychological study of America" had taken on greater relevance in the wake of a national crisis of faith and a concomitant desire by the United States to impose its will in Vietnam.

D. traveled to Europe in 1950–51 to recover from the painful breakup of a love relationship. When she returned she began a "fictional" chronicle of her emotional and physical "travail," but friends discouraged her from going beyond the first chapter. She turned to writing short stories. When D. returned to the novel in 1972 she realized that it, like others of her rejected works, held great promise—the lesbian protagonist, like her powerful social commentaries, made friends (and publishers) uncomfortable, but the story was strong. *A Humming under My Feet: A Book of Travail* was published in 1985.

In 1959, D. discovered the writings of Mahatma Gandhi while she was traveling through India. The following year she went to Cuba, and then attended a Peacemakers workshop. These experiences launched D. into a new phase of her life marked by public activism and a commitment to practicing and writing about nonviolence. Her personal activism made it easier for her to empathize with the struggles of other people (Cuban, Vietnamese, African American) and she joined a community that Leah Fritz describes as "cling[ing] to a whole complexity of political truths."

Active in the New England Committee for Nonviolent Action and the War Registers League, D. demonstrated, sat in, walked for peace and social justice, went to jail for acts of civil disobedience, and wrote about her experiences. *Prison Notes* (1966) grew out of her participation in the Quebec-Washington-Guantanamo Walk for Peace and Freedom and her arrest and imprisonment in Alabama. *Revolution and Equilibrium* (1971) includes essays that stemmed from her journeys to Cuba and to North Vietnam (1966–67). The essays in both volumes provide "a series of studies of nonviolent action and its possibilities" as well as a history of "The Movement" for peace and social change as it evolved during the 1960s. D.'s essays remain among the most significant writings on nonviolence. In 1971, a near-fatal car crash curtailed her physical activism, but her writings continued to be publicly political for the rest of her life.

In the mid-1970s, D. became a radical feminist and "came out" publicly during a Catholic Worker meeting. Through letters, several of which were then printed as "dialogues," she debated women's rights and sexuality with such civil rights and peace activists as Dave Dellinger and Arthur Kinoy and nonviolent tactics with feminist Jane Alpert. *We Cannot Live without Our Lives* (1974) reprints these and an exchange of letters on "confronting one's own oppression," which recognizes the common roots of racism, sexism, and homophobia, and the importance of claiming one's own identity. The book is dedicated to "all those seeking the courage to assert "I am—and especially to my lesbian sisters"; it makes clear D.'s defiance of the attempts of a homophobic and sexist society to define her. In 1983 she took part in actions organized by the Women's Encampment for a Future of Peace and Justice near Seneca Falls, New York, and served her final jail term.

D. died in her home on Sugarloaf Key of cervical cancer. She was survived by partners in two longterm relationships: painter and writer Mary Meigs (D.'s companion in the late 1950s and early 1960s) and artist Jane Gapen (Watrous) Verlaine, D.'s lover since the late 1960s.

OTHER WORKS: *Wash Us and Comb Us: Stories by Barbara Deming* (1972). *Remembering Who We Are: Barbara Deming in Dialogue with Gwenda Blair, Kathy Brown, Arthur Kinoy, Bradford Lyttle, Susan Sherman, Leah Fritz, Susan Saxe* (1981). *We Are All Part of One Another: A Barbara Deming Reader*, Jane Meyerding, ed. (1984). *Prisons That Could Not Hold: Prison Notes 1964—Seneca 1984* (1985). Articles in the 1940s and 1950s in *New Directions, Chimera, Wake, Voices, Partisan Review, The New Yorker, Charm, City Lights, Paris Review, Hudson Review, Tulane Drama Review*; in the 1960s and 1970s in the *Nation*, the *Catho-*

lic Worker, Liberation (of which she was an editor), *WIN, Kalliope,* and other magazines. The major collection of D.'s papers is in the Schlesinger Library, Radcliffe College; additional papers are in the Twentieth Century Collection of Boston University.

BIBLIOGRAPHY: *Broadside* 5:5 (1984). [Boston] *Gay Community News* (25 Aug./1 Sept. 1984, obituary). *Kalliope: A J. of Women's Art* 6:1 (1984). *NYT* (4 May 1984, obituary). *Ms.* (Nov. 1978, article by Leah Fritz).

KIMBERLY HAYDEN BROOKES

Toi Derricotte

B. 12 April 1941, Hamtramck, Michigan
D. of Antonia (Baquet) and Benjamin Sweeney Webster; m. Bruce Derricotte, 1964; c.: Anthony Webster, b. 1962

In 1983, having published two books of poetry and more than two-hundred poems and several articles in periodicals and anthologies, given countless readings, and conducted numerous seminars for students of all ages, D. remarked, "I want my work to be a wedge into the world, as what is real and not what people want to hear." In 1991 she flatly declared, "Definitely my teaching and writing is about making change," yet in a "Letter to an Editor Who Wants to Publish a Black Writer" worried, "To be published as a woman of color makes me fear I will be ignored by most white people, treated as if I don't exist" *(Callaloo).*

Happily, D. has been far from ignored and her writing acknowledged as much too compelling to be treated as if it does not exist. Publishing widely in journals and anthologies, she was recognized by **Maxine Kumin** as a poet who "transforms the raw stuff of experience into a language we can all treasure and continue to draw on." The *Village Voice* review of *Captivity* (1989), her boldest examination of contemporary black female

experience, proclaimed it an "outstanding example of personal exploration yielding truths that apply to all of us—if we admit them." An
African American feminist poet, D. speaks from a position particularly
attuned to American culture's racism and sexism. Yet in doing so, she
speaks to men as well as to women, to whites as well as to blacks; indeed,
the profound paradox in D.'s work is that by repeatedly examining states
of poverty, abuse, motherhood, and sexual pleasure that could only be
known by women, she manages also to explore experiences of fear,
pain, struggle, and ecstasy common to people of all races, sexes, nations,
and creeds.

At twenty-one D. was sent to a home for unwed mothers to bear a
son; seventeen years later she wrote a book of poems about that experience, *Natural Birth* (1983). After receiving her B.A. in Special Education
from Wayne State University in 1965, and marrying Bruce Derricotte,
she moved to New York City. There she continued her education by
participating in numerous writers' workshops and by studying English
literature and creative writing at New York University (NYU; M.A.
1984). An associate professor of English at the University of Pittsburgh
since 1991, she was a visiting professor of creative writing at NYU in
1992. D. lived for nearly two decades in New Jersey before moving to
Maryland in 1986. Between 1974 and 1991, she held diverse teaching
positions, including Poet-in-the-School in both New Jersey (1974–88)
and Maryland (1987–88), writer in residence for Cummington Community and School of the Arts (1986), associate professor of English literature at Old Dominion University (1988–90), and Commonwealth
Professor of English at George Mason University (1990–91).

Since her first book in 1978, D. has courageously examined the powers
and influences, agonies and ecstasies of family relations. Dedicated to a
grandmother who owned a funeral home and who never offered her
Cadillac Fleetwood to drive her granddaughter and daughter-in-law home
after their weekly visits, *Empress of the Death House* (1978) does more than
relay the pathos of mother and daughter being forced always to take
the bus, always to remember their lower status. In this book, formal
experimentations abound—"disappeared" punctuation, radically staggered lines, stanzas of varying and unpredictable length, ampersands and
abbreviations employed for suggestively casual diction ("yr"), capitalization used only for emphasis. These disruptive techniques complement
the volume's forbidden topics—deep and abiding anger toward the family
all black women are expected to protect and raw articulations of being
hurt and stifled by one's own people.

Natural Birth explores subjects considered too "low" and socially transgressive for poetry—childbirth and an unwed mother's responses to being hidden away from public knowledge in a special home, to being pummeled by an impatient doctor's procedure, and to being separated from the life her womb had protected for nine months. Though she incorporates the period into her technique much more frequently than before, D. uses italics, prose segments, staggered and rhythmically commanding schemes for lineation, and titles that underscore conflations of objective and subjective time so that readers are reminded that meanings are never simply a matter of word choice. When she reads from this collection, the texts are transformed into rocking, rolling, rhythmic, erotic performances. Through her near ecstatic readings, D. implicitly reminds her audience of the truth of the situation: what is *un*natural is not the birth out of wedlock but society's systematically abetted brutal, slashing response to it.

In *Captivity* D. speculates more boldly on the debilitating effects of a status that is perpetually powerless. Though her technique is somewhat more conventional than in the previous two volumes, prose segments, arresting lineation, and unpredictable stanzaic division still underscore subject matter that is even more unconventional. In the prose poem "Abuse" D. portrays a daughter seeking maternal protection by speaking out about abuse by the janitor and abuse by "Daddy." "Mama" seeks to fend off consciousness, responding: "Don't tell me that, you / make me suffer." "On the Turning up of Unidentified Black Female Corpses," a nine-stanza poem of regular, never disrupted four-line stanzas, mirrors "Mama's" attitude of desperate resignation. Poignantly, D.'s most radical subject is examined in the most formally regularized poem, as if to emphasize the fact that the victims are held captive even in death where they are scrutinized anonymously and only within the confines of the television tube. Yet this poem's speaker dares to ask the type of question "Mama" refuses her battered little girl: "Am I wrong to think / if five white women had been stripped, / broken, the sirens would wail until / someone was named?" The speaking of lost lives long overlooked, their tragedies denied, is equated with exhuming those rendered a "living dead" through neglect.

Tackling bloody, bruising, and bruised subjects in her poetry, D. launches complex and caring critiques of American society in her persistent poetic attention to lives of disenfranchised African American women. In doing so, she forces readers to grapple with her contention, proclaimed in her 1991 *Callaloo* interview, that "a lot of what doesn't get talked about gets translated into violence—racism, sexism—and gets worked out in families as physical and emotional abuse." She still believes that "we are prisoners of what we don't know, of what we don't acknowledge, what we don't bring out, what we aren't conscious of, deny." And thus D. has dedicated her formidable talents to producing poetic work that is indisputably "a wedge into the world."

OTHER WORKS: Creative Writing: A Manual for Teachers (1985, with Madeline Tyger). Selected excerpts from *The Black Notebooks*, "July 1977," "December 1977," "May 1978," in *Ariadne's Thread: A Collection of Contemporary Women's Journals*, Lyn Lifshin, ed. "At an Artist's Colony," in *Daily Fare: Essays from the Multicultural Experience*, Kathleen Aguero, ed. (1993).

BIBLIOGRAPHY: Reference works: *CA* 113 (1985). *CANR* 32 (1991). *WW Wr, Eds, Poets* (1989).
    Other references: *Callaloo* 14:3 (1991, interview, special section on D.). *Ikon* 2:5 + 6 (1986). *Kenyon Rev.* 13:2 + 4 (1991). *Paris Rev.* (1992, interview).

                                                    MARTHA NELL SMITH

Alexis De Veaux

B. 24 Sept. 1948, New York City
D. of Mae de Veaux and Richard Hill

Feminist, poet, playwright, fiction and children's book writer, illustrator, and political journalist, D. places African Americans, most often black women, at the center of her artistic world. Her work concentrates on the personal struggles and resolve of women, especially as they deal with love and sexuality. D. focuses on intimate relationships, whether they involve lesbian lovers ("The Sister"), contending forces in a love triangle (*Don't Explain*, 1980), or a daughter and her parent ("Adventures of the

Dread Sisters"). Because she believes that an understanding of the self in relationship with the intimate other leads to an understanding of the community, the nation, the world, D.'s work also gives testimony to black culture. As Mary Helen Washington notes, Nigeria, the central character in "Dread Sisters" (1989), is then not "an isolated teenager but a collective protagonist." D.'s writing projects her feminist perspective that the personal is the political.

D. grew up in Harlem and the South Bronx, which serve as the settings for most of her work. Both *Na-Ni* (1973), which received an Art Books for Children Award from the Brooklyn Museum (1974–75), and *Spirits in the Streets* (1973) are set in Harlem and revolve around the theme of "preserving spiritual vitality in a ghetto environment." While D.'s stories often embrace the harsh realities of poverty and exploitation, they are also infused with hope and beauty.

Spirits in the Streets (1973) reflects D.'s array of artistic talents. It integrates innovative use of language within narrative, lyric, and dialogue, with illustrations and variations of typography. *Spirits* is at once a poem, a mural, and a song.

Music has a great influence on D.'s writing. "The Riddles of Egypt Brownstone" (1977), D. explains, "is like jazz, each instrument/character playing variations on the melody so that the story is told not as a linear experience but as a holistic one." Jazz and language come together fully in *Don't Explain: A Song of Billie Holiday* (1980), a fictionalized biography of the singer, written in lyric form for young adults.

D. earned a B.A. from SUNY-Empire State College (1976) and a Ph.D. from the State University of New York at Buffalo (1992). She has been a community worker, an instructor of reading and English, and a teacher of creative writing and theater workshops in New York and Connecticut. A freelance writer since 1974, she is also a contributing editor of *Essence* magazine. D. has written a number of essays for *Essence* in which she reasserts her global feminist perspective, calling for the political and social liberation of black and third-world women. Her stories and poems have appeared in several publications, including *Black Creation, Conditions: Five,* and the *Iowa Review.*

OTHER WORKS: *Nani, a Story and Pictures* (1973). *Li Chen/Second Daughter, First Son* (1975). *Blue Heat: a Portfolio of Poems and Drawings* (1985). *An Enchanted Hair Tale* (1987). See also: *Home Girls: A Black Feminist Anthology,* Barbara Smith, ed. (1983, includes "The Sisters"). *Black-Eyed Susans. Midnight Birds,* (1990), Mary Helen Washington, ed. (1900, includes "The Riddles of Egypt Brownstone" and "Remember Him an Outlaw"). *Memory of Kin: Stories about Family by Black Writers*, M. H. Washington, ed. (1991, includes "Adventures of the Dread Sisters"). Play productions: *Circles* (1973, Frederick Douglass Creative Arts Center, New York City). *The Tapestry* (1976, Harlem Performance Center, New York City, and KCET-TV, New York City). "A Season to Unravel" (1979, Negro Ensemble Company, New York City).

BIBLIOGRAPHY: *Black Women Writers at Work*, Claudia Tate, ed. (1983). Washington, Mary Helen, "Commentary on Alexis De Veaux," *Memory of Kin*. Reference works: *Black Authors and Illustrators of Children's Books* (1988). *Black Writers* (1989). *CA* 65–68 (1977). *CANR* 26 (1989). *DLB* 38 (1985).
    Other references: *Ms.* 8 (June 1980).

DALE A. DOOLEY

John Dexter. *See Marion Zimmer Bradley*

Joan Didion

See AWW 1, 502–3

Since 1979, most of D.'s work has been nonfiction; she has published only one novel, *Democracy* (1984), which has strong journalistic elements. She continues to contribute to a variety of magazines, particularly *The New Yorker* and the *New York Review of Books*, and to write screenplays with her husband, John Gregory Dunne. All of her work takes an honest, often-cynical view of politics, society, personal relationships, even of D. herself. A master of language and prose, she conveys ideas succinctly in a spare but eloquent style. Believing that "we tell ourselves stories in order to live," her work continues to be driven by her sense of moral urgency.

The White Album (1979) is D.'s second collection of essays, most of which were previously published in such magazines as *Esquire* and *Life*. The essays record her response to events of the late 1960s and early 1970s, including reflections on the Manson family, and a return to the subject of Hollywood, described here ironically as "the last extant stable society." The volume also reprints D.'s essay on the women's movement, which caused considerable controversy amongst feminists when it first appeared in 1972. D. takes less-political looks at Georgia O'Keeffe, writes about personal experiences with migraines and travels in Hawaii and Bogotá, and even includes her own psychiatric evaluation.

Salvador (1982) is a difficult, extended essay documenting D.'s two-week stay in that country. In one sense a travel diary, the book seeks to provide insight into the complexities plaguing Central America. D. presents the conflict in El Salvador with little explanation or background; the confusion of the narrative mirrors the senselessness of the violence and hate she finds there. Often the people she meets who are involved in the fighting do not seem to understand the conflict themselves. Quite scathingly critical of American involvement in the crisis, D. finds the "mechanism of terror" to be beyond irony. *Salvador* is D. at her most despairing.

Democracy (1984) is fiction appearing as nonfiction, even journalism. D. places herself in the book as a narrator recounting the story of the Christian and Victor families and of their rise and eventual fall. Deliberately blurring the distinctions between fiction and journalism, D. creates a convincing narrative, especially in its climax against the backdrop of the United States evacuation of Saigon and the fall of the city.

In *Miami* (1987), D. analyzes the many complexities of the society, culture, and politics of a city of exiles and racial groups deeply at odds. Within the context of the history of United States–Cuban relations and its many failures, she explores the diverse views and feelings of Cuban exiles and the impact of the experience of exile. The book richly demonstrates D.'s ability to see the many sides of a difficult and confusing situation.

D.'s ability to recognize, imagine, and capture a variety of viewpoints and her mastery of the language establish her as a major writer. As critic

Joan Zseleckzy concludes: "It is not any journalist who can write a novel. It is not any journalist who can tell a story."

OTHER WORKS: After Henry (essays, 1992).

BIBLIOGRAPHY: Friedman, E. G., Joan Didion: Essays and Conversations (1984). Hanley, L. T., Writing War: Fiction, Gender, and Memory (1991). Henderson, K. U., Joan Didion (1981). "Joan Didion" in American Women Writing Fiction, M. Pearlman, ed. (1989). Loris, M. C., Innocence, Loss, and Recovery in the Art of Joan Didion (1989). Merivale, P., "The Search for the Other Woman: JD and the Female Artist Parable," in Gender Studies: New Directions in Feminist Criticism (1986). Winchell, M. R., Joan Didion (1980). Reference works: CA 5–8 (1969). CANR 14 (1985). CLC 1 (1973), 3 (1975), 8 (1978), 14 (1980), 32 (1985). CB (1978). DLB 2 (1978). DLBY (1981, 1986). FC (1990). Maj Twent Cent Writers (1991). Modern Amer. Women Writers (article and bibliography by J. Zseleckzy, 1991).

Other references: Amer. Lit. 59:3 (Oct. 1987). Critique 25:3 (Spring 1984). Esquire (June 1990). Hollins Critic 24:4 (Oct. 1989). Mass. Rev. 24:1 (Spring 1983). NYTBR (17 May 1992). PW (13 Nov. 1987). Saturday Rev. (April 1982). South Carolina Rev. 21:2 (Spring 1989). Working Woman (April 1982). See also MLA on-line bibliography.

SHAUNA SUMMERS

Annie Dillard

See AWW 1, 505–7

Describing the "writing life" D. asserts that "the art must enter the body." From her Pulitzer Prize–winning Pilgrim at Tinker Creek (1974) she establishes this relationship with both her writing and the environment it reflects. Rather than objectively observing the scenes of her life, she experiences them as religious encounters. Her early work, up through Holy the Firm (1977), secured D. a place among both naturalist and mystical essayists. Within her natural descriptions, D. theologizes on creation and its creator. A searching spirituality tempers her acute physical perceptions to create works heavy in allusionary and abstract meaning.

After *Holy the Firm*, D. began to change her focus from external to internal environments. With the 1982 publications of *Living by Fiction* and *Teaching a Stone to Talk*, the grand spiritual abstraction that characterized her early natural vision gave way to a more personal and human intimacy. *Living by Fiction* explores the landscape of fiction as a natural sphere of influence and means of personal definition, while *Teaching a Stone to Talk* continues to rely on nature as landscape. While her earlier work suggests that meaning is present and observable in nature, D.'s later work begins to examine her personal interactions with the landscape, recognizing that most meaning is humanly imposed on a scene.

D. clarified this movement with the 1984 publication of *Encounters with Chinese Writers*, a collection of essays based on her experience as a member of the United States Cultural Delegation to China in 1982. Describing a foreign landscape and people, D. seeks personal definition within cultural difference. In her autobiography, *An American Childhood* (1987), D. brings that search back to the most primally familiar of all landscapes—childhood. The book was nominated for the National Book Critics Circle Award. Both works exhibit a fluid exchange between the writer and her landscape. The writing itself becomes more concrete and accessible.

By the time of publication of *The Writing Life* (1989) D. has struggled to identify the tracks of her thoughts and the fissures they leave in the observed landscapes. Her writing no longer exposes only the interaction of God and nature as creator and creation, but the human mind as both creator and creation. D.'s movement into fiction attests to her attempt to understand the complex relationship between the human mind and the natural world. *The Living* (1992) chronicles the growth of Bellingham Bay and its inhabitants. Although the novel is historical, D. concentrates on the parallel evolutions of the personal and the physical landscapes.

D. resides in Middletown, Connecticut, with her husband and daughter. A writer in residence and adjunct professor at Wesleyan University, she has been the recipient of fellowships from the National Endowment for the Arts (1980–81) and the Guggenheim Foundation (1985–86).

BIBLIOGRAPHY: Clark, Suzanne, "Annie Dillard: The Woman in Nature and the Subject of Nonfiction," in *Literary Nonfiction*, Chris Anderson, ed. (1989). Johnson, Sandra H., *The Space Between: Literary Epiphany in the Work of Annie Dillard* (1992). Scheick, William, "Annie Dillard: Narrative Fringe," in *Contemp. Amer. Women Writers: Narrative Strategies*, Catherine Rainwater and W. Scheick, eds. (1985).

Other references: *Amer. Lit.* 59:1 (March 1987). *Belles Lettres* 8 (Fall 1992). *J. Feminist Studies in Religion* 6 (Spring 1990). *LA Times* (25 May 1992). *LATBR* (25 Sept. 1988). *Ms.* (June 1985). *Nation* (16 Oct. 1989; 25 May 1992). *NYTBR* (9 May 1982; 23 Sept. 1984; 27 Sept. 1987; 18 Nov. 1990). *Sewanee Rev.* 92 (Winter 1984). *Signs* 15 (Spring 1990). *So. Atl. Q.* 85 (Spring 1986). *WRB* (Jan. 1988).

JULIE ANN FIORE

Diane DiPrima

B. 3 Aug. 1934, New York City
D. of Emma (Mallozzi) and Francis DiPrima; m. Alan S. Marlowe, 1962, div.
1969; m. Grant Fisher, 1972, div. 1975; c.: Jeanne, b. 1957; Dominique, b.
1962; Alexander, b. 1963; Tara, b. 1967; Rudi, b. 1970

Since the late 1950s, D. has earned recognition for writings marked by a spirit of rebellion and countercultural exploration. Perhaps best known as a poet and editor, she has also published novels, plays, and translations. Her early writing chronicles the experiences of the Beat Generation, with special attention to the female dimensions of that culture. Together with LeRoi Jones (Imiri Baraka), D. coedited *The Floating Bear* (1961–69), a monthly poetry newsletter that became one of the most influential publications of its kind, featuring many important Beat writers. In all her work, she has maintained a strong consciousness of her identity as a woman writer, depicting through personal relationships, political tensions, and mythological images, a particularly female experience or truth.

Enrolling in Swarthmore College at seventeen, D. dropped out two years later and returned to New York, to Greenwich Village and the emerging Beat scene there. She published her first book of poems, *This Kind of Bird Flies Backwards*, with LeRoi Jones's Totem Press in 1958.

These poems make generous use of the Beat idiom, in such lines as "Like man don't flip, I'm hip you / cooled this scene." The book also reveals D.'s early interest in myths and fables, which become central motives in *Loba: Parts 1–8* (1973), one of her major works of poetry.

D.'s autobiographical novel *Memoirs of a Beatnik* (1969) describes her experience among the Beats. Some critics consider her "female" experience circumscribed in comparison to the rambling adventures of such male Beats as Jack Kerouac. Others see D.'s work as adding an important dimension to our understanding of the Beat world, reminding us, George Butterick notes, "that the generation spent as much time in urban 'pads' as it did 'on the road,' and that one can travel as far by human relationships as by thumb."

Along with the *Floating Bear*, D. worked with several other influential poetry journals of the time, including *Kulchur* and *Yugen*. She and husband Alan Marlowe founded the Poets Press (1964–69) and the New York Poets Theatre (1961–65), which produced plays by Frank O'Hara, Robert Duncan, James Schuyler, and others. Her own plays were performed at the Living Theater in New York.

D.'s poetry is often highly accessible in language and emotion, revealing "a willingness to trust language with deep feelings even if it is to declare more than explore those feelings." Her most challenging poems use a complex symbolism that is both idiosyncratic and archetypal. These poems, Butterick writes, "represent private feelings revealed in the tradition of symbolism, if not in traditional symbols themselves." In "The Waiting Room" (*The New Handbook of Heaven*, 1963) she writes: "Every human skull / uncovered, is one more home / for the spirits of darkness. / I leave the dice at the rat hole every night / no one keeps score."

In *Loba*, D. turns her symbolizing to the task of creating an epic of the female principle. "Loba" is a protean character, transforming from spirit to beast to human, alternately representing a Lilith- and an Eve-figure. This mythic persona embodies female power in a variety of forms, as in these first lines: "O lost moon sisters / crescent in hair, sea underfoot do you wander / in blue veil, in green leaf, in tattered shawl do you wander / with goldleaf skin, with flaming hair do you wander / on Avenue A, on Bleecker Street do you wander."

Critic Armand Schwerner argues that D.'s verse is not always equal to her task: that "in the attempt to particularize within the context of 'the life of mankind,'" her language "sometimes falls into banality." Yet, he acknowledges, "the attempt, the order of inclusiveness, the mythopoetic reach are a contribution to that profound ongoing process of poetry which . . . continues the self-transformative aims of our alchemical fa-thers."

D. lives in California, writing, teaching, and practicing Buddhism and healing arts. Her life and work continue to exemplify the spiritual and cultural journeying of the Beat Generation, as seen through the eyes of a woman.

OTHER WORKS: Various Fables from Various Places (editor, 1960). *Murder Cake* (play, 1960). *Like* (play, 1960). *Paideuma* (play, 1960). *The Discontent of a Russian Prince* (play, 1961). *Dinners and Nightmares* (short stories, 1960, 1974). *The Monster* (1961). *Poets Vaudeville* (1964). *Seven Love Poems from the Middle Latin* (translator, 1965). *Combination Theater Poem and Birthday Poem for 10 People* (1965). *Haiku* (1967). *Earthsong: Poems, 1957–1959* (1968). *Hotel Albert: Poems* (1968). *New Mexico Poems, June–July 1967* (1968). *The Star, The Child, The Light* (editor, 1968). *War Poems* (1968). *Revolutionary Letters* (1969). *L.A. Odyssey* (1969). *New As . . . (1969)*. *Notes on a Summer Solstice* (1969). *Kerhonkson Journal 1966* (1971). *Prayer to the Mothers* (1971). *So Fine* (1971). *The Calculus of Variation* (novel, 1972). *Freddie: Poems* (1974). *Selected Poems, 1956–1975* (1975). *Loba as Eve* (1975). *Loba, Part 2* (1976). *Revolutionary Letters, etc.* (1979). *Pieces of a Song: Selected Poems* (1989). *Zipcode: The Collected Plays of Diane DiPrima* (1992).

BIBLIOGRAPHY: Waldman, Anne, "An Interview with Diane DiPrima," *The Beat Road*, A. W. Knight, ed. (1984). Reference works: *CANR* 13 (1984). *Contemp. Poets* (1991). *DLB* 16 (1983, article by George Butterick). *FC* (1990).

Other references: *Amer. Book Rev.* 2 (May 1980, rev. by Armand Schwerner); 13 (June/July 1991). *MELUS* 14:3–4 (Fall–Winter 1987). *Village Voice* (13 June 1974; 9 May 1989).

MARY BURGER

Rita Dove

B. 28 Aug. 1952, Akron, Ohio
D. of Elvira (Hord) and Ray Dove; m. Fred Viebahn, 1979; c.: Aviva Chantal
Dove-Viebahn

In 1987 D. became the second African American to win the Pulitzer Prize, awarded for her third book of poems, *Thomas and Beulah* (1986). At thirty-four she was also one of the youngest recipients. D. received her B.A. (1973) from Miami University in Ohio, attended the University of Tuebingen in West Germany (1974–75), and earned her M.F.A. from the University of Iowa (1977). She has traveled widely, finding "travel a good way to avoid complacency." Her work, described by Alfred Corn as "never content to rest in a winning formula," reflects this.

In a quiet, unadorned voice, D.'s poems reveal a broad range of interests with intelligence and precision. Though her first book is called *The Yellow House on the Corner* (1980) there is nothing stationary about it. The poems travel from Mexico, Tunisia, and the Sahara Desert, to Kentucky in 1833. They also move through many states of mind—from the first reluctant glints of sexuality in adolescence to the mature love expressed in the poem "His Shirt." In the third section, speaking in a number of voices, D. re-creates painful episodes of African American history, making them immediate and personal again. She speaks for slaves who were not allowed the powers of literacy and articulation in life: "It's a crazy feeling that comes through the night, as if the sky were an omen we could not understand, the book that if we could read, would change our lives."

Museum (1983) is again filled with her never-idle curiosity about history and the world. There are poems here about Catherine of Alexandria, Catherine of Siena, Boccacccio, Shakespeare, Hölderlin. Two poems, "Grape Sherbert" and "Parsley," express a tension that runs through all of her books. D. articulates both a sense of deep sensual gratitude—the orange who "tears herself apart to give us relief" (*The Yellow House on the Corner*)—and a sense of history that is never shallow, naive, or one-sided. Her understanding is inclusive, taking in opposing views of the conflicts with which she deals, bringing her talents to bear on men as well as women, on whites as well as blacks.

This is particularly true of *Thomas and Beulah*, based on the lives of D.'s maternal grandparents who married in 1924 in Akron, Ohio, and raised four daughters. The book tells "two sides of a story": Thomas speaks in the first half, Beulah in the second. In the background we hear historical echoes—the migration of rural Southern blacks to the industrial North, the March on Washington in 1963. But the book is primarily the history of a marriage and a feeling for personal detail and the particularity of ordinary people's lives dominates. "I'm not interested in the big moments. I was interested in the thoughts, the things which were concerning the small people," D. noted. Marriage, the birth of children, job changes, the purchase of a car, a new house, grandchildren—D. looks at all these with a gaze that is both "sweet and merciless" ("Pomade"). As Beulah's father gives her away in marriage he says, "Each hurt swallowed is a stone" ("Promise"). D. takes these stones out again and arranges them in the light of a new day. Trouble and regret are not erased or softened but raised to a new level of value and regard.

The promises of youth trail both Thomas and Beulah into their adult lives, becoming a "curdled sweetness" ("Pomade"), making them deeply uneasy at times, philosophical at others. "Daystar" speaks of Beulah's wish for "a little room for thinking." Not having one, she "lugged a chair behind the garage / to sit out the children's naps." Caught in a preordained life of marriage and children, Beulah develops a rich inner life and her story is often told in such meditative poems.

D. never minimizes the gap between the promises of youth and the sometimes cold, leaden gravity of her grandparents' adult lives. Neither is she melancholy or angry about it. Though the history behind the poem is troubled, the poems themselves radiate life untouched by manipulative impulses or reformist zeal.

Though D. is more comfortable speaking about others than about herself, autobiography and biography are closely linked in her work. *Grace Notes* (1989) begins with childlike images of white American silos and ends at an Old Folk's Home in Jerusalem. The book's third section includes several mother-daughter poems that are more relaxed and personal in tone and mark a new development in her work. Though they seem to approach a sense of home, at least tentatively, for D. "home" is not a place easily arrived at.

D.'s first novel, *Through the Ivory Gate*, appeared in 1992. Semiautobiographical, it brings puppeteer and cellist Virginia King back to her hometown of Akron to work in the Artist in the Schools program. Through flashbacks and meetings with her grandmother and elderly aunt, and a rejected offer of romance, Virginia comes to understand both the tensions in her family and her own commitment to a career in the theater. In 1993, D. was named poet laureate of the United States, the first African American woman so honored.

OTHER WORKS: *Fifth Sunday* (short stories, 1985).

BIBLIOGRAPHY: Reference works: *CA* 109 (1983). *CANR* 27 (1989). *CLC* 50 (1988).
Other references: *Virginia Q. Rev.* (Spring 1988). *Library J.* (Dec.1989). *Poetry* (Oct. 1990).

TAM LIN NEVILLE

Elizabeth Drew

See AWW *1, 542–43*

As a political journalist, D. has been described as "the American Boswell" and "the Samuel Pepys of Washington." Her "Letter from Washington" has appeared regularly in *The New Yorker* since 1973, and from 1973 to 1992 she continued her television broadcasting career as a commentator and panelist for "Inside Washington" (formerly "Agronsky and Company"). D. has received many awards including the Dupont-Columbia Award for Broadcast Journalism (1973), the Newswomen's Club of New York Award (1983), the *Washington Monthly* Political Books Award (1984), and the Edward Weintal Prize for Diplomatic Reporting (1988).

In *Senator* (1979), D. recounts ten days in the congressional life of John Culver in the Senate and in his home state, Iowa. The book is written as a case study, realistically detailing the trivial and morally problematic aspects of political life without offering synthesis or analysis. The book is frequently excerpted in anthologies assigned for college political science courses.

In *Portrait of an Election: The 1980 Presidential Campaign* (1981) D. explains that she is taking a journalistic approach that "constitutes a history of the period—an account of the realities of the time, unguided, and also undistorted, by hindsight." The goal is to show "how people in politics think, calculate, react" and to capture how it looks and feels. One reviewer applauded her "cool, lucid style" and "reasoned fair-minded approach" to her interviews with political actors and their advisors. Another reviewer, however, sees D. spending time "lovingly describing Democratic programs or tearing apart Republican rhetoric." A perception by D.'s colleagues that she is a "serious, humane, responsibly liberal, one-track-minded, mildly workaholic veteran" Washington insider, is especially borne out in *Politics and Money: The Road to Corruption* (1983). Here D. carefully synthesizes the intricacies of the "role of money in the American political system" and provides a specifically argued analysis of what should be done to "bring the nation back closer to the fundamental principles of democracy." Her investigation into the "great rivers of money that were essentially unaccounted for, and legally questionable, flowing into both our congressional and presidential elections" has been consistently credited as one of the first journalistic attempts to document the problems inherent in the process of reforming campaign finance laws.

In *Campaign Journal: The Political Events of 1983–1984* (1985) D. returns to the "detailed diary" recording of a presidential election campaign with much of the focus on strategies used by Democratic Party candidates trying to win back the White House. *Election Journal: Political Events of 1987–1988* (1989) offers more discursive judgments of events and people than her previous books on presidential campaigns, assigning to Ronald Reagan, for instance, the role of "dominant figure" in the 1988 election. Both books reflect what a reviewer called her "extraordinary capacity for eliciting the informed observations of insiders."

Since 1989, D. has continued to contribute the "Letter from Washington" for *The New Yorker* as well as to write articles for such publications as the *New York Times Sunday Magazine*. Her subjects have included the role of Congress in the post–Cold War era, politics in the Soviet Union, the 1992 presidential election campaign and the politics of campaign finance reform. In 1993, she began work on a book about the first year of the Clinton administration.

BIBLIOGRAPHY: Reference works: *CA* 104 (1982).

Other references: *J. Amer. Studies* (Aug. 1983). *National Rev.* (9 Aug. 1985). *New Republic* (30 Dec. 1981). *NYRB* (21 Jan. 1982). *NYTBR* (13 May 1979; 8

Nov. 1981; 11 Sept. 1983; 17 March 1985; 2 April 1989). *Wash. Journalism Rev.* (Dec. 1981). Additions to *AWW* 1: *Biographical.* M. J. Patterson Drew, 1964 (d. 1970); m. David Webster, 1981.

JENNIFER L. TEBBE

Rosalyn Drexler

B. 26 Nov. 1926, New York City
Writes under: Julia Sorel
D. of Hilda (Sherman) and George Bronznick; m. Sherman Drexler, 1946; c.: one
daughter, one son

D. writes plays and novels that share pathos and satiric wit, mundaneness and magic, comedy and the blunt grimness of newspaper tragedy. She describes her feminist blend of "reality and fantasy" as "in the tradition of the Russian absurdists/surrealists such as Zamyatin, Gogol, and Bulgakov." Her writing is structured by plot development motivated by character, located in a world like ours—though the rules differ, and characters sometimes follow the spotlight or turn into angels. D.'s drama has been well received critically, and three of her plays (*Home Movies*, 1967; *The Writer's Opera*, 1979; *Transients Welcome*, 1984) were awarded Obies. Her short story "Dear" won a *Paris Review* humor prize (1966), and in 1974 she received an Emmy Award for writing a television special for comedian Lily Tomlin. D. has been the recipient of fellowships from the Rockefeller Foundation (1965) and the Guggenheim Foundation (1970).

Largely self-educated, D. has worked as a wrestler, a singer, a college teacher, a director, and a sculptor; she is also a noted painter. All of these occupations are preoccupations in her writing, which she describes as "very much concerned with the artist, creativity, and the relationship of the artist to life," with "human relationships" and questions of "what is real life and who's trying to squelch it."

Critics have compared her to the Marx Brothers (whose movies she saw as a child), commenting on her honesty and the playfulness of her sight gags, song, silliness, and puns. But D.'s writing is not just farcical, as critics who have likened her to Kafka, Joyce, and Pynchon recognize. D. "loves Beckett" and Ionesco, and her worlds' darker ironies and isolation reflect this. Her irreverence is iconoclastic. Her use of stream of consciousness reveals characters who are not having fun, whose desires lead only to loss. Her writing focuses on the theatricality of life, the ways characters script each other and adopt roles, revealing in the process that much of human identity is artificial and implying that these roles are inadequate or damaging.

Verbal and physical violence are also important technical and thematic issues in D.'s work, animating her interest in dysfunctional families, gender relations, and the impact of the arts and media. Her later work includes *Bad Guy* (1982), a novel about a therapist who uses dream interpretation and psychodrama to treat a teenage rapist/murderer whose role models have all been television characters.

D.'s work is art and entertainment, and her characters resemble circus grotesques, paradoxically evoking tenderness and laughter. Her style is both compassionate toward them and merciless in detailing their lives. These criminals and victims, healers and patients, social misfits and apparently normal characters—whose psychological deformities and scars D. reveals—are both archetypal and idiosyncratic. Her writing is memorable for these characters and their wordplay; it is poignant when we see them achieve a momentary self-awareness or transcend their fragmentation in an act of intimacy or kindness—perhaps because the meanings of self and action remain ambiguous.

D.'s writing is almost always political. The point of view is often feminist, as when she focuses on the commodification of the female body (*Line of Least Existence*, 1967; *Cosmopolitan Girl*, 1974) or mythologizes male rule as the rape/murder of a queen who incarnates her country (*She Who Was He*, 1973). But D.'s social critiques are broader than any label, ranging from parodies of class and racial stereotypes and witty indictments of commercialism, materialism, and egotism to trenchant satire of such topical issues as the American involvement in Panama (*Cara Piña*, 1992).

OTHER WORKS: *I Am the Beautiful Stranger* (1965). *Hot Buttered Roll*, in *Theater Experiment*, M. Benedikt, ed. (1967). *Skywriting*, in *Collision Course*, Edward Parone, ed. (1968) and in *A Century of Plays by American Women*, Rachel France, ed. (1979). *The Investigation and Hot Buttered Roll* (1969). *One or Another* (1970). *Home Movies* in *The Off Off Broadway Book*, Albert Poland

and Bruce Mailman, ed. (1972). *To Smithereens* (1972). *Starburn: The Story of Jenni Love* (1979). Fiction as Julia Sorel: *Unwed Widow* (1975). *Dawn: Portrait of a Teenage Runaway* (1976). *Rocky* (1976). *Alex: The Other Side of Dawn* (1977). *See How She Runs* (1978). Short stories in *New Amer. Rev.* #7 (1969). *Paris Rev.* 38 (1966). *Wonder*, Jonathan Cott and Mary Gimbel, eds. (1980). *Black Ice #8* (1992). Essays in *Esquire* (May 1970); *Mademoiselle* (July 1973; April 1979). *NYT* (7 Nov. 1971; 22 Oct. 1972; 20 May 1973). *Village Voice* (4 April 1968). Unpublished plays in D.'s possession (dates are for first production): *The Ice Queen* (1965). *Was I Good?* (1972). *Vulgar Lives* (1979). *The Writer's Opera* (1979). *Graven Image* (1980). *The Mandrake* (1983). *Starburn* (1983). *Delicate Feelings* (1984). *A Matter of Life and Death* (1986). *The Heart That Eats Itself* (1987). *The Flood* (1992). "Naked Desire; or, An Exceptional Woman" (MS in circulation). "Occupational Hazard" (MS).

BIBLIOGRAPHY: Abraham, Teresa Taisha, "Carnivalesque and American Women Dramatists of the Sixties." Unpublished Ph.D. diss., SUNY-Stonybrook, 1990; *DAI* 51:6 (Dec. 1990). Betsko, Kathleen, and Rachel Koenig, *Interviews with Contemporary Women Playwrights* (1987). Brown, Janet, *Feminist Drama: Definition and Critical Analysis* (1979). Dasgupta, Gautam, "Rosalyn Drexler," in *American Playwrights: A Critical Survey*, G. D. and Bonnie Marranca, eds. (1981). Gottfried, Martin, *A Theater Divided: The Postwar American Stage* (1967). Keyssar, Helene, *Feminist Theatre* (1984). Sontag, Susan, "Going to Theater, Etc." in *Against Interpretation and Other Essays* (1966). Sonnenschein, Dana, correspondence and telephone interview with D., June 1992. Reference works: *AmerWomen Dramatists of the Twent Cent* (1982). *CA* 81–84 (1979). *Contemp. Dramatists* (1988). *CLC* 2 (1974), 6 (1976). *Notable Women in the American Theater* (1989).

Other references: *Art in America* 74 (Nov. 1986). *Art News* (March 1964; interview, Jan. 1971). *Mademoiselle* (interview, Aug. 1972). *Mass Rev.* 13:1 (interview, Winter 1972). *New Yorker* (23 May 1964). *NYT* (interview, 27 Feb. 1978). *Plays and Players* 17 (April 1970). *Theater* 17:1 (Winter 1985).

DANA SONNENSCHEIN

Andrea Dworkin

B. 26 Sept. 1946, Camden, New Jersey
D. of Sylvia (Spiegal) and Harry Dworkin; m. 1969, div. 1972

As a child, D. aspired to be a writer or lawyer to "really change society." Arrested at eighteen for demonstrating for civil rights, she was held four days in the New York Women's House of Detention and forced to undergo a painful internal examination. She hemorrhaged vaginally for two weeks then went to the media to publicize the atrocity. The experience informed her later passionate feminist militancy and polemical writing. Retreating to Crete (1965–66), D. published her first book, Child (1966). She completed her B.A. in literature and philosophy at Bennington in 1968.

D. then left for five years in Amsterdam, where she began Woman Hating: A Radical Look at Sexuality (1974), aiming to incite revolution in conventional sex roles and cultural institutions by tracing the roots of sexism through psychology and pornography as means by which men control and possess women. Her generalizations about all men as neurotically dominant brutes and all male-female relationships as pathological led critics to lambaste her extremist separatist ideology. D. emerged as one of the most strident voices of radical feminism, calling in a speech at a National Organization for Women (NOW) Conference on Sexuality for heterosexual sex without erection or penetration, leading opponents to coin the term "castrating feminists." D. developed this argument in Intercourse (1987).

Yet radical lesbians criticized her bisexuality. D. rejected political lesbianism as a personal politic reminiscent of biological determinism, an ideology "which justified atrocity" and attacked the militancy of "prescribers" who "enforce sexual conformity" that impels the search for new enemies, dividing women from women in the name of sexuality. While denying a biological basis for sexism, the "essentialist" D. universalizes concepts of women and motherhood, misogyny and sexism. She favors the concept of androgyny. The nine essays in Our Blood: Prophecies and Discourse on Sexual Politics (1976) describe destructive male dominance and artificial sex roles that permeate cultures in Asia, Europe, and America, citing manifestations of "gynocide" in fairy tales, customs, religion, pornography, and other literature as leading to deprivation of women's rights.

D. focuses on pornography as the chief agency perpetuating the violent male power system. Her essay in the volume *Take Back the Night: Women on Pornography* (1980) and her *Pornography: Men Possessing Women* (1981) reject the notion that pornography creatively expresses eroticism, seeing it as a violent instrument by which men subjugate women, deprive them of individuality, and keep them safe, secure, but subservient. Putting theory to practice, D. teamed with attorney Catharine MacKinnon in 1983 to draft a controversial model civil ordinance defining pornography as illegal sex discrimination. It passed in Indianapolis; but despite D.'s testimony before the Minnesota attorney general, published as *Pornography Is a Civil Rights Issue for Women* (1986), the law was overturned in Minneapolis as violating freedom of speech. D. and MacKinnon co-authored *Pornography and Civil Rights: A New Day for Women's Equality* (1988), outlining the history of women's legal status and describing their ill-fated law. New organizations like Women against Pornography drew upon D. for the slogan, "Pornography is the theory, rape is the practice." D. remained in the forefront of the antipornography movement with public appearances and *Letters from a War Zone, 1976–1987* (1988, rev. 1989).

Right-wing Women (1983) argues that the 1970s antifeminist backlash from the political right stemmed from status anxiety, fear of personal consequences that might result from feminism's questioning of traditional roles in which many American women had invested a sense of self, and even greater fears of what their status would be outside of the home. The political right "makes certain metaphysical and material promises to women that both exploit and quiet some of women's deepest fears. These fears originate in the perception that male violence against women is uncontrollable and unpredictable. Dependent on and subservient to men, women are always subject to this violence. The right promises to put enforceable restraints on male aggression, thus simplifying survival for women." D. worries about a "coming gynocide," a grim future for all women but particularly for the poor and elderly.

D.'s short stories in the *New Woman's Broken Heart* (1980) as well as her novel *Ice and Fire* (1986) are, like much new women's fiction, autobiographical, polemical, and experimental in style, sometimes finding black humor in the dilemmas of women's lives voiced from a militant feminist perspective. Critics faulted *Ice and Fire* for graphically describing sex, drugs, and urban violence, seeing her "calculated nastiness" as akin to pornography. Her intent was to shake up her readers' consciousness, contrasting the contemporary squalor to a woman's origins in a typical American childhood to underscore the impact of pornography on lives. *Mercy* (1991), her second novel, is equally caustic.

D. has contributed to periodicals such as *Ms.*, *Heresies*, *Social Policy*, *Village Voice*, *America Report*, *Gay Community News*, and *Christopher Street*. She served for a time as an editor of *Ms.* magazine.

OTHER WORKS: *Morning Hair* (1967). *Woman Hating* (1974). *Marx and Gandhi Were Liberals: Feminism and the "Radical" Left* (1977). *Why So-called Radical Men Love and Need Pornography* (1978). *The Reasons Why: Essays on the New Civil Rights Law Recognizing Pornography as Sex Discrimination* (1985).

BIBLIOGRAPHY: Reference books: *CA* 77–80 (1979). *CANR* 16 (1986). *CLC* 43 (1987). *FC* (1990). *Maj Twent Cen Writers* (1991).

Other references: *Choice* (Oct. 1974). *Ms.* (Feb. 1977, June 1980, March 1981, June 1983, April 1985). *New Republic* (21 Feb. 1983, 15 June 1984). *New Statesman* (6 Nov. 1981, 29 July 1983). *NYTBR* (12 July 1981). *TLS* (1 Jan. 1982). *Village Voice* (15–21 July 1981). *Wash. Post Book World* (21 June 1981). *WRB* (May 1986).

BLANCHE LINDEN-WARD

Edith Maud Eaton

B. 1865, England; d. 7 April 1914, Montreal, Canada
Wrote as Sui Sin Far
D. of Grace (Trefusius) and Edward Eaton

The daughter of an English father and a Chinese mother, E. neither spoke nor wrote Chinese. According to her autobiography, "Leaves from the Mental Portfolio of a Eurasian," published in the *Independent*, 21 Jan.

1909, she could have passed as Caucasian. At a time when it was not advantageous to be Chinese, E. embraced her missionary mother's nationality and through her writings in magazines in Canada and the United States, became the champion of Chinese-American culture, taking the pen name Sui Sin Far. Her younger sister, Winnifred (1875–1954), adopted the Japanese pen name of Onoto Watanna; she published several popularly successful romances set in Japan and also wrote for films.

E. was the first Chinese-American to publish fiction. Her writing was widely read and, for the most part, received favorable reviews. Unlike her contemporaries, she did not create stereotypical Chinese characters. Instead, her characters are based on the people she met as a newspaper woman enlisting subscribers in Chinatown throughout the western United States.

E. wrote sketches and vignettes about common Chinese Americans, many of which were collected in *Mrs. Spring Fragrance* (1912). Others appeared in a variety of popular magazines. Her purpose in writing was to bridge the gap between Chinese immigrants and their descendants and North Americans by allowing Americans to see the Chinese as real people. She wrote about universal themes such as love between man and woman, parent and child, and the forces that attempt to obstruct this love. Some of her stories are intentionally charming and spirited, while others are ironic or bitter. She is most ironic when expressing her outrage at the conditions of the Chinese in the United States and especially the condition of the Chinese woman. In such pieces as "The Inferior Woman," (1910) and in stories of marriage, her interpretation is frequently feminist.

E. felt at odds with both mainstream American culture and Chinese culture. As a Chinese she was not accepted by American society, yet Americanized Chinese did not accept her as a member of their race. Rather than synthesizing the two cultures in herself, E. felt caught between East and West. Realizing that she could not survive this liminal existence, she claimed her mother's heritage as her own.

While a champion of her people, E. wrote about the universality of human experience. She was convinced that in the nature-versus-nurture argument, nurture or the environment was more influential than nature. She did not accept that differences in human beings were inherently due to race. Rather, she believed that the individual has the power to control his own behavior and that, in the end, all human beings are basically the same.

OTHER WORKS: Stories and sketches in *Century Mag.* (April 1904). *The Chataquan* (Dec. 1905). *Delineator* (Feb. 1910; July 1910). *Dominion Illustrated* (1888; 7 June 1890). *Good Housekeeping* (March 1909; May 1909; May 1910). *Hampton* (Jan. 1910; May 1910). *Independent* (21 Jan. 1909; 2 Sept. 1909; 10 March 1910; 18 Aug. 1910; 3 July 1913). *Land of Sunshine* (Jan. 1897; July 1900). *New England Mag.* (Aug. 1910; Sept. 1910; Dec. 1911; Jan. 1912; Feb. 1912). *Overland* (July 1899).

BIBLIOGRAPHY: Ammons, E., *Conflicting Stories: American Women Writers at the Turn into the Twentieth Century* (1991). Ling, Amy, *Between Worlds: Women Writers of Chinese Ancestry* (1990); "Chinese American Women Writers," *Redefining American Literary History*, A. LaVonne Brown Ruoff and Jerry W. Ward, eds. (1990). Reference works: *Dict. of North Amer. Authors Deceased before 1950* (1968). *FC* (1990). *Macmillan Dict. of Canadian Biog.* (1963, 1978). *CLHUS* (1988).

Other references: *Amer. Literary Realism* 16:2 (Autumn 1983). *Arizona Q.* 47:4 (Winter 1991). *MELUS* 8:1 (Spring 1981).

AMY D. STACKHOUSE

Barbara Ehrenreich

B. 26 Aug. 1941, Butte, Montana
D. of Isabel Oxley (Isley) and Ben Howes Alexander; m. John H. Ehrenreich, 1966; m. Gary Stevenson, 1983; c.: Rosa, Benjamin (first marriage)

Lecturer, journalist, feminist critic, and socialist activist E. is the daughter of "blue-eyed, Scotch-Irish Democrats" whom she credits as the "ultimate sources" of much of her "radicalism" and "feminism." She graduated from Reed College (1963) with a bachelor's degree in chemistry and physics and completed her Ph.D. in cell biology at Rockefeller University (1968). E. began her career as a writer and social justice activist as a research analyst for the Health Policy Advisory Center (Health-PAC) in New York City. Among the first social critics to speak of the "health-care crisis" in the late 1960s, E. spent much of the 1970s writing about women's health issues and teaching in the Health Sciences department at the State University of New York (SUNY) College at Old Westbury (1971–74) and at New York University (1979–81). During the 1980s she became a fellow at the New York Institute for the Humanities (1980–82) and the Institute for Policy Studies (1982–present) and broadened the scope of her social activism to encompass an analysis of the whole of American culture and society. E. has received a number of awards and honors including the National Magazine Award for Excellence in Reporting (1980), a Guggenheim Fellowship (1987), and honorary degrees from Reed College and SUNY, Old Westbury. She has held offices and board memberships in activist organizations including the Democratic Socialists of America, the National Women's Health Network, and the National Abortion Rights Action League and been on the editorial board of *Ms.*, *Mother Jones*, *Sociology of Health and Illness: A Journal of Medical Sociology*, and *Radical America*.

Long March, Short Spring: The Student Uprising at Home and Abroad (1969, with John Ehrenreich), the first of a number of coauthored books or "pamphlets" with a social activist agenda, focuses on student movements in Germany, England, France, Italy, and the United States. Eschewing any human interest or first-person accounts, her book analyzes student life in the late 1960s on a general level, including the "substratum of discontent" and the reasons why external issues, such as the Vietnam War, "set off the struggle," both violent and nonviolent.

The American Health Empire: Power, Profits, and Politics (1970, with John Ehrenreich) grew out of her work with Health-PAC. The book offers a critical analysis of such dramatic changes in the health-care system as the collapse of public hospitals, the rise of the "medical-industrial complex," the quest for national health insurance, and consumer attacks on the health system for its inhumanity. While careful in their analysis of data, the authors are clear in their polemical stance that the American health-care system is "not in business for people's health." In the debate over health-care reform that erupted in the 1970s and 1980s, *The American Health Empire* was consistently referenced as a starting point by academics and the media.

For Her Own Good: 150 Years of Experts' Advice to Women (1978) grew out of E.'s experiences as a college teacher and activist in the early women's health movement. "Working from a kitchen-table office," E. and Deirdre English coauthored a booklet, "Witches, Midwives, and Nurses: A History of Women Healers," which they paid to have printed and mailed to people who asked for it. The Feminist Press published the booklet as a pamphlet along with *Complaints and Disorders: The Sexual Politics of Sickness* in 1973. Reader response was diverse and enthusiastic. In *For Her Own Good* E. and English went on to develop a new "conceptual framework," demonstrating how "rationalist" scientific experts gained power over women's lives through their defense of sexual romanticism, a "systematic ideology" whereby women in the home became refuge and consolation to men engaged in the "savage scramble" of the marketplace. The book looks at nineteenth-century medical theory, the development of the domestic science movement, and twentieth-century notions of scientific motherhood within the context of a "sexual politics of health." It forces readers to look at the genre of "advice literature" from the new perspective of preventing women from competing with men in the larger world of economic labor, and urges them to "frame a moral outlook which proceeds from women's needs and experiences but which cannot be trivialized, sentimentalized, or domesticated."

The Hearts of Men: American Dreams and the Flight from Commitment (1983) is "about the ideology that shaped the breadwinner ethic and how that ideology collapsed as a persuasive set of expectations, in just the last thirty years" as men themselves revolted against their breadwinner roles. Examining documents from popular and elite cultural sources E. argues that men began rejecting "commitment" during the 1950s. Subsequently, the psychology of the human potential movement, the "do-your-own-thing" philosophy of the Age of Aquarius, as well as the search for a "liberated heart" by blue-collar men who abandoned "machismo" to achieve health and upward mobility outside their family, all reflected a new "moral climate that endorsed irresponsibility, self-indulgence, and an isolationist detachment from the claims of others."

E. warns readers against nostalgia: "Even if we wanted to return to the feminine mystique, to the tenuous protection of the family wage system, there is no going back . . . there is no male breadwinner to lean on—and probably not much use in waiting for one to appear." She hopes for a "reconciliation between men and women," resting on the "ethical basis" of feminism.

Also in 1983, E. worked with coauthors on two pamphlets sponsored by the Institution for New Communications. *Women in the Global Factory* (with Karen Stallard and Holly Sklar) and *Poverty in the American Dream: Women and Children First* (with Annette Fuentes), aimed at getting people involved in grassroots political organizations, to document and analyze the problems of exploitation of women and children and propose ways for women to unite and "resist" government and business powers that "exploit."

Re-Making Love: The Feminization of Sex (1986) grew out of an article E. coauthored with Elizabeth Hess and Gloria Jacobs for *Ms.* in 1980 to explore the suject of women's sexual liberation. Based on interviews with middle-class women and men and on popular media documents, the authors examine the sexual revolution not from the more predictable perspective of male sexuality, but as a revolution "of, by, and to a great extent, for women." Exploring the ways in which dramatic changes occurred in "women's sexual expectation and experience," they point to the increasing success from the 1960s on of purveyors in the marketplace who "institutionaliz[ed]" the sexual revolution, offering women from all classes and political persuasions left and right, numerous opportunities to become "consumers of sexual pleasure." In the context of feminist ideology similar to that which E. articulates in *The Hearts of Men*, the authors of *Re-Making Love* conclude that contemporary American women recognized that women's sexual revolution had become "unraveled from the larger theme of women's liberation. For women, sexual equality with men has become a concrete possibility, while economic and social parity remains elusive." As a political goal, women need to "reunite" sexual liberation and women's liberation for their mutual benefit.

E. contributed a lengthy essay on the subject of "The New Right Attack on Social Welfare" to *The Mean Season: An Attack on the Welfare State* (1987, with Fred Block, Richard Cloward, and Frances Fox Piven). She describes the New Right as presenting an "odd and even self-contradictory blend of themes and issues," trying at once to support the interests of the rich while also "champion[ing] the 'little man' against forces that would destroy his way of life," advocating "unfettered free-market capitalism" while also representing "a kind of moral authoritarianism that is reminiscent of European fascism." E. advocates "a reformed and expanded welfare state" that affirms "alternative values . . . the old small-R republican values of active citizenship, democratic participation, and the challenge and conviviality of the democratic process."

Fear of Falling: The Inner Life of the Middle Class (1989) focuses on the journey of the professional middle class from the "generosity and optimism" of the 1960s to the "cynicism and narrowing self-interest" of the 1980s. As in previous books, E. examines popular media artifacts—television, books, magazines, and movies. She argues that class tension had grown stronger between the professional middle class and the working class and that "nervous" professionals had isolated themselves from contact with those outside their ranks, turning to an increasingly conservative right-wing politics and adopting postures protective of their privileges and defensive of their status. Possibilities for "creating new opportunities or strengthening the U.S. economic system as a whole" have thus been lost, and E. encourages professionals to have faith in a "more egalitarian future," to pursue a "revival of conscience and responsibility" toward public life. She also urges that an allegiance to crass consumerism and economic growth be replaced with an effort to develop jobs across classes that offer "good and pleasurable and decent work: the work of caring, healing, building, teaching, planning, learning."

Reviewers praised *Fear of Falling* but differed in their perceptions of the book's ideological stance. While a critic from the right called her "anti-business bias" a "form of snobbery," a review from the left credited the author for "asserting the value of pleasurable work" for the professional and middle class as a "modest, humane and (I'm tempted to say) neoconservative suggestion."

In *The Worst Years of Our Lives: Irreverent Notes from a Decade of Greed* (1990), E. presents a selection of reprinted articles from publications as diverse as *Mother Jones*, *Ms.*, the *Nation*, the *New Republic*, the *New York Post*, the *New York Times*, and *New York Woman*. Essays with titles such as "The Unbearable Being of Whiteness," "The Unfastened Head of State," "Stop Ironing the Diapers," "Profile of a Welfare Cheat," and "How to Help the Uptrodden" illustrate E.'s analysis of the 1980s as a decade of greed, neglect, pain, racism, and class polarization as well as her ability to depict it in language that one critic described as "elegant, trenchant, savagely angry, morally outraged and outrageously funny."

E. has written numerous columns for newspapers and magazines, including the weekly "Hers" column for the *New York Times*, and monthly columns in *Ms.*, *New York Woman*, and *Mother Jones*. Since 1990, her essays have regularly appeared in *Time*. Frequently engaged as a public speaker at colleges and universities in the United States and abroad, E. also often appears on radio and television. A novel, *Kipper's Game*, appeared in 1993.

BIBLIOGRAPHY: Women, Health, and Medicine in America: A Historical Handbook, Rima D. Apple, ed. (1990). Reference works: *CANR* 16 (1986), 37 (1992). *WWA*, 47th ed. (1992–93).

Other references: *Atlantic Monthly* (Sept. 1986). *Commentary* (Jan. 1990). *Humanist* (Jan./Feb. 1992). *J. of Am. Hist.* (Sept. 1990). *J. of Marriage and the Family* (May 1984). *Nation* (24 Dec. 1983; 28 Feb. 1987). *New Republic* (11 July 1983). *New Statesman and Society* (17 May 1991). *NYRB* (1 July 1971).

NYT (16 Aug. 1983). *NYTBR* (7 March 1971; 5 June 1983; 14 Sept. 1986; 6 Aug. 1989; 20 May 1990). *Psychology Today* (Aug. 1986; Oct. 1989). *Signs* (Spring 1986). *Village Voice* (5 Feb. 1979; 23 Aug. 1983). *Vogue* (Sept. 1986).

JENNIFER L. TEBBE

Louise Erdrich

B. 6 July 1954, Little Falls, Minnesota
D. of Gorneau and Ralph Erdrich; m. Michael Dorris, 1981; c.: Abel, Sara,
  Madeline, Persia, and Pallas

E., a member of the Turtle Mountain Chippewa Tribe, grew up in Wahpeton, North Dakota, where her German-American father and her Chippewa mother were teachers for the Bureau of Indian Affairs. The eldest of seven children, E. spent much time on the nearby Turtle Mountain Chippewa Reservation visiting her maternal grandmother and learning about the conflict between the white and native cultures from which she had sprung. She attended the Wahpeton Indian Boarding School where both her parents taught, and throughout her childhood she wrote stories for which her father paid her a nickel and her mother bound into books.

In 1972, E. entered Dartmouth College where she met her future husband, Michael Dorris, also part Native American, who later became her agent and collaborator. After her graduation in 1976, she returned to North Dakota and conducted poetry workshops for the Poetry in the Schools Program. She attended Johns Hopkins University and received an M.F.A. in creative writing in 1979. In 1981 she was named writer in residence in Dartmouth's Native American Studies Program, which Dorris directs. E. credits her ability to address both sides of her heritage to her collaboration with her husband.

E. has published poetry, short stories, and three novels that have won critical acclaim. A series of short stories won the Nelson Algren Award in 1982 and a Pushcart Prize in 1983; one was anthologized in *Best Short Stories in 1983*. She also won an O. Henry Award in 1985. Her first volume of poetry, *Jacklight* (1984), shows the same narrative force and sense of place that make her fiction so powerful. E.'s poems have a mythic sense, gained from her Chippewa and German ancestry; they pay particular attention to the details of family, tribal history, and nature in connecting the individual to the universal experience. Writing about both her maternal grandmother and her Chippewa ancestors, E. attempts to integrate the two sides of her own experience in the poems. A second volume of poems, *Baptism of Desire*, appeared in 1989.

While the poems have strength, humor, and a sense of the past in the present, it is in the series of family chronicles, *Love Medicine* (1984), *The Beet Queen* (1986), and *Tracks* (1988), that E. fills in the canvas of Native American/Anglo experience. As **Alice Walker** made a crazy quilt of black women's experience, E. weaves a tapestry of Native American, half-breed, and Anglo experience. *Tracks,* chronologically the earliest (1912–24), sets much of the background for *Love Medicine.*

The conflict between Native American and Anglo beliefs in *Tracks* is highlighted by Fleur Pillager and Pauline Puyat. Fleur, who possesses life-giving and creative powers granted her by the water god for having twice drowned, acts as a counterbalance to the destructive power of the Catholic church as represented by Pauline, a part-Canadian, part-Chippewa, who has forsaken her Native American past and her grasp on reality to study to become a nun with an order that does not take Indian girls. When the loggers of the Anglo logging companies, helped by the government, defraud the Indians of their land, Fleur disappears into the wilderness with her shamanic possessions and Pauline takes her final vows. *Tracks*, like E.'s other novels, is told by several narrators, adding light and shadow to the story of loss of the land, loss of loved ones, loss of heritage.

Some critics have said that E.'s women are fiercer, more focused, and sharper than her men. There is in old Nanapush, however, a gentle power that allows him to understand Fleur and the strength that even endures the manipulations of his common-law wife, Margaret Kashpaw.

The Beet Queen focuses mainly on the white settlers of Argus, North Dakota, but there is a connection with the other books and with E.'s own past. The central action takes place in the town where Fleur Pillager had worked briefly and much of the story revolves around a butcher shop like the one where Fleur worked. The shop also recalls E.'s own German ancestors who were butchers. Further, ancillary characters from *Love Medicine* populate the center of *The Beet Queen*, which covers the years from 1932, when the eleven-year-old abandoned Mary Adare hops on a freight train to find her aunt and uncle who are butchers in Argus, to 1972, when her grandniece is elected Beet Queen of the town. More than the other two novels, *The Beet Queen* is a woman's book. The men father children, die or have strokes, but essentially lack the enduring power of Mary, her friend Celestine, and their child Wallacette (Dot) Adare.

Love Medicine, E.'s first novel, has a cast of characters who have endured, despite the deprivations of reservation life, and have become, like many of the poor the world over, rich in humanity. The large extended families of the Kashpaws, the Lamartines, and the Morrisseys add color to the North Dakota landscape. The novel begins with the death of June Kashpaw and proceeds through a series of minor tragedies to the announcement by Lulu Lamartine that Lipsha Morrissey is June Kashpaw's son. All the characters are interconnected.

E. finds a humorous vantage point that takes the despair out of her characters' lives. It is, as she says, survival humor. She also has a mythic perspective that enriches even the smallest acts. Like **Leslie Marmon Silko** and James Welch, E. portrays the painful and destructive side of Native American life, but she is also able to create those moments of true love and enrichment that give people's lives meaning—the moment when Lipsha finds his mother, the moment when Grandma Kashpaw serves up the Love Medicine with a garnish of lettuce and peas. Within the prose of the novels the characters can escape the alcohol sold to them by whites, the convents forced upon them in place of their gods, the wars they have been sent to by the army, and the ever-present prisons to which they are taken by their white jailers. Sometimes painful, sometimes surrealistic, and always honest, E.'s language frees all her characters from the death that whites would impose upon them—the denial of their heritage.

In *Tracks* and *Love Medicine* E. has successfully begun to chronicle the tragedy and the glory of the Chippewa nation. *The Beet Queen* shows that E. is also well aware of the special tragedies that befall strong and enduring women no matter what their race, and her writing gives a lasting voice to them all.

E.'s collaboration with Michael Dorris on *The Crown of Columbus* (1991) is the culmination of her own critical approach to her work. The story of two Dartmouth professors, the novel seems in many ways to parallel the lives of its authors, although both have insisted that the narrators,

Roger Williams and Vivian Twostar, are the products of a truly collaborative effort. Both writers wrote sections for both characters, read each other's drafts, and worked, revised, and edited together to create a seamless whole. The tone of the book quite closely resembles both E.'s *Beet Queen* and Dorris's *A Yellow Raft in Blue Water*, so it might be argued that the two authors have submerged their individual voices into one voice that speaks for both.

BIBLIOGRAPHY: "A Bibliography of Writing by Louise Erdrich," in *American Women Writing Fiction: Memory, Identity, Family, Space*, Mickey Pearlman, ed. (1989). Reference works: *CA* 114 (1985). *CLC* 30 (1984), 54 (1989). *CLCY* (1985). *CB* (1989). *FC* (1990). *Maj Twent Cent Writers* (1991).

Other references: *American Audio Prose Library* (interview, 1986). *Mother Jones* (May/June 1991). *Nation* (26 Nov. 1990). *NYT Mag.* (21 April 1991). *Western Amer. Lit.* 22:1 (1987).

MARY A. MCCAY

Mari Evans

B. 16 July 1923, Toledo, Ohio
C.: William Evan, Derek Reed

Poet, dramatist, short-story writer, and author of children's books, E. has made significant contributions to the tradition of twentieth-century African American literature. Influenced as a child by the writing of Langston Hughes, her own poetic voice emerged out of the civil rights movement of the 1960s, exploring both personal and political struggles within the black community. Dedicated to the promotion of black pride, E. uses vibrant images and powerful language to analyze, inform, and inspire.

E.'s first story, written when she was in the fourth grade, appeared in her school newspaper. Her father, an upholsterer who was E.'s primary caretaker after the death of her mother when E. was seven, saved the story, showing her "an impressionable Black youngster . . . the importance of the written word." She discovered Langston Hughes's *The Weary Blues* when she was ten and was greatly inspired by his words. He later became a mentor and a friend, and, with her father, encouraged her to aspire to become part of the black American literary tradition.

As an undergraduate at the University of Toledo E. wrote a column for a black-owned weekly. Her discipline as a writer was further enhanced by an apprenticeship as an editor at a predominantly white manufacturing plant, despite the racism that plagued her while there. Her first published poetry appeared in 1963 in *Phylon, Negro Digest,* and *Dialog.* In 1965 E. received the John Hay Whitney Fellowship, the first of her many writing awards.

The poems in *Where Is All the Music?* (1968), E.'s first collection, explore individual struggles for human closeness in direct language and powerful images. Her second and best-known poetry collection, *I Am a Black Woman* (1970), shows a shift in theme from personal struggles to the wider political issues of the African American community and asserts black pride: "Who can be born / black / and not exult." Highly praised for its sense of realism and authentic voice, the book received many awards including the Black Academy of Arts and Letters First Poetry Award (1970). Like Hughes, E. draws on African American oral traditions to make her poems speak to and for the community. A third collection, *Nightstar: Poems from 1973–1978* (1981), contains powerful exploration of earlier themes and contemporary tragedies.

While primarily a poet—with poems appearing in over two hundred anthologies, textbooks, and periodicals—E. is also known for her stories and contributions to theater, television, and other media. She has written six children's books and seven plays including *Eyes* (1979), a musical adaptation of **Zora Neale Hurston**'s *Their Eyes Were Watching God.* Much of her writing has appeared on record albums and in television specials and Off-Broadway productions. In 1968 E. began to produce, direct, and write a highly acclaimed weekly television series "The Black Experience." The series, which focused on political and social issues from an African American perspective, aired on WTTV, Indianapolis, from 1968 to 1973. It was one of the first television shows produced by an African American woman.

E. is also known as editor of an extensive anthology of biographical and critical essays entitled *Black Women Writers, 1950–1980: A Critical Evaluation* (1984). This collection highlights fifteen black women poets, novelists, and playwrights, including **Toni Morrison, Alice Walker,** and **Audre Lorde.** *Black Women Writers* was welcomed by critics as a much-needed addition to African American literary study. Since 1969 E. has taught or been writer in residence at a number of colleges and universities including Purdue, Indiana University, Northwestern, Washington University at St. Louis, Cornell, SUNY, Albany, and, most recently, Spelman College.

In 1975 E. received an honorary doctorate of humane letters from Marion College. Among her other awards and honors are a Woodrow Wilson Foundation grant, 1968; Indiana University Writers Conference Award, 1970; and a National Endowment for the Arts Creative Writing Award, 1981–82. She lives in Indianapolis, and is working on a new novel.

OTHER WORKS: J. D. (1973). *I Look at Me!* (1974). *Rap Stories* (1974). *Singing Black* (1976). *Jim Flying High* (1979). *Whisper* (1979). Unpublished plays include "River of My Song" (produced 1977), "Boochie" (produced 1979), "Portrait of a Man" (produced 1979), "Glide and Sons," "A Hand Is on the Gate," and "Walk Together Children."

BIBLIOGRAPHY: Edwards, Solomon, "Affirmation in the Works of Mari Evans"; Evans, Mari, "My Father's Passage," and Dorsey, David, "The Art of Mari Evans," in *Black Women Writers, 1950–1980: A Critical Evaluation.* Reference works: *CANR* 27 (1989). *Contemp. Poets* (1991). *DLB* 41 (1985). *FC* (1990). *Negro Almanac,* 5th ed. (1989). *NBAW* (1992). *WW Black Americans* (1992). *WW, Wrs Eds. Poets* (1992).

MARY E. HARVEY

Mary Frances Kennedy Fisher

B. 3 July 1908, Albion, Michigan; d. 22 June 1992, Glen Ellen, California
Wrote under: M. F. K. Fisher; Mary Frances Parrish (1939–41); Victoria Berne
   (collaborative novel with Dillwyn Parrish)
D. of Edith Oliver (Holbrook) and Rex Brenton Kennedy; m. Alfred Young Fisher,
   1929, div. 1938; m. Dillwyn Parrish, 1939, d. 1941; m. Donald Friede,
   1945, div. 1951; c.: Anne, b. 1943; Mary Kennedy, b. 1946

That the complexity and style of gastronomical writing in America has profoundly changed is due in no small measure to the efforts of F. Her twenty books and many magazine articles enhanced the art of eating, created metaphors of food and wine, and dazzled readers with what W. H. Auden characterized as "one of the best prose styles" in contemporary letters.

The oldest child of an Iowan "prairie princess" and a newspaper publisher, F. and her family left Michigan when she was two years old and settled in Whittier, California, where she grew up as an Episcopalian in a Quaker community and a precocious child in a household devoted to the printed word. From early on she was the one chosen to look up words in the dictionary, and because the kitchen was her favorite place, she prepared meals in the cook's absence. Both activities assured her a unique place in a family where attention was centered on an ailing younger sister, on a grandmother who suffered various gastric disorders, and on the special needs of her mother before, during, and after her confinements.

F. attended public schools in Whittier and private boarding schools in southern California. She spent a semester at Illinois College, Occidental College, and the University of California. Before completing her college education, she married Alfred Young Fisher and went to France where they both studied at the University of Dijon. Although F. gained proficiency in the language, and took classes at the École des Beaux Arts, she did not earn a degree and later regretted that she did not pursue her formal education more vigorously. The three years in Burgundy and Strasbourg, nevertheless, were seminal in the development of her literary career. She learned to understand the ways and prejudices of French acquaintances, gained a considerable knowledge of French literature, cinema, wine, and food, recorded her experiences in journals and letters, and wrote short stories.

F. and her husband returned to California in 1932. She published her first article, "Pacific Village," in *Westways* and began writing essays based on old cookbooks she discovered and read at the Los Angeles Public Library. At the urging of her neighbor, Dillwyn Parrish, she wove personal essays of secret indulgences, restaurants revisited, and the rituals of food preparation among the historical essays. The pieces originally intended as literary *amuse gueule* for her husband and Parrish were submitted to Harper and published as *Serve It Forth* in 1937.

By that time, F. and her husband had separated, and she was living with Parrish near Vevey, Switzerland. They created an idyllic home, cultivated a vineyard, and collaborated on a novel, *Touch and Go.* In 1939, Parrish was stricken with a fatal disease. He and F. left Switzerland, bought a ranch in Hemet, California, and married. When Parrish died in 1941, F. began writing to support herself, adding *Consider the Oyster* (1941), *How to Cook a Wolf* (1942), *The Gastronomical Me* (1943), and *An Alphabet for Gourmets* (1949) to her first title. The five books, republished in 1954 as *The Art of Eating*, are the core of her gastronomic works.

After her marriage to Donald Friede, F. began an edition of literary "banquet and feasting" pieces, translated Brillat-Savarin's *Physiology of Taste* (1949), published a novel, *Not Now but Now* (1947), and wrote articles and stories for *Gourmet, House Beautiful,* and *McCalls.* The press of deadlines, the care of her two daughters, the death of her mother, and her husband's financial and health problems led to the deterioration of her own health and to separation from Friede in 1949. F. and her daughters moved to the family ranch in Whittier where they lived until her father's death in 1953.

When the ranch was sold, they moved to the Napa Valley. F. concentrated on her daughters' education, moving with them to Aix-en-Provence and Lugano for over five years while they studied and became proficient in French and Italian. In Provence, F. wrote a small book of folk cures and superstitions called *A Cordiall Water* (1961), and worked on many of the sketches and stories that would create her "inner map" of Aix, Marseille, and Dijon, the cities that often lured her back to the south of France.

In the 1960s the pace of F.'s writing accelerated. *The New Yorker* contracted for exclusive right to her articles, and she wrote of unforgettable meals and of recipes she had collected over the years. Undoubtedly influenced by Colette, she re-created her Whittier childhood in a series of stories republished as *Among Friends* (1971). And she wrote incisive essays of places that had deeply affected her life. Using the kitchen in Whittier, the restaurants of Los Angeles, boarding schools as far away as Illinois, and the cities and villages of France, she wrote about places as they *were* to her. Reconfiguring characters within familiar settings, she re-created the sights, smells, and tastes that were irrevocably linked to those scenes. Eating was F.'s metaphor for living, though she took care to let her readers know that her other appetites were also ingenious, powerful, and erudite.

In a writing career of more than fifty years, no subject eluded her attention. The tried-and-true recipes of her mother's kitchen and the cooking of provincial France, youthful strategies of survival in Quaker-dominated surroundings, sea changes, and old age are all written about in that curious blend of detachment and subjectivity, storytelling and reflection, that distinguishes her style. That she wrote about eating and not about love, peace, and war is incidental. It is simply another way of dignifying human hunger in one of its many guises. In her refusal to be labeled a cookbook writer and her insistence on the pleasures of the table, F. stood apart from the mainstream of culinary writers while remaining their avatar. She is like no other writer in the American Academy and National Institute of Arts and Letters. "But then," as the *New York Times* noted in 1991, "M. F. K. Fisher is like no other writer anywhere."

OTHER WORKS: *Here Let Us Feast: A Book of Banquets* (1946). Brillat-Savarin's *Physiology of Taste; or, Meditations on Transcendental Gastronomy* (trans. 1949). *The Story of Wine in California* (1962). *Map of Another Town: A Memoir of Provence* (1964). *The Cooking of Provincial France* (1968). *With Bold Knife and Fork* (1969). *A Considerable Town* (1978; reptd. 1985, with *Map of Another Town*, as *Two Towns in Provence*). *As They Were* (1982). *Sister Age* (1983). *Spirits of the Valley* (1985). *The Standing and the Waiting* (1985). *Dubious Honors* (1988). *Answer in the Affirmative and The Oldest Living Man* (1989). *Boss Dog* (1990). *Long Ago in France: The Years in Dijon* (1991). *Stay Me, Oh Comfort Me: Journal and Stories, 1933–1945* (1993). The papers of M. F. K. Fisher are at the Schlesinger Library, Radcliffe College.

BIBLIOGRAPHY: Fussell, Betty, *Masters of American Cookery* (1983). Painter, Charlotte, *Gifts of Age* (1985). Ferrary, Jeannette, *M. F. K. Fisher and Me* (1991). *Magazine Index Online: 1959–1970, 1973–1991*, 127 articles and reviews. Reference works: *CA* 77–80 (1979). *CB* (1983). *The Women's Book of World Records and Achievements* (1983).

Other references: *LA Times* (obituary, 24 June 1992). *NYT* (obituaries, 23 June 1992; 24 June 1992).

JOAN REARDON

Frances Fitzgerald

See AWW *2, 39–41*

F. spent her childhood in America and England, graduated magna cum laude from Radcliffe College in 1962, and subsequently lived in Paris for two years, publishing magazine articles for the Congress for Cultural Freedom. After her return to New York in 1964, she wrote a series of profiles, including one about Amelia Peabody, her maternal grandmother who had been jailed for participation in a civil rights demonstration at the age of seventy-two, for the *New York Herald Tribune Magazine.* For nearly a year in 1966, F. worked as a freelance journalist in South Vietnam, producing articles for the *Atlantic Monthly, New York Times Magazine, Village Voice,* and *Vogue.* Returning to America, she spent five years researching and writing *Fire in the Lake: The Vietnamese and the Americans in Vietnam* (1972), which earned her (among other honors) the Pulitzer Prize for Contemporary Affairs Writing (1973), the National Book Award (1973), and the Bancroft Prize for History (1973).

In 1979, F. again explored changing representations of American culture and national identity through a study of elementary and secondary American history textbooks. In *America Revised: History Schoolbooks in the Twentieth Century,* she focuses on the special functions and traditions of schoolbooks for American children for the nineteenth and twentieth centuries, emphasizing how texts of the 1960s and 1970s were not "written" but "developed" within a context of conflict and compromise among publishing, educational, and political institutions. She concludes that contemporary efforts to present "the world, or the country, as an ideal construct," or a "utopia of the eternal present"—a place "without conflicts, without malice or stupidity"—rather than achieving the purpose of "creating good citizens" may "give young people no warning of the real dangers ahead."

In 1986, F. published *Cities on a Hill: A Journey through Contemporary American Culture,* an effort to understand change in America since 1960 by looking at four "communities or cultural enclaves" in which individuals "deny the power of the past" by seeking to "cut all ties." These include the "first gay neighborhood in the country," the Castro in San Francisco; the "separatist" Liberty Baptist Church ministered by Jerry

Falwell in Lynchburg, Virginia; the retirement community of Sun City Center in Tallahassee, Florida, "radical in the sense that never before in history had older people taken themselves off to live in isolation from the younger generation"; and Rancho Rahneesh, an eastern Oregon "New Age Commune" of "doctors, lawyers, accountants, and the like led by an 'Indian guru.'" The book studies the complexities of everyday life and moral conflicts for individuals in each community and illustrates F.'s consistent focus on the role of family in the relationship of individuals and communities in American life. While critics saw the book as a contribution to the study of the changing "American Dream," they often disagreed with her effort to find similarities among the four groups in their expression of "quintessentially American behavior and values," or to discover valid roots in nineteenth-century utopian social experiments. Since 1986, F. has continued to write regularly for *The New Yorker,* as well as *Atlantic Monthly, Esquire, Harper's,* the *New York Review of Books,* the *Nation, Rolling Stone,* and *Vogue* on subjects such as the rise and fall of evangelists Jim and Tammy Bakker, Oliver North and Iran-Contra, and corruption in the Reagan administration.

BIBLIOGRAPHY: Reference works: *CANR* 32 (1991). *CBY* (1987). *WW Wr, Eds, Poets (1989).*

Other references: *New Republic* (29 April 1985; 20 Oct. 1986). *NYRB* (29 Jan. 1987). *NYTBR* (12 Oct. 1986). *Vogue* (Oct. 1986).

JENNIFER TEBBE

Carolyn Forché

B. 28 April 1950, Detroit, Michigan
Writes under: Carolyn Sidlosky
D. of Louise Nada (Blackford) and Michael Joseph Sidlosky; m. Harry Mattison, 1984; c.: Sean Christoph, b. 1986

Poet, translator, essayist, activist, and teacher, F. was raised in rural Michigan and educated at Justin Morell College of Michigan State University (B.A. 1972) and Bowling Green State University (M.F.A. 1975). She won the Yale Younger Poets Award the year of her graduation from Bowling Green, for *Gathering the Tribes* (1976), a ceremonial, sometimes-cosmic collection of lyrics about people and places, written in a densely simple language centered on nouns and names. She has published frequently and fairly steadily since then—poems, translations, essays, reviews, interviews, and prefaces—and won many prizes and fellowships, including the Lamont Poetry Selection Award for her best-selling second book of poetry, *The Country Between Us* (1981). Appropriately for a distinguished translator and reader of many languages, her own poetry has been translated into German, Swedish, Russian, Spanish, Czech, Greek, Dutch, and Japanese.

F.'s status as an international figure in the arts and politics is based in her identification as a "poet of witness": she has lived in and written about many areas of the world where poverty and oppression are social norms, from the Mojave Desert to Johannesburg and, perhaps most crucially for her work, El Salvador. After spending the summer of 1977 on Mallorca with the self-exiled Salvadoran poet Claribel Alegria, translating Alegria's poems for the volume *Flowers from the Volcano* (1982), F. was encouraged by Alegria's cousin to go to El Salvador as a journalist and to bring back testimony to North America. This she did, in many forms: in magazine articles; in speeches, radio programs, panel discussions, international conferences; in her teaching and in the poems of *The Country Between Us*.

F.'s interest in other languages, other cultures, has been a constant, starting perhaps from the important childhood relationship with her grandmother Anna, an immigrant Slovak peasant about whom F. has written regularly since her death in 1968 (see especially "Burning the Tomato Worms" in *Gathering the Tribes*). Her first book of poems includes a long section based on her experiences living close to Native Americans in the Southwest and British Columbia. This urge toward contact and empathy with those outside her own region, nation, and native tongue, took on the focus of a mission once she began the "moral and political education" ("El Salvador") offered by her harrowing years in El Salvador. As she put it in a 1987 essay ("Letters to an Open City"), "there are . . . two human worlds and the bridges between them are burning."

Two of these bridges are poetry and translation: in addition to that of Claribel Alegria, F. has also brought the poet Robert Desnos into English (*The Selected Poems of Robert Desnos*, with William Kulik, 1991) and completed an anthology, *Against Forgetting: Twentieth Century Poetry of Witness*

(1993). She has also written prefaces and forewords to a number of books by lesser-known poets as well as translations. Photography is another important, if problematic, medium of "translation." F., who is married to the war photographer Harry Mattison, has written prose texts for two collections of photographs, *El Salvador: Work of Thirty Photographers* (1983) and *Shooting Back: Photography by and about the Homeless* (forthcoming). Her poem, "In the Garden of Shukkei-en," provided the text for a 1991 exhibit of photographs at the Arizona State University School of Art.

Last but emphatically not least, F. is a teacher. Like many contemporary poets she has held visiting positions at colleges and universities across the country. Since 1989 she has been a tenured faculty member at George Mason University, where she teaches the literature of witness as well as the craft of writing. In her public life F. has claimed every available forum for her testimony: speeches, conferences, readings, classrooms, radio, television, film, photography, arts journals, newspapers, and newsweeklies. Hers is a voice apparently compelled to speak, coming from the heart of one who has seen much that is unspeakable in places where, often enough, speech is against the law. Her work in progress, *Angel of History*, begins with a long poem, "The Recording Angel," which aptly names the function F. has come to share with other "poets of witness" in the global village of a genocidal century.

OTHER WORKS: *Women in American Labor History, 1825–1935: An Annotated Bibliography* (with Martha Jane Soltow, 1972). *History and Motivations of U.S. Involvement in the Control of the Peasant Movement of El Salvador* (with Rev. Philip Wheaton, 1980). Essays (selected): "El Salvador: An Aide Memoire," *American Poetry Rev.* (July–August 1981). "A Fantasy of Birches," *Singular Voices: American Poetry Today*, ed. Stephen Berg (1985). "A Lesson in Commitment," *The Writer in Our World*, Reginald Gibbons, ed. (1986). Foreword to Janet Levine, *Inside Apartheid* (1988).

BIBLIOGRAPHY: Reference works: *CA* 109 (1983), 117 (1986). *CLC* 25 (1983). *Contemp. Poets* 4 (1985). *DLB* 5 (1980). *FC (1990)*. *WWAW, 11th ed.* (1979). Interviews: *Book Forum* 2:3 (1976). *Five Fingers Rev.* 3 (1985). *Nightsun* 9 (Fall 1989).

Other references: *APR* 22:2 (March/April 1993). *Commonweal* (Nov. 1977). *Ms.* (Jan. 1980, Sept. 1982). *Nation* (May 1982, Oct. 1982). *Rolling Stone* (April 1983). *Salmagundi* (Spring 1984). *TVAR: Literarni Tydenik* 10 ([Prague] 1990). *Time* (March 1982). Films: "Carolyn Forché" (1990); "Witness in El Salvador" (1982).

MARY B. CAMPBELL

María Irene Fornés

B. 14 May 1930, Havana, Cuba
D. of Carmen Hismenia (Collado) and Carlos Luis Fornés

F. has been a powerful moving force in the experimental theater scene since the early 1960s. "A major voice in American drama" according to Scott Cummings and "the truest poet of the theater" according to Erika Munk, F. has won seven Obies. Although never explicitly feminist, F.'s plays explore women's role in society, examining power relations inherent in sexuality, households, and in all human relationships.

Trained early in American Method acting under Lee Strasberg in the Playwrights' Unit of the Actors Studio, F. soon began developing plays in collaboration with performers, often in workshop. She decided that it was important to direct her own works, a part of a natural, continuing process that she likens to cooking and then eating the same meal. "I never saw any difference between writing and directing," she said in a 1985 interview. "Of course, they are different things, but they are sequentially and directly connected."

The workshops F. designs and leads are aimed at "inducing inspiration." "I have invented exercises that are very effective and very profound," she told David Savran. Her own work "does not present a formulated thesis" but rather arrives as "messages that come" to her out of the inarticulate parts of her conscious or unconscious.

F.'s plays do not revolve around clear plots but instead present moments of intense engagement among characters. *Fefu and Her Friends* (1977) was performed, under F.'s direction, with the audience divided into groups that moved around a loft that served as theater space, seeing the scenes in different sequences. "From the first," John Kuhn writes, "F.'s broad and playful sense of attention and of verbal and visual images poked audiences with freakishly or theatrically exalted characters, both innocent and experienced." These characters are often limited by constricted environments or by their inability to articulate their experience, but even her simplest characters have a wisdom that transcends these limitations. And whatever their limitations, one senses in F. a great compassion and deep respect for the characters.

F. says that her plays become "crystallized" when she "feels the presence of a character or person. . . . I get it like *click*." Then, she sees "a picture of the set with the characters in it." Having begun as a painter and textile designer, she says, "The colors are very, very important for me. And the clothes that people wear. When it finally happens, the play exists; it has taken on its own life life." The result is a style most often described as realism, a realism that **Susan Sontag** says eschews both the "reductively psychological" and "sociological explanations" and that Bonnie Marranca characterizes as "emphasizing the interior lives of her characters, not their exterior selves."

F.'s plays often present an unromanticized sexuality, raw and violent and at the same time casual. Sexuality is rarely the subject, however. The subject is rather the ramifications of sexuality on human relationships, sexuality as power and as fact of life, another part of her characters' natural existence.

Her best-known plays include *Promenade* (1969), *Fefu and Her Friends* (1977), described by the playwright as "a breakthrough for me," and *Mud* (1983), which Bonnie Marranca calls a play centering on "the act of a woman coming to thought." Largely because they are products of workshops and have been performed Off- and Off-Off-Broadway, F.'s plays are often difficult to come by, many never having made it to publication.

Born and educated in Cuba, F. came to the United States in 1945 and became a naturalized citizen in 1951. Since then, her work has earned her such accolades as official citation as a "national treasure" by the American National Theatre, which commissioned her to write a play. She has received awards from the Rockefeller (1971) and Guggenheim (1972) foundations, the National Endowment for the Arts (1974, 1984, 1985), the American Academy and Institute of Arts and Letters (1985). She has also won six of her seven Obies since 1977, including one (1982) for Sustained Achievement. F. was a founding member of the Women's Theatre Council and of New York Theatre Strategy, an organization of Off-Off Broadway playwrights; she served as president of Theatre Strategy from 1973 until it disbanded in 1980.

OTHER WORKS: [Note: first or single date indicates production, second date indicates publication.] *The Widow* (1961, published as *La Viuda*). *Tango Palace* (also produced as *There! You Died*, 1963, 1966). *The Successful Life of 3: A Skit for Vaudeville* (1965, 1971). *The Office* (1966). *A Vietnamese Wedding* (1967, 1971). *The Annunciation* (1967). *Dr. Kheal* (1968, 1971). *The Red Burning Light; or, Mission XQ3* (1968, 1971). *Molly's Dream* (1968, 1971). *Promenade and Other*

Plays (1971, includes *Dr. Kheal; The Successful Life of 3; A Vietnamese Wedding; The Red Burning Light;* and *Molly's Dream*). *The Curse of the Langston House* (1972). *Dance* (1972). *Aurora* (1974). *Cap-a-Pie* (1975). *Lines of Vision* (lyrics, 1976). *Washing* (1976). *Lolita in the Garden* (1977). *In Service* (1978). *Eyes on the Harem* (1979). *Evelyn Brown (a Diary)* (1980). *Blood Wedding* (translation and adaptation of García Lorca, 1980). *Life Is a Dream* (translation and adaptation of Calderón, 1981). *A Visit* (1981). *The Danube* (1982, 1986). *Sarita* (1984, 1986). *Abingdon Square* (1984). *No Time* (1985). *The Conduct of Life* (1985, 1986). *Cold Air* (translation and adaptation of Pinera, 1985). *Drowning* (1985, 1986). *Lovers and Keepers* (1986). *The Trial of Joan of Arc on a Matter of Faith* (1986). *The Mother* (title later changed to *Charley*, 1986). *Art* (1986). *María Irene Fornés: Plays* (1986, includes *The Danube; Mud; Sarita; The Conduct of Life*). *Hunger* (1985). *Three Pieces for a Warehouse* (1988). *Springtime* (1989, 1991). "I Write These Messages That Come," *Drama Review* 21:4 (Dec. 1977). "Notes on *Fefu*," *SoHo Weekly News* (12 June 1978). "Creative Danger," *American Theatre* (Sept. 1986).

BIBLIOGRAPHY: Arnold, Stephanie K., "Multiple spaces, simultaneous action and illusion," in *Theatrical Space*, James Redmond, ed. (1987). Betsko, Kathleen, and Rachel Koenig, "María Irene Fornés," *Interviews with Contemporary Women Playwrights* (1987). Gilman, Richard, introduction to *Promenade and Other Plays* (1971). Sontag, Susan, preface to *Plays* (1986). Worthen, W. B., "*Still Playing Games:* Ideology and Performance in the Theater of María Fornés," *Feminine Focus*, Enoch Brater, ed. (1989). MSS collection, Lincoln Center Library of the Performing Arts, New York City. Reference works: *Amer. Women Dramatists of the Tw Cent* (1982). *CA 25–28* (1977). *CANR* 28 (1990). *Contemp. Dramatists* (1973, 1977, 1982, 1988). *CLC* 39 (1986), 61 (1990). *DLB* 7 (1981). *FC* (1990). *Hispanic Writers* (1990). *Maj Twent Cent Writers* (1991). *Notable Women in Amer. Theatre* (1989).

Other references: *New Republic* (25 Feb. 1978). *Newsweek* (4 June 1969). *New York* 18:28 (18 March 1985). *NYT* (5 June 1969; 14, 22 Jan. 1978; 25 Oct. 1983; 13 March 1984). *Performing Arts J.* 7:3 (1983); 8:1 (1984). *Studies in Amer. Drama, 1945–Present* 4 (1989). *Theater* 17:1 (Winter 1985). *Village Voice* (25 Jan. 1973; 23 March 1977; 23 Jan. 1978; 29 Aug. 1986).

MARCIA HEPPS   WILLIAM KEENEY

Paula Fox

See AWW 2, 75–77

Since 1980 F. has produced six books for young readers and two novels for adults. Reviewers and critics have praised her ability to depict the inner life of young protagonists, to create realistic characters and authentic settings, and to write clear, graceful prose. F. excels in portraying the emotions and perceptions of children and adolescents as they grow in understanding themselves, their peers, and the adults around them. In *A Servant's Tale* (1984), F. skillfully records the childhood experiences and relationships of Luisa de la Cueva while evoking the locale and lore of the West Indies. The adult Luisa, however, is less interesting and less believable than the child.

In her juvenile fiction F. never stints on complexity nor avoids difficult, even tragic, themes. The novels of this period explore guilt, grief, divorce, alcoholism, and death. In each book the protagonist confronts a complicated individual who exhibits attractive qualities but who also causes another discomfort, unhappiness, humiliation, injury, or loss. Each carefully crafted plot leads to a resolution in which the young person comes to terms with this individual in a manner that will foster future growth and happiness.

The "difficult" person in *A Place Apart* (1980) is a talented, arrogant, and wealthy high school student who befriends newcomers—and attempts to control their lives. Victoria Finch escapes his manipulation, but another student, who tries to regain his self-respect by driving up a dangerous, snow-covered mountain road, is seriously injured. In *One-Eyed Cat* (1984), eleven-year-old Ned believes that he has injured a wildcat when he disobeyed his father and fired his new air rifle. F. examines how Ned's burdened conscience affects his relations with his parents, his friends, an elderly neighbor, and the cat. On one level, the discordant character in the novel is the housekeeper, but the tale also demonstrates that a genuinely good person (Ned's father, Reverend Wallis) can cause discomfort for those who exhibit less patience and forbearance.

When fifteen-year-old Catherine Ames (*The Moonlight Man*, 1986) spends a month in Nova Scotia with her charming but irresponsible alcoholic father, she gains insight into her parents' divorce and realizes that she cannot change her father's behavior. While the Corey family (*Lily and the Lost Boy*, 1987) is living on a Greek island, twelve-year-old Lily feels left out when her older brother becomes friends with Jack, a rootless American youth whose father dances superbly but drinks too much. While riding his bicycle near the edge of a cliff, the reckless Jack causes the death of a Greek child. Despite her dislike for Jack, Lily overcomes her fear and goes out alone at night to befriend him. Obsessed with old family jealousies, ten-year-old Emma's acid-tongued Aunt Bea (*The Village by the Sea*, 1988) has an unkind word for everyone. At the climax of the novel, the elderly woman destroys the miniature village Emma and her friend have painstakingly built from debris found on the beach. Emma's uncle restrains her from immediate retaliation, and she later gains greater understanding of her unhappy aunt.

One of America's outstanding writers for young readers, F. has received numerous literary awards including an American Book Award for *A Place Apart* and Newbery Honor awards in 1985 and 1989.

OTHER WORKS: *The God of Nightmares* (1990). *Money Island* (1992). "A Childhood of Sermons and Sonnets," *NYTBR* (12 July 1981).

BIBLIOGRAPHY: Townsend, John Rowe, *A Sounding of Storytellers: Essays on Contemporary Writers for Children* (1979). Reference works: *CLR* 1 (1976). *CA* 73–76 (1978). *CANR* 20 (1987). *CLC* 2 (1974), 8 (1978). *Dict. of Am. Children's Fiction, 1960–1984* (1986). *DLB* 52 (1986). *Fourth Book of Junior Authors and Illustrators* (1978). *SATA* 17 (1979), 60 (1990). *Values in Selected Children's Books of Fiction and Fantasy* (1987).

Other references: *The Alan Rev.* (Winter 1987). *Horn Book* 60 (April 1984). *NYRB* (27 June 1985). *NYTBR* (9 Nov. 1980; 11 Nov. 1984; 18 Nov. 1984; 5 Feb. 1989; 8 July 1990; 10 Nov. 1991). *PW* (interview, 6 April 1990). *TLS* (21 Feb. 1986; 15 Jan. 1988).

ALICE BELL

Marilyn French

B. 21 Nov. 1929, New York City
Writes under: Mara Solwoska
D. of Isabel (Hazz) and D. Charles Edwards; m. Robert M. French, Jr., 1950,
   div. 1967

F. worked her way through Hofstra University to a B.A. and M.A. in English (1951–64), regretting that she did not major in philosophy. While supporting her husband through law school, she began to write seriously. After her divorce, she returned to Harvard for her doctorate (1972) and taught at Holy Cross College (1972–76).

In *The Book as World: James Joyce's Ulysses* (1976), literary criticism adapted from her dissertation, F. suggests a new reading of *Ulysses* focusing on its deliberately diverse successive styles and the role of the "scandalously unreliable" narrator as malevolent, contemptuously refusing "to mediate the events in the book for the reader who is thereby forced to engage in that process himself." F.'s argument is schematic, focusing on *Ulysses'* rhetorical effect.

Her first political novel of ideas, *The Women's Room* (1977), was a bestseller, called representative of the 1970s "women's renaissance" and the major novel of the women's liberation movement. Although a bitter, cynical, semiautobiographical fiction and polemic about how heterosexual relations exploit and manipulate women, it touched a chord in a generation of women disillusioned by the failure of early marriages, the suburban ideal, and problems of motherhood in a changing age. The novel details its protagonist's struggle over four decades for identity, intellectual independence, and a career, from the conformity and submissiveness of 1950s New Jersey suburbanites to the difficulties of a divorced older woman coming to Harvard as a graduate student, struggling to be taken seriously, liberated but lonely. Mira expresses the author's own perspective: "Sometimes I get as sick of writing this as you may be in reading it. . . . I get sick because, you see, it's all true, it happened, and it was boring and painful and full of despair." The Cambridge feminist Val voices a more militant feminist rhetoric informed by consciousness raising. Male characters are one-dimensional, revealing F.'s belief "that the white middle-class male is really hollow: a sort of walking uniform, making the expected jokes, maintaining the expected postures." She believes there is a chasm of exploitation, incomprehension, and mistrust between women and men; while women were "expectant in the 40s, submissive in the 50s, enraged in the 60s, they have arrived in the 70s independent but somehow unstrung, not yet fully composed after all they've been through." *The Women's Room* was made into a movie for television in 1980.

In F.'s novels, the reader hopes for a happy ending despite her powerfully stated thesis that there is little future for coexistence between men and women. The narrative rambles as characters appear and disappear. F. deliberately loosens control over her narrative, seeing her books as more documentary than fiction, thus strengthening their political impact, making them more autobiographical than creative, and confronting the reader's preconceptions mercilessly. *The Bleeding Heart* (1980) is a polemical story about an affair between two Americans living in Britain for a year, overcoming their individual barriers for mutual growth yet separating in the end.

F. returned to literary criticism with *Shakespeare's Division of Experience* (1981), examining his "horror at female sexuality." She has also provided introductions for reprints of novels by **Edith Wharton.**

In *Beyond Power: On Women, Men, and Morals* (1985), F. shifted to a long, encyclopedic, interdisciplinary, feminist theoretical analysis of the demise of matriarchy, the origins of social organization, and the rise of patriarchy lusting for power and its consequences over the last 2,500 years. F. draws on anthropology, philosophy, and history as well as literature "to urge the creation of a new morality," based on feminism's ancient origins: "a new 'world' does not imply that we will invent new values." It is a jeremiad, predicting dire economic, environmental, and even criminal consequences unless the value system is revised.

A later novel, *Her Mother's Daughter* (1987), probes the experience of four generations of women over half a century, examining the relationships of mothers and daughters and the desire to overcome fears to be autonomous. Like F.'s more theoretical works, it calls for a reassessment of values. F. also published books in Israel in 1980, 1989, and 1991. *The War against Women* (1992) continues F.'s analysis of the inevitable conflict between women's needs and societal norms.

BIBLIOGRAPHY: Reference works: *CA* 69–72 (1978). *CLC* 10 (1979), 18 (1981), 60 (1990). *FC* (1990). *Maj Twent Cen Writers* (1991).

Other references: *Library J.* (15 Nov. 1977). *Modern Language Rev.* (Jan.

1979). *Modern Philology* (May 1979). *Ms.* (Jan. 1978, April 1979). *NYT* (17 Oct. 1977, 9 March 1980, 10 March 1980, 17 Jan. 1990). *NYTBR* (16 Oct. 1977, 13 Nov. 1977). *People* (20 Feb. 1978). *TLS* (18 Feb. 1977, 21 April 1978, 9 May 1980). *Wash. Post Book World* (9 Oct. 1977, 9 March 1980).

BLANCHE LINDEN-WARD

Betty Friedan

See AWW 2, 90–92

Credited with having begun the current women's movement with her earliest book, *The Feminist Mystique* (1963), F. has remained active and has taken a middle ground in the various ideological differences that have characterized the movement since the 1970s. She describes the different stages of the movement as part of an evolutionary force. Writing in 1983 in her introduction to the twentieth-anniversary edition of *The Feminist Mystique*, she claims that she has become "increasingly convinced that the whole process [the women's movement] . . . is not really a revolution at all, but simply a stage in human evolution, necessary for survival."

Whereas in her groundbreaking first book she had argued that women had become socialized to accept the idea that they could only fulfill themselves through the roles of mother and wife, in her second book, *It Changed My Life: Writings on the Women's Movement* (1976), F. argued that women had demanded and received new opportunities and more equality. She warned, however, that women's gains were threatened by polarization amongst themselves and that the women's movement must focus on transcending divisiveness and work for "human liberation."

In *The Second Stage* (1981), F. pursued this line of thinking further. She states that the failures of the women's movement are due to "our blind spot about the family." After years of activism, research, and observation of women's lives, she concludes that many women are now caught in a new "feminist mystique" where they are doing two demanding jobs: the work of the family and the work of a career. They are forced to be "superwomen," juggling two roles and feeling guilty about both. The solution, she argues, is to take control of family policy agenda and to restructure family and work so that both men and women are freer to share roles. She insists that men will become allies when they see that the changing of outmoded institutions will also improve their lives. Citing the specific issues of flexible work schedules, parental leave, and child care as the new agenda for the women's movement, she calls for reclaiming the family as "the new feminist frontier." Reaction to her new agenda ranged from calling her a "repentant feminist" to reaffirming her importance in the movement and to recognizing, as **Marilyn French** did in an *Esquire* article in December 1983, that the affirmation of the family in *The Second Stage* was a "passionate plea for general awareness of the inclusive nature of feminism."

In the 1983 anniversary edition of *The Feminist Mystique* F. angrily denies the media's pronouncements that the "postfeminist generation" had abandoned feminist ideas: "Of course the postfeminist generation is in a different place. The women's movement put it there." Sounding the theme of evolutionary change, she writes, "It's hard to go on evolving, as we all must, just to keep up with a revolution as big as this when some . . . want to lock it in place forever, as an unchanging ism." In this new stage of her life, she sees the importance of linking the redefinition of the family with issues and interests of single women and older women. In *The Fountain of Age* (1993) she urges older people to draw on their strengths and not "forfeit these years with a preoccupation with death." She also notes her feelings of déjà vu when she hears geriatric experts talk about the aged "with the same patronizing, 'compassionate' denial of their personhood" that she heard twenty years before when the experts talked about women.

During the 1980s F. saw the defeat of the Equal Rights Amendment in Congress but despite that setback she was hopeful about the new political power of women represented by the vice presidential nomination of Geraldine Ferraro at the 1984 Democratic National Convention to which she was a delegate. In "Back to the Feminist Mystique," published in the *Humanist* in 1991, F. notes that the decade of the eighties had made it more difficult to move to the "second stage" because the support systems and social programs so necessary to restructure work and home had been almost destroyed in a political environment hostile to change. She challenges the leaders of the women's movement to heal divisions amongst themselves and to join together once again to fight for these changes. "Yes, my sisters and daughters," she writes, "into the breach again—and march, march, so that we can have real choices."

OTHER WORKS: "Twenty Years After," introduction to twentieth-anniversary edition of *The Feminist Mystique* (1983).

BIBLIOGRAPHY: Reference works: *CANR* 18 (1986). *CB* (1989).

Other references: *Esquire* (Dec. 1983, article by Marilyn French). *Feminist Rev.* (Autumn 1987). *LA Times* (26 April 1992, interview). *Nation* (14 Nov. 1981). *National Rev.* (5 Feb. 1982). *New Republic* (20 Jan. 1982). *NYT* (5 July 1981, 25 April 1983, 27 Feb. 1983). *NYTBR* (22 Nov. 1981). *TLS* (30 July 1982).

MARY GRIMLEY MASON

Jean Fritz

B. 16 Nov. 1915, Hankow, China
D. of Myrtle (Chaney) and Arthur Minton Guttery; m. Michael Fritz, 1941; c.: David, Andrea

F. has been heralded for her work in several genres of children's literature, but she is best known for her lively, engaging biographies. She has won numerous prestigious awards including the Children's Book Guild Non-Fiction Award for "total body of creative writing" (1978), and Boston Globe/Horn Book awards in 1984 for *The Double Life of Pocahontas* (1983), and in 1990 for *The Great Little Madison* (1990).

F. graduated from Wheaton College in 1937 and continued with graduate studies at Columbia University. She worked as a researcher, book reviewer, and editor while her husband served in the army during World War II. A prolific writer, F. began late; her first book was published when she was thirty-nine. In 1952, while working as a children's librarian at her local library in New York she discovered she not only wanted to read children's books, but write them as well. F.'s first picture book, *Fish Head* (1954), had its genesis in the fantasies of escape she invented when feeling overwhelmed by the task of caring for her two young children.

F. expected to continue writing picture books, but simple curiosity along with her awareness of textbook inadequacies motivated her to begin writing biographies. "Textbooks are so often both inaccurate and dull, a place where dead people just stay dead," she told an interviewer. "I think of my job as bringing them back to life." Critics have praised her for her success at this task; she is noted for her ability to captivate a young audience not only by focusing on the accomplishments of historical figures, but also by revealing them as the idiosyncratic, imperfect, and often humorous people that they were. F. shares interesting anecdotes and reveals weaknesses while still paying meticulous attention to accuracy and maintaining the integrity of both the reader and the subject. In her biographies she is "always looking for out-of-the-way details, for the little things that seem so trivial but throw such light on a personality."

F.'s devotion to the exploration of American history stems from her childhood, which she shares in one of her most critically acclaimed novels, *Homesick: My Own Story* (1982). F. lived in China with her missionary parents until the age of eleven. Despite her loneliness and isolation during this unstable time in China, F. was a thoughtful, often precocious child, writing once in a letter to her grandmother, "I'm not always good. Sometimes I don't even try." She was also extremely patriotic. On one occasion, she sang the words to *America* while all of the other children in her British classroom sang *God Save the King*. Reflecting on this experience in 1988, she explained: "No one is more patriotic than the one separated from his country; no one is as eager to find roots as the person who has been uprooted." Over a long career, F. has translated that eagerness into biographies for children of such quintessential American figures as George Washington, Ben Franklin, Sam Houston, and Theodore Roosevelt.

OTHER WORKS: 121 Pudding Street (1955). Hurrah for Jonathan (1955). Growing Up (1956). The Late Spring (1957). The Cabin Faced West (1958). Champion Dog, Prince Tom (1958). The Animals of Doctor Schweitzer (1958). How to Read a Rabbit (1959). Brady (1960). Tap, Tap Lion, One, Two, Three (1962). San Francisco (1962). I, Adam (1963). Magic to Burn (1964). Early Thunder (1967). George Washington's Breakfast (1969). And Then What Happened, Paul Revere?

(1973). *Why Don't You Get a Horse, Sam Adams?* (1974). *Where Was Patrick Henry on the 29th of May?* (1975). *Who's That Stepping on Plymouth Rock?* (1975). *Will You Sign Here, John Hancock?* (1976). *What's the Big Idea, Ben Franklin?* (1976). *Can't You Make Them Behave, King George?* (1976). *Brendan the Navigator* (1979). *Stonewall* (1979). *The Man Who Loved Books* (1980). *Where Do You Think You're Going, Christopher Columbus?* (1980). *Traitor: The Case of Benedict Arnold* (1981). *The Good Giants and the Bad Pukwudgies* (1982). *China Homecoming* (1985). *Make Way for Sam Houston* (1986). *Shh! We're Writing the Constitution* (1987). *China's Long March* (1988). *Bully for You, Teddy Roosevelt!* (1991). *George Washington's Mother* (1992). *The Great Adventure of Christopher Columbus* (1992). *Surprising Myself* (1992). *Around the World in a Hundred Years* (1993). *Just a Few Words, Mr. Lincoln* (1993). Contributing editor, *Worlds of Childhood: The Art and Craft of Writing for Children* (1990). Contributor, *The World of 1492* (1992). Contributor of short stories to *Seventeen*, *Redbook*, and *The New Yorker*.

BIBLIOGRAPHY: Hostetler, Elizabeth. *Jean Fritz: A Critical Biography* (1982). *Children's Literature Review*, Gerard J. Senick, ed. (1988). Other references: *Boston Sunday Globe* (6 Jan. 1991).

DIANE E. KROLL

Mariam Gardner. *See Marion Zimmer Bradley*

Sally Miller Gearhart

B. 15 April 1931, Pearisburg, Virginia
D. of Sarah and Kyle M. Gearheart

A feminist utopian novelist and professor of speech and communication studies, G. describes her politics as lesbian-feminist and her religion as

Philogyny. She received her B.A. from Sweet Briar College (1952) and continued her education at Bowling Green State University where she received an M.A. in 1953. In 1956 she was awarded a Ph.D. from the University of Illinois.

In 1974, G. edited and coauthored with William R. Johnson a piece entitled *Loving Women/Loving Men: Gay Liberation in the Church.* Her only novel, *The Wanderground: Stories of the Hill Women* was published in 1978 and has been reprinted several times. *Wanderground* depicts a lesbian utopian society of "hill women"—a group of antiviolent people who have escaped "in City" in a revolt against technology and male domination. Offering an essentialist portrayal of men and women as polar opposites, G. writes of the hill women's relationships to each other and to the planet Earth, which is depending on them for its survival. Critic Bonnie Zimmerman calls the novel "an extreme example of the idealization of the lesbian myth of community." She regrets the occasional artistic lapses that result from G.'s idealism, but notes the strength with which G. "and those inspired by her revere the virtues of equality, balance, harmony, and complete respect for all entities."

G. has held a variety of teaching positions including assistant professor of speech at the Stephen F. Austin State University in Texas (1956–59), and associate professor of speech and drama and department head at Texas Lutheran College from 1960 to 1970. She has been assistant professor of speech at San Francisco State University since 1972. She has also served as a member of the board of directors of the San Francisco Family Service Agency; as cochairperson of the Council on Religion and the Homosexual; as lecturer and consultant for the national Sex Forum; and as member of the San Francisco Women's Centers.

OTHER WORKS: *A Feminist Tarot: A Guide to Intrapersonal Communication* (1977).

BIBLIOGRAPHY: Rosinsky, Natalie, *Feminist Futures: Contemporary Women's Speculative Fiction* (1987). Zimmerman, Bonnie, *Safe Sea of Women* (1990). Reference works: *CA* 57–60 (1976). *FC* (1990).

MARY E. HARVEY

Kaye Gibbons

B. 5 May 1960, Nash County, North Carolina
D. of Alice (Gardner) and Charles Bennett Batts; m. Michael Gibbons, div.;
c.: Mary; Leslie; Louise

Born and raised in North Carolina, G. attended Rocky Mount High School and started college on a scholarship at North Carolina State University. She transferred to the University of North Carolina at Chapel Hill where she studied American literature with Louis Rubin and began writing her first novel. While she never finished her degree at Chapel Hill, she did receive the university's Distinguished Alumna Award. She became writer in residence at the Library of North Carolina State University in 1993.

All of G.'s novels are steeped in a sense of place and history, and they reveal an understanding of women's struggles to "shoulder extraordinary burdens" and to maintain their compassion, humor, and self-esteem in a culture that values those qualities very little in women. Understanding, strong, resourceful, and independent, all the women in G.'s fiction represent what one critic has called "a fictional oral history of female wishes [and] hopes." Generations of G.'s women share the vision of finding a place for themselves in the world without compromising their sense of self.

Ellen Foster (1987), which G. herself says is "emotionally autobiographical," won the Sue Kaufman Prize for First Fiction from the American Academy and Institute of Arts and Letters and a special citation from the Ernest Hemingway Foundation. Its particular strength lies in the resilient character of Ellen herself who endures the suicide of her mother, her father's sexual advances, and the meanness of her grandmother and aunt to emerge triumphant in a happy home. Her quest for place is determined and persistent: she will find a safe harbor. In her search she is forced to throw off her own racial prejudice and realize that, despite her poverty, her black friend Starletta has something she envies—a loving family.

Women are the center of all of G.'s novels, and *A Virtuous Woman* (1989) carefully orchestrates past and present so that the voice of a dead woman becomes the center of the novel. Ruby Pitt Woodrow has left her freezer stocked with food for her husband, Blinking Jack Ernest Stokes. She knew that, while some would think it morbid, men cannot really do all that much for themselves, and "if you want to see a man afraid just put him in a room with a sick woman who was once strong."

Women's strength resonates throughout the pages of G.'s work, from the strength of eleven-year-old Ellen Foster to the power of Charlie Kate, medicine woman of *Charms for the Easy Life* (1992). G. grounds her fiction in the knowledge that "this world is built up on strong women, built up and kept up by them too, them kneeling, stooping, pulling, bending, and rising up when they need to go and do what needs to get done."

A Cure for Dreams (1991), which won the Pen/Revlon Award for the best work of fiction by a writer under thirty-five, is, like her fourth book, *Charms for the Easy Life*, a generational novel. Grandmothers, mothers, and daughters all share the same hopes for themselves. Their struggles to endure hard times are given meaning by their stories. Told as gossip, recounted as family history, and preserved as the marrow of family life, these stories are the lives of the Randolph women. Marjorie Polly Randolph cherishes the stories told by her mother, Betty Davies Randolph, and her grandmother, Lottie O'Cadhain Davies. Marjorie need only say to her mother: "'Tell me about your mother and you, and Kentucky and Virginia and the wild way I was born. Tell me about the years that made you.' Then she would talk. Talking was my mother's life."

Women talking to each other, remembering the talents of their foremothers, surviving—all of G.'s women endure and pass on their power to the next generation. In *Charms for the Easy Life*, Charlie Kate, midwife and healer, leaves her legacy of herbs and cures with her granddaughter, Margaret, the narrator, who chooses her grandmother's calling as part of her heritage.

The women in G.'s novels represent a large extended family of Southerners who have not been defeated; their stories represent a history of the South that deconstructs the history of Southern womanhood and revitalizes the traditions of independence and self-reliance.

BIBLIOGRAPHY: Reference works: *CLC* 50 (1988).

Other references: *Kenyon Rev.* 10 (Winter 1988). *NYTBR* (30 April 1989; 12 May 1991; 11 April 1993). *PW* (Feb. 1993, interview). G. P. Putnam's Sons, "News" (1993). *Southern Q.* 30:2–3 (Winter/Spring 1992).

MARY A. MCCAY

Sandra M. Gilbert

B. 27 Dec. 1936, New York City
D. of Angela (Caruso) and Alexis Joseph Mortola; m. Elliot Lewis Gilbert, 1957;
*   c.: Roger, Katherine, Susanna*

G. is a widely published and influential feminist literary critic; she is also a poet with four collections of poetry. Her major critical works, beginning in 1979 with *Shakespeare's Sisters: Feminist Essays on Women Poets* and *The Madwoman in the Attic: The Woman Writer and the Nineteenth-Century Imagination*, have been written in collaboration with Susan Gubar. The collaboration has been a fruitful one and is ongoing, with a third volume of *No Man's Land: The Place of the Woman Writer in the Twentieth Century* due for publication. Also forthcoming by G. are *Mother Rites: Studies in Literature and Maternity* and editions of Virginia Woolf's *Orlando* and of the writings of **Kate Chopin.**

Shakespeare's Sisters marked the beginning of G.'s wide-ranging examination of what it has meant to be a woman writing in English in a culture whose literary values have been determined by men, and in which "woman poet" has been considered a "contradiction in terms." The book is a compilation of nineteen essays about women poets, from prenineteenth-century writers to contemporary. The effort is to recover lost poets, to reassess women's poetry, and to trace the outlines of a distinctively female poetic tradition.

In *The Madwoman in the Attic* G. and Gubar scrutinized problems of literary heritage, of women writers' alienation from male predecessors who depicted women as either "angels or monsters." They explore the "anxiety of authorship" that confronted women novelists of the nineteenth century: Jane Austen, Mary Shelley, Emily and Charlotte Brontë, George Eliot, and poets **Emily Dickinson** and Elizabeth Barrett Browning. As critic Walter Kendrick noted, the madwoman image serves "as an emblem of the confinement inflicted on Victorian women who wished to write."

The Norton Anthology of Literature by Women (1985), edited by G. and Gubar, was designed to serve as a "core-curriculum" text for courses in literature by women. While the principle of selection of this comprehensive and somewhat unwieldy volume has been challenged by some reviewers, it is a valuable compilation of women's work in every period and genre and provides useful editorial material.

No Man's Land: The Place of the Woman Writer in the Twentieth Century continues G.'s and Gubar's reassessment of the literary landscape, using "the battle of the sexes" metaphor as a way to approach changes in the modern period. A reviewer described the first volume, *The War of the Words* (1987), as documenting "a war on women's words waged by male writers who felt their tradition invaded by alien female talents." The second volume, *Sexchanges* (1989), approaches the post–World War I territory more intensively, comparing texts by men and women, and providing studies of **Kate Chopin, Edith Wharton,** and **Willa Cather** and a chapter on **Gertrude Stein** and lesbian writers of the 1920s.

G. received a B.A. from Cornell University in 1957, an M.A. from New York University (1961), and a Ph.D. from Columbia University (1968). Since 1989 she has been professor of English at the University of California at Davis, where she had taught earlier (1975–80). She held a similar position at Princeton University from 1985 to 1989. Prior to that she was an associate professor at Indiana University (1973–75), where her collaborative work with Susan Gubar began. From 1963 to 1972 she taught at colleges in New York and California. G. has also published more than fifty essays in a wide range of scholarly and literary journals and essay collections.

G. has received numerous awards and fellowships, including an honorary D. Litt. from Wesleyan University in 1988, a Guggenheim fellowship in 1983, a Rockefeller Foundation fellowship in 1982, and a National Endowment for the Humanities fellowship in 1980–81. She received the International Poetry Foundation's Charity Randall Award in 1990 and *Poetry*'s Eunice Tietjens Memorial Prize in 1980. With Susan Gubar she shared the "Woman of the Year" Award from *Ms.* magazine in 1986.

OTHER WORKS: *Acts of Attention: The Poems of D. H. Lawrence* (1973; 2nd ed. 1990). Kate Chopin, *The Awakening and Selected Stories* (editor, 1984). *In the Fourth World* (poems, 1979). *The Summer Kitchen: Poems* (chapbook, 1983). *Emily's Bread* (poems, 1984). *Feminism and Modernism* (1987). *Blood Pressure* (poems, 1988).

BIBLIOGRAPHY: Reference works: *CA* 41–44 (1979). *CANR* 33 (1991). *FC* (1990).

Other references: *Amer. Lit.* (March 1990). *College English* (Nov. 1988). *Commentary* (July 1988). *Comparative Lit.* (Spring 1991). *Contemp. Sociology* (July 1990). *Criticism* (Fall 1989). *English Language Notes* (Sept. 1990). *J. of*

Amer. Studies (April 1991). *J. of Modern Lit.* (Fall–Winter 1989). *J. of English and Germanic Philology* (July 1989). *Modern Fiction Studies* (Winter 1988; Winter 1989). *Nation* (2 July 1988). *National Rev.* (28 Oct. 1988). *NYRB* (31 May 1990). *NYTBR* (7 Feb. 1988; 19 Feb. 1989; 12 March 1989). *Studies in the Novel* (Spring 1989; Winter 1990). *Texas Studies in Lit. and Lang.* (Fall 1990). *TLS* (3 June 1988; 2 June 1989). *Tulsa Studies in Women's Lit.* (Spring 1989).

KINERETH GENSLER

Ellen Gilchrist

B. 20 Feb. 1935, Vicksburg, Mississippi
D. of Aurora (Aford) and William Garth Gilchrist; m. Marshall Walker (twice);
m. Freddie Kullam; c.: Marshall; Garth; Pierce [Walker]

Although she calls herself a poet and philosopher, G. is best known for her short stories and novels. The daughter of an engineer, G. spent some of her childhood in Indiana during World War II, but has lived most of her life in the South of her ancestors and of her own creation. Her childhood is a series of memories of the Hopedale Plantation where her mother's family lived and where G. was born. It is, she says, "THE RICHEST LAND IN THE WORLD and we are happy there." G. attended Mill-saps College (B.A. 1967), and has worked as a journalist and as a weekly commentator on National Public Radio's "Morning Edition."

Mother of three sons and several times a grandmother, G. asserts that children are much more important than writing and that she would burn all her books to save one finger joint of one of her children or grandchildren. It is not surprising, then, to find many of her stories peopled by adolescents who are struggling to find themselves, parents who live only to help their children survive, and family retainers who create an optimistic perspective on the possibility of family endurance. G. herself says she is a happy person and an optimist.

G.'s first book of short stories, *In the Land of Dreamy Dreams* (1981), was published by the University of Arkansas Press because G. was afraid to let her teacher give it to a New York agent; the underground success of the book led Little, Brown to reissue it in 1985. The stories are set among the vacuous rich of New Oreland or the dying aristocracy of the Mississippi Delta where G. spent much of her childhood. Stories about surviving, and sometimes not surviving, they all have a quality of vision about them. They are rampant with children whose lives are sprinkled with moments from G.'s own childhood; even those who die live a rich moment in her fiction.

Two other short-story collections, *Victory over Japan* (1984), which won the American Book Award for fiction, and *Drunk with Love* (1986) brought G. further recognition as a writer in control of her Southern material. In these volumes, some characters from *In the Land of Dreamy Dreams* return and G. writes about their lives with perception and humor. Perhaps the most important character in *Victory over Japan* is Traceleen, a black maid who, despite the fact that G. often waxes too poetic about the dedication of servants, is wise beyond G.'s own wisdom.

The Annunciation (1983), G.'s ambitious but flawed first novel, features Amanda McCamey, who is too stereotypically New Orleans rich, too egotistical. Finally, when she retreats to Arkansas to live simply and be a writer, she is simply unbelievable. The eternally dedicated Lavertis, another version of Traceleen and Amanda's ever-faithful maid, strains the book's credulity, but the effort is grand, and G. tries to deal with large issues of loss (Amanda was forced, as a teenager, to give up a child for adoption) and creativity. Her pictures of New Orleans capture the heart of the city's richness and vacuity.

With the publication of *The Anna Papers* (1988), *Light Can Be Both Wave and Particle* (1989), and *I Cannot Get You Close Enough* (1990), G. has begun to transcribe what her characters tell her to and thus to lose the control she had over her best fiction. There are some excellent adolescent characters in the Hand family who people much of *The Anna Papers* and *I Cannot Get You Close Enough*, but the artist character, Anna Hand, who seems to be a side of G. herself, is too self-advertising and often too self-absorbed to see how her actions affect her family.

In *Net of Jewels* (1992) G. once again incorporates pressing issues into her fiction. She asks, through the character of Rhoda Manning, how a woman can save herself from drowning in the limited and limiting culture of the South. A cousin of Anna Hand, Rhoda struggles through a series of attempts to find herself in marriage, affairs, diet pills, booze, and political movements—none of which can help her dispel her desperate sense that she is not really alive.

G. has a fine talent for capturing the voices of rich dissatisfied Southern ladies; she has a real empathy for her adolescents; and she has a Southerner's eye for the landscape outside and inside her characters. The author of one book of poetry, *The Land Surveyor's Daughter* (1979), she told an interviewer that soon she would stop writing fiction and return to poetry, a way, perhaps, for her to regain the control she demonstrated in her earlier work.

OTHER WORKS: Falling through Space: The Journals of Ellen Gilchrist (1987).

BIBLIOGRAPHY: Bonetti, Kay, interview with Ellen Gilchrist. American Audio Prose Library (1986). Reference works: *CA* 113 (1985), 116 (1986). *CLC* 34 (1985), 48 (1988). *CLCY* (1984). *FC* (1990). *Maj Tw Cent Writers* (1991).

Other references: [New Orleans] *Times Picayune*, 14 Oct. 1990.

MARY A. MCCAY

Nikki Giovanni

See AWW 2, 135–37

Her book jackets call G. "our most widely read living Black poet," and indeed her many volumes of poetry, a book of essays, and several recordings attest to her continued popular appeal. G.'s controversial poetry has not always fared so well with critics, however. Her first book, *Black Feeling, Black Talk* (1967), stunned an American public on the verge of social revolt when it asked, "Nigger / Can you kill / Can a nigger kill / Can a nigger kill a honkie / Can a nigger kill the Man." Today, her alternately provocative and elegant speeches keep her in demand as a public speaker and have helped earn her the title "Princess of Black Poetry."

G. grew up in a close family enriched by loving relatives, a few of whom she sketches in *Sacred Cows and Other Edibles* (1988). After her 1967 graduation from Fisk University, she planned the first Black Arts Festival in her hometown of Cincinnati, Ohio. As an extension of her community activism, with assistance from a Ford Foundation grant she attended the University of Pennsylvania School of Social Work; she later enrolled in Columbia University's School of Fine Arts. In 1968, G. received a National Foundation for the Arts grant; she was then teaching English at Queens College and continuing her activist work in the black community. In 1969, G. became an associate professor at Livingston College, Rutgers University.

Although G. desired children, she had no wish to be married; in 1969, determined to succeed as a single mother, she bore her son Thomas Watson G. Her 1971 book, *Spin a Soft Black Song*, written for black American children, was dedicated to him. A subsequent book of poems for children (*Vacation Time*, 1980) and poems in other books reveal her intense dedication to her family life. In *Sacred Cows and Other Edibles*, she devotes a large section of an autobiographical essay to the joys and frustrations of living with her then fourteen-year-old son.

Those Who Ride the Night Winds (1983) is composed primarily of meditations, on public figures, personal friends, social injustice throughout American history, and loved relationships. The book is an innovative experiment in form. The pieces are written in short paragraphs, punctuated with ellipses. As such, they have the telegraphic immediacy of **Emily Dickinson**'s dash-punctuated poems, as if the poet's thoughts are scribbled down as they flash across her mind. At the same time, the form implies an uncertainty, a care lest the reader miss a subtlety of thought or image. Dedicated to those courageous people "who in sonic solitude or the hazy hell of habit know—that for all the devils and gods . . . life is a marvelous, transitory adventure," these poems are written for **Lorraine Hansberry**, John Lennon, Robert Kennedy, Billie Jean King, Martin Luther King, Jr., and **Phillis Wheatley.** Of the latter, G. writes, "The critics . . . from a safe seat in the balcony . . . disdain her performance . . . reject her reality . . . ignore her truths. . . . How dare she. . . . Why couldn't she . . . be more like . . . more like. . . . The record sticks. . . . Phillis was her own precedent."

G., too, has had her share of critics. Paula Giddings, who wrote the introduction to *Cotton Candy on a Rainy Day* (1978), is disturbed that "as her persona matured, her language, craft, and perceptions did not." William J. Harris concedes that "at times she does not seem to think things through with sufficient care," but argues that G. is "a good popular poet: she is honest, she writes well-crafted poems, and she pushes against the barriers of the conventional."

Sacred Cows and Other Edibles is a quirky collection of essays previously published in newspapers and magazines. G. examines subjects from Spam to Miss America, from the aftereffects of the civil rights movement to termites, game shows, televised sports, furniture shopping, and the writing profession. Her tone is alternately sassy and introspective, strident and gentle, the style conversational, digressive. **Marita Golden** calls it "quintessential Nikki Giovanni—sometimes funny, nervy and unnerving with flashes of wisdom," although she wishes for a more stringent editor.

Whether in prose or poetry, G. continues to create an honest, charming, idiosyncratic, and alert persona. Her voice now marks the pulse, not only of black America, but of the country's diverse peoples and cultures.

OTHER WORKS: *Appalachian Elders: A Warm Hearth Sampler* (editor, with Cathee Dennison, 1991). Sound recordings: *The Reason I Like Chocolate* (1976). *The Poet Today* (1979). *The American Arts Project: Nikki Giovanni Reading from Her Works* (1984). Visual recordings: *Spirit to Spirit: The Poetry of Nikki Giovanni* (1987). Corrections and additions to AWW 2: *Black Judgment* (1968). *Re: Creation* (1970). *Night Comes Softly: An Anthology of Black Female Voices* (editor, 1970). *Ego-tripping and Other Poems for Young People* (1973).

BIBLIOGRAPHY: *Black Women Writers (1950–1980): A Critical Evaluation*, Mari Evans, ed. (essays by W. J. Harris and P. Giddings, 1984). *Conversations with Nikki Giovanni*, Virginia Fowler, ed. (1992). *Black Women Writers at Work*, Claudia Tate, ed. (1983). *Belief vs. Theory in Black American Literary Criticism*, J. Weixlmann and C. J. Fontenot, eds. (1986). Reference works: *Black Lit. Crit.* (1992). *DLB* 41 (1985).
Other references: *MELUS* (Winter 1982).

LISA CARL

Louise Glück

B. 22 April 1943, New York City
D. of Beatrice (Grosby) and Daniel Glück; m. John Dranow, 1977; c.: Noah (from earlier marriage), b. 1973

G.'s parents lost their first child, a daughter, seven days after her birth. This loss irrevocably altered the family that might have been, and in her poetry G. examines the intimate dramas of family life as loss reverberates across generational lines. She treats private pain with relentless, lyrical intensity, yet maintains a paradoxical reticence. In G.'s work confessional poetry meets restrained classicism; her poems are tragic in a traditional sense, yet imbued with the psychological awareness of Freud and Jung.

During the years she might have been at college, she undertook psychoanalysis. She attended Sarah Lawrence College for six weeks and later took courses, almost entirely poetry workshops, at Columbia University's School of General Studies. She worked with Leonie Adams, with Stanley Kunitz, and briefly with **Adrienne Rich.**

G. is one of the foremost American lyric poets. She has taught in a variety of institutions, including Goddard College, the universities of North Carolina, Virginia, Iowa, Cincinnati, and California (Berkeley, Davis, and Los Angeles), Columbia University, and Williams College. She has received grants from the Rockefeller and Guggenheim foundations and from the National Endowment for the Arts. G.'s work has been recognized with many awards and prizes, including the *Poetry Magazine* Eunice Tietjens Prize, the American Academy and Institute of Arts and Letters Award in Literature, the National Book Critics Circle Award, the *Boston Globe* Literary Press Award for Poetry, and the Poetry Society of America Melville Kane Award.

Firstborn, published in 1968, bears the imprint of the confessional sensibility, and G. assumes the stance of the embittered outsider. She uses short, trenchant sentences, rhyme and off-rhyme, and colloquial diction, much like Robert Lowell, **Sylvia Plath,** and **Anne Sexton.** In her late twenties, G. wrote nothing for over a year. In the poems that follow this silence she abandons her more formal approach with its implied harmony and its authorial virtuosity. The hot drama of the confessional style yields to increasing control and plainness of speech. Calvin Bedient says of *The House on Marshland* (1975): "Its ornament proved chastely limited; besides, the figurative . . . simply and hallucinatingly asserted itself as the real." The poems, authoritative, beautiful, and reticent, resemble folktale and myth. In "The School Children" the mothers must offer their children to the schools, like propitiatory apples, and are helpless to keep them from hurt: "And the teachers shall instruct them in silence / and the mothers shall scour the orchards for a way out, / drawing to themselves the gray limbs of the fruit trees / bearing so little ammunition."

In *Descending Figure* (1980) and *The Triumph of Achilles* (1985) she draws heavily on what **Helen Vendler** calls an "eclectic mythology" to elucidate private matters. In *Ararat* (1990), a series of lyrics that composes a balanced narrative about the death of her father, bereavement, and the surviving family, the mythic references are less explicit, but the resonances remain. Her family of origin appears as the archetypical family over which looms an ancient, unalterable tragedy. In *Wild Iris* (1992), which won the Pulitzer Prize for Poetry, G. explores questions of faith and the place of the human in the natural order through a series of meditative poems in the tradition of **Emily Dickinson** and George Herbert. Framed by the diurnal and seasonal cycles, the book locates itself in G.'s own garden, where everything has a voice. Characteristically, these voices are not gentle but tough and demanding.

OTHER WORKS: The Garden (chapbook, 1976). "Whole and Not Final: The Art of George Oppen," *Ironwood* 13:2 (Fall 1985). "On Stanley Kunitz," *APR* 14:5 (Sept.-Oct. 1985). "Symposium of Poets on T. S. Eliot," *The Southern Rev.* 21:4 (Autumn 1985).

BIBLIOGRAPHY: Vendler, Helen, *Part of Nature, Part of Us: Modern American Poets* (1980). Williamson, Alan, *Introspection and Contemporary Poetry* (1984). Dodd, Elizabeth, "Reticence and the Lyric: The Development of a Personal Classicism among Four Women Poets of the Twentieth Century," unpublished Ph.D. diss., Univ. of Indiana, 1989; *DAI* 50:12 (June 1990). Reference works: *CA* 73–76 (1978). *CLC* 7 (1977), 22 (1982), 44 (1989). *Contemp. Poets* (1970, 1975, 1980, 1991). *DLB* 5 (1980). *World Authors* (1970).

Other references: *Bull. of Bibliography* 44:4 (Dec. 1987). *Contemp. Lit.* 31:1 (Spring 1990). *Hollins Critic* 19:4 (Oct. 1982). *The Literary Rev.* 31:3 (Spring 1988). *Midwest Q.: A J. of Contemp. Thought* 24:4 (Summer 1983). *Parnassus: Poetry in Rev.* 9:1 (Spring–Summer 1981).

NORA MITCHELL

Gail Godwin

See AWW 2, 148–50

G. has continued to examine the inner workings of the family, especially those families with some connection to the American South. Many of her recent works open with the death or removal of a family member. This loss drives G.'s characters to create new and more meaningful families around the resulting void. In *A Mother and Two Daughters* (1982) the sisters Lydia and Cate Strickland help their mother, Nell, through the aftermath of the death of their universally loved father. Cate, an English professor teaching in the Midwest, returns to the North Carolina town of Mountain City where Lydia has remained.

Mountain City is also the setting of *A Southern Family* (1987); Clare Quick, a successful author in New York City, visits her childhood home and becomes embroiled in the travails of her family after the violent death of her brother Theo. In the novella *Mr. Bedford and the Muses* (1983), another expatriate Southerner, Carrie Ames, attempts to build a new family in an old house in London. This story and the five that were published with it address issues surrounding familial bonding and the creation of art. Each work in this volume concerns the inspiration of the artist, and G. includes an author's note identifying her own inspiration for each story.

The themes of family, art, and inspiration reappear in *The Finishing School* (1985), in which Justine Stokes, a successful actress, looks back on the summer when her father's death caused her and her mother to move from Virginia to the suburban North. There Justine meets and is fascinated by Ursula De Vane, a middle-aged woman who introduces her to the beauty and treachery of art.

Father Melancholy's Daughter (1991) also takes the perspective of a grown woman looking back on her girlhood. In this richly textured work Margaret Gower reflects on life changes precipitated by her young mother's unexpected decision to leave her and her father, an Episcopalian priest, to explore the art world. Margaret's recollections blend religion and ritual with G.'s ideas about art, inspiration, and family.

In addition to her published fiction, G. has provided the texts for musical compositions by composer Robert Starer and the libretto for his "musical morality play," *The Last Lover* (1977). Since the 1980s, her work has received increasing critical attention. *Violet Clay* and *A Mother and Two Daughters* both had National Book Award nominations. In 1981 G. received an Award in Literature from the American Institute and Academy of Arts and Letters.

BIBLIOGRAPHY: Hill, Jane, *Gail Godwin* (1992). Brownstein, Rachel, "Gail Godwin: *The Odd Woman* and Literary Feminism," in *American Women Writing Fiction: Memory, Identity, Family, Space*, Mickey Pearlman, ed. (1989). Rogers, Kim Lacy, "A Mother's Story in a Daughter's Life: Gail Godwin's *A Southern Family*," in *Mother Puzzles: Daughters and Mothers in Contemporary American Literature*, M. Pearlman, ed. (1989). Reference works: *CANR* 15 (1985). *CLC* 22 (1982), 31 (1985). *DLB* 6 (1980).

Other references: *Contemp. Lit.* 24:1 (Spring 1983). *Hollins Critic* 25:2 (April 1988). *Iowa English Bull.* 35:1 (1987). *Iowa J. of Lit. Studies* 3:1–2 (interview, 1981). *Miss. Q.* 42:1 (Winter 1988–89). *NYTBR* (9 Sept. 1990; 3 March 1991). *Southern Lit. J.* 21:2 (Spring 1989). *The Southern Q.* 21:4 (Summer 1983). G.'s papers are in the Southern Historical Collection, Univ. of North Carolina at Chapel Hill.

E. M. NIX

Marita Golden

B. 28 April 1950, Washington, DC
D. of Beatrice (Reid) and Francis Sherman Golden; c.: Michael Kayode

G. was educated in the 1960s, a time of great political turmoil and change in America. The daughter of a taxi-driver father and landlord mother, G.'s African American background and the tumultuous times of her schooling years influenced her writing. Though originally trained as a journalist, she has written novels, poetry, and an autobiography. In her own words, "I write essentially to complete myself and to give my vision a significance that the world generally seeks to deny."

G. entered American University in Washington, DC, in 1968, the year the black consciousness movement in America was reaching its peak. After receiving her B.A. in 1972, she interned at the *Baltimore Sun* newspaper. In 1973, she received a master's degree from Columbia University School of Journalism and worked as associate producer at WNET, Channel 13 in New York City, from 1974 to 1975, before her marriage to a Nigerian man led her to Africa. In Lagos, Nigeria, she taught as assistant professor of mass communication at the University of Lagos from 1976 to 1979.

Upon G.'s return to the United States, a literary agent who was impressed with her writings about Africa encouraged her to write her first book, an autobiography entitled *Migrations of the Heart* (1983). While G. found the prospect of writing an autobiography at the age of twenty-nine somewhat scary, she explains that she wanted "to meditate on what it meant to grow up in the sixties, what it meant to go to Africa for the first time, what it meant to be a modern black woman living in that milieu. I had to bring order to the chaos of memory." One of the first accounts of a contemporary African urban experience by a young black American, the book focuses on her years in Africa and on her marriage and its dissolution, but also tells of her relations with her family. It met with mostly favorable reviews.

G.'s first novel, *A Woman's Place* (1986), traces the lives of three black women who meet and become friends at a prestigious American college in the 1960s. The novel explores their relationships and the numerous problems and challenges that confront them during fifteen years of friendship. *A Woman's Place* was widely praised, especially for its believable characters.

Long Distance Life (1989) illustrates the transformation of black American culture throughout the twentieth century by tracing the lives of four generations of a black American family. G. traces the changes and growth of this family as they move from North Carolina in the 1920s, to Washington, DC, in midcentury, through the civil rights movement of the 1960s and 1970s, and finally into the tragedies and promises of contemporary America.

G. has also written poetry and her work has been included in many anthologies. Her writing has appeared in *Ms., Essence, National Observer, Black World*, the *New York Times*, the *Washington Post*, and many other publications. Executive director of the Institute for the Preservation and Study of African American Writing from 1986 to 1987, G. is also a founding member of the African American Writers' Guild and has been president of the guild since 1986. She has taught at Roxbury (Massachusetts) Community College (1979–81) and was professor of journalism at Emerson College, Boston, from 1981 to 1983.

OTHER WORKS: *Keeping the Faith: Writings by Contemporary Black American Women* (1974, contributor). *And Do Remember Me* (1992). *Wild Women Don't Wear No Blues; Black Women Writers on Love, Men, and Sex* (1992, editor).

BIBLIOGRAPHY: Reference works: *Black Writers* (1989). *CA* 111 (1984). *WW Black Americans* (1992).

Other references: *Black Amer. Lit. Forum* 24 (Winter 1990). *Wash. Post* (22 May 1983; 4 June 1983; 30 July 1986).

MARY E. HARVEY

Ellen Holtz Goodman

B. 11 April 1941, Newton, Massachusetts
D. of Edith (Wienstein) and Jackson Jacob Holtz; m. Anthony Goodman, 1963,
div. 1971; m. Robert Levey, 1982; c.: Katherine Anne

Syndicated columnist G. has lived all but a short period of her life in the Boston area and uses her family, neighbors, politics, the daily news, and social change as her subject matter. She is an observer and commentator who tries to make sense of the world; she explores and questions, and although she offers opinions, she does not always present answers.

G.'s social conscience and curiosity were honed in a family that valued the individual's decisions and political action. Her father was a lawyer and politician who served as a state legislator while in his twenties and later ran for Congress. Her mother, a homemaker, had a strong sense of the importance of fostering the individual. G. and her sister Jane (Holtz Kay), who became an architecture critic and journalist, were encouraged to do whatever they wanted to do, but doing well in school was expected.

G. grew up in Brookline, Massachusetts, attended the private Buckingham School in Cambridge, and graduated cum laude from Radcliffe College with a degree in history (1963). A week after graduation she married
a medical student and moved to New York where she was hired at *Newsweek* as a researcher. All the researchers were women, G. notes. Only
men received reporter jobs, a fact she found disturbing. During her
two years at the magazine she did some freelance work for the New
York weeklies.

When the couple moved to Michigan G. became a reporter for the
Detroit Free Press. They returned to Boston in 1967, where she was hired
by the *Boston Globe* and assigned to the women's pages. Her daughter was
born shortly after. After her divorce in 1971, G.'s ties with Boston,
family, and friends tightened. In 1972 she began her column, "At Large,"
in the *Globe*. It attracted broad readership and in the 1990s appeared in
syndication in over four hundred newspapers.

G. chronicles the changing society in which she lives and tries to make
sense of a complicated world. Her 750-word column is like a conversation
with a friend whose opinions are open-ended and who waits for your
response. After receiving the Pulitzer Prize in 1980 G. wrote that she
"had a sense of how much things had changed. Ten years ago, what I
write about—values, relationships, women's issues, families, change—
would not have been taken seriously by the newspaper world." Later, in
the same piece she wrote that her articles "deal with life-and-death issues
in my own home and in the Congress. They discuss matters which are
both public and private, argued in the bedroom and the boardroom, the
kitchen and the court: love, work, sexuality, children, war, peace. . . .
The one constant is a desire to find a context and a meaning."

In 1973–74 G. spent a year at Harvard University as a Nieman Fellow,
researching the dynamics of social change in personal lives. Subsequently,
between 1975 and 1978 she interviewed more than 150 people. The result
was *Turning Points: How People Change through Crisis and Commitment*
(1979), a book that examines how change affects people's lives, particularly the changes brought about by a reexamination of traditional sex
roles. It is her only publication that is not a compilation of previously
published newspaper columns.

G. won the New England Women's Press Association Woman of the
Year Award in 1968, the Catherine L. O'Brien Award in 1971, the Media
Award of the Massachusetts Commission on Status of Women in 1974
and the New England Women's Press Association Columnist of the Year
Award in 1975. In 1980 she won the Pulitzer Prize for commentary, as

well as the Distinguished Writing Award from the American Society of Newspaper Editors and the Headliners Best Local Column Award. In 1988 G. received the Hubert H. Humphrey Civil Rights Award for dedication to the cause of equality.

OTHER WORKS: *Close to Home* (1979). *At Large* (1981). *Keeping in Touch* (1985). *Making Sense* (1989). *Value Judgments* (1993).

BIBLIOGRAPHY: Braden, Maria, *She Said What? Interviews with Women Newspaper Columnists* (1993). Mills, Kay, *A Place in the News* (1988). Reference works: *CA* 104 (1982). *WWC* (1989–90).

Other references: *Boston Women* (Winter 1990). *Christian Science Monitor* (10 Nov. 1981). *Harvard Independent* (April 9–15, 1981). *Harvard Magazine* (March–April 1979).

JANET M. BEYER

Mary Catherine Gordon

B. 8 Dec. 1949, Far Rockaway, New York
D. of Anna (Gagliano) and David G. Gordon; m. James Brain, 1974 (annulled);
m. Arthur Cash, 1979; c.: Anna Gordon Cash, b. 1980; David Dess Gordon
Cash, b. 1983

Described as a "humane, masterly novelist," G. combines a rich moral imagination with a prose style whose sentences "burst with metaphoric energy." Writing within the contexts of Roman Catholicism, the Irish-American experience, and feminism, G.'s work poses increasingly complex problems, often centering on the struggle to balance the competing claims of the sacred and the profane, of particular and universal love, of the need for personal freedom and connection. "The Church of my childhood that was so important for my formation as an artist," she noted in 1988, "is now gone." Although she regrets the loss of connections with the past—in *The Other Side* (1989) the power of the Irish immigrant experience has been dissipated by the fourth generation—she often looks to children as the hope of the future.

The only child of an Italian-Irish Catholic mother and a Jewish father who converted to Catholicism, G. attended Catholic schools in Valley Stream, Long Island. Her father died when she was seven, but his faith and commitment to the intellectual life were long-lasting influences. In 1967, G. entered Barnard College (B.A. 1971), where **Elizabeth Hardwick** encouraged her to write fiction rather than poetry. After Barnard, G. earned an M.A. (1973) at Syracuse University and began work toward a Ph.D. in English. While teaching freshman composition at Dutchess Community College, in Poughkeepsie, New York, she began writing *Final Payments* (1978), which was accepted for publication after Hardwick suggested that she change the point of view from third to first person.

G.'s work often chronicles the attempt to find a moral center in a decentered age. In *Final Payments*, Isabel Moore, an Irish-American woman, puts her own life aside to minister to her ailing father. When he dies, she reenters the world and adapts to the new sexual mores, but seeks expiation for the guilt this causes her by taking responsibility for the care of her father's former housekeeper, a selfish and difficult woman. Ultimately, Isabel frees herself from the moral imperative of "loving the unlovable" by making a less costly but hopefully final payment.

The demands of charity are also addressed in *Men and Angels* (1985), but with greater complexity and outside the Catholic context. Anne Foster, who is not religious, hires Laura, a fundamentalist Christian, to care for her children while she works on an exhibition catalog. Anne tries to like Laura, but cannot; Laura, out of affection, plots Anne's religious conversion. The chapters alternate between Anne's and Laura's points of view, providing a compelling counterpoint between and among the requirements of the flesh and the spirit.

G.'s characters are also faced with the social expectations of women in a patriarchal society. Anne struggles to balance motherhood with scholarship, Isabel to escape the grudging self-sacrifice of the caretaker role. In *The Company of Women* (1980) five women are united in friendship by their devotion to a conservative priest, Father Cyprian, who grooms Felicitas, the daughter of one of the women, to be his intellectual heir. At college, however, Felicitas joins another company, also led by a male guru, a professor who believes in free love. When Felicitas becomes pregnant, she returns to the company of women, though no longer an acolyte, and her child becomes the group's hope for the future.

Good Boys and Dead Girls (1991), a collection of more than two dozen reviews, essays, and journal entries written between 1978 and 1989, manifests clearly what the *Economist*'s reviewer calls G.'s "fierce intelligence" and her own struggle to define the moral life. Her ambivalence toward Catholicism—a rejection of authoritarianism and patriarchy but an acceptance of mystery—as well as her insights into contemporary social and literary issues are evident here. The title essay extends Leslie Fiedler's observation that in literature by American males, men avoid domesticity by heading for the frontier in the company of other men. In a review, Wendy Martin points out that antinomianism—"the conviction that subjective experience is as important as religious doctrine"—not only explains this phenomenon more fully, but also reflects G.'s own tendency to trust experience over dogma. G. has also written introductions for reprints of writings by Virginia Woolf, Stevie Smith, and **Edith Wharton.**

G.'s short fiction, most of it collected in *Temporary Shelter* (1987), has been received somewhat less enthusiastically than her novels and criticism. Several of the short stories, including the title story, are memorable, however, as are the three novellas included in *The Rest of Life* (1993).

Mary McCarthy, Ford Madox Ford, J. F. Powers, and Virginia Woolf are among the writers G. admires, John Updike among those she finds dispensable. Although a few critics find some of her plotting a bit contrived, some of her characters lacking in development, and some of her prose uneven, G.'s intelligence, her deep and passionate moral sense, and her keen eye for nuance and detail have earned her a large following among the reading public. She received the Janet Kafka Prize for Fiction in 1979 and 1982 and her books have been widely translated.

OTHER WORKS: "The Parable of the Cave; or, In Praise of Watercolors," in *The Writer on Her Work*, ed. Janet Sternburg (1980). "Getting Here from There: A Writer's Reflections on a Religious Past," in *Spiritual Quests: The Art and Craft of Religious Writing*, ed. William Zinsser (1988).

BIBLIOGRAPHY: *Interviews with Contemporary Novelists*, Dianna Cooper-Clark, ed. (1986). Reference works: *CA* 102 (1981). *CBY* (1981). *DLB* 6 (1980). *DLBY* (1981). *FC* (1990).

Other references: *Christian Century* 102 (20 Nov. 1985). *Commentary* 79 (June 1985). *Commonweal* 115 (12 Aug. 1988); 118 (17 May 1991). *Critique* 27 (Summer 1986). *Cross Currents* 37 (Summer/Fall 1987). *Economist* 319 (15 June 1991). *Essays in Lit.* 17 (Spring 1990). *Lit. Rev.* 32 (interview, Fall 1988).

Newsweek (1 April 1985). *NYTBR* (28 April 1991, 8 Aug. 1993). *Sewanee Rev.* 87 (Spring 1979).

ANGELA DORENKAMP

Lois Gould

See AWW 2, *163–64*

In her novels since 1980, G.'s style has continued to move toward the fanciful, a mix of reality and fantasy. As she turns to historical figures and mythical kingdoms, her language becomes rich and sensuous, her imagery deeper and more obscure.

Mythology acted out for the love of the lower middle class was Jorge Luis Borges's description of the power of Juan and Eva Perón over Argentina. Referencing this observation and reflecting the magic realism of contemporary Latin-American fiction, in *La Presidenta* (1981) G. follows the progress of an impoverished, beautiful girl detailing her power over the media, her life with the president, her hold over her country, her untimely death. Corruption, sex, abuse, intrigue, and violence play against a background of poverty and wealth, hope and despair. G.'s rich use of language and imagination and of history that borders on fantasy and her vivid characterizations make it possible to put truth at a distance without judgment. We know we are not meant to take the story literally.

Subject to Change (1988) is entirely myth; least like G.'s other novels, it was accurately called by one critic an "adult fairy tale." A childish king, a childless queen, an aging mistress, a mystical dwarf, and a wandering sorcerer inhabit a medieval kingdom. The marks of a classical fairy tale are here: magical herbs, potions, secret gardens, labyrinths, foolish battles, stolen property, and a mysterious birth. The pope and a heretical cult play a mysterious role. The dwarf Morgantina—"A tiny monster. A gargoyle"—is sent to the queen as a gift: Morgantina is the queen's toy and she is cruelly treated. Her limbs are severed by the queen in sport, and grow back. Morgantina also has the significant power and great cunning of a sorceress. G.'s language and syntax add to the intrigue. Questions are asked and not answered. The ending, the last line tells us, is subject to change.

Medusa's Gift (1991) combines the styles of *La Presidenta* and *Subject to Change*. Fame, sex, power, history, and myth are again the means G. uses to tell the story. Marilyn Monroe could, but might not be the lead character, Magdalen. Medusa, the coldly beautiful Gorgon, swims in the waters off an Aegean island; her poisonous sting can be fatal. The island is the reality where playboys, power brokers, has-beens, artists, and writers live and where Magdalen comes seeking privacy. Or is it Magdalen? Filmmakers and movie historians follow, pursuing the rumor and her legend or myth. Sex, mystery, and carefully placed hints are the tools she uses to keep them interested. Medusa, the myth, strikes and apparently destroys the vulnerable Magdalen. G. again asks questions that have no answers, plays with syntax, illuminates and hides through lush language.

BIBLIOGRAPHY: Reference works: *CANR* 29 (1990). *Maj Twent Cent Wr* (1991). *WW Wr Ed Poets* (1989).

Other references: *Ms.* (July 1981). *NYTBR* (31 May 1981; 10 July 1988; 27 Oct. 1991). *Time* (4 July 1988). *Wash. Post Book World* (24 May 1981; 17 July 1988).

JANET M. BEYER

Jorie Graham

B. 9 May 1950, New York City
D. of Beverly (Stroll) and Curtis Bill Pepper; m. James Galvin, 1983; c.: Emily Van-Waning Galvin, b. 1983

G. grew up in Europe; she attended the Sorbonne, New York University (B.F.A. 1973), Columbia, and University of Iowa (M.F.A. 1978). She has taught at Murray State, Humboldt State, and Columbia universities; since 1983 she has been on the faculty of the Writer's Workshop, University of Iowa. Her first book, *Hybrids of Plants and of Ghosts* (1980), won the Great Lakes Colleges Association Award, and her work has generally been well received; John Ashbery describes her as "one of the finest poets writing today." G.'s work has been compared to that of Laura Jensen, Wallace Stevens, and Rainer Maria Rilke, and her poems have won prizes from the Academy of American Poets, *Poetry Northwest*, the *American Poetry Review*, and Pushcart Press. She has been awarded grants from the National Endowment for the Arts, from the Guggenheim, Whiting, Ingram Merrill, and MacArthur Foundations, and a fellowship from the Bunting Institute, Radcliffe College (1982). G.'s poems have been frequently anthologized and have appeared in such journals as the *Iowa Review*, the *Nation*, *The New Yorker*, *Paris Review*, and *Ploughshares*.

G.'s study of philosophy and her love of art are central to her poetry, which is both imagistic and abstract, rejecting the confessional for the metaphysical and rhyme and meter for variable length lines whose enjambment stresses and fractures syntax but creates the shapes of stanzas. Her subjects range from quotidian experiences (sewing, drawing, gardening, looking in a mirror) to investigations of historical violence and complicity, from explorations of identity through mythical figures to meditations about saints, artists, and philosophers. But her true focus is always the "spiritual questing" of writing itself, which gives her poetry the ascetic passion of the visionary or mystic. Images fragment into ideas; specific details and words are transcended in visions of light, of infinity, of what cannot be said. Consequently, these insights must be felt or intuited; her language is simultaneously flattened and allusive or, like T. S. Eliot's, interwoven with others' words.

In *The End of Beauty* (1987) she incorporates ——s, underlined spaces that may be blanks the reader is to fill in, or signs for an inability to speak, an "accurate failure" ("Some Notes on Silence"), or for what escapes language—consciousness, the world. Each —— may also be read as "line," in much the same way that her algebraic variables may be puns (y on "why" and x as "ex-" or "cross"), though they also function as markers (and disruptions) of the schematic nature of narrative.

These signs, like the dashes and ellipses that permeate and end some of her poems, also function as an acknowledgment of silence, into and against which the poet speaks. G. defines silence as existing in consciousness and the world, as "doubt, madness, fear," "awe or astonishment," and as all "forms of death and mystery."

This idea is suggested by the poems' synaesthetic figures, where sound (including the poetic line) is a fabric, tapestry, scrim, or shroud that she weaves and sees woven (by Penelope, for example) and, more importantly, sees cut, torn, or unraveled to reveal the silence all around it. Because G. perceives the most important task of poetry as enacting a struggle with silence, her imagery of gaps, rents, wounds, and openings is invested with sacred language and an oracular tone. Silence is her Kali, her Great Mother, giving birth to and destroying the line ("Imperialism," *The End of Beauty*), her home's inaudible "voice-over keeping on (come in, *in*)" to a pair of juncoes who may die trying to escape, "aiming for the brightest spot, the only clue," a sunlit window or white space ("The Phase after History," *Region of Unlikeness*).

OTHER WORKS: *Erosion* (1983). "Some Notes on Silence" in *New American Poets of the Golden Gate*, ed. Philip Dow (1984). "Pleasure," in *Singular Voices: American Poetry Today*, ed. Stephen Berg (1985). Editor, *The Best American Poetry, 1990* (1990). *Region of Unlikeness* (1991).

BIBLIOGRAPHY: Reference works: *CA* 111 (1984). *CLC* 48 (1988). *Contemp. Poets* (1985). *FC* (1990).

Other references: *APR* 11:1 (Jan.–Feb. 1982); 12:6 (Nov.–Dec. 1983). *Black Warrior Rev.* 15:2 (Spring 1989). *Boston Rev.* 8:4 (Aug. 1983). *Georgia Rev.* 37:4 (Winter 1983). *Hollins Critic* 24:4 (Oct. 1987). *Literary Rev.* 31 (Spring 1988). *Nation* (5 Sept. 1987). *New Yorker* (27 July 1987). *NYTBR* (17 July 1983; 26 July 1987). *Parnassus* 11:1 (Spring/Summer 1983). *Poetry* (April 1982). *Southwest Rev.* 67:3 (Summer 1982). Personal communication, G. to D. Sonnenschein, 28 Aug. 1992.

DANA SONNENSCHEIN

Judy Grahn

B. 1940, Chicago, Illinois
D. of Vera (Davis) and Elmer August Grahn
See AWW 2, 170–71

Remaining powerfully woman-identified, G.'s writings have become more diverse in form and content. Her reimagining of ancient myths of the goddess and of a civilization that preceded patriarchy, what critic Sue-Ellen Case calls "taking back the myths," has deepened and transformed her work.

G. has written in a variety of forms—poetry, fiction, and scholarship. Perhaps most important of her work since 1980 are the first two books of a projected four-book series, *A Chronicle of Queens*. In an introductory note to the first book, *Queen of Wands* (1982), G. tells of her first discovery of this mythological figure in a 1913 translation of a Babylonian "Tablet of Lamentation." The legend is of "the queen who has been stolen, of cities and temples ravaged by soldiers, of lamentation for a female power gone," the story most familiarly of Helen of Troy. It is, G. says, an "astonishing worldwide myth of a female god of beauty, fire, love, light, thought and weaving."

G. interprets this story as the shift from matriarchal power to the advent of patriarchy and offers, in *Queen of Wands*, a remarkable poetic celebration of the many names and manifestations of Helen/El-Ana from ancient images of creation goddesses to modern film stars. (The book is dedicated to Marilyn Monroe.) Through the weaving of the poet's language, this figure is reimagined both in her fall under the weight of patriarchy and her subversive reconnection, "the weaving tree / and Mother of the people."

The Queen of Swords (1987), the second volume of the *Chronicle of Queens*, includes a long verse play, "The Queen of Swords: A Play with Poetic Myth," and two related poems. The play continues the retelling of the Helen myth: the Helen figure here is Inanna, the Sumerian "goddess of heaven and earth." G. retells the myth of Inanna's descent into the underworld and experience of death and rebirth in the modern setting of an underground lesbian bar. The bar is owned by Ereshkigal, the "Queen of Swords," a figure of death and transformation; the seven judges who attend her are refigured as "Crow Dikes." G. comments that "in the spirit of the paganism" that had sustained the story over the centuries, she "made the play as funny as [she] could without losing its profound center of gravity."

The two poems in this volume are also based on the Inanna legend. "Descent to the Roses of the Family" records a white American woman's conversation with her brother, seeking help to prevent herself from making the descent into the alcoholism, madness, and the white supremacist convictions of their parents. Because that poem took her "down to the bottom of my heart," G. chose to end the volume with "Talkers in a Dream Doorway," a poem about love and women's collective powers.

G.'s anger at the lack of published writing by and respect for gays/lesbians sparked the research that led to *Another Mother Tongue: Gay Words, Gay Worlds* (1984). Winner of the 1985 Gay Book Award of the American Library Association, *Mother Tongue* traces the historical roots of gay culture. *The Highest Apple: Sappho and the Lesbian Poetic Tradition* (1985) reaches into the history of the lives and work of lesbian women and asserts the richness of women's heritage. Beginning with Sappho, G. writes of nine women, poets who seize language and, as lesbians, reform it. In G.'s work, the poets create a map and a center that demonstrate the importance of lesbian poetry for all women.

A utopian novel, *Mundane's World*, also appeared in 1985. It tells the story of four racially mixed clans who live in a peaceful balance, each serving a purpose the others need and living in harmony with all of nature. G. traces many journeys into life and death in her woman-centered world, culminating in a ritual passage to womanhood for five girls.

A colletion of essays and excerpts, *Really Reading Gertrude Stein* (1989), provides a critical look at Stein's work. G.'s work on women and mythology informs *Blood, Bread, and Roses* (1993), a study of the influence on contemporary culture of ancient beliefs and rites about menstruation. The book also looks at stories that draw on the idea of menstrual power.

In addition to her writing, G. lectures and reads her work on radio stations and at colleges. She has also made several recordings. G. lives in San Francisco, where she teaches Gay and Lesbian Studies.

BIBLIOGRAPHY: Case, Sue-Ellen, "Judy Grahn's Gynopoetics: *The Queen of Swords*," in *Studies in the Literary Imagination* 21:2 (Fall 1988). *Women Writers of the West Coast: Speaking of Their Lives and Careers*, Marilyn Yalom, ed. (1983).
Other references: *Quarterly J of Speech* (August 1986).

SUZANNE GIRONDA

Valerie Graves. *See Marion Zimmer Bradley*

Joanne Greenberg

See AWW 2, 177–78

In her fiction, G. makes the extraordinary accessible. Although she has been criticized on occasion for lacking in art, or seen as merely a special-interest author (her most famous novel, *I Never Promised You a Rose Garden*, concerns a young, female schizophrenic), G.'s consistently understated style lends a matter-of-fact quality to characters and experiences far from the ordinary reader's experience. However odd her characters, they exist within complex networks of interpersonal relationships; families, especially, are never far from the center of her stories. Her books are as much about connections as about isolation, as much about rich identities as about fractured selves.

While her prose hesitates to announce itself, G.'s plotting and narrative devices are prominent. In *Simple Gifts* (1986) G.'s use of multiple points of view is appropriate for a novel that explores the endless emotional and moral valences of a family who find themselves transformed when a government program turns their dilapidated farm into a vacation spot for jaded yuppies. *A Season of Delight* (1981) also examines the dynamics of competing family values.

Vivian Sanborn in *Age of Consent* (1987) embarks on a pilgrimage to find out about the life of her adopted, recently assassinated brother Daniel, healer, saint, and a man incapable of ordinary human interaction. Attempts at fixing one meaning to an event or person prove as fruitless as finding the incinerated pictorial documentation of Sanborn's work. Yet the plotting of this intricate novel is so tidy as to conflict with the complexity of the characters and events. Another perhaps overly plotted but richly textured novel is *The Far Side of Victory* (1983), which constructs itself around two focal points—the car accidents that mold Eric Gordon's life.

Of Such Small Differences (1988) departs from G.'s other works in its creation of a different language, appropriate for the reality experienced by the deaf-blind. G. returns here to an old concern—how "unfamiliar" worlds intersect with, conflict with, and question other realities. The poet John, deaf-blind and independent, falls into a relationship with the hearing and sighted Leda.

Isolation, disability, and even "the self" as static, limpid categories have no place in G.'s fiction, which always finds people striving among others, choosing among conflicting ideas of duty and fulfillment. The extraordinary inheres in both everything and nothing in works that treat the "oddest" and most "normal" of characters and events not from a stance of wonder or condescension but from the perspective of familiarity.

Formerly an elementary school teacher, G. is a professor of anthropology at the Colorado School of Mines.

OTHER WORKS: *High Crimes and Misdemeanors* (1979). *With the Snow Queen* (1991). *No Reck'ning Made* (1993).

BIBLIOGRAPHY: Reference works: *CANR* 14 (1985), 32 (1991). *CLC* 7 (1977), 30 (1984). *SATA* 25 (1981).
Other references: *PW* (23 Sept. 1988, interview). *NYTBR* (27 Dec. 1987; 30 Oct. 1988).

FAYE HALPERN

Eloise Greenfield

B. 17 May 1929, Parmele, North Carolina
D. of Lessie (Jones) and Weston W. Little; m. Robert J. Greenfield, 1950,
separated; c.: Steven, Monica

Early in her career, G. commented that "it has been inspiring . . . to be part of the struggle" to create quality books for African American children. In picture books, novels for young readers, biographies of famous African Americans, memoirs of childhood, and poetry, G.'s work has been infused with warmth, hope, and joy. Her vision has always pointed in two directions: back to a past rich with strength and courage and forward to a future brimming with possibilities.

G.'s young protagonists are often dreamers whose quiet time spent imagining and dreaming is growing time. In *Nathaniel Talking* (1988), her third Coretta Scott King Award winner, young Nathaniel B. Free raps philosophically about his family, his friends, his life. Despite losing his mother, Nathaniel feels strongly connected to his father and his extended family. Familial connections are always important in G.'s writing, and she lovingly explores alternatives to the traditional nuclear family.

Family provided G. with personal strength as she faced societal hostility and rejection. With her mother, Lessie Jones Little, she wrote *Childtimes: A Three Generational Memoir* (1979) dedicated to the memory of her grandmother who had dictated material for the book. This autobiography, which many consider G.'s best work, traces the history of the three women against the landscape of their times. An intimate personal history shapes the book's quiet theme that childhood can and should be happy, a time of building self-esteem supported by a caring family and community: "a childtime is a mighty thing." The book received the Boston Globe–Horn Book Award for nonfiction and the Carter Book Award for outstanding merit.

G. created her first book, a scrapbook put together with household paste, when she was three and views that act as the beginning of her life. As a creator, she thrilled to the sentence "Home is where the music is," and continues to feel a mission to celebrate those words. Home and music continue as constant themes, anchors to which she and her characters return. Her first book of poetry, *Honey I Love and Other Poems* (1978), a Reading Rainbow selection, includes the music of skipping rope and the rhythm of riding trains; all poems are home bound, safe and secure. *Nathaniel Talking* (1989) contains the literal music of "bones" and blues.

Most of G.'s picture books address everyday traumas and delight: the arrival of a new sibling, parent separation, a grandmother's sadness about moving, buying a present for a mother's birthday. Sometimes the resolution seems too easy and predictable, but G.'s determination that children feel good about themselves transcends these considerations. Two novels for young readers, *Sisters* (1974) and *Talk about a Family* (1978), record the anger and sadness of their young female protagonists as they try to make sense of their fears and confusion. Both novels conclude realistically: with a potential for a better future, but with no facile solution to present difficulties.

Her commitment to providing good role models for African American children has drawn G. toward biography. Lucid writing and artful selection of detail makes her books on heroic Americans Mary McLeod Bethune, Rosa Parks, and Paul Robeson accessible to young readers, and she has won numerous awards for these documents of resilience and courage. They are an important part of G.'s share in building a significant body of excellent literature for all children.

OTHER WORKS: Sister (1969). *Bubbles* (1972). *Rosa Parks* (1973). *She Come Bringing Me That Little Baby Girl* (1974). *Me and Nessie* (1975). *Paul Robeson* (1975). *First Pink Light* (1976). *Africa Dream* (1977). *Mary McLeod Bethune* (1977). *I Can Do It Myself* (with Lessie Jones Little, 1978). *Darlene* (1980). *Grandmama's Joy* (1980). *Daydreamers* (1981). *Alesia* (with Alesia Revis, 1981). *Grandpa's Face* (1988). *Under the Sunday Tree* (1988). *My Doll, Keshia* (1991). *Night on Neighborhood Street* (1991). *Big Friend, Little Friend* (1991). *Daddy and I* (1991). *I Make Music* (1991). *Kaya Delaney and the Good Girl* (1992). *William and the Good Old Days* (forthcoming). "Something to Shout About," *Horn Book Mag.*, Dec. 1975.

BIBLIOGRAPHY: Reference works: *Tw. Cent. Children's Writers* (1983, 1989). *SATA* 61 (1990). *CLR* 4 (1982).

SUSAN P. BLOOM

Susan Griffin

See AWW 2, 181–82

G.'s career has included a range of genres: poetry, plays, stories, and essays. By 1980, after almost a decade of publication, she had garnered such awards as the Ina Coolbrith Prize in poetry and a National Endowment for the Arts grant, as well as an Emmy for her radio drama, "Voices" (1975). Her work in the 1980s and 1990s engaged with subjects of a global nature—rape, pornography, and war.

Emphatically feminist in politics and writing, G. has increasingly become a theorist and interpreter of women's condition. This trend is especially clear in *Rape: The Power of Consciousness* (1979), a collection of essays, and *Pornography and Silence: Culture's Revolt against Nature* (1981). *Rape* includes a version of her well-known 1971 essay, "Rape: The All-American Crime," in which, like Susan Brownmiller, G. analyzes rape as the chief tool of patriarchy in maintaining power: a crime carried out by a few men on behalf of many. Calling it "a male protection racket" where a woman is made to feel unsafe and, therefore, dependent on "her man," she also connects the crime of rape with national aggressions, such as American imperialism, particularly in Vietnam. Her other essays look at encouraging changes in the attitude toward the prosecution of rape since the women's movement in the 1970s but warn that the crime of rape is still statistically increasing. In *Consciousness* she closes on a hopeful note, choosing "hope over dread," with a vision of the possibility of change for women when they learn to confront and overcome fears that keep them from full self-realization: "I have tasted freedom from fear, a world we imagine, and this small taste means more to me than large fears."

In *Pornography and Silence* (1981), a ground-breaking work, G. denies the conventional notion that women are subservient and enjoy subservience and argues forcefully that women do not welcome domination—a necessary message at that time. She also interprets the male psyche, perceiving it as separated from emotion and, ultimately, from women. This disassociation, as well as the belief in the subservience of women, creates the environment for pornography. Although some critics argued that the ferocity of

G.'s tone and language diminished the impact of her message, her work was prophetic, opening the way to a feminist analysis of pornography.

A Chorus of Stones: The Private Life of War (1992) is´a moving and profound multilayered meditation on history, especially the history of war and weapon making, on family secrets and the connections between public and private, and on the destructiveness that silence and denial create, in war and in families. Firmly joining the personal to the global, G. ranges over wars and countries to demonstrate connection. "As social concepts, war and gender evolved together," G. told an interviewer. "To change either, we have to change both." The stones of the title are a paradoxical symbol: though silent, they "reveal traces from fires suffered thousands of years ago." So, too, human beings carry "our own history and the history of the world embedded in us, we hold a sorrow deep within and cannot weep until that history is song."

G. has also published essays on such topics as chronic fatigue syndrome. In addition to writing, she is working toward a doctorate at the Starr King School of Ministry.

OTHER WORKS: *Made from This Earth: An Anthology of Writings* (1983). *Unremembered Country* (1987). Contributor of articles and essays to *Ms.*, *Whole Earth Review*, and other periodicals.

BIBLIOGRAPHY: Reference works: *CA* 49–52 (1975). *CANR* 3 (1981), 27 (1989). *Women Writers of the West Coast* (1983).

Other references: *NYTBR* (22 Nov. 1992). *PW* (10 Aug. 1992). *Whole Earth Rev.* (Summer 1989). *LJ* (July 1987).

LINDA BERUBE

Doris Grumbach

See AWW 2, 192–94

G.'s active, reflective spirit is especially obvious in *Coming into the End Zone* (1991), a memoir and a reflection on the seventieth year of her life.

"Growing old means abandoning the rituals of one's life, not hardening into them as some people think," she writes. And so, in the summer of 1989, the year following her seventieth birthday, G. and her longtime companion, Sybil Pike, moved from Washington, DC, to Sargentville, Maine.

Her active mind is not hardened against new ideas. The computer provides both assistance and simile: "My memory is diminished, like a hard disk that suddenly fails to deliver . . . I operate with floppy intelligence." She continues to believe that to help students learn you "hold their coats while they go at it."

G. collects, she says, metaphors for death—caged lions, a dead goldfish. Young friends are dying of AIDS, older ones are becoming frail. She is starting a new life, this time on the ocean, much as she and Sybil Pike did in 1972 when they moved to Washington to start their life together. Reflecting the freedom of form that memory enables, the book moves through sadness and loss to affirmation in a voice that is distinctively G.'s own.

During the 1980s, G. published three novels. *The Missing Person* (1981) traces, through second-person references, the life of Franny Fuller, a movie queen much in the Jean Harlow and Marilyn Monroe molds. Although reviewers frequently assume that the subject is Monroe, G. has said, "I really was not writing about Marilyn Monroe, as everyone assumed, but simply about someone who might have been almost anyone. I erred in staying too closely to the biographical facts." The missing person is a Hollywood star, manipulated, used, abused, superficial, and enormously beautiful. We do not hear her speak, but see her only through narrators, just as we see movie stars only through their pictures; she is a prototype for all people who are missing, especially to themselves.

The Ladies (1984) fictionalizes historical figures. Two Irish-born women, Lady Eleanor Butler and Sarah Ponsonby, move to a small Welsh village so they can live as they wish to, as a married couple, rather than as society wishes them to. The women become renowned for their independence and their visitors include such people as William Wordsworth, who dedicated a poem to them, Edmund Burke, and Walter Scott. Lonely, they are forbidden by Eleanor's father to step foot inside Ireland again; they farm their land, make friends with and enemies among the local townfolk, become sick, aged, and die. Their marriage has all the incumbent difficulties and pleasures. Eleanor, tutored and bright, teaches the shy, unlettered Sarah; as Eleanor becomes crotchety and loses her sight, Sarah is increasingly in charge. While some critics argue that the novel is an admirable departure from more pessimistic lesbian novels, others see it as predetermined, placing joy where it may not have existed.

The Magician's Girls (1987) tells of three college roommates in the 1940s. The title is taken from a line from Sylvia Plath, "I am the magician's girl who does not flinch." G. is acutely aware of the pains endured unflinchingly by young women: Maud, poor and unattractive, Minna, middle-class and overprotected, haunted by fears, and Liz, whose parents were Communist sympathizers, scoffing at the world outside their apartment. This is the first direct use of autobiographical material in G.'s work. Liz, the photographer who does not flinch, who survives, has G.'s socialist, Jewish, New York childhood. She is the survivor, recording the world through her lens.

In addition to her work as a novelist, G. has had a distinguished career as a teacher and a critic. In 1972 she became literary editor for the *New Republic,* a position that occasioned her move to Washington from Upstate New York where she had taught at the College of St. Rose. After two "magical" years at the *New Republic* she returned to teaching, becoming professor of literature at American University. G. retired from teaching in 1984, but remained very active as a reviewer for both print and radio. From 1982 to 1990, her distinctive voice and carefully considered reflections on books were familiar to listeners of National Public Radio. G. has completed a second volume of memoirs, *Extra Innings,* published in 1993.

BIBLIOGRAPHY: For articles in reference books, see *CAAS* 2 (1985). *CANR* 9 (1983). *CLC* 22 (1982), 64 (1991).

Other references: *Key Reporter* 57:1 (Autumn 1991). *WRB* 9:3 (Dec. 1991).

JANET M. BEYER

Rosa Guy

B. 1 Sept. 1925, Trinidad
D. of Audrey (Gonzales) and Henry Cuthbert; m. Warner Guy, ca. 1941
   (deceased); c.: Warner

When G. was seven, she and her sister left Trinidad to join their parents in Harlem. The adjustment from island life to city life was difficult. Although black, G. found herself set apart by other children because of her West Indian dialect and customs. When her mother became ill shortly after her arrival, G. was sent to the Bronx to stay with cousins. Here she was introduced to Marcus Garvey's fervent views extolling the dignity of all blacks and his belief in black nationalism, themes that proved to be major forces stimulating G. intellectually and politically.

Her mother's death two years after the family was reunited in New York, followed by her father's remarriage, financial failure, and death, left G. and her sister orphans. Experiences in a series of institutions and foster homes intensified her feeling of being an outsider. By fourteen G. had dropped out of school and had become a factory worker. At sixteen she married Warner Guy.

In searching for ways to enrich her life and to express her creativity, G. found herself drawn to the American Negro Theatre, then to the Committee for the Negro in the Arts. Experiences with the latter group led G. to write and to become a cofounder of the Harlem Writers Guild. Affiliation with the guild deepened G.'s commitment to black affairs by giving her the opportunity to meet and work with influential members of the community.

Her response to the waste of bright minds being "channeled into a life of crime and self-destruction by the crushing confinement of prejudice and poverty" inspired her first book, *Bird at My Window* (1966). Then, wanting to know how the death of Dr. Martin Luther King, Jr., and the turmoil of the 1960s affected Southern black children, G. collected taped interviews and essays that became *Children of Longing* (1971). This work, cited as bringing together G.'s activism and writing interests, advanced her writing skills to a new level.

G.'s theme of trying to find one's place in a hostile environment while struggling for self-identity and self-affirmation arises from her early child-hood and adolescent experiences. Her forte is her compassionate ability to portray the adversity ghetto children face. In her acclaimed trilogy, *The Friends* (1973), *Ruby* (1976), and *Edith Jackson* (1978), G. insightfully presents the lives of three adolescents as they mature fighting the odds in a deteriorating community.

The Disappearance (1979), which won G. the American Library Association Award for best book for young adults, and its sequels, *New Guys around the Block* (1983) and *And I Heard a Bird Sing* (1987) complete a second trilogy, each with a mystery involved. The protagonist is Imamu Jones, a young man determined to vindicate himself and escape the hopelessness of a now-corrupt Harlem.

In her first picture book, G. translated the Senegalese folktale *Mother Crocodile* (1981), successfully dipping her pen into the richness of African folklore. G. has also written two juvenile books, *Paris, Pee Wee, and Big Dog* (1985) and *The Ups and Downs of Carl Davis, III* (1989), which confirm the need for parental acceptance.

G.'s tightest and most poignant story, however, is one written for a general readership, *My Love, My Love; or, The Peasant Girl: A Fable* (1985). In this short tale G. expresses all the mystique of her West Indian heritage while carefully showing the impenetrable barriers of color and caste. This book was the basis for a musical by Lynn Ahrens, *Once on This Island*, which opened in New York in 1990. G.'s ventures into African tradition, which flow with a special warmth and seamlessness, add a new depth and dimension to her writing.

G.'s acute sensitivity to issues inner-city children face has made her a successful young-adult author who gives hope and books to a readership too frequently overlooked.

OTHER WORKS: Venetian Blinds (1954). "Wade," in *Ten Times Black*, ed. Julian Mayfield (1972). "Black Perspective: On Harlem's State of Mind" (1972). *Mirror of Her Own* (1981). *Mother Crocodile: An Uncle Amadou Tale from Senegal* (translator and adaptor, 1981). *A Measure of Time* (1983). *Billy the Great* (1991). *The Music of Summer* (1992).

BIBLIOGRAPHY: Norris, Jerrie, *Presenting Rosa Guy* (1988). Reference works: *Black Amer. Writers Past and Present* I (1975). *Black Amer. Fiction: A Bibliography* (1978). *BW* (1988). *CA* 17 (1976). *CANR* 34 (1991). *CLC* 26 (1983). *DLB* 33 (1984). *FC* (1990). *SATA* 14 (1976).

Other references: *Essence* (Oct. 1979). *Horn Book* (March/April 1985). *NYT Mag.* (16 April 1972). *Top of the News* 39:2 (Winter 1983).

SANDRA RAY

Marilyn Hacker

See AWW 2, 202–3

H.'s *Taking Notice* (1980) continues the formal and thematic concerns of her earlier work. Utilizing various traditional forms, particularly the sonnet sequence, and often using a colloquial diction, H. investigates private relationships of love, the semiprivate relationship of mother and daughter, and the public relationships among women in society. In this book H. begins clearly to articulate a lesbian eroticism that becomes an increasingly important part of her later works.

H.'s fourth collection, *Assumptions* (1985), again considers questions of family, love, sexuality, and the place of a woman among other women in the world. The section "Inheritances" deals specifically with the poet's history and her legacy to her daughter and from her mother, as well as her daughter's inheritance from her father's family. "Open Windows" is a sequence of love sonnets to other women. The book ends with "Ballad of Ladies Lost and Found," which invokes a repressed history of women, recalling the losses and erasure of women ranging from "the gym teacher, the math-department head" to such important writers as **H. D.** [Hilda Doolittle] and **Zora Neale Hurston.**

Love, Death, and the Changing of the Seasons (1986) is a verse novel describing a love affair between two women. This sonnet sequence is rooted in the mundane events of life—eating, drinking, shopping—as transformed by romantic longing and anxiety. *Going Back to the River* (1990), a largely autobiographical collection of poems, traces the poet's departure from the United States and her return to confront her often-difficult past and present as an American. This journey is perhaps best epitomized by the first poem, "Two Cities," where for the first three sections the poet in Paris is "the inventor / of my own life, / an old plane tree in new leaf, / a young woman almost forty-five." In the final section, the poet and her daughter sit in a New York restaurant watching a scene of seemingly random street violence, a cry of despair addressed to nobody in particular.

Like **Adrienne Rich,** whose work serves as epigraph for many of H.'s poems, H. surveys the emotional and social terrain of women who love women. She skillfully mixes traditional, or even archaic, poetic forms with various levels of diction from the most formal to the colloquial, producing one of the most powerful voices of contemporary poetry.

OTHER WORKS: *Woman Poet: The East* (editor, 1982). *The Hang Glider's Daughter: New and Selected Poems* (1991).

BIBLIOGRAPHY: Reference works: *CA* 77–80 (1979). *CLC* 23 (1983). *Contemp. Poets* (1985, 1991). *FC* (1990).

Other references: *Denver Q.* 20:1 (Summer 1985). *Frontiers* 3 (interview, 1980). *Hudson Rev.* 40 (Summer 1987). *LJ* (15 April 1990). *Nation* (21 Jan. 1991). *NYTBR* (21 June 1987). *Poetry* (July 1991). *TLS* (10 July 1987).

JAMES SMETHURST

Virginia Hamilton

See AWW 2, 232–34

Widely recognized as a writer who has raised the level of sophistication in books for young people, H. continues to stand at the forefront of children's literature. The granddaughter of a slave, she depicts the richness of African American life while presenting situations that are relevant for all human beings. Her ten books between 1967 and 1977 included five widely acclaimed novels. *M. C. Higgins, the Great* (1974) was awarded the Newbery Medal, the National Book Award, and the Boston Globe–Horn Book Award.

A prolific writer, H. has published thirteen novels since 1976. Like her earlier works, they present black adolescents who face problems common to all young people. In most of them strong extended families help the young protagonists to work out their problems. Sheema (*A Little Love*, 1984) learns that the meaning in her life must come from herself, not from others. In *A White Romance* (1987) Talley is drawn into a world of drugs, heavy metal music, and turbulent first love. Cammy's grandmother (*Cousins*, 1990) helps her to put behind her the guilt associated with the death of a detestable cousin and to focus on the present. Helped by the ghost of her dead uncle, Tree (*Sweet Whispers, Brother Rush*, 1982) learns about her family's past and is able to cope with a desperate present. The book won both the Coretta Scott King Award and the Boston Globe–Horn Book Award in 1983; it was also a Newbery Honor Book.

In the Justice trilogy (*Justice and Her Brother*, 1978; *Dustland*, 1980; *The Gathering*, 1981) H. sets a challenge for herself and her readers as the four young protagonists venture into Dustland in a science fiction allegory, which becomes a journey toward identity and black confidence and a powerful plea for social action. The trilogy has been compared to Ralph Ellison's *Invisible Man* in themes and use of language.

H.'s several folktale volumes are creative retellings of stories from a wide range of cultures. Folklore is also woven into several of her novels, notably *The Magical Adventures of Pretty Pearl* (1983), a mixture of black folklore and the author's own family history.

Critics frequently praise H.'s ear for language, describing her prose as musical, smooth, and liquid. Most find her use of black English superb; a few see it as a stumbling block for young readers. While sometimes expressing impatience with the complexity of her work and hesitancy about its accessibility to children, most critics see H. as a gifted and influential storyteller with remarkable imagination and vision.

OTHER WORKS: Willie Bea and the Time the Martians Landed (1983). *Junius over Far* (1985). *The People Could Fly: American Black Folk Tales* (1985). *The Mystery of Drear House* (1987). *Anthony Burns: The Defeat and Triumph of a Fugitive Slave* (1988). *The Bells of Christmas* (1988). *In the Beginning: Creative Stories from around the World* (1988). *The Dark Way* (1990). *The All-Jadhu Story* (1991). *Many Thousand Gone* (1992). *Dry Longso* (1992). *Plain City* (1993).

BIBLIOGRAPHY: Townsend, John Rowe, *A Sounding of Storytellers* (1979). Reference works: *BW* (1990). *CLC* 26 (1983). *CLR* 11 (1986). *CANR* 37 (1992). *DLB* 52 (1986). *Maj Twent Cent Writers* (1991). *SATA* 56 (1989).

Other references: *Horn Book Mag.* 57 (Dec. 1981). *Children's Lit. in Education* 14:4 (Winter 1983). *English J.* 73:7 (Nov. 1984).

MARY E. FINGER

Elizabeth Hardwick

See AWW 2, *241–44*

In 1986, H. commented, "As I have grown older I see myself as fortunate in many ways. It is fortunate to have had all my life this passion for studying and enjoying literature and for trying to add a bit to it as interestingly as I can. This passion has given me much joy, it has given me friends who care for the same things, it has given me employment, escape from boredom, everything."

H., who continues to enjoy a glowing reputation in the New York literary world, has not lost this "passion." She was nominated to the National Book Critics Circle in 1980 for her third novel, *Sleepless Nights* (1979). A founding editor of the *New York Review of Books* and the first woman to win the George Jean Nathan Award (1966) for drama criticism, she published her third collection of essays, *Bartleby in Manhattan and Other Essays*, in 1983. Since then, she has been honored with a Mayor's Award for Honor in Arts and Culture in 1986, election to the American Academy of Arts and Letters in 1989, and an honorary degree from Bard College in the same year.

The subjects of *Bartleby in Manhattan* range from Thomas Mann to the civil rights movement of the 1960s, from nudity to John Reed to a French production of Shakespeare's *Timon of Athens*. The title essay combines a close reading of Melville's "Bartleby the Scrivener" with a modern-day reinterpretation. Like her past essays, these blur the lines between life and art, using a fictional character to prove a point about everyday life and reading historical and political events as though they themselves are texts.

The collection received favorable reviews, many from critics who have themselves looked up to H. for years as an inspiration. William MacPherson noted that "Miss Hardwick's interests are both varied and deep: the ways of God and the ways of men, eschatology and Auschwitz, manners and morals, love and marriage as these things are revealed to us in life and in literature, and her insights make us stop a moment as they make us smile (but wryly)."

The *New York Review of Books* was sold to Rea Hederman in 1984, presumably providing the original owners with both money and leisure. H. has continued to publish, editing *The Best American Essays of 1986* and writing criticism and essays. She is also reported to be working on another novel.

In interviews H. is frequently asked more about her late former husband, poet Robert Lowell, and his influence on her work, than about the work itself. H. fields these questions gracefully, rarely alluding to Lowell's mental illness and praising his genius freely and generously. Recognized in her own right as both a writer and critic, and buoyed by her deep love of writing and reading, H. remains an active and valuable member of the literary community.

OTHER WORKS: "Its Only Defense: Intelligence and Sparkle," *NYTBR* (14 Sept. 1986).

BIBLIOGRAPHY: Pinckney, Darryl, "Elizabeth Hardwick" in *Writers at Work: The Paris Review Interviews* (1986). Reference works: *CANR* 32 (1991). *CLC* 13 (1980). *DLB* 6 (1980). *Modern Amer. Women Writers* (1991).

Other references: *Manchester Guardian Weekly* (18 Sept. 1983). *Newsweek* (30 May 1983). *NYT* (24 May 1983; 17 Aug. 1986). *NYTBR* (12 June 1983). *Wash. Post Book World* (29 May 1983).

LISI SCHOENBACH

Joy Harjo

B. 9 May 1951, Tulsa, Oklahoma
D. of Wynema (Baker) and Allen W. Foster; c.: Phil Dayn, b. 1968; Rainy Dawn, b. 1973

H. is a poet, screenwriter, and musician, and is a member of the Muskogee (Creek) Tribe. Raised in Oklahoma until leaving to attend high school at the Institute of American Indian Arts in Sante Fe, New Mexico, she received her B.A. from the University of New Mexico (1976) and an M.F.A. from the University of Iowa (1978).

H.'s Creek identity is central to her poetry. Her work is based on a doubleness that she argues is distinctly Indian: to be Native American is to experience acutely the banality and injustice of the present and, at the same time, to have privileged access to the mythic world and its resources for empowerment and survival. H. beautifully indicates these resources in "Javelina," where she gives voice to herself at seventeen: "I was born of a blood who wrestled whites for freedom, and I have lived dangerously in a diminished system." She consoles this earlier desperate woman with a prediction of a future already achieved: "The mythic world will enter with the subtlety of a snake the color of earth changing skin . . . you who thought you could say nothing, write poetry." Poetry directs self-destructive dangerous living into creatively dangerous struggle, dissent, and survival.

In her first book, *What Moon Drove Me to This?* (1980), H. demonstrates a variety of understandings of the mythic world in relation to present experience. Her palpable sense of the mythic both unites and separates her from the community of Indian peoples. Whereas much of H.'s early poetry labors on behalf of a social community, her later poetry finds her listening to the voices of those who also experience the power of myth, and needing that community for consolation and survival.

She Had Some Horses (1983) is a successful exorcism of personal, poetic, and historical fears that she describes intensely at the book's opening. H. drives doubleness inward, into an intense vacillation between hope and despair that she indicates by the doubling of her poetic endings. The survivor poem, "The Woman Hanging from the Thirteenth Floor

Window," ends with the woman both falling to her death and pulling herself off the ledge into life. By the book's end, H. embraces doubleness and argues that the triumph and tragedy of her personal and collective history are inseparable: "She had some horses she loved. / She had some horses she hated. / These were the same horses."

In Mad Love and War (1990) tells the story of powerful women—mythic and real—and their struggle to bring the world out of its current diminished state. The mythic deer dances naked in a bar, transforming the tawdry moment with the promising presence of the ancestors. In elegies extolling the transformative power of memory, H. (who renamed herself after her grandmother) keeps alive the work of Anna Mae Pictou Aquash, a woman active in the American Indian movement who was murdered in 1976, and Jacqueline Peters, a writer and activist lynched in California by the Ku Klux Klan in 1986. Being part of a community of women is as central to H. as her Creek identity and she counts among her mentors **Audre Lorde, Leslie Marmon Silko, Meridel LeSueur,** and **June Jordan.**

H. has written a series of prose poems on the Southwestern landscape, *Secrets from the Center of the World* (1989), which accompany photographs by Stephen Strom, and several screenplays. A teacher of poetry and Native American literature, she has taught at the Institute of American Indian Arts (1978–79), Arizona State University (1980–81), the University of Colorado (1985–88), and the University of Arizona, Tucson (1988–90). She joined the English department of the University of New Mexico in 1991. H. has served as a writer and consultant for the Native American Public Broadcasting Consortium, the National Indian Youth Council, and the National Endowment for the Arts (1980–83). She also plays tenor saxophone with jazz, rock, and big bands.

Notable among H.'s numerous awards are the American Book Award, Before Columbus Foundation (1991); the William Carlos Williams Award from the Poetry Society of America for the best book of poetry (1990); the American Indian Distinguished Achievement in the Arts Award (1990); and the Oakland PEN Josephine Miles Award (1990). She has held fellowships from the National Endowment for the Arts (1978) and from the Arizona Commission on the Arts (1989).

OTHER WORKS: *The Last Song* (chapbook, 1975). "Apache Mountain Spirits" (film script, 1985). "When We Used to Be Humans" (filmscript, 1990). *Furious Light* (audiocassette, 1986).

BIBLIOGRAPHY: *This Is About Vision: Interviews with Southwestern Writers*, William Balassi, John F. Crawford, and Annie O. Eysturoy, eds. (1990). Bruchac, Joseph, "The Story of All Our Survival: An Interview with Joy Harjo," in *Survival This Way: Interviews with American Indian Poets* (1987). Crawford, John, "Notes toward a New Multicultural Criticism: Three Works by Women of Color," in *A Gift of Tongues: Critical Challenges in Contemporary American Poetry*, Marie Harris and Kathleen Aguero, eds. (1987). Smith, Patricia, and Paula Gunn Allen, "Earthly Relations, Carnal Knowledge: Southwestern American Indian Women Writers and Landscape," in *The Desert Is No Lady: Southwestern Landscapes in Women's Writings and Art*, Vera Norwood and Janice Monk, eds. (1987). Reference works: *CA* 114 (1985). *CANR* 35 (1992). *FC* (1990).

Other references: *Amer. Indian Q.* (Spring 1983). *Amer. West* (Dec. 1989). *Christianity and Crisis* (22 Oct. 1990). *MELUS* (interview, Spring 1989). *Ms.* (July 1983). *WRB* (Oct. 1983; July 1990). *World Lit. Today* (Winter 1991).

DARIA DONNELLY

Carolyn G. Heilbrun

See AWW 2, 273–74

For more than twenty years H. has been actively promoting feminist scholarship and the discussion of women's issues particularly pertaining to the academic world. A central reason for her decision to retire from the faculty of Columbia University's department of English in 1992 was the resistance she met to feminist scholarship by the "old boys' network." Feminist critic Nancy Miller calls H. a women ahead of her generation and notes that she had a passion "for the life in texts" and "from the beginning . . . has been writing the biography of literature." In addition to her scholarly writing, H. has created an alternate identity as Amanda Cross, the writer of ten mystery novels.

In 1983 H. was coeditor of *The Representation of Women in Fiction*, a collection of papers from the first English Institute program (1981) devoted to feminist criticism. Her own work at this time began to focus on women's lives and particularly women's autobiographies and biographies. In an important article, "Women's Autobiographical Studies: New Forms" (1985), she argues that until the 1960s women had written only preautobiography, where "the individual . . . does not feel [her]self to exist outside of others." This interest culminated in *Writing a Woman's Life* (1988). In her characteristic combination of critical and textual analysis with autobiographical and biographical material, her essays focus on the necessity for women to write about their lives or to record the lives of others who have not been heard of before. She credits women poets, such as **Denise Levertov, Jane Cooper, Maxine Kumin, Adrienne Rich,** and **Sylvia Plath,** born between 1923 and 1932, with transforming "the autobiographies of women's lives" and notes that Rich, writing in prose, actually "practiced the new female autobiography directly" in her essay on her father, a subject, H. argues, that women must write about in order to confront the patriarchal world. Other new forms and plots of women's lives must be established, she argues, especially around marriage patterns and the story of friendship and love between women. H. also points out that in writing detective stories under a pseudonym, she was creating for herself another identity and another "possibility of female destiny." Kate Fansler, the woman detective of her novels, was unmarried (she later married the district attorney) and without children (H. has three children). She was also, H. notes, "unconstrained by the opinions of others, rich and beautiful."

In the foreword to *Hamlet's Mother and Other Women* (1990), Nancy Miller notes that H. has always identified with Virginia Woolf's "Society of Outsiders." In this collection of essays, beginning with her first published essay, "The Character of Hamlet's Mother" (1957), H. reveals that from the beginning she was writing and thinking as "an opposing self" opposed to the male-centered culture of the university. All of the other pieces were written between 1972 and 1988, during her life as a "declared and dedicated feminist." They thus record her own history in the women's movement as well as the spirit of "the revolution in its earlier years." Most central in her literary criticism are the essays on Virginia Woolf, in one of which she argues that Woolf is a more revolutionary figure in modernism than James Joyce. H. includes two essays given at formal professional occasions, one her president's address to the Modern Language Association and the other a University Lecture at Columbia. The two were, "collectively and separately, the bravest acts of my professional life" because in them she confronted the male academic culture and spoke as a woman and not as "a genderless member" of the profession. In "The Politics of the Mind," H. argues that "much of what passes for the life of the mind is, in fact, no more than the politics of the mind," a politics that has wasted the energies of women by too often silencing or hampering them.

H. produced five detective novels between 1981 and 1990. *Death in a Tenured Position* (1981), set at Harvard University's English department and featuring a victim who is the first tenured woman in the department, is characteristic of her novels in that it combines sharp social commentary with detective work and often solves the mystery through an analysis of literary texts. *No Word from Winifred* (1986), more than earlier novels, focuses on the effects of feminism on women's lives, while *The Players Come Again* (1990) features literary detective work in the service of revealing a woman's role in the work of a famous male writer. In *Writing a Woman's Life*, H. notes that alter ego Amanda Cross is no longer a fantasy figure "but an aging woman who battles despair" and who uses wit and humor and "the analysis of our ancient patriarchal ways" to find "a reason to endure." In all of her writing H. offers much more than mere endurance: she celebrates the lives and work of women who have the courage to live beyond convention and to tell their own stories.

OTHER WORKS: *Sweet Death, Kind Death* (1984). *A Trap for Fools* (1989). Important essays include "Bringing the Spirit Back to English Studies," in *The New Feminist Criticism: Essays on Women, Literature, Theory*, Elaine Showalter, ed. (1985). "Women's Autobiographical Writings: New Forms," *Prose Studies* (Sept. 1985). "Non-Autobiographies of Privileged Women: England and America," in *Life/Lines: Theorizing Women's Autobiography*, Bella Brodzki and Celeste Schenck, eds. (1988).

BIBLIOGRAPHY: *Designs of Darkness*, Cooper Clark, ed. (interview, 1983). Reddy, M., *Sisters in Crime* (1988). Reference works: *CANR* 28 (1990). *CLC* 25 (1983). *FC* (1990).

Other references: *Chronicle of Higher Ed.* (11 Nov. 1992). *Clues: A J. of Detection* 3:2 (Fall/Winter 1982). *NYT Mag.* (15 Nov. 1992). *WRB* (Dec. 1986).

MARY GRIMLEY MASON

Beth Henley

B. Elizabeth Becker Henley, 8 May 1952, Jackson, Mississippi
D. of Lyndy (Elizabeth Josephine Becker) and Charles Boyce Henley

The eldest of three daughters of an attorney and an actress, H. started out as an actress before beginning to write plays during a dry spell in her acting career. She is one of the first women to have been acknowledged as a playwright on the national level since **Lillian Hellman** and **Lorraine Hansberry.** H.'s plays, often described as Southern gothic or grotesque, are set in the Mississippi in which she was raised; they portray women and men and their complex, tragicomic relationships both within a family and between the family and the outside society that frequently disapproves of it. Her female characters are at their indecorous best when they gleefully or grimly sabotage societal expectations, and when they manage not to harm themselves too much.

As a Southern writer whose characters are frequently grotesque and obsessive, H. has been frequently compared with **Eudora Welty, Flannery O'Connor,** and William Faulkner. Several sources note that H. first read the work of O'Connor only after the resemblances between their work had been commented upon by reviewers.

H. achieved early success with *Crimes of the Heart* (produced 1979, published 1981), which won the Pulitzer Prize and was later made into a movie. *Crimes* introduces several themes and characters that appear in H.'s later work: the Magrath sisters, although they argue among themselves, bond together to defend themselves fiercely against all comers. Their social-climbing cousin Chick is mortified by Lenny, Meg, and Babe's family skeletons (including suicides, false pretenses, and illicit sexuality); the sisters themselves are busy trying to recoup lost chances. *Crimes* has been compared to plays of Chekhov for its realism, its mixture of tragedy and comedy, and its portrayal of the force of the family against outsiders.

That H. began her career as an actress may in part account for the liveliness of her characters and dialogue and for the ensemble quality of many of her plays. Her characters onstage are obsessive, identified by their quirkiness. We see them at awkward or unpleasant moments (at a wake, having lost a beauty contest), and we see them inflicting pain on themselves senselessly, while imparting to their actions a kind of logic (such as in *Debutante Ball* [1985, 1988] when Teddy stabs her face and legs repeatedly with any sharp object at hand). H.'s characters also tell stories of revelatory moments or formative experiences. In *The Miss Firecracker Contest* (1980, 1985), for example, Popeye tells the story of her nickname, which is also the story of her partial blindness and the beginning of her ability to hear voices in her eyes. Sometimes the grotesquerie or absurdity seems unfounded or unexplored, or to be only a hint at an unstated truth beneath the surface, as when Babe in *Crimes* explains she shot her husband "because I didn't like his looks."

Efforts by characters to change society's disapproval of them and their attempts at self-redemption recur in several of H.'s subsequent plays. Carnelle in *Miss Firecracker* tries to restore her bad reputation with the locals by winning a beauty pageant. *Debutante Ball* focuses on a woman who is determined to distract the town from her reputation as a murderess by providng her awkward misfit daughter Teddy with the ideal debut night. *The Wake of Jamey Foster* (1982, 1985) is another ensemble piece in which each character is looking for love and disappointed at his or her inability to live up to others' expectations.

H.'s later plays, *The Lucky Spot* (1986, 1987) and *Abundance* (1990, 1991), further her interest in characters' lost loves and broken dreams while moving her focus to settings beyond Mississippi and the New South, and to characters in circumstances not solely brought about by family commitments. Several of H.'s plays have been turned into movies, and she is the author of both unproduced and produced screenplays, notably as coscreenwriter with David Byrne and Stephen Tobolowsky of *True Stories* (Warner Brothers, 1986).

OTHER WORKS: Am I Blue (1982). *Beth Henley: Four Plays* (1992). *Monologues for Women* (1992).

BIBLIOGRAPHY: Betsko, Kathleen, and Rachel Koenig, *Interviews with Contemporary Women Playwrights* (1987). *Mississippi Writers Talking*, John Griffin Jones, ed. (1982). Karpinski, Joanne B., "The Ghosts of Chekhov's *Three Sisters* Haunt Beth Henley's *Crimes of the Heart*," in *Modern American Drama: The Female Canon*, June Schlueter, ed. (1990). Smith, Lucinda, *Women Who Write: From the Past and Present to the Future* (1989). Reference works: *CANR* 32 (1991). *Contemp. Dramatists* (1988). *CLC* 23 (1983). *DLBY* (1986b). *Notable Women in the Amer. Theatre* (1989).

Other references: *Conference of College Teachers of English Studies* 54 (Sept.

1989). *Southern Q*. 22:4 (Summer 1984); 25:3 (Spring 1987). *Studies in Amer. Drama* 3 (1988); 4 (1989). *Women and Performance: A J. of Feminist Theory* 3:1 (1986).

KATHRYN MURPHY ANDERSON

Josephine Herbst

B. 5 March 1892, Sioux City, Iowa; d. 28 Jan. 1969, New York City
D. of Mary (Frey) and William Benton Herbst; m. John Herrmann, 1925; div. 1940

H., a proletarian writer, is a major figure in the history of twentieth-century literature and radicalism. Although less well known than her friends Ernest Hemingway, **Katherine Anne Porter,** and John Dos Passos, critics have often regarded her as their peer. Her most important work is a trilogy, a sweeping reconstruction of the life of an American family from the Civil War through the 1930s. Other works include four more novels, reports from the crisis areas of the 1930s, and numerous short stories and critical essays.

H. grew up in Sioux City, where her father sold farm implements. Neither of her parents had much formal education, but her mother, a strong influence in H.'s life, imparted a love of books to her four daughters, and the stories that she told about her ancestors formed the beginning of H.'s trilogy. The family was always poor. Consequently H.'s college education spread out over nine years and four different institutions, as she alternated periods of work with periods of study, eventually receiving her degree from the University of California at Berkeley in 1919.

After graduation she moved to New York City and there became a part of the intellectual and political ferment of the 1920s. Maxwell Anderson, then a socialist journalist and poet, was her first serious lover; a pregnancy resulted, and, at Anderson's insistence, H. had an abortion.

A few months later her favorite sister died from an abortion. The pain from these two events was devastating for H.

Unable to resume her life in New York, she left her job as a reader for H. L. Mencken's magazines and went to Europe to write. There she met and fell in love with John Herrmann, an expatriate writer, whom she later married. The farm that they bought in Erwinna, Pennsylvania, continued to be H.'s home for the rest of her life. During the first ten years at Erwinna H. produced five novels. Herrmann, never as ambitious a writer as H., began to write less and to increase his involvement in the Communist Party. Although H. never formally joined the Communist Party, her beliefs and activities were sympathetic to it.

The trilogy, *Pity Is Not Enough* (1933), *The Executioner Waits* (1934), and *Rope of Gold* (1939), both tells the story of the Trexler and Wendel family, and reveals the development of H.'s ideas. Walter Rideout points out that she views the families' decline as a "tiny part of the dialectical process of world history," and juxtaposes the deterioration of capitalism with the possibility of power for the proletariat. The political message is carried mainly in vignettes about farmers and workers, which give added breadth and force to the main story.

Most of H.'s fiction is strongly autobiographical. The family of the trilogy is her own family thinly disguised. Two of the characters, Victoria and Jonathan Chance, closely resemble H. and Herrmann, and sometimes events in the author's life were being written into the book almost as soon as they occurred. In *Rope of Gold* Victoria and Jonathan are growing apart, as were H. and Herrmann, and the novel records the pain of their deteriorating relationship, which for H. and Herrmann resulted in divorce in 1940.

During the thirties H.'s reports from crisis areas of the world were widely published. She talked with farm pickets in Iowa, reported on the sit-down strike in Flint, Michigan, went to Nazi Germany shortly after Hitler took power, was in Spain with the Loyalists in 1937, and visited Cuban radicals in their mountain hideout.

Fired from a wartime job in Washington for political reasons, H. spent much of the 1940s and early 1950s at Erwinna, alone and suffering privately over the outcome of her marriage. The two novels published during this period were not given the attention of her previous books. Gradually she renewed old friendships, and Erwinna became a gathering place for writers and intellectuals. A lesbian relationship with the poet **Jean Garrigue** began during this period.

From the mid-1950s until the time of her death, she was preoccupied with her memoirs, which were never completed because she could not arrive at a portrait of her times that was satisfying to her. Elinor Langer's excellent biography is titled *Josephine Herbst; the Story She Could Never Tell.*

OTHER WORKS: *Nothing Is Sacred* (1928). *Money for Love* (1929). *Satan's Sergeants* (1941). *Somewhere the Tempest Fell* (1947). "Hunter of Doves," *Botteghe Oscure* (1954). *New Green World* (1954). "The Starched Blue Sky of Spain," *The Noble Savage* (1960). "A Year of Disgrace," *The Noble Savage* (1961). "Yesterday's Road," *New Amer. Rev.* 3 (1968); reptd. as *The Starched Blue Sky of Spain: And Other Memoirs* (1991). H.'s papers are at the Beinecke Library, Yale University, as is "A Bibliography and Checklist of Josephine Herbst," prepared by Martha Elizabeth Pickering in 1968.

BIBLIOGRAPHY: Langer, Elinor, *Josephine Herbst; the Story She Could Never Tell* (1984). Rideout, Walter, *The Radical Novel in the United States* (1966). Bevilacqua, Winifred Ferrant, "The Novels of Josephine Herbst," Unpublished Ph.D. diss., Univ. of Iowa, 1977. Gourlie, John M., "The Evolution of Form in the Works of Josephine Herbst," unpublished Ph.D. diss., New York Univ., 1975. Kempthorne, Dion Quintin, "Josephine Herbst: A Critical Introduction," unpublished Ph.D. diss., Univ. of Wisconsin, 1973.

Reference works: *DAB:* Supp. 8 (1988). *DLB* 9:2 (1981). *FC* (1990). *NAW:MP* (1980).

Other references: *NYT* (obituary, 29 Jan. 1969). *NYRB* (27 March 1969).

MARY E. FINGER

Patricia Highsmith

See AWW 2, 302–4

Since 1977 H. has continued to write psychological crime fiction. However, it is not only the criminal mind that attracts her. Rather, it is the mind of the person battling against stronger enemies; the shift in emphasis from good and evil to weakness and strength is an important one in much of H.'s later fiction.

Edith's Diary (1977) and *Little Tales of Misogyny* (1977, published in German in 1974) both focus on the lives of women who are trapped by circumstances, and by their own unwise choices in powerless situations. In Edith's case, the powerlessness is compounded by the character's need to pretend. Edith escapes into her diary in which she creates a happy family with a successful and loving son. The diary becomes more fictitious as the events and the people in Edith's life become more and more disappointing. Many of the sketches of women in *Little Tales of Misogyny* also highlight the failure of characters to look at reality squarely and to take control of their lives. The stories, in Andrew Macdonald's words, seem "medieval misogynist tracts," but they are also examinations of how women who are already socially stereotyped accept and abet their limited and limiting classifications. The two books illustrate H.'s clear eye for the ways in which power is used to entrap and destroy women, and the author's sense of menace, a hallmark of much of her earlier fiction, is present sometimes in physical, but mostly in psychological brutalization.

With *Ripley under Water* (1992) H. returned to the Ripley stories begun in 1955. In that novel almost the entire emphasis is on psychological one-upmanship as Pritchard, a full-blown sadist, torments Ripley about the one crime Tom wishes he had not committed, the murder of Dickie Greenleaf. The emphasis on weakness and power again displaces the conflict between good and evil, as Tom Ripley (remembered from the earlier books) is far more charming and sympathetic than Pritchard. While this latest Ripley novel is not nearly so satisfying as the earlier ones, it does create a sense of menace and psychological anxiety. The Ripley stories are, according to Julian Symons, H.'s most popular because contemporary readers feel "that crime is more interesting than its detection, and that intelligent criminals are to be congratulated or at least admired."

Other books by H. since 1977 include *Slowly, Slowly in the Wind* (1979), a series of stories including tales of revenge, murder, and muggings, and *Black House* (1981), another collection of tales focusing on violence and the seemingly ordinary people who commit bizarre and outlandish acts. A novel, *People Who Knock at the Door* (1983), shifts her focus from crime to religion and analyzes the behavior, often malignant, of a fundamentalist religious colony.

OTHER WORKS: *The Boy Who Followed Ripley* (1980). *Mermaids on the Golf Course* (1985). *The Mysterious Mr. Ripley* (1985). *Found in the Streets* (1986).

Tales of Natural and Unnatural Catastrophes (1987). "Not Thinking with the Dishes," *Writers Digest* 26 (Oct. 1983).

BIBLIOGRAPHY: Reference works: *Concise Survey of Short Fiction* (1991). *CANR* 20 (1987). *CLC* 2 (1974), 4 (1975), 14 (1980), 42 (1987). *Contemp. Novelists* (1991). *FC* (1990). *Maj Tw Cent Writers* (1991).

Other references: *Armchair Detective* 14:4 (Fall 1981, interview). *Clues* 5:1 (Spring/Summer 1984). *Midwest Q.* 25 (April 1984). *NYTBR* (29 Jan. 1989; 18 Oct. 1992, rev. by Julian Symons). *TLS* (4 Oct. 1991; 17 April 1992).

MARY A. MCCAY

Alice Hoffman

B. 16 March 1952, New York City
M. Tom Martin; c.: Jake, Zack

H. grew up in Franklin Square, New York, where she began writing at an early age. Her parents, who divorced when she was eight years old, worked in real estate and social work. She attended Adelphi University (B.A. 1973), received a fellowship to the writing program at Stanford University (M.A. 1975), and shortly thereafter began to publish stories. In 1976 she was awarded a fellowship at Breadloaf; her first novel, *Property of*, appeared in 1977. In addition to writing fiction, H. is also a scriptwriter and reviewer.

H. is particularly noted for infusing her realistic stories with the mythical, lyrical, and metaphorical. Settings, even the most ordinary, take on a surrealistic, dreamlike atmosphere where the reader is prepared for anything to happen. And almost anything does, for H. has tackled a wide range of issues in her novels: gangs, incest, AIDS, suicide, promiscuity, aging, agoraphobia, cancer. Her mystical treatment of emotionally charged issues allows the reader a measure of distance where judgment may be suspended for a time and even the most painful or objectionable subject can be contemplated.

In *Property of,* set in the depths of the New York underground of drugs and gangs, H. introduces a theme that recurs in subsequent novels: the outsider searching to belong in impossible situations. The narrator, a seventeen-year-old girl in love with a gang leader, tries initially to resist him and his world, where all the girlfriends are designated as property. Falling under the spell of violence and of heroin, she succumbs but ultimately extricates herself from this primitive and chaotic atmosphere. H.'s second novel, *The Drowning Season* (1979), takes the reader to the other end of the social spectrum. Its eighteen-year-old protagonist, Esther the Black, struggles for identity and connection against the forces of her wealthy Long Island family, and specifically against her formidable grandmother, Esther the White.

H. explores irony in plot and setting in *Angel Landing* (1980), a romance about love in the face of destruction set at a nuclear power plant. Like *Property of, White Horses* (1982) places an outsider in pursuit of an impossible person in an impossible situation. Teresa Connors waits, as her mother had, for a savior, an "Aria" (her mother's term) to lift her out of the uneventfulness of her life. She believes that her brother, the odd and elusive Silver, is her Aria; the novel traces the dangerous attraction between them. The feeling of suspension, so dominant in Teresa's life, is pursued through *Fortune's Daughter* (1985). Tracing the stages of women's lives on both a literal and symbolic level, H. again explores the relationship between two women.

Illumination Night (1987) focuses on the inner workings of the family, and the stresses from outside that threaten it. H. uses agoraphobia to symbolize not only the powerlessness of Vonny, the novel's primary female character, but also the other characters' loss of control in their lives.

In *At Risk* (1988), her most realistic novel to date, H. recounts the isolation and fragmentation of her family that results when Amanda, an eleven-year-old star gymnast, contracts AIDS from a blood transfusion. Making use of a social issue that comes complete with its own power of myth, H. transforms AIDS to the level of metaphor, detailing the stress not only to the family but also to the community.

The community struggling against what is foreign is also explored in *Seventh Heaven* (1990). *Turtle Moon* (1992) moves away from this pattern to assemble what seems to be an entire town of outsiders, some new to Verity, Florida, some who have lived all their lives there. H. again presents the readers with a surreal setting—a town in the grips of excruciating heat, its roads littered with fallen fruit and dying turtles following the moonlight—where anything might happen. It is not a total shock when a young mother is murdered, her baby daughter is missing, and Keith, a troubled adolescent boy, disappears. The novel follows the search of Keith's mother for her son, a search that reveals both the truth of the dead woman's past and of her own.

H. has described the predominant theme of many of her novels as the search for identity and connection. By raising this quest to the mythical and metaphorical level, H. allows the reader to look into the deepest fears and problems that are obstacles in the search.

OTHER WORKS: *Independence Day* (screenplay, 1983).

BIBLIOGRAPHY: Reference works: *CA* 77–80 (1979). *CANR* 34 (1991). *CLC* 51 (1989). *Maj Tw Cen Writers* (1991).

Other references: *BM* (Oct. 1988). *NYT* (14 July 1977; 25 July 1987). *NYTBR* (10 July 1977; 15 July 1979; 28 March 1982; 24 March 1985; 9 Aug. 1987; 26 April 1992). *Boston Rev.* (Sept. 1985; Oct. 1987). *Yale Rev.* (Winter 1978). *TLS* (21 April 1978). *Ms.* (2 Aug. 1979; 8 Feb. 1981). *Newsweek* (20 Aug. 1979; 12 April 1982; 1 Aug. 1988). *Wash. Post* (21 Dec. 1980; 19 May 1985; 2 Aug. 1987). *Observer* (29 May 1983). *New Yorker* (15 May 1985).

LINDA BERUBE

Linda Hogan

B. 16 July 1947, Denver, Colorado
D. of Cleona Florine (Bower) and Charles Colbert Henderson; m. Pat Hogan,
*   div.; c.: Sandra, Dawn Protector; Tanya, Thunder Horse*

Although born in Colorado, H. has her Chickasaw roots in south central Oklahoma; she is descended from a family of storytellers, who influence her writing. Poet, novelist, and essayist, she writes and tells her story from a Native American perspective. H. began to write in her late twenties while working with orthopedically handicapped children. Reading Kenneth Rexroth's work during her lunch hours gave her confidence to start writing. For her the process of writing tapped into her own life; she told an interviewer, "I write because the poems speak what I can't say in my normal language."

H. received an M.A. from the University of Colorado at Boulder (1978), where she is currently a member of the faculty. Previously she taught American Studies/American Indian Studies at the University of Minnesota in Minneapolis (1982–84) and at Colorado College (1980–84). H. was awarded both the Pushcart Prize and a National Endowment for the Arts grant in 1986. She has also been the recipient of a Guggenheim Fellowship and of the Five Civilized Tribes Museum Playwriting Award (1980) for *A Piece of Moon*. She was the D'Arcy McNickle Fellow at the Newberry Library in 1981, a faculty fellow at the University of Minnesota (1985), and the recipient of state arts grants from both Colorado (1984) and Minnesota (1985).

H.'s first book of poetry, *Calling Myself Home* (1978), is about discovering herself. In her introduction she writes: "These first poems were part of that return for me, an identification with my tribe and the Oklahoma earth, a deep knowing and telling how I was formed of these two powers, called ancestors and clay. Home is in the blood, and I am still on the journey of calling myself home." In "Heritage" she deals with the "painful and also inescapable reality and knowledge of being mixed." A later volume of poems, *Seeing through the Sun* (1985), received an American Book Award for poetry from the Before Columbus Foundation in 1986.

In *That Horse* (1985), a collection of notable short stories, H. incorporates both her own and her father's story about the same horse, pointing out that they are very different stories. Her goal is to show the history of the time: "*That Horse* deals with the historical fact of fiction and what's happened with Chickasaw people and what's happened in my own family particularly." *Red Clay: Poems and Stories* (1991) brings together work previously published in *Calling Myself Home* and *That Horse*.

Mean Spirit (1990), H.'s first novel, received the Oklahoma Book Award for fiction (1990) and the Mountains and Plains Booksellers Association Fiction Award. In this long, sad, historical novel, set in the early 1920s, H. chronicles the experience of two Osage Indian families during a time when "oil barons and government agents in Oklahoma swindle oil-rich, landowning Indians out of their land and rights." Her writing style is spare and compact but rich in detailed descriptions of Native American rituals and customs. To write this novel H. drew again from the history of her family. Like many Chickasaw and Choctaw people in the 1930s her family lost everything when the government and the banks foreclosed on their land. When H. was growing up she was very conscious of the land her family had lost and points out that the Ardmore Airport in Oklahoma was "my family's ranch land."

H. re-creates Native history and stories in her fiction; starting from the Native American spiritual foundation her poems seek images to embody its understanding of life and nature. Just as horses, turtles, birds, and small insects are prominent carriers of her poetic images, so too are "pollen blowing off the corn," "yellow flowers," "yellow sun," "red clay," and "brown earth." Her poetry, with its distinctive drive and rhythm and life, is constantly manifesting its respect for the natural world.

H. volunteers at wildlife rescue clinics to rehabilitate and to care for eagles, owls, and other birds of prey. She considers caretaking the basic work of living on earth, and "sees a direct relation between how we care for the animal-people and the plants and insects and land and water, and how we care for each other, and for ourselves."

OTHER WORKS: *Daughters, I Love You* (1981). *Eclipse* (1983). *The Stories We Hold Secret: Tales of Women's Spiritual Development* (coeditor, 1986). *Savings* (1988). *Wind Leans against Those Men* (1990). *Book of Medicines* (1993). "Who Puts Together," in *Studies in American Indian Literature: Critical Essays and Course Designs*, Paula Gunn Allen, ed. (1983). Also see *Frontiers* 6:3 (Fall 1981).

BIBLIOGRAPHY: Béranger, Jean, *L'Ici et l'ailleurs: Multilinguise et Multiculturalisme en Amérique du Nord* (1991). *Survival This Way: Interviews with American Indian Poets*, J. Bruchac, ed. (1987). Smith, P. C., "Linda Hogan," in *This Is about Vision: Interviews with Southwestern Writers*, W. J. Balassi et al., eds. (1990). Reference works: *CA* 120 (1987). *WW Writers, Eds., Poets* (1989).

Other references: *Amer. Indian Q.* (Fall 1991). *J. of Ethnic Studies* 16:1 (Spring 1988). *LJ* 115:125 (1 Nov. 1990). *NYTBR* (24 Feb. 1991). *Prairie Schooner* 57 (Fall 1983). *Studies in Amer. Indian Lit.* 2:4 (Winter 1990). *WRB* 8 (April 1991).

SHARI GROVE

Nicole Hollander

B. 25 April 1939, Chicago, Illinois
D. of Shirley (Mazur) and Henry Garrison

H.'s cartoon character, Sylvia, has changed the way women are portrayed in mainstream comic strips. Sylvia scrutinizes politics and society, fiftyish wisecracking woman from her bathtub, her easy chair, a barroom stool, or lunch table. Her foils are conventional Beth Ellen, her lunch partner; Harry, the cynical bartender; Rita, her patient, health-conscious daughter; and her all-knowing pets. Rita's father is away; where and why varies. She casts a critical eye on most men and on the occasional female such as conservative spokeswoman Phyllis Schlafly.

Although newspaper editors were wary of publishing this hefty woman in bathrobe, backless mules, and dyed hair, the public recognized a folk heroine. Unlike other women in comics, Sylvia is neither glamorous nor upwardly mobile. Her wardrobe is limited, her tastes tend to pizza and beer, and her politics are liberal; she casts a jaundiced eye on the world and says so in ten words or less.

Sylvia is not an analyst; she is an observer and commentator. In one strip, a television announcer notes: "Studies show that women with 'sexy names' like Dawn and Cheryl are less likely to be promoted to managerial jobs than women with names like . . ." "Bill or Roger," Sylvia comments from the bar stool.

The strip's characters also include a cast of Cops who have their own sets of rules and fly about the country trying to inflict them on other people; a fairy godmother, who anticipates women's needs; Gernif the Venusian who questions the habits of earth people; bright-eyed Patty Murphy, a fallible television commentator; Alien Lover, a sensitive male; the Devil, who bargains for souls; angels who determine who will enter heaven based on their behavior in the neighborhood supermarket and taste in movies; and Grunella, a fortune-teller whose crystal ball forecast can change to accommodate the listener. Sylvia's cats, who do not speak, but listen, think, write, and act, play a large role. In 1992 H. published a book of their advice to cat owners, *Everything Here Is Mine: An Unhelpful Guide to Cat Behavior.*

H. was educated in Chicago public schools. She received a B.F.A. from the University of Illinois (1960) and an M.F.A. from Boston University (1966). Growing up in a working-class Chicago neighborhood where the women had all the funny lines, she learned to read, she says, because she wanted to read the comics. As an adolescent H. realized that the comics were not relevant to her life because they were written by men and filled with male characters. Her first comic strip was published in *Spokeswoman*, a national feminist newsletter. The mainstream press resisted: men held decision-making positions in most newspapers and Sylvia was too feminist, too outrageous; she did not speak to or for the male point of view.

As feminist humor began to command a wider audience, St. Martin's Press printed the first book of Sylvia cartoons in 1979 and continued as her publisher until 1991. H. was first syndicated by the Toronto Syndicate in 1979, and by Field Syndications in 1981. She has been self-syndicated since then, doing both administrative and creative work for the strip. In the late 1980s Sylvia appeared in over fifty newspapers.

H. was given a national Wonder Woman Award in 1983, an honor given to women over forty who have advanced the cause of women. In 1985, she received a Yale University Chubb Fellowship for Public Service. H. was one of four cartoonists featured in the film *Funny Ladies: A Portrait of Women Cartoonists*, by Pamela Briggs. *Sylvia's Real Good Advice*, a musical comedy, first performed in 1991 in Chicago, won a 1991 Joseph Jefferson Award and a Chicago After Dark Award.

OTHER WORKS: *I'm in Training to Be Tall and Blonde* (1979). *Hi, This Is Sylvia; Ma, Can I Be a Feminist and Still Like Men?* (1980). *That Woman Must Be on Drugs* (1981). *My Weight Is Always Perfect for My Height—Which Varies* (1982). *Mercy, It's the Revolution and I'm in My Bathrobe* (1982). *Sylvia on Sundays* (1983). *Drawn Together: Relationships Lampooned, Harpooned, and Cartooned* (editor, with Skip Morrow and Ron Wolin, 1983). *O.K., Thinner Thighs for Everyone* (1984). *Never Tell Your Mother This Dream* (1985). *The Whole Enchilada* (1986). *Never Take Your Cat to a Salad Bar* (1987). *You Can't Take It with You, so Eat It Now* (1989). *Tales from the Planet Sylvia* (1990). Also, yearly calendars, the Sylvia Book of Days, mugs, dolls, and greeting cards.

BIBLIOGRAPHY: Alley, Patricia Williams, "Hokinson and Hollander: Female Cartoonists and American Culture," in *Women's Comic Visions*, June Sochen, ed. (1991). Cantarow, Ellen, "Don't Throw Away That Old Diaphram," *Mother Jones* (June–July, 1987). O'Sullivan, Judith, *The Great American Comic Strip: One Hundred Years of Cartoon Art* (1990). Walker, Nancy, and

Zita Dresner, eds. *Redressing the Balance: American Women's Literary Humor from Colonial Times to the 1980s* (1988).

JANET M. BEYER

bell hooks

B. Gloria Jean Watkins, 25 Sept. 1952, Hopkinsville, Kentucky
D. of Rosa Bell Watkins

Born in Kentucky to a Southern black working-class family, Gloria Jean Watkins grew up "talking back"—childhood punishments left her feeling exiled from the adult community and thus she turned to books and discovered an imaginary community. In "Black Is a Women's Color," she says that she began writing poetry, "using the poems to keep on living." h. has transformed the paradigm of "talking back" into an empowering metaphor for speech: "It is that act of speech, of 'talking back,' that is no mere gesture of empty words, that is the expression of our movement from object to subject—the liberated voice." Bell Hooks was the name of Watkins's maternal great-grandmother, "a sharp-tongued woman" who "talked back." h. chose to write using this pseudonym in lower case because "claiming this name was a way to link [her] voice to an ancestral legacy of women speaking." Demonstrating her own ability to "talk back" with authority and eloquence, h. has published several volumes of social, cultural, and autobiographical criticism, a book of poetry, and numerous critical articles.

h. was educated at Stanford, the University of Wisconsin-Madison, and the University of California, Santa Cruz, where she received her Ph.D. in 1983. Her first and most polemical book, *Ain't I a Woman: Black Women and Feminism* (1981), is a self-proclaimed "book of the heart, expressing the deep and passionate longing for change in the social status of black women, for an end to sexist domination and exploitation." For h. the book is a political gesture toward liberating the colonized mentality that fosters racism and sexism. The book provoked much critical commentary and debate and (although it took seven years to find a publisher) launched her prolific writing career as a "cultural worker" and social critic.

In *Feminist Theory: From Margin to Center* (1984), h. articulates the need for a feminist theory that addresses the mechanics of marginalization. Her consciousness of the impact of marginalization upon groups who exist outside of the center of white, middle-class, heterosexual feminism emerged from her own experience of the dividing railroad tracks in the small Kentucky town where she grew up. There, the tracks "were a daily reminder of [her] marginality" from the affluent world of the white middle class. The book articulates the need to bring women who have existed only marginally in the feminist movement into dialogue with those in the center.

Talking Back: Thinking Feminist, Thinking Black (1989) articulates African American women's struggle to emerge from silence: "Moving from silence into speech is for the oppressed, the colonized, the exploited . . . a gesture of defiance that heals, that makes new life and new growth possible." The essays in this book "talk back" by addressing the politics of domination in institutions of cultural production. The politics of cultural production is also h.'s subject in *Yearning: Race, Gender, and Cultural Politics* (1990). The essays in this collection range across film, television, music, the consumer culture, the community, and postmodernism. h. locates a yearning for radical social change in postmodern representations of race, class, gender, and sexual practice.

A dialogue with the philosopher Cornel West, published as *Breaking Bread: Insurgent Black Intellectual Life* (1991), is an intense and wide-ranging discussion of black intellectuality and the crises of both African American women and men. With their discussion, h. hopes to create a "community of comrades who are seeking to deepen our spiritual experience and our political solidarity." In *Black Looks* (1992), "a series of essays about identity," h. extends her critical interest in representations of blackness in the media, particularly in film.

h. is a prolific public speaker who has lectured all over the country; she is also an accomplished teacher and a member of the faculty at Oberlin College. She demonstrates in her writing, speaking, and teaching an activism that testifies to her engagement with the community of whom she speaks so eloquently whenever she "talks back."

OTHER WORKS: *And There We Wept* (1978). *Sisters of the Yam: Black Women and Self-Recovery* (1992). Important articles include: "Black Women's Sexuality in the New Film," *Sage* 2:1 (1985); "Writing the Subject: Reading *The Color Purple*," in *Modern Critical Views: Alice Walker*, ed. Harold Bloom (1987); "Black Is a Woman's Color," *Callaloo* 12:2 (Spring 1989); "Essentialism and Experience," *Amer. Literary History* 3:1 (Spring 1991); "Democracy, Inc.: The Hill-Thomas Hearings," *Artforum* 30 (Jan. 1992).

BIBLIOGRAPHY: Feminist Rev. 33 (Autumn 1989). *Signs* 11 (Summer 1986).

LISA MARCUS

Maureen Howard

See AWW 1, 335–37

Prize-winning writer of memoirs, short stories and novels, reviewer, and academician, H. writes in a way that calls readers' attention to her works as written texts, documents of life. It is not just that she often writes both about writing and writers—Margaret Flood, protagonist of *Expensive Habits* (1986) is a writer; Jack, a character in *Natural History* (1992), is a would-be screenwriter; and almost all of the characters of her recent novels are compilers and editors of their own memories. It is also that H.'s circling, sometimes-jagged, often-poetic narrative structures and prose augment our understanding of the setbacks, start-ups, and rich, enigmatic moments of her characters' lives.

Almost all of H.'s recent critics see her as a superb craftsperson, and many of them cite her precision of perception, her abundance of feeling, and occasionally, her tendency to judge. Her few negative reviews stem from what the critics see as her excessive ellipses and her penchant for leaping from person to person (both in terms of character and narrative point of view) and from story line to story line. In an interview, H. commented, "The most exciting thing in the world to me is the idea of audience. The knowledge that someone has had to do some work on the other side—to understand what you've implied, to imagine something in a new way."

Grace Abounding (1982) features Maude Dowd, widow, childlike mother of Margaret, fantasizer, and finally, child psychologist. Maude's character remains as unfixed as H.'s narrative, which alights on Margaret, the eccentric LeDoux sisters, and an abused little boy, among others.

Expensive Habits centers on, but hardly restricts itself to, another multi-faceted, intelligent, struggling woman. Margaret Flood battles, perhaps tritely, an injured heart. The novel chronicles her attempted rewritings of her life, rewritings that are beautifully crafted and perceptive, and that can never tell the whole story. In this and her other novels, H. creates the paradox of adding more and more details that increase our understanding of the novel while simultaneously expanding the parameters of what we have to understand.

Natural History is H.'s biggest novel, both in scope and ambition. It chronicles the development of Bridgeport, Connecticut, and some of its inhabitants, especially the Bray family. One critic names H.'s native Bridgeport as the protagonist, a good choice for those who insist that every good, big novel have one. The novel's lack of a main character, and of linear chronology and a consistent mode of storytelling (it includes prose narrative, screenplay, and civic diary), challenges notions about the necessities of novel writing. H.'s experimentalism is not merely for its own sake: her characters are also experimenting—adding meaning to the mystery of their lives and vice versa.

OTHER WORKS: *The Penguin Book of Contemporary American Essays* (editor, 1984). "Retrospect: Fiction in Review," *Yale Rev.* (Autumn 1985). Numerous book reviews in such publications as *Yale Rev.*, *NYTBR*, the *Nation*, and the *Virginia Q*.

BIBLIOGRAPHY: Reference works: *CANR* 31 (1990). *CLC* 46 (1988). *Contemp. Novelists* (1991). *DLBY* 1983 (1984). *Maj Twent Cent Wr* (1991).

Other references: *New Republic* (4 Oct. 1982). *NYTBR* (26 Sept. 1982; 21 Nov. 1982; 8 June 1986; 18 Oct. 1992). *PW* (27 Aug. 1982; 15 Oct. 1982).

FAYE HALPERN

Florence Howe

See AWW 2, 337–39

H. has been a driving force behind the establishment and success of The Feminist Press (founded in 1970) and of the development of women's studies programs nationwide. In addition to being a tireless advocate for women's writing and a theoretician, she is also a teacher, developing her philosophy and theories on the front lines. In all her work, development of the consciousness and the voices of women has been her primary goal. Widely respected for her work, H. received the Mina Shaughnessy Medal from the Modern Language Association (1982–83).

A predominant theme in H.'s work has been that education teaches society's rules; thus the only way to change society is to change education. H. started to make changes early. From 1960 to 1971 she taught at Goucher College in Baltimore, where she introduced women's literature into her courses, a revolutionary act for the time. Her experience as a teacher in a Mississippi Freedom School in 1964 as well as her involvement in the antiwar and student movements of the 1960s and 1970s further inspired her to focus her energy on societal reforms, especially reforms concerning women. Through education, H. hoped to expose the myths that kept women in their place and that prevented them from seeking the commonalities that would unite them.

Often using her own experience to illustrate the process of enlightenment, H.'s publications have consistently reflected this goal. In *The Impact of Women's Studies on the Curriculum and the Disciplines* (1980, with Paul Lauter) and in *The New Scholarship on Women: Issues and Constraints in Institutional Change* (1981), H. analyzes the effects the new empowerment of women has had on institutions and critiques the pace of change. *Everywoman's Guide to Colleges and Universities* (coeditor, 1982), a project conceived by H., advises young women who are choosing a college about the climate and opportunities for women in various institutions. *Myths of Coeducation: Selected Essays, 1964–1983* (1984) includes a detailed account of her summer with the Freedom School; she connects that experience not only to her personal development, but also to an analysis of the sources of political power. She also served as coeditor (with John Farragher) of *Women and Higher Education: In Celebration of Mount Holyoke's 175th Birthday* (1987), a collection of ten essays that not only reviews the myths about women in higher education, but also records triumphs over them.

H. has also served as editor of the *Women's Studies Quarterly* (1972–82) and as a member of the editorial boards of *Women's Studies: an Interdisciplinary Journal*, *SIGNS*, and *Research in the Humanities*. Continuing her deeply felt concern in giving voice to those who have been absent from, or excluded from, the literary canon, she coedited (with Marsha Saxton), *With Wings: An Anthology of Literature by and about Women with Disabilities* (1987).

Although much of her energy has been focused on education, H.'s primary interest remains literature by women. In *Tradition and the Talents of Women* (1991), dedicated to the feminist scholar Mary Anne Ferguson, H. reviews the decades of publishing and literary history of women since the founding of The Feminist Press. She notes that although critics may claim there are many traditions in women's literature, she herself insists on a singular tradition in her title for two reasons: "Never again to allow the disappearance of women writers from history, and never again to cease insisting on their appearance inside the curriculum, the formal manner in which 'tradition' becomes 'canonized.'" While acknowledging their diversity, H. argues, women can support one another in a tradition of their own.

Evoking her mentor, Virginia Woolf, whose work she has studied and written about since the 1960s, H. notes that in *A Room of One's Own* Woolf "charged women to work as a community on behalf of all women whose voices have not yet been heard." In her own work as publisher, writer, and teacher, H. has made Woolf's charge her own.

OTHER WORKS: *No More Masks: An Anthology of Twentieth-Century American Women Poets* (ed. 1993).

BIBLIOGRAPHY: Reference works: *CA* 109 (1983), 124 (1988). Other references: *Education Digest* (March 1986). *PW* (15 Apr. 1988). *Wilson Library Bull.* (Nov. 1985).

LINDA BERUBE

Tina Howe

B. 21 Nov. 1937, New York City
D. of Mary Lincoln (Post) and Quincy Howe; m. Norman Levy, 1961; c.: Eben,
  b. 1967; Dara, b. 1970

Born in New York City to a family of writers, H. writes plays that stretch
the dramatic forms and evoke her self-professed "obsession" with art.
While these plays often feature artists as characters, their concerns are
the integration of art and daily life, her themes the renewal and regeneration that only art and children provide.

After graduating from Sarah Lawrence College (B.A. 1959), where she
wrote her first play, H. spent a year in Paris, where she "wrote around
the clock . . . and the infatuation [with playwriting] began." After returning, she earned her teaching credentials at Columbia Teachers College and Chicago Teachers College, then began teaching high school first
in Monona Grove, Wisconsin, and later in Bath, Maine. There, she says,
she learned her craft while running the drama department, a task she
took on with the agreement that only her plays be produced. *The Nest*
(1970) was H.'s first professionally produced play.

Often innovative and even experimental, H.'s most critically successful
works to date have been *Painting Churches*, which won the Outer Critics
Circle Award for best Off-Broadway play, 1983–84, and was produced
by PBS's American Playhouse series in 1986, and *Coastal Disturbances*,
which received a Tony nomination for best play, 1987. In 1983, H. received an Obie for distinguished playwriting.

H. has always claimed an affinity with the absurdists. Her work, however, in its playful exploration of the absurd in a realistic setting, resembles more the early absurdists, Pirandello and especially Giraudoux, than
it does later, more minimalist absurdists such as Beckett and Genet.

H.'s plays typically work through theme and variation based on musical
forms rather than linear plot development. She moves her characters to
epiphany incrementally, through accretion, in a series of large and small
moments that build into a final, resonant image. This led to some unfounded accusations of formlessness in early reviews by critics more used
to obvious moments of crisis and resolution. H.'s plays develop a rhyth-

mic energy that carry them beyond the ordinary and into a heightened realism that borders on the fantastic or absurd, ending in a release: unexpected silliness, poignant ecstasy, what she calls "the flamboyant in everyday life."

H.'s plays are notable as well for their imaginative use of settings, from a full working kitchen in *Art of Dining* (1978) to the complete art exhibit of *Museum* (1983). Perhaps influenced by her mother's work as a watercolorist, H.'s stage directions often provide visual tableaux, as in the strikingly pictorial *Coastal Disturbances*, and an emphasis on the final image in the stage directions of each play. In *The Art of Dining*, H.'s personal favorite, the characters huddle around a bonfire inside a restaurant "purified of their collective civilization and private grief" as they feast and the curtain falls. And in *Approaching Zanzibar* (1990), a young girl bouncing on a trampoline made up to look like a bed chants, "Paradise . . . Paradise," as she bounces higher and higher, until she "looks like a reckless angel challenging the limits of heaven."

Since the late 1970s, H.'s plays have been produced around the country and abroad and have premiered in such prestigious venues as the Los Angeles Actors Theatre, the New York Shakespeare Festival, the Kennedy Center, and the Second Stage. H. has also received a Rockefeller grant (1984), a National Endowment for the Arts Fellowship (1985), and a Guggenheim Fellowship (1990), and has been awarded an honorary degree at Bowdoin College. Although her family has its roots in the Boston area, H. has spent most of her life in and around New York City. She has taught playwriting as a visiting professor at Hunter College, and as adjunct professor at New York University, as well as the Sewanee Writers' Conference, University of the South, Tennessee.

OTHER WORKS: "Birth and after Birth," in *The New Women's Theatre*, Honor Moore, ed. (1977). *Swimming* (1991). "Teeth," in *Best American Short Plays* (1990) and in *Antaeus Plays in One Act*, Daniel Dalpern, ed. (1991). "Antic Vision," *American Theatre Magazine* (Sept. 1985). "Stepping through the Frame," *Art and Antiques* (Jan. 1987). "The Reluctant Exhibitionist," *Allure Magazine* (Sept. 1991). *One Shoe Off* (produced 1993).

BIBLIOGRAPHY: Backes, Nancy, "Body Art: Hunger and Satiation in the Plays of Tina Howe," in *Making a Spectacle: Feminist Essays on Contemporary Women's Theatre*, Lynda Hart, ed. (1989). Barlow, Judith, "The Art of Tina Howe," in *Feminine Focus: The New Women Playwrights*, Enoch Brater, ed. (1989), and "An Interview with Tina Howe," in *Studies in American Drama, 1945–Present* 4 (1989). Betsko, Kathleen, and Rachel Koenig, *Interviews with*

Contemporary Women Playwrights (1987). Di Gaetani, John L., *A Search for a Post-Modern Theatre* (1991). Reference works: *CA* 109 (1983). *CLC* 48 (1988). *Contemp. Dramatists* (1988). *CBY* (1990). *FC* (1990).

Other references: *New York Mag.* (28 Nov. 1983; 22–29 Dec. 1986). *NYT* (1 May 1983; 28 Nov. 1983; 16 Nov. 1986; 30 April 1989; 7 May 1989). *Otherstages* (27 Jan. 1983). *Theatre Week* (12 June 1989).

MARCIA HEPPS   WILLIAM KEENEY

Humishuma. *See Mourning Dove*

Kristin Hunter

B. 12 Sept. 1931, Philadelphia, Pennsylvania
D. of Mabel (Manigault) and George Lorenzo Eggleston; m. Joseph Hunter, 1952;
* m. John I. Lattany, 1968; c.: two stepsons*

One of the most prominent writers for the often-neglected audience of African American youth, H. provides a message of optimism and hope in her stories of inner-city black life. From a middle-class background herself, H. was greatly influenced by the poorer inhabitants of Philadelphia among whom she grew up in the 1930s and 1940s; it is they who later became the focus of most of her fiction. Known for their realism and vitality, H.'s novels and short stories for both adolescents and adults celebrate the positive values of black culture and encourage unity, self-reliance, ingenuity, and courage in the face of adversity. In the tradition of the women writers of the Harlem Renaissance, H. explores particularly the African American female experience and provides new instruction and inspiration for contemporary black women writers.

The only child of a school-principal father and a schoolteacher mother, H. became an avid reader and writer in early childhood, commenting later: "I believe these circumstances—onliness, loneliness and resultant fantasizing and omnivorous reading—are the most favorable for producing writers." H. wrote poetry and articles for school publications and in 1946, at fourteen, she began a teenage social column for the Philadelphia edition of the *Pittsburgh Courier*. Continuing as a columnist and feature writer for the *Courier* until 1952, she later drew on her coverage of a story on the annexation by the city of Camden, New Jersey, of the all-black town of Lawnside to provide the basis for her novel *The Lakestown Rebellion* (1978). The novel depicts a black community's unified resistance to the construction of an interstate highway that is to run through their town.

H. received a B.S. in Education from the University of Pennsylvania in 1951. At her parents' request, she taught elementary school but quit in less than a year to pursue a writing career. In 1952 she began working as an advertising copywriter with the Lavenson Bureau of Advertising in Philadelphia, the first of several similar positions that allowed her enough stability and spare time to continue to write. In 1955 she won a national competition for a television documentary produced by CBS, entitled "A Minority of One." This recognition launched her career.

H. began her first novel, *God Bless the Child* (1964), while she was still at Lavenson. A poignant tale of a young black woman's struggle to raise herself and her family out of poverty, it establishes many themes for H.'s later works, particularly the importance of inner strength and self-sufficiency. As in much of her later fiction, H. explores the dangers and vitality of the city and the complex social and economic forces that oppress families there. The novel won the prestigious Philadelphia Athenaeum Award in 1964, went into a third printing within a month of its publication date, and had four subsequent softcover printings in the 1970s.

While working as an information officer for the city of Philadelphia, H. produced *The Landlord* (1966), her most successful novel to date. In this comical story about a young white landlord of an inner-city tenement building and his relationships with his tenants, H. uses slapstick, caricature, and parody to explore class distinctions and racial tensions. The "lightness" with which she treats serious issues here, along with her exaggerated, seemingly stereotypical portrayals of blacks, led to mixed reviews. H. was praised nonetheless for uniqueness of expression and in 1970 United Artists adapted her story for film.

The success of H.'s witty, comic style in *The Landlord* prompted her publishers to suggest she write books for children and adolescents. *The Soul Brothers and Sister Lou* (1968), inspired by young street singers who performed in an alley below H.'s inner-city apartment, tells the story of a young singing group's struggle for survival and success. With honesty and compassion, H. tackles such issues as police violence, gang warfare, and racial injustice as her protagonists demonstrate courage and strength of character. Widely praised for its affirmation of black culture and for providing hopeful alternatives to the violence and deprivation of the ghetto, *Soul Brothers* received many honors including the National Council on Interracial Books for Children Award (1968) and the Lewis Carroll Shelf Award (1971).

H. married for the second time in 1968 and became a stepmother to her husband's two sons. She credits them with greatly influencing her understanding of children and encouraging her works for young people. Among these are *Guests in the Promised Land* (1973), a collection of short stories that won several awards, and the critically acclaimed *Lou in the Limelight* (1981), a sequel to *Soul Brothers*.

Since early in her career, H.'s poems, short stories, book reviews, and articles have appeared in such publications as *Philadelphia Magazine, Philadelphia Bulletin*, the *Nation, Essence, Rogue, Black World, Good Housekeeping*, and *Seventeen*. H. was writer in residence at Emory University in 1979. She has taught English and creative writing at the University of Pennsylvania since 1972, and since 1983 has held the title of senior lecturer in English.

OTHER WORKS: "The Double Edge" (play, 1965). *Boss Cat* (1971). *The Pool Table War* (1972). *Uncle Daniel and the Raccoon* (1972). *The Survivors* (1975).

BIBLIOGRAPHY: Harris, Trudier, *From Mammies to Militants: Domestics in Black American Literature* (1982). *Black Women Writers at Work*, Claudia Tate, ed. (1983). Reference works: *Black Writers* (1989). CLR 3 (1978). CANR 13 (1984). *Contemp. Novelists* (1991). DLB 33 (1984). FC (1990). SATA 12 (1977). *Tw Cent Children's Writers* (1989).

Other references: *Black Literature Forum* 20 (Winter 1986). *Phila. Inquirer* (24 Nov. 1974).

MARY E. HARVEY

Morgan Ives. *See Marion Zimmer Bradley*

Rebecca Cox Jackson

B. 15 Feb. 1795, Hornstown, Pennsylvania; d. 24 May 1871, Philadelphia, Pennsylvania
D. of Jane (Cox), later Wisson or Wilson; father's name unknown; m. Samuel S. Jackson (date unknown, before 1830; separated 1836)

J. was a charismatic itinerant preacher, the founder of a religious communal family in Philadelphia, and a religious visionary writer. Though an important example of African American female religious leadership and spirituality in the nineteenth century, she was virtually unknown from her death until the rediscovery and publication of her manuscript spiritual autobiography, *Gifts of Power*, in 1981. Virtually all that is known of her life is recorded in this autobiography and in Shaker archives.

As the result of the powerful religious awakening experience in a thunderstorm in 1830 with which her spiritual autobiography begins, J. became active in the early Holiness movement and came to challenge the African Methodist Episcopal (AME) church of her upbringing. She moved from leadership of praying bands to public preaching, stirring up controversy within AME circles not only as a woman preacher, but also because she had received the revelation that celibacy was necessary for a holy life. She criticized the churches, including the AME church and its leaders, for "carnality." Her insistence on being guided entirely by the dictates of her inner voice led ultimately to her separation from husband, admired older brother (Joseph Cox, an AME preacher with whom she had lived since her mother's death), and church.

After a period of itinerant preaching in the later 1830s and early 1840s, in June 1847 J. joined the United Society of Believers in Christ's Second Appearing (the Shakers), at Watervliet, New York. She was attracted to their religious celibacy, their emphasis on spiritualistic experience, and their dual-gender concept of deity. With her younger disciple and lifelong companion, Rebecca Perot, J. lived at Watervliet until July 1851. Increasingly disappointed in the predominantly white Shaker community's failure to take the gospel of their founder, Ann Lee, to the African American community, J. left Watervliet on an unauthorized mission to Philadelphia, where she and Perot experimented with séance-style spiritualism. They returned to Watervliet for a brief second residence in 1857, and at this time Jackson won the right to found and head a new Shaker "outfamily" in Philadelphia. This predominantly black and female Shaker family survived her death by at least a quarter of a century.

Like several other African American women preachers in the nineteenth century, J. achieved her religious leadership role largely through visionary experience and her ability to communicate such experience to others, at first solely through oral testimonial. Illiterate into her middle age—"the only child of my mother that had not learning"—she depended immediately after her conversion on her literate elder brother to help her religious correspondence. Her autobiography records her increasing frustration with this dependency and her joy when she prayed for literacy and received it by divine gift.

Gifts of Power records her spiritual journey as a woman with a divine calling, from her awakening through her discovery of Shakerism and the founding of her own community. She describes a wide variety of visionary experiences, including mysterious prophetic dreams and supernatural "gifts of power" (such as the ability to control the weather by prayer). The dream visions give access to a world in which laws of nature are violated with ease. The physical body left behind, the dreamer soars into the air, and is given flashes of understanding about both the physical universe and the spiritual world. J.'s visionary dreams also show her confronting fears of racial and sexual violence; working out an understanding of the mother aspect of the godhead; and even resolving conflicts that arose in her relationships with brother, husband, spiritual companions, and Shaker leaders.

Alice Walker has described *Gifts of Power* as "an extraordinary document," which "tells us much about the spirituality of human beings, especially of the interior spiritual resources of our mothers." Writing of Jackson's relationship to Perot, Walker coined the term "womanism" to distinguish a specifically black feminist cultural tradition that includes women's love for other women but is not "separatist."

OTHER WORKS: Gifts of Power: The Writings of Rebecca Cox Jackson, Black Visionary, Shaker Eldress, Jean McMahon Humez., ed. (1981). Manuscript writings include an autograph version of her incomplete autobiography in the Berkshire Athenaeum at the Public Library, Pittsfield, Massachusetts. A short booklet containing Perot's dream accounts dictated to J. and a few of J.'s dreams, and a rough draft anthology of all J.'s extant writings, produced by her Shaker historian, Alonzo Hollister, are in the Shaker Collection, Western Reserve Historical Society, Cleveland, Ohio. A fair copy of this anthology is in the Library of Congress Shaker manuscript collection.

BIBLIOGRAPHY: Braxton, Joanne, *Black Women Writing Autobiography* (1989). Gates, Henry Louis, Jr., *The Signifying Monkey: A Theory of African-American Literary Criticism* (1988). Williams, Richard E., *Called and Chosen: The Story of Mother Rebecca Jackson and the Philadelphia Shakers* (1981). Duclow, Geraldine, "The Philadelphia Shaker Family," *The Shaker Messenger,* forthcoming. Humez, Jean M., "Visionary Experience and Power: The Career of Rebecca Cox Jackson," *Black Apostles at Home and Abroad,* David M. Wills and Richard Newman, eds. (1982). McKay, Nellie Y., "Nineteenth Century Black Women's Spiritual Autobiographies: Religious Faith and Self-Empowerment," *Interpreting Women's Lives: Feminist Theory and Personal Narratives,* the Personal Narrative Group, ed. (1989). Sasson, Diane, "Life as Vision: The Autobiography of Mother Rebecca Jackson," *The Shaker Spiritual Narrative* (1983). Walker, Alice, "Gifts of Power: The Writings of Rebecca Cox Jackson," *In Search of Our Mother's Gardens* (1983). Reference works: *NBAW* (1991). *Black Women in the United States: An Historical Encyc.* (forthcoming). *Encyc. of African American Culture and History* (forthcoming). *Amer. Nat. Biog.* (forthcoming).

Other References: *J. of Feminist Studies in Religion* (Fall 1989). *Tulsa Studies in Women's Lit.* (Fall 1982).

JEAN MCMAHON HUMEZ

Harriet Jacobs

B. *Autumn 1813, Edenton, North Carolina; d. 7 March 1897, Washington, DC*
Wrote under: Linda Brent
D. *of Delilah Horniblow and Daniel Jacobs; c.: Joseph, b. 1829; Louisa Matilda,*
  b. 1833

The process of identifying J. and constructing her relation to a place, people, and time by presentation of the place and dates of her birth and death, documentation of her parentage, and information about her marriage and children generates as many questions about Harriet Jacobs, the author, as it answers. It is not even clear how and when her last name became established as Jacobs. Her mother was a slave owned by a tavern keeper, John Horniblow. J.'s father was reputed to be Daniel Jacobs, a carpenter whose owner was Dr. Andrew Knox. A slave was not characteristically given his/her father's last name, however, since paternity of a slave was often disputed or disregarded. J.'s "naming" conformed neither to the prevailing convention of ascribing to slaves their master's surname nor to the convention of "self-naming" common in male-authored slave narratives such as *Narrative of the Life of Frederick Douglass.*

Like other slave narratives J.'s *Incidents in the Life of a Slave Girl* (1861) utilizes standard abolitionist rhetoric to provide an account of her life as a slave, her efforts to resist her master, and her eventual achievement of freedom for her children and for herself. Unlike other (male-authored) slave narratives that tend to foreground a cause-and-effect relation between the acquisition of literacy and the slave's desire for freedom, J. simply documents that her first mistress taught her to read, write, and sew, and represents her desire for freedom within the specific terms of her experience as a slave woman. She presents herself in *Incidents* as sexual object and as mother, registering her attempts to resist the sexual advances of her master, her selection of her children's father (both were the children of Samuel Tredwell Sawyer, a white lawyer), and her attempts to procure her children's freedom as exercises both of her agency and the collective agency of her community.

In addition to this gendered difference in narrative content, J.'s writing style engages the conventions of sentimental fiction (typically classified as women's fiction), marking *Incidents* as a woman's narrative. As black feminist scholars such as Hazel Carby and Valerie Smith have noted, J.'s use of conventions of sentimental fiction became, for many male literary critics and historians, the grounds for challenging the authenticity of *Incidents* as a slave narrative. Biographical details about J. and her author-ship of *Incidents* were only definitively established in 1980 with the publi-cation of Jean Fagan Yellin's research. Prior to the publication of Yellin's discoveries, authorship of J.'s narrative had been attributed to Linda Brent, the first-person narrator who claimed that the autobiographical *Incidents* had been "written by herself."

In addition to establishing the authenticity of J.'s narrative, Yellin traces its complex publishing history and provides information about the intri-cate editorial relations between Jacobs and such prominent abolitionist activists and writers as Amy Post, **Harriet Beecher Stowe, Lydia Maria Child,** and Frederick Douglass. She also documents J.'s years as a fugitive from slavery, her flight to the North in 1842 and her settlement in Roches-ter, New York, where she was active in abolitionist politics. Between 1862 and 1868, with her daughter, Louisa Matilda, J. participated in relief efforts in Alexandria, Virginia, Washington, DC, and Savannah, Georgia. They also returned to Edenton, to bring relief supplies. She moved to Washington, her daughter's residence, sometime before 1885, and died there in 1897.

OTHER WORKS: "Letter from a Fugitive Slave," *New York Tribune* (21 June 1853). *The Deeper Wrong* (British edition of *Incidents,* ed. Lydia Maria Child, 1862). Letters from Harriet Jacobs to Amy Post are in the Isaac and Amy Post Family Papers, Univ. of Rochester, Rochester, New York.

BIBLIOGRAPHY: Baker, Houston, *Blues Ideology and Afro-American Literature* (1984). Blassingame, John, *The Slave Community: Plantation Life in the Antebel-lum South* (1979). Carby, Hazel, *Reconstructing Womanhood* (1987). Davis, An-gela, *Women, Race, and Class* (1981). Smith, Valerie, *Self-discovery and Authenticity in Afro-American Narrative* (1987). Yellin, Jean Fagan, "Written by Herself: Harriet Jacobs' Slave Narrative," *Amer. Lit.* 53 (Nov. 1981); introduction to *Incidents in the Life of a Slave Girl, Written by Herself* (1987). This edition also contains a selection of J.'s letters to Amy Post. Reference works: *FC* (1990).

BEVERLY HORTON

Jane Jacobs

See AWW 2, 383–85

America's leading urbanist, J. grew up in Scranton, Pennsylvania. After high school, she worked on the Scranton *Tribune*, exhibiting an interest in working-class urban areas. She later took courses at Columbia University and married architect Robert Hyde Jacobs, Jr. In the 1940s, J. produced articles on architecture for the Office of War Information. As a New York–based freelance writer, she wrote essays on subjects ranging from metallurgy to geography, increasingly focusing on inner-city problems. From 1952 to 1962, J. was associate, then senior, editor of *Architectural Forum*, probing problems of cities. She also contributed to the *Reporter, Harper's,* and other periodicals, and brought a new approach to the study of city life with her essay, "Downtown Is for People," included in *The Exploding Metropolis* (1958).

The Death and Life of Great American Cities (1961) rejects the conventional "wisdom" of professional urban and regional planners and developers in a clarion call to preserve the vitality of cities despite prevailing trends of suburbanization and urban renewal that devastated neighborhoods and the historic urban fabric. Her incisive criticism, common sense, jargon-free prose, and wit strengthened her highly readable arguments for city life. J. praises urban parks, sidewalks, density, diversity, and mixed residential and commercial uses. She assesses the damage resulting from the loss of goods and services that undermines urban commerce and leads to decreased domestic spirit and even to crime. J. sought realistic solutions in economics to preserve cities as "intricate working organisms." The book's power is its simplicity in arguing for the "real life" of cities. She sounds an influential prourbanist note in an era that abandoned cities, helping turn the tide against modernism.

The Economy of Cities (1969) is an insightful account of the growth of cities, ancient and modern, as sources of civilization, not mere outgrowths of rural culture. Nourished on diversified manufacturing and trade, cities brought growth and prosperity to agricultural communities through industrial and technological innovations. J. celebrates "the invaluable inefficiencies and impracticalities of cities" as the only environment "where one kind of work leads inefficiently to another." A city "cannot be a work of art" because it needs "ugly, discordant, chaotic elements" in order to function. Challenging conventional ideas about cities, J. formulated "a badly needed urban myth" that had an immense influence on later design and planning.

As an urban environmentalist reformer and community activist, J. practiced what she preached, defending neighborhoods and businesses from obliteration by expressway construction. She opposed large, standardized, dehumanizing public housing, calling for "infill" human-scale building. J. inveighed against a 1961 New York zoning law permitting huge skyscraper towers in empty plazas and organized local opposition to "slum-clearance" for highways. In 1962 her Committee to Save the West Village preserved a fourteen-block historic district. Arrested once, she was also named to Mayor John Lindsay's Task Force on Housing and President Johnson's Task Force on Natural Beauty. The United Nations Conference on Human Settlements endorsed her ideas in 1976.

J. immigrated to Toronto in 1968 and was naturalized a Canadian citizen. *The Question of Separation: Quebec and the Struggle over Sovereignty* (1980) developed from a series of 1979 Massey Lectures broadcast nationally. Refusing to favor French or English factions, J. argues that separatism would not be tragic but would end the strain on Canada's political and cultural resources and institutions. Regions, she argues, are viable entities. J. tackles national economic patterns as related to urban competition between the "capitals" of Montreal and Toronto.

Cities and the Wealth of Nations: Principles of Economic Life (1984) expands J.'s iconoclastic challenge to prevailing economic theories across the political spectrum. It argues that modern, centralized nationalist policies everywhere "interrupt and distort the organic growth of cities," thus endangering the sources of national economic productivity and prosperity. Citing diverse examples ranging over time and over the globe, J. finds all development regionally uneven, failing to integrate agricultural and industrial sectors and leading to stagnation and decline of many areas. Again, she finds hope in the chaotic growth of the "city region," the natural mechanism for creating and distributing wealth. The "goofy" systems of the nation-state produce only recipes for failure, feeding local decline and even civil war. The only solution is in strengthening cities to form "a family of smaller sovereignties" that will reestablish intercity trade.

In *Systems of Survival: A Dialogue on the Moral Foundations of Commerce and Politics* (1992) J. uses the Platonic dialogue to analyze fundamental human behavior governed by two ethical systems—the guardian values associated with governmental entities and the commercial syndrome. Conflict occurs when the two cultures mix, causing ethical problems in everyday life, government, business, and politics. J.'s fictional but deeply philosophical conversations tap a wide variety of historic and recent documentation for diverse international examples, showing how these two fundamentally different and inflexible mentalities contribute to contemporary moral dilemmas. Fighting fatalism, J. calls for a new civilizing agent in "the guardian-commercial symbiosis" and for institutional self-examination to reevaluate and revise codes of ethics, to revitalize moral awareness, and to eliminate corruption.

Through her blunt, informal, and even entertaining prose laced with slang, J. criticizes the theories and work of orthodox experts, professionals, and planners. Her incisive, interdisciplinary diagnoses of problems have been called "spunky and informative cautionary documents." A maverick independent intellectual, she challenges credentialism and renews a tradition of nonspecialist participation in academic and professional realms.

BIBLIOGRAPHY: *Atlantic* (March 1984, April 1984). *Boston Globe* (3 Jan. 1993). *Commentary* (2 Nov. 1984). *Nation* (3 March 1962; 2 Feb. 1970; 2 June 1984). *New Rev.* (2 July 1984). *NYRB* (20 Nov. 1980). *NYT* (18 April 1968; 19 May 1969; 14 June 1969; 24 May 1984). *NYTBR* (5 Sept. 1980; 5 Oct. 1980; 27 May 1984; 16 Feb. 1992). *Sat. Rev.* (Aug. 1980). *TLS* (9 Nov. 1962; 6 April 1970; 4 Sept. 1981).

BLANCHE LINDEN-WARD

Diane Johnson

See AWW 2, 404–7

Novelist, biographer, and essayist, J. does not categorize her novels as "feminist fiction" yet often writes of the conflicts attractive and intelligent women face when they confront cultural ideals of femininity. In the late 1960s and 1970s her novels' satiric comments on this confrontation became grimmer in their portrayal of female survival.

While J. continues this theme in her fiction her work has lightened in tone. *Persian Nights* (1987), set in Iran just before the shah's fall, demonstrates both her characteristic rich use of symbol and an incisive humor toward her heroine and the other characters who are perplexed by both political and personal revolutions. *Health and Happiness* (1990) relies on a triple focus to include the perspective of a male physician with those of the two heroines. Humorous and ironic, and written with graceful clarity, the novel avoids any biting commentary on its characters who meet in a San Francisco hospital, and offers a softened satire on individual integrity, contemporary California culture, and the politics of the medical profession.

In 1980 J. collaborated with Stanley Kubrick on the screenplay of Stephen King's *The Shining*. She has been a frequent contributor to the *New York Times Book Review* and writes regularly for the *New York Review of Books*; many of her essays from the late 1970s and early 1980s were collected in *Terrorists and Novelists* (1982). A second biography, *Dashiell Hammett: A Life*, appeared in 1983 to mixed reviews. J. has also co-authored articles on the medical profession and on AIDS with her physician husband. *Natural Opium* (1993) is a collection of travel essays and what J. calls "auto-fiction."

J. has received an impressive number of literary prizes and grants: a Woodrow Wilson Foundation grant in 1965, an American Association of University Women grant in 1968, and a Guggenheim Fellowship for 1977–78. Her biography *Lesser Lives* (1972) was nominated for a National Book Award in 1973. *Lying Low* was similarly nominated and won a Rosenthal Foundation Award in 1979. In 1987 J. was a recipient of a five-year Mildred and Harold Strauss Livings grant. She is a professor of English at the University of California-Davis.

OTHER WORKS: "Do Doctors Mean What They Say?" (with John F. Murray) in *Fair of Speech: The Uses of Euphemism*, D. J. Enright, ed. (1985). "AIDS without End" (with John F. Murray), *NYRB* 35 (18 Aug. 1988).

BIBLIOGRAPHY: Portraits of Marriage in Literature, A. C. Hargrove and M. Magliocco, eds. (1984). LeClair, T., and L. McCaffery, *Anything Can Happen: Interviews with Contemporary American Novelists* (1983). *Women Writers of the West Coast: Speaking of Their Lives and Careers*, M. Yalom, ed. (1990). Reference works: *CANR* 17 (1986). *CLC* 48 (1988). *DLBY*:1980 (1981). *Maj Twent Cent Writers* (1991). *WW Wr, Ed, Poets* (1991).

Other references: *Clues* 9:1 (Spring–Summer 1991). *Critique: Studies in Modern Fiction* 26:1 (1974). *Modern Fiction Studies* 31 (Winter 1985). *Partisan Rev.* 55 (Fall 1988). *Sewanee Rev.* 92 (Fall 1984).

JOELLEN MASTERS

Jill Johnston

B. 17 May 1929, London, England
Writes under F. J. Crowe
D. of Olive Margaret Crowe and Cyril Frederick Johnston; m. Richard John
*   Latham, 1958, div. 1964; c.: Richard Renault, b. 1959; Winifred Brook,*
*   b. 1960*

J.'s mother, an American nurse, and her father, an English bell founder, lived together for four years but never married. Raised in England, J. was educated in an exclusive Episcopalian boarding school. In *Mother Bound: Autobiography in Search of a Father* (1983), the first of two autobiographical volumes, J. details the pain of her early life. As a result of Johnston's failure to marry Olive Crowe, J.'s mother lived a life of deception and lies to hide her daughter's illegitimacy. Led by her mother to believe that he had died years before, J. never met her father. Her perception of reality shifted in 1950 when she read of his death that year. By then he had married and had other children. From that moment on J. focused on discovering an identity, yearning to fill the paternal void.

J. attended college in Massachusetts and in Minnesota, and received an M.F.A. (1954) from the University of North Carolina before making her home in New York City. She went to Columbia University to study dance, and, she says, worked in the "female slave market" to support herself. Trying to fight the desire she felt for women, J. conceded to societal pressure and married in 1958. The marriage did not last because of J.'s resistance to convention and Latham's infidelity.

The *Village Voice* launched J.'s career as a writer and public figure, publishing her weekly "Dance Journal" column from 1960 to 1970; *Marmalade Me* (1974) is a collection of the columns. One of the original free spirits of the sixties, J. used the column as a medium to celebrate nonconformity. Her debut article was the first review of the new avant-garde dance and choreography group at the Judson Memorial Church. Gradually, she reviewed less dancing and more of her private life, using the column one week to "come out" as a lesbian and increasingly converting it to an open theater of the wild behavior and public disturbances that by then had come to be expected of her. J.'s writing took on a confessional, fractured style that led eventually to the termination of her career as a critic. She was later hospitalized for an emotional breakdown.

Paper Daughter (1985), the second of her autobiographical series in search of a father, begins with an account of her first nervous breakdown and commitment to Bellevue Hospital. The book depicts her journey to gain control over her life, and the experience of another breakdown, as she tries to move in new directions.

In 1973 *Lesbian Nation: The Feminist Solution* had brought J. into the feminist/women's movement. This collection of journal entries and stories tracks her evolving consciousness as a political lesbian. Her attempts to force the issue of lesbianism into the public forum resulted in establishment portrayals of her as an anarchist outcast.

Gullible's Travels (1974) reflects J. after her second breakdown, in motion, open to revolutionary ideas. Feminism and lesbianism create the backdrop for a mixture of fiction and true stories. An experimental style is used to disrupt the readers' preconceived ideas about fiction, sex, and reality.

Between 1984 and 1991, J. wrote a review column for *Art in America*, covering artistic events and books on the arts. She remains on the cutting edge of the dance and art world, covering the latest events and happenings.

OTHER WORKS: "Twentieth Century Sappho" (audio cassette, 1979).

BIBLIOGRAPHY: Reference works: *CA* 53–56 (1975). *FC* (1990).
Other references: *New York Mag.* (24 May 1971). *Art in America* (Jan. 1986).

SUZANNE GIRONDA

Gayl Jones

See AWW 2, 421–22

Admirers of J.'s novels of the 1970s assert that her construction of black women questions the "naturalness" of racist and sexist attitudes. Others, however, have faulted what they see as her lack of positive images of African American characters, especially of black men.

In the 1980s J.'s work changed substantially, although it is unclear whether the transformation stemmed from criticism of her novels. Her three collections of poetry have received little attention. Still interested in the slave history of colonial Latin America, J. continues to use mutilation themes as well as the richness of the oral tradition to create accounts of female subjectivity and the continuity of history. Set in seventeenth-century Brazil, *Song for Anninho* (1981) tells of the atrocities committed by the Portuguese in their attacks on Palmares, an independent settlement of escaped African slaves. The poem is told by a young African woman who also relates others' stories. Similarly, the title poem in *Xarque and Other Poems* (1985) weaves the voices of three women into a history told by a single female, the granddaughter of Almeyda from *Song for Anninho*. Thus tales of survival and oppression become a matrilineal heritage that finds its voice in song.

The Hermit-Woman (1983), which also develops voices from colonial Brazil, includes two self-referential pieces. One of these, "Stranger," closes the book with a couple's love-making, "fierce/strong/soaring," so that the joy of sexual union heals an African past of sundered relationships. The theme of tenderness in all three books is a departure from the brutality between black women and black men that critics had objected to in her fiction. While that tenderness exists often only in memory and is experienced through the pain of recollection, it closes the gap between women and men and locates violence in racist atrocities. By exploring memory's painful burden as a necessity for the survival of the African race, J. alters the feminist polemic many had noted in her novels to a dialogue of racial unity.

In the 1970s J. received a number of literary awards, including fellowships from Yaddo (1974) and from the National Endowment for the Arts

(1976), and the Henry Russell Award from the University of Michigan (1981), where she was professor of English from 1975 to 1983.

OTHER WORKS: *Liberating Voices: Oral Tradition in African American Literature* (1991).

BIBLIOGRAPHY: *Afro-American Literary Study in the 1990s*, Houston A. Baker and Patricia Redmond, eds. (1989). *Black Women Writers at Work*, Claudia Tate, ed. (1983). *Sturdy Black Bridges: Visions of Black Women in Literature*, Roseann P. Bell, Bettye J. Parker, and Beverly Guy-Sheftall, eds. (1979). Robinson, Sally, *Engendering the Subject: Gender and Self-Representation in Contemporary Women's Fiction* (1991). Reference works: *Black Writers: A Selection of Sketches* (1989). *DLB* 33 (1984). *FC* (1990). *WW Black Americans* (1992).

Other references: *Ariel* 23:3 (1992). *Callaloo* 7:1 (Winter 1984). *CLA J.* 28:1 (1984), 29:4 (1986). *MELUS* 7:4 (Winter 1980).

JOELLEN MASTERS

Erica Jong

See AWW 2, 425–26

J.'s work since 1979 has been prolific and varied. The travels and travails of Isadora, heroine of *Fear of Flying* and *How to Save Your Own Life*, are continued in *Parachute Kisses* (1984) and *Any Woman's Blues* (1990). The first takes Isadora through the breakup of her marriage to Josh Ace, her recovery from the divorce, and rediscovery of love—all while raising her toddler daughter. The next begins with the breakup of the love affair begun at the end of the previous novel. *Any Woman's Blues* diverges from its predecessors by continuing Isadora's saga from Isadora's point of view one step removed. The novel's conceit is that another author has organized and finished the semiautobiographical novel Isadora had been working on shortly before her death. The author's voice now interacts with the character she bases on herself.

This structure reflects J.'s new interest in experimenting with the borders between fiction and reality. *Fanny: Being the True History of the Adventures of Fanny Hackabout-Jones* (1980) and *Serenissima: A Novel of Venice* (1987) represent her work in this vein. The genesis of *Fanny* is J.'s imagined response of the heroine of Cleland's *Fanny Hill; or, Memoirs of a Woman of Pleasure* to his portrayal of her. Fanny responds by writing her own version of her life to reclaim it for herself. In this way, J. confronts the issues not addressed at the time, of incest, prostitution, and woman's powerless position in society, and does so from within, by giving the very source of Cleland's novel a voice. In *Serenissima* J. continues to appropriate and rework older styles and language. The heroine is an actress at a Venice film festival who is about to play Jessica in a new film production of *The Merchant of Venice*. Becoming feverishly ill, she begins to hallucinate and dreams she is a Jew in Venice around Shakespeare's time—in fact, the very woman who will inspire Shakespeare to write *The Merchant of Venice*. Accidents of fate bring her together with Shakespeare and, naturally, adventures ensue. J.'s attempts to meld and confuse the border of time greatly test her reader's suspension of disbelief. *Serenissima* could have used more of the refinement of *Fanny* in concept as well as structure; and the contrast between the critical and popular receptions of the two novels reflect these discrepancies.

J. has also ventured into two new genres: nonfiction and children's literature. *Witches* (with Joseph Smith, 1981), a book about witches and witchcraft, utilizes poetry and illustrations—in addition to the expected prose—to educate its readers. Clearly the result of much research, it even includes a few spells and rites that one might practice, if one dared. *Megan's Book of Divorce* (1984), a self-proclaimed "kid's book for adults," takes on divorce, presumably from J.'s daughter's point of view. The view, however, seems a little unrealistically rosy.

J. considers herself primarily a poet. Since 1979 she has published two books of poetry: *Ordinary Miracles* and *Becoming Light: Poems New and Selected* (1991). The first covers the themes of motherhood and divorce, while the second is a comprehensive compilation, including poems from each of her previous collections as well as some early unpublished poems, poems included in other prose works, and her newest poems.

OTHER WORKS: The Devil at Large: Erica Jong on Henry Miller (1993).

BIBLIOGRAPHY: Boston Rev. (March 1992). *Denver Q.* (Winter 1983). *LATBR* (24 Nov. 1991). *NYTBR* (5 June 1988). *Novel* (Winter 1987). *U. of Dayton Rev.*

(Winter 1985–86). (Additional biographical information: m. Jonathan Fast, 1977; div. 1983; m. Kenneth David Borrows, 1989; c: Miranda [Molly], b. 1979).

GINA BIANCAROSA

June M. Jordan

B. 9 July 1936, New York City
Wrote under: June Meyer
D. of Mildred Maude (Fisher) and Granville Ivanhoe Jordan; m. Michael Meyer,
  1955, div. 1965; c.: Christopher David Meyer

Born in Harlem, of Jamaican parents, J. began writing at the age of seven. Demonstrating her belief that "language is power," she has published six volumes of poetry, an equal number of books for younger readers, three collections of political essays, two novels (for young adults), several plays, and numerous articles and columns for various journals and periodicals.

Educated at Barnard College and the University of Chicago, J. was the recipient of Rockefeller Foundation grants in creative writing in 1969 and 1970. In 1970, she also received the Prix de Rome in environmental design for a project originating, in part, from a plan for the architectural redesign of Harlem—a collaboration with Buckminster Fuller for *Esquire* magazine. The other impetus for the prize was her novel, *His Own Where* (1971), a work written entirely in African American vernacular speech or "Black English." The projects for J.'s year in Rome included the adaptation of the novel into a film scenario and a study of alternative urban designs for the promotion of flexible and pacific communal street life. J. has also held a Poetry Fellowship from the National Endowment for the Arts (1982).

J.'s poetry reflects her diligent attention to the works of poets she has read and admired from Shelley and Whitman to Langston Hughes, Robert Hayden, and Imari Baraka, to **Adrienne Rich** and **Audre Lorde.**

It reflects a writer who defines her role as both personal and communal. She is, as she has written and stated often, "one Black woman poet."

J.'s choice of language has been a source of praise and criticism. Her use of "Black English" caused many attempts to ban *His Own Where* from various schools and libraries. J.'s eloquent defense of a "verbally bonding system" of language provides valuable critical insights—both cultural and linguistic. Her poetic voice is both lyrical and exhortatory: it proclaims and laments, sounds battle cries and alarms, sings and shouts. As an essayist, focusing primarily on political topics, she demands also to be read aloud. Her works demonstrate an acute awareness of the sounds and rhythms of the language.

J. is also a teacher. She has conducted workshops for young writers and taught at Sarah Lawrence College, City College of New York, Yale, and the State University of New York at Stony Brook before joining the English faculty at the University of California at Berkeley. She articulates in her poetry and essays an aesthetic and an ethics that encompass a worldview to which "nothing is alien." This stance allows her a range of subjects and a choice of languages that is expansive. In her singularity, "one Black woman poet," she achieves the universal.

OTHER WORKS: *Who Look at Me* (1969). *Soul Script: Afro-American Poetry* (editor, 1970). *The Voices of the Children* (coeditor, 1970). *Some Changes* (1971). *Dry Victories* (1972). *Fannie Lou Hamer* (1972). *New Days: Poems of Exile and Return* (1973). *New Room, New Life* (1975). *Things That I Do in the Dark: Selected Poetry* (1977). *Passion: New Poems, 1970–1980* (1980). *Kimako's Story* (1981). *Civil Wars* (1981). *Living Room: New Poems, 1980–1984* (1985). *On Call: New Political Essays, 1981–1985* (1985). *Naming Our Destiny: New and Selected Poems* (1989). *Moving Towards Home* (1989). *Technical Difficulties: African-American Notes on the State of the Union* (1992). "The Difficult Miracle of Black Poetry in America," *Massachusetts Rev.* 27 (Summer 1986). J.'s papers are at the Schlesinger Library, Radcliffe College.

BIBLIOGRAPHY: *In the Memory and Spirit of Frances, Zora, and Lorraine: Essays and Interviews on Black Women and Writing*, Juliette Bowles, ed. (1979). Davenport, Doris, "Four Contemporary Black Women Poets: Lucille Clifton, June Jordan, Audre Lorde, and Sherley Ann Williams," unpublished Ph.D. diss., Univ. of Southern California, 1985; *DAI* 47:7 (Jan. 1987). Reference works: *CANR* 25 (1989). *CLC* 5 (1976), 11 (1979), 23 (1983). *CLR* 10 (1986). *DLB* 38 (1985).

Other References: *Callaloo* 9:1 (Winter 1986). *Feminist Rev.* 31 (Spring 1989). *High Plains Literary Rev.* 3:2 (Fall 1988).

FAHAMISHA PATRICIA BROWN

Pauline Kael

See AWW 2, 431–32

"It is unlikely that anyone in the world has reviewed more movies than Pauline Kael," William Shawn noted. "The quintessential movie lover" retired in 1991 at the age of seventy-one after a long and distinguished career. K.'s announcement that she would be leaving *The New Yorker* after twenty-four years as its film critic was a shock to the movie industry.

K. raised expectations for criticism as well as moviemaking. She was the primary advocate of the "cinematic pleasure principle," as she called it, and she truly believed that moviegoers should not settle for mediocrity. Her reviews bashed the Hollywood "cloning process" where filmmakers try to sell the same film over and over again under a different title.

In the 1970s, many films had risen to K.'s heightened expectations of them. She praised bright young innovators such as Martin Scorsese and Francis Ford Coppola in her book of collected reviews, *When the Lights Go Down* (1980), as "directors who weren't afraid to excite your senses." If the seventies proved that someone was listening to K., the 1980s seemed to prove that no one was listening but everyone was making money.

K.'s reviews during the 1980s responded to the film standards of the decade. She criticized Hollywood for trying no bold undertakings, instead producing only cheap imitations of old clichés with overexposed actors regurgitating mass-produced messages. Four books assembling her 1980s reviews reflect her disgust, while noting the occasional successes. *Taking It All In* (1984) and *State of the Art* (1985) cover the early 1980s. *Hooked* (1989) includes reviews from 1985 to 1988, a period that occasioned some of her most congratulatory comments. In the author's note, she comments that the films "began rather lamely, and then suddenly there's one marvelous movie after another," citing as examples *Blue Velvet* and *Unbearable Lightness of Being*. *Movie Love* (1991), incorporating her reviews from the late 1980s to her retirement, contains only a few complimentary reviews and many examples of her distaste for the films of the eighties. Although she was criticized for overbashing the popular film about Native Americans, *Dances with Wolves*, her response to it is a good example of her attractive irreverence and intolerance for films made simply to be "do-gooders."

Although many viewers have disagreed with K.'s opinions, her reviews have had an important impact on the way movies are viewed. She has forced moviegoers to react instead of merely to watch. K.'s contributions to the movie industry will continue to affect both moviemakers and moviegoers.

OTHER WORKS: *5001 Nights at the Movies* (1991).

BIBLIOGRAPHY: *Amer. Scholar* 58 (Winter 1989). *Boston Globe* (8 Sept. 1991). *Kaleidoscope* 19 (interview, April 1989). *Mirabella* (interview, August 1992). *Newsweek* (18 March 1991).

SARAH E. MASON

Adrienne Kennedy

B. 13 Sept. 1931, Pittsburgh, Pennsylvania
D. of Etta (Haugabook) and Cornell Wallace Hawking; m. Joseph C. Kennedy, 1953, div. 1966; c.: Joseph, b. 1954; Adam, b. 1961

K. had a middle-class upbringing in Cleveland, Ohio, and what she has described as an excellent public school education. After high school (Glenville, 1949) she went to Ohio State University, where she briefly studied social work (her father's profession) before majoring in elementary education (her mother's). A few weeks before graduation (1953) she married, eventually moving with her husband and child to New York City. There she studied writing at Columbia University (1954–56), the New School for Social Research, the American Theatre Wing, and Circle in the Square (1962), where she was a member of playwright Edward Albee's workshop and saw her first play performed, *Funnyhouse of a Negro*. This play won an Off-Broadway Obie Award in 1964; she followed it with *The Owl Answers* (1965), her favorite among her works. By this time she had developed her own intense one-act style, among whose literary influences she credits, besides Albee, Tennessee Williams and Federico García Lorca.

Since the 1970s K. has taught at universities around the country, among them Yale, Princeton, Brown, Berkeley, Rutgers, and Harvard. She has been on the PEN board of directors, and was a founding member of the Women's Theatre Council (established 1972). K. has been commissioned to write for, among others, the Juilliard School of Music, the Royal Court Theatre in London, the New York Shakespeare Festival, the Alvin Ailey Dance Company, and the Empire State Youth Theatre Institute. Her many awards include Rockefeller (1967–69, 1973) and National Endowment for the Arts (1973) grants, a Guggenheim Fellowship (1967), and a Yale Fellowship (1973). In March 1992 K.'s work was celebrated in a month-long Adrienne Kennedy Festival organized by the Great Lakes Theatre Festival in her hometown of Cleveland.

Her work has been described as gothic, expressionist, and surrealist, but K.'s writings are also, as her interviews and autobiographical writings demonstrate, personal and introspective. It is difficult to keep the writer and her writing separate; and the absence of boundaries for establishing separate identities is a common theme and tactic in her work. Movie stars, dreams, her mother's scrapbooks, political figures, paintings, music, and statues are as alive in her writing as her own memories of childhood, her own rooms, her neighborhood. Commenting on the Wolf Man in her *People Who Led to My Plays* (1987), she writes, "Soon the characters in my plays and stories would be changing personae at an alarming rate." The strange, blinding vividness of her stage images—animals, people who turn into animals, people with smashed heads, people with worms in their hair, exploding body parts, blood pouring out of a fractured moon—images of violent brilliance unleash the possibilities of imaginative juxtapositions on the stage, the complex beauty and horror of dreams, the power of memory, and the transforming magic of the movies, theater, art, beauty, and fame.

K.'s later plays seem more directly concerned with the filmic properties of her work. In *A Movie Star Has to Star in Black and White* (1976) a black woman named Clara is partly spoken for by the female stars of classic Hollywood movies. In *An Evening with Dead Essex* (1973) a group of performers rehearses a production based on Mark Essex's life and death, using music and photographs exhibited by a projectionist—the only white character in the play, and the only one dressed in black.

K.'s insistence on images of black on white, and her blazing use of color, are "typical" in more ways than one: race is both visual and felt in her work as the image and the tone of identity and conflict, which she suggests are complementary impulses. Her adaptations from Euripides, *Electra* and *Orestes* (1980), like her "Theatre Mystery" *Deadly Triplets* (1990), dramatize these tensions in somewhat more linear works about family loyalty and sibling rivalry. In *The Alexander Plays* (1992), K.'s alter ego from *Deadly Triplets*, "Suzanne Sand . . . playwright," seems to reappear as "Suzanne Alexander, a Writer." These plays continue her exploration of narrative, while also experimenting with sound in their use of radio, offstage noise, and music. *The Film Club* is a monologue by Suzanne, and *The Dramatic Circle* is a radio play. Meanwhile, the mise-en-scène in *She Talks to Beethoven* and *The Ohio State Murders* is less violent than in K.'s early work, and the narrator, Suzanne, seems more in control of the events she remembered. K.'s American Eurocentric influences—from Charlotte Brontë to Bette Davis—were released into her plays, interestingly, after she visited Africa in 1960. There she "discovered the place of my ancestors," bought an African mask, "a woman with a bird flying through her forehead," listened to the owls at night and was afraid, and thought about herself as a separate person: "The solitude under the African sun had brought out a darkness in me. I wanted to be more separate." This journey was a turning point in her writing and its influences are clear in the works that followed.

OTHER WORKS: *Cities in Bezique* (1969). *The Lennon Play: In His Own Write* (1969, with John Lennon and Victor Spinetti). "A Growth of Images," *Drama Rev.* 21:4 (1977). *Adrienne Kennedy in One Act* (1988). "Becoming a Playwright," *American Theatre* (Feb. 1988). Plays by Kennedy are included in: *Poet Lore* (1965). *Collision Course* (1968). *New American Plays* (1968). *New Black Playwrights* (1968). *Best Short Plays of 1970*. *Black Drama: An Anthology* (1970). *Black Theater* (1971). *Scripts One* (1971). *More Plays from Off-Off-Broadway* (1972). *Broadway Book* (1972). *Spontaneous Combustion* (1972). *Kintu Drama* (1974). *Woman as Writer* (1978). *Wordplay Three* (1984).

BIBLIOGRAPHY: Reference works: *Black Writers* (1989). *CA* 103 (1982). *CANR* 26 (1989). *Contemp. Dramatists* (4th ed. 1988). *Dict. of the Black Theatre* (1983). *DLB* 38 (1985). *Notable Women in the Amer. Theatre* (1989). *Women in Amer. Theatre* (1981).

Other references: *Amer. Lit.* 63:3 (Sept. 1991). *College Lang. Assoc. J.* 20 (1976). *MELUS* 12:3 (Fall 1985). *Modern Drama* 27:4 (Dec. 1985); 28:1 (March 1986); 32:1 (March 1989). *Negro Amer. Lit. Forum* 9 (1975). *NYT* (reviews of first productions: 14 Jan., 20 June, 9 July, 14 July 1964; 13 Jan., 19 Jan., 1 Nov. 1969; 11 March 1976; 21 May 1980; 20 Sept.1985). *Studies in Amer. Drama, 1945–Present* 4 (1989). *Studies in Black Lit.* 6:11 (1975). *Theatre J.* 44:1 (March 1992). *Theatre Southwest* (April 1989).

ANNE FLECHE

Jamaica Kincaid

B. Elaine Potter Richardson, 25 May 1949, St. John's, Antigua
D. of Annie Richardson; m. Allen Shawn, 1979; c.: Annie, Harold

Until she was sixteen, K. spent her life on the nine-by-twelve-mile island of Antigua. Her father was a carpenter; her mother ran the household and became the dominant figure in K.'s childhood. K. excelled in her government schools and was an avid reader and library user. However, she felt stifled and isolated on her small island, and at sixteen she left for New York City as an au pair. Realizing she would need a high school diploma, she obtained one in New York and subsequently attended Franconia College for one year. She then moved back to New York City and began writing. With the publication of her first story in 1973, she changed her name to Jamaica Kincaid.

In the mid-1970s K. became a staff writer for *The New Yorker*, where editor William Shawn provided immense help and support. Ten of the stories she wrote for the magazine became her first book, *At the Bottom of the River* (1983). K. married Shawn's son Allen and in 1985 the couple moved to North Bennington, Vermont. They have two children, and K. divides her life between her family, writing at home, and giving lectures and readings.

K.'s books closely reflect her island culture and experience, and are a blend of fiction and autobiography. Her fictional style has progressed from the dreamlike images in her early stories to a more linear narrative form in the novels *Annie John* (1985) and *Lucy* (1990). Her voice, however, remains uniquely lyrical and exotic. Often her sentences repeat phrases in musiclike cadences, lulling the reader into K.'s very special poetic rhythms. Critics have heard in her work the voices of Caribbean folktales.

At the Bottom of the River begins with her most frequently anthologized story, "The Girl," a one-page sentence of combative dialogue between mother and daughter. This love-hate relationship continues in others of these stories and throughout K.'s work. Fantastic folklike images appear and disappear: a mother becomes a lizard, yet she also makes her daughter a mat from her own hair. The book is both a child's nightmare and a vision of bliss and innocence. As in all of K.'s writing the sense of place and the rhythms and colors of the Caribbean are powerful.

Annie John, a penetrating look at a perceptive and vulnerable adolescent's world, recollects similar childhood images and themes, but it is written in a simpler, more narrative style. The intimacy ten-year-old Annie feels with her mother evolves into anger and fear as Annie is told by her mother that she can no longer be "a little me." She rebels, trying on new "forbidden" relationships, deciding finally to depart from her island home. The end of the novel finds her on a boat headed north.

Antigua is seen from a different, and far more bitter perspective in *A Small Place* (1988), K.'s only book of nonfiction. The reader is a tourist, the "you" of the essay who plucks the beauty of the island, yet remains blind to the reality of its poverty and foreign domination. K. describes Antigua as a "prison of beauty" where, despite the end of slavery and the departure of the English "criminals," political corruption persists. She sees little hope for positive change.

K.'s anger continues to ferment in her second novel, *Lucy* (1990), told through the eyes of a young woman newly arrived from "an island" and now an au pair to four blond sisters. Lucy's penetrating observations of the family's white world relentlessly uncover their mirages and self-deception. She sees the family's white culture as domineering, both within their home and as far-reaching as the domination of her own island, and suffers as she discovers that she is just as detached from this family as she was from her own. Lucy remains critical and separate. Her mother's letters are unopened, and even after her father's death, she chooses to stay away from her mother. At novel's end, she begins to write.

K.'s career has developed and expanded into new forms, including an adaptation of a Chekhov short story for public television. She has also written for the newly revamped journal *Transitions* and continues to publish frequently in *The New Yorker*.

BIBLIOGRAPHY: Perry, Donna, "An Interview with Jamaica Kincaid," in *Reading Black, Reading Feminist*, Henry Louis Gates, Jr., ed. (1990). Reference works: *CA* 125 (1989). *CLC* 43 (1987), 68 (1991). *Contemp. Novelists* (1986). *CB* (March 1991). *FC* (1990).

Other references: *Bennington Banner* (27 April 1991). *Commonweal* (4 Nov. 1988). *Nation* (18 Feb. 1991). *NYT* (7 Oct. 1990). *WRB* (Nov. 1985).

SUSAN SWAN

Barbara Kingsolver

B. 8 April 1955, Annapolis, Maryland
D. of Virginia (Henry) and Wendell R. Kingsolver; m. Joseph Hoffman, 1985, div. 1993; c: Camille, b. 1987

K., then working as a journalist, drove into the mining town of Clifton, Arizona, in 1983 to cover the strike against the Phelps Dodge Copper Corporation. Her book, *Holding the Line: Women in the Great Arizona Mine Strike of 1983* (1989), was K.'s tribute to the women who kept the strike alive. It was also her introduction to the way politics work for women— down and dirty.

Born in Maryland, K. grew up in eastern Kentucky and subsequently moved to Arizona. She graduated from DePauw University (B.A., 1977) and later completed a master's degree in biology at the University of Arizona. Her work as a journalist and political rights activist has been the source of many of the themes of her poetry and fiction, but her central concern in all of her writing is the way women relate to the world.

The twelve stories of *Homeland and Other Stories* (1989) depict enduring women who seek to reconcile their quest for individual fulfillment with their sense of responsibility to the community. Their progress is often thwarted by political, social, or economic circumstances. Magda of "Island on the Moon" is a woman who would have been an artist "if her life had been better." Instead, she "just has to ooze out a little bit of art in everything she does."

K.'s three novels focus on women seeking their place in community while developing a sense of self. In her first, *Bean Trees* (1988), protagonist Taylor Greer flees rural Kentucky and entrapment in what happens to all her friends—pregnancy. Her odyssey includes finding a Cherokee baby, whom she names Turtle, in her car. They settle in Tucson, finding a place in the Jesus Is Lord Used Tire Shop, whose proprietor offers sanctuary to Central American refugees. In that world, Taylor and Turtle find their own sanctuary and become a family.

In *Pigs in Heaven* (1993), the sequel to *Bean Trees*, the community Taylor and Turtle have forged is under threat. Annawake Fourkiller, a Cherokee lawyer dedicated to returning Indian children to the custody of the tribe, starts proceedings to gain custody of Turtle. The struggle for the child sends Taylor on another odyssey to escape her responsibility to Turtle's people. Finally, she returns to the reservation and finds that, because of a Cherokee great-grandmother, it is also her tribe.

Animal Dreams (1990) combines the personal quest for identity with the larger quest for human rights. Codi Noline, a medical doctor turned high school teacher, returns to Grace, Arizona, to understand her family's past. Her sister, Hallie, chooses commitment to the politics of the future and goes to Nicaragua while Codi retreats into herself to try to understand her place in the cosmos of Grace.

The balance of the personal and the political is a hallmark of K.'s fiction and has parallels in her poetry. *Another America* (1992), a dual-language text with Spanish translations by Rebeca Cartes, captures women's entry into the arena of politics, violence, and survival. K.'s poems chronicle the struggle for community that keeps women strong.

Throughout her work, K. seeks a dialogue among women of the many cultures of the United States—Native American, Latino, Anglo—as they encounter each other and find ways to establish community in difference. Among these women is the Cherokee great-grandmother who appears again and again in K.'s work and who, like the Great Mother, watches the unfolding history of all her children.

BIBLIOGRAPHY: Reference works: *CA* 129 (1989). *CLC* 55 (1992). Other references: *Ms.* 16:10 (April 1988). *NYTBR* (10 April 1988; 5 June 1988; 11

June 1989; 7 Jan. 1990; 2 Sept. 1990; 28 July 1991). *Time* (24 Sept. 1990). *WRB* 5:8 (May 1988).

MARY A. McCAY

Maxine Hong Kingston

See AWW 2, 461–62

Since the publication of *The Woman Warrior* (1976), K. has become one of the most critically praised and best-known contemporary writers in the United States and by far the most studied Asian-American writer. Devoting herself wholly to her writing since the late 1970s, she won the 1981 nonfiction American Book Award for her narrative *China Men* and the American Academy and Institute of Art and Letters Award for literature in 1990.

A series of biographical/autobiographical narrations, *China Men* recounts the encounters of several generations of K.'s male ancestors with the United States and graphically examines the difficult questions of race, ethnicity, and nationality in America. These men often work in menial or marginal jobs—as a farmworker clearing land in Hawaii, as a laborer building the transcontinental railroad, as the owner of a small laundry. Yet these jobs are often at the foundation of the communities in which these men and their families live. The men whose stories are told remain outside "mainstream" United States society in many respects, victims of virulent racist discrimination, culturally enforced silence, and violence. Their identification as "Chinese" is also called into question, however: one uncle, deranged by dreams of the United States and the Communist Revolution in China, goes there, to a "home" that he may never have previously seen, and disappears; the narrator's father is cheated by his Chinese partners in a laundry. As in K.'s earlier work, dreams of China and American dreams collide with American racial constructions and the actual conditions of immigrant life in the United States, producing an unstable story of hope, disappointment, and disquiet in which neither side of the hyphen in "Chinese-American" can be either erased or made to remain fixed.

K.'s first novel, *Tripmaster Monkey: His Fake Book* (1989), also deals with the unstable and inescapable categories of race and nationality in the United States. The protagonist of the novel, Wittman Ah Sing, is a fifth-generation Chinese-American living in San Francisco's Chinatown during the 1960s. He can speak, though not read much Chinese, as well as recognize and speak a number of Chinese-American vernaculars produced by various Chinese encounters with American English in the "Chinatowns" of the United States. He is also familiar with Chinese folklore and traditional culture. At the same time Wittman (named for Walt Whitman) is a poet, storyteller, and graduate in English at the University of California at Berkeley, familiar with both the "high" literary culture of Rilke and Joyce and the counterculture that seems on the cusp of the transformation from the period of the Beats, especially Jack Kerouac, to the hippies. He is also saturated and obsessed with American popular culture, particularly the images of Asians and Asian-Americans promoted in such movies as *Flower Drum Song* and *The World of Suzie Wong*. The son of Chinese-American vaudevilleans who traveled the country performing largely African American music, Wittman is at home, if not exactly comfortable, with theatrics, illusion, and ethnic types and stereotypes that can sometimes seem completely different and at other times strangely conflated. He frequently invokes and identifies with the trickster King of the Monkeys of Chinese folklore, which becomes an "American Monkey" by the end of the book.

K. has been criticized by some for promoting a fake exotic Asian-American image or for catering to "mainstream" tastes at the expense of ethnic authenticity. It is precisely the notion of "authenticity" that K. questions while she affirms the existence and significance of tradition and history. She is one of the premier interpreters of the fluctuating and persistent nature of those racial and ethnic categories in the United States that are impossible both to escape and to fix with any certainty.

OTHER WORKS: Hawaii One Summer (1987, originally published 1978). *Through the Black Curtain* (1987). "Cultural Mis-readings by American Reviewers," in *Asian and Western Writers in Dialogue*, ed. Guy Amirthanayagam (1982).

BIBLIOGRAPHY: Eakin, Paul John, *Fictions in Autobiography: Studies in Self-Invention* (1985). Frye, Joanne S., *"The Woman Warrior:* Claiming Narrative

Power, Recreating Female Selfhood," in *Faith of a (Woman) Writer*, Alice Kessler-Harris and William McBrian, eds. (1988). Lau, Joseph, "Kingston as Exorcist," in *Modern Chinese Women Writers: Critical Appraisals*, Michael S. Duke, ed. (1989). Ling, Amy, "Chinese-American Women Writers: The Tradition behind Maxine Hong Kingston," and Sledge, Linda Ching, "Oral Tradition in Kingston's *China Men*," in *Redefining American Literary History*, A. Lavonne Brown Ruoff and Jerry Ward, eds. (1990). Reference works: *CANR* 13 (1987). *FC* (1990). *Modern Amer. Women Writers* (1991).

Other references: *Amer. Lit. History* 2:3 (1990). *Biography* (Winter 1983, Spring 1986, Spring 1989). *MELUS* (Winter 1982, Winter 1983, Fall 1985, Spring 1987, Spring 1988). *Ms.* (June 1989). *Michigan Q. Rev.* 26:1 (1987). *PMLA* 103 (1988). *NYTBR* (23 April 1989). *Village Voice Lit. Supp.* 74 (May 1989).

JAMES SMETHURST

Carolyn Kizer

B. 10 Dec. 1925, Spokane, Washington
D. of Mabel (Ashley) and Benjamin Hamilton Kizer; m. Charles Stimson Bullitt, 1948, div. 1954; m. John Marshall Woodbridge, 1975; c.: Ashley, Scot, Jill

In the second half of the twentieth century, K. emerges as one of a powerful group of women poets for whom motherhood is a crucial aspect of identity. These women, **Adrienne Rich, Denise Levertov, Audre Lorde, Anne Sexton,** and **Sylvia Plath,** among others, helped expand the range of metaphor and the depth of meaning for all poets and for all women. Not simply a feminist poet, not simply a gifted translator, not simply a committed internationalist, K. has an inclusive generous intellect that offers a strong stand against the petty visions attributed to "women" poets of the past.

Born when her politically active biologist mother was in her forties and her distinguished planner-lawyer father fifty, K. flourished on the attentions afforded an only child with extraordinary parents. Her father introduced her to a parade of accomplished friends such as Lewis Mumford, Percy Grainger, and Vachel Lindsay, and her mother gave up her own work to encourage her daughter's talents. When K. later garnered much praise for her "interpretations" of Chinese poetry, she remarked that her mother (credited in *Yin: New Poems* [1984] as her Muse) had read Arthur Waley's translations to her when she was as young as eight. High-minded and intense, K. missed other children, but her childhood and her remarkably individual education suggest the freedom available to many important creative personalities. Living in the Western United States may also have contributed to the sense of possibility essential to becoming a writer. In a valuable brief autobiography K. captures the bravery and the variety of her ancestors' achievements as they struggled toward the far edge of the continent. Similar pride might have also inspired her first public success: a patriotic poem published in the *Ladies' Home Journal* and set to music for radio when she was just fifteen.

Looking for a college far from home that would match the seriousness and eccentricity of her upbringing, K. settled on Sarah Lawrence, a school that challenged her self-image but also provided encouragement for her writing. When *The New Yorker* published one of her poems, the seventeen-year-old author received over five hundred letters—public endorsement for an unsure commitment. Going on to Columbia University after graduation to study comparative literature on a Chinese Cultural Fellowship, K. subsequently continued her studies in China. But her poetic inspiration remained more imaginative than linguistic. Waley's translations suggested the imitations included in her second collection of poems, *Knock upon Silence* (1965). Praising her sensitivity to the spirit of the Chinese poems, critics admired her ability to include many perspectives in her work. Comparisons with Waley suggest entirely new dimensions of psychological insight.

It was, K. said, her study of craft with Theodore Roethke at the University of Washington in the early 1950s that finally turned her into a self-assured poet. *The Ungrateful Garden* (1961), her first volume, was a polished offering reflective of the highly valued stress on workmanship that characterized the earlier decade. Poems like "The Great Blue Heron" and "The Death of a Public Servant" hold up as elegantly crafted artifacts. Perhaps reacting to Roethke's mocking hostility to women poets as much as she admired his teaching techniques, K. also began to record the range of women's sensibilities finally included in her assembled poems for women, *Mermaids in the Basement* (1984). But the idea that women writers were the custodians of the world's best-kept secret, "merely the private lives of one-half of humanity," has always been with her. A proto-feminist, as were many of her gifted contemporaries (women poets trained by men), she early saw beyond the college English Department into life. With the "Pro Femina" sequence in *Mermaids* she distinguished herself as a pioneer in forging new traditions in American women's writing.

The roles K. has played as poet are various and international. In 1959, she became an editor and founder of *Poetry Northwest*, which she served until 1965. She acted as cultural ambassador to Pakistan in 1964–65 and continued a life of public service as the first director of Literary Programs for the National Endowment of the Arts, where good sense distinguished her choices. During these years she managed to raise three children who make their presence felt in a number of moving poems. And she has continued to share her knowledge of poetry as a teacher: from North Carolina to Ohio to Iowa to Stanford to Arizona and Princeton, young writers have profited from her critical advice. Fellow professionals have appreciated her talents enough to award her a Pulitzer Prize in 1985 and a Robert Frost medal in 1988.

What we continue to value most highly in K.'s work is her deep sense of engagement with life on every level, personal, political, and aesthetic, an involvement that makes all readers more human by sharpening our awareness of the possibilities in every kind of experience.

OTHER WORKS: Midnight Was My Cry (1971). *The Nearness of You* (1986). *Carrying Over, Translations from the Chinese, Urdu, Macedonian, Yiddish, and French African* (1989). *The Shattered Mirror: Poems from the Chinese Democracy Movement* (1991). *The Essential John Clare* (editor, 1992).

BIBLIOGRAPHY: An Answering Music: On the Poetry of Carolyn Kizer, David Rigsbee, ed. (1990): includes references to all other published written work as well as criticism, interviews, reviews, and available tapes. Reference works: *CAAS* 5 (1987). *CA* 65–68 (1977). *CANR* 24 (1988). *CLC* 15 (1980), 39 (1986). *DLB* 5 (1980). *FC* (1990).

EUGENIA KALEDIN

Elisabeth Kübler-Ross

See AWW 2, 488–89

Although she does not administer medication or perform surgery, few people have K.-R.'s power to heal. *On Death and Dying* (1969), K.'s groundbreaking book, and her subsequent lectures, writings, and workshops, have helped, as Anne Hudson Jones noted, to revolutionize "the way Americans think about death and dying, and consequently, about living as well."

K.'s early experiences in war-torn Europe and her work with terminally ill patients at the University of Chicago led her to write *On Death and Dying*. Since then, K. has established many retreats worldwide where she holds her Life, Death, and Transition Workshops. In these intense and intimate five-day gatherings, participants attempt to cope with the traumas of death and dying. In *Working It Through* (1982), K.'s second collaboration with photographer Mal Warshaw, she briefly recounts the history behind these retreats (known as Shanti Nilaya, Sanskrit for "home of peace") and then describes the workshops, integrating photographs and letters from former participants.

In *AIDS: The Ultimate Challenge* (1987) K. recounts her ongoing efforts to help AIDS patients accept their condition with strength and serenity. She believes that AIDS presents "the ultimate challenge" because the stigma attached to the disease has been as devastating as the disease itself. In one fascinating section, K. reprints a transcript of a town meeting held to discuss the founding of a hospice for babies with AIDS; she encounters hostile resistance from town members, whose concerns and prejudices reflect the fear and uncertainty shared by many across the country. Contrasting society's support for victims of "acceptable" illnesses such as cancer to the isolation and condemnation faced by AIDS sufferers, K. addresses her book to those who would still deny or ignore the tragedy of AIDS and withhold compassion from its sufferers.

OTHER WORKS: *Living with Death and Dying* (1981). *Remember the Secret* (1982). *On Children and Death* (1983). *Psychoimmunity and the Healing Process: A Holistic Approach to Immunity and AIDS* (1987). *On Life after Death* (1991).

BIBLIOGRAPHY: Reference works: *Biog. Directory of the Amer. Psychiatric Assoc.*, A. Gammons et al., eds. (1991).

Other references: *Book World* (17 Oct. 1982). *New Statesman* (9 July 1982). *NYTBR* (10 April 1988). *Psychology Today* (Oct. 1982).

JEROME CHOU

Maxime Kumin

See AWW 2, 490–92

K.'s considerable output attests to the power of nature and mortality as literary subjects. Between 1961 and 1978, she published six books of poetry, four novels, and many children's books, as well as making regular contributions—essays, poetry, and fiction—to a number of journals. Focusing primarily on country living and farming, she derives many of her subjects from her own experience of living on a farm in New Hampshire. The critics and the public alike showed their appreciation of her contributions: in 1976 she received the Borestone Mountain Award for best poems, and she was awarded the Pulitzer Prize for poetry in 1973 for *Up Country: Poems of New England* (1972). During the same period she was the recipient of two honorary doctorates of humanities, and contributed her time and talent to such institutions as Washington University, the University of Massachusetts, Columbia, Princeton, and Brandeis universities, and the Breadloaf Writers' Conference.

K.'s work remains impressive. The well-received *Retrieval System* (1978) was followed by *To Make a Prairie: Essays on Poets, Poetry, and Country Living* (1979), five books of poems, and a book of stories, *Why Can't We Live Together like Civilized Human Beings?* (1982). Although K.'s work makes much of the positive coexistence with nature, these works pursue another common theme: "loss" and "relinquishment," especially as experienced in intimate relationships such as family. K. communicates these themes by juxtaposing scrupulous attention to the detail of everyday life with transcendent communion with the natural world.

While K. amuses readers with characterizations of her neighbors in New Hampshire in *Our Ground Time Here Will Be Brief* (1982), the willfulness, almost maliciousness of nature that seems not to care for connections, familial or neighborly, is a powerful presence. Henry Manley, a recurring character in K.'s poems, provides a way of exploring both sides: the little foibles of day-to-day existence and the large specter of mortality that looms over everyone. Paradoxically, nature allows for continuation and extinction at the same time, and K. is determined readers will understand both.

In her ninth book of poems, *The Long Approach* (1985), K. not only continues with the subject of farm living, but also takes on social issues such as pollution, religious persecution, nuclear holocaust, and famine. These poems mark somewhat of a turning point in K.'s career in that her essentially personal, intimate voice transforms into one that is more public and critical. The critics were quick to notice this alteration, and not all of them were pleased. Although K.'s appraisal of these issues was sometimes perceived as underdeveloped, the growth into new areas of expression was welcome from a poet who had brought such understanding to the paradoxes of nature.

K. continued to mix the personal with the globally relevant in *Nurture* (1989). The intimate voice recurs in such autobiographical poems as "Marianne, My Mother, and Me." But she further develops the socioecological voice that expresses concern over pollution and consequent extinction. K. understands animals' perceived cruelty to each other; conflict inherent in survival is one of the foundations of nature. But the argument for survival does not extend to humanity's abuse and neglect of animals.

This concern for animals and their relationship with human beings is also important in *Looking for Luck: Poems* (1992). But animals do not take center stage in this collection; K. is equally interested in the universalities of her own personal relationships, with her daughter who has departed to another country and with fellow writers **Flannery O'Connor** and her close friend **Anne Sexton.** K.'s relationships with family, friends, and nature are the settings for a deeper consideration of nature and mortality.

K.'s productivity has not been confined to poetry. She continues to write essays, specifically *In Deep: Country Essays* (1987), and children's books, such as *The Microscope* (1984). An accomplished horsewoman, she makes regular contributions to equestrian journals. Her essays and columns also encompass such topics as organic gardening. She has continued to teach, at New England College, Claremont Graduate School, and the University of New Hampshire. Among K.'s many honors are the American Academy and Institute of Arts and Letters Award (1980) and the Academy of American Poets Fellowship (1986).

BIBLIOGRAPHY: Reference works: *CANR* 1 (1981), 21 (1987). *CAAS* 8 (1989). *CLC* 5 (1976), 13 (1980), 28 (1984). *DLB* 5 (1980). *Maj Twent Cent Wr* (1991). *Modern AmerWomen Writers* (1991).
    Other references: *America* (18 Nov. 1989). *Belles Lettres* 8 (Fall 1992). *Commonweal* (29 Nov. 1985). *Hudson Rev.* (Winter 1982–83). *LJ* (1 March 1989). *Nation* (24 July 1982). *NYTBR* (8 Aug. 1982; 5 Nov. 1989; 21 March 1993). *Virginia Q. Rev.* 67 (Summer 1991). *WRB* 9 (May 1992). *Yankee* (Dec. 1987).

LINDA BERUBE

Ursula K. Le Guin

See AWW 2, 546–47

L. is a prominent writer of fantasy and science fiction, publishing short stories, novels, and novellas in these genres. She also writes essays, poems, and "realistic" stories of invented countries.

The Beginning Place (1980) is a mixture of realism and fantasy that made some critics feel that L. was joining the mainstream. The fantasy element consists of fantasies in the psychological sense, rather than the construction of an alternate reality. *The Compass Rose* (1982) is a collection of short stories similar to those in *The Wind's Twelve Quarters* (1975), except that the sad stories are sadder and the funny stories are funnier and more inventive. The concluding story, "Sur," describes a team of women conducting a successful expedition to the South Pole but keeping it a secret so as not to embarrass the men.

The gentle, humorous feminism that characterizes this story reappears in *Always Coming Home* (1985), an account of a matrilineal society that may exist in the Napa Valley some time in the future. The girls and women who tell their stories are gentle, persevering, and close to the earth. One goes briefly to live in the patriarchal society of her father, but returns gladly to the valley. In great part a tribute to the traditional lifestyle of the Native people of California, *Always Coming Home* bears the imprint of L.'s anthropologist father. A combination of poetry and music with narrative and illustrations, the book received an American Book Award nomination.

L.'s earlier books, the young-adult Earthsea trilogy (1968, 1971, 1972), *The Left Hand of Darkness* (1969), and *The Dispossessed* (1974), continue to receive considerable critical attention. Some feminist critics saw *The Left Hand of Darkness* as a betrayal of their cause. L. takes her critics seriously enough to be affected by this, and she has moved gradually to a rather more militant stance. Her views on magic and politics have aroused less controversy.

Buffalo Gals and Other Animal Presences (1987) is another collection of stories. The first story, "Buffalo Gals, Won't You Come Out Tonight," reflects the belief of the Native American people that the first people in the world had animal shapes and great wisdom and intelligence. It won the Hugo Award for the best novelette in 1988.

Tehanu: The Last Book of Earthsea (1990) is quite strongly feminist. The wizard Ged, having lost his magic in his last, great deed, is miserable and humiliated. His old friend Tenar, who had opted for the life of an ordinary woman years before, comforts him. But it is her adopted child, mysteriously both a dragon and a little girl, who saves both of them from their enemies. L. depicts women as having a strength of their own, different from that of men, on which men have to rely when their own strength fails them.

OTHER WORKS: *The Eye of the Heron* (1978, also in *Millennial Women*, ed. V. Kidd). *Leese Webster* (1979). *The Language of the Night* (1979). *Malafrena* (1979). *Edges: Thirteen New Tales from the Borderlands of the Imagination* (ed., with V. Kidd, 1980). *Interfaces* (ed., with V. Kidd, 1980). *Hard Words and Other Poems* (1981). *Solomon Leviathan's Nine Hundred and Thirty-first Trip around the World* (1983). *King Dog: A Screenplay* (1985). *Catwings* (1988). *A Visit from Dr. Katz* (1988). *Wild Oats and Fire Weed* (poems, 1988). *Fire and Stone* (1989). *Catwings Return* (1989). *Dancing at the Edge of the World: Thoughts on Words, Women, Places* (1989). *The Way of the Water's Going* (1989). *Searoad: Chronicles of Klatsand* (1991). *Fish Soup* (1992). *Nine Lives* (1992). *The Norton Book of Science*

Fiction (ed., with Brian Atteberry, 1993). Addition: "The Word for the World Is Forest," in *Again, Dangerous Visions*, H. Ellison, ed. (1972).

BIBLIOGRAPHY: Bittner, J. W., *Approaches to the Fiction of Ursula K. Le Guin* (1979, 1984). Bucknall, B. J., *Ursula K. Le Guin* (1981). *Ursula K. Le Guin: Voyager to Inner Lands and Outer Space*, J. De Bolt, ed. (1979). Lefanu, S., "Inner Space and the Outer Lands: Ursula K. Le Guin," in *Feminism and Science Fiction* (1988). *Ursula K. Le Guin*, J. D. Olander and M. H. Greenberg, eds. (1979). Selinger, B., *Le Guin and Identity in Contemporary Fiction* (1988). Reference works: *CANR* 32 (1991). *CLC* 8 (1978), 13 (1980), 22 (1982), 45 (1987). *DLB* 8 (1981), 52 (1986). *FC* (1990). *Maj Twent Cent Writers* (1991). *SATA* 4 (1973), 52 (1988).

Other references: *Extrapolation* (Fall 1980, Spring 1985, Summer 1987, Spring 1988). *Science-Fiction Studies* 7 (1980), 14 (1987).

BARBARA J. BUCKNALL

Madeleine L'Engle

See AWW 2, 548–50

Novelist, poet, playwright, autobiographer, and essayist, L. writes for both children and adults. Her novels for young people combine a good story with theological, scientific, and philosophical ideas. Her works for adults challenge and reward the reader's mind and spirit. The innovative fantasy *A Wrinkle in Time* (1962) continues to receive more attention than L.'s other children's books, but critics find later books more successful.

L.'s children's novels published since 1978 relate further adventures of the Austin, O'Keefe, and Murry families. In *A Ring of Endless Light* (1980) the Austin family gathers to be with the dying grandfather on an island in Maine, and Vicky, the young protagonist, learns to come to terms with death. Polly O'Keefe, in *A House like a Lotus* (1984), experiences an almost devastating homosexual advance but eventually is able to put it in perspective. The Murry twins return to the days of Noah in *Many Waters* (1986) and the O'Keefes to prehistoric times in *An Acceptable Time* (1989).

Two Part Invention (1988), the story of L.'s almost forty-five-year marriage to the actor Hugh Franklin, written after his death from cancer, chronicles the shared joys and difficulties of their marriage, as well as the silent communion that develops between two people who live together for many years. The book is a tribute both to the memory of her husband and to L.'s faith as a Christian.

In keeping with her passionate belief in the strength of the human spirit, L. has written the introductions to twenty-five volumes in a series called *Triumphs of the Spirit in Children's Literature*.

Critics are sometimes bothered by weakly drawn characters in L.'s works, overcrowded plots, and stories burdened by an excess of theological, scientific, and philosophical ideas. She is generally regarded, however, as an accomplished writer, admired for her virtuosity, her respect for the intelligence of young readers, her portrayal of caring families, her concern for individual dignity, and her insistence upon the redemptive power of love.

OTHER WORKS: *The Weather of the Heart* (1978). *Ladder of Angels* (1979). *Walking on Water* (1980). *The Anti-Muffins* (1981). *The Sphinx at Dawn* (1982). *A Severed Wasp (1982)*. *And It Was Good* (1983). *Dare to Be Creative* (1984). *Trailing Clouds of Glory* (1985, with Avery Brook). *A Stone for a Pillow* (1986). *Cry Like a Bell* (1987). *The Glorious Impossible* (1989). *Certain Women* (1992). *The Rock That Is Higher: Story as Truth* (1993).

BIBLIOGRAPHY: Reference works: *CANR* 21 (1987). *CLC* 12 (1980). *CLR* 14 (1988). *DLB* 52 (1986). *Maj Twent Cent Writers* (1991). *SATA* 27 (1982).

MARY E. FINGER

Gerda Lerner

See AWW 2, 555–57

L. is a prominent and influential scholar in the field of women's history. Since publication of the collection *The Female Experience: An American Documentary* (1977) her work in women's history has been essentially theoretical, redefining the discipline of history from a feminist perspective. While she has tirelessly worked to integrate women's experiences into the study of history, she also challenges traditional assumptions about the past and how it has been conceptualized. She continues to express her belief that "historical periodization" is inadequate for understanding women's past; by freeing women's lives from the rigid periodization defined by the experiences of men, she believes, a more complete picture of women's past may be found. *The Majority Finds Its Past: Placing Women in History* (1979), a collection of many of L.'s essays and addresses, demonstrates how her ideas about the discipline of history have changed and evolved.

L.'s controversial work, *The Creation of Patriarchy* (1986), is the first volume of a two-volume work, *Women and History*. In this important book, L. delves into prehistory to uncover the roots of patriarchial domination. Studying the cultures of the Sumerians, Babylonians, Hebrews, and Greeks, she uses historical, archaeological, artistic, and literary evidence to demonstrate that patriarchy is a cultural creation. This study provided an entirely new approach to understanding the position of women in world history. Though criticized by some historians for its selective use and interpretation of sources, it has led many to rethink traditional assumptions about the origins of patriarchy and to reevaluate women's place in the past.

In the final volume, *The Creation of Feminist Consciousness: From the Middle Ages to 1870* (1993), L. traces women's efforts to free themselves from patriarchal thought, discover their past, and achieve a feminist consciousness. In her exploration of the many ways women worked to achieve equality and autonomy, L.'s study of feminist criticism of biblical authorities is noteworthy. Most valuable is her discovery of the discontinuity of women's history, requiring each generation of women to rediscover its own past.

L. has asserted: "Women's History is indispensable and essential to the emancipation of women. . . . [It] changes their lives." To assist others in their efforts to bring women's history into the classroom, she wrote *Teaching Women's History* (1981). She has also created an extensive bibliography, *Women Are History: A Bibliography in the History of American Women* (1975; 4th revised edition, 1986), which is regularly updated and is a valuable resource for teachers of history.

L. has also fostered the development of undergraduate and graduate programs in the field of women's history. At Sarah Lawrence she was instrumental in creating one of the first graduate programs in the field and served both as the program's director (1972–76, 1978–79) and as educational director of summer institutes in women's history (1976, 1979). She also sponsored an oral history conference on the Midwestern Roots of the Modern Women's Movement at the University of Wisconsin-Madison (1992). In 1980, L. was appointed the Robinson-Edwards Professor of History at the University of Wisconsin-Madison; she was named senior distinguished research professor by the University of Wisconsin-Madison Alumni Research Foundation in 1984 and was granted emerita status by the university in 1991. Her election by her peers in the historical profession as president of the Organization of American Historians (1981–82) was an acknowledgment of both her work and the validity of women's history.

L. has been the recipient of several honorary degrees and numerous honors and awards. She was a scholar in residence at the Rockefeller Foundation Conference Center in Bellagio, Italy, in 1975, and has received fellowships from the National Endowment for the Humanities (1976), the Ford Foundation (1978–79), the Lilly Foundation (1979), and the Guggenheim Foundation (1980–81), and a grant from the Organization of American Historians (1980–83). She was also corecipient of a Department of Education-FIPSE grant for Promoting Black Women's History (1980–83). Sarah Lawrence College established the Gerda Lerner Scholarship Fund (1983) in her honor, and the American Association of University Women Educational Foundation granted her its Achievement Award (1986).

In addition to her activities in the historical profession, L. was a founding member of the National Organization for Women, and has served on the advisory board of the Elizabeth Cady Stanton Project and on the National Advisory Committee for Women, Education, and Culture Task

Force. She continues to be an important influence on a generation of students and scholars. Rewriting and reinterpreting the past to shape the future of history, L. has left her mark on the historical profession.

OTHER WORKS: A History of the Coordinating Committee on Women in the Historical Profession—Conference Group on Women's History (1989, with Hilda Smith and Nupur Chaudhuri). Important articles include "The Necessity of History and the Professional Historian," *J. Amer. Hist.* 69 (June 1982); "The Origin of Prostitution in Ancient Mesopotamia," *Signs* 11 (Winter 1986); "A View from the Women's Side," *J. Amer. History* 76 (Sept. 1989).

BIBLIOGRAPHY: Reference works: *CANR* 26 (1989).
    Other references: *J. Amer. Hist.* 70 (June 1983), 77 (Sept. 1990). *Ms.* (May 1986). *NYTBR* (17 Nov. 1985; 20 April 1986; 2 May 1993). *Signs* 13 (Summer 1988). *WRB* (Jan. 1987).

                                                    PAULA A. TRECKEL

Meridel Le Sueur

See AWW 2, 563–65

In her nineties, L. is still writing about the America that is often ignored or overlooked, and her message is as timely as when she started to write at age thirteen. Though she can no longer travel the country in her Volkswagen van or by Greyhound bus, she remains a significant interpreter of the heart of American life and a model for younger feminists.

Ripening (1982) is a collection of journalism, poetry, fiction, history, and autobiography spanning the years from 1927 to 1980. Represented is what Elaine Hedges describes as "fifty years of faithful and passionate witness to many of the central economic, political, and social realities of twentieth century American life." L.'s title is a metaphor for her belief in the continuum of her work and her sense of literary fulfillment. The volume contains such important earlier pieces as "Women on the Bread-lines" and "The Girl," and excerpts from *North Star Country* and from her personal journal.

Class-conscious writing blends together art and ideology in *I Hear Men Talking* (1984), three stories published originally in the thirties. Striking workers, natural disasters, and human nature are the themes of the stories, which have contemporary relevance as well as historical interest. L.'s short story "Jelly Roll" appeared in the anthology *Walt Whitman: The Measure of His Song* (1982). Whitman's poetry encouraged a young L. to write in spite of the fact that she would be blacklisted for her ideas. She also recalls Whitman's impact on Midwestern farmers and workers of the Great Depression.

Winter Prairie Woman (1990), written when L. turned ninety, is a six-part story of the end of a very old woman's life. She must leave the farm where she has lived all her life as it is falling apart around her. Instead of fearing or rejecting death, L.'s character, with a powerful resemblance to L. herself, goes toward it, welcoming it as a new start.

L. challenges and informs the reader about the atrocities of American history in *The Dread Road* (1991). A woman, a semiautobiographical figure, makes a trip every year from El Paso to Denver on a Greyhound bus to visit the institution that holds her son. He is "dead but not buried," a victim of earlier nuclear weapons testing in the West. Intricately written, three narratives share each page: quotations from Edgar Allan Poe, the main story, and excerpts from L.'s journal.

L.'s literary voice speaks for the common person in America. Many of her earlier writings, including novels, a number of children's books, and a family memoir, have been reissued and gained a new popularity. Living in Hudson, Wisconsin, with her family, she will continue to write.

OTHER WORKS: Reissues: *For My Time* (1982). *Crusaders: The Radical Legacy of Marian and Arthur Le Sueur* (1984). *North Star Country* (1984). *Little Brother of the Wilderness: The Story of Johnny Appleseed* (1987). *Salute to Spring* (1989). *Sparrow Hawk* (1989). *The Girl* (1990). *Chanticleer of Wilderness Road: A Story of Davy Crockett* (1990). *Nancy Hanks of Wilderness Road: A Story of Abraham Lincoln's Mother* (1990).

BIBLIOGRAPHY: *Unless Soul Clap Its Hands: Portraits and Passages* (1984). Gelfant, Blanche, *Women Writing in America* (1984). Oktenberg, A., "From the Bottom Up: Three Radicals of the Thirties," in *A Gift of Tongues: Critical Challenges in Contemporary American Poetry*, Marie Harris and Kathleen Aguero, eds. (1987). *Women of Valor: The Struggle against the Great Depression as Told in Their Own Life Stories*, Bernard Sterusher and Judith Sealander, eds. (1990). Reference works: *CANR* 30 (1990). *Encyc. of the Amer Left* (1990). *FC* (1990). *Tw Cent Western Writers* (1991).

Other references: *Book Forum* 6:1 (1982). *WRB* 9:7 (April 1992). *Women's Studies* 14:3 (1988).

SUZANNE GIRONDA

Denise Levertov

See AWW 2, 567–69

L., one of America's foremost contemporary poets, was born in England in 1923. She emigrated to the United States in 1948 and has taught at a number of American colleges and universities; until 1992 she taught for part of each year at Stanford University. L. is the author of over twenty volumes of poetry and essays and has received numerous awards for her work, including the Jerome J. Shestack Prize (*American Poetry Review*, 1989) and a 1990 National Endowment for the Arts Senior Fellowship.

L. was influenced by the poetry and poetic theory of William Carlos Williams. Though she was considered an "aesthetic compatriot" of some of the poets of the Black Mountain School, she does not consider herself today part of any "school" of poetry. She brings her own unmistakably distinct voice to poems concerned with several dimensions of the human experience: love, motherhood, nature, war, the nuclear arms race, the environment, mysticism, poetry, and the role of the poet.

In "Poetry, Prophecy, Survival" (*New and Selected Essays*, 1992) L. tells us that we need poets whose "witness" will inspire "hope." She recalls the words of the Inuit poet Orpingalik, "We make poems when ordinary speech no longer suffices" and cites Williams's lines: "It is difficult / to get the news from poems / yet men die miserably every day / for lack / of what is found there." People turn to poems, L. believes, "for some kind of illumination, for revelations that help them to survive, to survive in spirit, not only in body." These revelations are usually not of the unheard-of, but of what lies around us, unseen and forgotten ("Flowers of Sophia," *Evening Train*, 1992). And she believes that poems and/or dreams, as she poignantly muses in "Dream Instruction," can illuminate "what we feel but don't *know* we feel until it is articulated."

"Poetry, Prophecy, Survival" reiterates a theme that L. has addressed on several occasions; the poet or artist's "vocation," the call "to summon the divine." Her awareness of the truly awesome nature of the poet's task is evident in a 1984 essay "A Poet's View":

> To believe, as an artist, in "inspiration" or the "intuitive," to know that without Imagination . . . no amount of acquired craft or scholarship or of brilliant reasoning will suffice, is to live with a door of one's life open to the transcendent, the numinous. Not every artist, clearly, acknowledges that fact—yet all, in the creative act, experience mystery. The concept of "inspiration" presupposes a power that enters the individual and is not a personal attribute; and it is linked to a view of the artist's life as one of obedience to a vocation.

L.'s poems, most notably those since *The Jacob's Ladder* (1958), reflect her commitment to this concept of a personal sense of "calling." In her essays "Work That Enfaiths" (1990) and "An Autobiographical Sketch" (1984), and in her poem "Dream Instruction," one also feels the poet's heightened awareness of the rich depth of her inheritance and the important influence of the "cultural ambiance" of her family—those other "travellers / gone into dark." Her father's Hasidic ancestry, his being steeped in Jewish, and after his conversion, Christian scholarship and mysticism, and her mother's Welsh intensity and lyric feeling for nature are priceless threads in the texture of some of the poet's finest works.

L.'s reflections on the "vocation" of the poet should also be examined in light of the notable influence of the poetry and poetics of Czech poet Rainer Maria Rilke—an influence that she tells us in "Rilke as Mentor" predated by seven or eight years her coming to America and her reading of Williams, Ezra Pound, and Wallace Stevens. In "Levertov and Rilke: A Sense of Aesthetic Ethics" (*Twentieth Century Literature*, Fall 1992), Edward Zlotkowski offers an astute, probing analysis of Rilke's impact on L.'s understanding of her personal sense of calling as poet.

An interest in humanitarian politics came early into L.'s life. Her father was active in protesting Mussolini's invasion of Abyssinia; both he and her sister Olga protested Britain's lack of support for Spain. Long before those events, her mother canvassed on behalf of the League of Nations Union and all three worked on behalf of German and Austrian refugees from 1933 onwards. L. has long blended an activist career of opposition to war and injustice with her commitment to her calling as a poet. It is not surprising when she speaks out against prejudice, injustice, and war in "Poetry, Prophecy, Survival," "Paradox and Equilibrium" (1988), and "Poetry and Peace: Some Broader Dimensions" (1989). Her poems in the "Witnessing from Afar" section of *Evening Train* are testimonies to her belief that "[a] passionate love of life must be quickened if we are to find the energy to stop the accelerating tumble . . . toward annihilation. To sing awe—to breathe out praise and celebration—is as fundamental an impulse as to lament." This strong blend of the mystical with a firm commitment to social issues has undoubtedly contributed to L.'s placement by critics in the American visionary tradition. Rather than deliberately attempting to integrate social and political themes with lyricism, her approach is to fuse them, believing as she does that they are not antithetical. As is evident in her poetry and prose of the last several years, though L.'s range of subject matter remains by no means exclusively "engaged," she has continued with other poets, such as Pablo Neruda and **Muriel Rukeyser,** to confront the social issues of our time.

OTHER WORKS: *Life in the Forest* (1978). *Collected Earlier Poems, 1940–1960* (1979). *Pig Dreams: Scenes from The Life of Sylvia* (1981). *Candles in Babylon* (1982). *Light up the Cave* (essays, 1982). *Poems, 1960–1967* (1983). *Oblique Prayers* (1984). *Poems, 1968–1972* (1987). *Breathing the Water* (1987). Editor, *The Collected Poems of Beatrice Hawley* (1989). *A Door in the Hive* (1989).

BIBLIOGRAPHY: Breslin, James E. B., *From Modern to Contemporary American Poetry, 1945–1965* (1984). Felstiner, Joan, "Poetry and Political Experience," in *Coming to Light: American Women Poets in the Twentieth Century*, Diane Middlebrook and Marilyn Yalom, eds. (1985). Gilbert, Sandra, "Revolutionary Love," in *Conversant Essays*, James McCorkle, ed. (1985). Marten, Harry, *Understanding Denise Levertov* (1988). Ostriker, Alicia, *Stealing the Language: The Emergence of Women's Poetry in America* (1986). *Critical Essays on Denise Levertov*, Linda Wagner-Martin, ed. (1990). Reference works: *Benet's* (1991). *CANR* 29 (1990). *CLC* 15 (1980), 28 (1984), 66 (1991). *Contemp. Poets* (1991). *DLB* 5 (1980). *FC* (1990). *Maj Twent Cent Wr* (1991). *WW Wr Eds Poets* (1991).

Other references: *Amer. Poetry* 7 (Spring 1990). *APR* 20 (Nov.–Dec. 1991); 21 (Sept.–Oct. 1992). *Contemp. Lit.* 27 (Summer 1986). *MELUS* 9:4 (Winter 1982). *Michigan Q. Rev.* 24 (Fall 1985, interview). *Parnassus* 12–13 (Spring–

Winter 1985). *Sagetrieb* 8:1–2 (Spring–Fall 1989); 8:3 (Winter 1989). *Studies in Amer. Jewish Lit.* (1990).

JOAN HALLISEY

Bette Bao Lord

B. 3 Nov. 1938, Shanghai, China
D. of Dora (Fang) and Sandys Bao; m. Winston Lord, 1963; c.: Elizabeth Pillsbury, Winston Bao

Born in China and raised in the United States, L. explores her dual identity through novels and nonfiction that acknowledge both her Asian and her American sides as integral parts of one self. In this respect, perhaps, she differs from slightly younger contemporaries who have sought to give voice more directly to ethnic and gender concerns. Eldest child of a middle-class family (her father was a Nationalist Chinese government official while her mother descended from an illustrious clan of scholars), L. accompanied her parents to America in 1946. They left behind L.'s youngest sister, Sansan, who was forced to remain in China after the Communist victory. L. spent a happy childhood in Brooklyn, where she eagerly (and apparently easily) adapted to American ways. She later attended Tufts University (B.A. 1959; Fletcher School of Law and Diplomacy, M.A. 1960).

L. inadvertently began her writing career with *Eighth Moon* (1964), the straightforward account of how Sansan, who was reunited with the family in 1962, grew up amid the extreme hardships of the People's Republic. Despite the book's favorable reception, it did not prompt L. to define herself as a writer; for several years she occupied herself with family and modern dance. Inspired by a 1973 trip to China, however, L. produced two extraordinarily successful novels in middle age. Centered on strong female characters, both books examine different aspects of L.'s heritage. *Spring Moon* (1981), which began as a journal based on family history, is set during the years between the Boxer Rebellion and the Communist Revolution, and evokes traditional China with a mixture of sympathy and distance characteristic of all of L.'s work. Her decision to reshape the material as fiction allows her to displace onto her characters emotions that might be too intimately exposed in a memoir. Similarly, L.'s own childhood is described from a mature and balanced perspective in the autobiographical *In the Year of the Boar and Jackie Robinson* (1984), a novel for young readers. The America young Shirley Temple Wong encounters is basically a welcoming one; the book's focus is on the positive experience of achieving an identity, not on the adverse effects of racism.

From 1987 to 1989 L. and her husband lived in Beijing, where he served as United States Ambassador. Here L. presided over a sort of *salon* at the embassy, attracting large numbers of artists and intellectuals eager to share their stories of life during the Cultural Revolution. These accounts became the foundation of *Legacies: A Chinese Mosaic* (1990). Published soon after the 1989 student uprising in Tiananmen Square, the book weaves together these histories with stories of L.'s own extended family. Again, her choice of genre is apt: the fragmented material allows L. both intimacy and distance, enabling her to write engagingly from both a Chinese and an American perspective.

In addition to her writing career, L. has been assistant director of the University of Hawaii East-West Cultural Center (1960–61); program officer, Fulbright Exchange Program (1961–63); conference director for the National Conference for the Associated Councils of the Arts (1970–71); lecturer with the Leigh Bureau; member of the selection committee, White House Fellows; and member of the board of the National Committee on U.S.–China Relations, Inc. She received an honorary LL.D. from Tufts University in 1982.

OTHER WORKS: *Eighth Moon: The True Story of a Young Girl's Life in Communist China*, by Sansan as Told to Bette Bao Lord (1964).

BIBLIOGRAPHY: Wu, Wei-hsiung Kitty, "Cultural Ideology and Aesthetic Choices: A Study of Three Works by Chinese-American Women—Diana Chang, Bette Bao Lord, and Maxine H. Kingston." Unpublished dissertation, University of Maryland, 1989. Reference works: *CA* 107 (1983). *CLC* 23 (1983).

Other references: *PW* (30 Oct. 1981). *Time* (12 March 1990). *NYTBR* (15 Oct. 1990).

ELIZABETH SHOSTAK

Audre Lorde (Giamba Adisa)

B. 18 Feb. 1934, New York City; d. 17 Nov. 1992, Christiansted, St. Croix,
Virgin Islands
Wrote under: Rey Domini
D. of Linda Gertrude (Belmar) and Frederick Byron Lord; c.: Elizabeth Lorde-
Rollins; Jonathan Rollins

Born in Harlem of Barbadian and Grenadian parents (her father was a real-estate broker), L., one of three sisters, overcame muteness and sight problems to become one of the most eloquent, outspoken, and visionary poets, teachers, and orators of her times. Her writing was inseparable from her life as a "Black Lesbian, Feminist, mother, lover, warrior poet doing her work."

While a student at Hunter College High School L. joined the Harlem Writers' Guild founded by John Henrick Clarke, where she met Langston Hughes, **Rosa Guy,** and others. Her poems were published in the *Harlem Writers' Quarterly* and *Seventeen* magazine. After studying at the National University of Mexico in 1954, L. received her B.A. in American literature from Hunter College in 1959 and her M.L.S. from Columbia University in 1960. She married Edward Rollins in 1962; they divorced eight years later.

L. worked as a librarian for eight years before beginning her teaching career at Tougaloo College. Subsequently she taught at Herbert Lehman College and at John Jay College of Criminal Justice in New York City, and at Atlanta University. In 1987 L. became Thomas Hunter Professor of English at Hunter College.

L.'s poetry expresses her profound interest in the power of difference, the responsibility of the individual in the community, women loving women, connections among people of African descent, and the bond between parents and children. A recurring theme in all of L.'s writing is breaking silence and speaking out. In "A Litany for Survival" (from *The Black Unicorn*, 1978), a rich and lyrical work considered to be a high point of her poetic achievement, she writes, "And when we speak we are afraid / our words will not be heard, / nor welcomed / but when we are silent / we are still afraid. / So it is better to speak / remembering / we were never meant to survive." L. developed a new fictional form, the biomythography, an amalgam of fiction, biography, and myth in her 1982 work *Zami: A New Spelling of My Name*. The book remains one of the most powerful and provocative evocations of black lesbian life.

L. battled serious health problems beginning in the late 1970s and incorporated those struggles into her work, challenging traditional Western notions about illness and women's ability, responsibility, and right to make decisions regarding their health. *The Cancer Journals* (1980), named the 1981 Gay Book of the Year by the American Library Association, was L.'s first book-length prose work and greatly expanded her readership.

L. never shied away from facing difficult and painful subjects. *Sister/Outsider* (1984) includes the essay "Eye to Eye: Black Women, Hatred, and Anger." "Manchild," in the same volume, discusses her long interracial relationship with Frances Clayton, with whom L. raised her two children. In the poem "Sisters in Arms" from *Our Dead behind Us* (1986) she explores what it means for black women to live and love within the horror and obscenity of the South African apartheid regime. The title essay in *A Burst of Light* (1988) is subtitled "Living with Cancer." Despite, or perhaps because of all that she experienced, L. had a remarkable ability to communicate her great compassion and generosity of spirit through her writing.

L.'s work has had wide impact as evidenced by the many awards and honors she received during her energetic and prolific career. Her third book of poetry, *From a Land Where Other People Live* (1973), received a nomination for the National Book Award. *A Burst of Light* won the 1989 Before Columbus Foundation American Book Award. L. was named state poet of New York (1991–93) by Governor Mario Cuomo and the New York State Writers Institute and received the Astrea Foundation's Sappho Award and the Bill Whitehead Award for Lifetime Achievement in Gay and Lesbian Literature, presented by the Publishing Triangle. (She accepted the award and declined the money.) She held fellowships from the National Endowment for the Arts in 1968 and 1990. There is an Audre Lorde Women's Poetry Center at Medgar Evers College; an international feminist "celeconference," "I Am Your Sister," based on the principles of her work, was held in Boston in October 1990. L. received honorary degrees from Oberlin College (1989) and Haverford College (1990).

L.'s commitment to justice and empowerment for all was expressed through her involvement in the civil rights movement, the women's movement, the lesbian and gay rights movement, and the international antiapartheid movement. She served on the editorial boards of the *Black Scholar, Amazon Quarterly*, and was a founding member of Kitchen Table: Women of Color Press; SISA (Sisters in Support of Sisters in South Africa); and the St. Croix Women's Coalition. L. played a key role in the development of the Afro-German Movement and in the publication of *Farbe Bekennen (Showing Our Colors: Afro-German Women Speak Out*, 1992) for which she provided the introduction. Her work has been translated into seven languages and she lectured, read, and taught throughout the United States and around the world. L. died in St. Croix, in the home she had shared for many years with her companion, Dr. Gloria I. Joseph.

OTHER WORKS: The First Cities (1968). *Cables to Rage* (1970, 1972). *New York Headshop and Museum* (1974, 1977, 1981). *Between Ourselves* (1976). *Coal* (1976). *The Uses of the Erotic: The Erotic as Power* (pamphlet, 1978). *Chosen Poems Old and New* (1982). *Undersongs: Chosen Poems Old and New Revised* (1992). *The Marvelous Arithmetics of Distance* (1993).

BIBLIOGRAPHY: "Audre Lorde: A Special Section," *Callaloo* 14:1 (1991). "Revolutionary Hope: A Conversation between James Baldwin and Audre Lorde," *Essence* 15 (December 1984). Annas, Pamela, "A Poetry of Survival: Unnaming and Renaming in the Poetry of Audre Lorde, Pat Parker, Sylvia Plath, and Adrienne Rich," *Colby Library Quarterly* 18:1 (March 1982). "Before Stonewall: The Making of the Gay and Lesbian Community" (video, 1986). Davenport, Doris, "Four Contemporary Black Women Poets: Lucille Clifton, June Jordan, Audre Lorde, and Sherley Anne Williams." Unpublished Ph.D. diss., Univ. of Southern California (1985); *DAI* 47:7 (Jan. 1987). *Black Women Writers (1950–1980): A Critical Evaluation*, Mari Evans, ed. (1984). *Black Women Writers at Work*, Claudia Tate, ed. (1983). Zimmerman, Bonnie, *Safe Sea of Women: Lesbian Fiction, 1969–1989* (1990). Reference works: *Black American Writers Past and Present (1975). Black Amer. Women in Literature: A Bibliography, 1976–1987* (1989). *Black Women in Am.: an Hist. Encyc.* (1993). *CANR* 26 (1989). *CLC* 18 (1981). *DLB* 41 (1985). *FC* (1990). *Maj Twent Cent Writers* (1991). *NBAW* (1992).

Other references: *Advocate* 619 (29 Dec. 1992, obituary). *NYT* (20 Nov. 1992, obituary).

KATE RUSHIN

Lois Lowry

B. 20 March 1937, Honolulu, Hawaii
D. of Katharine (Landis) and Robert E. Hammbersberg; m. Donald Grey Lowry,
1956, div. 1977; c.: Alix, Grey, Kristen, Benjamin

One of the most popular children's novelists, L. combines a perceptive sense of humor with a sure understanding of children and childhood. Although best known for her comic novels about a girl named Anastasia growing up in the Boston area, L. has also received widespread critical acclaim for her more serious novels, including the 1990 Newbery Award winner, *Number the Stars* (1989).

L. lived in Pennsylvania during World War II, while her father was on active duty. After the war, she moved with her family to Japan, where she finished junior high. When they returned to the United States, L. graduated from high school in New York City. She taught herself to read at an early age and always loved books. "I remember the feeling of excitement that I had the first time that I realized each letter had a sound, and the sounds went together to make words, and the words became sentences, and the sentences became stories. I was very young—not yet four years old. It was then that I decided that one day I would write books." Determined to fulfill her dream, L. entered Brown University at seventeen. She left after two years to marry and had four children by the time she was twenty-seven. Returning later to college she received her B.A. from the University of Maine in 1973 at the age of thirty-six.

After a successful career as a freelance writer and photographer, L. published her first novel, *A Summer to Die*, in 1977. Written in memory of her sister Helen, who died young, the book received the International Reading Association's Children's Book Award for the best book of the year by an author "who shows unusual promise in the children's book field."

L.'s other novels also draw on personal and family experience. Her years in Pennsylvania, where she lived in her grandparents' home, inspired *Autumn Street* (1980), the moving story of a child's response to a war being waged far away and her growing understanding of the curious inequities that existed in her own home and town. The Appalachian community in which her brother works as a physician is the setting of the 1987 Boston Globe–Horn Book Award winner for fiction, *Rabble Starkey*, while a friend's experiences in Copenhagen during World War II led directly to L.'s Newbery Award–winning novel *Number the Stars*. This is a vivid portrayal of friendship and courage in which a gentile family helps its Jewish neighbors escape when their safety is threatened by Hitler's planned roundup of Denmark's Jews.

Humor forms the backbone of L.'s novels about the precocious Anastasia Krupnik, whom critic Eric A. Kimmel calls L.'s "supreme creation, the most formidable child since Ramona Quimby." Beginning with *Anastasia Krupnik* (1979) and continuing through *Anastasia at This Address* (1991), the series details the myriad changes and comic moments that mark the life of a girl between the ages of ten and thirteen.

All about Sam (1988), focusing on Anastasia's younger brother, describes with broad humor and flashes of genuine insight the world as seen through the eyes of an extremely curious, extremely verbal little boy. Underneath the humor, however, lies a serious theme, one L. herself identifies as pivotal to her work: "If I go on writing books as I hope to for years and years . . . probably everyone of those books will have the same basic theme . . . the importance of human beings to one another." A sequel, *Attaboy Sam!*, was published in 1992.

Original characters, brilliant plotting, and a finely tuned ear for the comic touch combine to give L.'s novels for children a permanent place in the history of children's literature.

OTHER WORKS: *Anastasia Again!* (1981). *Anastasia at Your Service* (1982). *Taking Care of Terrific* (1983). *The One Hundredth Thing about Caroline* (1983). *Anastasia, Ask Your Analyst* (1984). *Us and Uncle Fraud* (1984). *Anastasia on Her Own* (1985). *Switcharound* (1985). *Anastasia Has the Answers* (1986). *Anastasia's Chosen Career* (1987). *Your Move, J.P.* (1990). *The Giver* (1993).

BIBLIOGRAPHY: Kimmel, Eric A., "Anastasia Agonistes: The Tragicomedy of Lois Lowry," *Horn Book Mag.* 63 (March/April 1987). Reference works: *CA* 69–72 (1976). *CANR* 13 (1984). *CLR* 6 (1984). *DLB* 52 (1986). *SATA* 23 (1981). *SATA Autobiog. Series* 3 (1978).
Other reference: *Horn Book Mag.* 66 (July/August 1990).

AMY L. COHN

Alison Lurie

B. 3 Sept. 1926, Chicago, Illinois
D. of Bernice (Stewart) and Harry Lurie; m. Jonathan Peale Bishop, Jr., 1948,
sep. 1976, div. 1985; c.: John, Jeremy, Joshua

The daughter of a sociology professor father turned Jewish-welfare administrator, and a mother who had been a journalist, L. was encouraged to explore her creativity at an early age. An "odd-looking," partially deaf child, L. predicted that she would become one of the "old maids" she voraciously read about in Victorian and Edwardian children's books.

After graduating from Radcliffe (B.A. 1947), L. worked as a manuscript reader for Oxford University before marrying in 1948. Although she had sold three poems and a short story while in college, L. published nothing until her privately printed memoir of her friend Violet Ranney (Bunny) Lang appeared in 1959. The memoir, reprinted commercially in 1975, focuses on Lang's career and the beginnings of the Poets' Theater of Cambridge.

L.'s first novel, *Love and Friendship* (1962), explores the academic milieu that figures prominently in her life and her novels. A member of the English faculty at Cornell University since 1969, L. sets several of her multilayered satirical novels at universities. In *Love and Friendship*, Emily Turner suddenly realizes that she no longer loves her adoring professor-husband.

L.'s characters are well-educated middle- or upper-middle-class people who have, for a brief time, taken themselves or what they do too seriously. *The Nowhere City* (1966) explores several dichotomies: east-west, male-female, and past-present. In *Imaginary Friends* (1967) L. satirizes both religious cults and academia, exploring the pressure on professors to publish as well as the apathy some exhibit regarding their power over students. *Real People* (1969) draws on L.'s experiences at Yaddo, an upstate New York artists' retreat, to describe Illyria, where "one becomes one's *real* self."

The title of L.'s fourth novel, *The War between the Tates* (1974), works on various levels: it refers to Erica and Brian Tate's marital problems, to the difficulty of their children's budding adolescence, and to the parallel between the war in Vietnam and the battle between the sexes and the generations. In *Only Children* (1979), L.'s narrative point of view alternates between that of eight-year-old Mary Ann and an objective third person. The novel satirizes adult responsibility, love, beauty, and moral values.

L. masters the use of metaphor in *Foreign Affairs* (1984) in which a little dog represents self-pity. Vinnie Miner, an Anglophile professor of children's literature on sabbatical in England, resembles her creator. An affair between Vinnie and Chuck Mumpson, a stereotypical Oklahoman tourist, forces her to reconsider her concept of reality. The novel won the Pulitzer Prize (1985). L.'s other awards include fellowships from the Guggenheim (1965) and Rockefeller (1967) foundations.

In *The Truth about Lorin Jones* (1988), museum curator Polly Alter undergoes a journey toward self-discovery while trying to learn about Lorin Jones, a painter who had died many years before. Although some critics dismissed the novel as frivolous, it explores difficult choices, and has many satirical moments. By ostensibly stereotyping both gender roles and sexual preference, L. speaks profoundly about the backlash against feminism. The novel also reflects on the futility of seeking *the* truth: as Polly struggles to sort out the myriad perceptions she has gathered about Lorin, she realizes no one she interviewed was "lying . . . : everyone had told her the truth as he or she knew or imagined it."

L.'s long-term interest in children's literature is illustrated in such gatherings and translations of children's tales from around the world as *The Heavenly Zoo* (1970), *Clever Gretchen and Other Forgotten Folktales* (1980), and *Fabulous Beasts* (1981). In *Don't Tell the Grown-ups: Subversive Children's Literature* (1990) she examines underlying texts in children's stories, ranging from folk- and fairy tales and Gothic novels through such modern writers as J. R. R. Tolkien and Richard Adams. According to L., most children's literature maintains the status quo, but the books in which she takes pleasure undermine current assumptions and express alternate views of the world.

L.'s diversity of interests takes yet another form in *The Language of Clothes* (1981). Explaining fashion as a nonverbal language of signs, she shows the influence that political climates have historically had on dress and costume.

OTHER WORKS: *V. R. Lang: A Memoir* (1959; reprinted as *Poems and Plays/ V. R. Lang with a Memoir by Alison Lurie*, 1975). Editor, *The Oxford Book of Modern Fairy Tales* (1993).

BIBLIOGRAPHY: Reference works: *CANR* 2 (1981), 17 (1986). *CLC* 4 (1975), 5 (1976), 39 (1986). *CBY* (1986). *DLB* 2 (1978). *FC* (1990). *Maj Twent Cent Writers* (1990).

Other references: *Commonweal* (16 Dec. 1988). *Human Ecology* (Spring 1991). *Ms.* (Oct. 1988). *Nation* (21 Nov. 1988). *New Leader* (16 April 1990). *New Statesman and Society* (8 July 1988; 25 May 1990). *NYRB* (24 Nov. 1988; 23 Nov. 1989; 26 April 1990; 20 Dec. 1990; 25 April 1991). *NYTBR* (4 Sept. 1988; 25 Feb. 1990; 11 March 1990). *PW* (9 Feb. 1990). *Redbook* (Oct. 1990). *Vogue* (Oct. 1989; Aug. 1991).

PHYLLIS S. GLEASON

Mary Therese McCarthy

See AWW 3, 65–69
D. 25 Oct. 1989, New York City

A prolific writer for more than half a century, M. was known as America's "First Lady of Letters." At the time of her death M. had published nineteen books, including fiction, criticism, journalism, and autobiography. Declaring in 1985 that it is not possible to write a successful novel "after a certain age," she devoted the last decade of her life to writing literary and cultural criticism and autobiography. *Cannibals and Missionaries* (1979) was her last novel.

Ideas and the Novel (1980) consists of the Northcliffe Lectures that M. delivered earlier that year at University College, London. In this brief book she argues that the twentieth-century novel has failed to engage in a meaningful discussion of socially significant ideas. The model for writers is no longer the nineteenth-century "novel of ideas," with its focus on public issues and moral questions, but rather the Jamesian novel, with its inward focus on private relationships. *Ideas and the Novel* had a mixed critical reception but generated a lively debate on the health of the twentieth-century novel.

Occasional Prose (1985) is a diverse collection of M.'s essays written since 1970. It includes a discussion of a 1968 demonstration in London against the war in Vietnam, a "postface" to her friend Nicola Chiaromonte's *Paradox of History*, as well as a tribute to her late friend **Hannah Arendt.** In addition there are critical essays, lectures, book reviews, obituaries, and a retelling of *La Traviata. Occasional Prose* was received more favorably than *Ideas and the Novel*, although it prompted less discussion.

In 1987 M. published the first of what she had hoped would be a three-volume autobiographical work. Like her earlier *Memories of a Catholic Girlhood* (1957), *How I Grew* covers the years from her childhood through her graduation from Vassar College and her marriage to Harold Johnsrud, both in 1933. Unlike the earlier work, however, *How I Grew* chronicles the intellectual development of its subject, beginning, "I was born as a mind during 1925, my bodily birth having taken place in 1912." The book was widely criticized for returning to the material of her earlier memoir and generally compared unfavorably with it. Written as a narrative monologue, the style of *How I Grew* is discursive, at times even deliberately antiquated. The tone is one of comic detachment. Even while relating the abuse she suffered during her orphan years, or her teenage attempts at suicide, M. remains emotionally distanced from her material. "Laughter is the great antidote for self pity," she explains. As a result the emotional force of the work is somewhat diminished.

In 1980, M.'s zeal for truth telling landed her in the midst of a legal battle. On the Dick Cavett television show that year she accused **Lillian Hellman** of being a "dishonest writer." Hellman responded with a two-and-a-quarter-million-dollar libel suit. When Hellman died in 1984, the case was dropped, much to M.'s disappointment; she had been looking forward to the public trial.

In 1984 M. was awarded both the Edward MacDowell Medal for outstanding contributions to literature and the National Medal for literature, only the third woman to have been honored with the National Medal. She sold her papers—more than 6,500 pages of manuscripts, legal documents, notes, and letters—to Vassar College in 1985.

M. died of cancer in New York City at the age of seventy-seven. At the time of her death she was working on a study of Gothic architecture and on the second volume of her autobiography. *Intellectual Memoirs: New York, 1936–1938* (1992) was published posthumously by the Mary McCarthy Literary Trust. In addition to writing, M. had also been teaching at Bard College, the same institution that first invited her to teach in the 1940s.

OTHER WORKS: Papers and MSS are at Vassar College, Poughkeepsie, New York.

BIBLIOGRAPHY: Brightman, Carol, *Writing Dangerously* (1992). Gelderman, Carol, *Mary McCarthy: A Life* (1988). *Conversations with Mary McCarthy*, Carol Gelderman, ed. (1991). Reference works: *CA* 129 (1990). *FC* (1990). *Modern Amer. Women Writers* (1991).

Other references: *Hudson* Rev. (Spring 1981; Spring 1989). *NYRB* (4 Dec. 1980; 11 June 1987). *NYT* (1 May 1985; 5 May 1985; 29 March 1987 [*Magazine*]; 26 Oct. 1989 [obituary]; 18 Nov. 1989). *NYTBR* (18 Jan. 1981; 19 April 1987; 24 May 1992). *Partisan Rev.* 57 (Winter 1990). *TLS* (6 March 1981; 31 Jan. 1986; 18–24 Sept. 1987).

MELISSA BURNS

Alice McDermott

B. 27 June 1953, Brooklyn, New York
D. of Mildred (Lynch) and William J. McDermott; m. David M. Armstrong,
1979; c.: Willie, b. 1986; Eames, b. 1989.

Credited in a review of *At Weddings and Wakes* (1992) with "transfiguring everyday life," M. draws deeply from her childhood memories of suburbia to detail those "deceptively ordinary elements" that are integral to formulating an adult moral vision. Writing from the perspective of an Irish-American, Roman Catholic woman and mother, M. masterfully integrates into her harmonious prose the tragedies and complexities that arise from the ambiguous nature of morality, the delicacies of the extended family relationship, the malleability of children's memories, and the constancy of women's pain. Along the continuum of feminist writings, M. identifies with the cadre of female authors who balance the demands of motherhood and of writing. Devoted to her own family, M. writes her critically acclaimed novels about women and families downstairs, adjacent to the laundry room, while her children are at school. Fascinated by the suburban subject, she sees the church as the spiritual center of family life and the impetus for improving the lives of one's children. M.'s parents had excluded stories of Ireland from her rearing, yet she attributes to genetics her elegiac writing within the Catholic context, which, a reviewer comments, "neither attacks the church or proselytizes."

M. spent her childhood on Long Island where she attended parochial grammar and high school and claims never to have missed the ten o'clock Sunday Mass. In 1975, she received her B.A. from the State University of New York. After a year of working in publishing, an experience that forms the backdrop to one of her novels, M. enrolled at the University of New Hampshire (M.A. 1978) where her goals as a writer were encouraged by teacher Mark Smith, and by the tangible affirmation of her talent—publication of short stories in *Ms.*, *Redbook*, *Seventeen*, and *Mademoiselle* magazines. Her first novel, *A Bigamist's Daughter* (1982), was accepted, unfinished, for publication six months after its initial submission; assured of her career as a writer M. relinquished her original desire to attend law school and committed her time to writing, editing, lecturing, and, later, teaching writing workshops at American University.

M. honestly chronicles the pain, confusion, and yearning of childhood from the later, infringing perspective of adulthood. *A Bigamist's Daughter* examines these memories and stories of youth and the essential part that fiction plays in life. In a review, Jean Strouse praised the human depth of M.'s "wise, sad, witty novel about men and women, God, hope, love, illusion and fiction itself."

The characters in M.'s novels struggle with the choices that either define and determine happiness or impose the realities of sorrow. In *That Night* (1987) the characters are caught in the seamless intractability of suburbia, unable to achieve their dreams within this limited space. Nominated for a National Book Award, the novel was later made into a film.

At Weddings and Wakes (1992) transports the reader into the heart of Irish-Catholic family life on Long Island, through the eyes of children. From the female vantage point of four middle-aged sisters and their stepmother, M. interrogates the common aspects of life that hold extraordinary significance for her characters—joy and grief, mortality and faith, illusion and reality. According to reviewer Jill Smolowe, the novel secures M.'s "reputation as a mesmerizing and innovative storyteller." In addition to her novels, M. has published dozens of short stories as well as articles and reviews.

BIBLIOGRAPHY: Reference works: *CA* 109 (1983).
    Other references: *LATBR* (26 April 1987). *Ms.* (May 1987). *Newsweek* (22

March 1982, review by Jean Strouse). *New Yorker* (17 Aug. 1987). *NYTBR* (21 Feb. 1982; 19 April 1987; 12 April 1992). *PW* 239 (30 March 1992, interview). *Time* (20 April 1992, review by Jill Smolowe). *Wash. Post* (21 April 1992, interview).

AMY HOLBROOK

Shirley MacLaine

See AWW 3, 100–102

In the public mind, M. is first and foremost a Hollywood star. Prior to 1983, her reputation as a writer was based on two candid, colorful travel memoirs. But the publication in 1983 of *Out on a Limb* brought M. into a new arena. In that book, which was to become a best-seller, she recounts her search for her own spiritual identity, ending in her embracing such New Age concepts as reincarnation, trance channeling, and astral projection. For the spiritually unconvinced, her best writing here details her trip to the remarkable Mantaro River Valley, high in the Peruvian Andes. But the bulk of the book is divided between M.'s tortuous love affair with a married British politician and her ongoing movement from skepticism to spiritual certainty.

Dancing in the Light (1985) opens in 1984, with M., at the top of her profession, looking back on a year that included the Academy Award for best actress for *Terms of Endearment*, the overwhelming success of *Out on a Limb*, and the record-breaking run of her one-woman musical show on Broadway. Amid all this joy, she must contend with the health problems of her aging parents. She speculates on their complex interrelationship and why they chose to spend this lifetime as a couple. To probe the mystery of the entangled lives of her parents and other family members, she journeys to Santa Fe for a session with a spiritual acupuncturist. The book climaxes with her multiple visions of herself in previous incarnations—as an elephant princess in Africa, a desert nomad swept away by a marauding chieftain, a helpless liberal in czarist Russia. Ultimately she meets her own androgynous Higher Self, who will serve as her personal inspiration and spiritual guide.

Some of the most convincing passages of *Dancing in the Light* deal with the life of a working dancer. Similarly, *It's All in the Playing* (1987) effectively brings the reader behind the scenes into the filmmaker's self-absorbed world. The book also probes M.'s further spiritual development during the filming of a television miniseries based on *Out on a Limb*.

Going Within: A Guide for Inner Transformation (1989), inspired by seminars M. has given from coast to coast, introduces the reader to additional spiritual possibilities. They include forms of meditation, the Seven Chakras, and something called psychic surgery. The book extends the optimistic vision of each individual's godlike potential that has marked M.'s earlier works. M. is always a refreshingly honest writer, but the intensity of her spiritual beliefs may try the patience of many readers.

In *Dance While You Can* (1992) M. returns to explorations of her relationships with her parents, her mother's ambitions for her children and her father's anxieties, and to the struggle to resolve the tensions she has faced with her own daughter. Beginning with memories of Hollywood, the book details M.'s experience of aging, as an actress in *Postcards*, coping with injury and pain, more often alone. Less insistent on detailing her spiritual development, the book continues M.'s account of her search "to become harmonious with the music of the universe."

BIBLIOGRAPHY: Reference works: *CA* 103 (1982). *CANR* 32 (1991).

Other references: *LJ* (1 July 1983; 1 Nov. 1985). *New Statesman* (14 Oct. 1983). *NYTBR* (18 Sept. 1983; 13 Oct. 1985). *Time* (14 Oct. 1985).

BEVERLY GRAY BIENSTOCK

Terry McMillan

B. 18 Oct. 1951, Port Huron, Michigan
D. of Madeline Washington (Tillman) and Edward McMillan; c.: Solomon Welch

The oldest daughter of five children born into a middle-class working family, M. spent her childhood in Port Huron. Her father was often forced to be away from the family because he suffered from tuberculosis and needed sanitorium care. When M. was thirteen, her parents divorced, and three years later, her father died. During M.'s childhood, her mother, who never finished high school, provided for her family by working in jobs as diverse as auto worker, domestic, and pickle-factory employee. In a 1992 interview, M. claimed that her mother is "one of the strongest women I've ever met in my life" who "taught us to test ourselves in every way."

M. left Michigan at seventeen to attend Los Angeles City College, but soon transferred to the University of California at Berkeley (B.S. 1979), attending classes at night while working as a typist. It was during this time that she began to write, initially for *Black Thoughts,* an African American campus newspaper. Her foray into creative writing was inadvertent: a roommate's friend discovered a poem M. had written about a heartbreak romance and published it in the literary magazine of which he was editor. M.'s intrigue with the idea of being a published writer was fueled by a workshop with Ishmael Reed, "a very encouraging and nurturing teacher" who, M. says, gave her "the courage to write." Following his injunction not to distract herself by pursuing an advanced degree in writing, M. left for New York City after graduation to enter a master's degree program in film at Columbia University.

In New York she joined the Harlem Writers' Guild where members encouraged her to extend the short story she read them into what became her first novel, *Mama* (1987). M. undertook her own publicity tour, sending out over three thousand letters to independent bookstores, bookstore chains, and universities, inviting them to purchase her book and offering to give readings. Much to the surprise of her publishers, her strategy worked— her novel sold out its first hardcover printing of five thousand copies.

Of her own writing, M. has said, "All I've ever wanted was to tell a story in the best way I possibly could, with the hopes that other people would share and identify with my characters and find the same kind of gratification or redemption from the reading that I found in the writing." Her central figures are all African American; they are poor single mothers, enterprising and gifted young girls passing into womanhood, or middle-class single women coming to terms with themselves as adults, as well as with relationships with parents, lovers, and husbands who are sometimes extremely trying, humiliating, and unempowering. In addition, M.'s narratives are often peopled with young children who are being influenced, alienated, and decidedly shaped by their homelives, their family's encounter with American culture. Portraying strong African American characters with honesty, insight, and love, M. details the intense emotional and psychological bonds her characters are trying to unearth or flee, as well as the vital bonds of friendship and love they are trying to sustain.

In *Mama*, her most autobiographical novel, M. explores the tensions and frustrations experienced by a poor African American family in the 1960s and 1970s. The protagonist, Mildred Peacock, is an indefatigable, imaginative woman and mother of five who reacts with untempered rage and ingenuity to the variety of demands made of her whether from bill collectors, the U-Haul company from whom she has stolen a truck to move her family cross-country, or her alcoholic husband.

Disappearing Acts (1989) is a tense, explosive love story set in Brooklyn in the early eighties. M.'s real-life lover sued her, claiming that the male character was a libelous version of him and his relationship with M. He did not win the case. The book proceeds as two first-person narratives, those of Zora and Franklin. Zora is M.'s deliberate attempt to honor the voice and spirited writing of **Zora Neale Hurston.** In creating the voice of Franklin, M. says that "all [she] wanted to show was that he was a really good person with a lot of anger." The novel received favorable reviews and sold more than 100,000 copies in paperback.

Waiting to Exhale (1992) has built upon M.'s early self-promotion. Charting the friendships between four women in Arizona, it offers their explicit, funny, indulgent analyses of social politics, and their frustration with aspects of their personal lives and choices. As with her earlier novels, *Waiting* has been criticized for coarse language—something M. describes as simply realistic rendering. Defending the placement of men at the novel's periphery, M. explains that for her, this was a book about women, to be told from women's points of view, with women at its center.

In addition to her fictional works, M. has published a critical analysis of the films of Spike Lee and edited the first collection of contemporary African American fiction to appear since the 1970s; she is developing a screenplay of *Disappearing Acts*. A visiting writer at the University of Wyoming in 1987–88, she received a literary fellowship from the National Endowment for the Arts in 1988, and then went on to a tenured position at the University of Arizona-Tucson. She is also a vocal member of PEN and member of the Author's League. Despite having achieved a dynamic literary profile, this feisty and unapologetic writer remains frustrated by what she calls the lack of respect from other prominent African American women writers. Some critics have labeled M. a pulp writer: nonetheless, her reading public is celebrating the ways in which her works attend to and affirm contemporary African American women and the worlds in which they live.

OTHER WORKS: *Breaking Ice: An Anthology of Contemporary Black American Fiction* (1990). *Five for Five: The Films of Spike Lee* (1991).

BIBLIOGRAPHY: Reference works: *CLC* 50 (1986), 61 (1990). *WW Black Wr* (1992).
    Other references: *Callaloo* 11:3 (Summer 1988). *Essence* 23:6 (Oct. 1992). *NYT* (1 May 1992, 1 July 1992). *NYTBR* (22 Feb. 1987; 6 Aug. 1989; 31 May 1992). *NYT Mag.* (9 Aug. 1992). *Poets and Writers Mag.* (Nov./Dec. 1992, interview). *PW* (11 May 1992). *TLS* (6 Sept. 1991). *Wash. Post* (11 April 1991; 2, 3 July 1992).

LOIS M. BROWN

Sandra McPherson

B. 2 Aug. 1943, San Jose, California
D. of Frances (Gibson) and William James McPherson; m. Henry D. Carlile, 1966, div. 1985; c.: Phoebe, b. 1967

Raised in California, M. attended Westmont College and San Jose State (B.A. 1965) and went on to graduate study under David Wagoner and

Elizabeth Bishop at the University of Washington. M. shares Bishop's unsentimental love of nature and precision in observing it, though what Bishop complimented in her former student's work was its voice—"original, surprising, and clean." M.'s evolving combination of colloquialism and what poet Gary Snyder terms "linguistic accuracy," of natural speech rhythms and poetic forms, as well as her gift for the unexpected and tonally complex metaphor, have continued to win praise for her poetic voice.

M. has received numerous grants, including three from the National Endowment for the Arts (1974, 1980, 1985) and a Guggenheim Fellowship (1976); her poems have received prizes from *Poetry, Poetry Northwest*, and the Poetry Society of America. *The Year of Our Birth* (1978) was nominated for a National Book Award, and *Streamers* (1988) was nominated for two major regional awards, while *Radiation* (1973) won the Pacific Northwest Booksellers Prize. In 1987, M. received the Award in Literature of the American Academy and Institute of Arts and Letters. In addition to her several chapbooks and volumes of poetry, M.'s work is widely anthologized.

M. has taught at the University of California at Davis since 1985, where she also served as the director of creative writing (1987–90). Previously, she taught at the University of California at Berkeley, the Writers Workshop at the University of Iowa, and the Oregon Writers Workshop at Pacific Northwest College of Art. Her teaching has influenced both her writing process and subject, as "Sonnet for Joe" suggests: "I would rather you describe a clock than time." But M. does not generally write dicta; more typical is her feminist reenvisioning of a student's essay, "Sentience," and her dreamlike meditation on a fellow teacher's miscarriage, "A Coconut for Katerina." Though she continues "to learn from" her "students' work," in her later books her interest shifts to her own teachers and role models.

Relationship, the flux of intimacy and isolation, is a central theme of M.'s work, though the poems always locate their lovers, mothers and daughters, and women friends in a figurative and literal natural world. Her poems are also concerned with the art of writing and vision itself; she describes writing as a way to "think, learn, make discoveries."

M.'s early work has been compared to **Sylvia Plath**'s and her late work to **Marianne Moore**'s, but her vision and voice have always embodied aspects of both, in the use of slant rhyme, in rhythm, image, and tone, and in the impulse to revise myths of female identity. Though her later poems are less private and slightly more abstract, all her work exhibits a tension between objective and subjective views, between description and symbol, between seeing wildflowers, seaweed, or jellyfish as uniquely themselves, or as other, and finding in them objective correlatives for the poet's emotions. Her careful eye, her quirky sense of humor, her hope, and her delicate modulations of idea through image make reading her poems a way for the reader, too, to think, learn, and make discoveries—about the natural world and human nature.

OTHER WORKS: *Elegies for the Hot Season* (1970, reprinted 1982). *Sensing* (chapbook, 1979). Editor, *Journey from Essex: Poems for John Clare* (1981). *Patron Happiness* (1983). *Pheasant Flower* (chapbook, 1985). *Responsibility for Blue* (chapbook, 1985). *Floralia* (chapbook, 1985). *The God of Indeterminacy* (1993).

BIBLIOGRAPHY: Turner, Alberta T., "A Coconut for Katerina," *Fifty Contemporary Poets: The Creative Process* (1977). Reference Works: *CA* 29–32 (1978). *CANR* 12 (1984). *Contemp. Poets* (1985, 1991). *DLBY* (1986).

Other references; *APR* (May/June 1978; July/Aug. 1978; Sept./Oct. 1981, interview; May/June 1989; May/June 1991; July/Aug. 1991). *College English* 42 (Oct. 1980). *LJ* (15 Feb. 1978). *New Republic* (9 Dec. 1978). *NYTBR* (17 Nov. 1974). *Northwest Rev.* 20:2/3 (1982). *Poetry* (Aug. 1971; May 1975; April 1989). Letter from M. to D. Sonnenschein, 13 Aug. 1992.

DANA SONNENSCHEIN

Nancy Mairs

B. 23 July 1943, Long Beach, California
D. of Anne Pedrick (Cutler) and John Eldredge Smith, Jr.; m. George Anthony Mairs, 1963; c.: Anne Pedrick, b. 1965; Matthew Anthony, b. 1969

M. is among a new and growing group of disabled women writers telling long-hidden stories. She believes in experience as her primary source material and works in the genres of essay and memoir writing. She chooses to interpret theory through experience and writes as precisely as she can about herself as a disabled feminist with the conviction that others will find some commonality in their own experiences.

Born by "accident of war" in California where her father was stationed, at five months of age she became a New Englander, the origin of both of her parents. She was raised a middle-class Yankee Congregationalist, categories she considers significant when placing her essays in context. In addition to designating her writing as gender specific she also feels it is informed by her conversion to Catholicism.

M. began her writing career as a poet and first completed a chapbook, *Instead It Is Winter* (1977). A 1984 collection of poems, *In All the Rooms of the Yellow House*, won that year's Western States Book Award.

M. completed her B.A. at Wheaton College (1964) and later received an M.F.A. (1975) and a Ph.D. (1984) from the University of Arizona. Her first collection of essays was *Plaintext: Deciphering a Woman's Life* (1986). She discusses such topics as sexuality, motherhood, and work, with the overlay of her disability ever present. This is not a term she likes; she prefers to call herself crippled, as one of the essays, "On Being a Cripple" attests. She feels that word accurately, rather than euphemistically describes her physical condition: chronic progressive multiple sclerosis (MS). The disease first moved slowly and with minor consequences but eventually accelerated rapidly and M. feels it is critical for her to keep working fast before she loses her ability to communicate.

In 1989 she published *Remembering the Bone House: An Erotics of Place and Space*, a memoir chronicling her childhood in Massachusetts. The work invites us into the physical as well as the emotional dimensions of her life as she marries, becomes a mother, experiments with other sexual partners, and discovers and begins to live with a disability. She addresses her nervous breakdowns, beginning at age twenty-three: numerous hospitalizations and extensive electroconvulsive therapy. In 1980 she finally found a good therapist who assisted her during a breakdown and diagnosed her "moodiness" as depression, an illness that could be successfully treated with medication. M. considers her depression a disease like MS only more treatable. She discounts the notion that one must be "crazy," drunk, or in any other unhealthy state in order to write. "Not writing was killing me . . . writing was my way of staying alive."

The essays in *Carnal Acts* (1990) further explore her roles—disabled mother/wife/traveler/writer. In her essay, "I'm Afraid. I'm Afraid. I'm Afraid," she acknowledges that her life is difficult, a fact she wants known in all its graphic physical and psychological dimensions. Although not a disability rights activist, M. does consider herself part of the disabled community. *Ordinary Time: Cycles in Marriage, Faith, and Renewal* (1993) continues to confront the progression of her disability as well as her struggle to reconcile her feminism and her catholicism.

Mindful of the continuity of the historical mode of women artists, she prefers both her essays and her poetry to be read aloud. She denounces the title "author" with its inherent association to "authoritarian" and refers to herself as a writer or a workwoman. The oral tradition of women sharing stories about their lives endures; she wants her readers to imagine themselves sitting around a table with her, rather than picturing her delivering essays at an ever distancing podium.

OTHER WORKS: Four essays in *With Wings*, Marsha Saxton and Florence Howe, eds. (1987).

BIBLIOGRAPHY: LJ (1 April 1989; 1 Sept. 1990). *NYTBR* (27 April 1986; 21 June 1987; 6 Aug. 1989; 2 Sept. 1990). *Psychology Today* (Oct. 1989). Reference works: *CA* 136 (1992). *WW Wr, Eds and Poets* (1989). *Biography Index* 16 (1990).

KAREN SCHNEIDERMAN

Paule Marshall

See AWW 3, *125–27*

All of M.'s major fiction reveals the author's preoccupation with the history of blacks dispersed throughout the Western hemisphere, a history of struggle and resistance to oppression but also a history of independence and self-determination. M. firmly believes her task as a writer is to "reinvent" the images that define African peoples. To this end, she builds upon African myth in her fiction to illustrate the relevance of history to the modern world. In *The Chosen Place, the Timeless People* (1969) she centers the theme of the novel around the legend of Cuffee Ned. In *Praisesong for the Widow* (1983) she includes the "unwritten" history of the Ibo people.

Praisesong takes on surreal, ethereal qualities emanating from dreams and memories. Those dramatically overlap opposing time frames and conflicting modes of thought. Having forgotten the "nurturing ground from which she sprang," the widow embarks on a journey. Her destination is not as intended, however; she arrives instead at her symbolic cultural home. M. describes in this novel a common history of separation and loss among peoples of African descent. Despite this physical separation, the heroine learns, it is possible to sustain spiritual (mental) ties. This, in part, is the message of the Ibos.

Reena and Other Short Stories, also published in 1983, is a collection of some of M.'s early short fiction. It includes commentary by the author and her seminal essay, "The Making of a Writer: From the Poets in the Kitchen." This important essay describes M.'s indebtedness to her mother and other Barbadian women who taught her the power of the spoken word as both a tool of communication and as a weapon of survival. Two selections from *Soul Clap Hands and Sing* (1961) make up a part of the volume as well as a new novella, entitled "Merle." Many will recognize that story as an adaptation and condensation of the story of the pivotal character in *The Chosen Place, the Timeless People*. In some respects, the short selections in *Reena* introduce the reader to themes M. develops more fully in her novels. They certainly indicate her early exploration of the ways in which women, especially, define themselves and actively engage in battling the double forces of racism and sexism.

In *Daughters* (1991) M. returns to the complex, changing parameters of a female persona living and growing in the two worlds that have formed her: the Caribbean and the United States. The novel, while contemporary in focus, also moves backward and forward in time to underscore enduring relationships between women. The novel is about black female-male relationships as well—particularly a young woman's struggle to sever emotional ties with her overpowering father. Once again M. turns to myth to insinuate the dominant motif. The story of Congo Jane and Will Cudjoe teaches that despite overwhelming odds, men and women can work together in mutual support. Through a series of subplots that involve intimate human relationships and corrupt political practices, M. shows how exacting this ideal may be. Yet for the common good, the ideal must become the standard.

M. offers no easy solutions in her fiction, but she does suggest models for change and possibility. Because she develops those possibilities through the characterization of black women, she celebrates female agency and empowerment. Indeed, black women become representative of the larger black struggle for individual autonomy and communal wholeness.

BIBLIOGRAPHY: Braxton, J., and A. McLaughlin, *Wild Women in the Whirl-wind: Afra-American Culture and the Contemporary Literary Renaissance* (1990). *Black Women Writers (1950–1980): A Critical Evaluation*, Mari Evans, ed. (1984). Pryse, M., and H. Spillers, *Conjuring: Black Women, Fiction, and Literary Tradition* (1985). Willis, S., *Specifying: Black Women Writing the American Experience* (1987). Reference works: *African-American Writers* (1991). *CANR* 25 (1989). *CLC* 27 (1984). *DLB* 33 (1984). *FC* (1990).

Other references: *Black Amer. Lit. Forum* 20 (Winter 1986). *Callaloo* 10:1 (Winter 1987); 16:2 (Spring-Summer 1986). *Freedomways* (first quarter, 1970). *World Lit. Written in English* (Autumn 1985). *SAGE: A Scholarly J. on Black Women* 1:2 (Fall 1984).

Additional biog. information: one son, Evan Keith Marshall

DOROTHY L. DENNISTON

Valerie Martin

B. 14 March 1948, Sedalia, Missouri
D. of Valerie (Fleischer) and John Roger Metcalf; m. Robert Mark Martin, 1970,
  div.; m. James Watson, 1986, div.; c.: Adrienne Metcalf Martin, b. 1975

Though born in Missouri, M. was raised and educated in New Orleans. Having earned a B.A. from the University of New Orleans in 1970, she enrolled in the graduate writing program at the University of Massachusetts (M.F.A. 1974). Subsequently she held a series of teaching posts at New Mexico State University, the University of New Orleans, the University of Alabama, Mount Holyoke College, and since 1988, at the University of Massachusetts-Amherst.

The title of her first book, a little-known but powerful collection of stories called *Love* (1977), announced M.'s one consuming subject. Over the course of her career, she has examined its complexities in intense and widely admired novels and short stories. Her first novel, *Set in Motion* (1978), recounts the uneasy progress of Helene Thatcher's passionate relationships with the husbands of her two best friends and the gentle but passionless friendship with a drug addict to whom she always returns. Winning praise from Walker Percy and others, *Set in Motion* was quickly followed by *Alexandra* (1979).

Less well received, *Alexandra* relates the melancholy tale of Claude Ledet's abandonment of his life in New Orleans to follow a beautiful woman into the bayou country, where they attend to the needs of her wealthy and pregnant friend. M. takes the bold step of narrating this novel about memory and mystery from the man's point of view. Such experimentation with narrative perspective culminates in *A Recent Martyr* (1987), an intense meditation on the relationship of the profane to the sacred. Widely praised, the novel tells the story of a highly charged erotic affair in a New Orleans beset by plague. The two lovers, yielding to more and more dangerous sexual play, engage in a struggle over a saintly young novice on leave from her convent. In a display of technical virtuosity, the point of view in *A Recent Martyr* shifts throughout the novel from first to third person as the scene shifts from the woman to the man.

Similarly concerned with structural experimentation and love on the edge of doom, M.'s second collection of short fiction, *The Consolation of Nature and Other Stories* (1988), juxtaposes lovers in crisis with animals of both domestic and fantastic species. The obviously gothic character of this volume finds even clearer expression in *Mary Reilly* (1990).

Widely hailed as a major achievement, M.'s fourth novel retells Robert Louis Stevenson's *The Strange Case of Dr. Jekyll and Mr. Hyde* from the point of view of Dr. Jekyll's devoted maid. Though certainly related to M.'s earlier work, the book strikes out in many new directions. A historical novel set in London, *Mary Reilly* abandons the triangle of two women and one man that forms a basic unit of conflict in some of the earlier novels. Also, the explicit sexuality of her other fiction yields to an implied (though menacing) eroticism here. Even the narrative voice is unlike any other in M.'s work.

Reviewing *The Consolation of Nature and Other Stories*, Michiko Kakutani summarized the characteristics of M.'s work: "A preoccupation with the dark underside of life, a taste for disturbing, even macabre imagery, and a tendency to use that imagery to delineate turning points in people's lives—the moment when innocence is replaced by an acute awareness of death and pain." Though all this continues to be true of *Mary Reilly*, the novel also promises increasingly complex and subtle strategies for the expression of these qualities.

OTHER WORKS: "Waiting for the Story to Start," *NYT* (7 Feb. 1988).

BIBLIOGRAPHY: Fischer, John Irwin, "Masochists, Martyrs (and Mermaids) in the Fiction of Valerie Martin," *The Southern Rev.* 24 (Spring 1988).
   Other References: *NYT* (23 June 1978; 21 July 1979; 5 Aug. 1979; 7 June 1987; 13 Jan. 1988; 31 Jan. 1988; 26 Jan. 1990; 4 Feb. 1990).

JOHN BIGUENET

Bobbie Ann Mason

B. 1 May 1940, Mayfield, Kentucky
D. of Christi Anna (Lee) and Wilber A. Mason; m. Roger B. Rawlings, 1969

M. writes of the world of the changing South that she inhabited during her childhood. It is a world of people who shop at K mart, listen to rock and roll, and go to shopping malls for entertainment. She grew up on her parents' dairy farm near Mayfield, Kentucky, reading Nancy Drew and the Bobbsey Twins. When she was ten, she began to write her own mysteries. Her writing career took off briefly when she was a teenager and became the national president of the Hilltoppers Fan Club. She wrote their monthly newsletter and corresponded with the presidents of other fan clubs.

When she entered the University of Kentucky in 1958, M. began to read more classical literature, but, she claims, she related to none of it. She knew she wanted to be a writer, but received no encouragement. Upon graduation in 1962, M. went to New York and wrote for fan magazines such as *Movie Stars*, *Movie Life*, and *T.V. Star Parade*. She returned to graduate school and received her Ph.D. from the University of Connecticut in 1972. Her dissertation on Nabokov's *Ada* became her first published book, *Nabokov's Garden: A Guide to Ada* (1974). Returning to her childhood reading, M.'s second book was *The Girl Sleuth: A Feminist Guide to the Bobbsey Twins, Nancy Drew, and Their Sisters* (1975). She taught English for several years at Mansfield College in Pennsylvania.

M. was in her midthirties before she began to write serious fiction. In 1980, *The New Yorker* accepted her story "Offerings," which later became a part of *Shiloh and Other Stories* (1982). That first book of fiction was nominated for the National Book Critics Circle Award, the American Book Award, and the PEN/Faulkner Award for fiction, and received the Ernest Hemingway Foundation Award in 1983. The title story, "Shiloh," was anthologized in *Best American Short Stories* for 1981, and "Graveyard Day" was reprinted in the 1983 edition of *The Pushcart Prize: Best of the Small Presses*.

While "Shiloh" is the most anthologized, M. feels that the central story of the book is "Residents and Transients," which focuses on her fascination with the conflict between those who stay home and those who run away. The story highlights the tensions between the old and the new South and between the world of mass, popular culture, and the world of academic, elite culture. M. has her most scathing words for the elite who disdain those who shop at Kmart and spend their leisure time at shopping malls, and she treats her drugstore workers and truck drivers with love and respect. While they pay their bills and eat at McDonald's, they often dream of something more in their lives, and these dreams lead them to paint watermelons, build log cabins out of popsicle sticks, use fennel toothpaste, and, like M. herself, dream of returning home to Kentucky. M.'s regional sense and her eye for the details and detritus of everyday life enrich *Shiloh and Other Stories*, while her love for her characters lends them dignity.

M.'s first novel, *In Country* (1985), began with a set of characters much like those in her short stories. They live marginal lives on the fringe of the middle class and spend time listening to rock and roll and driving secondhand cars and trucks to the mall. As M. wrote, the story of Samantha (Sam) Hughes's loss emerged. Sam's father was killed in Vietnam before she knew him. Her mother has remarried and just had a new baby, and Sam is living with her uncle, Emmett Smith, a Vietnam veteran. The Vietnam War is the biggest thing that has happened in the lives of all the characters, and in America's life as well. While rejecting didacticism, M. creates the texture of the Vietnam experience. After spending the night in a swamp with her father's diary, Sam emerges knowing that she will never really experience being "in country," but her search for her father leads her to the Vietnam Memorial in Washington, DC, where she sees not only her father's name, Dwayne E. Hughes, but also her own—Sam A. Hughes. The memorial represents America for Sam, just as it did for M. when she first saw it. *In Country* records America's tragedy in Vietnam and reminds readers of the continuing loss from such Vietnam dangers as Agent Orange.

M.'s second novel, *Spence and Lila* (1988), follows the personal tragedy of Lila Culpepper's cancer. Married for over forty years, Spence and Lila have reared their children and farmed their rural Kentucky farm. Now their future is threatened by a lump in Lila's breast. With the same unerring ear for dialogue that characterized her earlier work, M. reveals the impatience, fear, loneliness, and love that wash over ordinary human beings as they try to deal with family and with old age, disease, and death. Lila's encounter with mortality helps her see that many people "won't or can't come out with their feelings," but despite their inability, M. is able to reveal her inarticulate characters' emotions. Nancy, Spence, and Lila's daughter, who also appears in "Nancy Culpepper" and "Lying Doggo" in *Shiloh and Other Stories*, is one of M.'s transients while her sister, Cat, and her brother, Lee, are residents who stay close to their parents' farm.

With *Love Life* (1989) M. returned to the short-story form. The collection, which focuses on varying responses to love, has, like *Shiloh and Other Stories*, thematic interconnections that make it almost novelistic. Like those in her earlier work, the characters listen to rock and roll and watch MTV and live on the margins of the middle class in small-town Kentucky. Here, as in all of her work, M. takes lives that seem on the surface to be barren and devoid of interest and invests them with will, dignity, and grace.

M.'s third novel, *Feather Crowns* (1993), is a tribute to Kentucky and to Christine Wheeler, mother of the first quintuplets born in North America. Like *In Country*, the novel records America's choices and the conflicts these choices create.

BIBLIOGRAPHY: *A World Unsuspected, Portraits of Southern Childhood*, Alex Harris, ed. (1990). Ryan, Maureen, "Stopping Places: Bobbie Ann Mason's Short Stories," *Women Writers of the Contemporary South*, Peggy Whitman Prenshaw, ed. (1984). Interview with Bobbie Ann Mason by Kay Bonetti, Amer. Audio Prose Library (1985). Reference works: *CA* 53–56 (1975).

CANR 11, (1984), 31 (1990). *CBY* (1989). *CLC* 28, 43 (1984, 1987). *DLBY* (1987). *Maj Twent Cent Writers* (1991).
Other references: *NYT Mag.* (15 May 1988). *Southern Literary J.* 19 (Spring 1987).

MARY A. MCCAY

Eve Merriam

B. *Eva Moskovitz, 19 July 1916, Philadelphia, Pennsylvania; d. 11 August 1992, New York City*
D. *of Jennie (Siegel) and Max Moskovitz; m. Erwin Spitzer, 1939, div. 1946; m. Martin Michel, 1947, div. 1960; m. Leonard Lewin, 1963, div. 1980; m. Waldo Salt, 1983 (d. 1987); c.: Guy Michel., b. 1951; Dee Michel, b. 1952*

Best known for her many exuberant and language-loving books for children, M. was primarily a poet. She was also a successful playwright, and well before the emergence of the contemporary women's movement, a feminist who wrote, often bitingly, about the relations between women and men. M. grew up in Pennsylvania where her parents, who had emigrated from Russia as children, owned a chain of women's clothing stores. She attended Cornell for two years, graduated from the University of Pennsylvania (B. A., 1937), and moved to New York to attend Columbia University. Unsuccessful in her attempts to publish her poems, she reluctantly agreed with one of her professors that anti-Semitism might be the cause and changed her name: Merriam was borrowed from the Merriam-Webster dictionary.

During the early 1940s, M. worked in New York City as a copywriter and feature editor on fashion magazines; she later published a wittily critical book on the fashion industry (*Figleaf: The Business of Being in Fashion*, 1960). She was also a writer for radio and from 1942 to 1946 moderator of a weekly radio program on poetry. A long-sought goal was reached in 1946 when her first book, *Family Circle*, won the Yale Series of Younger Poets Award. In his introduction to the collection, poet Archibald MacLeish praised the distinctiveness of M.'s voice and diction: "If Miss Merriam can continue in her own person, speaking her own tongue, with the courage of her own carelessness, she may well survive."

M. continued speaking her own tongue in more than sixty books and plays for children and adults. Her work was consistently motivated by two passions: a love of language and wordplay and an abiding concern for social justice. In "How to Eat a Poem" (*It Doesn't Always Have to Rhyme*, 1964), she urged children to understand poems as nourishment: "Bite in. / Pick it up with your fingers and lick the / juice that may run down your chin. / It is ready and ripe now, whenever you are." *Finding a Poem* (1970) includes a series of poems on punctuation marks: "Semicolon" pictures the diver who "lunges toward the edge; / hedges; / . . . hesitates; / plunges." Describing herself in "Writing a Poem" as "fooling around with images and rhymes simultaneously," M. unlocks the process, leading her readers through the evolution of "Landscape" from the original image, a rusting car, to its final musing on "what you will find at the edge of the world."

M.'s delight in the potential and joy of language made her unusually successful as both poet and educator; in her work pleasure and learning are simultaneous. Her poems never speak down to children but offer them ideas to imagine and consider: "Fantasia" *(Finding a Poem)* invites them into her "dream" of giving birth to a child who will have to ask, "Mother / what was war?" In addition to poems, M. also wrote biographies for young readers, including *The Voice of Liberty: the Story of Emma Lazarus* (1959), and books that raised issues of gender equality. The ground-breaking *Mommies at Work* appeared in 1961; it celebrates all the kinds of work that women do. *Boys and Girls, Girls and Boys* (1972) inventively calls gender roles into question. M. received the 1981 Award for Excellence in Poetry for Children from the National Council of Teachers of English, and continued throughout her life to travel to talk with children and teachers. She also taught writing at City College of New York in the 1960s and at New York University in the 1980s.

Long committed to a progressive political outlook, M.'s concern for social justice and her anger at society's failure to overcome the prejudices of race and gender permeate her writing. In the 1950s, she wrote about the civil rights struggle and its leaders: *Montgomery, Alabama, Money, Mississippi, and Other Places* (1956) contains poems praising Rosa Parks, Martin Luther King, Jr., and Autherine Lucy. *The Inner City Mother Goose* (1969, 1982) draws powerfully on the rhythms and language of nursery rhymes to indict a society that destroys its youth by racism and violence. The controversial book provided the basis for two theatrical productions: *Inner City: A Street Cantata*, with lyrics by M. (produced on Broadway in 1971), and *Sweet Dreams*, which premiered at La Mama Experimental Theatre Company in February 1984. Satire and anguish predominate in *The Nixon Poems* (1970), a response to the implications of Nixon's election for the continuation of both the war in Vietnam and injustice at home.

No subject more consistently drew M.'s attention than relationships between women and men and their inequities. As early as the 1940s she collaborated with historian **Gerda Lerner** on "Singing of Women: A Dramatic Review," which offers a panoramic view of women's history and women's struggle for justice. *The Double Bed from the Feminine Side*, published in 1958, is a series of poetic sequences tracing the story of a marriage from passion to alienation. The bride dreams "He'll make me free / And we'll hold our marriage forever"; the wife finally breaks free of the "monotonous round," and dreams of "becoming her own horizon." When it was published in a new edition in 1972, M. noted her hope that *The Double Bed* might become "a consciousness-raising book." A later book of poems, *A Husband's Notes About Her* (1976), is wryly subtitled *Fictions*.

After Nora Slammed the Door: American Women in the 1960s: The Unfinished Revolution appeared to almost no notice in 1964, perhaps overshadowed by the popular success of **Betty Friedan**'s *The Feminine Mystique* (1963). Combining social and economic analysis of "relations between the middle-class sexes" with poetry and the deconstruction of myths about women, M. offers no simple solutions for the modern Nora (the reference is to the heroine of Ibsen's *A Doll's House*). She argues for the need to alter the gender-bound nature of language, education, and social relations so women might imagine themselves, and so that both sexes might break free of the roles that keep them "bent over, stooped." M.'s several contributions to the effort of reeducation include *Growing up Female in America: Ten Lives* (1971, rept. 1987), a selection of autobiographical writings edited with a historical introduction by M. The subjects range from Eliza Southgate, an eighteenth-century schoolgirl, to **Susie King Taylor** and Mountain Wolf Woman. The stories were later made into a play, *Out of Our Father's House* (1975; first New York production 1977), which had a White House performance in 1978 and was adapted for public television.

From the early 1970s on, M. was deeply involved with theater projects. Probably best known of M.'s dramatic work is the OBIE Award winning *The Club* (1976). In this satirical feminist commentary set in an "exclusive men's club in 1903 . . . when male chauvinist behavior and banter were in full flower," M. made her devastating point by casting women, dressed in formal male attire, in all of the roles. Other theatrical productions include *At Her Age* (1979; published 1983), first staged at the Theatre for Older People in New York, and *Plagues for Our Time*, produced by Tom O'Horgan (who also staged "Inner City") at La Mama in 1983. *Plagues*, one critic noted, is "a pointed critique of a society that offers its pets hundreds of varieties of food, yet won't adequately feed all its elderly."

In the last year of her life, M. focused her writing on a remarkable series of poems that confront death. "Poems Purgatorio" will appear with the Plague poems and the "Jack Dark" sequence in a forthcoming volume *Embracing the Dark*. The "Jack Dark" poems are the saga of a fierce and painful struggle: Jack, rapist, murderer, cruel jokester, holds all of the cards, except for that of the poet's language which, still inventive, outwits and outlasts him.

OTHER WORKS: Juvenile: *The Real Book about Franklin D. Roosevelt* (1952). *The Real Book about Amazing Birds* (1955). *Emma Lazarus: Woman with a Torch* (1956). *A Gaggle of Geese* (1960). *There Is No Rhyme for Silver* (1962). *Funny Town* (1963). *What's in the Middle of a Riddle?* (1963). *Inside a Poem* (1964). *What Can You Do with a Pocket?* (1964). *Do You Want to See Something?* (1965). *Don't Think about a White Bear* (1965). *Small Fry* (1965). *The Story of Ben Franklin* (1965). *Catch a Little Rhyme* (1966). *Andy All Year Round* (1967). *Miss Tibbett's Typewriter* (1967). *Independent Voices* (1968). *Epaminondas* (reteller, 1968; republished 1972 as *That Noodle-Headed Epaminondas*). *I Am a Man: Ode to Martin Luther King, Jr.* (1971). *Project 1-2-3* (1971). *Bam! Zam! Boom!; a Building Book* (1972). *Male and Female under 18: Frank Comments from Young People about Their Sex Roles Today* (coeditor, 1973, with Nancy Larrick). *Rainbow Writing* (1976). *Ab to Zogg: A Lexicon for Science-Fiction and Fantasy Readers* (1977). *The Birthday Cow* (1978, illus. Guy Michel). *Unhurry Harry* (1978). *Good Night to Annie* (1980). *A Word or Two with You* (1981). *If Only I Could Tell You: Poems for Young Lovers and Dreamers* (1983). *Jamboree: Rhymes for All Times* (1984). *Blueberry Ink* (1985). *A Book of Wishes for You* (1985). *The Birthday Door* (1986). *Fresh Paint: New Poems* (1986). *A Sky Full of Poems* (1986). *Alligator in the Attic* (1987). *Halloween ABC* (1987). *You Be Good and I'll Be Night: Jump on the Bed Poems* (1988). *Chortles: New and Selected Wordplay Poems* (1989). *Daddies at Work* (1989). *Poem for a Pickle: Funnybone Verses* (1989). *Where Is Everybody?* (1989). *The Wise Woman and Her Secret* (1991). *Fighting Words* (1992). *Singing Green: New and Selected Poems* (1992). *Train Leaves the Station* (1992). *Shhh!* (1993). *12 Ways to Get to 11* (1994). *Higgle Wiggle* (1994). Adult: *Tomorrow Morning* (poems, 1953). *The Trouble with Love* (poems, 1960). *Basics: an I-Can-Read Book for Grownups* (1962). *Man and Woman: the Human Condition*

(1968). *Equality, Identity, and Complementarity: Changing Perspectives of Man and Woman*, ed. Robert H. Amundson (contributor, 1968). "We the Women" (television documentary, 1975). "Viva Reviva" (play, produced 1977). "Woman Alive: a Conversation Against Death" (opera with music by Patsy Rodgers, produced 1977, 1981). "The Good Life: Lady Macbeth of Westport" (play, produced 1979). *Dialogue for Lovers: Sonnets of Shakespeare Arranged for Dramatic Presentation* (1981). *And I Ain't Finished Yet* (play, 1981). "The World Outside My Skin [on writing "social poetry"]," in *Fanfare: The Christopher Gordon Children's Literature Annual I* (1993).

BIBLIOGRAPHY: Heffer, Helen, "A Checklist of Works by and about Eve Merriam." Unpublished M. A. thesis, Univ. of Maryland, 1980 (includes biographical introduction). Reference works: *CA* 137 (1992, obituary). *CANR* 29 (1990). *CLR* 14 (1988). *DLB* 61 (1987). *SATA* 3 (1972), 40 (1985). *Tw Cent Childrens' Wr* (1989). *WW Wr, Eds, Poets* (1989).

Other references: *Language Arts* 58 (Nov./Dec. 1981). *Learning 85* (Sept. 1985). *Nation* (31 Jan. 1959; 21 Mar. 1959; 23 June 1962; 14 Dec. 1964; 7 June 1965; 7 Oct. 1968; 7 Feb. 1972). *NYT* (22 Dec. 1963; 23 July 1976; 30 May 1980; 17 April 1983; 9 Dec. 1987; 13 Aug. 1992, obituary). *NYTBR* (16 Aug. 1964; 2 Mar. 1969; 1 Nov. 1970; 25 June 1972; 13 Mar. 1977; 15 Nov. 1981; 25 Nov. 1984; 8 Dec. 1985; 25 Oct. 1987; 26 Mar. 1989). *Working Woman* (March 1982). Mss. and correspondence at Schlesinger Library, Radcliffe College; Kerlan Collection, University of Minnesota (materials relating to juvenile works).

Biographical information confirmed by Dee Michel and Guy Michel.

CAROL HURD GREEN

June Meyer. *See June M. Jordan*

Josephine Miles

See AWW *3, 169–71*
D. 12 May 1985, Berkeley, California

M. was descended from an English business family that came to America on the *Mayflower*. Her mother studied history and education with John Dewey at the University of Chicago. M. attended public schools in Los Angeles and graduated Phi Beta Kappa from the University of California at Los Angeles in 1932. She received an M.A. (1934) and Ph.D. (1938) from the University of California at Berkeley and joined the Berkeley faculty in 1940. She retired, university professor emerita, in 1978.

M., who began writing poems at age eight, developed her compelling interests in poetic language and form during early graduate study. The metaphysical poets and Yeats led her early verse in a direction counter to that of her contemporaries. Later, the writing of Neruda and Rilke offered modern alternatives to the more oblique expression of the metaphysical poets. The contemporary poets she regarded most highly included Richard Eberhart, **Muriel Rukeyser, Denise Levertov,** William Stafford, and A. R. Ammons. Those characteristics M. identified as important in their verse—incisiveness, factualness, simplicity, and lyricism—are evident in her own finest poems. M. received distinguished awards for her poetry and literary scholarship, among them a National Institute of Arts and Letters Award for poetry (1956), the Fellowship of the American Academy of Poets (1978), and election to the American Academy and Institute of Arts and Letters (1980).

M.'s approach to what she called "verse composition" was often determined by "the idea of speech . . . people talking . . . as the material from which poetry is made." In an early poem, "Speaker," the voice admits: "My talking heart talked less of what it knew / Than what it saw." What is known in many of M.'s poems is conveyed by what is observed in commonplace landscapes. Long a city resident, M. includes in these landscapes the repeated sights of urban life. Noting in her work a subtle satiric gift, **Louise Bogan** pointed to the indirect way M. drew meaning from "the parking lot, the motel . . . the supermarket, and the service station."

M.'s poetry has not received the critical attention it deserves, although reviews of her last two books, *Coming to Terms* (1979) and *Collected Poems, 1930–1983* (1983), were uniformly laudatory. It is difficult to generalize about M.'s writing except to note its condensation, craft, unexpected juxtaposition of images, pleasure in "the space and active interplay of talk," and—in later volumes—willingness to employ more irregular forms and an increasingly more direct political and ethical stance.

OTHER WORKS: *The Primary Language of Poetry in the 1640s* (1948).

BIBLIOGRAPHY: Reference works: *CANR* 2 (1981). *CA* 116 (1986, obituary). *CLC* 34 (1985), 39 (1986). *DLB* 48 (1986). *FC* (1990).
 Other references: *Hudson Rev.* (Autumn 1984). *LJ* (Aug. 1983). *Southern Rev.* (July 1983).

THEODORA R. GRAHAM

Isabel Miller. *See Alma Routsong*

Kate Millett

See AWW 3, 188–90

One of the founding members of the "second wave" feminist movement, M. remains an influential artist and scholar, providing inspiration to another generation of women and men committed to the goals of what may broadly be termed radical feminism. Since the publication of *Sexual Politics* (1970), now considered a classic in feminist criticism, M. has struggled to overcome the oftentimes intense resistance of many within the major

American publishing houses to see her work in print. Largely through her own tenacity, with the assistance of several dedicated colleagues, M. has in recent years published two largely autobiographical volumes, *Going to Iran* (1982) and *The Loony-Bin Trip* (1990). She has also completed work on another manuscript, which she terms "purely literary," on the subject of her family; as of this writing it is unpublished.

Going to Iran is a little-noted account of M.'s experiences in that country during some of the most turbulent months of the Iranian Revolution. Her primary interest throughout is the evolving status of women, which she observes as having deteriorated markedly as what began as a popular revolution was gradually transformed into fundamentalist reaction. Imbued with the penetrating insight and critical awareness that are emblematic of M.'s work, *Going to Iran* offers a poignant and disturbing perspective on the myriad issues confronting contemporary Iranian women. Predictably, M. was viewed with considerable suspicion and animosity by the Iranian authorities, and thus, for political reasons, was officially detained and ultimately deported.

The Loony-Bin Trip concerns her ordeals as a psychiatric patient forced, on multiple occasions, to suffer the trauma and indignities of involuntary hospitalization. One of the greatest strengths of the book lies in the unflinching honesty with which M. portrays the inner workings of her mind as she endures not only the vagaries of manic-depressive disorder, her clinical diagnosis, but also the well-intended though nonetheless devastating treatment she received at the hands of family, friends, and physicians.

In addition to her writing, M. is an accomplished visual artist, whose sculpture and painting have frequently been exhibited in cities throughout the United States. M. also continues to operate a cooperative artists' colony in Poughkeepsie, New York, a venture she embarked upon several years ago. Participants include writers, sculptors, photographers, and painters, all of whom receive studio space in exchange for their contributions to the maintenance of the colony. Moreover, M. lectures widely on an array of feminist and humanist issues. Through these diverse means, M. continues her efforts to raise public consciousness of persisting social injustices and contribute to the continued elevation in the quality of women's lives.

BIBLIOGRAPHY: Cohen, Marcia, *The Sisterhood* (1988). *The Traditions of Women's Autobiography: From Antiquity to the Present*, Estelle Jelinek, ed. (1986). Mills, Sara, et al., *Feminist Readings/Feminists Reading* (1989). Moi,

Toril, *Sexual/Textual Politics* (1985). Reference works: *CANR* 32 (1991). *CLC* 67 (1992). *FC* (1990).

Other references: *Ms.* (March 1988; May 1988). *NYTBR* (3 June 1990). *WRB* (Oct. 1990).

Additions/corrections to AWW 3: D. of James and Helen Feely Millett; m. Fumia Yoshimura, 1965; div. 1985.

LISA CARDYN

Valerie Miner

B. 28 Aug. 1947, New York City
D. of Mary (McKenzie) and John Daniel Miner

Journalist, novelist, essayist, editor, and critic—M. could be any one of her main characters. They are all a type of everywoman—Liz, Susan, Beth, Polly, Teddy, Anne, Gerry—who mirror not only M.'s life, but the life and struggle of many women. Educated at the University of California at Berkeley (B.A. 1969) where she also earned a graduate degree in journalism (M.A. 1970), M.'s accomplishments include a founding membership in the National Feminist Writers Guild, a position on the board of directors of Women against Violence in Pornography and Media, a twenty-year teaching career including ten years at UC-Berkeley, and many awards including the Pen Syndicated Fiction Award.

M.'s dedication to political causes, especially feminism, is reflected in her fiction as well as her career. Her characters are fiercely independent, fiercely political and, for the most part, fiercely alone. And these women need to be ferocious, for they must weather wars, terrorism, exile, imprisonment, marriage, divorce, and complex relationships, both heterosexual and lesbian. Each situation, each relationship is approached with hope and trepidation. Sometimes, all the women are left with is their hope and fear. But the perseverance to change their world survives.

Perseverance is indeed the legacy left to Liz and Beth, daughters of the

Irish-born twin sisters, Polly and Gerry, in *Blood Sisters: An Examination of Conscience* (1981). Liz and Beth, although only cousins, are mirror images of each other; their twinning going beyond biological ties is established in blood, the blood shed from IRA bombings in England. War of a different kind challenges the perseverance of the bonds of women in *All Good Women* (1987). A desire for careers and independence is what brings Teddy, Ann, Moira, and Wanda together in the first place. But the endurance not only of their friendship but also of their dreams is tested by United States involvement in World War II and the internment of Wanda, a Japanese-American. Ann cannot sit still with the knowledge that some of her family in Europe may be the victims of concentration camps and sets off to work with war orphans in London. Teddy and Moira are left to handle their own personal struggles with the war effort at home, in addition to the realization and consummation of their feelings for each other. M. takes on a whole host of social issues aside from those related to war: the lesbian lifestyle, pregnancy and birth outside of marriage, women living on their own and working in male-dominated jobs, sexual harassment. The bond of the four women is what sustains them all, much as the bond of blood and kin sustains Liz, Polly, and Beth, despite the death of Gerry and the imprisonment of Beth.

Winter's Edge (1984) is somewhat of a departure from the above novels in that the focus is on a couple—two elderly women, Chrissie and Margaret—whose bond survives Margaret's flirtations with men, Chrissie's jealousy, Margaret's passiveness, and Chrissie's activism. The reader sees the world of San Francisco, replete with dirty politics, greedy developers, and bombings, through the eyes of each woman. If the novel reads like a mystery for senior citizens, perhaps M.'s previously published novel, *Murder in the English Department* (1982), is responsible for her further experimentation with the genre. The title conjures up an old-fashioned scholarly atmosphere, but the reality of the setting and plot focuses on violence, not only physical, but the emotional kind that can undermine reputation and self-confidence. The reader follows Nan Weaver as she is implicated in the murder of a university colleague, and is treated to a good dose of examples of sexual harassment and tenure woes.

In another kind of examination of the academic world, *Competition: A Feminist Taboo* (1987), coedited with Helen Longino, M. explores the one area of female experience that is steeped in denial. Aimed specifically at academia, the collection of essays examines what happens to sisterhood in atmospheres that dictate rivalry. *Rumors from the Cauldron: Selected Essays, Reviews, and Reportage* (1992) looks back on M.'s career, pulling together various writings in order to report on her own development as a writer and a woman. As in *Competition,* she examines sisterhood and its endurance in the face of career and art, but in *Tales* rivalry cedes to sisterhood in the last section of the book where M. reviews the work of other women writers, taking care to spotlight those who are lesser known. It is clear from this book that, indeed, M. has been on an odyssey of her own and has more than merely survived.

OTHER WORKS: *Her Own Woman* (with M. Kostash et al., 1975). *Tales I Tell My Mother* (with Z. Fairbairns et al., 1978). *More Tales I Tell My Mother* (1987). *Trespassing* (1989).

BIBLIOGRAPHY: Reference works: *CA* 97–100 (1981). *CLC* 40 (1986). *FC* (1990).

Other references: *New Statesman* (24 July 1981). *NYTBR* (19 Jan. 1986, 22 Aug. 1987). *PW* (9 July 1982, 27 Sept. 1985, 11 Sept. 1987, 7 Aug. 1987, 8 Aug. 1986). *TLS* (17 July 1981, 5 Nov. 1982, 27 July 1984, 12 July 1989). *WRB* (April 1986, Dec. 1986, Nov. 1987, March 1988).

LINDA BERUBE

Janice Mirikitani

B. 5 Feb. 1942, Stockton, California
D. of BelleAnne Matsuda and Ted Mirikitani; m. (2nd) Cecil Williams, 1982;
  c: Tianne Tsukiko Miller, b. 1967

Poet, editor, anthologist, teacher, choreographer, and political activist, M. is an important figure in the Asian American community and in the literary world. A third generation Japanese American whose grandparents immigrated from Hiroshima, incarcerated at birth with her family in the Rohwer, Arkansas, concentration camp during World War II, M. has spoken out with persuasive and lyrical militancy against racism, violence, and containment. She has urged others, particularly women of color, to shed their silences and find the power of collective voice.

M. received her B.A. (cum laude) from UCLA in 1962 and her teaching credentials from U.C.-Berkeley in 1963. She taught English, speech, and dance at the Contra Costa Unified School District (1964–65) and enrolled in graduate studies in creative writing at San Francisco State University, where she was later (1972) a lecturer in Japanese American literature and creative writing. In 1966 M. began work at the Glide Church/Urban Center in San Francisco. Since becoming program director there in 1969, she has overseen meal and housing projects, rape and abuse recovery programs for women, and a volunteer program offering computer services to the poor and homeless. She was elected president of the Glide Foundation in 1983.

M. has been involved in efforts for reparations for Japanese Americans who were interned during World War II and she has served on many Bay Area boards, including the Zellerbach Community Arts Distribution Committee and the United Tenderloin Community Fund. With her husband, Rev. Cecil Williams, she compiled a book of children's writings on the crack cocaine crisis, *I Have Something to Say about This Big Trouble: Children of the Tenderloin Speak Out* (1989). She has also choreographed and produced more than thirty-five dance productions with social themes. These include "A Tribute to King"; "Who Among the Missing" (in honor of Central Americans missing, tortured, and imprisoned); "Hiroshima, California," an antiwar statement that had a national tour; "Lonnie's Song," which focuses on a community of people affected by the AIDS crisis; and "Revealing Secrets, Releasing Fear," dances and poetry about addiction, incest, and recovery.

M.'s writing, like her community work, is largely informed by her history and her politics. Committed to helping third-world and women artists and writers to publish, M. has served as an editor for several magazines and anthologies, including *Aion Magazine*; *Time to Greeze!: Incantations from the Third World* (1975); *AYUMI: A Japanese American Anthology* (1980); and *Making Waves: An Anthology of Writings by and about Asian American Women* (1989). She also published two collections of her own poetry and prose, *Awake in the River* (1978) and *Shedding Silence* (1987), and her work has appaeared in numerous anthologies, textbooks, magazines, and journals in the United States and Japan.

In pieces dedicated to war veterans and to comrade sisters, in poems written in response to the assassinations of Steve Biko and of Orlando Letelier, and in remembrance of relatives, M. speaks out against legally sanctioned racism and brutality. She links the devastation of Hiroshima with Vietnam and the internment camp at Tule Lake, and further connects war atrocities with such assaults and invasions as sexual harassment, child molestation, incest, rape, and battering (see "Zipper," "Tomatoes," "The Winner," "Crazy Alice," and "Spoils of War"). She also writes of racial exoticization, cultural misogyny, and self-erasure ("Doreen," "Recipes," "Suicide Note"). Other poems note the injunction to women of color to bleach their stories, starch their thoughts, and curb desire ("Healthy Choices"), and the cost of political passivity and silence. In a second version of "Spoils of War," included in *Shedding Silence*, M. powerfully links racism, colonialism, and the militarization of people's consciousness with misogyny and violent sexuality in the story of the rape and mutilation of a young woman by a Vietnam veteran.

M's writings, however, are not about victimization as much as they are about survival, rebirth, and affirmation of self. While many remain silent about their violent pasts, M. refuses to bow to a history of violation; instead, she voices her anger and acts for change. In "Shedding Silence," a dramatic presentation that developed out of the agitation propaganda theater of the 1960s, M. uses the image of a discarded obi to symbolize rejection of the containment of women and of prescriptions for "proper" (traditional Japanese, feminine) behavior and writing. Not fearful or powerless, not quiet or demure, she takes memory and creativity as her weapons and becomes a word warrior, deftly wielding her pen to rewrite Japanese American women's roles (see especially "Without Tongue" and "Slaying Dragon Ladies"). She is, she affirms, a "saboteur of stereotypes" ("Who Is Singing this Song?").

Recognizing that real power lies not in oppression but in sharing, M. celebrates legacies of strength and claims her place among generations of Asian American women and their "loud, yellow" and "dangerous" protest against injustices and violence ("Generations of Women," "Prisons of Silence"). As she writes in "Breaking Silence": "We must recognize ourselves at last. / We are a rainforest of color and noise." Difficult though it may be for women of color to break free of "prisons of silence," it is important, M. insists, to "give testimony," for, as she says repeatedly, "We survive by hearing."

Direct, vitally angry, and politically impassioned, M. breaks taboos, writing against expectations of her as a woman and as an Asian American to speak decorously. Without apology, dimunition, self-deprecation, or conciliation, she validates her voice and places its power, its passion, and its rage in the context of large and violent truths. While some have found her writings too angry and blunt, many have felt empowered by her explosive poetry and prose and her clear political commitment. In all that she does, M. insists on the collective power of voice and vows to do her part to stop violence: "Count our numbers, / harvest our strength, / breathe between the rain. / We shall not go into their camps again."

In recognition of the exceptional commitment and impact of her writings and her life work, M. received the Woman Warrior in Arts and Culture Award from the Pacific Asian American Women Bay Area Coalition (1983). She was also honored, along with **Alice Walker, Alice Adams, Judy Grahn, Josephine Miles,** and **Tillie Olsen,** with the Woman of Words Award (1985). In 1988 she and Cecil Williams received the U.C.-San Francisco Chancellor's Medal of Honor. The California State Assembly named her "Woman of the Year" in the Seventeenth Assembly District (1988) and she was the recipient in 1990 of the Outstanding Leadership Award of the Japanese Community Youth Council.

BIBLIOGRAPHY: Crawford, John F., "Notes toward a New Multicultural Criticism," in *A Gift of Tongues*, Marie Harris and Kathleen Aguero, eds. (1987). Kim, Elaine H., *Asian American Literature: An Introduction to the Writings and Their Social Context* (1982).

Other references: *Feminist Studies* 14:3 (Fall 1988). Brief biog. notes in *Ayumi, Making Waves,* and *The Heath Anthol. of Amer. Lit.* (1990). Résumé and biographical sketches from Janice Mirikitani.

ANN E. REUMAN

Jessica Mitford

See AWW 3, 195–97

In the 1980s M. returned in her writings to explore her English youth, first in *Faces of Philip* (1984) and then in *Grace Had an English Heart* (1988). *Faces of Philip* purports to be a memoir of Philip Toynbee, son of the historian Arnold, and originally a friend from the time of M.'s first marriage. In writing about the "many faces" of Philip Toynbee, however, one senses that M. is actually writing about herself—her lost aristocratic youth, her lost marriage, her ambivalence toward the many roles she has played in her own life. As a portrait of one man, the book is adequate albeit a bit sentimental. A more ambitious writer might have tried to depict Toynbee as a representative of his class, the embodiment of a declining aristocratic tradition. Instead, M. is content to portray his life simply through his personal relationships, in particular his relationship with her.

In *Grace Had an English Heart* M. dissects a young woman who became a cultural icon and legend of female heroism in Victorian England. Grace Darling, daughter of a lighthouse keeper off the coast of Northumberland, assisted her father in the rescue of nine shipwrecked passengers in September 1838, and became the first Victorian media sensation, an almost totally created media heroine. The episode allows M. to meditate on the rise of journalism as a profession, and its complicity in promulgating the values demanded in women of the period—virginity, courage, selflessness, and a tendency to die young. Although written with humor, the book fails to probe in any scholarly or sustained manner how "femininity" became an ideological construction during the Victorian period. The published reviews of this volume note its humor and light touch, M.'s trademarks, but they also sense that such humor wears thin when M. attempts to present herself as a "cultural historian."

Echoing the title of her popular 1963 book, *The American Way of Death*, M. returned to observations of American culture with *The American Way of Birth* (1992). Here, however, her tone is primarily indignant rather than satirical as she details the growing crisis in American obstetrics and excoriates the male medical establishment. Based on her journey across the United States to observe both standard and alternative methods of birth, M. urges a return to traditional "direct-entry" midwifery and home birth. More directly feminist than her earlier work, the book has been variously received, with reviewers acknowledging the justice of her accusations and the attractiveness of her solutions while questioning her right to claim expertise.

BIBLIOGRAPHY: Reference works: *CANR* 1 (1981).

Other references: *LJ* (1 March 1989). *NYTBR* (16 April 1989; 8 Nov. 1992).

TLS (7 Oct. 1988). *Twentieth Cent. Lit.* (Fall 1988). *Times Educational Supp.* (9 Sept. 1988).

DIANE LONG HOEVELER

Nicholasa Mohr

B. 1 Nov. 1938, New York City
D. of Nicholasa (Rivera) and Pedro Golpe; m. Irwin Mohr, 1958 (d. 1978);
  c.: David, Jason

The youngest child in a family with six brothers, M. was born in El Barrio, Spanish Harlem, where her parents had moved from Puerto Rico at the height of the Depression of the 1930s. Like several of her young characters, M.'s artistic abilities were recognized at an early age. In spite of her talent, she attended a trade high school, a decision made by a grade-school counselor who felt that "because I was a child from a poor Puerto Rican family, I most likely could not go on to higher education." Subsequently, she studied at the Art Students League of New York (1957), Brooklyn Museum Art School (1961–63), and Pratt Center for Contemporary Printmaking (1966–70), and established an active career as a graphic artist.

M. began writing when the words, phrases, and bold figures of her prints caught the eye of one of her collectors, the head of a publishing house. Through her agent, he suggested that M. try writing stories about her experiences. After some encouragement, she took the suggestion seriously and in 1973 published her first novel, *Nilda*. Since that time, she has written fiction, short stories, screenplays, and articles for both children and adults. She is best known for her novels and short-story collection for children and young adults.

M. is the first Puerto Rican woman on the mainland to write in English about the experiences of first-generation Puerto Rican–Americans. Her writing is characterized by simplicity in its structure and in its choice of words. Short sentences and a matter-of-fact, episodic style paradoxically create vivid, detailed scenes of streets and neighborhoods, and introduce complex, sometimes controversial, characters and themes. The individual experiences and feelings of her characters demonstrate the clash between white and Puerto Rican cultures as well as the tensions between Puerto Ricans from the mainland and those from the island. Other themes explored in her work include the resilience of the human spirit, the role of ritual and celebration in family life, the difficulty of moving from the country to the city, and the effects of institutionalized racism.

Together, *Nilda* and M.'s two short-story collections, *El Bronx Remembered* (1975, 1986) and *In Nueva York* (1977), comprise a history of the everyday struggles of Puerto Ricans in New York City over a thirty-year period (1941–70). Written for the general public, the books were published as juvenile trade books and marketed as young-adult literature. They continue to spark controversy over their appropriateness for young people because M. incorporates homosexuality, teenage pregnancy, graphic language, racist violence, and shocking effects of poverty in these stories of urban life.

Nilda, a coming-of-age story, is set in El Barrio during World War II. Told from the point of view of Nilda Ramirez who is nine at the outset of the novel, the story's parameters expand as Nilda's understanding of life expands. Nilda's struggle to become herself is the foreground as her mother's struggles to nurture and maintain a family of six is the background. The two stories come together when Nilda is left confused and overwhelmed after her mother's death. With only the legacy of her mother's final words, "I have never had a life of my own . . . hold onto yourself. . . . A little piece inside has to remain yours always," Nilda turns to her art for solace.

Many of the women in M.'s short stories struggle to keep that "little piece inside" intact. The importance of self-determination and self-expression for women is most explicitly explored in *Rituals of Survival: A Woman's Portfolio* (1985), a short-story collection for adults. Zoraida, Carmela, Virginia, Amy, Lucia, and Inez contend with poverty, rigid role expectations, racism, and internal confusion as they fight to maintain their inner lives. Whether triumphant or defeated, each is transformed as she steps toward self-identity.

With *Felita* (1979) and its sequel, *Going Home* (1986), M. began writing specifically for children. The fresh outlook and lively, independent spirit of each of these books rests in the characterization of Felita. In both, the harsher realities of the world are balanced by the ordinary events and crises of growing up. In *Felita*, her family is driven from a white neighborhood by violent racist harassment and Felita and her best friend experience jealousy and misunderstanding over the lead in the class play. In *Going Home*, Felita's summer in Puerto Rico is marred by being an outsider on her "own" island while she works on sets for a local youth group's play.

Providing an animated and loving, yet uncompromising portrayal of the Puerto Rican-American community, M.'s writing focuses on details, in both setting and experience, to capture the spirit and resilience of individuals and their community. This illumination of details and incidents effectively shapes itself into compelling portraits of individuals as well as of the whole in many stories, although it sometimes creates narratives that lack drama or depth. Overall, M.'s literature for both children and adults is valuable as a unique and significant artistic rendering of the experiences of Puerto Rican-Americans.

OTHER WORKS: All for the Better (1993). *Old Letivia and the Mountain of Sorrows* (1994). Short stories in *Revista Chicano-Riqueza* 8:2 (Spring 1980); 9:2 (Spring 1981); 11:3–4 (1983). "Puerto Ricans in the U.S.: The Adopted Citizen," in *Ethnic Lifestyles and Mental Health*, Gloria Valencia-Weber, ed. (1980). "Their America," *Perspectives: The Civil Rights Quarterly* 14 (Summer 1982). "On Being Authentic," *The Americas Rev.* 14:3–4 (Fall–Winter 1986). "Puerto Rican Writers in the United States, Puerto Rican Writers in Puerto Rico: A Separation beyond Language," *Americas Rev.* 15:2 (Summer 1987). "Puerto Ricans in New York: Cultural Evolution and Identity," in *Images and Identities: The Puerto Rican in Literature*, Asela Rodriguez de Laguna, ed. (1987).

BIBLIOGRAPHY: Reference works: *Biog. Dict. of Hispanic Writers in the US* (1989). *CANR* 32 (1991). *CLR* 22 (1991). *Fifth Junior Book of Authors* (1983).

Other references: *MELUS* 5 (1978). *Revista/Review Interamericana* 9 (1979–1980). *Revista Chicano-Riqueza* 8 (1980). *English J.* 67 (1978). Turner, Faythe, "The Myth of the American Dream in the Works of Nicholasa Mohr," unpublished paper, Amherst College, Amherst, Massachusetts. Biographical information verified by Mohr, Dec. 1992).

SUSAN GRIFFITH

A. G. Mojtabai

See AWW 3, 202–3

Since her early training in science and philosophy, M. has continued to be influenced by Cartesian dualism, which was central to her first novel, *Mundome* (1974), and by the moral and ethical consequences of scientific achievement, which was her concern in *The 400 Eels of Sigmund Freud* (1976). Since that time, M.'s interest in what separates or connects the human community has often been related to religion.

A Stopping Place (1979), a political novel set on the border of India and Pakistan, is a fictional account of the 1963 crisis for the newly partitioned states that occurs when a holy relic—a hair of the prophet Muhammed—is stolen. It is a tale of growing suspicion and division between religions, nations, and individuals. "A hair, and then a blade" is the dominant image. One character, an American writer on a cultural tour, is known as "a poet of lost connections," identifying a theme central to M.'s fiction.

Autumn (1982), a virtual prose poem set on the bleak Maine seacoast, is a meditation on loss and grief by a recent widower who refuses to leave his summer house after the summer is ended. He is lost between the physical and spiritual realms.

M. had a Guggenheim Fellowship in 1981–82. In 1983, she gave up a lectureship at Harvard, where she had taught since 1978, to become writer in residence at the University of Tulsa. This position served as a base from which to research the religious debate surrounding the United States's nuclear weapons final assembly plant in Amarillo, Texas. *Blessed Assurance* (1986), which won the Lillian Smith Award that year for the best book about the South, is a nonfiction account of the peculiar tension between two kinds of futurism M. found in Amarillo: the frontier optimism of a business community set in a "fertile but bare, expectant land, where anything could happen," and a largely fundamentalist religious community that passively accepts the implications of the bomb by relying on an apocalyptic "Rapture" when God will rescue the saved. There was some hostile local reaction to the book, but not from the Pentecostals, who praised her accurate reporting of their message of salvation.

Ordinary Time (1989), named for the Roman Catholic liturgical season, is a novel that grew out of M.'s west Texas experience. Protagonists are Henrietta, a Pentecostal who searches for religious faith and human love, and Father Gilvary, an aging Catholic priest whose eyesight and religious certainty are growing dim. Characters hunger for miracles they do not find in ordinary life, but Henrietta realizes that she and the priest share a common ground: they are alone, yet not alone.

Recent comparisons of M. to **Flannery O'Connor** and T. S. Eliot suggest the ironic mixture of grotesque humor with the poetic expression of a moral vision she achieves in *Ordinary Time*. Each book has been a new experiment with prose form. Her narratives focus on the solitary voice, but the quiet affirmation of *Ordinary Time* represents a new sense of optimism.

BIBLIOGRAPHY: *America* (Feb. 1990). *Christian Science Monitor* (27 June 1986). *Commonweal* (20 Oct. 1989). *NYTBR* (8 June 1986; 24 Sept. 1989). *Rev. of Contemp. Fiction* (Spring 1990). *Southern Q.* 29:1 (Fall 1990). *Tulsa Women* (Spring 1990).

RUTH D. WESTON

Cherríe Moraga

B. 25 Sept. 1952, Whittier, California
D. of Elvira and Joseph Lawrence Moraga

M. is the daughter of a Chicana mother and a European American father. When M. was nine, the family settled in the Los Angeles area. A poor reader as a child, she affirms that listening to the women of her mother's family instilled in her the art of telling a story and the blend of Spanish and English that characterizes her writing. She received a B.A. in English (1974) and a M.A. in feminist writings (1980) from San Francisco State University. M. joined the Chicano Studies department at the University of California, Berkeley, in 1986, and taught there until 1991.

M.'s work is courageous and polemical in both Chicano and feminist communities. Speaking as a Chicana feminist lesbian, she has broken the silence surrounding taboo topics such as sexuality and lesbianism; sexism and homophobia in Chicano culture; racism and classism in the white women's movement; and the urgent need for a feminism defined by women of color. M.'s effort to "think through" what it means to be Chicana and lesbian in essays that are collages of dreams, journal entries, and autobiographical reflection are an important foundation on which to build further Latina feminist theory.

With **Gloria Anzaldúa,** M. coedited *This Bridge Called My Back: Writings by Radical Women of Color* (1981), a groundbreaking feminist anthology that provides an analysis of interlocking systems of oppression. Besides the important prefatory material, including the introduction defining the concept of "theory in the flesh," M.'s work is represented by two poems and an essay. "La Guera" explains how M.'s light skin allowed her to "pass" until she came out as a lesbian. Only then did she understand oppression. The essay documents her painful journey to "my brown mother—the brown in me," and calls for an awareness of the ways in which all women internalize the values of the oppressor.

Cuentos: Stories by Latinas (1983), edited by M. with Alma Gomez and Mariana Romo-Carmona, is the first anthology of fiction by Latina feminist writers. "Sin luz," one of M.'s two stories, is a frank depiction of a young girl's attitudes about sexuality. In *Lo que nunca paso por sus labios (Loving in the War Years,* 1983) M. gathered together seven years of poetry and continued to work out in essays the contradictory aspects of her identity. The book focuses on the intersections of race and sexuality (the *light-skinned* Chicana, the Chicana *lesbian*). In "A Long Line of Vendidas," M. traces the ways in which Chicanas are both damaged and empowered as sexual subjects by their cultural experience, a theme that runs throughout her writing. She analyzes the pervasive influence on gender roles of the myth of "La Malinche," Cortés's mistress and tactical advisor who represented the equation of female sexuality and betrayal and contributed to the cultural construction of woman as passive object.

Women's fear of betrayal, because of the cultural mandate to put men first, is echoed throughout M.'s writing. Many of the pieces in *Loving* also explore women's desire to "prove their faith," not in God or men, but in each other. In her exploration of her complex heritage, M. characteristically (and iconoclastically) infuses Mexican and Catholic archetypes with the "heat" of lesbian desire.

M.'s first work for the theater, the two-act verse play *Giving up the Ghost*

(1986), juxtaposes the poetic monologues of three characters: Marisa, a Chicana lesbian; Corky, Marisa's younger self; and Amalia, a heterosexual Chicana. Corky's fierce attempts to escape the definition of her female self as passive object are defeated when she is raped at the age of eleven. The adult Marisa is left with her rage, unable to open herself in her love for women, and crippled by the betrayal of women who always put men first. Through Amalia's love for her, Marisa experiences what it is like to surrender to the woman she desires. But this sexual love does not bring salvation and at the end of the play both women are still struggling with the private ghosts that torment them, although Marisa dreams of a community based on the love and loyalty of women for women.

M.'s second play, *Shadow of a Man*, performed in 1990 at San Francisco's Eureka Theatre, explores the harmful impact of machismo on Chicano men. Set in the late 1960s in Los Angeles, the play tells the story of the Rodriguez family, torn apart by the dark "secret" of the father Manuel's obsession with his *compadre* Conrado, who represents the masculine ideal Manuel both desires and fails to embody. The play asks the Latino community to think about sexuality and desire beyond rigid heterosexual roles and to explore the intersections and contradictions of homosociality and homosexuality.

M.'s third play, *Heroes and Saints* (first production 1991), combines consideration of the pesticide poisoning of farmworkers, sexuality, and female subjectivity. With it, M. continues the project of creating a "healing" theater that offers the possibility of transformation by addressing Chicano reality in all its complexity.

OTHER WORKS: *The Last Generation* (1993).

BIBLIOGRAPHY: Alarcon, Norma, "Interview with Cherríe Moraga," *Third Woman* 3 (1986). Sternbach, Nancy Saporta, "'A Deep Racial Memory of Love': The Chicana Feminism of Cherríe Moraga," in *Breaking Boundaries: Latina Writing and Critical Readings*, Asunción Horno-Delgado et al., eds. (1989). Yarbro-Bejarano, Yvonne, "Cherríe Moraga's *Giving up the Ghost*: The Representation of Female Desire," *Third Woman* 3 (1986); "De-constructing the Lesbian Body: Cherríe Moraga's *Loving in the War Years*," in *Chicana Lesbians. The Girls Our Mothers Warned Us About*, Carla Trujillo, ed. (1991); "Cherríe Moraga's *Shadow of a Man*: Touching the Wound in Order to Heal," in *Acting Out: Feminist Performances*, Lynda Hart and Peggy Phelan, eds. (1993). Reference books: *CA* 131 (1991). *DLB* 82 (1989). *Hispanic Writers* 15:3–4 (1987).

Other references: *Americas Rev.* 14 (Summer 1986), 15 (Fall 1987). *Monographic Rev./Rev. Monográfica* 6 (1990). *off our backs* (Jan. 1985, interview).

YVONNE YARBRO-BEJARANO

Robin Morgan

B. 29 Jan. 1941, Lake Worth, Florida
D. of Faith Berkeley Morgan; m. Kenneth Pitchford, 1962; c.: Blake Ariel
Morgan-Pitchford

As a child, M. played Dagmar on the popular television series "I Remember Mama" but quit acting at age sixteen. She left Columbia University in 1962 to marry a fellow poet and work as a literary agent and freelance editor. Becoming an antiwar "politico" activist in the New Left, M. met Ellen Willis and Jane Alpert and like many female colleagues made a quick transition to radical feminism. She was a founding member of New York Radical Feminists (NYRF, 1967) and the Women's International Conspiracy from Hell (WITCH, 1968). M. helped organize and publicize the 1968 WITCH demonstration at the Miss America Pageant and was an early participant in NYRF consciousness-raising sessions.

M. and Alpert engineered the January 1970 women's takeover of the New Left magazine *Rat*, publishing a women's issue in retaliation for the male staff's "sex-and-porn special." M's essay, "Good-Bye to All That," a bitter indictment of male chauvinism among leftist activists and a call for a women's revolution, was "the shot heard round the Left," and became a feminist classic signaling gender fragmentation, the rise of the Women's Liberation Front, and the demise of the New Left. M.'s rage, with characteristically emotional leftist rhetoric punctuated by obscenities, proclaimed the beginning of a new era critical of patriarchal, sexist, racist, imperialist, and capitalist "Amerika." M. and other radical women published *Rat* for two years as a feminist periodical before Alpert fled "underground" to avoid prosecution for Weatherman activities. M.'s "Letter to a Sister Underground" revealed that she remained Alpert's mentor despite intense controversy over Alpert among feminists.

M. became a major theorist for cultural feminism, urging creation of alternative women's institutions as "concrete moves towards self-determination and power" and "an absolute necessity." She emphasized women's essential sameness and connections, their difference from men. *Sisterhood Is Powerful: An Anthology of Writings from the Women's Liberation Movement* (1970), edited by M. and proclaimed as the radical feminist "bible," compiled documents on race, class, sexuality, and cultural representation from over seventy women and organizations. M. believed the process of creating the book through "collectivity, cooperation, and lack of competition" to be "proof of how radically different the women's movement is from male-dominated movements."

M.'s essays in *Going Too Far: The Personal Chronicles of a Feminist* (1977) exemplify a personal struggle to compromise tensions between heterosexuality and radical feminism. Recounting the early years of her marriage to a bisexual, marital tensions, motherhood, and the beginnings of the women's liberation movement, the book is an account of personal growth spanning the transition from prefeminism in 1962 to "transformative" feminism by 1977, a process of discovering that personal problems are intrinsic in gender relationships related to larger cultural issues. M. declared herself a lesbian in the midseventies, yet vilified male values in lesbianism in her attempt to end the gay-straight split in the women's movement. "The Rights of Passage" in *Ms.* (September 1975) epitomized her unsuccessful crusade to reconcile fragmentation in the movement through "pluralistic tolerance."

In her poetry M. often uses a feminist, polemical voice more celebratory of Jungian matriarchal archetypes than simply countering patriarchy, ranging in form from sonnets and villanelles to forms of her own invention. In *Monsters* (1972) and *Lady of the Beasts* (1976), she finds female identity in a universal self, mundane aspects of the eternal Creatrix, and ends with hope for cultural transformation. Her third volume, *Depth Perception: New Poems and a Masque* (1982), is an almost novelistic progression from self-affirmation to a call for transcendent unification. The one-act verse play with which it ends, featuring archetypal woman and man speaking truths spanning the comic and the tragic, was first performed in New York in 1979 with her husband's complementary one-act play, *The Dialectic*, under the joint title *Love's Duel*. Rejecting "this century's divisions between thought and action, art and politics, thinking and feeling," M. means her poems to "shock, infuriate, terrify, move, heal, release." *Upstairs in the Garden: Poems, Selected and New, 1968–1988* (1990) contains works that have appeared in many literary magazines, anthologies, and feminist journals. "The Two Gretels" provided feminists with slogans for banners, posters, buttons, and T-shirts.

The Anatomy of Freedom: Feminism, Physics, and Global Politics (1982) argues for human freedom based on erratic motion in quantum physics and a historic perspective. Here M. describes creating a logo for the women's movement, a clenched fist inside the universal sign for the female as inclusive of "women and men together" and a "sign of hope." M. also edited *Sisterhood Is Global: The International Women's Movement Anthology* (1985), full of demographic, economic, and political facts from seventy counties and including an extensive bibliography. Critical of patriarchy, the volume argues that "the world's problems are *women*," rarely consulted for solutions or considered by those in power. Critics lambasted it as left leaning. Contributors met in 1984 in the Sisterhood Is Global Institute to "address the problems of women everywhere," including care for the elderly, poverty, population, education, religion, and women's rights, status, and problems.

M.'s first novel, *Dry Your Smile* (1987), is the self-conscious account of a woman writer, expressing many of the concerns seen in *Going Too Far.* For *The Demon Lover: On the Sexuality of Terrorism* (1989), describing herself as a feminist "apostate Jew" trying to understand the Middle East conflict, M. interviewed women in the Gaza Strip and on the West Bank. The book continues earlier themes of "metaphysical feminism" in theoretical essays. A longtime contributing editor to *Ms.* magazine, M. became its editor in 1990. She received the Front Page Award for distinguished journalism in 1982 and is an active lecturer.

OTHER WORKS: *Poems by Seven: Robin Morgan and Others* (1959). *Women's Liberation* (1969, reprinted from *WIN* magazine, 2/15/69). *The New Woman: A Motive Anthology on Women's Liberation* (editor, with Charlotte Bunch-Weeks and Joanne Cooke, 1970). *Our Creations Are in the First Place Ourselves* (audiocassettes, Iowa State University of Science and Technology, 1974). *Death Benefits* (1981). Text for *Manpower: Photographs by Sally Soamer* (1987). *The Mer-Child: A Legend for Children and Other Adults* (1991). *The Word of a Woman: Feminist Dispatches, 1968–1991* (1992). M.'s papers are in the Schlesinger Library, Radcliffe College.

BIBLIOGRAPHY: Alpert, Jane, *Growing Up Underground* (1981). Cohen, Marcia, *The Sisterhood: The Inside Story of the Women's Movement and the Leaders Who*

Made It Happen (1988). Echols, Alice, *Daring to Be Bad: Radical Feminism in America, 1967–1975* (1989). *Between Ourselves: Letters between Mothers and Daughters, 1750–1982*, Karen Payne, ed. (1984). Reference works: *CA* 69–72 (1978). *CLC* 2 (1974), 29 (1990). *Maj Twent Cent Writers* (1991). *FC* (1990).

Other references: *Choice* (May 1985). *Commonweal* (2 April 1971; 15 Jan. 1973). *Ms.* (Sept. 1975, March 1977, Jan. 1991). *Nation* (14 Dec. 1970; 2 March 1985). *NYT* (29 Oct. 1970). *NYTBR* (22 Nov. 1970; 21 Feb. 1971; 19 Nov. 1972; 27 Jan. 1985; 27 Sept. 1987). *off our backs* (April 1989). *Partisan Rev.* (10 Jan. 1980). *Poetry* (Dec. 1973, Aug. 1975, Aug. 1977). *Progressive* (Jan. 1977, Aug. 1977). *TLS* (12 Nov. 1982). *WRB* (8 July 1987).

BLANCHE LINDEN-WARD

Hilda Morley

B. 19 Sept. 1918, New York City
Wrote under Hilda Auerbach
D. of Sonia (Kamenetsky) and Rachmiel Auerbach; m. Eugene Morley, 1945, div. 1949; m. Stefan Wolpe, 1952 (d. 1972)

M., who began writing poems at nine and who as a young woman living in London both corresponded with W. B. Yeats and became friends with **H[ilda]. D[oolittle].**, is frequently associated with the Black Mountain poets. With her husband, Stefan Wolpe, she taught at Black Mountain College in North Carolina from 1952 to 1956, and published in the *Black Mountain Review*. She was a friend of Charles Olson, as poems such as "For Constance Olson (January 1975)" and "Charles Olson (1910–1970)" recall. Influenced by Olson's ideas on Projective Verse, she mastered and went beyond his theories of "composition by field" for, as **Denise Levertov** states, M. "is one of the few who know exactly how to notate, or score, the words on the page so that emphasis, nuance, pace, all get *into the reader's ear*." Black Mountain poet Robert Creeley wrote the introduction to her first collection of poems, *A Blessing outside Us* (1976). Levertov wrote the preface for *What Are Winds and What Are Waters* (1983); M. opens the first section, "Makers," of *To Hold in My Hand: Selected Poems, 1955–1983* (1983) with a poem "for Denise" called "Psalm," and she has written long essays for *Ironwood* about Levertov (Spring 1985) and George Oppen (Fall 1985).

A highly visual person, whose poems are filled with a sense of place and landscape, M. has also been influenced by painters. *Cloudless at First* (1988) contains "Eye of Pissarro" and "Matisse: Large Red Interior" as well as "Yeats at Seventy" and "A Voice Suspended," on H. D.: "Hilda Doolittle / like myself American / in London."

Born of parents who had emigrated from Russia, M. received a rich and varied education. As a youngster, she attended the experimental Walden School in New York City. In 1934 she moved with her parents to Palestine, where she completed high school at the Haifa Realschule. In autumn 1936, she moved to London, where in 1939 she took an Honors B.A. in English language and literature at University College. Subsequently, M. earned graduate degrees and taught at New York University, and was a faculty member at Queens College (New York) and Rutgers University. At Black Mountain College, known for its experimentation in the arts, M. taught seventeenth-century English literature, late nineteenth- and early twentieth-century literature, and Hebrew.

M.'s experiences in Palestine and her Jewish heritage have been important to her life and writing. During World War II, she worked with the Office of War Information and later with the American Jewish Congress. She also translated modern Hebrew poetry, which appeared in *The Jewish Frontier* and *Israel Life and Letters*. Her translation of M. Mosenson's *Letters from the Desert* won the Lamed Award for best translation. "I am a daughter of the daughters of Jerusalem," she writes in "Untitled."

Central to M.'s life and poetry has been her twenty-four-year relationship with the avant-garde composer Stefan Wolpe, whom she met in the United States in September 1948. During her early years of marriage, M. subordinated her own artistic career to her husband's, and in "La Belle Otero" speaks of herself as "Being one of those who postponed / her real self so much, / letting others lead me (or not) / being loved / & loving so much." In 1962 Wolpe was diagnosed as terminally ill with Parkinson's disease; he died in 1972. M. describes Wolpe in "Letter for Stefan Fifteen Years Later" as "most gifted / of all the men I've known in making / life more alive, more charged with / pride." She is currently writing a prose biography of her husband; many, even most, of her poems are about Wolpe—their love, her loss.

In 1983, M. received a Guggenheim Fellowship and also became the first recipient of the Capricorn Award, sponsored by the Writer's Voice of the West Side YMCA in New York City and "given to a poet over forty in belated recognition of excellence." In 1989, she won awards from the New York Foundation for the Arts and from the Fund for Poetry; she was a nominee for the Poets Prize in 1990. Critics speak admiringly of M.'s courage and self-effacing modesty, of her unflinching determination to experience all of life fully, of her "combined lyricism and intelligence." Her poems are permeated with the sense of loss, yet filled with a sensuous joy.

OTHER WORKS: *Between the Rocks* (1992).

BIBLIOGRAPHY: *Amer. Book Rev.* 2 (Feb. 1980), 8 (Jan. 1986). *Book List* 81 (15 Sept. 1984). *Boston Rev.* 14 (Aug. 1989). *Georgia Rev.* 39 (Spring 1985). *Ironwood* 20 (featured: Nov. 1982). *LJ* 109 (1 June 1984). *Parnassus* 14:2 (1988). *Poetry* 146 (Aug. 1985). *PW* 225 (27 April 1984). *Small Press Rev.* 7 (Aug. 1989). *TLS* (18 April 1986). *Village Voice* 29 (16 Oct. 1984).

JEAN TOBIN

Toni Morrison

See AWW 3, 223–24

Widely considered the leading American novelist of the late twentieth century, M. received the Nobel Prize for Literature in 1993, the first African American woman to be thus honored. Her later novels extend M.'s conscious effort, begun in *Song of Solomon* (1977), to "write it all out" by moving into a more discursive style. The resulting lyricism of *Tar Baby* (1981), *Beloved* (1987), and *Jazz* (1992) has been widely praised.

Though each of her novels has accumulated some mixed reviews, by far the majority have been very positive. Appearances of her recent titles on best-seller lists demonstrate public as well as critical admiration for her work.

Song of Solomon received the National Book Critics Circle Award in 1978 and *Beloved* received the Pulitzer Prize in 1988. *Beloved* failed to win the National Book Award for that year although it was on the short list, prompting concern that M. was not receiving adequate recognition. In the 24 January 1988 issue of the *New York Times Book Review,* a group of black writers and critics published a "testament of thanks" to M., noting that her works have "advanced the moral and artistic standards by which we must measure the daring and the love of our national imagination and our collective intelligence as people." An accompanying piece by **June Jordan** and Houston A. Baker, Jr., suggested a parallel between M.'s situation and that of James Baldwin, who was never nominated for the "keystones to the canon of American literature: the National Book Award and the Pulitzer Prize." Subsequently, when *Beloved* did win the Pulitzer Prize, the prize committee stressed that merit was the only standard upon which the award was granted. The controversy raised questions about the effect of racism on American life similar to the questions M. consistently addresses in her work.

M.'s most recent novels extend the exploration of a key theme of her first works—the effect on the individual of the presence or the absence of love—just as they continue to examine relationships between parents and their children. From these perspectives, M. considers the impact of others' responses upon her characters' attitudes, emotions, and behavior. The sources of those responses are themselves crucially powerful subjects in her work, for almost all of the problems that her protagonists confront stem from the racism so pervasive in American history and culture.

As M. brilliantly and painfully depicts it, racial injustice has not only poisoned relationships within the community but has also damaged individuals to the point that they may contribute to their own destruction. Only by confronting personal and social history and by considering— sometimes embracing—the magic, folklore, and myths that illuminate it can an individual empower herself to face the future with more confidence than fear. Understanding eases the crippling pressure of self-blame, though sadly, not all of her characters have strength enough to achieve it.

Tar Baby, which reinvents the old tale of the fox and the rabbit, depicts intraracial as well as interracial conflict, here dramatized in the story of Jadine and Son—she beautiful, educated, nearly assimilated into the white culture, he angry, violent, at odds with her world. Passionate lovers, each is also a threat to—a trap for—the other. M. contrasts these lovers with a white couple, wealthy, "cultured" Valerian and Margaret Street, and with the Streets' butler, Sydney, and his wife.

Beloved, like *Song of Solomon*, is an especially powerful rendering of the control the past can exert over the present until an emotional exile achieves community with his or her own people. Based on a true story, *Beloved* depicts the life of Sethe, a slave who escaped to Cincinnati to find freedom for her children. When slave catchers close in, she succeeds in murdering one daughter, though three other children survive. Much later, in the guise of a grown woman, the dead daughter's ghost takes over Sethe's household, symbolizing the guilt and grief that have crippled her spirit. To survive, Sethe must come to believe what Paul D. tells her, that she is "her own best thing," as she finds her way through her surviving daughter, Denver, into the life of the community.

In *Jazz*, an unidentified first-person narrator recounts the story of Joe Trace, a middle-aged cosmetics peddler who murders his teenaged mistress, and of his wife, Violet, who attempts to deface the corpse in its coffin. The narrative style echoes a jazz performance, and the scene riffs fluidly from one time period to another. Though the community knows all about the murder and the attack upon the corpse, no one informs the authorities, and the Traces are left to confront one another, to acknowledge their deeds and misdeeds, and to attempt to repair their lives. More successful than *Tar Baby*, not so powerful as *Beloved*, *Jazz* is most effective in its bluesy evocation of New York in 1926.

By her vivid, telling depictions of African American experience in various periods and settings, M. has cast new perspectives on the nation's past and even suggests—though she makes no promise—that people of strength and courage may be able to achieve a somewhat less destructive future. In a theoretical work, *Playing in the Dark: Whiteness and the Literary Imagination* (1992) she examines the impact of race, racism, and the Africanist presence on several works by prominent American writers. The book is a stimulating companion to M.'s fiction.

OTHER WORKS: *Race-ing Justice, En-gendering Power: Essays on Anita Hill, Clarence Thomas, and the Construction of Social Reality* (editor, 1992).

BIBLIOGRAPHY: Lee, Dorothy H., "'The Quest for Self': Triumph and Failure in the Works of Toni Morrison," in *Black Women Writers (1950–1980): A Critical Evaluation*, Mari Evans, ed. (1984). Reference works: *Benet's* (1991).

Black Writers (1989). *CANR* 27 (1989). *CLC* 22 (1982), 55 (1989). *DLB* 33 (1984). *FC* (1990). *Handbook Amer. Women's Hist.* (1990). *Maj Twent Cent Wr* (1991). *NBAW* (1992). *Negro Almanac* (1989). *SATA* 57 (1989). *WW Wr, Eds, Poets* (1989).

Other references: *Amer. Lit.* 52:4 (1981). *Black Amer. Lit. Forum* 22:1 (1988). *MELUS* 17 (1991–92). *Modern Fiction Studies* 34:1 (1988). See MLA on-line bibliography.

JANE S. BAKERMAN

Mourning Dove (Humishuma)

B. April 1882–88, near Bonner's Ferry, Idaho; d. 8 Aug. 1936, Medical Lake, Washington
D. of Lucy Stuikin (Colville Tribe) and (father or stepfather) Joseph Quintasket (Okanogan Tribe); m. Hector McLeod, 1908; m. Fred Galler, 1919

M. D. is a grandmother of the Native American Renaissance in literature. Among the first generation to live their entire lives on a reservation, she balanced assimilation pressures with the need to comment on her times through fiction and recollection, as well as to record the Okanogan legends of her people. Her final manuscripts, published as *Mourning Dove, a Salishan Autobiography* (1990), include stories of her early childhood when the family followed traditional migration routes, her experiences of being sent off to mission and then Bureau of Indian Affairs schools, the settlement of Indians onto farm plots, and a mineral rights and homesteaders' run on the Colville Reservation. Her novel, *Cogewea, the Half-Blood* (1927), one of the first by an American Indian woman, explores young adulthood for a mixed-blood on the Montana frontier during the first decade of this century, and her collection of tribal legends, *Coyote Stories* (1933), is an important act by a Native American storyteller to preserve some of her cultural heritage in the face of what then appeared to be inevitable cultural genocide.

The history of the Northwest and the assimilation period form the background for appreciation of Mourning Dove's achievement. In the decade before her birth, Custer met his death (25 June 1876) and Chief Joseph fled to Canada (1877). The massacre at Wounded Knee, South Dakota (December 1890), occurred soon after her birth. In 1883 the federal government established a Court of Indian Offenses that made it a crime for Native Americans to speak their own languages, to practice traditional religious rituals, even to wear traditional dress. By 1887 the General Allotment, or Dawes Act opened up reservations to white settlement and initiated an even more intense period of suppression of Native cultures. Children were removed from their homes and sent to mission and government schools to eradicate their Indian ways and to teach them to imitate the dominant culture.

M. D. received such an education, attending the Goodwin Mission School from 1895 to 1899 and the Fort Spokane School for Indians in 1899–1900. She pursued a white education of her own volition when she became a matron of the Fort Shaw Indian School in exchange for classes (1904–7), and she attended a secretarial school in Calgary, Canada, from 1912 to 1914. Yet she ultimately chose to use that education to preserve the knowledge of her people and her times. She also became a recognized elder of the Colville Reservation.

Two events triggered her life's work—witnessing the last roundups of the buffalo on the Flathead Reservation in 1907–8, and meeting L. V. McWhorter in 1914, a father figure who became her mentor, collaborator, and friend. When she met him, M. D. already had the rough drafts for *Cogewea* and twenty-two legends. Enthusiastic about her writing, McWhorter worked tirelessly to edit her Indian English and to add the ethnographic and historical information to "enhance" the novel. He went too far, however, and the novel is torn by two voices: M. D.'s story about the dilemma of being a half-breed woman on the Northwest frontier, and McWhorter's diatribes against the greed and Christian hypocrisy of his own people. Yet the work is important. It conveys both white and Indian concern about the racism and exploitation in the settlement of the West.

McWhorter's editorial work on *Okanogan Sweathouse*, which came to include thirty-eight stories, is restrained, and thus the work remains its author's. It is a rich collection of Okanogan tales. Dean Guie, who joined the project in 1928, is responsible for reducing the number of stories and editing the selections toward a juvenile audience. The manuscript was retitled *Coyote Stories*.

Unfortunately, as Mary Dearborn explains in *Pocahontas's Daughters*, women of color have often come to print through white male editors who "interpret" and "alter" the material to make the texts palatable to publishers and the dominant culture. Jay Miller has continued that role in his edition of *Mourning Dove, a Salishan Autobiography*. Nonetheless, M. D.'s storytelling gifts are powerful enough that her core themes survive and direct readers to the devastating impact of Manifest Destiny on Native people's lives.

Late in her life M. D. achieved recognitions that meant much to her. She was the first Indian to be made an honorary member of the Eastern Washington Historical Society (1927), and later a life member of the Washington State Historical Society. Moreover, she was the first woman elected to the Tribal Council on the Colville Reservation (1935).

OTHER WORKS: Tales of the Okanogans (1967). Most of M. D.'s unpublished letters are included among the Lucullus Virgil McWhorter collection, Holland Library, Washington State Univ. Her final manuscripts are included in the Erna Gunther materials, Archives Division, Univ. of Washington.

BIBLIOGRAPHY: Brown, Alanna, articles in *Plainswoman* 11:5 (Jan. 1988); *The Wicazo Sa Rev.* 4:2 (Fall, 1988); *Legacy* 6:1 (Spring 1989); *Canadian Lit.* 124 and 125 (Spring–Summer 1990); *Native Writers and Canadian Writing*, W. H. New, ed. (1990); *WRB* 8:2 (Nov. 1990); *Studies in Amer. Indian Lit.* 4:2&3 (Summer–Fall 1992). Dearborn, Mary, *Pocahontas's Daughters: Gender and Ethnicity in American Culture* (1986). Fisher, Alice Poindexter, "The Transformation of Tradition: A Study of Zitkala-Sa (Bonnin) and Mourning Dove, Two Transitional Indian Writers." Unpublished Ph.D. diss., City University of New York, 1979; portions rpt. in an article [under Dexter Fisher] in *Critical Essays on American Literature*, Andrew Wiget, ed. (1985). Miller, Jay, *On Being and Becoming Indian: Biographical Studies of North American Frontiers*, James A. Clifton, ed. (1989). Reference works: *FC* (1990). Information also available from tribal enrollment records, marriage licenses, allotment records, and from family descendants who live on the Colville Reservation, Washington, and on Reserves around Penticton, British Columbia. M. D. appears under the name Christal Quintasket in some references.

ALANNA KATHLEEN BROWN

Gloria Naylor

B. 25 Jan. 1950, New York City
D. of Alberta (McAlpin) and Roosevelt Naylor

In four novels published in only six years, N. demonstrated a talent to match her ambition. Her elaborately detailed, precisely drawn fictional worlds represent the complex social worlds of late twentieth-century African Americans. Always conscious of class and gender distinctions, as well as racial difference and sexual preference, N. crafts nuanced and varied representations of black life. All reflect a particular concern with black female character and with the problem of preserving a distinctive cultural heritage during a period of social and cultural assimilation. Larded with literary allusions to both classical Western texts and African American fiction, N.'s novels deliberately call attention to themselves as literary artifacts. They have enjoyed critical and commercial success.

Among their most striking elements is the keen evocation of place. N. maps a fictional geography that encompasses Brewster Place, an inner-city neighborhood that is home to those with nowhere else to go; Linden Hills, a suburb to which successful blacks aspire; and Willow Springs, a mythical island off the coasts of South Carolina and Georgia that constitutes an ancestral home. Geographically disparate, these sites are connected through the genealogies of the characters who inhabit them. With each novel, the dimension of N.'s project becomes clearer.

The Women of Brewster Place (1982) was published one year after N. graduated from Brooklyn College and embarked on a career as a writer. Subsequently, she earned an M.A. in Afro-American Studies from Yale (1983). Earlier she had been a missionary for Jehovah's Witnesses (1968–75) and a switchboard operator. *Women* won the 1983 American Book Award for best first novel. In 1989, without N.'s involvement, it was adapted for television.

Walled off from the rest of society, Brewster Place is a literal and figurative dead end; yet its women (each, "an ebony phoenix") have the will to make it home. Their poverty imposes a familiarity—the buildings are too cramped for privacy—that they mold into community. Mattie Michael, a Southern-born, hardworking, religious woman, is the book's moral center. A failed mother, whose spoiled son's betrayal has compelled her move to Brewster Place, Mattie redeems herself and her maternal power. In a powerful scene, she saves a young woman's life by "rocking" her through the pain of a lost child. Like racism and poverty, sexism fractures families. Under the weight of these interlocking oppressions, the novel asserts, black women must rely on each other to survive. When they fail, as in the story of the lesbian couple whom the community ostracizes, the consequences are fatal.

Kiswana Browne is the character who provides the link to N.'s second novel, *Linden Hills* (1985). This daughter of the bourgeoisie moves to Brewster Place to be with "the people." *Women* gently mocks her naive idealism; *Linden Hills* illuminates its source. Founded by an ex-slave as a challenge to racism, "a beautiful, black wad of spit right in the white eye of America," Linden Hills has been passed down through five generations of Luther Nedeed's heirs and namesakes. Despite its subversive intent, it is a monument to patriarchal power and materialism. Kiswana could find no community here.

Within a structure borrowed from Dante's *Inferno*, N. inserts the voices and perspectives of the Nedeed wives, whose legacies are buried in the letters, recipe books, and photograph albums that Willa Nedeed discovers in the family cellar. Their words and images empower Willa. Similarly, through a series of allusions to, and revisions of, texts by **Paule Marshall, Toni Morrison,** and **Alice Walker,** N. pays homage to the literary predecessors who enable her work.

Mama Day (1988) confirms N.'s consciousness of participating in multiple literary traditions. Echoes of Shakespeare's *The Tempest* resound against the mythic voice of the slave woman, Sapphira, whose rebellion secured Willow Springs for her descendants. Prominent among these are the title character, Miranda (Mama) Day, a healer, conjure woman, and dispenser of wisdom, and her grandniece Ophelia; Willa Nedeed is their kinswoman. The plot depicts Ophelia's courtship and marriage to George Andrews, by birth an orphan, by training an engineer, and by inclination a rationalist. The couple's sojourn on the island builds to a climax in which the forces of faith and reason, history and progress, collide.

As *Linden Hills* draws on Dante and *Mama Day* on *The Tempest*, *Bailey's Cafe* (1992) reimagines biblical women—Eve, Mary, Jezebel, Mary Magdalene—in a late twentieth-century netherworld. A novel "'about sexuality,'" according to N., it is "'structured . . . like a jazz set.'" Using a kaleidoscopic point of view, N. tells stories of sin and redemption, love and hate, damnation and salvation. The cafe, presided over by Maestro

Bailey, is both the end of the world and the beginning of new life for those who gather there.

Some critics question whether N.'s characters are strong enough to carry the historical and philosophical burdens she imposes on them. They point to elements of melodrama and sentimentality as well. But N.'s strengths transcend these occasional weaknesses. Through lyrical yet gritty prose and sharply delineated characters, she advances a vision too challenging to ignore.

OTHER WORKS: "Love and Sex in the Afro-American Novel," *Yale Rev.* 78:1 (Autumn 1989). "A Message to Winston," *Essence* (Nov. 1982). "A Conversation," *Southern Rev.* 21 (Summer 1985, with Toni Morrison).

BIBLIOGRAPHY: Awkward, Michael, *Inspiriting Influences* (1989). Christian, Barbara, "Gloria Naylor's Geography: Community, Class, and Patriarchy in *The Women of Brewster Place* and *Linden Hills*," in *Reading Black, Reading Feminist*, Henry Louis Gates, Jr., ed. (1990). Reference works: *African American Writers* (1991). *CA* 107 (1983). *CANR* 27 (1989). *CLC* 28 (1984), 52 (1989).

Other references: *Black Amer. Lit. Forum* 24 (Spring 1990). *Boston Globe* (interview, 21 Oct. 1992). *CLA J.* 33:1 (Sept. 1989); 34:3 (March 1991). *Contemp. Lit.* 28:1 (1987); 29:3 (1988); 29:4 (1988).

CHERYL A. WALL

Lorine Niedecker

B. 12 May 1903, Fort Atkinson, Wisconsin; d. 31 Dec. 1970, Fort Atkinson, Wisconsin
D. of Theresa Daisy (Kunz) and Henry E. Niedecker; m. Frank Hartwig, 1928, div. 1942; m. Albert Millen, 1963

Although a relatively obscure and secluded Wisconsin author and poet, N.'s reputation crossed the Atlantic and her list of admirers is long. In 1978 she posthumously won the Notable Wisconsin Writers Award.

N. is best known as a poet of the people. Her various occupations as a librarian's assistant, a research editor in the 1930s for the Works Progress Administration's Federal Writers' Project helping to produce the *Wisconsin Guide*, a radio scriptwriter, a stenographer and proofreader in a print shop, a landlady, a washerwoman for a local hospital, and a housewife allowed her insight into small-town working people.

N.'s literary work was highly influenced by her childhood on Blackhawk Island, a small island near the little town of Fort Atkinson. Her father was an alcoholic who had a boisterous personality with a cruel streak. Her mother was deaf and going blind, a silent sufferer of her husband's philandering and alcoholism. As a result of her parents' chaotic relationship, N. learned the importance of balance that is reflected in her volume *My Life by Water: Collected Poems, 1936–1968* (1970).

N. graduated from Fort Atkinson High School in 1922 and left home for Beloit College to study literature. Two years later she abandoned her studies to care for her ailing mother. In 1928 she married Frank Hartwig from whom she was permanently separated two years later. During this period N. wrote relatively little.

In 1931, N. discovered the poetry of Louis Zukofsky and the objectivist movement that included among others William Carlos Williams. Impressed by a poetry that condensed details to create a sense of completeness, she began a correspondence with Zukofsky that lasted until her death. He introduced her into the world of literary journals and his critical suggestions helped her develop into a mature poet.

In the 1930s, N. began to publish an avant-garde experimental poetry that attempts to discover meaning in everyday life. Her first book, *New Goose* (1946), was filled with the quotidian, such as moving into a new house and visiting neighbors. Although the people were N.'s poetic muse, she does not naively glorify them. Politically aware, she realized that the common person was often provincial and that this lack of awareness could be dangerous for the world. It was the common folk, one poem points out, who were manufacturing the bomb.

N.'s next book, *My Friend Tree* (1961), deals with the same themes as her earlier work, but it places the poet in the natural world. As before, N. does not glorify her subject. Rather, the poetry in her second book shows the bleak as well as the bright in the relationship between human beings and nature.

In *North Central* (1968) N. explores her own sense of poetics, moving beyond Objectivism and Imagism into what she calls "Reflectivism." A 1967 letter to Gail Roub explains her purpose: "The visual form is there in the background and the words convey what the visual form gives off after it's felt in the mind." In this work, the poet mentally explores the world and records her experiences.

Ironically, the people of N.'s community did not know that the poet of the people was a poet. N. felt that she had to hide her poetry from the community because of the small town's mistrust of literary and intellectual activity. The people were her poetic muse; to be ostracized by them would dry up her wellspring of poetry. It was not until after her death that the community discovered and began to appreciate its poet.

OTHER WORKS: *T & G: The Collected Poems, 1936–1966* (1969). *Blue Chicory* (1976). *The Granite Pail: The Selected Poems of Lorine Niedecker* (1985). *From This Condensery: The Complete Writing of Lorine Niedecker* (1985). *Between Your House and Mine: The Letters of Lorine Niedecker to Cid Corman, 1960–1970,* Lisa Pater Faranda, ed. (1986). *Harpsichord and Salt Fish* (1991).

BIBLIOGRAPHY: *The Full Note: Lorine Niedecker,* Peter Dent, ed. (1983). Walsh, Phyllis, *Lorine Niedecker: Solitary Plover* (1992). *Epitaphs for Lorine,* Jonathan Williams, ed. (1973). Reference works: *Benet's* (1991). *CA* 25–28 (1977). *CA Perm. Ser.* 2 (1978). *CLC* 10 (1979), 42 (1987). *DLB* 48 (1986).

Other references: *Arts in Society* 3 (Summer 1966). *Belles Lettres* 2:5 (May–June 1987). *Line* 6 (Fall 1985). *New Directions in Prose and Poetry* 1 (1936), 2 (1937), 12 (1950), 13 (1951). *Origin* 3:2 (July 1966), 4:16 (July 1981). *Parnassus* 5 (Spring/Summer 1977), 12–13 (Spring/Winter 1985), 14 (1987). *Quarterly Rev. of Lit.* 8 (Spring 1956). *Truck* 16 (Summer 1975).

AMY STACKHOUSE

Marsha Norman

B. 21 Sept. 1947, Louisville, Kentucky
D. of Bertha Mae (Conley) and Billie Lee Williams; m. Michael Norman, 1969, div. 1974; m. Dann C. Byck, Jr., 1978, div. 1986

N. is one of the first women to receive national acknowledgment as a playwright since **Lillian Hellman** and **Lorraine Hansberry.** With

Beth Henley and **Wendy Wasserstein,** she has won the Pulitzer Prize and has "made successful inroads on a still very much male-dominated reserve."

The first of four children of an insurance salesman and a homemaker, N. was raised in a fundamentalist home in Louisville. She received a B.A. in philosophy at Agnes Scott College (1969) and an M.A.T. at the University of Louisville (1971). N. taught school in Kentucky and also worked with disturbed children in a state hospital. Her award-winning first play, *Getting Out* (1977), received national attention. It portrays the first days of freedom of a young woman, Arlene, in jail for murder; N. has said that the character of Arlie (Arlene's younger, unrehabilitated self) is based on a young woman she encountered while working in the hospital. The play explores Arlene/Arlie's relationship with her mother, a precursor relationship for those in N.'s later works.

Several subsequent plays failed to receive critical acclaim, although they ring changes on many themes important to N.'s work. *Third and Oak* (1978), consisting of one-acts *The Laundromat* and *The Pool Hall*, involves characters coming to terms with various types of bereavement and loss, and with their debts to the people in their past and present. Richard Wattenburg describes *The Holdup* (produced 1980, published 1987) as a "feminist perspective on the frontier experience."

Although some critics describe *The Holdup* as a comedy, most of N.'s work is tragic or serious, punctuated by comic moments. Several critics have called *'Night, Mother* (1982, published 1983), which won the Pulitzer Prize and was made into a film, an excellent example of Aristotelian tragedy. N. told Irmgard Wolfe that she looks to classic Greek tragedies as playwriting models. *'Night, Mother,* which portrays daughter Jessie's preparations and conversations with her mother, Thelma, on the night Jessie plans to commit suicide, is N.'s most complete exploration of mother-daughter relations. N. is one of the first female dramatists to make relationships in women's lives and the social and economic constraints on middle- and lower-class women into appropriate matter for powerful plays.

Characters in several of N.'s plays wrestle with issues of religious faith and redemption. In *Getting Out* Arlene remembers the prison chaplain who told her that Arlie was the evil inside her, which could be banished for Arlene's salvation. In *Traveler in the Dark* (produced 1984, published 1988) Sam, a surgeon, struggles to come to terms with the death of a family friend his surgical talent could not save and with his fears that his son is being wooed away from the logical thinking Sam so values by his reading fairy tales and by the influence of Sam's father, an evangelical preacher.

Frequently in N.'s plays women and men have conflicting expectations and understandings; their conversations are characterized by misunderstanding, manipulation, or hostility. In *Traveler* Sam and his wife, Glory, never connect. Even in *'Night, Mother,* where there are no male characters onstage, the men in Thelma and Jessie's lives are remembered and discussed with a mixture of hurt, confusion, and contempt.

Although N. is primarily known as a playwright, she has published a novel, *The Fortune Teller* (1987), and wrote the book and lyrics for a musical adaptation of **Frances Hodgson Burnett**'s *The Secret Garden* (1991). *The Fortune Teller* further explores mother-daughter relationships and the inescapability of human fate. Fay, the title character, has roots and a past similar to that of Thelma in *'Night, Mother.* She undergoes a symbolically similar process of separation and loss, described by Fay as inescapable events on the turning wheel of fortune, while she reconciles herself to her daughter's adulthood and maturing sexuality. The novel deals more overtly with contemporary political themes, particularly abortion, than any of N.'s previous work; it also shows a more developed and intimate relationship between a female and a male character (Fay and her lover Arnie) than in any other of N.'s works.

OTHER WORKS: *Circus Valentine* (1979, unpublished). *Merry Christmas* (1979, unpublished). "Ten Golden Rules for Playwrights," *Writer* (Sept. 1985).

BIBLIOGRAPHY: Betsko, Kathleen, and Rachel Koenig, *Interviews with Contemporary Women Playwrights* (1987). Burkman, Katherine H., "The Demeter Myth and Doubling in Marsha Norman's *'Night, Mother,*" in *Modern American Drama: The Female Canon,* June Schlueter, ed. (1990). Carlson, Susan L., "Women in Comedy: Problem, Promise, Paradox," in *Drama, Sex, and Politics,* James Redmond, ed. (1985). Dolan, Jill, *The Feminist Spectator as Critic* (1988). Harriott, Esther, *American Voices: Five Contemporary Playwrights in Essays and Interviews* (1988). Kane, Leslie, "The Way Out, the Way In: Paths to Self in the Plays of Marsha Norman," in *Feminine Focus: The New Women Playwrights,* Enoch Brater, ed. (1989). Smith, Raynette H., "*'Night Mother* and *True West:* Mirror Images of Violence and Gender," in *Violence in Drama,* James Redmond, ed. (1991). For articles in reference works, see: *Amer. Playwrights Since 1945* (1980). *Amer. Women Dramatists of the Tw Cent* (1982). *CA*

105 (1982). *Contemp. Dramatists* (1988). *CLC* 28 (1984). *CB* (1984). *DLBY* (1984). *Writers Directory* (1992–94).

Other references: *Conf. of College Teachers of English Studies* (Sept. 1989). *Modern Drama* (Sept. 1987, March 1989, Dec. 1990). *Southern Q.* (Spring 1987). *Studies in Amer. Drama* 3 (bibliography, 1988). *Text and Performance Q.* 9:3 (July 1989). *Theatre J.* 35:3 (Oct. 1983). *Western Amer. Lit.* 23:4 (Feb. 1989).

KATHRYN MURPHY ANDERSON

Naomi Shihab Nye

B. 12 March 1952, St. Louis, Missouri
D. of Miriam (Allwardt) and Aziz Shihab; m. Michael Nye, 1978; c.: Madison Cloudfeather Nye, b. 1986

N.'s poetry celebrates moments of grace when, through ordinary acts, people confirm each other. She asserts that poetry itself and poetic voice depend upon these ordinary acts of recognition. In "Coming into Cuzco," the closing poem of N.'s first collection, *Different Ways to Pray* (1980), the poet describes herself as a newly arrived and disoriented traveler, unable to speak—"That morning my mouth was a buried spoon"—until she is noticed on the bus by the young girl she has noticed: "And she handed me one perfect pink rose, / because we had noticed each other, and that was all." N.'s attention to the simple acts of human communion wherever and however they occur springs from a generosity and acuity forged by a sense of her own multifaceted identity.

The daughter of a Palestinian businessman and later journalist and an American painter, N. began to write when she was very young, publishing her first poem when she was seven. In 1966, with her brother and parents, she left Missouri and moved to Jerusalem. They left Jerusalem the next year, eventually settling in San Antonio, Texas, where N. received her B.A. from Trinity University (1974).

N. began working as a poet-in-the-schools in 1974 for the Texas Arts Commission. She has been Holloway Lecturer at the University of California at Berkeley, lecturer in poetry at the University of Texas at Austin, and visiting writer at the University of Hawaii. N. traveled in Asia and the Middle East for the United States Information Agency's "Arts America" program in 1983 and 1984 and made a second tour to the Middle East in 1992.

N.'s desire to be at home in multiple human communities, her experience of her father's exile and restless wandering, and her acute sense of place is reflected in all of her poetry. *Different Ways to Pray* attends to human landscapes, from a local Texas street to the Guatemalan jungle and to the human need for a sense of connection. *Hugging the Jukebox* (1982) continues her argument that the human voice finds its proper song by acts of orientation in a world both familiar and strange. A young boy in Honduras, separated from his land and his mother, clings to his grandparents' jukebox and sings love songs; trash pickers on Madison Street "murmur in language soft as rags." N. has a deep respect for human utterance and for each person's attempt to find a place in a world that is generous but cool, that does not grant identity until the attempt is made for it.

In *Yellow Glove* (1986) N.'s vision is darker and she records the enormous cost of not finding the objects or persons that ground you in the world: "Part of the difference between floating and going down." The book is filled with vulnerable people holding resolutely to objects so as not to fall apart, with broken and fallen objects, and with cries to earth about human cruelty: "Who calls anyone *civilized?*" Yet, N.'s vision of the world as filled with tenderness and wry comedy endures.

Both *Different Ways to Pray* and *Hugging the Jukebox* received the Voertman Award from the Texas Institute of Letters. *Hugging* was chosen by **Josephine Miles** as National Poetry Series Winner in 1982, and as one of the Most Notable Books by the American Library Association. N. is 1988 recipient of the Academy of American Poets' Lavan Award and corecipient (with Galway Kinnell) of the Charity Randall Award for spoken poetry.

In addition to her work as a poet, N. is a folksinger and has recorded two albums, *Rutabaga Roo* (1979) and *Lullaby Raft* (1981). N. is cotranslator for PROTA (Project of Translation from Arabic Literature) and her work appears in *Modern Arabic Poetry* (1987); she has also rendered into English the poems of Muhammad al-Maghut, *The Fan of Swords* (1991), and poems found in Fadwa Tuquan's autobiography, *A Mountainous Journey*. She has published an international anthology of poems for young readers, *This Same Sky* (1992), and is preparing a book of her short stories.

OTHER WORKS: Tattooed Feet (chapbook, 1976). *Eye to Eye* (chapbook, 1977). *On the Edge of the Sky* (chapbook, 1982). *Invisible* (chapbook, 1986). *Fifty Poems: A Personal Selection* (book and tapes, 1988). *"Twenty Other Worlds"* in *A Quartet: Texas Poets in Concert* (1990). *Tomorrow We Smile, The Miracle of Typing, Mint* (chapbooks, 1991). Short stories in *Virginia Q. Rev.* (Summer 1983); *Prairie Schooner* (Fall 1984); *Southwest Rev.* (Spring 1986); *Georgia Rev.* (Spring 1986, Spring/Summer 1990). Essays in *J. of Palestine Studies* (Winter 1984).

BIBLIOGRAPHY: Grape Leaves: A Century of Arab-American Poetry, Orfalea Gregory and Sharif Elmusa, eds. (1988).
Other references: *Booklist* (15 March 1982). *Georgia Rev.* (Spring 1989). *Kenyon Rev.* (Fall 1987). *LJ* (Aug. 1982, April 1989). *New Letters* (Winter 1981/82). *Village Voice* (18 Jan. 1983).

DARIA DONNELLY

Joyce Carol Oates

See AWW 3, 281–85
Writes also under: Rosamond Smith

One of the most prolific writers of our time, since 1980 O. has published more than twenty-five novels and story collections in addition to numerous short stories and critical reviews. Her work inspired by a consistent moral vision, O. has become a distinguished woman of letters. Despite its abundance, O.'s writing has not become predictable. The critically acclaimed *Bloodsmoor Romance* (1982) demonstrates her mastery of literary forms, as she provides in the story of five nineteenth-century Pennsylvania sisters what one reviewer describes as "an antiromance that provides the satisfaction of a romance," while also making feminist points about the limitations placed on women. The book is rather uncharacteristically lighthearted: much of her work continues to carry a heavy, gothic aura, as in *American Appetites* (1989) and *You Must Remember This* (1987). These, like others of O.'s books, warn that trouble, suicide, and murder lurk under the facade of average American life when human emotion is repressed.

Racism, child abuse, and madness are the subjects of *Because It Is Bitter and Because It Is My Heart* (1990) and *Rise of Life on Earth* (1991). Separated by racism in the 1950s, the protagonists of *Because It Is Bitter*, a white woman and a black man, fulfill their destinies apart, each hiding their turbulent feelings. *Rise of Life* tells the story of a victim of child abuse who buries her feelings very deeply only to have them emerge later in her life. As a nurse in rest homes she unobtrusively kills old people, moving every two years to new places.

Black Water (1992) is loosely based on the story of Chappaquiddick and the accusations leveled against Ted Kennedy in the drowning death of Mary Jo Kopechne. O.'s detailed account, told in the voice of the drowning victim in the last hours of her life, imparts a quality of truth to a story that will never be proven.

The precarious balance between sanity and madness is a frequent theme in O.'s short stories. The stories in *Sentimental Education* (1980), *Raven's Wing* (1986), and *Assignation* (1988), find paranoia, sexual obsession, abuse, and isolation lurking below the surface of the lives of Americans of all ages and economic strata. Here, as in the novels, O. turns an admonitory gaze on the failure of human beings to live up to their ethical capacities.

Two volumes of poetry, *Invisible Woman: New and Selected Poems, 1972–1982* (1982) and *Time Traveler* (1989), show a more personal and political side of O. In an interview, she describes poetry as "a rite involving language—at its very highest a sacred rite in that it transcends the personality of the poet and communicates its vision." *Invisible Woman* provides an insightful look at issues of invisibility and personal identification while *Time Traveler* offers spiritual reflections on feminism, nature, and the beauty of the world.

An astute and scholarly critic, in *Contraries* (1981) O. brings together essays on such figures as Dostoyevsky, Oscar Wilde, and James Joyce. In *The Profane Art: Essays and Reviews* (1983) O.'s concerns range from women in Yeats, to the writings of John Updike, Colette, **Flannery O'Connor,** and other moderns.

In an unexpected deviation from her past writing, O. documents the world of boxing in *On Boxing* (1987) and *Reading the Fights* (1988). She sees a common bond between boxers and writers—they both "invite pain, humiliation, loss and chaos" that others avoid—and delves into that predominantly masculine world of pain. In *On Boxing* she examines the sport's feminine aspects, seeing within the violent rituals a tender, loving quality. *Reading the Fights,* coedited with Daniel Halpern, collects the best writing about the controversial sport.

The Mysteries of Winterthurn (1984), a novel containing three separate tales, was O.'s first foray into the world of mystery stories. Very well received, the novel uses nineteenth-century narrative strategies to trace strange and never-solved crimes, all connected by the detective hero. O. has also written five mysteries under the pseudonym Rosamond Smith: *Lives of the Twins* (1987), *Kindred Passions* (1988), *Soul/Mate* (1989), *Nemesis* (1990), and *Snake Eyes* (1992) are popular and gripping stories full of intrigue and evil murderers.

O.'s private and professional life resembles a perpetual-motion machine. She teaches at Princeton University and works with the publishing company she helped create, the Ontario Review. In 1991 she had two one-act dramas playing in New York, a new collection of stories, another Rosamond Smith novel scheduled for publication, and films of *You Must Remember This* and the thriller *Snake Eyes* due in movie theaters.

OTHER WORKS: *Night Side* (1980). *A Middle Class Education* (1980). *Three Plays* (1980). *Night Walks: A Bedside Companion* (1982). *First Person Singular* (1983). *Last Days* (1984). *Luxury of Sin* (1984). *Marya: A Life* (1985). *Solstice* (1985). *Wild Nights* (1985). *Story: Fictions Past and Present* (with Boyd Litzinger, 1985). *(Woman) Writer: Occasions and Opportunities* (1988). *I Lock the Door upon Myself* (1990). *Winter's Stories* (1990). *Heat, and Other Stories* (1991). *The Best American Essays, 1991* (editor, 1991). *Twelve Plays* (1991). *The Bingo Master* (1992). *The Oxford Book of American Short Stories* (ed., 1992). *Where Is Here?* (1992). *The Sophisticated Cat* (comp., with Daniel Halpern, 1992). *Foxfire* (1993).

BIBLIOGRAPHY: *Conversations with Joyce Carol Oates* (1989). *Joyce Carol Oates: An Annotated Bibliography*, Francine LeCangée, ed. (1986). Reference works: *CANR* 25 (1989). *CLC* 19 (1981), 33 (1985), 52 (1989). *DLB* 2 (1978), 5 (1980). *DLBY* (1981). *FC* (1990). *Maj Twent Cent Wr* (1991).

Other references: *Boston Phoenix* (June 1992). *Georgia Rev.* (Winter 1988). *Michigan Q. Rev.* (Fall 1983). *New Statesman and Society* (1 Sept. 1989).

SUZANNE GIRONDA

Sharon Olds

B. 19 Nov. 1942, San Francisco, California

O. writes in the tradition of the confessional poets, especially of **Sylvia Plath** and **Anne Sexton,** but has turned their poetic idiom to new purpose. Where Plath and Sexton bitterly denounced the state of affairs for women, they paradoxically sought haven in the persona of the crazy lady and threatened harm to themselves rather than to the world. O. speaks with similar energy, vividness, and emotional urgency about her life as a woman, as both daughter and mother, but seeks catharsis and healing rather than destruction of the self. The raw power of her poetry, which caused the critic David Leavitt to remark "that I was inclined to turn my eyes from the page," is often leavened by a wry humor.

O. received a B.A. from Stanford University in 1964 and a Ph.D. from Columbia University in 1972. She has taught poetry in many places, including the Theodor Herzl Institute, the Poetry Center at the YMCA in New York City, Goldwater Memorial Hospital (Roosevelt Island, New York), and at many colleges and universities, including Sarah Lawrence, Columbia, New York University, State University of New York at Purchase, and Brandeis. The Guggenheim Foundation and the National Endowment for the Arts (1982–83) have awarded her fellowships. *Satan Says* (1980) received the San Francisco Poetry Center Award in 1981. *The Dead and the Living* (1984) was the Lamont Poetry Selection of the Academy of American Poets for 1984 and received the National Book Critics Circle Award in 1985.

Love—erotic, maternal, and compassionate—lies at the heart of her poetic project. Rage lies there too, but rage is to be exorcised in relation to her own past and to be deployed in the present in defense of the vulnerable, like her own children and people caught in political violence. She can even rage in defense of the father, who has hurt her deeply. In "Late Poem to My Father" she thinks of him as a child, "the / tiny bones inside his soul / twisted in greenstick fractures, the small / tendons that hold the heart in place / snapped. And what they did to you / you did not do to me." Her fourth book, *The Father*

(1992), is reminiscent of the deathwatch poetry of the nineteenth century. The poems lovingly and relentlessly detail the death of the father and the speaker's care for him.

O. celebrates the body in the tradition of Walt Whitman. Sex, as human connection, regeneration, and a source of great energy, is sacred. Likewise, all the functions of the body, male and female, are sacred: menstruation, childbirth, dying, nursing, miscarriage. She revels in sexual life and in the sensual poem. In O.'s world there are no dirty words; she uses the common names, *cock, sex, nipples,* and *fucking,* domesticates, and reclaims them. In the short lyric "The Pope's Penis," the pope cannot repress his penis, but O. converts failure into spiritual triumph: "and at night, / while his eyes sleep, it stands up / in praise of God."

This maternal and erotic love of the body determines O.'s straight-forward politic: love the body of the person, love the body of the world. To affirm the life of the human body stresses the preciousness of each and every life and our mutual belonging. O. transforms William Carlos Williams's famous imperative, as poet Linda McCarriston notes: "No ideas but in beings." The poet asserts an intimate connection with others, no matter how distant, who are hurt. O.'s refusal to maintain a conventional poetic distance from her subjects conveys what **Alicia Ostriker** calls a "tacit moral imperative." She serves as a clear-eyed, compassionate witness; where others retreat behind irony, she confronts horror directly.

OTHER WORKS: The Gold Cell (1987). "George and Mary Oppen: Poetry and Friendship," *Ironwood* 13:2 (Fall 1985). "Silenced Voices: Turkey-Ismail Besikci," *APR* 15:4 (July–Aug. 1986).

BIBLIOGRAPHY: Matson, Suzanne, "Talking to Our Father: The Political and Mythical Appropriations of Adrienne Rich and Sharon Olds," *APR* 18:6 (Nov.–Dec. 1989).

Other References: *Amer. Book Rev.* (Jan.–Feb. 1982). *APR* (Sept.–Oct. 1984). *Georgia Rev.* (rev. by L. McCarriston, Winter 1984). *Iowa Rev.* (Winter 1985). *Nation* (13 Oct. 1984). *NYTBR* (18 March 1984, 21 March 1993). *Poetry* (June 1981, Oct. 1984; rev. by A. Ostriker, Jan. 1987). *Village Voice Lit. Supp.* (March 1984).

NORA MITCHELL

Mary Oliver

B. 10 Sept. 1935, Maple Heights, Ohio
D. of Helen M. (Vlasak) and Edward William Oliver

O. is widely regarded as one of America's finest nature poets. She writes in the Romantic tradition, recording discoveries about the self made through instructive and consoling communion with nature. Critic Janet McNew has argued persuasively that O.'s lyrics revise the traditional Romantic relation with nature by her reverence for—rather than terror or transcendence of—nature's ineluctable forces of decay and renewal.

O. attended both Ohio State University and Vassar College. Some have noted a resonance between her work and that of fellow Ohio poet James Wright, as well as the influence on her early poetry of **Edna St. Vincent Millay.** O. worked at "Steepletop," Millay's estate, as secretary to the poet's sister, Norma Millay. Since 1964 she has lived in Provincetown, Massachusetts, where for several years she was affiliated with the Fine Arts Work Center. She has been a visiting professor in creative writing at Case Western University (1980, 1982) and writer in residence at Case Western Reserve (1983), Bucknell University (1986), the University of Cincinnati (1986), and Sweet Briar College (1991–94).

In her first book, *No Voyage and Other Poems* (1963; England, 1965), O. counts the cost of withdrawing from human society into the world of nature. "A Dream of Trees" expresses doubt about her desire for nature over culture, and for the present tense of nature over the history of herself and her family that she fully explores in *The River Styx, Ohio, and Other Poems* (1972). She wonders, "Whoever made music of a mild day?" After the preparatory questions and exorcisms of her first two books, O. embraces the making of such music as her poetic vocation. Her poetry argues that she enters more deeply into the world by bearing witness to nature.

In her essay on poetic audience, "For the Man Cutting the Grass," O. asserts that poetry is meant "to reach the regions of shared experience." Her poetry creates such a region by being faithful to the self as it is transformed by patiently sitting with the natural world. The

effect of her insistence that the single receptive self is speaking, acting, and posing questions in a world of nature set apart from received
forms is that the reader chooses to meet the poem rather than being
swept into it by a collective voice. With each successive book, from
Twelve Moons (1979) to *American Primitive* (1983) to *Dream Work*
(1986), O.'s precise and fluid language has shaped a singular and
increasingly open voice. She received the 1984 Pulitzer Prize for
American Primitive, a book heralded for its calm and unsentimental
lyrics, produced by the difficult labor of accepting consolation from
nature, the very force that makes consolation necessary.

House of Light (1990), praised as a visionary work, questions the
form O. has previously mastered. Here she rejects the Romantic view,
present in her earlier work, that nature's exposition supersedes an
exhausted Christian account of the world. Following and invoking
Blake, O. investigates nature as it rejuvenates and subverts Christianity rather than competing with and usurping it.

She also returns to an old anxiety about whether the "music of a
mild day" is enough in the face of the injustice and ugliness of society.
In "Singapore," wondering whether her poetry is an escape from
the woman washing ashtrays in a toilet bowl, she discovers that the
woman herself brings nature into the poem. In her *New and Selected
Poems* (1992), O. continues to question the economy and effect of her
poetry, announcing in the opening poem, "Rain," "I do not want
anymore . . . to lead / children out of the fields into the text / of
civility, to teach them that they are (they are not) better / than the
grass." O. fears that her poetry, inherently and against her desire,
privileges human consciousness and receptivity to nature over nature
itself. The struggle between the visionary and the social, and the
wrestling with her vocation, evidences the ongoing honesty of O.'s
work and promises to take it in new directions.

In addition to the Pulitzer Prize, O. has received first prize from
the Poetry Society of America for the poem "No Voyage" (1962);
Devil's Advocate Award (1968) for "Christmas 1966"; the Shelley Memorial Award (1970); the Alice Fay de Castagnola Award (1973); the
American Academy and Institute of Arts and Letters Achievement
Award (1983); the Christopher Award and the L. L. Winship Award
for *House of Light* (1991); the National Book Award for *New and
Selected Poems* (1992). She held a National Endowment for the Arts
fellowship in 1972–73 and was a Guggenheim fellow in 1980–81.

OTHER WORKS: The Night Traveler (chapbook, 1978). *Sleeping in the Forest* (chapbook, 1978). "For the Man Cutting the Grass," *Georgia Rev.* (Winter 1981). "Some Thoughts on the Line," *Ohio Rev.* 38 (1987).

BIBLIOGRAPHY: Waggoner, Hyatt Howe, *American Poets: From the Puritans to the Present* (1984). *Our Other Voices: Nine Poets Speaking*, John Wheatcroft, ed. (1991, interview). Reference works: *CANR* 9 (1983). *CLC* 19 (1981), 34 (1985). *Contemp. Poets* (1985, 1991). *DLB* 5 (1980).

Other references: *Bloomsbury Rev.* (May/June 1990, interview). *Christianity and Crisis* (11 Jan. 1988; 22 Oct. 1990). *Christian Science Monitor* (5 Oct. 1990). *Contemp. Lit.* (Spring 1989, article by Janet McNew). *Kenyon Rev.* (Winter 1991). *LJ* (15 May 1990). *Michigan Q. Rev.* (Spring 1987). *NYTBR* (25 Nov. 1990; 13 Dec. 1992). *Poetry* (May 1987). *Prairie Schooner* (Spring 1989). *Virginia Q. Rev.* (Winter 1987). *WRB* (April 1993). *World Lit. Today* (Autumn 1990).

DARIA DONNELLY

Tillie Olsen

See AWW 3, 303–5

Writing for O. was one of many important activities that included political activism, work, and domestic life. During her career, she has often had to balance her writing against these other responsibilities, particularly motherhood. Never a prolific writer, part of O.'s lasting appeal has been the struggle she has gone through to continue writing. She has published little since *Silences* (1978), but she has become increasingly the subject of critical attention.

Mother and Daughter, Daughter to Mother: A Daybook and Reader (1984) consists of a daily calendar and monthly readings selected by O. The collection also contains an essay in which O. recounts the circumstances leading up to her mother's death. In her hands, this potentially depressing scenario becomes instead an inspirational scene, as she is able to see within her mother's dream visions signs of the wisdom she had obtained throughout a difficult life. It is this well-earned knowledge that O. keeps as her mother's legacy.

Similarly, in an introduction to *Mothers and Daughters, That Special Quality: An Exploration in Photographs* (1987, with Julie Olsen Edwards) O. celebrates the special bond between mothers and daughters. She finds "this crucial relationship still veiled in the unseen, the unexpressed, the unarticulated." In commenting on the photographs that follow, O. wishes for more pictures of women engaged in everyday activities, believing that it is these commonplace, shared experiences "which create, condition the relationship."

Among the critical studies of O., the most extensive is *Tillie Olsen* (1991) by Mickey Pearlman and Abby H. P. Werlock. This study aims to strike a balance between appreciation and evaluation of O.'s work. The authors devote chapters to each of her major published works, and critically examine her both as an inspirational figure and as a skilled writer.

O. continued in the 1980s to lecture and promote the rediscovery and publication of women's writing. Since 1980, she has received a number of honorary degrees, awards, and university fellowships. Her husband, Jack Olsen, died in 1989; O. continues to live in California near her daughters and grandchildren.

OTHER WORKS: Preface to *Black Women Writers at Work*, Claudia Tate, ed. (1983). "The Word Made Flesh," in *Critical Thinking, Critical Writing* (1984).

BIBLIOGRAPHY: Bauer, H. P., "A Child of Anxious, Not Proud Love: Mother and Daughter in Tillie Olsen's 'I Stand Here Ironing,'" in *Mother Puzzles*, Mickey Pearlman, ed. (1989). Coiner, C., "Literature of Resistance: The Intersection of Feminism and the Communist Left in Meridel Le Sueur and Tillie Olsen," in *Left Politics and the Literary Profession*, L. Davis and M. B. Mirabella, eds. (1990). Kamel, R. W., *Aggravating the Conscience: Jewish-American Literary Mothers in the Promised Land* (1988). Martin, A., *Tillie Olsen* (1984). Meese, E., *Crossing the Double Cross* (1986). Orr, E. N., *Tillie Olsen and a Feminist Spiritual Vision* (1987). Pearlman, M., and A. H. P. Werlock, *Tillie Olsen* (1991). Reference works: *CANR* 1 (1981). *CLC* 13 (1980). *DLB* 28 (1984). *DLBY* 1980 (1981). *FC* (1990). *Maj Twent Cent Writers* (1991).

JAMES O'LOUGHLIN

Judith Ortiz Cofer

B. 24 Feb. 1952, Hormigueros, Puerto Rico
D. of Fanny (Morot) Ortiz and Jesús Ortiz Lugo; m. Charles John Cofer, 1971;
c.: Tanya, b. 1973

O. C. moved from Puerto Rico to Paterson, New Jersey, in 1956 when her father enlisted in the United States Navy. Jesús Ortiz Lugo frequently traveled to Europe with the cargo fleet and sent his family back to Puerto Rico during these prolonged absences. Consequently, O. C. grew up in several cultures: peasant Puerto Rican society, the immigrant America of her tenement home, and the white middle-class world of her American Catholic school. Her poetry, novel, and memoirs reflect her need to reconcile her disparate and at times conflicting self-identities.

O. C.'s works usually describe Puerto Rican women—in Puerto Rico and in the United States—surviving harshly limited lives in either or both settings. Marisol, the semiautobiographical figure in *The Line of the Sun* (1989), must learn to make sense of two Americas, the "exclusive club" of her Puerto Rican tenement "expatriates" and the "white middle class world" of her classmates. In Puerto Rico, peasant women are burdened by poverty and large families, and often rejected from society. These characters endure ugly conditions yet they develop lives with an increasingly rich sense of human strength: "We are like the dead, / invisible to those who do not / want to see / and our only protection against / the killing silence of their eyes is color / . . . we will build our cities of light, / we will carve them / out of the granite of their hatred / with our own brown hands" ("What the Gypsy Said to Her Children," *Reaching for the Mainland*, 1987).

Like her metaphors, stories about the past give O. C.'s characters a nearly visible foundation that extends with time and generations. Praising *Silent Dancing* (1990), Aurora Levins Morales warmly claims: "for Puerto Rican women in the U.S. controlling language, telling our own stories, is central to our sense of territory, of having a place in the world." In this book, Morales says, she "has told a piece of our common story, added another room to our house." Trying to understand how she "came to be a writer," O. C. wrote *Silent Dancing*, a loosely autobiographical collection of short stories and poetry. Similarly, Marisol in *The Line of the Sun* searches for an identity by writing a story. The first half of the novel depicts the childhood of her mother, father, and unconventional uncle in Puerto Rico. Marisol completes her story, soothed by the realization that "the only way to understand a life is to write it as a story, to fill in the blanks left by circumstance, lapse of memory, and failed communication." O. C. thus suggests that through writing one can construct a history and an identity perhaps not yet recognized: "I wish I could write a poem . . . that would make you want to get up in / the middle of the night to search for things / you didn't know were lost" ("A Poem," *Reaching for the Mainland*).

Writing about the past, placing it into ordered and transferable terms, also permits O. C.'s characters to envision a future filled with repetitions of possibility. Past generations have suffered, but the younger generation can carry on perhaps more powerfully with a combined strength: while Ramona, Marisol's mother, "became Penelope, weaving her stories into a rich tapestry . . . [Marisol] held the threads for her" and Marisol eventually creates a novel out of the fragments. An elusive future grammatically anticipated even allows *Reaching for the Mainland*, a collection of poems depicting loss and alienation within American and Puerto Rican society, to conclude with lyrically echoing hope: "In Spanish the conditional tense is the tense of dreamers / of philosophers, fools, drunkards / of widows, new mothers, small children / of old people, cripples, saints, and poets. / It is the grammar of expectation / and the formula for hope: cantaria, amaria, viviria. / Please repeat after me" ("Lesson One: I Would Sing").

Although she received a B.A. from Augusta College in Georgia (1974), an M.A. from Florida Atlantic University (1977), and a scholarship to study at Oxford University (1977), O. C. attributes her writing talents to "the spoken word" and, most particularly, to the "stories" of her grandmother. O. C. began writing poetry when she started teaching high school and later college in southern Florida (1974). A Bread Loaf Writers' Conference scholar in 1981 and 1982, she repeatedly returns to Bread Loaf as part of the administrative staff. Since 1992, she has been writing and teaching full-time at the University of Georgia, having previously been a part-time lecturer there for several years. Her poems and short stories have appeared in many journals, including *Antioch Review, Kenyon Review, Georgia Review, Prairie Schooner,* and *Southern Exposure.*

OTHER WORKS: *Latin Women Pray* (chapbook, 1980). *The Native Dancer* (chapbook, 1981). *Among Ancestors* (chapbook, 1981). "Latin Women Pray" (play, with Rolando Ortiz, 1984). *Peregrina* (chapbook, 1986). *Terms of Sur-*

vival (poems, 1987). *Triple Crown: Chicano, Puerto Rican, and Cuban American Poetry* (includes *Reaching for the Mainland,* 1987).

BIBLIOGRAPHY: Reference works: *Biographical Dict. of Hispanic Lit. in the U.S.* (1989). *CANR* 32 (1991). *Hispanic Writers* (1990). *WW Hispanic Americans* (1991, 1992). *WW Wrs, Eds, Poets* (1989).

   Other references: *LATBR* (6 Aug. 1989). *NYTBR* (24 Sept. 1989). *WRB* (July 1989, Dec. 1990).

PAMELA VASQUEZ

Brenda Marie Osbey

B. 12 Dec. 1957, New Orleans, Louisiana
D. of Lois Emelda (Hamilton) and Lawrence Osbey, Sr.

A native of New Orleans, O. grew up in seventh ward, the largest downtown black community in the city, and attended McDonogh 35, an all-black examination high school in Faubourg Tremé. The area next to the French Quarter, Tremé had once been the site of Congo Square where, before the Civil War, slaves congregated, practiced their religions, and carried on what recreation was allowed them. The area was also the focus of free black life in the city. O. attended Dillard University (B.A. 1978), a historically black college, and the Université Paul Valéry at Montpellier, France. In 1986 she received an M.A. from the University of Kentucky.

   Writer in residence at Loyola University in New Orleans since 1989, O. has taught at Dillard University and the University of California at Los Angeles. She has been a fellow at the Fine Arts Work Center in Provincetown, the Kentucky Foundation for Women, the MacDowell Colony, the Millay Colony, and the Bunting Institute of Radcliffe College. A writer of narrative poetry, O. has published three books to critical acclaim. In 1980 she won the Academy of American Poets Loring-Williams Prize; in 1984 she was honored with an Associated Writing Programs Award; and in 1990 won an NEA Creative Writing Fellowship.

Her first book of poetry, *Ceremony for Minneconjoux* (1983), is about the women of New Orleans, and it is their voices that are heard in the poems. There is Lavinia, who lives in the tan house on Calliope Street and sings, as she says, "to tell the truth as i know it." And there is Minneconjoux whose mother named her that "so that people would not mistake / her indian blood." The women—Eliza, Minneconjoux, Ramona Véagis ("who fell off the earth in 1916"), Eileen—make connections with each other and with women from other generations. In their stories there is a map of the city and a tapestry of black New Orleans life.

In These Houses (1988) speaks again for generations of women. As in her earlier book, O. depends on many of the oral traditions of black New Orleans, and she appends a glossary to clarify phrases and to highlight the special traditions of the city. Divided into three sections, "Houses of the Swift Easy Women," "House of Mercies," and "House of Bones," the book is a chronicle of the spiritual lives of women, and hoodoo, or voodoo, is evident not simply in rituals but in the spiritual care people take of one another. Elvena in her madness has lost touch with her neighbors, as Ramona Véagis did in "Ceremony." It is the work of mothers or healers, central figures in O.'s poems, to bring them back to the community. As with the women, the houses have stories: if "you go inside for the first time / its stories come out to meet you." In the final poem in the book, O. sums up the intensely spiritual nature of the lives of women and urges her readers to connect themselves to houses: "this is the house / i have carried inside me / this is the house / made of artifact and gut / this is the house / all my bones have come from / *this is the house / nothing / nothing / nothing can tear down.*" Bodies and souls are one in the house of life, and nothing can destroy the spirit of the powerful women whom O. portrays.

Desperate Circumstance, Dangerous Women (1991) is a long narrative poem set, as is much of O.'s poetry, in the Faubourg Tremé. The speaker of the poem asks at the beginning, *"do you know what hunger is?"* and sets the tone for the rest of the narrative. It is the story of mothers and daughters, women and lovers; it is the story of rituals that heal and those that destroy; it is the story of obsession and loss; and finally, it is the story of the Faubourg and its "slave-bricked streets" and the rains that threaten to wash it all away.

All of O.'s poetry is redolent with a sense of place and time passing. Past and present mingle in the lives of her women and in the vibrant and exotic life of the city. It is in her memories that O. conjures up race memories of the Faubourg and of its people.

BIBLIOGRAPHY: *Louisiana Lit.* 4:2 (Fall 1987). *The Mississippi Q.* 40 (interview, Winter 1986–87). *Parnassus* (1985). McCay, Mary A., unpublished interview, May 1992.

MARY A. MCCAY

Martha Ostenso

B. 17 Sept. 1900, Haukland, near Bergen, Norway; d. 24 Nov. 1963, Seattle, Washington
D. of Lena (Tungeland) and Sigurd Briget Ostenso; m. Douglas Durkin, 1944

O. was born in a small village high in the mountains of Norway, and immigrated to the United States with her parents when she was two. Her childhood was spent in small towns in both Minnesota and South Dakota, where she first learned to speak English and, more importantly, where she developed an ear for the Scandinavian dialects of the Midwest, which she would later incorporate into her fiction. While she was still in her early teens, her father moved the family to Canada where they settled in Manitoba.

O. attended Brandon Collegiate School and in 1918 entered the University of Manitoba. Following graduation, she spent a year (1921–22) at Columbia University, where she studied the "technique of the novel" with Douglas Durkin, with whom she lived for many years and eventually married. From 1920 to 1923 she was a social worker in Brooklyn. Yet, what proved to have the greatest effect on her as a writer were her childhood years in the Midwest and then on Canada's northern frontier. In those rugged and at times harsh environments O. developed a deep appreciation for the men and women whose lives were spent working the land.

O.'s writing career began in 1924 with the publication of *A Far Land*, a book of verse. The following year she published two works of fiction, one of which was to become her most successful and highly regarded work, *Wild Geese* (1925, rept. 1989). Its inspiration was the lake district of Manitoba: "Here was human nature stark, unattired in the convention of a smoother, softer life." Although none of her later novels ever reached the acclaim *Wild Geese* attracted, most continued to explore a similar theme: the relationship between human beings and the land they work.

Wild Geese centers on the Gares and their struggle to reach a balance between making a living off the land and allowing their lives to become consumed by it. The family is headed by a domineering father who pushes his family to sacrifice everything to the farm. The women, particularly his daughter Judith, truly understand the cost to the family. "Living only for the earth, and the product of the soil, they were meager and warped."

A Man Had Tall Sons (1958) also focuses on a domineering father; like Caleb, Luke is just as willing to sacrifice the happiness of his family for the sake of running the farm. The novel ends with the death of his son Mark. At the graveside, Luke quotes Whitman, for his son's death illustrates the cyclical process of nature: "You will be given to the earth again and you will grow in beauty."

Like **Willa Cather,** O. portrays the lives of rural immigrants with dignity and respect and examines the "strange unity between the nature of man and earth." By the end of her career, O. had published sixteen works of fiction and a biography, *And They Shall Walk: The Life Story of Sister Elizabeth Kenny* (1943), which like a number of her other works was translated and reprinted several times.

OTHER WORKS: *The Passionate Flight* (1925). *The Dark Dawn* (1926). *The Mad Carews* (1927). *The Young May Moon* (1929). *The Water's under the Earth* (1930). *Prologue to Love* (1932). *There's Always Another Year* (1933). *The White Reef* (1934). *The Stone Field* (1937). *The Mandrake Root* (1938). *Love Passed This Way* (1942). *O River Remember!* (1943). *The Sunset Tree* (1943). *Milk Route* (1948).

BIBLIOGRAPHY: Harrison, Dick, *Unnamed Country* (1977). Northey, Margot, *The Haunted Wilderness* (1976). Reference works: *CA Permanent Series 1. Canadian Novelists, 1920–1945*, C. Thomas, ed. (1946). *DLB 92* (1990). *FC* (1990). *Tw Cent Authors* (1942, 1955).

CHRISTINE O'CONNOR

Alicia Ostriker

B. 11 Nov. 1937, Brooklyn, New York
D. of Beatrice (Linnick) and David Suskin; m. Jeremiah Ostriker, 1958;
  c.: Rebecca, b. 1963; Eve, b. 1965; Gabriel, b. 1970

It would be impossible to hierarchize the influences on O.'s work, but the poetry and thought of William Blake has been a significant and consistent one throughout her career as a poet and critic. Blake, whom she calls a "rule-breaker and revolutionary," had the courage and vision that for O. clearly characterize the best and most challenging poetry.

Raised in Manhattan, one of two daughters of working-class Jewish parents, O. did not always want to be a poet. Although her mother had read poetry to her throughout her childhood, and though she had written poetry since she was old enough to write, she first wanted to be a visual artist. By the time she graduated from Brandeis University in 1959, however, she knew that she wanted to do further work in English literature. In 1965, having received her M.A. (1961) and Ph.D. (1964) at the University of Wisconsin-Madison, O. was hired to teach literature and creative writing in the English Department at Rutgers University, where she is a full professor.

O.'s dissertation, *Vision and Verse in William Blake* (1965), became the first of her full-length critical studies. At that time, she also looked to a number of other poets as models, including Keats, Walt Whitman, and W. H. Auden. As varied as they were, all of the poets whose work she then admired were men.

Like many women poets of her generation, O.'s work was radically influenced in the 1970s by the women's movement and the new recognition it gave to women poets like **H.D.** [Hilda Doolittle], **Sylvia Plath,** and **Anne Sexton.** In their work and the work of such contemporaries as **Adrienne Rich, Lucille Clifton, May Swenson,** and **June Jordan** O. found complexity and challenge comparable to the work of Blake. She also found themes, motifs, and language that helped her begin to theorize a distinctly feminine sensibility in American poetry.

O.'s 1980 collection, *The Mother/Child Papers,* may be the best and most explicit marker of her own move into what she identifies in her critical study *Stealing the Language* (1986) as "women's poetry." Dominated by a specifically maternal voice, the poems reveal such a voice to be in fact many voices. Although the "I" of O.'s poems is always in some sense O. herself, the multiplicity of women's experiences and forms of expression is something that her poetry nevertheless emphasizes.

The courage to take risks and to break the silence of women partly defines O.'s project as a Blakean, feminist, and Jewish poet. Her work involves playing with new poetic forms as well as rewriting already established ones. When she works in traditional forms, she implicitly confronts a masculine poetic tradition with the assertion of a feminine (and often, feminist) one. More explicitly, O. often combines or interweaves the "public" discourses of politics with the "private" ones of the home and the body, as in her prose poem "Cambodia."

Throughout O.'s poetry are signs of struggle—with day-to-day life, with history, with language. Poems like "The War of Men and Women" and "Surviving," from *The Imaginary Lover* (1986; recipient in 1987 of the William Carlos Williams Prize from the Poetry Society of America) expose the subtle and not-so-subtle complexities of such struggles without providing any easy resolutions. In poems like "A Meditation in Seven Days," from *Green Age* (1989), she looks to alternative constructions of history and religion to locate women in both.

In addition to seven volumes of poetry and four critical works, O. has published many essays, articles, and reviews in a number of journals. Her poems have been published in *Ms., Poetry, The New Yorker,* the *Nation, Feminist Studies,* and many other publications. She has also received numerous honors and awards, including fellowships in poetry from the National Endowment for the Arts (1976–77) and the Guggenheim Foundation (1984–85), and three MacDowell Colony fellowships.

OTHER WORKS: *Songs: A Book of Poems* (1969). *Once More out of Darkness, and Other Poems* (1971). *William Blake: The Complete Poems* (editor, 1977). *A Dream of Springtime: Poems, 1970–1978* (1979). *A Woman under the Surface* (1982). *Writing like a Woman* (1983). *Feminist Revision and the Bible* (1993).

BIBLIOGRAPHY: Aal, Katharyn Machan, "An Interview with Alicia Ostriker," *Poets and Writers Mag.* (Nov./Dec. 1989). Reference works: *CANR* 10 (1983), 30 (1990). *FC* (1990).

MONICA DORENKAMP

Rochelle Owens

B. 2 April 1936, Brooklyn, New York
D. of Molly (Adler) and Maxwell Bass; m. David Owens, 1956, div. 1960; m. George Economou, 1962

O. is best known as a playwright and poet, although she has worked in all genres and with all forms of media. She professes to live a "middle-class existence" similar to her upbringing in Brooklyn. Her husband, a poet, has acted in O.'s plays and written about her work. O. never attended college; instead, after high school, she traveled to Greece, Egypt, Syria, Turkey, and Greenland; several of these became settings for her plays. She also took classes at the Herbert Berghof Studio, though never intending to act, and at the New School for Social Research. O. has taught at the University of Oklahoma at Norman, the University of California at San Diego, and Brown University. Besides her membership in several professional organizations, she is cofounder of the New York Theatre Strategy, the Women's Theatre Council, and *Scripts/Performance* magazine, a sponsor of the Women's Interart Center, and a member of the editorial board of *Performing Arts Journal*.

O.'s plays are almost always nonnaturalistic or surrealistic, refiguring time and space. In both the poems and plays, she manages a sharp, frequently sexual humor while challenging traditional notions of gender roles, examining power issues, and, using her own anthropology, exploring the myths of other cultures. O. sees herself as "belonging to the generation of experimental artists that gave rise to the present feminist movement."

Her poetry subverts language by dividing words, and by creating new words and unexpected combinations, juxtaposing biblical references and Hebrew, for example, with contemporary images and stark sexual language. The visual/verbal effect of the poems forces a reconsideration of these new word forms whose meaning assaults cultural conceptions of gender roles. "My writing is feminist," says O., "because it has much to do with my identity as a woman in a particular culture." In the four books of poems of *The Joe Chronicles* (1974–79), O. creates Wild-Man, who with violence and the assumption of superiority, submits Wild-Woman, who represents the possibility of change and new values, to his rule. In the third book, *Shemuel* (1979), the queen of the title subverts the progress women have been able to make by acting with as much cruelty as any male ruler, allowing the women in her society to remain oppressed.

O. credits the use of myth by William Blake, James Joyce, and Marcel Proust as influences. She frequently uses different personas, notably in *Discourse on Life and Death* (1990), which, according to the author, is "a loose personal narrative around the theme of Mona Lisa and Da Vinci. The constant shifting of gender as well as personal pronoun referents represents an advance in the knowledge of women being part of culture rather than alien to it."

O. has received numerous awards and honors for her plays including Rockefeller grants for playwriting (1965, 1974), a Yale School of Drama and American Broadcasting Fellowship (1968), a Guggenheim Fellowship (1971), grants from the National Endowment for the Arts, awards from the New York Drama Critics Circle, and several Obie nominations and awards. Both the New York Public Theatre and the New York Shakespeare Company have commissioned her works. Her first play, *Futz*, which focuses on a man's love for his sow, won the Obie award for best play (1967). O.'s plays have been translated into several languages and have successfully toured Europe, although *Futz* was nearly banned at the 1967 Edinburgh festival for its explicit sexuality.

O., who held jobs as a clerk, typist, and telephone operator, wrote *Futz* on office stationery when she was twenty-one. She sees it as a moral play, about society's improper need for individuals to conform. O. feels that the emergence of "feminist criticism adds a new dimension to my dramatic literature," encouraging expression of the woman's perspective that had been lost. Constantly shifting pronouns and gender in *He Wants Shih!* (1974), O. portrays a Chinese emperor abdicating his rule to pursue the "Shih," the "everything" in himself. "I have always drastically re-imagined and re-defined the relationships of female/male. [That] is why I am an avant-garde poet and playwright," O. explains. A failed artist hates his mother and ex-wife for their success in *Chucky's Hunch* (1982), which addresses feminist concerns of empowerment and victimization. *Beclch* (1968), set in Africa, precedes the poems in *Shemuel* with another cruel female ruler abusing power. The animal sacrifices and human violence in this play reflect the influence of Antonin Artaud.

In both *The Karl Marx Play* (1974), a musical comedy, and *Emma Investigated Me* (1976), eponymously titled from the nineteenth-century radical feminist/anarchist **Emma Goldman,** O. concentrates on the author's creative struggle. An African, Leadbelly, calling himself "the real revolutionary force," inspires Marx to write. Similarly, *Kontraption* (1974) tests the bounds of theater with speeches to the audience and time measured in duration rather than by a clock. Dealing further with racial issues in this play, O. stresses the concept of human community through a black character and a white character sharing their entire range of thoughts and emotions. In *Homo* (1968) O. questions Western racial superiority; *The String Game* (1968) and *Istanboul* (1968) show the negative results of cultural imperialism.

In the visual medium, O. write the screenplay for and acted in the movie *Futz* (1969). Her autobiographical art video, *How Much Paint Does the Painting Need* (1990), sharing title and subject matter with the poems, fuses disjointed images of paintings, sculptures, and photographs with video art. Her audio work includes recordings of her adaptations of primitive and archaic world poetry, radio plays, and hosting a public radio program in Norman, Oklahoma, "The Writer's Mind," for which she interviewed authors. While O. continues to write poetry, she has moved away from writing plays and more toward electronic media production in recent years.

OTHER WORKS: Poetry: *Not Be Essence That Cannot Be* (1961). *Salt and Core* (1968). *I Am the Babe of Joseph Stalin's Daughter* (1972). *Poems from Joe's Garage* (1973). *The Joe 82 Creation Poems* (1974). *The Joe Chronicles Part 2* (1979). *French Light* (1984). *Constructs* (1985). *Anthropologists at a Dinner Party* (1985). *W. C. Fields in French Light* (1986). *Paysanne: New and Selected Poems, 1961–1988* (1991). Poems by O. are included in over two hundred anthologies, magazines, and journals, from *Four Young Lady Poets* (1962) to *A. Bacus 59* (July 1991). *Spontaneous Combustion: Eight New American Plays* (1972, editor and contributor). *The Karl Marx Play and Others* (1974). *The Widow and the Colonel* (1977). *Who Do You Want, Peire Vidal?* (1986). Plays by O. are included in: *New American Plays*, vol. 2 (1968). *Methuen Playscripts* (1969). *Yale Theatre*, vol. 2, No. 2 (1969). *New Underground Theatre* (1968). *Scripts 2* (1971). *Best Short Plays: 1971*, 1977, and 1978. *Off-Off Broadway* (1973). *Performing Arts Journal* (1976). *Scenarios* (1980). *Wordplays 2* (1982). Translation: Atlan, Lillian, *The Passerby* (1990). Recordings: *From a Shaman's Notebook* (1968). *The Karl Marx Play*, songs, music by Galt McDermot (1974). *Totally Corrupt* (1976). *Sweet Potatoes* (1977). *Black Box* 17 (1979). Video: *Oklahoma Too* (1987).

BIBLIOGRAPHY: American Playwrights: A Critical Survey, Bonnie Maranca and Gautam Dasgupta, eds. (1981). Murray, Timothy, "The Play of Letters: The Possession of Writing in *Chucky's Hunch*," in *Feminine Focus: The New*

Women Playwrights, Enoch Brater, ed. (1989). Ostriker, Alicia, *Stealing the Language: The Emergence of Women's Poetry in America* (1986). Ratner, Rochelle, *Trying to Understand What It Means to Be Feminist: Essays on Women Writers* (1984). Rothenberg, Jerome, introduction to *Futz* (1968). Reference works: *CA* 17–20 (1976). *CAAS* 2 (1985). *Contemp. Dramatists* (1988). *Contemp. Poets* (1991). *FC* (1990). *Not. Women in Amer. Theatre* (1989). *WW Wr, Eds, Poets* (1989).

Other references: *Margins* 24/25/26 (1975). *Nation* (12 May 1969). *NYT* (21 July 1968, interview; 17 Dec. 1968; 25 Dec. 1968; 2 Feb. 1973; 3 April 1973; 28 May 1977; 19 March 1978; 25 March 1981; 5 Sept. 1982). *Parnassus* (1985). *Saturday Rev.* (7 Jan. 1967). *Theater* 20:2 (Spring 1989, interview). *Village Voice* (19 Dec. 1965). *Women's Wear Daily* (3 April 1973). *World*, no. 29 (April 1974). O.'s papers are at Boston University; other collections at the University of California at Davis, the University of Oklahoma, and the New York Public Library at Lincoln Center.

ANDREW SCHIAVONI

Cynthia Ozick

See AWW 3, 330–32

A distinctive voice in American literature, O. is known chiefly for her complex fiction centered on Jewish characters and Judaic themes. Widely recognized as an outstanding essayist, she is also a poet and translator. She has received many awards, including a Guggenheim Fellowship and, in 1982, a Mildred and Harold Strauss Living Award from the American Academy and Institute of Arts and Letters, to which she was subsequently elected (1983).

Success did not come early for O. After receiving her B.A. from New York University (1949) and her M.A. in English from Ohio State University (1950), she spent seven years working on a long novel called "Mercy, Pity, Peace, and Love," which was never published. O. then spent six and one-half years on yet another novel, *Trust*, which finally appeared in

1966. Writing with biting humor and poignancy about the painful years between her twenties and her "despairing middle thirties," when she was writing obsessively and publishing nothing, submitting work to magazines and being routinely turned down, she said in a 1984 essay, "Cyril Connolly and the Groans of Success," that she never "properly recuperated" from the "pounding of denigration and rejection."

Following the publication of *Trust*, which has received varying appraisals, O. turned from the long novel to the shorter fiction that won her critical acclaim. Between 1971 and 1982, she published three collections of stories and novellas: *The Pagan Rabbi and Other Stories* (1971), *Bloodshed and Three Novellas* (1976), and *Levitation: Five Fictions* (1982). Almost all of the tales in these collections revolve around Jewish themes, treated from cultural, historical, or theological perspectives: the Holocaust; Jewishness in America; "the corruptions and abominations" *(Bloodshed)* of the idolatry forbidden by the Second Commandment, whether it takes the form of worshiping ideas, nature, individuals, or poems. While some of O.'s stories are realistic, some are fantastic. "Puttermesser and Xanthippe," for instance, involves a Frankenstein-like creation of Jewish folklore known as a golem.

In the 1980s, O. returned to the novel with two rich, compressed works: *The Cannibal Galaxy* (1983) and *The Messiah of Stockholm* (1987). In 1989, she published *The Shawl*, comprised of the title story and a prizewinning novella, *Rosa*, both revolving around a Holocaust survivor.

O.'s work has been praised for its originality, its intelligence, and its superb craftsmanship. Her fiction has an intellectual, multilayered complexity, and critics have varied in both their interpretation and their assessment of individual works. Though O. has stated in her well-known preface to *Bloodshed* that "a story must not merely *be*, but mean," in some of her tales the meaning seems obscure. At its best, her fiction is at once philosophical and witty, thought-provoking and gripping—adjectives that can be applied to the best of her essays as well.

A contributor to many popular, literary, and Jewish periodicals, O. has gathered a selection of her essays into two collections: *Art and Ardor* (1983) and *Metaphor and Memory* (1989). Whether offering literary analysis or portraits of literary figures, exploring Judaic issues, or addressing feminist concerns, O. can be a superb essayist. Successful personal essays have included "Washington Square, 1946," which was included in *The Best American Essays: 1986*, and "A Drugstore in Winter," a childhood memoir that critic Katha Pollitt judged "as rich and dense as the best of her fiction."

In the "Forewarning" that opens *Metaphor and Memory*, O. warns readers against using her essays to "interpret" her stories, and the critic Harold Bloom has observed that O.'s "narrative art and her stance as an essayist seem not to be wholly reconcilable." Nonetheless, O.'s provocative, perceptive essays on Judaic and literary themes help define the religious and aesthetic issues central to her fiction, especially her views on idolatry.

Taking a strong stand against postmodernism, minimalism, art for art's sake—i.e., literature as idol—O. has argued that "literature is for the sake of humanity." Her essays provide an understanding of the moral seriousness that she believes should be central to all literature, and that clearly resides at the heart of everything she writes.

OTHER WORKS: *The Mystic Explorer* (1980). *Ink and Inkling: Mark Podwal, Master of the True Line* (1990). Translations in *A Treasury of Yiddish Poetry*, Irving Howe and Eliezer Greenberg, eds. (1969), and *Voices from the Yiddish: Essays, Memoirs, Diaries* (1972); *The Penguin Book of Modern Yiddish Verse*, Irving Howe, Ruth Wisse, and Khone Shmeruk, eds. (1987); *Voices within the Ark: The Modern Jewish Poets*, Howard Schwartz and Anthony Rudolf, eds. (1980).

BIBLIOGRAPHY: *Cynthia Ozick: Modern Critical Views*, Harold Bloom, ed. (1986). Currier, Susan, and Daniel J. Cahill, "A Bibliography of the Writings of Cynthia Ozick," in *Contemporary American Women Writers: Narrative Strategies*, Catherine Rainwater and William Scheick, eds. (1985). Friedman, Lawrence S., *Understanding Cynthia Ozick* (1991). Kauvar, Elaine, *Cynthia Ozick's Fiction: Tradition and Invention* (1993). Lowin, Joseph, *Cynthia Ozick* (1988). Pinsker, Sanford, *The Uncompromising Fictions of Cynthia Ozick* (1987). *The World of Cynthia Ozick: Studies in American Jewish Literature* 6, Daniel Walden, ed. (1987). Reference works: *CA* 17–20 (1976). *CANR* 23 (1988). *CLC* 3 (1975), 7 (1977), 28 (1984), 62 (1991). *Contemp. Novelists* (1991). *CB* (1983). *DLB* 28 (1984). *DLBY* (1982). *FC* (1990). *Maj Twent Cent Writers* (1991).

Other references: *Texas Studies in Lit. and Language* 25:2 (Summer 1983).

GAIL POOL

Grace Paley

See AWW 3, 334–36

Short-story writer, essayist, and poet, P. creates vivid portraits, especially of women struggling through love and familial relationships. Theirs is a world fraught with dependent, elderly parents; anxious, precocious children; distant men; as well as the global issues of nuclear arms and war. Between 1959 and 1974, P. published two books of short stories: *The Little Disturbances of Man* (1959) and *Enormous Changes at the Last Minute* (1974). Critics have made much of her spare narrative style, open-ended plot structure (if there is structure at all), and vivid imagery and characterizations.

Since *Enormous Changes* P. has continued publishing stories, as well as poetry, at her own laconic pace, continuing to experiment with structure. Her often-quoted protest against the well-plotted story (in "Conversations with My Father") remains the literary philosophy she follows. In *Later the Same Day* (1985), characters from earlier stories—most noticeably Faith—reappear, establishing a continuity that produces some of the best stories in the collection. Faith, considered to be P.'s alter ego, is middle-aged now, giving P. the opportunity to explore all the attending issues of that period of life. Her children have grown, and she must also face the death of her mother and her own aging.

In "Friends," Faith deals with middle age and mortality through the experience of visiting a seriously ill friend, Selena: "People do want to be young and beautiful. When they meet in the street, male or female, if they're getting older they look at each other's face a little ashamed. It's clear they want to say, Excuse me, I didn't mean to draw attention to mortality and gravity all at once."

To climb out of these depths, Faith says, requires a certain amount of strength; it is possible, but difficult. Other people offer assistance, and so P. fills her stories with new characters: Chinese tourists; the parents of kidnapped children; Cissy who is slipping into insanity and her father who gives up comfort in old age to save her; Ruthy who holds too tightly to her granddaughter Letty. Another way to climb out of the depths is global awareness, and especially, as P. herself has consistently done, acting on that awareness. In "Listening," Faith passes out leaflets calling for the United States to honor the Geneva Agreements. It is common for many of the characters to be at, or on their way to, or coming from some kind of political gathering or rally. *Later the Same Day* is not only a continuation of P.'s stories of life from youth to middle age, but also a reaffirmation of all the reasons to go on with life.

In her afterword to *Leaning Forward* (1985), a book of poems, **Jane Cooper** reminds readers that P. wrote nothing but poetry until the age of thirty and recommends that the poems be read as preparation for the stories. Indeed, the poems clearly outline the stages of life on both a personal and global level in a journal style of free association. "Middle Age Poem," "Note to Grandparents," "Old Age Porch," "The Sad Children's Song," and "Illegal Aliens," among others, reassert P.'s interest in how the everyday problems of life mirror on a smaller scale the cataclysms of world politics. *New and Collected Poems* (1992) offers more of the same economic style of observational poetry with the most clearly focused works dealing with P.'s experiences in El Salvador and Hanoi.

P.'s political activism inspired *Long Walks and Intimate Talks: Stories and Poems* (1991), which also contains drawings by Vera Williams. In this collection, P. moves away from her characteristic mixture of the global and the personal for works that are entirely issue-oriented: the Vietnam War draft, the nuclear power plant in Seabrook, New Hampshire, Mothers of the Disappeared in El Salvador, patriarchal government. The poems dealing with political problems have a sharp edge to them. But the stories are hardly fiction, more essays or sketches.

Living most of the time in Vermont, P. continues her political activism. It remains as much of a career and a way of life as her writing does.

OTHER WORKS: *The Little Disturbances of Man: Stories of Women and Men at Love* (1959), reptd. with new intro. by A. S. Byatt (1980).

BIBLIOGRAPHY: Arcana, Judith, *Grace Paley's Life Stories: A Literary Biography* (1993). Taylor, Jacqueline, *Grace Paley: Illuminating the Dark Lives* (1990). Reference works: *Benet's* (1991). *CA* 15–28 (1977). *CANR* 13 (1984). *CLC* 4 (1975), 6 (1976), 37 (1986). *Contemp. Novelists* (1991). *DLB* 28 (1984). *FC* (1990). *Maj Twent Cent Writers* (1991). *Modern Amer. Women Writers* (1991). *Short Story Crit* 8 (1991). *WW Wrs, Eds, Poets* (1989).

Other references: *Commentary* (Aug. 1985). *New Republic* (29 April 1985). *NYT* (10 April 1985). *NYTBR* (14 April 1985; 15 Aug. 1985; 22 Sept. 1991;

19 April 1992). *PW* (28 June 1991; interview, Oct. 1991). *Village Voice Lit. Supp.* (June 1985). *WRB* (Nov. 1991).

LINDA BERUBE

Mary Frances Parrish. *See Mary Frances Kennedy Fisher*

Linda Pastan

B. 27 May 1932, New York City
D. of Bess (Schwartz) and Jacob L. Olenick; m. Ira Pastan, 1953; c.: Stephen,
* b. 1956; Peter, b. 1957; Rachel, b. 1965*

P. studied at Radcliffe (B.A. 1954) and in her senior year won *Mademoiselle's* Dylan Thomas Poetry Award. (**Sylvia Plath** took second place.) She earned an M.L.S. from Simmons in 1955 and an M.A. from Brandeis in 1957. Her life as a mother and homemaker both interrupted and fueled her vocation as a writer. She suspended a writing career and carved out hours for writing when her children were at school; family life emerged as her major subject.

P.'s poetry explores the nuances and meaning of domestic life by recounting her daily transactions as mother, wife, daughter, and poet in light of older stories and myths (chiefly biblical and classical). Her oft-noted ironic vision rises out of the paralleling of familiar domestic experience and culturally privileged narratives.

P. is committed to writing accessible short lyrics of personal observation. Skeptical of the division between public and private poetry, she asserts that "the ability of the poet to make the reader see and feel always serves a political function." P.'s poems are built of finely wrought images and plainly articulated narratives and replete with references to a writer's tools. Her central emphasis is on labor: her labor to form words that meet experience; her labor against desolation and toward meaning in light of mortality. Death and the shadow that death casts on domesticity and life are major preoccupations.

A Perfect Circle of Sun (1971), *Aspects of Eve* (1975), *The Five Stages of Grief* (1978), *Waiting for My Life* (1981), and *PM/AM* (1982) consider events large and small—in light of death. The tension, comedy, and continuity of family experience is explored in poems such as "Passover" that blend the old and new family saga: "The wise son and the wicked / the simple son / and the son who doesn't act, are all my son / leaning tonight as it is written / slouching his father calls it." In *Aspects of Eve* P. asserts the writing of poems and the naming and nurturing of children as parallel and necessary acts of saving, although powerless against loss.

The Five Stages of Grief is the most thematic of her books, taking its name and its divisions from **Elizabeth Kübler-Ross**'s understanding of the grief process as sequential stages: denial, anger, bargaining, depression, acceptance. In this book of midlife P. explores these feelings and discovers that her pain emanates from the reality that within mutability, nothing can be definitively lost. The book is a process of making peace with her desires for an intensity of feeling and perception that has passed.

There is a permanent shift in the gravity of P.'s poems with *A Fraction of Darkness* (1985). Written during her mother's stroke and recovery, the book reflects P.'s heightened sense of mortality and renewed commitment to the search for sense. In *The Imperfect Paradise* (1988) and *Heroes in Disguise* (1991) P. focuses her attention on art objects: paintings, formal gardens, museums, The *Odyssey*. She remains concerned with passages in a woman's life and with the gleaning function of the poet in a world depleted of and hungry for meaning: "Look out the car window. / Hogs have been let loose / in the stubbled fields / like heroes in disguise / to find what grains of corn / are left."

P. was named poet laureate of Maryland in 1991. Cowinner with Naomi Lazard of the Poetry Society of America's di Castagnola Award (1977), she has also received the Bess Hoskins Prize of *Poetry Magazine* and the Maurice English Award.

OTHER WORKS: On the Way to the Zoo (chapbook, 1975). *Selected Poems of Linda Pastan* (1979). *Even as We Sleep* (chapbook, 1980). *Setting the Table* (chapbook, 1980). "The Place of Poetry: A Symposium," *Georgia Rev.* (Winter 1981). "Penelope—the Sequel: Some Uses of Mythology in Contemporary Poetry" in *The Bread Loaf Anthology of Contemporary American Essays*, Robert Pack and Jay Parini, eds. (1989). "Washing My Hands of the Ink," *Prairie Schooner* (Winter, 1991). "Writing about Writing" in *Writers on Writing*, R. Pack and J. Parini, eds. (1991). Sound recordings: *Linda Pastan and Dave Smith*, Academy of American Poets, 1981. *Linda Pastan*, The Spoken Page, Pittsburgh Poetry Forum, 1989.

BIBLIOGRAPHY: Isaac, Donna, et al., "Choosing the Poet Laureate: Were They Listening?" *English J.* (Nov. 1990). Reference works: *CA* 61–64 (1976). *CANR* 18 (1986). *CLC* 27 (1984). *DLB* 5 (1980).

Other references: *America* (21 Feb. 1976). *APR* (Jan. 1982). *Belles Lettres* (Fall 1988). *Christian Science Monitor* (30 July 1975). *Encounter* (April 1980). *English J.* (Dec. 1979). *Georgia Rev.* (Winter 1979, Spring 1983, Summer 1986, Summer 1988). *Hudson Rev.* (Autumn 1978). *Mass. Rev.* (Spring 1989). *Ms.* (Sept. 1976). *New Republic* (4 Feb. 1978). *NYT* (18 Aug. 1972). *NYTBR* (20 Feb. 1983; 18 Sept. 1988). *Poetry* (Sept. 1982, Jan. 1984, April 1986). *Prairie Schooner* (Summer 1976, Fall 1979, Spring 1991). *Sewanee Rev.* (July 1976). *Southern Rev.* (Winter 1992). *TLS* (18 Jan. 1980). *Tulsa Studies in Women's Lit.* 9:1 (Spring 1990). *Virginia Q. Rev.* (Winter 1981, Winter 1982, Spring 1983, Autumn 1988). *WRB* (June 1986, Oct. 1988).

DARIA DONNELLY

Katherine Paterson

B. 31 Oct. 1932, Qing Jiang, Jiangsu, China
D. of Mary (Goetchius) and George Raymond Womeldorf; m. John Barstow
Paterson, 1962; c.: Elizabeth Po Lin, John, David Lord, Mary Katherine

One of the foremost contemporary writers of children's books, P. has won numerous awards; they include two Newbery Medals, for *Bridge to Terabithia* (1972) and *Jacob Have I Loved* (1980), and two National Book Awards, for *The Master Puppeteer* (1975) and *The Great Gilly Hopkins* (1978). She also lectures and writes extensively about the importance of excellence in children's literature.

P. draws greatly from her own childhood experience to create multifaceted, realistic characters. Born in China, with the outbreak of war in 1941 she and her missionary parents fled to North Carolina. At the age of twelve, she was labeled an outcast by her peers because she spoke with a British accent, wore clothes from the missionary barrel (which some of the children recognized as their own contributions), and had peculiar mannerisms. She was painfully shy and, because of her parents' work, she had to move eighteen times during her growing-up years. She turned to books and her own elaborate fantasies for comfort.

Although P. suffered some lonely years as a child of missionary parents, she became a missionary herself. After graduating from King College (B.A. 1954) she earned an M.A. from Presbyterian School of Christian Education (1957) and served from 1957 to 1961 in Japan. There she studied at Naganuma School of the Japanese Language in Kobe. When she returned to the United States, she earned an M.R.E. (1962) from Union Theological Seminary.

P.'s deep interest in the culture and history of Japan inspired her first three novels for children, *The Sign of the Chrysanthemum* (1973), *Of Nightingales That Weep* (1974), and *The Master Puppeteer*. Despite her ability to capture the feel of Japanese culture and conventions, critics feel that she did not find her true voice and style until she began to write contemporary novels set in the United States.

P. never planned on becoming a writer. She says: "When I finally began to write books, it was not so much that I wanted to be a writer but that

I loved books and wanted somehow to get inside the process, to have a part in their making." One of her college professors noted her tendency to conform her writing style to that of the author they happened to be studying, a habit that turned out to be a great asset; critics note P.'s ability to modify her writing style to create the appropriate mood for a piece. She believes that "the very language, the metaphors, must belong to the world of the story." In *The Tale of the Mandarin Ducks* (1990) P. displays this talent through the economy of language and clarity appropriate for a traditional tale.

P. also draws from the experiences of her four children for her writing. She was moved to write the highly praised *Bridge to Terabithia* when her son David's close friend was killed by lightning. She says, "I seem to be in tune with the questions my children and their friends are asking. Is there any chance that human beings can learn to love one another? Will the world last long enough for me to grow up in it? What if I die?" Critics note the sensitivity and honesty with which she explores these questions in her writing.

P.'s talents as a writer for children are also reflected in her essays for adults collected in *The Gates of Excellence* (1981) and *The Spying Heart* (1989). She is noted for her candor and humor when speaking about her own experiences as well as for her stimulating and challenging scholarly opinions about children's literature.

OTHER WORKS: *Who Am I?* (1966). *Justice for All People* (1973). *To Make Men Free* (1973). *Angels and Other Strangers: Family Christmas Stories* (1979, published in England as *Star of Night*, 1980). *The Crane Wife* (translator, 1981). *Rebels of the Heavenly Kingdom* (1983). *Come Sing, Jimmy Jo* (with John Paterson, 1985). *Consider the Lilies: Plants of the Bible* (1986). *Once upon a Time: Celebrating the Magic of Children's Books in Honor of the Twentieth Anniversary of Reading Is Fundamental* (contributor, 1986). *The Tongue-Cut Sparrow* (translator, 1987). *Park's Quest* (1988). *Lyddie* (1991). *The King's Equal* (1992). *The Big Book for the Planet* (1993).

BIBLIOGRAPHY: Reference works: *CLR* 7 (1984). *CANR* 28 (1990). *CLC* 12 (1980), 30 (1984). *DLB* 52 (1986). *SATA* 51 (1988).

DIANE E. KROLL

Jayne Anne Phillips

B. 19 July 1952, Buckhannon, West Virginia
D. of Martha Jane (Thornhill) and Russell R. Phillips; m. Mark Brian Stockman, 1985; c.: one son, two stepsons

P. came of age during the Vietnam War and is one of the first American writers to deal explicitly with the social effects of this conflict at home. The daughter of a contractor father and schoolteacher mother, her rural roots situated her among ordinary people who were removed from the radical ferment of the 1960s and 1970s, but who nevertheless had to deal with many of the wrenching social changes of that time. P.'s work examines the effects of these changes, especially the disruption of family and the individual's search for both connection and transcendence.

P. began to publish poetry while a student at West Virginia University. After graduation in 1974, she lived in California and Colorado, working as a waitress and beginning to experiment with the intensely compressed, brief prose that culminated in *Sweethearts* (1976), published in the same year P. entered the University of Iowa writing program (M.F.A. 1978). Intrigued by the challenge of fiction, P. began to concentrate in that genre. Her first collection for a commercial press, *Black Tickets* (awarded the Sue Kaufman Award for first fiction), was published in 1979. Critics praised its poetic language and its sharp observations of socially marginal characters: street people, drug addicts, the emotionally disturbed and neglected. Many stories deal frankly with violence and sexuality; others, more traditional in structure, explore family relationships.

P.'s first novel, *Machine Dreams* (1984), set in a small West Virginia town, traces the history of the Hampson family from the Depression of the 1930s through Vietnam. The book received wide praise for its evocation of disillusionment, and for the sensitivity with which it portrayed the disparate members of a loving, but troubled, family. The novel's intimate sense of place—the rural and small-town South—again appears in some of the stories in *Fast Lanes* (1984; 1987). Other stories return, however, to the situations of rootless and confused young characters on the road. In them women as much as men have the need to wander and accumulate experiences, including erotic ones, in their search for themselves.

P. taught writing at Boston University and at Brandeis University during the 1980s, and was a fellow at the Bunting Institute at Radcliffe College in 1981. Subsequently, she has devoted herself full-time to writing and to her family. "In Summer Camps," part of a novel in progress published in *Granta* (Spring 1991), returns to P.'s familiar themes of sexual awakening and the violence of disturbed consciousness.

P.'s stories have been widely anthologized. In addition to the Sue Kaufman Award, P. has received the Pushcart Prize (1977, 1979); the Fels Award for fiction (1978); two fellowships from the National Endowment for the Arts (1978, 1985); the St. Lawrence Award for fiction (1979); the O. Henry Award (1980); a National Book Critics Circle Award nomination (1984); and a *New York Times* best books of 1984 citation.

OTHER WORKS: Sweethearts (1976). *Counting* (1978). *How Mickey Made It* (1981).

BIBLIOGRAPHY: Reference works: *CANR* 24 (1988). *CLC* 15 (1980), 33 (1985). *DLBY: 1980* (1981). *FC* (1990). Interviews in *PW* (8 June 1984); *Croton Rev.* (1986). See also Ann Hulbert, "Rural Chic," *New Republic* (2 Sept. 1985).

ELIZABETH SHOSTAK

Marge Piercy

See AWW 3, 389–91

Since 1980, P. has solidified her reputation as a powerful and politically committed writer while branching out into a variety of genres. Her frequent publications testify to an author who uses her writing to explore vital issues and ideas. *Braided Lives* (1982) is P.'s most autobiographical novel to date. She describes it as "more novel than memoir . . . a heightened fantasy on certain autobiographical themes." It follows the protagonist, Jill, from her youth in the 1950s through her growing radicalization in the late 1960s, and uses her relationship with a cousin to measure the psychic as well as geographic distances Jill has traveled. The book is concerned in great part with the difficulties Jill faces in becoming a writer.

Fly Away Home (1984) centers around Daria, a woman whose traditional domestic life is forever altered. Her security shaken by her divorce and the death of her mother, Daria makes a number of difficult decisions that transform her life and draw her back to the working-class values of her childhood.

Gone to Soldiers (1987) was P.'s most ambitious work to date. This epic World War II novel follows ten characters as their personal lives become intertwined with the war and its effects both on the battle front and the home front. Although the war novel would not initially appear to be well suited to a feminist and leftist writer such as P., she is able to work successfully within this genre to explore separation, friendship, and the overall impact of war on a varied cast of characters.

Summer People (1989) follows three artists as their decade-long *ménage à trois* begins to fall apart. Running alongside the development of these personalities is an examination of the effect of real-estate development on Cape Cod. In a 1984 autobiographical memoir, P. details her move to Cape Cod with her second husband, Robert Shapiro, whom she married in 1962, and her deep attachment to that area, which has remained her home. *Summer People* reflects her concern for the ecological survival of Cape Cod, threatened by overdevelopment.

In *He, She, and It* (1991) P. ventures into the world(s) of cyberpunk science fiction. Issues of individual identity and social responsibility are explored on a dystopian future Earth, primarily through the cyborg, Yod. Like much of cyberpunk writing, the future portrayed in this book is not so far away that we can easily distance ourselves from the questions P. forces her readers to ask.

The reactions to P.'s novels have always ranged across the critical spectrum. Admirers feel that she achieves the difficult balance between political motivation and aesthetic accomplishment. Critics have complained that her politics often lead to one-dimensional characterization. P.'s poetry, on the other hand, has met with a less-varied, and generally positive, response.

She credits her mother with making her a poet: "She taught me to observe sharply and to remember what I observed. She also taught me intense curiosity about other people." As with her prose, P.'s verse brings together political and personal issues that can include her deeply held feminism, concern over the impact of nuclear power, and an environmentalist's appreciation of nature. *Circles on the Water* (1982) is a collection of the best of P.'s early poems, reprinted along with seven new poems. Other recent volumes of poetry include *Stone, Paper, Knife* (1983), *My Mother's Body* (1985), *Available Light* (1988), and *Mars and Her Children* (1992).

In addition to these writings, P. has coauthored a play, *The Last White Class* (1980) with Ira Wood, whom she married in 1982. The play explores race relations in a changing Boston neighborhood. P. has also published a collection of essays on poetry, *Parti-Colored Blocks for a Quilt* (1982), and she has edited a poetry anthology entitled *Early Ripening: American Women's Poetry Now* (1988).

P. and Wood live on a small, almost self-sufficient farm on Cape Cod. She has proven herself both a prolific and a timely author whose work continues to be informed by her continually developing political consciousness.

OTHER WORKS: The Earth Shines Secretly: A Book of Days (1990). *Body of Glass* (1992).

BIBLIOGRAPHY: Future Females: A Critical Anthology, Marleen Barr, ed. (articles on P. by Susan Kress and Joanna Russ, 1981). *Women and Utopia*, M. Barr and N. Smith, eds. (1983). Hansen, E. T., "The Double Narrative Structure of *Small Changes*," in *Contemporary American Women Writers: Narrative Strategies*, C. S. Rainwater, ed. (1985). Reference works: *CAAS* 1 (1984). *CANR* 13 (1984). *CLC* 62 (1991). *FC* (1990).

Other references: *NYTBR* (5 Feb. 1984; 12 May 1985; 10 May 1987; 10 July 1988; 11 June 1989; 22 Dec. 1991). *WRB* 1 (Aug. 1984), 4 (July 1987), 5 (July 1988).

JAMES O'LOUGHLIN

Dawn Powell

B. 28 Nov. 1897, Mount Gilead, Ohio; d. 16 Nov. 1965, New York City
D. of Hattie B. (Sherman) and Roy K. Powell; m. Joseph Roebuck Gousha, 1920;
c.: Joseph Roebuck, Jr., b. 1921

P. grew up in Ohio, received her B.A. from Lake Erie College in 1918, and then moved to New York City. She made her home in Greenwich Village, did various kinds of commercial writing to earn a living, and published some stories, a few plays, and the fifteen novels that were her major work.

Most of P.'s early fiction is set in Ohio. Her later novels, which are her best, are witty satires set in a fast-paced, boozy New York world inhabited by artists, writers, and businessmen, by people out "to Live," and, above all, by provincial Midwesterners dealing with Manhattan.

Although in her lifetime P. had a following that included Ernest Hemingway, John Dos Passos, and Edmund Wilson, her novels won neither huge popularity nor much serious critical attention. After her death, they fell into obscurity. Interest in P. was revived in 1987, when Gore Vidal wrote an essay about her in the *New York Review of Books*. Vidal, who had known P., sketched in her life: her mother's early death; her marriage and the birth of her brain-damaged only son; her playwriting ambitions and failure; her social life, which figures in Edmund Wilson's *The Thirties*. But mainly he focused on the fiction of this forgotten writer whom he called "our best comic novelist," discussing both her Ohio novels and the New York works in which, he felt, "she came into her own." Five of P.'s New York novels were reissued within a few years after Vidal's essay: *Angels on Toast* (1940; revised as *A Man's Affair*, 1956; 1989), *The Locusts Have No King* (1948; 1990), *The Wicked Pavilion* (1954; 1989), *The Golden Spur* (1962; 1989), and *A Time to Be Born* (1942; 1991).

Edmund Wilson, writing in *The New Yorker* in 1962, remarked that women readers might "find no comfort in identifying" with P.'s female characters who, he said, "are likely to be as sordid as the men." Powell herself suggested that her critical obscurity might be the result of her satire of the middle class. "It is considered jolly and good-humored to point out the oddities of the poor or of the rich. . . . I go outside the rules with my stuff because I can't help believing that the middle class is funny, too."

As Vidal comments, neither reviewers nor readers knew quite how to take P.'s work. She was "that unthinkable monster, a witty woman who felt no obligation to make a single, much less a final down payment on Love or the Family." Americans have "never been able to deal with wit," Vidal notes, citing a reviewer who complained that P. viewed "the antics of humanity with too surgical a calm" and lacked a "sense of outrage."

Wit is certainly at the heart of P.'s novels, which are filled with astute observations rather than either outrage or sentimental comfort. In writing about lovers and spouses, insiders, outsiders, and eccentrics, Midwesterners at home or in the big city, P. does not make life or people out to be any better than they are. Her great talent was for evoking so precisely what—in all their comicality and sadness—they are.

Caught up in duplicity and self-deception, messy love affairs or miserable marriages, P.'s characters do not easily escape their predicaments—and not because she has set them up. P. is too fine a satirist for that. As she once said, "My characters are not slaves to an author's propaganda. I give them their heads. They furnish their own nooses."

Permeated as they are with their setting, P.'s New York novels chronicle the city over decades. *The Locusts Have No King* conveys a postwar culture run amok. In her last novel, *The Golden Spur* (1962), P. playfully links past and present, Greenwich Village of the late 1920s and the 1950s, through the story of a young man from Ohio who believes he was illegitimately conceived in Manhattan and arrives there in 1956, seeking his true father.

For all their urbane smartness, Powell's novels are extraordinarily intelligent; and for all their hilarity, as Wilson remarked, they are "more than merely funny." Filled with "psychological insights that are at once sympathetic and cynical," they give us stories that are poignantly true.

OTHER WORKS: *Whither* (1925). *She Walks in Beauty* (1928). *The Bride's House* (1929). *Dance Night* (1930). *The Tenth Moon* (1932). *Big Night* (play, 1933). *Jig Saw, a Comedy* (play, 1934). *The Story of a Country Boy* (1934). *Turn, Magic Wheel* (1936). *The Happy Island* (1938). *Lady Across* (play, 1941). *My Home Is Far Away* (1944). *Sunday, Monday, and Always* (short stories, 1952). *A Cage for Lovers* (1957).

BIBLIOGRAPHY: Pett, Judith Faye, "Dawn Powell: Her Life and Her Fiction," unpublished Ph.D. diss., University of Iowa, 1981; *DAI* 42:7 (1982).

Van Gelder, Robert, interview, *Writers and Writing* (1946). Vidal, Gore, "Dawn Powell: The American Writer," in *At Home: Gore Vidal, Essays 1982–1988* (1988). Warfel, Harry R., *American Novelists of Today* (1951). Reference works: *CA 5–8* (1969). *FC* (1990).

Other references: *Belles Lettres* (Fall 1990). *LJ* (1 May 1990; 15 April 1991). *LATBR* (25 March 1990). *The New Yorker* (17 Nov. 1962, article by Edmund Wilson). *NYT* (16 Nov. 1965, obituary). *NYTBR* (1 April 1990). *Vanity Fair* (Feb. 1990). *Village Voice Lit. Supp.* (April 1990, June 1990). *Wash. Post Book World* (18 March 1990). *WRB* (July 1990).

GAIL POOL

Nancy Gardner Prince

B. 15 September 1799, Newburyport, Massachusetts; d. after 1856
D. of Thomas Gardner and his wife (d. of Tobias Warton); m. Nero Prince, 1824

P. was born of free parents of African and American Indian descent. Called "a colored woman of prominence in Boston" by a contemporary, she was a member of the Anti-Slavery Society in Boston, a missionary, a reformer and, during her marriage that took her to Russia for years, a businesswoman and a world traveler.

Narrative of the Life and Travels of Mrs. Prince, P.'s only published work, is the first African American woman's narrative to combine the traditions of the spiritual autobiography, the slave narrative, and the travel narrative. P. used all three forms to validate her identity as a free black woman and also to extend the conventions of these forms. Her work was first published in 1850 (a portion of it appeared in 1841) and had two more editions. Written primarily "to obtain the means to supply my necessities," as P. noted in her 1856 preface, the narrative tells of a childhood full of hardship and of overwhelming responsibilities. From the age of thirteen, P., along with her brother George, was the main support of her family. After a series of exploitive domestic service jobs and years of "anxiety and toil," she went in 1822 "to learn a trade" in Boston, but she met and married Nero Prince, a widower of standing in the New England black community and a sailor who had served the Russian czar as a footman for twelve years. They left for St. Petersburg in 1824.

Although the first part of P.'s narrative reads more as a spiritual autobiography, framed in the preface with an invocation to "divine aid," P.'s account of her life in Russia becomes a travel narrative, including vivid observations on the customs and events of czarist Russia and sketches of members of the court of Emperor Alexander and Empress Elizabeth. While in Russia, P. was able to educate herself and to learn several languages and she was successful in starting a business, making fashionable children's clothes. She had to return to Boston in 1833 because of ill health.

In the next phase of her life P. became active in the abolitionist movement, later meeting the Quaker abolitionist Lucretia Mott in Philadelphia. After an unsuccessful attempt due to lack of funds to start a home for orphans in Boston, P., now a widow, was persuaded by the pastor of the Free Will Baptist Church to go to Jamaica as a missionary to teach the newly freed native population. Her account of her missionary life from 1840 to 1843 combines a description of the chaos of postslavery days in Jamaica with a short travelogue on the geography and history of the island. The story of her hazardous final journey home is in the tradition of the slave narrative as she relates her own experiences with racism to the evils of slavery in America. During this one-year journey from Kingston to Boston, the unscrupulous captain detoured his ship to Key West and, after a storm disabled the ship, abandoned P. in New Orleans without returning her passage money. Afraid to leave the ship in the Southern ports for fear that she might be seized as a slave, she was confronted constantly with images of her own oppressed people. Finally boarding another ship, she arrived in New York, penniless. She stayed there for months trying to pay her debts and recover her belongings before she could return to Boston.

Although P. does not tell much more about her life after her return, an eyewitness account confirms that she remained an activist and in 1847 helped to save a fellow African American from a slaveholder. Like other women in the slave narrative tradition, she tells about her trials obliquely, stating that she shared "in common the disadvantages and stigma that is heaped upon us, in this our professed Christian land." Her closing passages return to the traditional spiritual autobiography, citing her own suffering and the fearful "world's pilgrimage" as purification for the life to come.

BIBLIOGRAPHY: Braxton, Joanne M., *Black Women Writing Autobiography* (1989). Carby, Hazel V., *Reconstructing Womanhood* (1987). Barthelemy, Anthony, Introduction, *Collected Black Women's Narratives* (Schomburg Library Series, 1988). Shockley, Ann, *Afro-American Women Writers* (1988). *We Are Your Sisters: Black Women in the Nineteenth Century*, Dorothy Sterling, ed. (1984). Reference works: *FC* (1990).

MARY GRIMLEY MASON

Christal Quintasket. *See Mourning Dove (Humishuma)*

Margaret Randall

B. 6 Dec. 1936, New York City
Wrote under: Margaret Randall de Mondragon (1962–68)
D. of Elinor (Davidson) and John Philip Randall; m. Sam Jacobs, 1954, div.
1957; m. Sergio Mondragon, 1962, div. 1968; m. Floyce Alexander, 1984,
div. 1987; c.: Gregory Randall, b. 1960; Sarah Dyhana Mondragon, b. 1963;
Ximena Mondragon, b. 1964; Ana Laurette Cohen, b. 1969

Poet, essayist, oral historian, translator, photographer, and political activist, R. resists easy classification. Out of a politically committed life that has spanned several continents and extended over three decades, she has produced more than fifty works, works that embody her belief that "passion and reason, socialism and feminism, art and responsibility" all need one another. R.'s life and work are an eloquent testimony to this commitment.

R. grew up in Albuquerque, New Mexico, where she briefly attended the University of New Mexico, married, and divorced. In 1957 she moved to New York City, where she became closely associated with the Black Mountain poets and Abstract Expressionist artists, published two collections of poetry, and gave birth to her first child. In 1961, with her ten-month-old son, R. returned to Albuquerque for a brief visit and then headed south to Mexico. This was the first stage in an open-ended twenty-three-year journey that would take her to Mexico, Cuba, Nicaragua, and, finally, back to Albuquerque. In 1962 R. and the Mexican poet Sergio Mondragon (whom she married that year) began editing *El Corno Emplumado/The Plumed Horn*, a bilingual literary magazine that sought to publish the most exciting new voices of North and Latin America. In 1967, on the basis of poor legal advice, R. took out Mexican citizenship and relinquished her United States passport to American consular authorities—a decision that would have grave consequences when she returned to the United States in 1984. Her involvement with *El Corno Emplumado* brought her into association with a generation of artists and intellectuals deeply committed to the struggle against social and political injustice. R. traveled to Cuba in 1967, her first visit to a socialist country and one that was fundamental to her growing political commitments.

In 1968, the Mexican student movement erupted and was violently repressed. During the same year, R. separated from Mondragon and began to live with a United States poet, Robert Cohen. She took an active role in the Mexican student movement and *El Corno Emplumado* supported the student demands. As a result R. was harassed by the government and forced to live underground. In 1969 R. and her four children managed to leave Mexico and move to Cuba, where she lived for the next ten years. In Cuba R. immediately became interested in what a socialist revolution could mean for women. For the next two years she traveled around the country talking with women from all walks of life about their experiences under the Cuban variety of socialism. The result of this research, *Cuban Women Now* (1974), signaled yet another stage in R.'s multifaceted career, one marked by an increasing commitment to people's voices, testimony, and oral history. In 1979, shortly after the victory of the Sandinista revolution, the Nicaraguan minister of culture, Ernesto Cardenal, invited R. to visit the country and do field work on the experiences of Nicaraguan women. As a result R. produced *Sandino's*

Daughters (1981), her first work in which she created both the written and the photographic images. In 1980 R. and her daughter Ana moved to Nicaragua, where they were later joined by another daughter, Ximena. R. returned to the United States in 1984. After her marriage to Floyce Alexander, he petitioned the Immigration and Naturalization Service (INS) for her permanent resident status. In October 1985, R. was informed that the INS, invoking the 1952 McCarran-Walter Act, had denied her application because of the political nature of her writings; she was given thirty days to leave the country. During the next four years, with the assistance of the Center for Constitutional Rights and many supporters throughout the country, R. fought the deportation order. She also continued to write, publishing six books and completing one novel between the date of the deportation order and the end of the case. She also launched a career as a teacher: at the University of New Mexico, Trinity College, Oberlin College, Macalester College, and the University of Delaware. In the summer of 1989 the Board of Immigration Appeals finally ruled that R. had never lost her American citizenship. A resident since of Albuquerque, New Mexico—the setting that continues to nourish her life and imagination—R. lives with her companion, Barbara Byers, and continues to teach and write.

OTHER WORKS: Giant of Tears (1959). *Ecstasy Is a Number* (1961). *Poems of the Glass* (1964). *Small Sounds from the Bass Fiddle* (1964). *October* (1965). *Twenty-five Stages of My Spine* (1967). *Water I Slip into at Night* (1967). *So Many Rooms Has a House but One Roof* (1967). *Getting Rid of Blue Plastic* (1968). *Los hippies: analisis de una crisis* (1968). *Let's Go!* (1971; translation 1984). *Part of the Solution* (1972). *This Great People Has Said "Enough!" and Has Begun to Move* (translator, 1972). *Day's Coming* (1973). *La Situatión de la Mujer* (1974). *With Our Hands* (1974). *Spirit of the People: Vietnamese Women Two Years from the Geneva Accords* (1975). *All My Used Parts, Shackles, Fuel, Tenderness, and Stars* (1976). *Carlotta: Poems and Prose from Havana* (1978). *Doris Tijerino: Inside the Nicaraguan Revolution* (1978). *These Living Songs/Estos cantos habitades* (translator, 1978). *El pueblo no solo es testigo: la historia de Dominga* (1979). *Sueños y realidades de un Guajiricantor* (1979). *No se puede hacer la revolución sin nosotras* (1980). *Todas estamos despiertas: testimonios de la mujer nicaraguense de hoy* (1980). *Breaking the Silences: Poems by Twenty-five Cuban Women Poets* (translator, 1982). *A Poetry of Resistance* (1983). *Testimonios* (1983). *Christians in the Nicaraguan Revolution* (1983; translation, 1985). *Carlos, the Dawn Is No Longer beyond Our Reach* (1984). *Risking a Somersault in the Air: Conversations with Nicaraguan Writers* (1984). *Women Brave in the Face of Danger* (photographs, 1985). *Nicaragua Libre!* (photographs, 1985). *Albuquerque: Coming Back to the USA* (1986).

The Coming Home Poems (1986). *This Is about Incest* (1987). *Memory Says Yes* (1988). *The Shape of Red: Insider/Outsider Reflections* (1988). *Photographs by Margaret Randall: Image and Content in Differing Cultural Contexts* (1988). *Coming Home: Peace without Complacency* (1990). *Walking to the Edge: Essays of Resistance* (1991). *Dancing with the Doe: New and Selected Poems, 1986–1991* (1992). *Gathering Rage: The Failure of Twentieth Century Revolutions to Develop a Feminist Agenda* (1992). *Sandino's Daughters Revisited* (forthcoming, 1994).

BIBLIOGRAPHY: Crawford, John, and Patricia Smith, *This Is about Vision: Interviews with Southwestern Writers* (1990). Miller, James, "The Writer and Artistic Freedom: Interview," in *Reimaging America: The Arts of Social Change,* Mark O'Brien and Craig Little, eds. (1990). Nathan, Debbie, "Adjustment of Status: The Trial of Margaret Randall," in *Women and Other Aliens: Essays from the U.S. Mexican Border* (1991). Reference works: *CA* 41–44 (1979).

Other references: *Conceptions Southwest* 9:1 (Spring 1986). [Santa Cruz] *Express* (24 Oct. 1985). [Albuquerque] *Impact Mag.* (14 Jan. 1986). *Minnesota Rev.* 6:2 (1966). *Ms.* (interview, June 1986). [Berkeley] *Poetry Flash* (Dec. 1985). *WRB* (Jan. 1993).

JAMES A. MILLER

Kit Reed

B. Lillian Hyde Craig, 7 June 1932, San Diego, California
Writes under: Kit Craig, Shelley Hyde
D. of Lillian (Hyde) and John Rich Craig; m. Joseph Reed, 1955; c.: Joseph
  McKean Reed, John Craig Reed, Katherine Hyde Reed

Although R. has published in several fields, she is best known for her novels of self-discovery and for her science fiction. From her earliest novel, *Mother Isn't Dead, She's Only Sleeping* (1961), set in St. Petersburg, Florida, and satirically confronting the pieties around aging, R. has defied convention. The source of her defiance is moral indignation, even outrage; her most typical response is edgy humor and satire.

Disillusionment is a common theme in R.'s portrayal of character. Often outsiders seeking acceptance, her characters invariably come to recognize their own romanticism as well as the shallowness of the conventions that they have been pursuing. They realize as well the need to create their own world to make up for the failures of what exists. R.'s characters are sometimes overburdened with meaning, cast into allegorical structures that reflect her concern with the moral subtext of her fictions.

R.'s ventures into novels of self-discovery have been most warmly received by critics. *The Better Part* (1967) and *Tiger Rag* (1973) are stories of adolescent girls coming into maturity under very difficult circumstances, acutely aware of their status as outsiders. *Tiger Rag*, like the earlier *Cry of the Daughter* (1971), focuses on struggles between children and a mother who is proud, stubborn, and controlling, although perhaps not intentionally so.

In *The Ballad of T. Rantula* (1979), one of R.'s most critically successful coming-of-age novels, her speaker, the adolescent Futch, uses a relaxed colloquial voice reminiscent of Holden Caulfield. Futch's voice is both difficult and believable as he narrates a year of his life during which his parents split up and his two best friends go through changes which he can neither understand nor control. Those with whom he has been most close are moving away from him and no adult will level with him; they can neither handle the craziness nor tell him the truth. The contrast between the adults and the children is somewhat overdrawn; the adults are oblivious and foolish, the children remarkably sensitive and conscious of what is happening around them. *T. Rantula* was named to the American Library Association list of Best Books for Young Adults for 1979.

Self-discovery is also the theme of one of R.'s best-known adult novels, *Catholic Girls* (1987), the story of four graduates of a Catholic women's college who reconverge at a bizarre funeral. Like an earlier work, *Captain Grownup* (1976), the book focuses on middle-aged characters whose internal growth seems incomplete; R. allows each to come to a comfortable catharsis by the end. The success of the novel rests in the ambiguous Kath, the one of the four who has consciously abandoned Catholicism. She is spiritually hungry, filled with nagging, inescapable remnants of her Catholic past; in the end, she is inspired toward her own freedom and vision although it remains unclear whether this is a sign of something deep and powerful or is merely delusionary.

Although R.'s style has remained essentially consistent through her many books, she has experimented widely with formulas, especially in science fiction. In *Magic Time* (1980), the story of four characters attempting to escape a violent and fascist Disneyworldlike vacation park, she creates a prefabricated, allegorical world of concentrated authoritarianism. The novel is written in four voices, following the thoughts of the characters as they seek a way out of "Happy Habitat." Here, as elsewhere, R.'s attraction toward allegory controls the characters and their setting.

Critics consistently note the intensity of R.'s fictions. John Klute has described R.'s style as "prepubescent in its clean, clear tone, and . . . ominously pregnant with meaning." Frank Kermode praised an early science fiction novel, *Armed Camps* (1969), for offering a "new imaginative intensity and a power of communicating insights as dark as they are compassionate." Like others of R.'s science fiction tales, *Armed Camps* imagines a near future, full of horror, made to seem chillingly possible. R. has a particular ability, one reviewer noted, to "metamorphose the ordinary into the macabre."

In two novels published in 1993, R. appears to have embarked in a different direction. *Gone* and *Twice Burned*, both written under Kit Craig, are in a genre new to her work, the "psychological thriller." The jacket of *Gone* makes no mention of R.'s previous work, noting only that this is Craig's "first psychological thriller."

A graduate of the College of Notre Dame of Maryland (B.A., 1954) and a former journalist, R. is a longtime resident of Middletown, Connecticut, where she regularly teaches creative writing at Wesleyan University. She has held Guggenheim Foundation grants (1964, 1968) and in 1965 became the first American recipient of a five-year literary grant from the Abraham Woursell Foundation. In addition to novels, short story collections, and *Fat* (1974), an anthology of personal writings about obesity edited with an introduction by R., she has provided direct, sensible advice to writers in handbooks, the central theme of which is characterized by the title of a 1989 volume, *Revision*.

OTHER WORKS: *At War as Children* (1964). *Lighthouse: A Story* (1966). *When We Dream* (1966). *Mister da V., and Other Stories* (1967). *Love Story* (1971). *The Killer Mice* (1976). *Other Stories and . . . the Attack of the Giant Baby* (1981). *The Savage Stain* (as Shelley Hyde, 1982). *Story First: the Writer as Insider* (1982), republished as *Mastering Fiction Writing* (1991). *George Orwell's 1984* (1984). *Fort Privilege* (1985). *The Revenge of the Senior Citizens* (1986). *Thief of Lives: Stories* (1992).

BIBLIOGRAPHY: Reference works: *CANR* 16 (1986), 36 (1992). *Tw Cent Sci Fi Wr* (1986). *Sci Fi Sourcebook* (1984). *New Encyc of Sci Fi* (1988). *WW Wr*,

Eds, Poets (1989). Other references: *Mag of Fantasy and Sci Fi* (Dec. 1980, article by John Klute). *Newsweek* (19 April 1976). *New Leader* (4 June 1979). *Analog Science Fiction/Science Fact* (29 March 1982). *America* (26 Dec. 1987). *PW* (24 July 1987). *NYTBR* (17 June 1979, 1 Nov. 1987, 12 July 1992).

ROBERT BONAZOLI

Anne Rampling. *See Anne Rice*

Anne Rice

B. Howard Allen O'Brien, 4 Oct. 1941, New Orleans, Louisiana
Writes under: Anne Rice, Anne Rampling, A. N. Roquelaure
D. of Katherine and Howard O'Brien; m. Stan Rice, 1961; c.: Michelle (deceased), Christopher

New Orleans and the Catholic church have been central to R.'s life. She was born and brought up in the Irish Channel, a working-class, ethnic neighborhood in the city. Her father, after whom she was named (she changed her name to Anne when she began school), was a post-office worker, and her mother maintained a strictly Catholic and very Southern household. Born not in but on the fringe of the wealthy Garden District, R. spent her childhood wandering the distinct neighborhoods of New Orleans, and many of her novels capture the sense of the old creole city.

Shortly after her mother's death R. left the Catholic church and New Orleans. She attended Texas Women's University (where she met her husband) and then San Francisco State College. She received her B.A. in 1964 and her M.A. in 1971 and did further graduate work at the University of California, Berkeley.

After the death of her daughter from leukemia, R. took up writing at her husband's suggestion, and her first novel, *Interview with the Vampire* (1976) became an instant publishing success. All of her books have continued to sell at a phenomenal rate. While she did not immediately return to the Vampire Chronicles after the success of the first, R. later added three more to the series: *The Vampire Lestat* (1985), *Queen of the Damned* (1988), and *The Tale of the Body Thief* (1992). The vampire series is responsible for much of R.'s fame as a cult writer; there are elements in the novels, however, that touch on the deeper issues of good and evil, salvation and damnation. Louis, the vampire of her first novel, is a tormented creature who longs for companionship. He finds it briefly in a child vampire, Claudia, whom he creates and in a vampire community that gives him the illusion that he is almost human. *Interview with the Vampire* brings out the best in R.'s writing. It captures her impeccable sense of place and her sense of how people become haunted and lost, and integrates these elements with the implacable sense of loneliness that one feels after great loss. Claudia's death in the novel is almost an elegy for her own daughter.

For almost ten years after her first success, Rice turned away from the Vampire Chronicles and wrote historical fiction, popular novels, and erotica. *Feast of All Saints* (1980) and *Cry to Heaven* (1982) are carefully researched historical novels that examine respectively the lives of free people of color in New Orleans in the decades before the Civil War and of castrati in eighteenth-century Italy. Both deal with people on the outside and R.'s empathy for the outcast is palpable. Culturally, the free blacks of *Feast of All Saints* are as restricted in their movements as R.'s vampires who can only come out at night, and the castrati of *Cry to Heaven* long for normal human lives as much as Louis the vampire does.

In *The Vampire Lestat*, R. brings back Louis's teacher/father, Lestat, the powerful vampire figure of the first novel. Unlike Louis, Lestat has no moral ambivalence about his condition, and in fact seems to revel in the power it gives him. Powerful physically, intellectually, and emotionally, he challenges not only the boundaries of the human world, but of the vampire world as well.

The third novel of the series, *Queen of the Damned*, seems weak, unfocused, and sometimes even silly by comparison with the first two. The same problem affects the fantastical novel. *The Mummy; or, Ramses the Damned* (1989), which makes a joke out of the issues R. once handled seriously.

With *The Witching Hour* (1990), R. returns to New Orleans both literally and metaphorically. After almost three decades in San Francisco, she and her family moved back to New Orleans to settle in the Garden District house that became the center of the novel. The novel chronicles a family of witches who, for thirteen generations, have called forth a spirit named Lasher who wants desperately to attain humanity. Once again, R. grapples with the nature of humanity, the tension between good and evil, and the mystery of life.

In *The Tale of the Body Thief* R. returns to the Vampire Chronicles and Lestat, her most enduring and possibly most perceptive character, undertakes an amazing journey into contemporary philosophy and the meaning of existence. In this book, R.'s writing exhibits the power of her two earliest chronicles.

There is no doubt that R. is more than a popular novelist. Both her historical fiction and her vampire and witch novels focus on issues central to modern culture, and she deftly integrates larger philosophical and theological issues into her fiction. Even her potboilers and erotic fiction squarely confront the issues of fate and free will in ways that less serious novels simply ignore.

OTHER WORKS: As A. N. Roquelaure: *The Claiming of Sleeping Beauty* (1983). *Beauty's Punishment* (1984). *Beauty's Release* (1985). As Anne Rice: *Exit to Eden* (1986). *Belinda* (1986). *Lasher* (1993).

BIBLIOGRAPHY: Reference works: *CA* 65–68 (1977). *CANR* 12 (1984). *CLC* 41 (1987).

Other references: *New Orleans Times-Picayune* (28 Oct. 1990). *NYTBR* (4 Nov. 1990). *NYT Mag.* (14 Oct. 1990).

MARY A. MCCAY

Adrienne Cecile Rich

See AWW 3, 462–64

In the 1980s, R. became a poet who at times received standing ovations *before* she read—from audiences sometimes numbering in thousands, not hundreds. By the early 1990s, although some still deplored her work as "polemical," she was acclaimed as both critic and poet, and forty years after the publication of her first book of poems (*A Change of World*, 1951), R. was beginning to be assigned her permanent niche in American literature. R. is "widely recognized as the preeminent American poet-critic of the post–World War II years," wrote Elaine Showalter. R. "will be remembered in literary history as one of the first American women to claim a public voice in lyric," wrote **Helen Vendler.** Further, among many living women, R. came to be held in affectionate esteem as more than poet and critic: "This complex and controversial writer, who began as poet-ingenue, polite copyist of Yeats and Auden, wife and mother," wrote Carol Muske, "has progressed in life (and in her poems, which remain intimately tied to her life's truth) from young widow and disenchanted formalist, to spiritual and rhetorical convalescent, to feminist leader, lesbian separatist and *doyenne* of a newly-defined female literature—becoming finally a Great Outlaw Mother."

Certainly the honors flowed. The National Gay and Lesbian Task Force gave R. the Fund for Human Dignity Award in 1981. She was a nominee for the 1982 *Los Angeles Times* Book Prize for *A Wild Patience Has Taken Me This Far* (1981) and made an Honorary Fellow of the Modern Language Association in 1985. In 1986 R. won the Ruth Lilly Poetry Prize of the Modern Poetry Association and American Council for the Arts, in 1987 the Brandeis University Creative Arts Medal, in 1989 the Elmer Holmes Bobst Award, and in 1992 the Lenore Marshall/Nation Prize for poetry. She received honorary doctor of letters degrees from Brandeis University (1987), City College of New York (1990), and Howard University (1990). Meanwhile, from 1980 to 1984 she coedited *Sinister Wisdom* with long-time companion **Michelle Cliff** and served after 1989 as a member of an editorial collective for *Bridges, a Journal for Jewish Feminists and*

Our Friends. She taught, becoming White Professor at Large at Cornell University (1981–85), Clark Lecturer and distinguished visiting professor at Scripps College (1983), visiting professor at San Jose State University (1985–86), Burgess Lecturer at Pacific Oaks College (1986), and since 1986 Professor of English and Feminist Studies at Stanford University.

During the 1980s, R. published a new volume of selected prose and five books of poetry, including *The Fact of a Doorframe: Poems Selected and New, 1950–1984* (1984). *An Atlas of the Difficult World: Poems, 1988–1991* appeared in 1991. As before, a dominant theme in her works is the search for integrity and meaning in her own identity. Echoing an early poem in which she had described herself as "split at the root / neither Gentile nor Jew, / Yankee nor Rebel" ("Reading of History," 1960) and others such as "The Spirit of Place" (in *A Wild Patience Has Taken Me This Far*), she asks in "Sources": *"From where does your strength come, you Southern Jew? / split at the root. . . . With whom do you believe your lot is cast? . . . /* I think somehow, somewhere / every poem of mine must repeat those questions." In "Sources," a long, moving autobiographical poem published first as a chapbook (1983, reprinted in *Your Native Land, Your Life,* 1986), R. places her own past under "a powerful, womanly lens," addressing several of the twenty-three parts of the poem to her father or her husband, both Jews at last seen to be similar. A woman born of a gentile mother and thus not a Jew under Jewish law, yet fully aware Nazi logic would have made her "a *Mischling, first-degree*—nonexempt from the Final Solution," R. reflects on her "own ambivalence as a Jew; the daily, mundane anti-Semitisms of [her] entire life." Repeating her key phrase in "Split at the Root: An Essay on Jewish Identity," R. increasingly sees herself as fragmented and conflicted: "Sometimes I feel I have seen too long from too many disconnected angles: white, Jewish, anti-Semite, racist, antiracist, once-married, lesbian, middle-class, feminist, exmatriate southerner, split at the root— that I will never bring them whole" (1982, reprinted in *Blood, Bread, and Poetry: Selected Prose, 1979–1985,* 1986).

In bringing these multiple selves together, R. has in the last decade developed an extraordinary empathy with others, particularly with the outsiders of the world. She uses her increasingly damaged body (see "The Skier") as a means to understanding: "I'm already living the rest of my life / not under conditions of my choosing / wired into pain . . . the body pain and the pain on the streets / are not the same but you can learn / from the edges that blur" ("Contradictions: Tracking Poems," *Your Native Land*). A lesbian who in 1976 came out in print with *Twenty-One Love Poems*, R. has continued to demonstrate in her poetry that "Two women sleeping / together have more than their sleep to defend" ("Images," *A Wild Patience*). In important prose essays—such as "Compulsory Heterosexuality and Lesbian Existence" (1979) and "Invisibility in Academe" (1984)—she warns that "invisibility is not just a matter of being told to keep your private life private; it's the attempt to fragment you, to prevent you from integrating love and work and feelings and ideas, with the empowerment that that can bring." A radical feminist, R. has continued to write about a range of women, identifying passionately with victims and merging with them: "She is carrying my madness. . . . She walks along I.S. 93 howling / in her bare feet / She is number 6375411 / in a cellblock in Arkansas / She has fallen asleep at least in the battered / women's safe-house and I dread / her dreams that I also dream." Often she extends her empathy to the world, as in the poem "In the Wake of Home": "What if I tell you your home / is this planet of warworn children / women and children standing in line or milling / endlessly calling each other's names" *(Your Native Land)*.

In a major essay, "Notes toward a Politics of Location" (1984), R. discusses how she came to experience "whiteness as a point of location for which I needed to take responsibility." Born female in a segregated hospital, she was likewise born into whiteness, "though the implications of white identity were mystified by the presumption that white people are the center of the universe." Extending her insight to criticism, R. challenges those feminists who have formulated a largely "white-centered theory." Moreover, she newly urges a greater understanding of "differences among women, men, places, times, cultures, conditions, classes, movements."

Increasingly, R. has broadened her sense of what it means to be a poet. Drawing the mantle of public poet more closely about herself in "North American Time" (1983), she acknowledges and accepts responsibility: "One line typed twenty years ago / can be blazed on a wall in spraypaint. . . . We move but our words stand / become responsible / all you can do is choose them / or choose / to remain silent." In *Time's Power* (1989), in the short poem "Dreamwood," R. fashions a "dreammap" for the "last age of her life" by which to "recognize that poetry / isn't revolution but a way of knowing / why it must come."

OTHER WORKS: *Collected Early Poems* (1993). *What Is Found There: Notebooks on Poetry and Politics* (1993).

BIBLIOGRAPHY: *Engendering the Word*, Temma Berg, ed. (1989). *Reading Adrienne Rich: Reviews and Revisions, 1951–81*, Jane Roberta Cooper, ed. (1984). Keyes, Claire, *The Aesthetics of Power: The Poetry of Adrienne Rich* (1986). *Points of Departure: International Writers on Writing and Politics*, David Montenegro, ed. (1991). *World, Self, Poems: Essays on Contemporary Poetry from the "Jubilation of Poets,"* Leonard M. Trawick, ed. (1990). Werner, Craig, *Adrienne Rich: The Poet and Her Critics* (1988). See MLA on-line bibliography. Reference works: *Benet's* (1991). *CANR* 20 (1987). *CLC* 18 (1981), 36 (1986). *Contemp. Poets* (1991). *DLB* 5 (1980), 67 (1988). *FC* (1990). *Handbook of Amer. Women's History* (1990). *Maj Twent Cent Wr* (1991). *Modern Amer. Women Writers* (1991). *WW Wrs, Eds, Poets* (1989).

JEAN TOBIN

Alfrida Rivers. *See Marion Zimmer Bradley*

Carolyn M. Rodgers

B. 14 Dec. 1942, Chicago, Illinois
D. of Bazella (Colding) and Clarence Rodgers

R. grew up on Chicago's South Side, a member of a vibrant urban black community that has served as one source for her poetry. She spent much of her younger years as an active member of an AME (African Methodist

Episcopal) church congregation. Those experiences, as well as the continuing influence of her mother's religious faith, would make themselves into the materials of poetry.

As a child, R. was an avid reader. In addition, her father, an aspiring singer, encouraged her musical talents. In her second year at Hyde Park High School, R. converted to Roman Catholicism. During her high school and college years, she began writing, primarily for herself. While attending Roosevelt University, R. attended a poetry reading by and a reception for the Pulitzer Prize–winning poet **Gwendolyn Brooks.** This meeting stimulated R.'s reading of black writers. She dropped out of Roosevelt University in 1963 and began to work with high school dropouts. Returning to school several years later, she received a B.A. from Chicago State University in 1981 and an M.A. from the University of Chicago in 1983.

Although R. had been writing throughout her high school and college years, it was while she was working in the dropout program that she decided she was a writer. Quitting her job in 1968, with some financial and moral encouragement from her first mentor, Gwendolyn Brooks, she began her career as a writer. A subsequent encounter with Hoyt W. Fuller, editor of *Negro Digest* (later *Black World*) provided a direct stimulus to R.'s literary career. Soon after meeting him, she submitted several pieces to *Negro Digest.* Her poems and a short story were published and R. became a regular contributor to the magazine. Shortly afterwards, Fuller and several other artists founded the Organization of Black American Culture (OBAC [oh-bah-see]), including a musicians' workshop, a theater workshop, an artists' workshop, and a writers' workshop. It was the OBAC Writers' Workshop that would thrive and R., along with Johari Amini (then Jewel Latimore), Haki Madhubuti (then Don L. Lee), Walter Bradford, Mike Cook, Rhonda Davis, and others provided the nucleus of the leadership of what became a center for the New Black Poetry movement. The same group met as the Gwendolyn Brooks Writers Workshop at Brooks's home.

R.'s first books of poems, *Paper Soul* (1968), selected with Brooks's assistance and featuring an introduction by Fuller, was self-published. The book was later distributed by the newly established Third World Press, publishers in 1969 of *Songs of a Blackbird.* R. also published single poems in broadside form with the young Broadside Press. Described early on by a young actor fan as a "new Langston Hughes," R. translated black vernacular idioms into poetic language and won immediate response from her community and from college audiences. In the introduction to her first book, Fuller wrote of R.'s language as "honed with bitterness and tipped with grace, [one that] swaggers along the brutal street and prances into the parlors: it does not know its bounds."

R.'s poetry has been widely anthologized and since the later 1960s she has been in demand as a reader of her own work. OBAC helped pioneer the poetry reading as cultural event, popularizing a style of presentation called "rise and fly" in which each poet briefly presented that material that she/he felt would elicit the greatest crowd response. OBAC writers attempted to institutionalize poetry readings that functioned in the community in the same ways as presentations of black music. The New Black Poets were also frequently characterized as Black Revolutionary Poets, an aspect of their writings that became something of a straitjacket for R. and several of her colleagues who had a wider range of subjects than the "revolution."

As a published writer of some acclaim, R. began to serve as writer in residence and creative writing teacher at many colleges and universities. She has also taught African American literature. Since 1989, R. has taught at Columbia College in Chicago, location of her first teaching position in 1969.

In 1975, R. published her first volume of poems with a "mainstream" publisher, *how i got ovah: New and Selected Poems*. Since 1980, all of R.'s books have been privately published under her own imprint, Eden Press. Her poems have been widely anthologized and her critical essays, short stories, and reviews have appeared in numerous journals.

In the introduction to *Black Bird*, David Llorens describes R. as a "storyteller of the highest order." She has also been praised for her sensitive lyrics and musical lines. Angela Jackson, a sister OBAC poet, celebrated R. as a "singer of sass and blues. . . . everytime you look at her u see somebody u know. . . . she a witness. humming her people / to the promis/d land."

OTHER WORKS: Two Love Raps (1969). *Now Ain't That Love* (1969). *For H. W. Fuller* (1970). *For Flip Wilson: Long Rap/Commonly Known as a Poetic Essay* (1971). *Poems for Malcolm* (1972). *The Heart as Ever Green: Poems* (1978). *Translation: Poems* (1980). *Love* (play, produced 1982). *Eden and Other Poems* (1983). *A Little Lower than Angels* (fiction, 1984). *Finite Forms* (1985). *Morning Glory: Poems* (1989).

BIBLIOGRAPHY: Jamison, Angelene, "Imagery in the Woman Poems: The Art of Carolyn Rodgers," and Bettye Parker-Smith, "Running Wild in Her Soul: The Poetry of Carolyn Rodgers," in *Black Women Writers (1950–1980)*, Mari Evans, ed. (1984). Russell, Sandi, *Render Me My Song: African-American Women Writers from Slavery to the Present* (1990). Reference works: *CAAS* 13 (1991). *CANR* 27 (1989). *Contemp. Poets* (1991). *DLB* 41 (1985).

Other references: *CLA J.* 25:1 (Sept. 1981).

FAHAMISHA PATRICIA BROWN

A. N. Roquelaure. *See Anne Rice*

Judith Rossner

B. 31 March 1935, New York City
D. of Dorothy (Shapiro) and Joseph George Perelman; m. Robert Rossner, 1954;
* div.; m. Mordeccai Persky, 1979, div.; c.: Jean, b. 1960; Daniel b. 1965*

R. grew up in New York City, where she attended public schools and City College (1952–55). After marrying Robert Rossner, she dropped out. Though she has written a few short stories, R. applies her skill to novels that continue to support her early assertion that her "abiding theme is separations." Drawing on the nineteenth century as a fount for ideas, R. uses contemporary urban settings to explore, with increasing sensitivity, the difficulty of establishing and sustaining boundaries: between self and other, past and present, fiction and reality. She especially examines the complicated emotions of women-in-relationship who strive to negotiate "the dangers in attaching oneself to others out of sheer terror of the alternatives." R.'s women characters, rejected or abandoned early in life, usually struggle emotionally. Acknowledging the influence of **Tillie Olsen** and especially **Grace Paley,** in whose voice she found her own, the "confirmed New Yorker" told Jean Ross that she reaps reward from the "chaos and energy" of the city.

After leaving college, R. took jobs that would not tax the mental energy she needed to write before work each morning. The result was an unpublished novella and two novels, *To the Precipice* (1966) and *Nine Months in the Life of an Old Maid* (1969). The Rossners moved to New Hampshire to begin a free school, but R. returned to New York in 1971, "unsuited" to rustic living (and marriage). *Any Minute I Can Split* (1972), set in a commune of tenuous relationships and family "ties," resulted.

Her fourth novel received popular and critical acclaim and was made into a successful film that brought her earlier work into recognition. R. wrote *Looking for Mr. Goodbar* (1977) after *Esquire* lawyers rejected her article about an incident upon which the novel is based— the murder of Roseann Quinn, a teacher killed by a man she had met in a bar and brought home. Success allowed R. to resign secretarial work for her "real work," writing. Her perception of herself as a writer had from earliest memory been encouraged by her "never critical" teacher-mother, who had desired but failed to write.

Attachments (1977) was criticized as merely sensational. In this unique analysis of the marriage of friends to Siamese-twin brothers, R. sensitively uses the physical to get at complex emotional "attachments" between friends as well as within marriage and family. Also hurt by reviews, *Emmeline* (1980) differs radically in style, setting, and period from the rest of R.'s work. Yet the terse, true narrative of a nineteenth-century Lowell factory girl still pivots on separation, recounting the distortion of a displaced need for love.

R. constructs her characters and reveals their complicated motivations through colloquial yet pointed dialogue. She often re-creates "recorded" conversation—trial proceedings, analyst sessions, or film dialogue. Further, each work evidences the "steady attention to character and psychological probability" that Walter Clemens found in *Emmeline.* This concern with authentic character development is especially apparent in *August* (1983) and *His Little Women* (1990). *August* emerged from R.'s reading of Freud and Anna O. and focuses on the *process* of attachment and separation; R. literally transcribes painful emotional growth and addresses gendering. *His Little Women* self-consciously examines the difficulty of the writer's own processes of emotional separation that spur creativity and blur boundaries between fiction and reality.

BIBLIOGRAPHY: Reference works: *CA* 17–20 (1976). *CANR* 18 (1986). *DLB* 6 (1980). *Maj Twent Cent Writers* (1991). *CLC* 6 (1976), 9 (1978), 29 (1984).

Other references: *Hudson Rev.* (Winter 1983–84). *NYTBR* (22 April 1990). *TLS* (4 Nov. 1983).

NANCY L. BOISVERT

Alma Routsong

B. 26 November 1924, Traverse City, Michigan
Wrote under: Isabel Miller
D. of Esther (Miller) and Carl Routsong; m. Bruce Brodie, 1947, div. 1962;
  c.: Natalie, Joyce, Charlotte, Louise

As Isabel Miller, R. wrote *A Place for Us* (1969, later published as *Patience and Sarah*), one of the first American novels to deal openly and optimistically with lesbianism. Raised in the Midwest, R. received her B.A. from Michigan State University in 1949. She married Bruce Brodie after a brief stint as a hospital apprentice in the United States Navy (1945–46) and "lived the straight life to the hilt" for fifteen years, her life roughly paralleling that of Henrietta in her first novel, *A Gradual Joy* (1953).

Considered at the time to be something of a model for happy heterosexuality, *Joy* chronicles the evolving marriage of Henrietta and Jim, children of the depression drawn together more by a desire for stability and security than by love or passion. By mutual agreement they continue to pursue their own interests: Jim as a teacher, Henrietta as a medical student. After some initial difficulties, they suddenly discover what a *New York Times* reviewer called "the real meaning of love." Jim becomes more concerned with the marriage, Henrietta with homemaking. With the arrival of their daughter, she abandons her professional aspirations to become "a real wife and mother." Her decision goes without comment.

Central to heterosexual union for Jim and Henrietta are sacrifice and compromise. Central to Patience and Sarah's union in *A Place For Us*, on the other hand, are freedom and fulfillment. This may be less a comment on heterosexual convention than on the author's experience of it. What makes *A Place For Us* remarkable, however, is not how it differs from *A Gradual Joy*, but how it differs from other literary portrayals of lesbian existence available at the time of its publication.

Set in the early 1800s, *Place* is a rather conventional love story: two people discovering themselves and each other in the context of evolving love and intimacy. The uniqueness of the novel lies in its portrayal of women lovers, who are neither seen as tragic nor subjected to other popular stereotypes about lesbians.

The women are, to some extent, misfits. Patience, well educated and left with an inheritance that allows her a modicum of independence, is on her way to becoming an "old maid," as she puts it. Coming from a family with no sons, Sarah was reared by her father to perform traditionally male tasks, so the family might be able to eke out its living. Their respective eccentricities cause some distrust and disapproval but they remain fully integrated in their rural Connecticut community until they eventually fall in love with each other. The point at which they begin to desire a life together is the point at which they realize that they must create a space for themselves elsewhere.

Each woman wavers in her commitment to this goal at different moments in the novel. Patience eventually forces the issue—covertly, but cleverly. The two set out for New York State to make a life together and their relationship continues to evolve, and their intimacy deepen, as they go. They buy a farm and build a home together as the novel comes to a close.

Many readers have felt that the story leaves off where it ought to be beginning. Yet given the time when it was written and the era it is written about, *Place* must concern itself less with a life together than with the need to find—or make—a safe space in which that life can unfold. For this reason, the original title is more accurate than the sanitized, isolating *Patience and Sarah*, under which McGraw-Hill published the work in 1972 and as it is generally known today. The original title defies stereotype,

Us implying a community, if only a community of two, rather than solitary individuals.

R. also refused to typecast her lesbian protagonists. Their identities are complex, as is their relationship. Sarah is more overtly masculine and Patience is more overtly feminine. Read carefully, however, this is not simply "butch/femme" role playing. The women need Sarah's "masculine" skills—the tasks she learned as "boy"—in order to survive on their own. They also need Patience's "feminine" wiles to survive when dealing with the straight world. Within their relationship they value and desire each other as women. As they do not internalize preconceived roles, nor deliberately rebel against them, they must negotiate their identities and their relationship.

The history of the novel runs parallel to its plot. Dissatisfied with available representations of women loving women, R. sought to create a new one. Unable to find a publisher at first, she printed the manuscript herself and sold the book out of shopping bags at meetings of burgeoning gay/lesbian rights groups. Such was the climate of fear that R. had to ask the editor of *The Ladder*, America's first and then only lesbian periodical, to vouch for the fact that R. was not an "FBI fink." R. distanced herself from her previous works by publishing *Place*, and such later lesbian-themed works as *The Love of Good Women* (1988), *Side by Side* (1990), and *A Dooryard Full of Flowers* (1993) under the pseudonym "Isabel Miller." (Miller was her maternal grandmother's surname; Isabel is an anagram for "Lesbia.") She told Jonathan Katz, "By using a new name, I wanted to start a new thing."

OTHER WORKS: as Alma Routsong, *Round Shape* (1959).

BIBLIOGRAPHY: Katz, Jonathan, *Gay American History* (1976). Zimmerman, Bonnie, *The Safe Sea of Women: Lesbian Fiction 1969–1989* (1990). Reference works: *CA* 49–52 (1975). Other references: *The Ladder* (Dec. 1969–Jan. 1970, Oct.–Nov. 1971, Aug.–Sept. 1971). *New Statesman* (26 Feb. 1988). *NYT* (23 Aug. 1953). *NYTBR* (6 Sept. 1959, 23 April 1972). *Sat. Rev.* (26 Sept. 1953). *TLS* (26 Feb. 1988). *VV* (20 April 1972).

BETH GRIERSON

Rosemary Radford Ruether

See AWW 3, 514–15

R., a Catholic feminist liberation theologian, has written prolifically, lectured widely, and served in numerous advisory and editorial capacities to periodicals and social justice agencies. Her scholarship has three distinct strands. First is the historical work of documentation, retrieval, and revision. R.'s focus on women's experience in Western Christian traditions throughout history also includes the documentation of contemporary women's experiences, her contribution toward a new canon that she hopes will emerge from the contemporary Christian community. The second strand is her work toward the development of a feminist systematic theology. The third is her interest in the connection between Christianity and anti-Semitism and the religious and political issues of the Middle East.

Of the six anthologies R. has published since 1980, four have contributed to her work of feminist historical retrieval. With Rosemary Skinner Keller, she edited the three-volume *Women and Religion in America* that spans the colonial period through 1968. Each volume contains essays with selected documents that address women's religious experiences in the designated time period with attention to various denominational, racial, and ethnic specificities. In 1985 R. published *Womanguides*, a compilation of historical and contemporary documents by and about women, including items that had existed either at the margins of Western Christian theological writing, such as the work of black Shaker eldress **Rebecca Cox Jackson,** or, like Aristotle's statement on "woman as defective male," had been central in proliferating patriarchal definitions. R. also included several contemporary stories that she hoped would encourage other women to record their experiences as a legacy for future generations. In twelve chapters, each with its own introduction, R. organized the documents into theological topics that span systematic theology.

Women-Church also appeared in 1985. The first part of the book is a descriptive essay of the women-church movement, a network of women gathering in small groups to pray, reflect, discuss, and act. The second part is a collaborative effort to record liturgies devised by women for various occasions, such as creating community and healing wounds due to patriarchal violence, and life passages.

During the 1980s R. wrote three topical theological volumes reflecting her interest in the revision of systematic theology. *To Change the World* (1981) develops Christological themes based on an analysis of political theology from Europe, Latin-American liberation theology, and feminism. This work also relates Christology to her long-standing interests in Jewish–Christian relations and ecology. In *Disputed Questions: On Being a Christian* (1982), her most autobiographical piece, R. connects her personal experience to her investigation of the credibility of Christianity, Jewish–Christian relations, feminism, and politics and religion in the United States and delineates the critical dimensions of each of these issues. *Contemporary Roman Catholicism* (1987) examines three critical issues for the church at the end of the twentieth century: "1) the challenge of democratic values and human rights in the church's institutional life; 2) the demands of women for full participation in the church's ministry, and the crisis over the church's teachings on sexual morality; and 3) the challenge of the Third World liberation struggles and the church's alignment with the poor."

To date, R.'s feminist systematic theological reflections culminate in *Sexism and God-Talk* (1983). Here, R. uses a topical outline similar to *Womanguides* but also including Christology and Mariology. She follows a consistent methodological pattern of tracing the history of the topic and calling the question for the contemporary situation. Noted for expanding the resources used in theological reflection, including pre-Christian, pagan, heterodox, and post-Christian sources, R.'s goal is to undo the dichotomous thinking that theology has inherited through Western philosophy and to unravel the deformations of the prophetic tradition at the heart of the biblical message.

R. established her interest in anti-Semitism in her early work *Faith and Fratricide* (1974). In 1989 she collaborated with her spouse Herman J. Ruether, a political scientist and former acting director of the Palestinian Human Rights Campaign, on *Wrath of Jonah*. Convinced that an accurate historical portrayal of the Israel–Palestine conflict is key to a just settlement of the tensions, the Ruethers discuss the attitudes of exclusivity in Judaism, Christianity, and Islam; the development of Zionism and Palestinian nationalism; and the Christian relations to Judaism, the Holocaust, and Zionism. Not without its critics, it was generally well reviewed. R. provided a brief synopsis of the historical analysis in "The Occupation Must End" in *Beyond Occupation,* an anthology she edited with Marc H. Ellis. Her concluding essay, "Beyond Anti-Semitism and Philo-Semitism," urged the distinction between anti-Semitism and critical analysis/criticism of Israeli policy.

Faith and Intifada: Palestinian Christian Voices (1992), an anthology of papers given at the First International Symposium on Palestinian Liberation Theology, includes R.'s essay "Western Christianity and Zionism," in which she discusses the deficits in "four key religious arguments that are still operative in linking Christians in America to Israel."

OTHER WORKS: *Women and Religion in America*, editor with Rosemary S. Keller: *vol. 1* (1981); *vol. 2: The Colonial and Revolutionary Periods* (1983); *vol. 3: 1900–1968* (1986). *Gaia and God: An Ecofeminist Theology of Earth Healing* (1992).

BIBLIOGRAPHY: Ramsay, William, *Four Modern Prophets: Walter Rauschenbusch, Gustavo Gutierrez, Martin Luther King, Jr., Rosemary Radford Ruether* (1986). Snyder, Mary Hembrow, *The Christology of Rosemary Radford Ruether: A Critical Introduction* (1988; includes chronological bibliography of R.'s works to 1987). Vaughan, Judith, *Sociality, Ethics, and Social Change: A Critical Appraisal of Reinhold Niebuhr's Ethics in the Light of Rosemary Radford Ruether's Works* (1983).

BARBARA ANNE RADTKE

Joanna Russ

See AWW 3, 521–22

R., whose parents were teachers, spent her childhood "half in The Bronx Zoo and half in the Botanical Gardens." She attended Cornell University

(B.A. 1957) and then Yale University School of Drama (M.F.A. 1960). She taught at Cornell, the State University of New York at Binghamton, and the University of Colorado, before becoming professor of English at the University of Washington.

Although usually described as a writer of science fiction, over half of R.'s output has been outside of the genre. She has written a mainstream lesbian novel, *On Strike against God* (1980); *Kittatinny: A Tale of Magic* (1978), a children's fantasy; *Magic Mommas, Trembling Sisters, Puritans, and Perverts* (1985), a collection of feminist essays; and *How to Suppress Women's Writing* (1983), a witty indictment of the male-centered publishing and academic establishment.

R.'s short fiction has been collected in *The Zanzibar Cat* (1983), *The Adventures of Alyx* (1983), and *The Hidden Side of the Moon* (1987). Her most famous story, "When It Changed," first appeared in the groundbreaking anthology *Again: Dangerous Visions*, edited by Harlan Ellison (1972). It describes the planet Whileaway, where the women have developed a utopian society after all the men have died in a plague. The women lead happy, independent, and fulfilled lives until men from Earth rediscover them. The downbeat ending implies that their freedom is at an end and their accomplishments will again be made subordinate to masculine power.

R. studied with Vladimir Nabokov at Cornell, and her science fiction reveals his influence. She is a fine stylist who does not hesitate to use experimental techniques or deal with themes like feminism and homosexuality that were ignored in science fiction until she began to write. *And Chaos Died* (1970) features a homosexual hero and a utopian telepathic society. *The Female Man* (1975), admired by most women and dismissed by many male readers, has four different heroines: the pliable, suppressed Jeanine; Janet, who comes from the planet Whileaway; Joanna, a woman much like the author herself; and the man-destroying assassin Jael. It is angry, iconoclastic, surrealistic, and funny. *We Who Are About To* (1977) is a much darker novel. In it, the survivors of a wrecked spaceship are murdered one by one by a bitter and rebellious woman who refuses to go along with their survivalist attempt to establish a colony. *The Two of Them* (1978), in which two time-traveling agents rescue a young woman poet from a repressive male-dominated world, is more optimistic, as is *Extra(Ordinary) People* (1984), an interlocking series of meta-science-fiction tales.

R.'s strong lesbian-feminist stance has often caused her to be described as "controversial" and "radical," and she has not always found it easy to get her work published. However, she has received both the Nebula

(1972) and Hugo (1983) awards for her fiction, and the Science Research Association Pilgrim Award in 1988 for her contributions to science-fiction scholarship. Her essays and critical papers, mostly on aspects of feminism and science fiction, have appeared in such varied places as *Science Fiction Studies*, the *Village Voice*, *Signs*, *Sojourner*, *Ms.*, and *Chrysalis*. "When It Changed" and *The Female Man* have been reprinted many times. R.'s literate prose, dry humor, and unstereotyped characters have made her an influential writer whose example has encouraged other women to explore science fiction and fantasy as venues for serious writing about hitherto-taboo themes.

OTHER WORKS: Picnic on Paradise (1968).

BIBLIOGRAPHY: LeFanu, Sarah, *In the Chinks of the World Machine: Feminism and Science Fiction* (1988). *Across the Wounded Galaxies: Interviews with Contemporary American Science Fiction Writers*, Larry McCaffrey, ed. (1990). Platt, Charles, *Dream Makers II* (1983). Shinn, Thelma J., "Worlds of Words and Swords: Suzette Haden Elgin and Joanna Russ at Work," *Women Worldwalkers: New Dimensions of Science Fiction and Fantasy*, Jane B. Weedman, ed. (1985). Reference works: *CANR* 31 (1990). *CLC* 15 (1980). *DLB* 8 (1981). *FC* (1990). *Maj Twent Cent Writers* (1991).
  Other references: *Chrysalis* 4 (1977). *Science Fiction Studies* 19 (Nov. 1979). *A Room of One's Own* 1–2 (1981).

LYNN F. WILLIAMS

Sonia Sanchez

B. 9 Sept. 1934, Birmingham, Alabama
D. of Lena (Jones) and Wilson L. Driver; c.: Anita, b. 1957; Morani Meusi and Mungu Meusi, b. 1968

Born in the South, S. moved north at the age of nine with her family to the Harlem community of New York City. She graduated from Hunter

College (B.A. 1955) and did postgraduate work at New York University where she studied with poet **Louise Bogan.**

S. worked in the civil rights movement and became further radicalized as a result of hearing Malcolm X. Becoming involved with the burgeoning black arts movement in Harlem during the 1960s and early 1970s as a poet and dramatist, S. became one of the most forceful and best known of the cultural nationalist African American writers of that period. In 1966, she began teaching at San Francisco State College where she was a founder of the nation's first black studies program. S. has since taught at a number of colleges and universities and has been a faculty member at Temple University since 1977.

Following in the tradition of such writers as Langston Hughes, Sterling Brown, and **Margaret Walker,** S. is widely credited as one of the writers most important in the establishment of "Black English" as legitimate literary diction. In addition to her use of a distinctly African American syntax and phonetic spelling, she often, particularly in her early work, broke the lines of her poems unusually and used unorthodox spellings that were not phonetic—leaving out certain vowels, for example—forcing the reader to look more carefully at the words themselves and to consider them as a distinctive African American cultural product. S. also constructs her poetry and her short fiction so as to emphasize the oral performative aspect that she sees both as an important part of the African American tradition and as more accessible to popular audiences. Some of S.'s best work engages with African American music as in "a / coltrane / poem" from *We a BaddDD People* (1970), in which S. literally attempts to re-create the structure and sound of John Coltrane's music while connecting it to the oppression of black people and the fight against that oppression.

S.'s poems and short stories both celebrate the survival and strengths of the black community in the United States and chronicle its losses. Since the beginning of her career, S. has gradually adopted a stance rooted in her experiences as an African American woman that addresses itself beyond a specifically black context to concern with all oppressed peoples. The powerful and moving "MIA's" in *homegirls and handgrenades* (1984), for example, links the disappearance of black children from the streets of Atlanta in the early 1980s to the death squad disappearances in El Salvador and the death of Stephen Biko in South Africa. The volume won the American Book Award for poetry in 1985.

Her concern with social justice has also led S. to write a number of books for children whom she sees as having been particularly poorly served by literature. These include a volume of inspirational poems, *It's a New Day: Poems for Young Brothas and Sistuhs* (1971); *The Adventures of Fat Head, Small Head, and Square Head* (1973); and a collection of stories, *A Sound Investment* (1980), which invites children to draw moral meaning from the tales.

Since the beginning of her career, S. has been a voice for the concerns of women even during the black arts era, when such concerns were generally muted. In this respect, S. consciously sets herself in the tradition of female blues, jazz, and rhythm and blues singers who are tough, strong, loving, and often betrayed by love in a harsh world. Several poems in *Wee a BaddDD People* reflect the suffering in her marriage to poet Etheridge Knight, who had a severe drug problem. *Love Poems* (1973) demonstrates the poet's lyricism, but here too the poems of man–woman relationships reflect their difficulty as well as their passion. S.'s work celebrates the power, pride, and solidarity of black women; she also portrays the personal betrayals of love—which often have a larger social implication—as in the poem "Blues" and the short story "After Saturday Night Comes Sunday." *A Blues Book for Blue Black Magical Women* (1974), written while S. was a member of the Nation of Islam (1972–75), praises black women, "Queens of the Universe," and urges them to turn away from false values to "embrace Blackness as a religion / husband." Her concern for women's lives and their freedom reverberates through such later volumes as *I've Been A Woman* (1978) and *Under a Soprano Sky* (1987).

S. has also written a number of significant plays including *The Bronx is Next* (1968, produced 1970) where she speaks "symbolically" about the need for blacks to destroy urban centers, "to move out of that which is killing them," and the autobiographical *Sister Son/ji* (1969). S. remains one of the most powerful writers, and readers, of poetry, drama, and prose in the United States. Her voice speaks forcefully, and at times bittersweetly, about racism, sexism, oppression, and the need for revolutionary change. She is also one of the most poignant chroniclers of the social and emotional experience of a woman in the late twentieth century in the United States.

OTHER WORKS: *Home Coming* (1969). *New Plays from the Black Theatre*, ed. Ed Bullins (1969). *Three Hundred and Sixty Degrees of Blackness Come at You* (editor, 1971). *Ima Talken bout the Nation of Islam* (1972). *We Be Word Sorcerers:*

Twenty-five Stories by Black Americans (editor, 1974). *Uh Huh: But How Do It Free Us?* (1975). *Malcolm Man Don't Live Here Anymore* (1979). *I'm Black When I'm Singing, I'm Blue When I Ain't* (1982). *Culture in Crisis: Two Speeches by Sonia Sanchez* (1983). *Generations: Selected Poetry, 1969–1985* (1986).

BIBLIOGRAPHY: Baker, Houston A., Jr., "Our Lady: Sonia Sanchez and the Writing of a Black Renaissance," in *Black Feminist Criticism and Critical Theory*, H. A. Baker, Jr., and Joe Weixlmann, eds. (1988). Curb, Rosemary, "Pre-Feminism in the Black Revolutionary Drama of Sonia Sanchez," in *The Many Forms of Drama*, Karelisa V. Hartigan, ed. (1985). Madhubuti, Haki, "Sonia Sanchez: The Bringer of Memories," in *Black Women Writers (1950–1980): A Critical Evaluation*, Mari Evans, ed. (1984). Melhem, D. M., *Heroism in the New Black Poetry: Introductions and Interviews* (1990). *Black Women Writers at Work*, Claudia Tate, ed. (1983). Reference works: *CANR* 24 (1988). *CLC* 5 (1976). *DLB* 41 (1985). *FC* (1990). *Maj Twent Cent Writers* (1991). *SATA* 22 (1981).

Other references: *MELUS* 12 (Fall 1985), 15 (Spring 1988). *Parnassus: Poetry in Review* (Spring–Winter 1985).

JAMES SMETHURST

May Sarton

See AWW 4, 20–22

S. has continued as a prolific writer in three major genres: poetry, fiction, and autobiography. Considered a romantic in her insistence on the individual and the connections between the individual self and some larger communion with others, she writes of solitude and friendship, of transcendent life-affirming moments, and the realities of illness, death, and grief.

While all the major themes continue, especially foregrounded and personalized are the traumas of illness and old age that S. has experienced, and the clearer focus on herself as a lesbian artist. Creating herself through her writing, she explicitly examines past and present attitudes that define her being.

The novel *Anger* (1982) portrays the intense emotions of anger and despair that arise between an artistic woman and the man she marries. Despite the consolations of love, relationships are inherently conflictive. The title character in *The Magnificent Spinster* (1985) is based on S.'s former teacher Anne Thorp. A woman narrator struggles toward a clear biographical tribute to her admired teacher. In the process, she considers the qualities of the single life and the varieties of female friendship. *The Education of Harriet Hatfield* (1989) is especially noted for its candid and sympathetic portrayal of lesbianism. Sixty-year-old Harriet Hatfield (unrelated to a character of that name in *As We Are Now*) opens a women's bookstore after the death of her longtime companion. As others react— some with support, some with intolerance—Harriet comes out of her closet of silence to affirm human dignity.

Three volumes of poetry, *Letters from Maine* (1984), *The Phoenix Again* (1987), and *The Silence Now* (1988), continue S.'s themes of openness and silence. She prefers formal poetic boundaries, often with a definite meter and rhyme, but a spare, quintessentially lyric quality infuses the language in the later works. Images of light, solitude, and silence lead both inward and outward, toward and beyond self.

The journals, which have brought S. the widest audience, continue with *At Seventy* (1984), in which she details her daily routines, including her pets, her gardening, and most noticeably here her relationship with the readers who correspond with her. *After the Stroke* (1988) traces her recovery from the first major health blow, a stroke in February 1986. In *Endgame: A Journal of the Seventy-Ninth Year* (1992) she struggles with the crises of severe health problems and old age. By *Endgame* S. must adjust to dictating with a tape recorder rather than writing, but the journal itself becomes a motive for survival, a method of sustaining her sense of self.

Other endeavors indicate the increased critical focus on S. Collections of her work include *Selected Poems* (1978, edited by Sue Hilsinger and Lois Byrnes); a group of essays, *Writings on Writing* (1980, edited by Constance Hunting); and *Sarton Selected* (1991, edited by Daniel Dalziel). *May Sarton: A Self-Portrait* (1986) emerged from an outstanding film, *A World of Light: A Portrait of May Sarton* (1979), made by Marita Simpson and Martha Wheelock. Other films, videos, and recordings of her readings attest to the appeal of her works, and several of her novels have been optioned for feature films. During the 1980s S. published various limited editions and collector volumes through small presses, including her portrait of her lover of many years, Judith Matlock, titled *Honey in the Hive* (1988).

S. has been repeatedly honored for her work. Her several honorary degrees include one from Westbrook College in Portland, Maine, also the site of a major national conference, May Sarton at Eighty: A Celebration of Her Life and Work (1992). S. has selected Margot Peters as her official biographer.

Although S. has often expressed concern over the neglect of her work by the literary establishment, critical attention and reevaluation have increased, and her work continues to attract both new and loyal readers.

OTHER WORKS: *Letters to May* (by Eleanor Sarton), May Sarton, ed. (1986). *Coming into Eighty* (1992). *Collected Poems: 1930–1993* (1993). *Encore: A Journal of the Eightieth Year* (1993). *May Sarton: Among the Usual Days: A Portrait. Unpublished Poems, Journals, and Photographs*, ed. Susan Sherman (1993).

BIBLIOGRAPHY: Evans, E., *May Sarton Revisited* (1989). *May Sarton: Woman and Poet*, C. Hunting, ed. (1982). *Conversations with May Sarton*, E. G. Ingersoll, ed. (1991). *A House of Gathering: Poets on May Sarton's Poetry*, M. Kallet, ed. (1993). Miner, V., "Spinning Friends: May Sarton's Literary Spinsters," in *Old Maids and Excellent Women*, L. Doan, ed. (1990). *That Great Sanity: Critical Essays on May Sarton*, S. Swartzlander and M. Mumford, eds. (1992). Films/videos: Robitaille, S., and W. Suchy, *Writing in the Upward Years* (1990). Saum, K., *She Knew a Phoenix* (1981). Reference works: *CANR* 34 (1981), 41 (1989). *CLC* 14 (1980), 49 (1988). *DLB* 48 (1986). *FC* (1990).

LOIS A. MARCHINO

Susan Fromberg Schaeffer

See AWW *4, 32–34*

Although discussion of S.'s fiction has labeled her a Jewish-American writer, her recent novels do not deal with Jewish feminism. *The Madness of a Seduced Woman* (1983) involves a young woman in nineteenth-century Vermont; *Mainland* (1985) and *The Injured Party* (1986) use Brooklyn writers and academics of no discernible ethnic heritage as their heroines. *Buffalo Afternoon* (1989) focuses on a teenage Vietnamese girl and an Italian-American soldier.

As in her earlier novels S. writes of women who face the power wielded by memory and the often paralyzing trauma inflicted by family. Human inconstancy and vision and blindness are prevalent images that complement themes of enclosure, and S.'s rich development of spatial metaphors stresses depression and isolation as female more than male conditions. S.'s novels are filled with "ghosts": *The Madness of a Seduced Woman* and *Buffalo Afternoon*, for instance, have narrators who are themselves dead. Voices from the past and dreams haunt her characters. While some have described her fusion of time as "Faulknerian," S. claims this approach as a feminist one: trapped in the present, her heroines must deal with the unresolved past by rejecting their roles as wives and mothers and often by facing the aggression S. portrays as a given between mother and daughter. Her peripheral male characters aid the heroines' epiphany because of their constant, albeit marginal, roles. Although *Mainland* and *The Injured Party* depict women who are healed by this recovery and acceptance process, *The Madness of a Seduced Woman* shows the violent consequences when a passionate woman rejects family history in favor of shaping a unique present. *Buffalo Afternoon* departs from these novels in several ways. While it continues S.'s interest in memory, death, and identity, its male protagonist faces the chains of generational influence after the horror he undergoes as a soldier in Vietnam. Thus, the hero learns to understand a political as well as a familial past.

S. is a frequent contributor to the *New York Times Book Review*. She has published new poems in *Prairie Schooner*, the *Southern Review*, and the

Literary Review, and two novels for young adults: *The Dragons of North Chittendon* (1986) and *The Four Hoods and Great Dog* (1988).

S. has received many literary awards: the O. Henry Award (1978); the Lawrence Award (1984), the Friends of Literature Award (1984); and the *Prairie Schooner*'s Edward Lewis Wallant Award (1984). She received a Guggenheim Fellowship for 1984–85 and the *Centennial Review*'s Poetry Award in 1985. S. is Broeklundian Professor of English at Brooklyn College where she began the M.F.A. program in creative writing.

OTHER WORKS: "The Unreality of Realism," *Critical Inquiry* 6:4 (Summer 1980). *First Nights* (1993).

BIBLIOGRAPHY: Gottschalk, Katherine K., "Paralyzed in the Present: Susan Fromberg Schaeffer's Mothers, or Daughters," in *Mother Puzzles: Daughters and Mothers in Contemporary American Literature*, Mickey Pearlman, ed. (1989). *American Women Writing Fiction: Memory, Identity, Family, Space*, M. Pearlman, ed. (1989). Reference works: *CANR* 18 (1986). *CLC* 22 (1986). *DLB* 28 (1984). *Maj Twent Cent Writers* (1990). *WW Wrs, Eds, Poets* (1989).
Other references: *APR* 5:1 (Jan./Feb. 1976). *Centennial Rev.* 22 (1978). *MELUS* 7:4 (Winter 1980). *Southwest Rev.* 69 (Winter 1984).

JOELLEN MASTERS

Lynne Sharon Schwartz

B. 19 March 1939, Brooklyn, New York
D. of Sarah (Slatus) and Jack Sharon; m. Harry Schwartz, 1957; c.: Rachel, Miranda

S. grew up in Brooklyn, the subject of her most important work to date, *Leaving Brooklyn* (1989), which she describes as an autobiographical memoir. She graduated from Barnard College (1959), received an M.A.

in literature from Bryn Mawr College (1961), and did further graduate study at New York University between 1967 and 1972. S. worked as associate editor for the magazine *Writer* from 1961 to 1963, and as a writer for Operation Open City, a civil rights–fair housing organization in New York City from 1965 to 1967. She was a lecturer in English at Hunter College of the City University of New York from 1970 to 1975.

S.'s other major works include three highly acclaimed novels and two collections of short stories. Her fiction is remarkable for its sharply delineated portraits of the everyday life of the urban middle class; skillfully piercing through the surface of the comfortable, familiar worlds of her characters, she exposes the dreams, anxieties, and absurdities that lie beneath. The rich images with which she paints her characters' foibles and eccentricities have led critics to compare her to the painter Goya, or to **Flannery O'Connor.** Yet while she often deals with idiosyncrasies of personality and behavior, S. strives to portray the universal motivations that channel human desires. She succeeds unusually well in depicting the complex emotional and psychological underpinnings of the "dailiness of life," as one reviewer noted, while at the same time exploring the moral and philosophical dilemmas that confront her characters. Her work is distinguished by its broad intellectual range as well as by its clear style, graceful elegance, and wit.

Much of S.'s writing probes the contradictory pull between security and risk, order and change, the "safety of rules and traditions" and the "thrill of defiance." This theme is prominent in *Leaving Brooklyn,* a novel about Audrey, a fifteen-year-old girl coming of age just after World War II. Narrated by the protagonist, now a mature writer struggling to understand and accept her own history, the story concerns discovery of her physical differences—a "wandering" eye that gives her a special "double vision"—and her seduction by her eye doctor, a seduction in which she is a willing participant. By telling "the story of an eye, and how it came into its own," S. reveals the development of her own "I," as the girl Audrey begins to "see" the truths beneath Brooklyn's surface comforts, its rules, and its order, and to distance herself from the conventions of her parents, immigrants-once-removed, and of Brooklyn. "Leaving Brooklyn" becomes a metaphor for reaching beyond custom, convention, and rules, for risk taking, experience, and passion.

In *Disturbances in the Field* (1983), the comfortable, upper-middle-class lives of Victor Rowe, a painter, and his talented, well-educated wife, Lydia, a chamber pianist, are suddenly split apart after the deaths of two of their children in a school-bus accident. Unable to respond to her husband's emotional needs in the wake of the tragedy, Lydia sets in motion the "disturbances" of the title—when "something gets between the expressed need on the one hand and the response on the other." This unsettling, compelling story is told crisply and compassionately: through the accumulation of detail, character, and event, S. compiles a stunningly realistic portrait of an intelligent, but ultimately ordinary woman seeking to find meanings in the terrible loss that wrenched the "placidity" from her life.

Rough Strife (1980), S.'s first novel, is a chronicle of the emotional dynamics of a marriage over twenty years; S., in Katha Pollitt's words, "registers the fluctuations of marital feeling with the fidelity of a geiger counter." The attention paid to detail and to exposing the jumbled, countrapuntal realities beneath the surface of what appears to be a successful conventional relationship predicts the course of much of S.'s later fiction.

The theme is realized most vividly in S.'s masterful short story collection, *Acquainted with the Night* (1984). In the title story, a successful forty-seven-year-old architect, given to insomnia, confronts terrifying demons of his past, his psyche, and even beyond, something more "cosmic"—as he seeks sleep in the middle of the night. The characters in the fifteen other stories of this anthology also wrestle with the terrors, illusions, and fantasies that compose their reality. For S., true knowledge is based on an understanding of night—the hidden fears, secrets, and reversals of life—as well as of day.

The characters in the stories collected in *The Melting Pot and Other Subversive Stories* (1987) also confront "the unending cycles of light and darkness" that shatter complacency. Nuances of shifting relationships, marriage, and divorce are once again illuminated; S. also writes poignantly, and with great good humor, of other subjects—a middle-aged woman undergoing a hysterectomy; another reflecting on the life and death of her opinionated, tempestuous father; a homeless family finding shelter in a Manhattan TV studio. She is particularly concerned with the impact of dream and memory on consciousness: exploring the present, she reaches back to "subversive" impulses—among them, tradition, illusion, and fantasy—that guide contemporary lives. Here, as in *Leaving Brooklyn* and other stories, the daughter of Americanized Jews must confront the meaning of that heritage.

OTHER WORKS: *Balancing Acts* (1981). *We Are Talking about Homes: A Great University against Its Neighbors* (1985). *Four Questions* (text for paintings by Ori

Sherman, 1989). *A Lynne Sharon Schwartz Reader: Selected Poetry and Prose* (1992). "Remembrance of Tense Past," *New England Rev. and Bread Loaf Q*. 10:2 (Winter 1987).

BIBLIOGRAPHY: *Amer. Book Rev.* (Nov./Dec. 1989). *Hudson Rev* . 37 (Spring 1984). *NYTBR* (6 Nov. 1983; 26 Aug. 1984; 24 Nov. 1985; 16 April 1989). *Newsweek* (14 Jan. 1985). *Sewanee Rev.* 93 (Spring 1985). *WRB* (Sept. 1989). Reference works: *CA* 103 (1982). *CLC* 31 (1985).

JOYCE ANTLER

Ruth Seid

Writes under: Jo Sinclair
See AWW *4, 51–53*

The fifth and youngest child of Jewish immigrants, S. moved to Cleveland from her birthplace in Brooklyn, New York, at the age of three. Growing up as a Jewish working-class lesbian in a society that was anti-Semitic, homophobic, and hostile to values not perceived as middle-class, S. has devoted her output as a writer to the battle against prejudice and to the reclamation of those whose lives have been crippled by the role of outsider. Her novels, short stories, and plays focus on the human potential for change.

Between graduating from a vocational high school in 1930 and becoming a freelance writer in 1946, S. held various factory and office jobs. In the mid to late 1930s, she submitted stories to a wide range of political and general interest magazines. *Esquire,* in 1938, was the first to pay for a short story by "Jo Sinclair." She aired a number of radio plays throughout the 1940s; a stage play, *The Long Moment* (1951), about a black musician contemplating passing for white to get work, had an eight-week run in Cleveland. Her experiences with the Works Progress Administration (1936–41) and the American Red Cross (1942–46) were significant influences on her writing. Many of her Red Cross stories are about donating blood, a practical contribution to the war effort that also symbolized for S. the breaking down of ghetto walls.

Donating blood is a central image near the end of the Harper Prize novel *Wasteland* (1946) in which "John Brown" learns to accept himself as Jake Braunowitz, an assimilated American Jew, through the help of his strong, caring sister who has learned to accept herself as a lesbian. *Wasteland,* which pioneered the use of psychotherapy as a narrative device, is also remarkable both for its focus on a Jewish family at a time when anti-Semitism was peaking in America, and in its presentation, possibly for the first time in twentieth-century American fiction, of a lesbian as a positive role model.

In *Sing at My Wake* (1951) S. pursued her theme of the importance of finding and nourishing abandoned souls who hunger for love and security. Though that novel was not a commercial success, *The Changelings* (1955), a fictionalized urban history in which whites fear a takeover of their neighborhood by blacks, restored the author's reputation. John Weigel has noted that the female protagonists in *Wasteland* and *The Changelings,* S.'s two most autobiographical novels, "anticipate contemporary liberation movements." *Anna Teller* (1960) depicts another strong female protagonist, a woman of seventy-four who escapes to America during the 1956 Hungarian uprising. In 1969 S. completed the still-unpublished *Approach to the Meaning,* dedicated to her sister Fannie, the author's constant emotional and financial supporter. The novel depicts a fragmented woman who must discover herself in order to save her adopted daughter from imitating her own wasted life.

S. herself was saved from the emotional wastelands of her youth when she met Helen Buchman in 1938. Although Buchman was married with two children, S. lived in her household for almost thirty years, including seven years with Helen's widower. The Feminist Press launched a series of women's autobiographies with a reprinting of S.'s *The Seasons: Death and Transfiguration* (1972, 1993), which describes the author's attempt to keep her own creative death at bay when Helen, her muse and best editor died. In 1973, Joan Soffer, who began their correspondence with a fan letter after *Wasteland,* asked S. to move in with her in Jenkintown, Pennsylvania. There, S. has continued gardening and writing in her lifelong attempt to save walking wastelands with her changeling language.

BIBLIOGRAPHY: Sandberg, Elisabeth, "Jo Sinclair: Toward a Critical Biography," unpublished Ph.D. diss., University of Massachusetts, 1985. Reference works: *Amer. Novelists of Today* (1951). *CA* 5–8 (1969). *Contemp. Novelists* (1986, article by John Weigel). *DLB* 28 (1984). *Tw Cent Authors* (1951).

ELISABETH SANDBERG

Mary Lee Settle

B. 29 July 1918, Charleston, West Virginia
D. of Rachel (Tompkins) and Joseph Edward Settle; m. Rodney Weathersbee, 1939;
   m. Douglas Newton, 1946; m. William Littleton Tazewell, 1978;
   c.: Christopher Weathersbee, b. 1940

Although she draws heavily from memories of her Kentucky and West Virginia childhood for her important novel sequence, the Beulah Quintet, S. defies the regional writer pigeonhole. *Blood Tie* (1977), for which she won the National Book Award in 1978, is set principally in Turkey. *Celebration* (1986) is set all over the world—London, Kurdistan, Africa, Hong Kong, Virginia—settings that reflect S.'s seventeen years of living and working abroad.

The Beulah Quintet, composed of *O Beulah Land* (1956), *Know-nothing* (1960), *Prisons* (1973), *The Scapegoat* (1980), and *The Killing Ground* (1982), traces four centuries of family networks as they affect the development of what is now West Virginia. Charleston, S.'s birthplace, appears as the fictional town of Canona. The novels reflect S.'s mixed reactions to growing up in the South where, she wrote, children are taught to "ridicule the delicate qualities in ourselves and in others that might interfere with that hard, polite drifting acceptance. The punishment for choosing another path . . . is brutal and unconscious."

Although *The Love Eaters* (1954), *The Kiss of Kin* (1955), *The Clam Shell* (1971), and *Charley Bland* (1989) are usually considered apart from the quintet, all are set in or near Canona; the latter three include families familiar from the quintet. S. has called *The Clam Shell* her one autobiographical novel; it is drawn from her years (1936–38) at Sweet Briar College.

S.'s characters, whatever their age, race, sexual preference, or national origin, are psychologically informed by their physical environments. In *Blood Tie*, Ariadne, a middle-aged American divorcee who is diving off the coast of Turkey, discovers a new world, both physical and psychic. "For once, Ariadne realized, I am not searching for someone else's words, only my own will do. Nothing is new in this kneeling in this place. It is the most ancient of homecomings, astonishing familiar water fields of light."

Much of S.'s work is distinctively visual, almost cinematic, although grounded in the psychological. She traces this concentration to her partial blindness, a result of a childhood bout with whooping cough that precipitated a premature eye-straightening operation: "I had consciously to develop a visual sense and that psychic awakening was to me like seeing for the first time." Much of S.'s work similarly echoes her own experiences, both obliquely and, as in *The Killing Ground*, rather slyly.

S.'s casts are often large. Some critics have complained that she sometimes tempts the reader with an intriguing portrait, then fails to develop the character satisfactorily. Nevertheless, she has a remarkable eye for texture, for the interweaving of points of view to create transcendent meaning. Plus Deng, the physically imposing African priest who is the hero of *Celebration* appears first as an iconic figure. Later, however, we learn through a shift in the limited omniscient point of view that "he was the youngest of his father's children, a prince in his own tribe, a nigger in Washington, D.C., *ageeb* in Khartoum, nignog in London, and priest everywhere."

In the majority of her novels, S. uses the omniscient point of view, not to imply a central authority, but to express the irony of discrepancies between various characters' worldviews, and to demonstrate their basic misunderstandings of each other, sometimes despite their best intentions. Her style is conventional only on its surface, profound and innovative in its final effect.

S.'s nonfiction includes *All the Brave Promises: Memoirs of Aircraft Woman Second Class 2146391* (1966), an account of experiences with the Women's Auxiliary of the Royal Air Force during World War II, and *The Scopes Trial: The State of Tennessee vs. John Thomas Scopes* (1972), an intense account of the famous "monkey trial," written for young adults. Over the years, she has supplemented her writing career by teaching, at Bard College in New York, and at the University of Virginia.

OTHER WORKS: *Fight Night on a Sweet Saturday* (1964). *The Story of Flight* (1967, juvenile). *Prisons* (1973; also published as *The Long Road to Paradise*, 1974). *Water World* (1984, juvenile). *The Search for Beulah Land: The Story behind the Beulah Quintet* (1988). *Turkish Reflections: A Biography of a Place* (1991).

BIBLIOGRAPHY: Garrett, G., *Understanding Mary Lee Settle* (1988). Joyner, N. C., "M. L. S.'s Connections: Class and Clothes in the Beulah Quintet," *Women Writers of the Contemporary South*, P. W. Prenshaw, ed. (1984). Rosenberg, B., *Mary Lee Settle's Beulah Quintet: The Price of Freedom* (1992). Shattuck, R., introduction to paperback edition of *The Beulah Quintet* (1982). Reference works: *CAAS* 15 (1992). *CA* 89–92 (1980). *CLC* 19 (1981), 61 (1990). *DLB* 6 (1980). *Cycl. of World Authors Two*, vol. 4 (1989). *FC* (1990).

LISA CARL

Ntozake Shange

B. *Paulette Williams, 18 Oct. 1948, Trenton, New Jersey*
D. *of Eloise (Owens) and Paul T. Williams; m. David Murray, 1977; m. John Guess; c.: Savannah Thulani Eloise*

S. was named for her father, a surgeon. Her mother was a social worker and educator. In 1971, she renamed herself, taking the Zulu names "Ntozake—she who comes with her own things" and "Shange—she who walks like a lion." The name reflects some of the cultural and personal concerns of S.'s writings.

S.'s early life was a privileged one. Her home life brought her into contact with many of the giants of black intellectual and cultural life, including W. E. B. Du Bois, Josephine Baker, and musicians Charlie Parker, Dizzy Gillespie, Miles Davis, and Chuck Berry. The impact of black musical traditions remains characteristic of S.'s work today. An avid reader as a child, after the family's move to St. Louis she seems to have immersed herself in the world of her imagination: her novel *Betsey Brown* (1985) is semiautobiographical.

S. attended Barnard College, graduating in 1970 with honors in American studies. She completed an M.A. in American studies at the University of Southern California (1973) and began her academic career, teaching humanities, women's studies, and Afro-American studies at Sonoma State College, Mills College, and the University of California Extension. During these years, S. formed and worked with several performing arts groups and began performing her poetry in clubs across the country. Her transition from poet to dramatist began during this period.

In 1975, S. moved to New York City, a move that brought her work a wider audience. Her Obie Award–winning "choreopoem," *For Colored Girls who have considered suicide / when the rainbow is enuf* (1977) displayed what would come to be seen as characteristic of S.'s art, mixing dramatic interpretations of her poems with movement, dance, song, music, and lighting effects to forge a unified woman-centered statement. The poignancy, humor, and rage of the piece delighted some and infuriated others. The work's focus on relationships among women in the face of neglect and mistreatment by men brought attacks from drama, literary, and politico-social critics alike.

S. herself had attempted suicide in 1966 after separating from her first husband, a law student. In 1976, she described that and subsequent suicide attempts as the result of suppressed rage. Writing and artistic expression, among other things, provided a healthier outlet for that rage.

In subsequent theater pieces, S. continued the experiments of *For Colored Girls*, substituting poetry, music, and dance for straight plot narrative and character development. It is only in her adaptations, *Mother Courage and Her Children* (1980, from the Berthold Brecht work) and *Betsey Brown* (1991, from her own novel of the same name), that S. attempts something approaching conventional drama. And each of these plays makes use of several experimental devices, particularly in their use of music. None of S.'s subsequent work for the theater has received the praise of *For Colored Girls*.

S. is primarily a poet who works in the oral tradition. Her strength is in her artistic rendering of the spoken word emanating from her sure ear for the musicality of vernacular speech, its rhythms and intonations. Criticized for "distorting" the language in her written work, she has responded in characteristic language: "i cant count the number of times i have viscerally wanted to attack deform n maim the language that i waz taught to hate myself in / the language that perpetuates the notions that cause pain to every black child as he / she learns to speak of the world & the 'self' . . . / in order to think n communicate the thoughts n feelings i want to think n communicate / i haveta fix my tool to my needs."

S.'s creation of her own black, female image weaves together her prose and poetry. Her novels, *Sassafras, Cypress, and Indigo* (1982) and *Betsey Brown*, explore various aspects of the black woman's psyche from Betsey's youthful introspection through the trials of young womanhood of the three plant-named sisters. Fusing her personal and public concerns, S. also writes cultural criticism and social commentary for a wide variety of publications. In addition, she continues to lecture widely and perform her works as a soloist and in performing arts ensembles.

In addition to her 1977 Obie, S. also received nominations for the Tony, Grammy, and Emmy awards for the Broadway-recorded and televised versions of *For Colored Girls*. She has served as artist in residence for the New York State Council on the Arts (1977 and 1981). In 1981, additionally, she was awarded a Guggenheim Fellowship and the Columbia University Medal of Excellence as well as an Obie for the Off-Broadway production of *Mother Courage and Her Children*.

OTHER WORKS: *Natural Disasters and Other Festive Occasions* (1977). *Nappy Edges* (1978). *Three Pieces: Spell #7; A Photograph; Boogie Woogie Landscapes* (1981). *A daughter's geography* (1983). *From okra to greens: A different love story* (1984). *See no evil: prefaces, reviews, & essays, 1974–1983*; reissued as *See No Evil: Prefaces, Essays, & Accounts, 1976–1983* (1984). *Ridin' the moon in Texas: word painting* (1987). *The Love Space Demands* (1991). Other productions: *A Photograph: A Still Life with Shadow / A Photograph: A Study of Cruelty* (1977), revised as *A Photograph: Lovers in Motion* (1979). *Where the Mississippi Meets the Amazon* (with Thulani Nkabinda and Jessica Hagedorn, 1977). *From Okra to Greens* (1978). *Black and White Two-dimensional Planes* (1979). *Spell #7* (1979). *Note:* In addition, many sets of poems have been staged in workshop and small theater or college theater productions.

BIBLIOGRAPHY: Betsko, Kathleen and Rachel Koenig, *Interviews with Contemporary Women Playwrights* (1987). Deshazer, Mary K., "Rejecting Necrophilia" in *Making a Spectacle*, Lynda Hart, ed. (1989). Geis, Deborah, "Distraught Laughter: Monologues in Ntozake Shange's Theater Pieces," in *Feminine Focus: The New Women Playwrights*, Enoch Brater, ed. (1989). Keyssar, Helene, *Feminist Theatre* (1984). *Black Women Writers at Work*, Claudia Tate, ed. (1983). Reference works: *CA 85–88* (1980). *CANR 27* (1989). *CLC*

8 (1978), 25 (1983), 38 (1986). *DLB* 38 (1985). *FC* (1990). *Maj Twent Cent Writers* (1991). *Notable Women in the American Theatre* (1989).

FAHAMISHA PATRICIA BROWN

Gail Sheehy

See AWW *4, 74–75*

Pop psychologist and journalist, S. followed up her best-selling *Passages* (1976) with another popular success. *Pathfinders* (1981), a testament to the American public's need to fit their psyches into a schema, is rife with such generalizations as "What's wrong with me?" is the "archetypal female response." Nonetheless, the book demonstrates S.'s genuine concern for "the female psychology."

Pathfinders revives *Passages'* "Sexual Diamond," describing the gradual divergence of male and female character traits from eighteen to forty and the slow crossover each sex makes thereafter. Subsequently, S. redirected her analysis of the human personality toward politics, aiming at, in her words, an "X-ray of history." *Character: America's Search for Leadership* (1988) concerns the "character" of achievers: the cast includes Al Gore, George Bush, Ronald Reagan, Jesse Jackson, and Gary Hart, examined to substantiate her view on how achievers handle crises and develop. *Character* was followed by a long biography, *The Man Who Changed the World: The Lives of Mikhail S. Gorbachev* (1990). S. describes her journey to Gorbachev's hometown to talk to its residents, her time with the KGB, and her interviews with more than one hundred people. *The Man* received almost universally negative reviews across the political spectrum, with several critics noting the inadequacy of her preparation and her popular psychology approach to the massiveness of her subject. To S.'s credit, however, she charged into a complicated issue and attempted a comprehensive account; her relatively uncritical fascination is what makes her good at what she does—American journalism.

S. returned to the subject with which she seems most comfortable, female psychology, with *The Silent Passage: Menopause* (1992). The book immediately made the best-seller list although some women were critical in their reviews. **Barbara Ehrenreich,** in a review titled "All Aboard the Raging Hormone Express," claims that S.'s description of menopause "drive[s] women to whimper, 'Won't I ever be me anymore?'" Fortunately, as Ehrenreich points out, S. gives plenty of evidence within the book to refute this frightening image. Despite such mixed reviews, S. has received praise for her journalistic excellence; a March 1991 poll in the *Washington Journalism Review* gives her a high rating and she is widely published in newspapers and magazines. S.'s strong journalistic background infuses her pop psychology with a broad appeal and a sense of the drama of world affairs.

BIBLIOGRAPHY: Reference works: *CA* 49–52 (1975). *CANR* 1 (1981), 33 (1991). *Maj Twent Cent Writers* (1991).

Other references: *National Rev.* (11 Feb. 1991). *New Republic* (28 Sept. 1987; 27 May 1991). *NYTBR* (review by B. Ehrenreich, 7 June 1992). *PW* (1 June 1992).

KATHERINE L. KRETLER

Alix Kates Shulman

B. 17 Aug. 1932, Cleveland, Ohio
D. of Dorothy (Davis) and Samuel S. Kates; m. Marcus Klein, 1953, marriage
    dissolved; m. Martin Shulman, 1959; c.: (second marriage) Teddy, Polly

Spiritually, creatively, and professionally influenced by the Russian-born feminist, anarchist, and activist **Emma Goldman,** as well as by the women's liberation movement, S. feels obligated to focus her work primarily on the personal lives and sexual/political struggles of women. Writing as a Jewish-American, a radical feminist, wife, and mother, S. is concerned with the oppressive aspects of growing up as a female in America and with the lives of those considered marginal by society. Within these contexts, S. balances her complementary identities as a writer and a feminist to create intellectual, educational, and inspirational feminist books for children as well as adult novels that examine, as she states, the "relation between the sexes, the organization of society, and most profoundly, the connection between the two." Interested in the social and psychological roots of her characters, S. carefully checks her subjects' feelings against her own, thereby integrating her personal experiences and growth as a feminist with her professional literary career.

S. received an associate's degree from Bradford Junior College in 1951 and a B.A. from Western Reserve University in 1953. Moving to New York City, she briefly pursued graduate study in philosophy at Columbia University (1953–54) and math at New York University (1960–61), while supporting herself as an encyclopedia editor. These personal experiences form the backdrop to her first book, *Bosley on the Number Line* (1970), a children's mathematical fantasy, and *In Every Woman's Life . . .* (1987), a novel in which the protagonist struggles for professional recognition as the only female math instructor at a community college. Yet, S. marks her early research and writings on Goldman, culminating in *Red Emma Speaks: Selected Writings and Speeches by Emma Goldman* (1972), as the inspirational root of her career. She gained from Goldman's example the courage and confidence to write with conviction and to question all authority.

According to Lucy Rosenthal, S.'s first novel, *Memoirs of an Ex–Prom Queen* (1972), "is probably the first important novel to emerge from the Women's Liberation movement." Evoking the transitional years from the late 1950s into the 1960s, *Memoirs* illustrates the ways in which "ideology and social forces" determine the destiny of women: here, that of a beautiful Midwesterner who is at once "a prude and a sexpot; dumb and cunning." This comic novel offers an alternative view of marriage in which the heroine resists the "traditional passive female" role.

Adept at portraying the universal female character involved in a lifelong consciousness-raising process, S. is careful to record women's experiences in connection with historical events, as in *Burning Questions* (1978). Proclaimed as "up to date and desperately timely," this novel affectionately and energetically documents one woman's transformation into a radical feminist who finds fulfillment in her positive experiences with "lesbianism, dialectics, and activism."

On the Stroll (1981), reflecting Emma Goldman's concern for society's outcasts, compassionately presents the interconnected lives of a naive, yet experienced, runaway and an aging, homeless woman, both existing on the social fringes of New York City. Deemed by the reviewer Michelle Leber a feminist novel in the "best and broadest sense," it is a wise and moving story of life on the streets.

Offering what one critic described as "bold new ways of answering the perennial questions about marriage and monogamy," *In Every Woman's Life* richly examines the emotional and social choices women must confront concerning marriage. With insight and empathy, S. examines a major feminist struggle: balancing the desire to nurture one's family with the need for independence and personal growth. A significant chronicler of her times, in addition to her novels S. has published many short stories, articles, and reviews.

OTHER WORKS: *The Traffic in Women and Other Essays* (editor, 1970). *Women's Liberation: A Blueprint for the Future* (contributor, 1970). *Woman in Sexist Society: Studies in Power and Powerlessness*, Vivian Gornick and B. K. Moran, eds. (1971, contributor). Juvenile books: *Awake or Asleep* (1971). *To the Barricades: The Anarchist Life of Emma Goldman* (1971). *Finders Keepers* (1972).

BIBLIOGRAPHY: *Between Women: Biographers, Novelists, Critics, Teachers, and Artists Write about Their Work on Women*, Carol Ascher, et al., eds. (1984). Reference works: *CA* 29–32 (1978). *CLC* 2 (1974), 10 (1979). *SATA* 7 (1975).

Other references: *Booklist* (15 June 1971; 15 June 1987). *Children's Lit. in Education* 17 (1986). *Christianity and Crisis* 47 (28 Sept. 1987). *Commonweal* 94 (21 May 1971). *LJ* (15 June 1971; Aug. 1981). *Newsweek* (1 May 1972). *NYT* (25 April 1972). *NYTBR* (23 April 1972; 26 March 1978; 31 May 1987). *Saturday Rev.* (20 May 1972).

AMY HOLBROOK

Carolyn Sidlosky. *See Carolyn Forché*

Leslie Marmon Silko

See AWW 4, 81–83

Native American novelist, poet, essayist, and short-story writer, S. was raised in Old Laguna, New Mexico. The Spaniards had founded a mission there early in the eighteenth century, but old Laguna had been formed centuries earlier by cattle-keeping Pueblos, successfully repelling raids by the Navajos and the Apaches. S.'s heritage is complicated: her great-grandfather was Caucasian, while her mother was a mixed-breed Plains Indian; she also has Mexican ancestors. S. uses the heritage as a source of strength: "I suppose at the core of my writing is the attempt to identify what it is to be a half-breed or mixed blooded person; what it is to grow up neither white nor fully traditional Indian." She asserts, however, that "what I know is Laguna. This place I am from is everything I am as a writer and human being." S. draws from the oral traditions and folklore of her heritage to enrich her work and to relate Native American moral codes, values, and experiences. She insists that storytelling is integral to the oral tradition in order to store knowledge, and her themes include pride in transmitting an untouched heritage to scholars, aware that hers is a culture threatened with extinction. She recounts in her short stories and poems what happens when a way of life that has existed for centuries rapidly undergoes cataclysmic and brutal changes with the coming of the Anglos. Community and tribal life break down under the pressure of external conflicts, the advent of reservation life, and the introduction of English-based educational schools. She insightfully interprets her people's plight—disease, wars, broken treaties, relocation, alcoholism, promiscuity—but her characters are seldom embittered or defeated. Instead they cope with adversity, using survival tactics learned from their past to enrich and strengthen their resolution to triumph in spite of a harsh environment or Caucasian society abuse. For S., literature is an extension of an oral tradition based on the power of the word to maintain a sense of a Native American tribal and community culture. Although nostalgia and a sense of loss haunt her stories, they frequently end on an optimistic hope for a better future where diverse ethnic groups have learned respect for each other's unique life-styles.

S.'s first published story, "The Man to Send Rain Clouds" (1969) re-counts an actual event of an old man found dead and given a traditional Native American burial. Although the local priest sees this as heresy, he nonetheless wisely cooperates by sprinkling holy water on the corpse when Grandpa's relatives tell him that the water is necessary so that the old man would not be thirsty, and through some form of sympathetic magic "could send them big thunderclouds."

"Tony's Story" (1981), also a fictionalization of an actual event, describes the reasons for an embittered war veteran's killing of a racist state patrol-man. *Ceremony* (1977), the first full-length novel published by a Native American woman, also uses a World War II veteran in acute physical and emotional straits, managing to survive by reestablishing contact with his Native cultural roots. S. explained that the novel "is essentially about the powers inherent in the process of storytelling. . . . The chanting or telling of ancient stories to effect certain cures or protest from illness and harm have always been a part of the Pueblo's curing ceremonies."

There is strong moral connection between S.'s artistic delight in craft-ing a story and the therapeutic functional purpose she hopes it will serve in the Native American community. In both *Ceremony* and the aptly titled *Storyteller* (1981), which also includes poems and photographs as well as short stories, she sketches realistically sympathetic people living in har-mony with animals and with the forces of nature. "Lullaby" (1974), in-cluded in *The Best American Short Stories* (1975) and *Two Hundred Years of Great American Short Stories* (1975), shows the tough, devoted perseverance of an old woman, Ayah, sitting wrapped in a blanket with her husband, Chato, their backs against a rock as a storm beats down. Ayah sings a lullaby as the story ends: "The earth is your mother, she holds you. The sky is your father, he protects you. Sleep, sleep. Rainbow is your sister, she loves you. The winds are your brothers, they sing to you. Sleep, sleep. We are together always." Thus, S. draws upon religious and philo-sophic ideas from her Native American oral and cultural storytelling traditions to create poignant artistic creations.

One of S.'s best critics, Per Seyerstedt, believes that her achievement is to have "raised the life and problems of a minority to the level of general significance." *The Delicacy and Strength of Lace: Letters between Leslie Marmon Silko and James Wright* (1985) chronicles an eighteen-month ex-change of correspondence and friendship-through-the-mail; the letters interpret both writers' concept of brotherly love, sensitivity to nature's beauty, and the clarity of their courageous voices. S.'s sensitivity and humanity are displayed through language always rich, yet controlled and finely tuned, reminding us that the persistent drums of tradition reverberating down the generations powerfully shape lives today.

S.'s awards and honors include a grant from the National Endowment for the Arts and a poetry award from *Chicago Review*, both in 1974, the Pushcart Prize for poetry in 1977, and a Catherine T. MacArthur Foundation grant in 1983. She has written screenplays for public television and has taught at the University of New Mexico-Albuquerque and the University of Arizona. Her second novel, *Almanac of the Dead*, appeared in 1991.

OTHER WORKS: "Lullaby," in *The Ethnic American Woman: Problems, Protests, Lifestyle*, Edith Blicksilver, ed. (1978). "Gallup, New Mexico—Indian Capital of the World," et al., in *The Third Woman: Minority Women Writers of the United States*, Dexter Fisher, ed. (1980).

BIBLIOGRAPHY: Reference works: *CA* 115 (1985), 122 (1988), *CLC* 23 (1983). *Contemp. Novelists* (1986). *Contemp. Poets* (1985). *Encyc. of Frontier and Western Fiction* (1983). *FC* (1990).

Other references: *Amer. Indian Q.* (Winter 1977–78). *Amer. Studies in Scandinavia* 13 (1981). *Harper's* (June 1977). *LATBR* (4 Jan. 1987). *MELUS* (Winter 1978, Summer 1981). *Ms.* (July 1981). *New Leader* (6 June 1977). *Newsweek* (4 July 1977). *NYT* (25 May 1981). *NYTBR* (12 June 1977). *Prairie Schooner* (Winter 1977–78). *Saturday Rev.* (May 1981). *Southwest Rev.* (Spring 1979). *Time* (8 Aug. 1983). *Wash. Post Book World* (24 April 1977).

EDITH BLICKSILVER

Kate Simon

B. *Kaila Grobsmith, 5 Dec. 1912, Warsaw, Poland; d. 4 Feb. 1990, New York City*
D. *of Lina (Babicz) and Jacob Grobsmith; m. Robert Simon, 1947, div. 1960; c.: Alexandra, d. 1954*

S.'s passionate and daring life provided excellent material for her many popular travel books and the memoirs she produced in old age. Born in the Jewish section of Warsaw, she emigrated to New York with her family at age four and grew up in working-class neighborhoods in the city, where she excelled in the public schools and displayed unusual musical talent. Holding a series of odd jobs, she worked her way through the demanding James Monroe High School and Hunter College (B.A. 1935). A common-law marriage to Dr. Stanley Goldman ended with his death in 1942, leaving S. to support herself and their daughter, Alexandra, by working at various editorial and reviewing jobs.

After her marriage to Robert Simon, which apparently freed her from financial constraints, S. began to travel extensively throughout Europe and Mexico. She published her first book, *New York Places and Pleasures: An Uncommon Guidebook*, in 1959. Hailed as a landmark in the travel genre, it went through four revisions and sparked a successful career in travel writing. S. went on to produce guides to Mexico City, Paris, London, Rome, Italy, and England—all informed by her artistic tastes and graceful prose—as well as the more historically focused *Fifth Avenue: A Very Social History* (1978) and *A Renaissance Tapestry: The Gonzaga of Mantua* (1988).

Acclaimed as these works are, it is S.'s memoirs that distinguish her as more than an elegant and cosmopolitan stylist. *Bronx Primitive: Portraits in a Childhood* (1982) shocked readers with its revelation of intense emotional conflict and sexual abuse within her family. S. recounts the strong influence of her mother, who built her own business as a corset maker and encouraged her daughter to acquire an education and the means to be self-supporting. She describes her defiance of her shoemaker father, who insisted she leave high school to become a concert pianist and who, S. believed, tolerated the sexual abuse by relatives and acquaintances to which she was subjected from early adolescence. Leaving her family in her early teens, S. eagerly absorbed the influence of leftist politics, antibourgeois sentiment, artistic values, and free love among the 1920s New York City avant-garde. *A Wider World: Portraits in an Adolescence* (1986) reveals, however, that this life was scarcely romantic: S. was again the victim of sexual predators (sometimes her teachers) and was often desperately poor. She describes shabby lodgings and meager jobs, illegal abortions, and above all, her struggle to nourish her growing aesthetic and intellectual sensibilities.

The posthumously published *Etchings in an Hourglass* (1990) is the most digressive of her books, and also the most bitter and intimate. Here she confronts her grief and anger at the early deaths of Goldman and of her only child, and contemplates a long life filled with as much doubt as comfort: "At seventeen I was so enamored of life . . . that I promised myself I would experience everything, stipulating no qualities good or bad, and it has pretty much all happened. Little more than I knew at seventeen do I surely know who I am at seventy-five." S.'s work documents, through the consciousness of a complex and brave woman, the arduous process of living fully.

Also widely published in such magazines as *Harper's, Holiday*, the *National Geographic, Saturday Review*, and *Vogue*, S. received awards of honor from Hunter College and the English Speaking Union. The National Book Critics Circle listed *Bronx Primitive* as one of the most distinguished books published in 1982.

OTHER WORKS: *New York* (photographs by Andrea Feininger, 1964). *Mexico: Places and Pleasures* (1965, 3rd ed. 1979, rpt. 1984). *Kate Simon's Paris: Places and Pleasures* (1967). *Kate Simon's London: Places and Pleasures* (1968). *Italy: The Places in between* (1972). *England's Green and Pleasant Land* (1974).

BIBLIOGRAPHY: Reference works: *CA* 127 (1989), 130 (obituary, 1990). *Maj Twent Cent Writers* (1991).

Other references: *Feminist Studies* 17 (Spring 1991). *LA Times* (4 May 1982). *Ms.* (June 1982, July 1986). *NYT* (5 Feb. 1990, obituary). *NYTBR* (19 Aug. 1990). *PW* (14 May 1982). *Time* (14 July 1967; 19 April 1982; 24 Feb. 1986).

ELIZABETH SHOSTAK

Jo Sinclair. *See Ruth Seid*

Lee Smith

B. 1 Nov. 1944, Grundy, Virginia
D. of Virginia (Marshall) and Ernest Lee Smith; m. James E. Seay, 1967; m. Hal
Crowther, 1985; c.: Josh, Page

As a child, S. was convinced she was going to be a writer and chose to attend Hollins College because it offered an M.F.A. in creative writing. She took writing courses throughout college, and found that they taught her elements of a technique that helped her mature as a writer; two teachers, Louis D. Rubin and R. W. Dillard, were especially important to her. She graduated with a B.A. in 1967 and in that year the novel she wrote in college, *The Last Day the Dogbushes Bloomed* (1968), won a Book-of-the-Month Club Writing Fellowship.

S. calls herself a storyteller, and her stories range from humorous short stories to novels that seek to understand the artist's search for a self. Some of her characters, like Susan, the narrator of *The Last Day the Dogbushes Bloomed,* watch the world around them and try to transform it into something beautiful. Others, like Crystal of *Black Mountain Breakdown* (1981), cannot accept themselves and escape into a fantasy world.

Something in the Wind (1971), *Fancy Strut* (1973), *Black Mountain Breakdown* (1981), and *Cakewalk* (1981) all received positive reviews, and critics saw in S. a writer who could combine comic elements with a skilled narrative technique. The books did not sell well, however.

With *Oral History* (1983) S.'s acceptance by reviewers was translated into acceptance by the reading public, and the book, compared by critics to Faulkner's work, was the first to make a profit for her. While S. deprecates the comparison with Faulkner, the book is a tightly constructed examination of the Old and the New South for the benefit of Jennifer, a young college student who has returned to the Virginia mountains to find her roots. S. interweaves the history of Appalachia with the legends, songs, and folktales of the region in a way that makes the mountain people live again.

In *Family Linen* (1985) S. uncovers a family secret, the murder of Jewell Rife by his wife, Elizabeth Bird Hess, the family matriarch who is dying while all her children try to come to terms with her and with their lives.

Viewed from the perspective of several family members, the discovery of the secret murder counters the journal that Elizabeth Bird herself leaves to carry on the myth of her devotion to family and duty. Written in the orotund style of the Victorian South, the journal becomes a mockery when contrasted with the lives of Elizabeth's children and when set beside the murder she has hidden for almost half a century.

With *Fair and Tender Ladies* (1988) S. achieved real popularity as a teller of a wonderful story. The novel, written in the epistolary form, chronicles the life of Ivy Rowe and again reveals S.'s deep affection for the mountains of Virginia and for the mountain people who have lived, suffered, and endured. Like many of S.'s narrators, Ivy Rowe is chiefly an observer, and her letters vividly depict life in Sugar Fork, where her parents' homestead is, and in the two neighboring towns to which her hard life takes her. Throughout her long life, Ivy Rowe reveals her passions, secrets, hopes, and dreams to a long list of correspondents, but chiefly to her sister Silvaney, who has lived most of her life in an asylum and whom Ivy keeps alive through her letters. Here S. again reveals the truth behind the myths of Southern womanhood, and the reality is far more solid and enduring than the fantasy.

In *Me and My Baby View the Eclipse* (1990), a collection of stories, S. highlights the daydreams of average Southerners and weaves epiphany and loss in the stories of breakdowns, divorces, and death. The conflict is often between those like Rose Dee in "Tongues of Fire" who insist on keeping up appearance at all costs, and those like her daughter who learn to accept the tragedies in their lives and go on living. The stories are full of humor, empathy, and a sense of the irony of being a Southerner in the twentieth century. *The Devil's Dream* (1992) is a characteristic blend of Virginia history and wry and loving accounts of family held together by women. Moving back from Nashville to the roots of country music in the lives of the mountain people, the novel again demonstrates S.'s ability as a storyteller. Like generations of Southern writers before her S. has a sense of place, an ear for language, and a vision of a South that endures.

BIBLIOGRAPHY: Reference works: *CA* 114 (1985), 119 (1987). *CLC* 25 (1983). *DLBY* (1983). *FC* (1990).

Other references: *NYTBR* (19 July 1992). [New Orleans] *Times-Picayune* (11 March 1990; 12 July 1992). *Southern Q.* 5 (Fall 1983).

MARY A. MCCAY

Rosamond Smith. *See Joyce Carol Oates*

Mara Solwoska. *See Marilyn French*

Cathy Song

B. 1955, Honolulu, Hawaii; m. Douglas Davenport; two children

The selection in 1982 of S.'s *Picture Bride* (1983) as the winning manu-script in the Yale Series of Younger Poets competition marked the young poet's rather sudden literary emergence. In a review of *Picture Bride*, Shirley Geok-lin Lim hails S. as "a major figure on the Asian American literary scene." S. received her B.A. from Wellesley College (1977) and an M.F.A. from Boston University's creative writing program (1981).

In many of the poems in *Picture Bride*, S. writes about her family's history and interrelationships. In the title poem she imagines her grand-mother, joined to a stranger through a prearranged marriage, leaving home to meet her husband for the first time. Insightful and sensitive in capturing her evolving relationship with her mother, S. intimates in sev-eral poems that she must escape her mother's presence, but eventually realizes that what she draws from her mother is vital to her own identity. "When I stretch a canvas / to paint the clouds, it is your spine that declares itself."

The poems of *Picture Bride*, though driven by the specific details of S.'s past, also help to illuminate the Asian-American experience in general. In "Lost Sister," about a Chinese-American who finds herself alienated from both East and West, and in her unflinching portrayal of Chinatowns, S.

addresses the difficult realities faced by Asian-American immigrants. S. has expressed concern that critics encountering her acute cultural awareness may marginalize her work. Her strengths as a poet—startlingly clear description, lines quietly unfolding a story in short breaths, images running threadlike throughout a poem, weaving a unified work—stand independent of her Asian themes.

S. further explores her past in *Frameless Windows, Squares of Light* (1988), her second volume of verse. These poems, writes S., focus on "the mind . . . tunneling into memory, released by imagination. Out of that depth, squares of light form, like windows you pass at night." In these new poems, S. returns to many of the themes and scenarios introduced in *Picture Bride*. Also familiar are her characteristic straightforward diction and her strong sense of closure. "A Small Light" captures with rhythmic repetition the feel of a distant memory. In "A Child's Painting" S. reaffirms her ability to transform commonplace events into beautiful portraits.

In addition to her poetry, S. has edited (with Juliet Kono) *Sister Stew* (1991), an anthology of writings by Asian-American women. Her poems have also appeared in several anthologies and in such periodicals as *Asian-Pacific Literature, Hawaii Review, Poetry,* and *Seneca Review.*

BIBLIOGRAPHY: Cheung, King-Kok, *Asian-American Literature* (1988). Chock, Eric, *Talk Story: An Anthology of Hawaii's Local Writers* (1978).

Other references: *International Examiner* (2 May 1984). *MELUS* (Fall 1983, Spring 1988). *WRB* (Oct. 1988).

JEROME CHOU

Susan Sontag

See AWW 4, 127–29

S. has always insisted she is a fiction writer, labeling her essays a type of fiction and recalling that her first book was a novel. In most of her work in the 1970s and 1980s, however, S. investigated modes of criticism; her subjects have been European writers, thinkers, and filmmakers, photography, pornography, and the problems with assigning metaphorical meanings to epidemic illnesses. Throughout, S. has insisted that her work and the work of her models be allowed to stand on their own as art, to maintain their aesthetic, not decimated by interpretation: "Criticism in all the arts . . . treats the work of art as a statement being made in the form of a work of art."

In *Under the Sign of Saturn* (1980), which S. has described as "seven portraits in consciousness," she explores how modernism has become "the dominant tradition of high literary culture instead of its subversion" through essays on artists who are also her models, particularly Walter Benjamin, Paul Goodman, Antonin Artaud, Roland Barthes, and Elias Canetti. Making male European intellectuals not only available but relevant in the United States, both in these essays and in her Artaud collection (1976) and *A Barthes Reader* (1982), S. has disappointed some of the feminist community because of her lack of interest in feminist scholarship. Although she has been portrayed as elitist and attached to an outmoded canon, S.'s vision includes all things of intellectual value, from the moralism of high modernism to pop culture. But S. insists on aesthetic value, separates high culture from low culture, and judges all art forms independently of their popularity. Averse to labels and stereotypes, S. says her writing is "based on freedom and self-revelation."

In 1982, S. further showed her individualism when she spoke against martial law in Poland at Town Hall in New York City, calling communism a successful variant of fascism. She has befriended artists from the former Eastern bloc and was working into 1988 on an unpublished novel, "The Western Half," about Polish and Soviet emigrés in Paris, New York, and Midwest academe.

In other projects, S. has continued to look toward Europe for her subjects. Her fourth film, *Unguided Tour* (1983), from the short story of the same title, tells of a relationship that is fragmenting as the couple tours the decaying ruins of Italy. In *Sarah* (1988), a documentary film about Sarah Bernhardt, S. narrates the voice of the actress. She has directed three plays: *As You Desire Me* by Luigi Pirandello, whom she calls "the most influential playwright of the twentieth century," ran in Italy (1979–81); *Jacques and His Master* by Milan Kundera played at the American Repertory Theater in Cambridge, Massachusetts (1985); she directed Samuel Beckett's *Waiting for Godot* in Sarajevo in 1993 during the Serbian seige of the city. In addition to essays on dance, Dutch painting, and Robert Mapplethorpe, S. collaborated with Cesare Colombo on *Italy: One Hundred Years of Photography* (1988), and included ten of her poems, collectively entitled "In Memory of Their Feeling," in a catalog for a London exhibition entitled *Cage, Cunningham, and John: Dancers on a Plane* (1989).

In *AIDS and Its Metaphors* (1988), S. examines the language and interpretation surrounding the disease and argues against the degradation and guilt that AIDS patients suffer due to ill-chosen metaphors. As Angela McRobbie has suggested, however, in attempting to view this complex social phenomenon more objectively, S. may "evade the extent to which cultural meanings and metaphors about AIDS are inextricably connected with the politics of AIDS." D. A. Miller argues that despite her clear reasoning and erudition, S.'s language sometimes ratifies homophobic presumptions as well as prejudice against all AIDS sufferers, and silences the victims themselves.

"The Way We Live Now" (1986), one of S.'s two short stories published in *The New Yorker*, tells the story of a dying AIDS patient and was included in the anthology *The Best American Stories of the Eighties* (1991). In "Pilgrimage" (1987), a rare autobiographical retrospective piece, the voice of the adult narrates the teenage S.'s meeting with Thomas Mann, one of her early heroes. With *A Susan Sontag Reader* (1982), S. said she felt a closure to one part of her career, although this was not evident until the publication of her third novel *The Volcano Lover* (1992).

S. has called that book "a turning point" and plans now to concentrate on fiction. Subtitled "A Romance," *The Volcano Lover* tells the story of Sir William Hamilton, the "Cavaliere," his second wife Emma, and her lover, Lord Horatio Nelson. The story takes place in eighteenth-century Naples, Hamilton's diplomatic outpost, where he pursues his two passions, Mount Vesuvius and art collecting. By far S.'s best novel, this historical narrative speaking in many voices, including the author's, fully conceives minor characters and events as well as major ones. "If there's been a change in my views over the years, it's that I've had to give the historicist approach a more central role in my reaction to things," S. says. Her style includes aphorisms, fragmentation, and layers of erotic, immediate, moral, and cool tones: every page reflects her learning and knowledge.

As PEN's American Center President (1987–89), S. joined a protest at an international conference in Seoul, South Korea, against that government's treatment of writers and publishers. Among her other achievements and awards, she is a member of the American Academy and Institute of Arts and Letters. In 1984 the French government named her an Officier des Arts et des Lettres. In 1990 she was granted a five-year fellowship from the MacArthur Foundation.

BIBLIOGRAPHY: Bruss, Elizabeth, *Beautiful Theories* (1982). Sayres, Sohnya, *The Elegiac Modernist* (1990). Reference works: *Benet's* (1991). *CANR* 25 (1988). *Contemp. Novelists* (1986). *DLB* 67 (1985). *FC* (1990).

Other references: *Am. Lit. Hist.* 1:3 (Fall 1989). *Feminist Rev.* 38 (Summer 1991, article by A. McRobbie). *J.Am.St.* 24:1 (April 1990). *Midwest Q.* 29:2 (Winter 1988). *Nat. Rev.* (31 Aug. 1992). *New Republic* (7, 14 Sept. 1992). *NYTBR* (24 Oct. 1982; 9 Aug. 1992; 24 Oct. 1992). *NYTMag* (2 Aug. 1992). *October* 49 (Summer 1989, article by D. M. Miller). *Performing Arts J.* 9:1 (interview, 1985). *Sat. Rev.* 55:39 (Oct. 1972). *Sewanee Rev.* 92 (Fall 1984). *Time* (24 Oct. 1988). *VV Lit. Supp.* (Nov. 1990).

ANDREW J. SCHIAVONI

Elizabeth Spencer

See AWW 4, 139–41

S. continues to expand her vision of life both in terms of setting and ideas. Early identified as a Southern writer influenced by William Faulkner and **Eudora Welty** because of the regional themes and precise local details in her first three novels, she has kept on challenging her original identity both geographically and spiritually. Like many women writers trained by men she remains intensely aware of the importance of craft, and she has created as many heroes as heroines. She has also learned over the years, however, to identify and articulate the human problems that women's lives often exemplify more clearly than men's.

Critics distressed by the power of the manipulative American mother who arranges an Italian marriage for her brain-damaged daughter in S.'s most popular novel, *The Light in the Piazza* (1960),

saw S. following the international theme of Henry James. Few acknowledged the ironic force of the idea that many men might prefer
a pretty obedient woman with the mind of a ten-year-old. *Knights and
Dragons* (1965), also set in Italy, reflects a recurrent theme in S.'s
work: the tension between a woman's need for independence and
her social conditioning and psychological need to live for others.
Perhaps because critics considered this work too allegorical S.'s next
two novels, *No Place for an Angel* (1967) and *The Snare* (1972) are rich
in realistic detail. Both attempt to record the demoralized affluent
life of post–World War II America and each features a strong heroine who refuses to connect meaning in life with men.

The Stories of Elizabeth Spencer (1981; reprint 1983), thirty-three
stories written over more than thirty years, appeared with Eudora
Welty's foreword paying tribute to S.'s seriousness. Asked in a 1980
interview about recurrent themes in her writing, S. remarked that
many stories were "about liberation and the regret you have when
you liberate yourself." Such ambivalence might well isolate S. from
more ideological feminists but links her with the divided self that
remains a valued part of American literary tradition. *Jack of Dia-
monds* (1988), a shorter collection of stories that includes two
O. Henry Award winners, reveals S. to be one of our most skillful
literary artisans.

In *The Salt Line* (1983) S. returned to the novel to create a more
complex social reality. Here the academic upheavals of the 1960s and
the natural disaster of a hurricane help shape her characters' needs.
Once again using the South as a convincing background she explores
the problematic nature of marriage. *The Night Travellers* (1991), her
most political work to date, uses the war in Vietnam as a focus for
generational conflict. Beginning in the traditional South, perhaps
reflecting her personal growth toward a cosmopolitan conscience, S.
carries her characters to Canada and the Mid-Atlantic states and
finally even to Vietnam. Again, a mother-daughter relationship becomes the most unforgettable aspect of this record of social upheaval.

S. returned to the South from Canada in 1986 to teach at the
University of North Carolina in Chapel Hill. She is a writer who
continues to grow, and who struggles to give her readers more than
just a slice of life or a neat ideology. Although her effort to create
mythology and enhance themes may make her work seem old-fashioned, the precision of her observations, the subtlety of her style, and

the diversity of backgrounds she evokes should increase the number of her readers.

OTHER WORKS: *Marilee: Three Stories* (1987). *On the Gulf* (1991).

BIBLIOGRAPHY: Barge, Laura, "An Elizabeth Spencer Checklist, 1948 to 1976," *Mississippi Q.* 29 (Fall 1976). Prenshaw, Peggy Whitman, *Elizabeth Spencer* (1985); *Conversations with Elizabeth Spencer* (editor, 1991). Reference works: *CANR* 32 (1990). *CLC* 22 (1982). *DLB* 6 (1980).

EUGENIA KALEDIN

Gloria Steinem

B. 25 March 1934, Toledo, Ohio
D. of Ruth (Nuneviller) and Leo Steinem

As a child, S. moved around from city to city in a house trailer while her father Leo, who "never wore a hat and never had a job" looked for work. Her parents divorced when she was ten and S. became the sole caretaker of her mentally ill mother. As a teenager, S. was an avid reader who dreamed of "dancing [her] way out of Toledo," not of following in the footsteps of her pioneer feminist grandmother, Pauline Steinem, who was president of the Ohio Women's Suffrage Association and one of two United States representatives to the 1908 International Council of Women.

In her teens, S. worked part-time dancing for ten dollars a night at conventions. She left Toledo during her senior year in high school and moved to Washington, DC, to live with her older sister. Winning an academic scholarship to Smith College, she graduated with a B.A. in government, Phi Beta Kappa and magna cum laude (1956). Travel in southern India after graduation as a Chester Bowles Asian Fellow helped her develop a lifelong understanding and empathy for oppressed peoples and started her writing career freelancing for Indian newspapers. In India, she joined a group called the Radical Humanists and worked as part of a peacemaking team during the caste riots. Her first monograph, *The Thousand Indias*, a guidebook for the government in New Delhi, appeared in 1957. When S. returned to the United States in 1958, filled with an "enormous sense of urgency about the contrast between wealth and poverty," she became the codirector of the controversial Independent Research Service, an offshoot of the National Student Association.

S. moved to New York in 1960 to establish herself as a journalist. Her first job was as a writer of photo captions and celebrity liaison for *Help!*, a political satire magazine. In 1962, her first bylined article appeared in *Esquire*, a study of the contraceptive revolution called "The Moral Disarmament of Betty Co-ed." Her second monograph, *The Beach Book* (1963), a coffee-table semibook filled with excerpts from literature about beaches, featured suggestions of things to do while sunbathing, beach fantasies, and a foil jacket that could double as a sun reflector.

"I Was a Playboy Bunny," written in 1963 for *Show* magazine, helped to launch S.'s freelance writing career and celebrity status by bringing her assignments on fashion, culture, celebrities, and books from such mass-circulation magazines as *Glamour*, *McCall's*, and *Look* and from the *New York Times*. The essay, in the form of a diary, recounts S.'s undercover experiences working in the New York Playboy Club, waiting on tables with Kleenex-stuffed bosoms. It is full of the beginnings of her feminist consciousness, the recognition of power differences, and illustrations of indignities suffered by the body. Looking back, S. refers to this work as "schizophrenic." In 1968, she began taking on more serious writing assignments, becoming a cofounder, contributing editor, and political columnist for *New York* magazine. After attending a 1969 hearing on illegal abortions, organized by the radical feminist group Redstockings, S. wrote "After Black Power, Women's Liberation," her first openly feminist essay, which won her the Penney-Missouri Journalism Award. Having come to believe that only a magazine controlled by women would advance women's issues, in 1972 S. founded *Ms.*, the first feminist mass-circulation magazine.

S.'s first major collection of articles, essays, and diary entries, *Outrageous Acts and Everyday Rebellions* (1983), chronicles her twenty-year writing journey from prefeminist pretty "girl reporter," who never thought her work was good enough, to feminist editor of *Ms.* and spokeswoman-icon of American women's liberation. The collection begins with "I Was a Playboy Bunny," which was adapted for an ABC television movie, "A Bunny's Tale," in 1985.

Outrageous Acts also includes pieces on politicking with McGovern, McCarthy, Kennedy, King, and Chavez, the contradictory messages of the right-wing, the institution of marriage, the media, and the comical "If Men Could Menstruate." S. shows us where feminism has been and encourages women to network, find their sisters, and perform outrageous acts in order to advance the liberation of women and other powerless groups. Her personal journey to feminism is accompanied by empathic sketches of a diverse group of notable women that includes Marilyn Monroe, Jackie Onassis, **Alice Walker,** Pat Nixon, and Linda (Lovelace) Marchiano, and a moving tribute to S.'s mother in "Ruth's Song." Like herself, the women S. profiles are both victims and survivors, sexual objects and feminist protagonists.

S.'s biography of Marilyn Monroe, *Marilyn: Norma Jean* (1986), expands on her profiles of emblematic women. In a series of essays S. provides a feminist and psychological portrait of a multidimensional sex goddess who is a prisoner of her neglected childhood and of an age characterized by sexual exploitation. S. explores her own identification with the actress, remembering that as a teenager in 1953 she walked out of *Gentlemen Prefer Blondes* in embarrassment at the "whispering, simpering, big-breasted child-woman" who dared to be just as "vulnerable and unconfident" as she was. Focusing on the private, inner life of Norma Jean, not the mythical, public Marilyn Monroe, S.'s sensitive portrayal weaves together the story of a neglected, abused, unparented child with a vulnerable woman, an "interchangeable pretty girl," living behind a mask of sexuality, struggling for independence, wanting only to please others, but longing to be taken seriously.

Revolution from Within: A Book of Self-esteem (1992) is also a modern parable of a woman whose image of herself is very distant from the image others had of her. S. employs her autobiographical account of the search for identity and self-worth to help explore internal barriers to women's equality. She takes the reader from a rat-infested Toledo home where she is her mentally ill mother's caretaker to a television studio where her "impostor" self has become the mother of a movement. While supporting her argument that inner strength and self-esteem are the bases of liberation with extensive summaries of psychological research and exegeses of *Jane Eyre* and *Wuthering Heights,* she also makes central the voices of diverse people: a lesbian, a man-junkie, a Cherokee Indian, and others whose comparable journeys of personal growth are linked to social activism. She associates women's loss of self-esteem with such factors as stereotypical gender roles, a preoccupation with romantic love, and male-imposed standards of female beauty. S. encourages both men and women to find their inner child, un-learn, reparent themselves, and imagine a future self in order to begin their own positive personal and social change.

S. was chosen by the *World Almanac* as one of the Twenty-five Most Influential Women in America for nine consecutive years and has received the Front Page, Clarion, and ACLU Bill of Rights awards, the United Nation's Ceres Medal, and the first Doctorate of Human Justice awarded by Simmons College (1973). In 1978, she studied the impact of feminism on the premises of political theory as a Woodrow Wilson Scholar at the Smithsonian Institution. Arguing that "we teach what we need to learn and write what we need to know," she has been credited with inventing the phrase "reproductive freedom" and popularizing the usage of "Ms." to address women. S. continues to travel as a lecturer and feminist organizer and to work for the movement as consulting editor at *Ms.* and as a board member or advisor to the Ms. Foundation for Women, the National Women's Political Caucus, Voters for Choice, Women's Action Alliance, and the Coalition of Labor Union Women.

OTHER WORKS: Introductions to G. Chester, *Wonder Woman* (1972); Marlo Thomas, *Free to Be . . . You and Me* (1974); Suzanne Levine and Harriet Lyons, eds., *The Decade of Women: A Ms. History of the Seventies in Words and Pictures* (1980); Jean Shinoda Bolan, *Goddesses in Everywoman: A New Psychology of Women* (1984); Marilyn Waring, *If Women Counted: A New Feminist Economics* (1988).

BIBLIOGRAPHY: Cohen, Marcia, *The Sisterhood: The Inside Story of the Women's Movement and the Leaders Who Made It Happen* (1988). Davis, Flora, *Moving the Mountain: The Women's Movement in America since 1960* (1991). Diamonstein, Barbalee, *Open Secrets: Ninety-Four Women in Touch with Our Time* (1970). Echols, Alice, *Daring to Be Bad: Radical Feminism in America, 1967–1975* (1989). Gilbert, Lynn, and Gaylen Moore, *Particular Passions: Talks with Women Who Have Shaped Our Times* (1981). Henry, Sondra, and Emily Taitz, *One Woman's Power: A Biography of Gloria Steinem* (juvenile, includes afterword by S., 1987). Reference works: *CANR* 28 (1990). *CLC* 63

(1991). *Encyc. of Tw Cent Journalists* (1986). *CBY* (1988). *FC* (1990). *Maj Twent Cent Writers* (1991).

Other references: *Boston Globe* (17 Jan. 1973; 15 Jan. 1992; 22 Jan. 1992). *Chicago Tribune* (20 Jan. 1992; 26 Jan. 1992). *LA Times* (3 Feb. 1992). *NYT* (11 Dec. 1984). *NYTBR* (21 Dec. 1986; 2 Feb. 1992). *Newsweek* (16 Aug. 1971). *Time* (20 Jan. 1992; 9 March 1992). *TLS* (8 June 1984). *Wall Street J.* (6 March 1992). *Wash. Post* (9 Oct. 1983; 12 Jan. 1992; 1 Feb. 1992; 23 Feb. 1992). *WRB* (Dec. 1983, June 1992).

MELISSA KESLER GILBERT

Ruth Stone

B. 28 June 1915, Roanoke, Virginia
D. of Ruth (Ferguson) and Roger McDowell Perkins; m. Walter B. Stone (d.
   1960); c.: Marcia, Phoebe, Blue-Jay Abigail

S. is a poet, born in Virginia and raised in Indianapolis. She attended the University of Illinois and received her B.A. from Harvard University. The author of five books of poetry, she has also taught at universities across the country.

S.'s poems are fresh and original, quirky and funny. Gaiety and loneliness are all mixed up together and self-pity does not stand a chance. The poems are marked throughout by a strong sense of rhythm that never loses touch with the first primitive body rhythms, "the natural singing mind" she absorbed from her parents as a child. Her mother taught her poems by heart, and by the time she was two both the cadence of the language and the music of poetry and forms had become part of her body. Her father was a musician; hearing him play drums at home was another way she took in rhythms by ear at an early age. By the time she was six S. was writing poems and ballads with a strong, uninhibited attachment to form. This is particularly evident in her first book, *In an Iridescent Time* (1951). In her later books, though the feeling for rhythm remains, the poems become more elastic and are less often strictly rhymed.

S.'s life and work are closely bound together. Her second book, *Topography* (1970), begins with a strong rhymed love poem, "Dream of Light and Shade," a poem of young marriage, enchantment, and stability. "I watch him sleep, dreaming of how to defend / his inert form." But soon death, with a horrible abruptness, makes a mockery of normality and order. After the suicide of her husband the book becomes heavier, tilted and "chaotic with necessary pain" ("The Plan").

It is in *Topography* that S. begins the long letter to her deceased husband that in a sense becomes the body of the rest of her work. Sometimes, as in "Tenacity," he is addressed directly: "I sit for hours at the window / preparing a letter; you are coming toward me." At other times, as in the poem "Salt" ("I saw the long hair roots, / The long arms and the boots / of despair"), it is guilt and the impossibility of reconciliation that keep the wound open and drive the poet.

In an interview with Robert Bradley, S. says, "What is this living in the present? It seems your past drags behind you like a great huge snake or worm. . . . You can't help but live in your past." But S.'s particular past makes her present very vivid, intense with the work of seeing for two. Her vision, never subdued and dutiful, is shot through with a respect for the crazy perverse fertility of life.

The poses and props of "the literary life" hold no attraction for her and her poems work hard to demystify poetry. In her third book, *Cheap* (1972), the reader often glimpses the underbelly of life. In "Codicil" an ornithologist's widow recounts trips with her husband: "Yes, / he would send her up a tree / And when she faltered he would shout, / 'Put it [the egg] in your mouth. Put it in your mouth.' / It was nasty, she said." These glimpses are seldom "pretty" or decorative but they speak with their own bold vitality. The events of her life have made S. impatient with convention. She shrugs off distinctions between morbidity and fertility and chooses instead to walk, grieving fiercely, along the messy borders where decay and regeneration overlap ("Overlapping Edges").

S.'s development, with its wild quirky ups, downs, and turns, is exhilarating to follow. The pure girlish delight of her first book's title poem, "In an Iridescent Time," surfaces again in an odd, funny, matronly form in the title poem of *Second Hand Coat* (1987). In this book, and particularly in her 1991 book, the exuberant, irreverent *Who Is the Widow's Muse?*, S.'s strong survivor's instinct has brought her through. Confronting late middle age with buoyancy, she speaks in a rich, original voice of courage that makes you want to be near her. She has been many things—a young bride, an exasperated mother, a wild granny who has sat wailing with an apron over her head. S. gives us a fresh, unconventional eye with which to look at women's lives.

OTHER WORKS: *Unknown Messages* (1974). *The Solution* (1989).

BIBLIOGRAPHY: Reference works: *CANR* 2 (1981). *FC* (1990).
Other references: *Associated Writing Programs Chronicle* (Oct./Nov. 1990). *Hudson Rev.* (Summer 1988). *English Studies* (Oct. 1988). *Iowa Rev.* 12 (1981).

TAM LIN NEVILLE

Sui Sin Far. *See Edith Maud Eaton*

May Swenson

See AWW 4, 191–93
D. 4 Dec. 1989, Ocean View, Delaware

A prolific poet, translator, author of children's books, dramatist, and critic, S. enjoyed a career that spanned thirty-five years. Noted for poetry evocative of natural phenomena, she published, between 1954 and 1978, seven books of poetry, three children's books, and one book of translations of the works of Swedish author Tomas Tranströmer. She was also the recipient of many awards, including Guggenheim, Rockefeller, and Mac-Arthur Foundation fellowships and an award in literature from the National Institute of Arts and Letters. In her poetry, S. not only evinces an interest in nature and its metaphorical relationship to the human psyche, but also indulges in wordplay and innovative and startling uses of traditional literary devices. She even ventured into the area of visual poetry in *Iconographs* (1970), the shapes evolving after the poems were completed. Her sense of humor, combined with a serious study of the natural world, made S. one of the United States' foremost poets.

In the last decade of her life, S. continued to have fun with words and literary conventions; this wordplay translated into serious pronouncements on the world around her, for S. was no mere technician. In *In Other Words* (1987), her abiding interest in science is reinforced by a sharp eye for detail, much in evidence in poems like "In Florida," "Waterbird," "Shuttles," and "Banyan." Neither the technician nor the scientist predominates here, but rather the pure poetical meeting of music, words, and ideas. Often-quoted lines from "Goodbye, Goldeneye" illustrate this meeting perfectly: "And goodbye, oh faithful pair of swans that used to glide—god and goddess shapes of purity—over the wide water." S.'s interest in science also extended to technology. *In Other Words* includes poems on space travel and astronomy. The five-part "Shuttles" concludes with the subject of the *Challenger* disaster, where she illustrates not just an observer's reaction to the incident, but also the emotions of the doomed occupants of the shuttle.

S. published some 450 poems. Amid the many that speak of nature, science, and technology, there are also a number of love poems. Those originally published in earlier works, along with thirteen not previously published, have been collected in *The Love Poems of May Swenson* (1991). Included in this volume are visual and nature poems that treat love and sexuality while also interpreting the world through human hearts. S.'s metaphorical use of flowers to communicate a frank sexuality and sensuality has much in common with the more erotic interpretation of the Song of Songs. Love is not always pleasure, and S. is quick to point out the isolation that occurs in a life without love as an anchor. "In love we are set free" certainly, and S. implies that without love we are truly imprisoned in ourselves.

OTHER WORKS: *The Complete Poems to Solve* (juvenile, 1993). *The Centaur* (forthcoming, 1994). S.'s papers are at Washington University, St. Louis, Missouri.

BIBLIOGRAPHY: Reference works: *AWP* (1986). *CA* 5–8 (1969), 130 (obituary, 1990). *CANR* 36 (1992). *CLC* 4 (1975), 14 (1980), 61 (1990). *Contemp. Poets* (1985). *DLB* 5 (1980). *FC* (1990). *Maj Twent Cent Writers* (1991). *SATA* 15 (1979).

Other references: *Christian Science Monitor* (12 Feb. 1979). *Explicator* (Fall 1979). *Hudson Rev.* (Summer 1988). *New Republic* (7 March 1988). *NYT* (5 Dec. 1989, obituary). *NYTBR* (11 Feb. 1979; 19 Jan. 1992). *Parnassus* (1985, 1990). *Poetry* (Feb. 1980, July 1989).

LINDA BERUBE

Amy Tan

B. 19 Feb. 1952, Oakland, California
D. of Daisy (Tu Ching) and John Tan; m. Lou de Mattei, 1974

T.'s fiction, infused with the spirit of the fairy tales she read avidly as a child, earned for the author a fairy-tale success in real life. While still in her thirties, T. published two novels to spectacular critical acclaim and commercial gain. T. grew up in San Francisco, the child of Chinese immigrant parents who made it out of China just before Mao came to power. Drawing on the tensions and dislocations of this background, her novels depict a new aspect of an honored American literary experience, the immigrant adventure.

In the first, *The Joy Luck Club* (1989), and even more so in the second, *The Kitchen God's Wife* (1991), T. exhibits an extraordinarily satisfying storytelling gift: pacing, imagery, descriptive vividness, laced with suspense, humor, emotion, and psychological reality. Clearly a writer with a modern sensibility, she also includes acute social observations in the manner of the nineteenth-century novel, and the mix results in a masterful tapestry of individual and social anguish. Both novels describe mother-daughter relationships in which exotic elements of Chinese background clash against a contemporary feminist point of view. The mothers are oppressed, but not victims; the daughters strive to place themselves beyond the control of these strong mothers, claiming their own space and time, without losing the richness of their beginnings and their loyalties. The resolutions of the conflicts are emotionally satisfying, without a trace of romanticizing lies or sentimentality.

In "Two Kinds," a short story published in the February 1989 *Atlantic Monthly*, T. describes the narrator's mother's background: "She had come to San Francisco in 1949 after losing everything in China: her mother and father, her family home, her first husband, and two daughters, twin baby girls." T.'s fiction tells and retells variations of that story, while engaging a modern audience with the further labyrinthine irony and pain of mother-daughter love, complicated by dual, conflicting cultures and needs. Further, in *The Kitchen God's Wife*, the reader is swept into the detailed horrors of the havoc and devastation suffered by the Chinese people throughout the social upheavals of this century.

T.'s father was an engineer and Baptist minister. She knew her mother had been married before, but she learned only at twenty-six that she had half sisters from that marriage still living in China. T. herself was a middle child, and only daughter of her mother's second marriage. Both her father and her older brother died of brain tumors in the 1960s. Her remarkably resourceful mother took T. and her younger brother from the "diseased" house to Montreux, Switzerland, where she finished her high school years. When the family returned to the Bay Area, T. enrolled in Linfield College, a Baptist school in Oregon, but soon followed her boyfriend to San Jose State University (B.A. 1963), changing her major from premed to English. Her mother had harbored unrealistic hopes for her daughter. "Of course you will become a famous neurosurgeon . . . and, yes, a concert pianist on the side."

What T. had always wanted to be was a writer, ever since she won a writing contest at age eight. Disappointing her mother, she married her boyfriend, Lou de Mattei, earned a master's degree in linguistics (San Jose State, 1974), worked at a variety of freelance technical writing jobs, and wrote her stories on the side. She and her mother became more and more estranged until a trip to China resolved T.'s ambiguities about her past heritage and her present sense of herself. For the first time, she felt Chinese as well as American. "When I began to write [*The Joy Luck Club*], it was so much for my mother and myself," to explain the turbulent disagreements of their lives together. She has reported that the writing of her first novel was like "taking dictation from an invisible storyteller."

One is reminded of **Harriet Beecher Stowe**'s statement that God had dictated *Uncle Tom's Cabin*.

T.'s third published book is for children; *The Moon Lady* (1992) is "set in the China of long ago . . . a story of a little girl who discovered that the best wishes are those she can make come true herself." She is at work on a third novel.

BIBLIOGRAPHY: *Far Eastern Economic Rev.* (27 July 1989; 14 Nov. 1991). *LATBR* (12 March 1989). *New Statesman and Society* (30 June 1989; 12 July 1991). *Newsweek* (17 April 1989). *NYT* (4 July 1989; 31 May 1991; 11 June 1991; 20 June 1991). *NYTBR* (19 March 1989; 16 June 1991; 8 Nov. 1992). *Time* (27 March 1989; 3 June 1991). *Wash. Post* (8 Oct. 1989). *Wash. Post Book World* (5 March 1989; 16 June 1991). *WRB* (Sept. 1991). Reference works: *Bestsellers* 3 (1989). *CA* 136 (1992). *CLC* 59 (1990).

HELEN YGLESIAS

Mildred Delois Taylor

B. 1943, Jackson, Mississippi
D. of Deletha Marie (Davis) and Wilbert Lee Taylor

In writing realistic stories about the African American experience in the South, T. juxtaposes the warmth and safety of family love and community solidarity against the burning injustices of racism. Emotionally powerful and often graphic in its horrifying verisimilitude, T.'s small but critical body of work celebrates the physical and spiritual survival of her heroic black characters and the indomitability of the human spirit.

T. graduated from the University of Toledo and pursued graduate study in journalism at the University of Colorado, but her most valuable education took place at home and through life experiences. Storytelling was an integral part of T.'s family life. From her father, a master storyteller, she learned the black history that was absent from the textbooks she studied at school—a history that emphasized the pride, dignity, and values of African American life despite the sorrows and defeats experienced in an unjust society. During two years (1965–67) spent in Ethiopia with the Peace Corps, T. was frequently reminded of her father's stories and her determination to write the truth about the black experience further solidified.

T.'s first book, a novella called *The Song of the Trees* (1975), won first prize in the African American category of a competition sponsored by the Council on Interracial Books for Children. Told from the perspective of eight-year-old Cassie Logan, the book begins the saga of the proud Logan family, and in particular the children, which continues in much of T.'s subsequent work. The Logan books chronicle the family's hardships and joys in Depression-era Mississippi, exploring what it means to grow from childhood to adulthood as an African American in the United States. Themes of strength, dignity, determination, integrity, love of the land, and the importance of family are woven through works alive with drama and vivid with sure characterization, quick dialogue, and a skilled narrative style.

T. incorporates into her stories much of what she learned in her own childhood, and incidents about which she read or heard. The result are stories that bristle with life, read like autobiography, and have an aural, poetic quality. *Roll of Thunder, Hear My Cry* (1976), the first full-length novel about Cassie and her family, won the 1977 Newbery Medal, was chosen as a National Book Award finalist, and was named a Boston Globe–Horn Book honor book for 1977. *Let the Circle Be Unbroken* (1981) was nominated for the American Book Award and won the Coretta Scott King Award for 1981. *The Friendship* (1987), like *The Song of the Trees*, focuses on a single incident in the life of the Logans, and is also intended for a younger audience. It received the 1989 Boston Globe–Horn Book Award. *The Road to Memphis* brings the Logan children into explosive young adulthood, and was chosen as the 1990 Coretta Scott King Award winner.

In *The Gold Cadillac* (1987), a Christopher Award winner, T. introduces the reader to new characters, 'lois and her sister Wilma, who discover for the first time what it is like to be scared because of the color of their skin. *Mississippi Bridge* (1990) is written from the point of view of a white boy, Jeremy Simms, who witnesses a tragic bus accident that results in ironic justice for the blacks who have been ordered off the bus. Both books resonate with honesty and emotionally wrenching incidents.

In all of her work, T. draws upon the well of history and the "cauldron of story." As a writer, she considers herself only a link in the storytelling chain, drawing from a long tradition that has enabled her to write of herself, but ultimately to write of others. T.'s work rises above the personal to the universal, standing as a historical monument to how things used to be, and a contemporary reminder of how much work remains to be done in the eradication of racial discrimination.

In 1988 T. was honored by the Children's Book Council "for a body of work that has examined significant social issues and presented them in outstanding books for young readers." She is widely acknowledged as a talented voice whose groundbreaking contributions have greatly enriched the field of children's literature. Many critics consider *Roll of Thunder, Hear My Cry* already a classic work in the tradition of realistic fiction.

BIBLIOGRAPHY: Rees, Davis, "The Color of Skin," in *The Marble in the Water: Essays on Contemporary Writers of Fiction for Children and Young Adults* (1980). Reference works: *CA* 85–88 (1980). *CANR* 25 (1989). *CLC* 21 (1982). *DLB* 52 (1986). *Tw Cent Children's Writers*, 3rd ed. (1989). *CLR* 9 (1985). *SATA* 15 (1979). *Black Authors and Illustrators of Children's Books* (1988).

Other references: *Booklist* (1 Dec. 1990). *Horn Book Mag.* (Aug. 1977, March/April 1989).

CAROLYN SHUTE

Megan Terry

See AWW 4, 222–24

T. (born Marguerite Duffy) first earned nationwide notice with *Viet Rock: A Folk War Movie* (1967) and *Comings and Goings* (1967). She received a 1973 Obie, best play, for *Approaching Simone* (1973) and was instrumental in founding the New York Theatre Strategy and Women's Theatre Council in 1971. A member of the Open Theatre movement in New York City during the late 1960s and early 1970s, T. left for Omaha, Nebraska, in 1974, where she has made a home for herself as a playwright in residence at Omaha Magic Theater (OMT). She has since been, along with artistic director, founder, and longtime collaborator Jo Ann Schmidman, one of OMT's principal members. OMT tours extensively, especially in the Midwest, and is an eminently successful example of American theater's neoregionalism.

T. is a somewhat iconoclastic combination, an experimental dramatist who advocates entrepreneurial management and espouses the "pioneer values" of hard work and self-sufficiency. A designer early in her career, she still thinks of her work as "a kind of architectural process in which she 'builds' plays," and not only as a metaphor. She believes that theater is a hands-on-business, and that one must be willing to build sets, create audiences, and manage finances, as well as conceive of "Theater."

Called "The Mother of American Feminist Drama" by Helene Keyssar, T. writes plays characterized by rapid transformation of character and situation, by a great deal of physical action, and by a deep political commitment. The body of her work has continued to grow, as has the range of her styles. Critic David Savran has said that her plays constitute "a virtual compendium of the styles of modern drama, ranging from collaborative ensemble work to performance art to naturalism."

T. is a feminist whose critique of society is less "ideological" than it is grounded in humanist values and in a deep commitment to community. In her work she explores such issues as "production and reproduction, the language of patriarchy, gender roles . . . the victimization and heroism . . . and the pain and power of women," according to Keyssar and Jan Breslauer. Directing her critiques less at systems than "as protests against individual circumstances, institutional corruption, or verbal and conceptual distortions," her feminism, Keyssar says, is "a precise criticism of gender roles, an affirmation of women's strength, and a challenge for women to use their own power." T. puts these principles into practice in her own professional life, encouraging other women playwrights, collecting and distributing bibliographies, and building networks as she crosses the country.

One of her own best expositors, she says of the legacy of the Open Theatre in New York, "I feel we democratized the theater." She also feels that she contributed to the form of American musicals by proving "that rock music worked on the stage" and by "speed[ing] up exposition." Of her work now, she says that the playwright's responsibility is "to critique

[her] society," and that she wishes to convey through her plays "that life is possible."

OTHER WORKS: Fireworks (1979). *Pro Game* (1975, 1979). *Attempted Rescue on Avenue B* (1979). *Advances* (1980). *Maps: India Collage* (1980). *Running Gag* (lyrics, 1980). *Katmandu* (1982). *Flat in Afghanistan* (1982). *The Trees Blew Down* (1983). *Mollie Bailey's Traveling Family Circus: Featuring Scenes from the Life of Mother Jones* (1983). *Fifteen Million Fifteen-Year-Olds* (1974, 1984). *Objective Love* (1984). *Kegger* (1985). *Retro* (1985). *Disko Ranch* (1986). *Sleazing toward Athens* (1986). *Sea of Forms* (1987, with Jo Ann Schmidman). *Dinner's in the Blender* (1987–88, first version titled "Family Talk"). *Headlights* (1988). *Do You See What I'm Saying?* (1990). *High Energy Musicals from the Omaha Magic Theater,* (including *American King's English for Queens, Babes in the Bighouse,* and *Running Gag,* 1983). *Right Brain Vacation Photos: Omaha Theatre New Plays and Production Photographs,* Jo Ann Schmidman, Sora Kimberlain, and T., eds., with photographs by T. (1992). "Anybody Is as Their Land and Air Is," *Studies in American Drama, 1945–Present* 4 (1989). All of T.'s plays are available through the OMT self-publishing enterprise.

BIBLIOGRAPHY: Betsko, Kathleen, and Rachel Koenig, *Interviews with Contemporary Women Playwrights* (1987). Breslauer, J., and H. Keyssar, "Making Magic Public: Megan Terry's Traveling Family Circus," in *Making a Spectacle: Feminist Essays on Contemporary Women's Theatre,* Lynda Hart, ed. (1989). Keyssar, H., *Feminist Theatre* (1984). Marranca, B., "Megan Terry," in *American Playwrights: A Critical Survey,* B. Marranca and G. Dasgupta, eds. (1981). Savran, David, *In Their Own Words: Contemporary American Playwrights* (1988). Schlueter, June, "Megan Terry's Transformational Drama: 'Keep Tightly Closed in a Cool, Dry Place' and the Possibilities of Self," *Modern American Drama: The Female Canon,* J. Schlueter, ed. (1990). Reference works: *CA* 77–80 (1979). *Contemp. Dramatists* (1977, 1982, 1988). *CLC* 19 (1981). *Contemp. Theater, Film, and Television* 5 (1988). *DLB* 7 (1981). *FC* (1990). *Notable Women in American Theater* (1976). *Tw Cent Amer Dramatists,* pt. 2 (1981).

Other references: *Centennial Rev.* 32:3 (Summer 1988). *Mississippi Folklore Register* 22:1–2 (Spring–Fall 1988). *Modern Drama* 27:4 (Dec. 1984). *Studies in Amer. Drama, 1945–Present* 2 (1989), 4 (1989). Additions to *AWW* 4 (other plays before 1979): *The Gloaming, Oh My Darling* (1967). *Women and the Law* (1976).

MARCIA HEPPS WILLIAM KEENEY

Barbara Tuchman

See AWW 4, 263–65
D. 6 Feb. 1989, Greenwich, Connecticut

In the year before T.'s death this highly successful narrative historian had planned to write a book of a different genre, a murder mystery. She believed strongly that history should be readable, and her grounded attitude carried through in her fascinatingly plotted history books, sometimes researched on battlefields in a rented car.

T.'s first book, *The Lost British Policy: Britain and Spain since 1700*, appeared in 1938. By 1981 she had published nine more studies in history, with subjects ranging from fourteenth-century England to late twentieth-century America. Two won Pulitzer prizes, and several became best-sellers. Before embarking on her tenth volume, T. produced a significant paper on disarmament, entitled "The Alternative to Arms Control," for the Center for International Strategic Affairs at the University of California.

In *The March of Folly: From Troy to Vietnam* (1984) T. examines four episodes of evident governmental blunder across a broad sweep of time, attempting to discern their commonalities. Her subjects include the Trojans' decision to bring a mythical Greek horse within their city walls, the refusal of six Renaissance popes to arrest the church's growing corruption, British misrule under King George III, and the United States' mishandling of Vietnam. She notes three vital connections between these highly varied events: that those responsible were all forewarned of outcomes of "folly"; that feasible alternatives existed; and that a group rather than an individual perpetrated foolishness. Although the book was criticized for its lack of a true common thread, T. was praised for her thoroughness, imagination, and valuable insight into the political process.

In her final book, *The First Salute* (1988), T. returned to the subject of the American Revolution and the reasons for Britain's defeat. Focusing on the failure of famed British naval officer Sir George Brydges Rodney to pursue the French fleet from his base in the recently captured Dutch West Indian island of St. Eustatius, T. places the Revolution in international context. She draws parallels between the Dutch struggle for independence and that of the American colonies, and, with great admiration for the leadership of George Washington, examines the forces on both the British and American sides that resulted in the American victory.

T.'s many honors included honorary degrees from Yale, Columbia, Harvard, and New York University; the Regent Medal of Excellence from the State University of New York; and the Order of Leopold from the Kingdom of Belgium.

BIBLIOGRAPHY: *Atlantic* (Dec. 1988). *Nation* (6 March 1989). *NYRB* (22 Dec. 1988). *NYT* (7 March 1984; 7 Feb. 1989; 8 Feb. 1989; 13 Feb. 1989). *NYTBR* (11 March 1984, 2 Oct. 1988; 16 Oct. 1988; 12 Nov. 1989). *Time* (3 Oct. 1988; 7 Nov. 1988; 20 Feb. 1989). *Times* [London] (8 Feb. 1989).

MARGIT GALANTER

Linda Ty-Casper

B. 17 Sept. 1931, Manila, the Philippines
D. of Catalina Velasques-Ty and Francisco Figueroa Ty; m. Leonard Casper, 1956;
c.: Gretchen, b. 1958; Kristina, b. 1970

Although T.-C. has lived for over thirty-five years in the United States, with her husband, writer and critic Leonard Casper, and their two daughters, she has maintained her Philippine citizenship and makes frequent visits there. She has published nine novels and two collections of short stories, all of which focus on life in the Philippines, with a strong concern for historical and political crosscurrents and developments, particularly the long history of colonialism and revolution and the imposition of martial law. One of her recent novels, *Awaiting Trespass* (1985), could not be published there for political reasons during the last years of the dictatorship of Ferdinand Marcos, which came to an end in 1986 with the Peoples Revolution. Published in Britain and the United States, it recounts the mysterious death by torture of a prominent citizen.

Trained as a lawyer, with law degrees from both the University of the Philippines (1955) and Harvard University (1957), T.-C. began writing fiction almost immediately upon graduation from law school. She started her first novel in 1957, she says, "because I'd read some historical accounts which were derogatory to the Philippines and I wanted to answer them." The result was *The Peninsulars* (1964), in which T.-C. brings to life the impact of Spanish colonialism on the Philippines in the eighteenth century, heightened by the English invasion of Manila and early, unsuccessful attempts by various local factions at gaining independence.

With a precision of detail and observation, T.-C. documents in short stories and novels the personal and political lives of her characters with great subtlety. Moral choices are often at the center of the conflicts faced by her characters, but these choices evolve naturally out of the lives of the characters themselves; they are not imposed on them by the author. T.-C.'s writing often joins the precision of a legal brief with a poetry of brilliantly ambiguous imagery. With careful and understated language, she explores the difficult decisions encountered by ordinary people confronted with violence and political treachery.

T.-C.'s approach to writing and to her characters is that of the storyteller. Her writing takes on a cumulative trancelike quality that weaves the reader into the events that it recounts by maintaining a cool and distanced objectivity that is at the same time passionate and deeply felt. Her later work, such as *Wings of Stone* (1986), becomes almost surrealistic as her characters encounter the frenetic tensions of modern-day life in the Philippines and the United States. Her storyteller's voice, she says, was inherited from her grandmother, who told her stories during World War II.

T.-C.'s forthcoming *Dream Eden* is set in the Philippines during the 1986 Peoples Revolution. One of the most prominent Philippine writers, and yet in a very real sense binational, T.-C. documents the turmoil of past and present-day politics and social intrigue in the Philippines while also conveying the anxieties and uncertainties of the modern world in both the East and West. In 1993, T.-C. won a UNESCO-PEN short story prize and the Southeast Asia WRITE Award.

OTHER WORKS: Books: *The Transparent Sun and Other Stories* (1963). *The Secret Runner and Other Stories* (1974). *The Three-cornered Sun* (1979). *Dread Empire* (1980). *Hazards of Distance* (1981). *Fortress in the Plaza* (1985). *Ten Thousand Seeds* (1987). *A Small Party in a Garden* (1988). *Common Continent: Selected Stories* (1991). Her short stories and reportage have also appeared in:

Antioch Rev. (Summer 1958). *Asia Magazine* (June 1963, Nov. 1968). *Cuyahoga Rev.* (Fall 1985). *Descant* (Fall 1978). *Four Quarters* (Winter 1977). *Greensboro Rev.* 36 (1984). *Hawaii Pacific Rev.* (Spring 1990). *Hawaii Rev.* (Fall 1980). *Home to Stay: Asian-American Women's Fiction*, Sylvia Watanabe and Carol Bruchac, eds. (1990). *Literary Apprentice* (1961–63). *Manila Rev.* (Jan. 1975). *Mr. and Mrs.* (Nov. 1980). *Nantucket Rev.* (Summer 1979, Fall 1979). *New Mexico Q.* (Spring 1965, Autumn 1967). *Other Side* (March 1988). *Philippines Free Press* (June 1963, Feb. 1989). *Philippine Graphic* (27 Aug. 1990). *Prairie Schooner* (Fall 1977). *Solidarity* (March 1970, Oct. 1972; Third Quarter 1983). *Southwest Rev.* (Summer 1961). *Triquarterly* (Fall 1974). *Weekly Nation* (23 Dec. 1968). *Windsor Rev.* (Winter 1976). Essays: "Literature: A Flesh Made of Fugitive Suns," *Philippine Studies* 28 (1980). "Marcos's Revolution from the Top," *Christian Science Monitor* (28 July 1981). "Philippine Women Writers: A Room Shared," *Pilipinas* (Fall 1987). "The Question of Country, the Question of Self," *Philippine-American News* (June 1989). "Literature, a Common Country," *City Lights* 4 (1990).

BIBLIOGRAPHY: Bresnahan, Roger, *Conversations with Filipino Writers* (1990). Casper, Leonard, *New Writing from the Philippines* (1966). Montenegro, David, *Points of Departure: International Writers on Writing and Politics* (1991). Reference works: *CA* 107 (1983); *CANR* 24 (1988) *Encyc. of World Lit.* (1992). Other references: *Belles Lettres* (May–June 1987).

DAVID MONTENEGRO

Anne Tyler

See AWW 4, 275–77

T.'s critical and popular success has increased steadily. Since *Morgan's Passing* (1980) she has published four novels and many short stories. In 1988, *The Accidental Tourist* (1985) became a major motion picture; in the same year, T. received the Pulitzer Prize for fiction for *Breathing Lessons* (1988).

All of T.'s novels take place in Baltimore, where she has lived for many years. They are portraits of families who, behind the appearance of normality, shelter idiosyncrasies, pain, and secrets. *Dinner at the Homesick Restaurant* (1982) begins with eighty-five-year-old Pearl Tull looking back on her life and the three children she raised alone after being abandoned by her husband. Gradually the reader sees the profound effect this desertion has had on each character, and the inability of these children to escape their past, even as adults. In the end, however, the bonds of family overcome the pain of years of misunderstandings and lack of communication.

The Accidental Tourist is about the Learys, another abandoned family. Most of the story centers around Macon Leary, a man controlled by structure and routine. His apparent refusal to grieve after the brutal murder of his son drives away his wife, causing Macon to draw even more inward. Not until he meets Muriel Pritchett, whom he hires to train his unruly and sometimes vicious dog, does Macon finally begin to live. The Learys are an excellent example of T.'s ability to portray a seemingly ordinary family with all their quirks and hang-ups in a subtle, ironic, and humorous way. The novel won the National Book Critics Circle Award for fiction.

Breathing Lessons (1988) takes place in one day, with periodic flashbacks. During the journey to and from a friend's funeral, Ira and Maggie Moran come to certain realizations about their children and themselves, particularly how different from their expectations their life has become. Recognizing their regrets, they also come to know the importance of the bond they share.

The Bedloe family in *Saint Maybe* (1991) has also failed to live up to its own expectations. It is the "ideal" family, but through a series of tragic events the course of all their lives changes drastically and permanently. The novel focuses on Ian, the youngest son, who sacrifices his own goals and dreams in an effort to make amends for what has happened. With more sadness and less humor than T.'s previous work, the novel delves beautifully into the lives of ordinary people, and the necessity for endurance.

T.'s work retains its clarity of style; her ability to combine the tragic with the comic gives her characters a genuine humanity. She consistently addresses the individual struggle for identity, happiness, and fulfillment, and demonstrates that the simple, even the apparently trivial, is sometimes the source of what is most rich and complex in life, and well worth examination.

OTHER WORKS: Tumble Tower (1993).

BIBLIOGRAPHY: Petry, A. H., *Understanding Anne Tyler* (1990). *The Fiction of Anne Tyler*, C. R. Stephens, ed. (1990). Voelker, J., *Art and the Accidental in Anne Tyler* (1989). Reference works: *CA* 9–12 (1974). *CANR* 11 (1984), 33 (1991). *CLC* 7 (1977), 11 (1979), 18 (1981), 28 (1984), 44 (1987), 59 (1990). *CBY* (1981). *DLB* 6 (1980). *DLBY* (1982). *Maj Twent Cent Writers* (1991). *SATA* 7 (1975).

Other references: *Atlantis: A Women's Studies J.* (Fall 1987). *Classical and Modern Lit.* (Fall 1989). *English J.* (Fall 1987). *Hollins Critic* (April 1986). *Iowa J. of Literary Studies* (interview, 1981). *Mississippi Q.* (Winter 1988). *New England Rev. and Bread Loaf Q.* (Spring 1985). *People* (26 Dec. 1988). *Southern Literary J.* (Fall 1983). *Southern Q.* (Summer 1983). *Southern Rev.* (Fall 1984).

SHAUNA SUMMERS

Yoshiko Uchida

B. 24 Nov. 1921, Alameda, California; d. 21 June 1992
D. of Iku (Umegaki) and Dwight Takashi Uchida

A tenacious belief in the power of literature and education directed U.'s work as an author. A cum laude graduate of the University of California at Berkeley (1942), U. received an M.Ed. from Smith College (1944). Her publications included articles on folk arts and crafts for the *Nippon News* in Tokyo and columns for *Craft Horizons;* her diverse contributions to children's literature span the genres of picture book, chapbooks for young readers, adolescent novels, collections of folklore, and historical novels. In addition, an adult novel, a number of nonfiction titles, and countless short stories illustrate U.'s versatility.

Of her work, U. stated: "I try to write of meaningful relationships between human beings, to celebrate our common humanity." The realistic stories set in the United States often depict immigrant Japanese families and first-generation Japanese-Americans struggling to make a good life in a new land. *The Promised Year* (1959), *The Birthday Visitor* (1975), *A Jar of Dreams* (1981), *The Best Bad Thing* (1983), and *The Happiest Ending* (1985) especially portray the promises of America and the hopes of a better future.

Journey to Topaz (1971) and *Journey Home* (1978) never abandon that hope even as they chronicle a dark chapter of America's history. As a college student, U. was evacuated with her family from California to the Tanforan Racetrack with 8,000 other Japanese-Americans, and four months later moved to the Topaz concentration camp in Utah. In writing of the Japanese internment during World War II from an eleven-year-old child's perspective, U. not only describes the physical treatment of prisoners, but also captures the individual and collective bafflement at America's imprisonment of its own citizens. She also speaks openly about her experience in a Japanese relocation center, where she worked as a teacher. In her two novels, U. re-creates the family's sparse and crowded living quarters, and contrasts their physical humiliation and poverty with a triumphant spirit and tenacious belief in goodness.

Well-developed, complex characters, provocative situations, and gifted storytelling account for U.'s success with critics and readers alike. She garnered many awards and honors, including citations from the National Council of Teachers of English, the American Library Association, the California Association of Teachers of English, chapters of the Japanese-American Citizens League, the International Reading Association, the National Council for Social Studies, and the Children's Book Council. A Ford Foundation Fellowship in 1952 enabled U. to travel to Japan. This and later trips brought authority and authentic settings to her writing. Books set in Japan include the series about the endearing young Sumi, *Rokubei and the Thousand Rice Bowls* (1962), and *In-between Miya* (1967). An early work, *The Full Circle* (1957), is a compelling story of postwar peace in Japan, and of the dubious privilege of being Umeko Kagawa, the adolescent daughter of a prominent religious leader. Based on conversations between U. and Kagawa the novel is essentially a biography.

Ceremony, tradition, and revered customs influenced U.'s creations. Both old and young are respected; joyous friendships between young and old promote genuine intergenerational understanding. The centrality of family, and its unquestioning support of individual contributions and invaluable uniqueness, fosters the growth of all of U.'s characters. A strong sense of morality inhabits the center of her work, but it never overpowers nor seems artificial. U.'s early commitment to education flows through her books that teach in the best possible ways: answers are never simple, growth never easy but always possible. Her memoir, *The Invisible Thread* (1991), chronicles the relationship between her adopted country, her Japanese legacy, and her growth as a writer. Sharing her own cultural heritage, U. defeated stereotypes and presented to "Japanese-American young people an understanding of their own history and pride in their identity."

OTHER WORKS: *The Dancing Kettle and Other Japanese Folk Tales* (1949). *New Friends for Susan* (1951). *We Do Not Work Alone: The Thoughts of Kanjiro Kawai* (1953). *The Magic Listening Cap: More Folk Tales from Japan* (1955). *Takao and Grandfather's Sword* (1958). *Mik and the Prowler* (1960). *The Forever Christmas Tree* (1963). *Sumi's Prize* (1964). *The Sea of Gold and Other Tales from Japan* (1965). *Sumi's Special Happening* (1966). *Sumi and the Goat and the Tokyo Express* (1969). *Kisako's Mysteries* (1969). *Makoto, the Smallest Boy* (1970). *Samurai of Gold Hill* (1972). *The History of Sycamore Church* (1974). *Margaret de Patta* (exhibition catalogue, 1976). *The Rooster Who Understood Japanese* (1976). *Tabi: Journey through Time: Stories of the Japanese in America* (1981). *Desert Exile: The Uprooting of a Japanese American Family* (1982). *The Foolish Cats* (1987). *Picture Bride* (1987). *Bird Song* (1992). *The Bracelet* (1993). *The Magic Purse* (1993). *The Wise Old Woman* (forthcoming, 1994). U.'s manuscripts and papers are in the Kerlan Collection, University of Minnesota; University of Oregon Library (manuscripts prior to 1981); Bancroft Library, University of California, Berkeley (manuscripts, papers, and all published materials since 1981).

BIBLIOGRAPHY: Chang, C. E. S., *Language Arts* (1984). Dreyer, S. S., *The Bookfinder: A Guide to Children's Literature about the Needs and Problems of Youth Ages Two through Fifteen* (1981). Reference works: *CA* 13–16 (1975). *CANR* 6 (1982), 22 (1988). *Children's Book World* (1967). *Maj Twent Cent Writers* (1991). *SATA* 1 (1971), 55 (1989). *Tw Cent Children's Writers* (1989).

Other references: *NY Herald Tribune Book Rev.* (8 March 1949; 15 May 1955). *NYT* (4 Nov. 1942; 9 March 1958; 24 June 1992, obituary). *TLS* (3 Oct. 1968).

CATHRYN M. MERCIER

Jean Valentine

B. 27 April 1934, Chicago, Illinois
D. of Jean (Purcell) and John Valentine; m. James Chace, 1957, div.; m. Barrie
  Cooke, 1991; c.: Sarah, b. 1958; Rebecca, b. 1960

V. is a graduate of Radcliffe College (B.A. 1956). Her first book of poetry, *Dream Barker and Other Poems* (1965) won the Yale Series of Younger Poets Award and was chosen for publication by Dudley Fitts. She has taught at Yale, Massachusetts Institute of Technology, New York University, Bucknell, Swarthmore, and Hunter Colleges, among others, and since 1974 has been on the faculty of Sarah Lawrence College. Though over the years V. has not had the recognition accorded many of her contemporaries, she is considered by many to be among the finest contemporary American poets. Hayden Carruth has commented: "No other living poet gives me as keen a sense of intelligence, the mind at work there on the page, as [V.]. . . . Such poems are very, very rare." Her incomparable poems have won fellowships for her from the National Endowment for the Arts (NEA) and from the Guggenheim and Rockefeller foundations.

Her poetry makes of experience something deeply spiritual, spare and emblematic, like dreams. In lines that are metaphoric but rely on what is "sent" out by the image and not created by it, time and objects are haunting presences in a V. poem. She is always investigating what Richard Jackson calls the "hallowing of the everyday," using language in order to go places it seems most difficult or useless to go, to describe the moment things invisible become visible.

V.'s early poems are more formal and explore language in a simple way, in a manner that says she is delighted by it. Subjects at this time ranged from poems about the family to love poems (which make up a great percentage of her work). In these, as well as in many later poems, V. uses dialogue in a symbolic manner. The speaker in the poem speaks in an associative rather than linear way. People populate her poems much in the way they populate dreams, as figures floating between language. "Ask, and let your words diminish your asking" ("Waiting," *Dream Barker*).

In recent years V.'s poems have become more statement-oriented: "Everything starts with a letter, / even in dreams and in the movies. . . . Take *J.* / Juliana, on a summer afternoon." ("Everything Starts with a Letter," *Home. Deep. Blue.*, 1989). There is also more of a communal recognition in force here than in the earlier work. V. is now concerned by issues like AIDS, feminism, incest, alcoholism, and recovery. As Alberta Turner comments, all of her poems, in one way or another, address "the threat of an empty universe."

The later poems use the elliptical phrasing and spare cadence by which V. has long been identified, but they are more political, less personal. She has not become more accessible, necessarily, but more acute, aware of the "feeling" stages of life in America as an emotional process rather than a particularly historic one.

V.'s poems have appeared in *American Poetry Review, Ironwood, The New Yorker, Ploughshares,* and other journals. They have also been frequently anthologized.

OTHER WORKS: *Pilgrims* (1969). *Ordinary Things* (1974). *The Messenger* (1979). *The River at Wolf* (1992).

BIBLIOGRAPHY: *APR* 9 (Jan. 1980); 2:4 (July/Aug. 1991, interview by Michael Klein). *Field* 40 (Spring 1989). *Harper's* (Jan. 1980, article by Hayden Carruth). *NYTBR* (7 Nov. 1965; 2 Aug. 1970; 21 Oct. 1979). *Poetry* 127 (Oct. 1975), 161 (Dec. 1992). *VLS* 34 (23 May 1989). Reference works: *CANR* 34 (1991). *Contemp. Poets* (1991).

MICHAEL KLEIN

Mona Van Duyn

B. 9 May 1921, Waterloo, Iowa
D. of Lora (Kramer) and Earl George Van Duyn; m. Jarvis Thurston, 1943

The first woman named as poet laureate of the United States (1992), V. was educated at the University of Northern Iowa (B.A. 1942) and the

University of Iowa (M.A. 1943), where she was an instructor at the Writer's Workshop from 1943 to 1946. In 1946 she joined the faculty of the University of Louisville, leaving there in 1950 for a lectureship at Washington University in St. Louis. She later served as poetry consultant to the Olin Library Modern Literature Collection at Washington University, and was appointed Visiting Hurst Professor there in 1987. In 1973, she taught at the Salzburg (Austria) Seminar in American Studies. She has also taught at the Breadloaf Writers Conferences. V. and her husband founded *Perspective: A Quarterly of Literature* and coedited the journal from 1947 to 1967.

V. has received an impressive array of awards, including the Pulitzer Prize in poetry, 1991, and the prestigious Bollingen Prize (1971). She has been the recepient of fellowships from the National Endowment for the Arts (1966, 1985), the Academy of American Poets (1981), and the Guggenheim Foundation (1972). In addition to honorary degrees from Washington University and Cornell College, her honors also include the Shelley Memorial Prize (1987); National Book Award (1971); Harriet Monroe Memorial Prize, from *Poetry Magazine* (1968); Borestone Mountain Poetry Prize (1968); Hart Crane Memorial Award (1968); Helen Bullis Prize from *Poetry Northwest* (1964); and the Eunice Tietjens Memorial Prize (1956). In 1985 V. became a chancellor of the Academy of American Poets.

V. has been compared to such diverse poets as William Shakespeare, John Donne, Robert Browning, Wallace Stevens, Robert Lowell, and **Elizabeth Bishop.** Well received by critics, her work of almost four decades is frequently characterized as formalist. Examining the quotidian, her poetry is sometimes called "domestic," a designation she decries for its sexism. She writes of married life and ordinary people, and speaks of love and its losses, often using ventriloquism to speak the stories of her family members. Sweet but painful, her poems provide glimpses into suburban life. Conventional in subject matter, they lack postmodern cynicism. Drawing from Greek mythology, the Bible, and employing colloquial language, her poetry combines the usual with the unusual.

Her seventh book, *Near Changes* (Pulitzer Prize, 1991), asks, "How can human love be unfearing?" and asserts V.'s belief in an essential goodness in human community. Even as she accuses the earth of "uncaring" in the "The Accusation," she resolves that "no lie can conceal the truth / that our kind was built to be caring." This worldview permeates V.'s work. Praised for its seemingly effortless crafting of formality, storytelling, and wit into a poetics of transformation, *Near Changes* marks her passage from middle age.

To See, To Take (National Book Award, 1971) contextualizes the poet-speaker within a larger world, concentrating on observations of middle-class suburban life. *Merciful Disguises: Published and Unpublished Poems* (1973) acknowledges, in "Open Letter, Personal," that "We know the quickest way to hurt each other," but insists that nevertheless, "We love." V. reveals the disguises we use to distance ourselves from our deepest sorrows, to keep ourselves going despite the pain of living. In *Letters from a Father and Other Poems* (1983) V. projects an anecdotal, epistolary style as she explores relationships with aging parents. Autobiographical, the poems are without the high egocentricism of the confessional poets, and break through personal pain to celebrate joy and compassion.

Emphasis on the power of love and its healing properties remains a hallmark of V.'s poetry. Preferring hope to despair, her work offers a vision where love peers through rage as it confronts the impossibility of satisfying human desire, quietly bringing gentleness to a world accustomed to hardness.

OTHER WORKS: Valentines to the World (1958). *A Time of Bees* (1964). *Bedtime Stories* (1972). *If It Be Not I (Poems 1959–1982)* (1993). *Firefall* (1993).

BIBLIOGRAPHY: APR (Nov.–Dec. 1973). *Antioch Rev.* (Spring 1970). *Carleton Miscellany* (Spring/Summer 1974). *Nation* (4 May 1973). *New Republic* (6 Oct. 1973; 31 Dec. 1990). *NYT* (11 Jan. 1971; 21 June 1991). *NYTBR* (21 Nov. 1965; 2 Aug. 1970; 9 Dec. 1973; 18 Nov. 1990). *Parnassus* 16:2 (1991). *Poetry* (Oct. 1990). *Sewanee Rev.* (Winter 1973). *Va. Q. Rev.* (Spring 1965, Winter 1974). *Wash. Post* (10 April 1991; 15 June 1992). *Wash. Post Book World* (6 Jan. 1974). Reference works: *CANR* 7 (1982). *CLC* 3 (1975), 7 (1977), 63 (1991). *Contemp. Poets* (1991). *DLB* 5 (1980). *FC* (1990).

LOLLY OCKERSTROM

Helen Hennessy Vendler

See AWW 4, 298–99

Regarded by her fellow critics as America's best "close reader" of poetry, V. has published six books of criticism since her first study of Yeats appeared in 1963. She has also edited several collections of poetry. An active teacher as well as a prolific writer, V. is a professor of literature at Harvard University. She lectures frequently in the United States and around the world.

In *The Odes of John Keats* (1983), V. proposes that the odes are best understood when studied together, in sequence. When read this way, she argues, the odes raise and attempt to resolve a series of formal and philosophical questions about the nature of art. V.'s original treatment of the odes as an artistic unity was welcomed by critics as a full and persuasive study of Keats's great poems.

Wallace Stevens: Words Chosen Out of Desire (1984) grew out of the Hodges Lectures that V. delivered at the University of Tennessee at Knoxville in 1982. Discussing Stevens's shorter poems, V. hopes to correct what she considers to be a popular misconception—that his work is remote and cerebral. Instead, she focuses on the "disappointment of desire" in Stevens's work, revealing the warmth and loneliness that permeate many of the poems.

The Music of What Happens: Poems, Poets, and Critics (1988), essays originally published in *The New Yorker, New York Review of Books*, and the *New Republic,* includes discussions of contemporary poets, as well as articles on Wordsworth, Keats, and Whitman. In a particularly interesting introduction V. explains her critical methods. Dismissing interpretation-centered and ideological criticism as "paraphrase and polemic," she argues that a work of literature, like any work of art, can best be understood only through a thorough consideration of the work's formal elements and their relationship to meaning. She calls her own method "aesthetic criticism" and claims that too often critics involved in both hermeneutic and ideological criticism overlook aesthetic achievement, thereby missing the essence of the artwork itself.

V. edited the *Harvard Book of Contemporary American Poetry* (1985), published in England as the *Faber Book of Contemporary American Poetry* (1986), and served as poetry editor of the *Harper Anthology of American Literature* (1987). In 1987 she edited and contributed to *Voices and Visions: American Poets*, a companion work to the Public Broadcasting System television series of the same name. V. also edited and introduced Wallace Stevens, *Poems* (1985), and W. B. Yeats, *Selected Poems* (1990). She writes regulary for the *New York Review of Books* and the *New Republic* and has been the poetry critic for *The New Yorker* since 1978.

V. is the recipient of numerous professional awards including the National Book Critics Circle Award for Criticism (1980) and a fellowship from the National Endowment for the Humanities (1986–87). She was a Fulbright lecturer at the University of Singapore in 1986 and at Trinity College, Dublin, in 1988. For many years she served as a judge for the Pulitzer Prize in poetry and since 1990 has been a member of the board of that organization. Her work in progress includes a commentary on Shakespeare's *Sonnets* and a history of Yeats's poetic styles.

BIBLIOGRAPHY: Reference works: *CA* 41–44 (1979). *CANR* 25 (1989). *CB* (1986). *Maj Twent Cent Writers* (1991).

Other references: *J. of Amer. Studies* 23 (Aug. 1989). *New Boston Rev.* 9 (March 1984). *NYT* (27 Nov. 1983). *TLS* (2 March 1984; 24 May 1985; 8 July 1988). *Wilson Q.* 8 (Winter 1984).

MELISSA BURNS

Helena Maria Viramontes

B. 26 Feb. 1954, Los Angeles, California
D. of Maria Louise LaBrada and Serafin Viramontes; m. Eloy Rodriguez, 1983;
  c.: Pilar and Eloy Francisco

V. was born in East Los Angeles and graduated from Garfield High School. With eight brothers and sisters, she learned about hard work at an early age. Working twenty hours a week while carrying a full load at Immaculate Heart College (B.A. 1975) would have seemed like a vacation, were it not for the pressure involved in being one of only five Chicanas in her class.

V.'s first collection of stories, *Moths* (1985), presents Chicana subjects who are a contradictory blend of strenghts and weaknesses, struggling against lives of unfulfilled potential and restrictions forced upon them because they are women. While racial prejudice and the economic and social oppression of Chicanos form the backdrop, V. focuses her narrative lens on the cultural values that shape women's lives and against which they struggle with varying degrees of success.

Most of the stories develop a conflict between a Chicana and the man who represents the maximum authority in her life, either father or husband. In several texts, V. exposes the collusion of the Catholic church in the socialization of women. To assume more independence and responsibility in their lives, these women must break with years of indoctrination by the church. In "Birthday," Alice's abortion radically redefines her relationship to her religion. In "The Long Reconciliation," Amanda's decision to abort because she cannot bear to "watch a child slowly rot" in poverty defies the values of her husband as well as the dictates of the priest: "It is so hard being female, Amanda, and you must understand that this is the way it was meant to be." The main character in "The Broken Web" reveals her disillusionment with "a distant God." "Her children in time would forgive her. But God? He would never understand. He was a man, too."

In most cases, V.'s characters pay dearly for breaking with traditional values, and the exploration of their sexuality outside the bounds of cultural norms often brings negative consequences. The two women who abort are either wracked with guilt or ostracized by their communities. By murdering her husband, the nameless woman of "The Broken Web" breaks a cycle of use and abuse, but suffers both literal incarceration and the belief that she has condemned her soul to eternal punishment.

"Growing" and "The Moths" explore the relationship between the culture and female sexuality in that crucial phase in the life of a Chicana when she ceases to be girl and must accept her role as "woman." In "Growing," Naomi rebels against the mandate that her life must change because her body has changed. "The Moths" also depicts the coercive socialization of adolescent girls in femininity. The adolescent tomboy of the story is acutely aware that she is "different" from her "pretty" and "nice" older sisters. Estranged from her mother and sisters, she is close to her grandmother, whose body she bathes after her death in a cleansing ritual that is also a rite of passage. The words she whispers, "I heard you, abuelita . . . I heard you," suggest that she may have inherited from her grandmother the strength to alter her culture's definitions of "man" and "woman."

The language of V.'s stories is rich and varied. The cook's speech in "The Cariboo Cafe" contrasts with the style of "Snapshots," which captures the dilemma of a middle-aged woman with an offhand humor that is both wacky and moving. Ways of seeing and speaking typical of Chicano children and adolescents make up the stylistic texture of "Growing," "The Moths," and parts of "The Cariboo Cafe."

This vein dominates her more recent stories. They offer a more straightforward narrative structure unified by the point of view of a young girl, Champ, who talks about her fears and desires, her mother, brother, Tia Olivia, and other family members and friends. In their poetic elaboration of the language of a working-class Chicano family, the stories are an expressive tour de force mixing humor and poignancy. V.'s denseness of poetic imagery, her exploration of working-class Chicano speech, and her constant struggle with words to make them yield fresh insights create imaginative vehicles for these Chicanas' stories.

OTHER WORKS: "Spider's Face's," Americas 2001 1:5 (March/April 1988). "Dance Me Forever," Pearl (Spring–Summer 1988). "Miss Clairol," Chicana Creativity and Criticism: Charting New Frontiers in American Literature, M. Herrera-Sobek and H. M. Viramontes, eds. (1987). "Tears on My Pillow," New Chicano Writing, Charles Tatum, ed. (1992). "'Nopalitos': The Making of Fiction (testimonio)," in Breaking Boundaries: Latina Writing and Critical Readings, Asunción Horno-Delgado et al., eds. (1989).

BIBLIOGRAPHY: Alarcon, Norma, "Making 'Familia' from Scratch: Split Subjectivities in the Work of Helena Maria Viramontes and Cherríe Moraga," in Chicana Creativity and Criticism: Charting New Frontiers in American Literature. Franklet, Duane, "Social Language: Bakhtin and Viramontes," Americas Rev. 17:2 (Summer 1989). Yarbro-Bejarano, Yvonne, introduction, The Moths and Other Stories (1985).

YVONNE YARBRO-BEJARANO

Cynthia Voigt

B. 25 Feb. 1942, Boston, Massachusetts
D. of Elise (Keeney) and Frederick C. Irving; m. Walter Voigt, 1974; c.: Jessica
(from first marriage), Peter

A graduate of Smith College (1963), V. places independent, resilient, and intelligent young women at the center of all but two of her novels. She made her debut in the children's literature field in 1981 with *Homecoming*, the first of her Tillerman stories, which earned immediate critical applause.

The seven novels in the Tillerman family saga form the core of V.'s substantial contributions to realistic young-adult literature. Abandoned by her mother in a shopping mall parking lot, thirteen-year-old Dicey leads her siblings, intelligent James, reliable Sammie, and gifted Maybeth on a long search for family. *Homecoming* documents their arduous journey from Massachusetts to their grandmother's house in Maryland. *Dicey's Song* (1982), winner of the Newbery Medal, explores their new family constellation. *Sons from Afar* (1987) depicts James and Sammie's attempts to find their father, while *Seventeen against the Dealer* (1989) concludes the cycle with Dicey's encounter with her drifter father as she achieves a hard-earned focus on the future. The three satellite novels, *A Solitary Blue* (1983), *The Runner* (1985), and *Come a Stranger* (1986), maintain the Chesapeake Bay setting integral to the Tillerman books while each tells the story of a relative or friend connected to the family. *The Runner* completes an intricate portrayal of their grandmother before the arrival of Dicey and her siblings. *A Solitary Blue* develops the character of Jeff Greene, Dicey's first friend in Crisfield, who becomes her steadfast boyfriend. *Come a Stranger* concentrates on Dicey's schoolmate Mina Smiths, who feels the burn of racial prejudice when she is excluded from an all-white dance camp.

As she does with all of her characters, V. imbues each Tillerman with the fiber of individuality and the substance of family. Hard physical work, belief in positive change, and sheer will drive these determined characters. Love, generosity, and mutual respect temper them and deepen their emotional ties. Similar qualities within interdependent relationships characterize *The Vandemark Mummy* (1991) in which an intelligent, tenacious brother and sister team up to defeat a villain and solve a mystery in a small college town. *David and Jonathan* (1992) explores the ties of friendship as a Holocaust survivor disrupts a New England family.

Essential human bonds infuse not only V.'s realistic novels but also those that draw on fantasy and myth. A tense gothic novel, *The Callender Papers* (1983), unearths dark family secrets as Jean Wainwright discovers her inner resources. *Building Blocks* (1984) transports Brann Connell from modern times to a recent past where he confronts his father as boy. *Jackaroo* (1985) and *On Fortune's Wheel* (1990) share the same mythical setting of Kingdom but are separated in time by two generations. V. reshapes the well-known Robin Hood tale with vigor and freshness in *Jackaroo*, while the later book relates the escape and survival of spirited Birlie, Jackaroo's granddaughter, and her devoted companion Orien, in a riveting adventure and love story. *Orfe* (1992) casts the Orpheus myth into a contemporary setting. *Tree by Leaf* (1988) also includes elements of the fantastic as it tells the very real story of a World War I soldier's agonizing return to his neglected family in Maine.

V.'s consistency alone would win her readers. She can be counted on to tell a "rattlin' good tale"—one enlivened by unexpected plot twists but satisfying in its honest, complete resolution. Her portrayals of trustworthy, capable adolescents can empower readers to effect meaningful change, and she shares with them her vision of a better world, strengthened by human connectedness.

OTHER WORKS: Tell Me If the Lovers Are Losers (1982). *Izzy Willy-Nilly* (1986). *Stories about Rosie* (1986). *The Wings of a Falcon* (1993).

BIBLIOGRAPHY: Henke, J. T., *Children's Literature in Education* (1985). Sutherland, Z., *Newbery and Caldecott Medal Books: 1976–1985* (1986). Reference works: *CLR* 13 (1987). *CA* 106 (1982). *CANR* 18 (1986). *CLC* 30 (1984). *SATA* 48 (1987). *Tw Cent Children's Writers* (1989).

Other references: *Children's Lit. in Education* 16:1 (Spring 1985). *Christian Science Monitor* (13 May 1983; 7 June 1985; 1 Nov. 1985). *Horn Book Mag.* (Aug. 1983). *Language Arts* (Dec. 1983, Dec. 1985). *School Library J.* 30:3 (Nov. 1983). *Wash. Post Book World* (1 July 1985).

CATHRYN M. MERCIER

Ellen Bryant Voigt

B. 9 May 1943, Danville, Virginia
D. of Zue (Yeatts) and Lloyd Gilmore Bryant; m. Francis G. W. Voigt, 1965;
  c.: Julia Dudley, b. 1972; William Bryant, b. 1976

"The fight is on between the will to live and the nature to die," wrote **Ellen Glasgow** in *Vein of Iron* (1935), set in the Piedmont area of Virginia. V.'s poetry carries on that contest with passion and persistence.

V. grew up in a family of Southern Baptists rooted for generations in the foothills of the Blue Ridge, knowing rural life not as pastoral but as daily reality. Her mother was an elementary schoolteacher. Her own life growing up was mainly music, her most crucial teacher her music teacher; she worked her way through college and graduate school by playing the piano in various settings. She later wrote (in "The Chosen") that when a "clear melody / comes in to represent a grieving heart, / it will do so as a brook, rushing over stones, / approximates a flock of birds rising."

A graduate of Converse College (1964), V. earned an M.F.A. at the University of Iowa (1966), where she studied with Donald Justice. Settling in the rural Northeast Kingdom of Vermont, she joined the core literature and writing faculty of the Adult Degree Program at Goddard College. There, in 1976, she founded the country's first low-residency M.F.A. program for writers, believing that many writers, and particularly women, could benefit from a program that did not obligate them to be in residence throughout the term. In 1980 the faculty of the program transplanted itself as a body to Warren Wilson College in North Carolina, where V. continued to teach and, since 1984, to serve as chair of the academic board. She has held many other teaching positions and received many grants and awards, including fellowships from the Guggenheim Foundation and the National Endowment for the Arts.

In V.'s first book of poems, *Claiming Kin* (1976), a strong physical compassionateness asserts itself in and against the wrenchings and separations of family life. The poet is gifted with lucid perception, musical speech, and a controlling sense of shapely form, "following the taut strands / that span flower and drain spout, / down the long loops, moving / through the spider's whole house" ("Dialogue: Poetics"). But her moral imagination is with the drowned, buried, and violated; it springs from something vital and inarticulate. Of the flailing body of a decapitated hen, she writes, "I knew it was this / that held life, gave life, / and not the head with its hard contemplative eye" ("The Hen").

The Forces of Plenty (1983) is alert to the delicate balances and subtle patterns that preserve love and trust in the world and sustain life in the face of danger. Often, as in the marriage poem "Liebesgedicht" where recurring masculine and feminine half-rhymes support a meditation of selfhood and otherness, she dwells on the fragility of connection. Momentarily suspended between love and loss, these poems are filled with poignant longing for a world where we "are buoyed past our individuating fear, / and . . . memory is not, as now, a footprint filling with water."

V.'s third book, *The Lotus Flowers* (1987) leaves behind the stillness-in-motion of the lyric to embrace a more textured, inclusive, open world of narrative. It is a collection of elegies, but a newfound security of tone and richness of emotional, circumstantial, and symbolic reference enable the poems to reach beyond grief and loss toward a vision of community. The stars, which in an earlier poem for her father had failed to promise immortality, here are seen as constellations, even as the poet, learning to recognize her own mortality gains new access to the world around her. "Staring down into her losses," she "fills her throat with air and sings," and even, in the last poem, dances with "all those who cannot speak / but only sing."

Two Trees (1992) refuses to rest in the achieved vision and art of *The Lotus Flowers*. Seeking truth, wary of the beautiful, these elliptic and difficult, often angry, bitter, or sardonic poems refuse to mask the pain and cold-blooded savagery of the world. Art must get outside of itself, V. insists, must be "flung like a rope into the crater of hell" ("Song and Story"): only so can the knowledge of good and evil, in the myth of the title poem, lead us beyond our limits, toward a vision of the forever-inaccessible tree of everlasting life.

OTHER WORKS: Important essays include: "Poetry and Gender," *Kenyon Rev.* 9:3 (Summer 1987). "On Tone," *New England Rev./Bread Loaf Q.* 12:3 (Spring 1990), reprinted in *Writers on Writing*, Robert Pack and Jay Parini, eds. (1991). "Image," *New England Rev.* 13:3/4 (Spring/Summer 1991).

BIBLIOGRAPHY: *Hudson Rev.* 41:1 (Spring 1988). *Nation* (6 Aug. 1977). *New Letters Rev. of Books* 1:1 (Spring 1987, interview). *NYTBR* (1 May 1977; 17 July 1983; 23 Aug. 1987). *Partisan Rev.* 55:3 (Summer 1988). *Poetry*

43:5 (Feb. 1984). *Tri-Quarterly* 71 (Winter 1988). *Yale Rev.* 66:3 (Spring 1977). Reference works: *CA* 69–72 (1978). *CANR* 11 (1984), 29 (1990). *CLC* 54 (1989).

SARAH KAFATOU

Diane Wakoski

See AWW *4, 309–10*

Since 1976, W. has continued as poet in residence at Michigan State University, becoming University Distinguished Professor in 1990. She has maintained a steady outpouring of publications, primarily poetry and occasionally essays. Her collections, many of them published by Black Sparrow Press, consistently show concern for the quality of books as physical objects, and continue to be fine samples of the bookbinder's as well as the poet's art.

W.'s middle years have brought no extreme rupture with the poetics of her youth, but rather an organic process of refinement and development. As she says in "When Breakfast Is Brought by the Morning Star," from *Medea the Sorceress* (1991), "New day doesn't mean new life; / it means that you continue work out afresh / each day / the story you were always destined/ to tell." She continues to work with loose forms, free imagination, coherent narrative, tangential digression, reiteration of images, and personal history and mythology to add to the poetic mosaic she is constructing of her life. This life work is a self-portrait of a woman across time—aging—and space: the West, the Midwest, and Europe orient W.'s work like a three-cornered compass rose. Because her project is essentially the weaving of an autobiography consisting of many individual poems, these poems are tightly interconnected. The full strength of the work can best be appreciated by taking it as a unified whole, a life in progress.

In 1988, W. published *Emerald Ice*, a selection of her poems written between 1962 and 1987. This volume, like *The Collected Greed* (1984), shows the development of the poet's technique and themes over the decades. *Medea the Sorceress* entwines poems with prose in the form of letters and excerpts from quantum physics texts. In this volume, her dark focus—on the humiliations of aging, human ugliness in its many forms, and what she perceives to be her own failures—lightens toward a calmer self-appreciation and acceptance.

Although W. wholeheartedly engages many issues in contemporary women's lives she avoids being labeled as political. "I don't ever want a political point of view imputed to me," she says in a 1983 interview. Alliance with a political movement seems to run counter to her strong individualism: "One of the reasons I have not been wanting to be called a feminist poet is that the label seems to lump all women writers together, as if we have a common message. I am not sure that I have a message, but if I do, it is full of contradictions and paradoxes and perhaps even baffling" (*Medea the Sorceress*).

W. has received many awards and honors, including Guggenheim (1972), National Endowment for the Arts (1973), and Fulbright (1984) fellowships. She received a grant from the Michigan Arts Council in 1988 and both the Michigan Arts Foundation award and the William Carlos Williams prize in 1989.

OTHER WORKS: *Creating a Personal Mythology* (essays, 1975). *Cap of Darkness* (includes *Looking for the King of Spain* and *Pachelbel's Canon*, 1980). *Earth Light* (1981). *Saturn's Rings* (1982). *Divers* (1982). *The Lady Who Drove Me to the Airport* (1982). *Making a Sacher Torte* (1982). *The Magician's Feastletters* (1982). *Why My Mother Likes Liberace* (1985). *The Managed World* (1985). *The Rings of Saturn* (1986). *Roses* (1987).

BIBLIOGRAPHY: "A Colloquy with Diane Wakoski," *Gypsy Scholar* 6 (Summer 1979). Reference works: *CAAS* 1 (1984). *CANR* 9 (1983). *CLC* 40 (1986). *Contemp. Poets* (1991). *FC* (1990).

Other references: *boundary* 2:10:3 (Spring 1982). *Hudson Rev.* 38:3 (Autumn 1985). *LATBR* (18 July 1982; 4 Nov. 1984). Biog. additions to *AWW* 4: div. from Shepard Sherbell, 1967; m. Michael Watterlond, 1973, div. 1975; m. Robert J. Turney, 1982.

DONNA GLEE WILLIAMS

Alice Walker

See AWW *4, 313–15*

In the twenty years since publication of *The Third Life of Grange Copeland* W. became one of the best-known American writers. Among the numerous honors and awards she has won are the Pulitzer Prize and the American Book Award in 1983 for *The Color Purple*, the O. Henry Award in 1986 for the story "Kindred Spirits," and the Langston Hughes Award in 1988. She resides in northern California.

Set in the rural South in the early twentieth century, W.'s epistolary novel *The Color Purple* (1982) describes the spiritual, emotional, and practical growth of the protagonist Celie from a physically and emotionally repressed "slave" of black men and white men and women to a loving and loved, self-sufficient woman. This growth is largely a process of Celie's finding her own voice and learning to control it. In many respects *The Color Purple* is a tribute to the work of Walker's "foremother," **Zora Neale Hurston**, particularly Hurston's novel *Their Eyes Were Watching God*.

The autobiographical essays of W.'s *In Search of Our Mothers' Gardens* (1983) range in subject from the civil rights movement to the writer **Flannery O'Connor** to discussions of beauty and childbearing. The book discovers and articulates a black feminist sentiment and tradition that W. calls "womanist." W. recovers the work of African American women artists, locating art in the quilts and gardens of mothers and grandmothers, and reclaims writers, particularly black women writers, whose writing had been distorted or entirely ignored. It was in part due to this book that *Their Eyes Were Watching God* was elevated from a forgotten book to a near-canonical text.

A fourth collection of poems, *Horses Make a Landscape More Beautiful* (1984), attempts to come to grips with the complexities of what W. elsewhere has called her "triple-blood," her inheritance from African American, European-American, and Native American ancestors, within the political landscape of the contemporary United States. The language of these spare poems often appears prosaically simple and almost artless, but is in fact tightly bonded by slant rhymes, alliteration, and repetition.

Living by the Word: Selected Writings, 1973–1987 (1988) covers as wide a range of subjects as *In Search of Our Mothers' Gardens*. The overriding concern that runs through the diverse pieces of the later book is for a universal spirituality that W. hopes will redeem a world seemingly bent on destroying itself.

The novel *The Temple of My Familiar* (1989) represents 500,000 years of human history, investigating the cultural inheritance of black and white Americans through the medium of the oral tradition of storytelling. Instead of a linear narration, the novel consists of series of stories, many told from the perspective of Miss Lissie, an elderly African American woman who can recall earlier lives, and who switches back and forth in gender, race, nationality—even species. Miss Lissie is not the only storyteller in the novel; virtually all the characters tell stories in a variety of media: oral narratives, letters, diaries, songs. Some complete stories come from earlier books: the reader finds out more, for example, about the later history of Shug and Celie from *The Color Purple*.

In *Possessing the Secret of Joy* (1992), W. again returns to characters from *The Color Purple*, using Tashi, the young African girl who marries Adam, as her heroine. Her story is about her struggle to reconcile her African heritage with the modern world. In order to show her solidarity with her Olinka people's fight against colonialism, Tashi embraces their traditions, including female circumcision, a practice that had proven fatal to her own sister. Political in intent, W.'s novel focuses on this controversial subject of clitoridectomy to call attention to a practice that submits women to a patriarchal definition of sexuality that not only destroys their pleasure in sex but also endangers their health throughout their lives.

W.'s importance as a writer encompasses her skill as novelist, essayist, and poet as well as her role as a promoter and reclaimer of an African American women's cultural tradition. Her work has changed the shape of contemporary literature as her novels helped to put African American women fiction writers at the front of the American literary culture. W. has also changed literary scholarship, reviving the work of nearly forgotten writers and articulating a black feminist criticism that has had a major impact on the increase in critical writings by African American women scholars.

OTHER WORKS: *Her Blue Body Everything We Know: Earthling Poems, 1965–1990* (1991). *Warrior Marks: Female Genital Mutilation and the Sexual Blinding of Women* (1993, with Patibha Parmar).

BIBLIOGRAPHY: Alice Walker, Harold Bloom, ed. (1989). Butler-Evans, E., *Race, Gender, and Desire: Narrative Strategies in the Fiction of Toni Cade Bambara, Toni Morrison, and Alice Walker* (1989). Collins, G. M., "*The Color Purple*: What Feminism Can Learn from a Southern Tradition," in *Southern Litera-ture and Literary Theory,* Jefferson Humphries, ed. (1990). Christian, B., "Alice Walker: The Black Woman Artist as Wayward," and Parker-Smith, B. J., "Alice Walker's Women: In Search of Some Peace of Mind," in *Black Women Writers (1950–1980): A Critical Evaluation,* M. Evans, ed. (1984). Gates, H. L., Jr., *The Signifying Monkey* (1988). Hite, M., "Romance, Margin-ality, and Matrilineage: *The Color Purple* and *Their Eyes Were Watching God,*" and Hooks, Bell, "Writing the Subject: Reading *The Color Purple,*" in *Reading Black, Reading Feminist,* H. L. Gates, Jr., ed. (1990). *Black Women Writers at Work,* Claudia Tate, ed. (1983). Reference works: *African American Writers* (1991), *CANR* 27 (1989). *CLC* 5 (1976), 9 (1978), 19 (1981), 27 (1984), 46 (1988). *DLB* 6 (1980), 33 (1984).

Other references: *Callaloo* 12:2 (Spring 1989). *NYRB* (29 Jan. 1987). *NYTBR* (5 June 1988, 30 Aug. 1989). *Newsweek* (24 April 1989). *PMLA* 106:5 (Oct. 1991). *Time* (1 May 1989).

JAMES SMETHURST

Margaret Walker

See AWW 4, 315–16

W. was born and reared in the South, primarily in Birmingham and New Orleans. After graduating from Northwestern University (1935), she worked on the Federal Writers Project in Chicago. She was a member of the South Side Writers Group organized by Richard Wright, also a writers' project worker to whom she had been introduced by Langston Hughes, and an active participant in the "Chicago School" of African American writers that included Wright, Bontemps, William Attaway, **Gwendolyn Brooks,** Frank Marshall Davis, Willard Motley, and Theo-dore Ward.

After earning a master's degree at the University of Iowa (1940) W. returned to the South in 1941 to teach. From 1949 until her retirement in 1979, she was a professor of English at Jackson State College in Mississippi. There in 1968 she established the Institute for the Study of Black Life and Culture, one of the first centers for the study of African American culture and the first such center in the South. Since her retirement W.'s professional life has been devoted to writing and lecturing.

Writing poetry since childhood, W. received the Yale Younger Poets Award for her first book of poetry. *For My People* (1942) celebrates the lives of African Americans and their struggle for freedom and equality; she was the first African American to win the Yale award. Among the many other awards and honors W. has received is the Houghton Mifflin Literary Fellowship Award, for her novel *Jubilee* (1966). *For My People* generally employs three forms: long-lined free verse influenced by the Old Testament dealing with subjects of epic scope; sonnets often elegiac in tone; and ballads in an African American vernacular language frequently invoking the "badman" heroes of African American folklore—to which W. adds her own "badwomen." (Virtually all W.'s subsequent poetry would utilize one of these three forms.)

Prophets for a New Day (1970) is W.'s tribute to the civil rights movement of the 1950s and 1960s, particularly those activists killed in the course of the struggle for equality. The ten poems in *October Journey* (1973) were written over a period of forty years. They are for the most part occasional poems and elegies for and tributes to various black writers and activists such as Owen Dodson, Mary McLeod Bethune, and Gwendolyn Brooks.

This Is My Century: New and Collected Poems (1989) is a collection of autobiographical poems, elegies, historical portraits, and meditations on the state of African American life in the 1980s. It contains a new group of poems, "This Is My Century," and another, "Farish Street," previously published only in periodical form. "Farish Street" describes and commemorates an African American community in Jackson, Mississippi, portrayed both as a specific place and as an archetype of African American life in the United States.

W.'s novel *Jubilee*, written over many years, was conceived in part as an answer to **Margaret Mitchell**'s *Gone with the Wind*. *Jubilee* draws on both the modern form of historical fiction and the genre of the nineteenth-century slave narrative as well as oral African American traditions. Sometimes criticized for an overly conciliatory tone, the novel chronicles the survival and personal and spiritual growth of an African American woman, Vyre, in the face of slavery and incredible cruelty. Vyre not only withstands slavery but is able to transcend her hatred and forgive her former slave mistress, offering a vision of society without racism.

In *How I Wrote Jubilee and Other Essays on Life and Literature* (1990) W. writes about her own artistic development, her experience as a woman teacher in traditionally black colleges, African American literature, and Southern literature. W.'s essays especially chronicle the difficulties of African American women who teach in colleges dominated by men.

W.'s biography *Richard Wright, Daemonic Genius* (1988) attempts to analyze the complex influences that molded Wright's particular literary vision. W. brings to bear her skills as scholar and writer as well as her personal knowledge of Wright, with whom she had a close working relationship—W. did much of the primary research for Wright's novel *Native Son*.

W.'s work, particularly her poetry, shares many formal and thematic concerns with other African American writers of her generation, notably in her use of the sonnet, epic free verse, and vernacular-based ballads. In her fiction, she shares with such women writers of her generation as **Tillie Olsen** and **Meridel Le Sueur** a feminist sensibility, portraying strong female protagonists and suggesting that a more humane society is possible in the United States through the maternal power of women.

BIBLIOGRAPHY: Collier, E., and E. Traylor, "Margaret Walker," in *Black Women Writers (1950–1980): A Critical Evaluation*, Mari Evans, ed. (1984). Gwin, M. C., in *Conjuring: Black Women, Fiction and Literary Tradition*, Marjorie Pryse and Hortense Spillers, eds. (1985). *Black Poets between Worlds, 1940–1960*, R. B. Miller, ed. (1986). *Black Women Writers at Work*, Claudia Tate, ed. (1983). Reference works: *African-American Authors* (1991). *CANR* 26 (1989). *CLC* 1 (1973), 6 (1976). *DLB* 76 (1988).

Other references: *Christian Science Monitor* (22 Jan. 1990). *LATBR* (19 Feb. 1989). *WRB* (July 1990).

JAMES SMETHURST

Michele Wallace

B. 4 Jan. 1952, Harlem, New York City
D. of Faith Ringgold and Robert Earl Wallace

African American cultural critic and feminist theorist, W. received her B.A. (1974) and M.A. (1990) from the City College of New York, where she did graduate work in African American literature and feminist literary criticism. She has taught journalism at New York University, and creative writing and African American literature at the University of California at San Diego, the University of Oklahoma, and the University of Buffalo. W. Joined the faculty of the City College of New York and the City University of New York Graduate Center in 1989, teaching literature and women's studies.

W.'s articles, essays, short stories, and poetry have appeared in a number of anthologies, newspapers, and magazines. She is best known for her two books of cultural criticism, *Black Macho and the Myth of the Superwoman* (1979, reprinted with a new introduction by the author in 1990) and *Invisibility Blues* (1990).

Black Macho and the Myth of the Superwoman, published when W. was twenty-six, generated an enormous amount of controversy, and the debates it provoked continue to resonate. Using autobiography, psychohistory, literary and political criticism, sociological study, and feminist theory, she examines the ways in which racism and sexism distort relationships between black men and women. She argues that black leaders and writers give credence to the stereotypes of the black stud and the super matriarch imposed on them by whites. These myths, she says, perpetuate hatred and self-hatred and leave black men and women at odds with one another and politically powerless. W. contends as well that the black power movement failed because it equated manhood and masculinity with power and did not move beyond the sexual politics that play an important role in maintaining the oppression and marginalization of black women.

Some critics, like **June Jordan**, felt that W.'s youth invalidated her arguments, many of which were based on personal experience. Others criticized her for devaluing the civil rights and black power movements and for neglecting the additional factors that led to their demise, such as institutional racism, economic inequality, and political assassinations.

Many critics agreed with W., however, seeing her as a harbinger for change and praising her for urging black women to assert their own identity. Even those who thought her vision was limited agreed that it provoked important and necessary discussion about the future of African Americans in general and of black women in particular.

In *Invisibility Blues* (1990), W. turns her attention to questions of representation, examining popular culture and its limited representations of black womanhood from a black feminist perspective. She discusses the ways in which black artists, ranging from her mother, the artist Faith Ringgold, to pop superstar Michael Jackson, make a distinct contribution to American culture and, at the same time, challenge the status quo or disrupt the dominant discourse. W. repudiates the notion that black women are marginal to the production of culture or knowledge and explores the ways in which demands for their solidarity with black men often render women's contributions to the struggle for liberation invisible.

Invisibility Blues has been generally well received. W.'s unique combination of popular journalism and rigorous scholarship makes an important contribution to the field of cultural studies and to the formidable and growing body of black feminist criticism.

OTHER WORKS: *Black Popular Culture* (1992, "a project by Michele Wallace," edited by Gina Dent).

BIBLIOGRAPHY: Exum, Pat Crutchfield, *Keeping the Faith* (1972). Reference works: *CA* 108 (1983).

Other references: *Black Amer. Lit. Forum* 18 (interview, Winter 1984). *Essence* (Feb. 1979; Aug. 1979). *J. of Communication* 41 (Spring 1991, Autumn 1991). *The Nation* (17 Feb. 1979; 15 July 1991). *New Directions for Women* (Jan. 1992). *New Statesman and Society* (30 Nov. 1990). *Newsweek* (5 Feb. 1979). *NYTBR* (18 March 1979). *Wash. Monthly* (Feb. 1979).

MARJORIE BRYER

Mildred Pitts Walter

B. 9 Dec. 1922, De Ridder, Louisiana
D. of Mary (Ward) and Paul Pitts; m. Earl Lloyd Walter, 1947 (d. 1965);
c.: Earl L., Jr.; Craig

W. began writing because she "wanted to know why there were so few books for and about the children I taught who were black." She became an author "out of the need to share with all children the experiences of a people who have a rich and unique way of living that has grown out of the ability to cope and to triumph over racial discrimination."

Raised in Louisiana, W. has spent her adult life in California and Colorado. After graduating from Louisiana's Southern University with a B.A. in English (1944), W. accepted a position as a teacher and librarian in the Los Angeles Unified School System, where she taught for many years. She received an M.A. in Education from Antioch Extension in Denver (1947) and later (1950–52) attended California State College in Los Angeles. With her husband, a city chairman of the Congress on Racial Equality, W. worked with the American Civil Liberties Union and the National Association for the Advancement of Colored People toward desegregating the Los Angeles schools. She was also a consultant for the Western Interstate Commission of Higher Education and a consultant, teacher, and lecturer in Metro State College. In 1977 W. served as a delegate to the second World Black and African Festival of the Arts and Culture in Lagos, Nigeria.

In her books, which range from picture format to young-adult novels, W. sensitively incorporates issues of family, heritage, race relations, and change. She specifically builds her characters around "the dynamics of choice, courage and change." W. firmly believes that heritage is integral to identity: children must know their family and cultural heritage before they can know themselves.

Although she did not start her writing career until 1969, W. has written fifteen children's books and received numerous awards and honors. In 1987 *Justin and the Best Biscuits in the World* (1986) won the Coretta Scott King Award, and *Because We Are* (1983) and *Trouble's Child* (1985) were Coretta Scott King Honor Books. The nonfiction *Mississippi Chal-*

lenge (1992) relates the history of the African American in Mississippi from slavery through the Civil War and Reconstruction, to the inception of the Mississippi Freedom Democratic Party.

W.'s strength in writing for children is her ability to bring life to everyday situations. Children's literature has been enriched through the warmth, sensitivity, love, gentleness, and caring that speak out in her work.

OTHER WORKS: Contribution of Minorities to American Culture (n.d.). *Lillie of Watts: A Birthday Discovery* (1969). *Lillie of Watts Takes a Giant Step* (1971). *The Liquid Trap* (1976). *Ty's One-Man Band* (1980). *The Girl on the Outside* (1982). *My Mamma Needs Me* (1983). *Brother to the Wind* (1985). *Mariah Loves Rock* (1988). *Have a Happy . . .* (1989). *Little Sister, Big Trouble* (1990). *Mariah Keeps Cool* (1990). *Two and Too Much* (1990).

BIBLIOGRAPHY: "Social Responsibility," *Horn Book* (Jan./Feb. 1991). Reference works: *Authors of Books for Young People,* supp. to 2nd ed. (1979). *Black Authors and Illustrators of Children's Books* (1988). *CLR* 15 (1988). *Sixth Book of Junior Authors and Illustrators* (1989). *SATA* 45 (1986), 69 (1992). *Tw Cent Children's Writers* (1989).

SANDRA RAY

Wendy Wasserstein

B. 18 Oct. 1950, Brooklyn, New York
D. of Lola (Schleifer) and Morris W. Wasserstein

The plays that W. has written since the late 1970s capture with humor the hope and the despair, the joy and the anguish of her generation of well-educated, successful upper-middle-class women whose lives have defined, and been defined by, the progress of the women's movement in America during the last few decades of the twentieth century. The women of W.'s plays have ridden the exhilarating, yet sometimes disorienting, wave of the women's movement through college in the sixties and seventies only to come crashing ashore in the eighties to find the beckoning sands of professional success and personal fulfillment made rocky by the demands of relationships, family, and the "biological clock."

W. was raised in New York City, the youngest of four children of Jewish immigrant parents who prospered in the United States. She was educated at the Calhoun School (an exclusive Manhattan private school for girls), Mount Holyoke College (B.A. 1971), City College of New York (M.A. 1973), and the Yale School of Drama (M.F.A. 1976). For most of her life since Yale, she has lived in New York City in a world focused on the theater.

As a child, W. was introduced to dance and theater (she was especially fond of musicals) by her mother and wrote musical revues at the Calhoun School. While an undergraduate, she took a summer playwriting course at Smith College, and performed in campus theatrical productions. After W. graduated from Mount Holyoke, but before she enrolled at Yale, in 1973 her play *Any Woman Can't* was produced Off-Broadway by Playwrights Horizons.

While at Yale, W. collaborated on two musical works, *Montpelier Pazazz* and *When Dinah Shore Ruled the Earth*. She wrote a one-act version of *Uncommon Women and Others* as her master's thesis, and after completing her M.F.A., she expanded this play into two acts. The revised version was produced initially at the 1977 National Playwrights Conference at the O'Neill Theatre Center in Waterford, Connecticut, and then a few months later, by the Phoenix Theatre Company, at the Marymount Manhattan Theatre. *Uncommon Women and Others* (1978) was W.'s first successful play, receiving an Obie Award, among others. It was followed in 1981 by *Isn't It Romantic* (published 1984), also produced by the Phoenix at the Marymount Manhattan Theatre; a revised version opened Off-Broadway late in 1983.

W.'s most important work to date, *The Heidi Chronicles*, opened at Playwrights Horizons in New York in 1988; after three months, it moved to Broadway. This play "chronicles" the life of Heidi Holland from her adolescence in the 1960s to her adulthood in the 1980s. Heidi voices disillusionment with the women's movement ("I thought the point was that we were all in this together"), yet in her commitment to rearing her adopted daughter (she remains unmarried), she makes an active statement of hope for the future.

The Heidi Chronicles received the Pulitzer Prize for drama and the Tony

Award as best new play of the year in 1989, as well as "best play" awards from the New York Drama Critics Circle, Outer Critics Circle, and Drama Desk; W. also received the Susan Smith Blackburn Prize, and the 1988 Hull-Warriner Award from the Dramatists Guild. While her work has been criticized by some for lack of depth, it has been praised by many critics for its witty dialogue and honest insights into one particular contemporary social milieu.

W. has also written a one-act play, *Tender Offer*, produced in 1983, and collaborated on a musical, *Miami*, as yet (1993) unproduced. She has written several scripts for television, including an adaptation of the John Cheever story "The Sorrows of Gin" for public television; she was also a regular contributor to the CBS series *Comedy Zone* in 1984–85. She coauthored with Christopher Durang the screenplay *The House of Husbands*, wrote *Maids in America* for Steven Spielberg, and adapted Stephen McCauley's novel *The Object of My Affection* for Twentieth Century-Fox (all still unproduced). She also adapted her own *Uncommon Women* for television (broadcast on PBS in 1978 and rebroadcast in 1991), and wrote a screenplay for *Isn't It Romantic* (unproduced).

In 1991, W. published *Bachelor Girls*, a collection of her personal essays on contemporary women's lives; many critics found these nonfictional prose writings less compelling than her dramatic work. W. has received several fellowships and grants, including a 1983 Guggenheim Fellowship and a 1984 NEA grant for playwriting.

W.'s play *The Sisters Rosensweig* (1992), about the conflicts between Jewish ethnic/religious identity and cultural assimilation in the lives of three sisters, opened Off-Broadway to favorable reviews: it moved to Broadway in early 1993.

OTHER WORKS: *The Heidi Chronicles and Other Plays* (1991). Articles and book reviews in *New York Woman*, *New York*, *NYTBR*, and other publications.

BIBLIOGRAPHY: Betsko, Kathleen, and Rachel Koenig, *Interviews with Contemporary Women Playwrights* (1987). Carlson, Susan L., "Comic Textures and Female Communities 1937 and 1977: Clare Boothe and Wendy Wasserstein," *Modern American Drama: The Female Canon*, June Schlueter, ed. (1990). Keyssar, Helene, *Feminist Theatre* (1984). Reference works: *CB* 50 (July 1989). *CA* 121 (1987). *Contemp. Theatre, Film, and Television* 8 (1986). *WW Amer. Women*, 14th ed. (1984). *National Playwrights Directory*, 2nd ed. (1981).

Other references: *Modern Drama* 27 (Dec. 1984). *Women's Studies: An Interdisc. J.* 15 (1988, interview).

STEVEN F. BLOOM

Gloria Jean Watkins. *See bell hooks*

Sarah Appleton Weber. *See Sarah Appleton-Weber*

John J. Wells. *See Marion Zimmer Bradley*

Eudora Welty

See AWW 4, 353–59

Her work spanning a period of more than fifty years, W. ranks among the most extraordinary writers of the twentieth century. Her lyrical passages, her transcendence of conventional narrative form, and her concern for the inner stirrings of her characters have invited comparisons to Virginia Woolf. Into commonplace events and surroundings W. can infuse an illusory quality, invoking myths and interweaving shades of memory. In this dreamlike light, she strikes what is true and concrete in human relationships. The unbridgeable gulfs that separate us, the experiences that draw us together—these, she writes, are her "true subjects."

In the last fifteen years, W. has rounded our her life's work with two major collections, *The Eye of the Story* (1978) and *The Collected Stories of Eudora Welty* (1980, winner of the 1981 American Book Award), and the 1984 autobiography *One Writer's Beginnings*. In this book, W. celebrates the clarifying power of memory, capturing her past in a stream of individual moments and events. With all the humor and attention to detail that W. exhibits in her fiction, the author re-creates the Jackson, Mississippi, of her childhood, once again painting a lasting portrait of the American South.

Throughout *One Writer's Beginnings*, W. focuses on her development as a writer. As a young girl, surrounded by books, reading constantly, W. had begun to attune her ear to the rhythms and cadences of the written word. In addition, the gossip and anecdotes flying recklessly about her small hometown provided a fertile environment in which she learned the art of telling tales. W. devotes the third and final chapter of *One Writer's Beginnings* to reflections on her career and on writing in general, offering a window on both the forces that move a master artist and the act of creation itself. The book achieved universal acclaim, and received an American Book Award. In 1989, W. published *Photographs*, her second collection of what she likes to refer to as "snapshots." She has also continued to contribute articles to such publications as the *Atlantic*, *The New Yorker*, and the *New York Times Review of Books*, and to garner prestigious awards for a lifetime of distinguished achievement: the National Medal for literature (1980), the Presidential Medal of Freedom (1980), the Commonwealth Award for distinguished service in literature from the Modern Language Association (1984), the Chevalier de l'Ordre des Arts et Lettres (1987), and the National Medal of Art (1987).

Entering her nineties, W. lives, as she has for over sixty years, in a house her father built in Jackson. From that vantage point, she continues to unfold her own experiences and to search for connections in her work and her life. "As we discover, we remember; remembering, we discover," she writes in *One Writer's Beginnings*. Readers can be sure that W. continues to make discoveries—and that she has not yet finished telling stories about them.

OTHER WORKS: *A Worn Path* (editor, with Ronald A. Sharp, 1991).

BIBLIOGRAPHY: Bloom, H., *Eudora Welty (1986)*. Devlin, A., *Eudora Welty's Chronicle: A Story of Mississippi Life* (1983). *Welty: A Life in Literature*, A. Devlin, ed. (1987). Gygax, F., *Serious Daring from Within: Feminine Narrative Strategies in Eudora Welty's Novels* (1990). Kreyling, M., *Eudora Welty's Achievement of Order* (1980); *Author and Agent: Eudora Welty and Diarmuid Russell*

(1991). Manning, C., *With Opening like Morning Glories: Eudora Welty and the Love of Storytelling* (1985). Prenshaw, P., *Conversations with Eudora Welty* (1984). Schmidt, P., *The Heart of the Story: Eudora Welty's Short Fiction* (1991). Spacks, P., *Gossip* (1985). *Eudora Welty: Eye of the Storyteller*, D. Trouard, ed. (1989). *Critical Essays on Eudora Welty*, W. Turner and L. Harding, eds. (1989). Westling, L., *Sacred Groves and Ravaged Gardens: The Fiction of Eudora Welty, Carson McCullers, and Flannery O'Connor* (1985); *Eudora Welty* (1989). Reference works: *FC* (1990).

Other references: *Atlantic* (March 1984). *Boston Globe Mag.* (29 Nov. 1992). *Mississippi Q.* (Fall 1986 et seq.). *The New Yorker* (20 Feb. 1984). *Newsweek* (20 Feb. 1984). *NYTBR* (19 Feb. 1984; 22 Oct. 1989; 22 April 1990). *Southern Lit. J.* (Spring 1989). *Southern Q.* (Fall 1990). *Southern Rev.* (Spring 1990). *TLS* (20 July 1984).

JEROME CHOU

Ruth Whitman

B. 28 May 1992, New York City
D. of Martha Harriet (Sherman) and Meyer David Bashein; m. Cedric Whitman, 1941, div. 1958; m. Firman Houghton, 1959, div. 1964; m. Morton Sacks, 1966; c.: Rachel Claudia Whitman, Leda Miriam Whitman, David Will Houghton

Poet, translator, editor, teacher, W. has won literary awards for thirty years, but she is best known for the imagined journals of two real women—Tamsen Donner and Hanna Senesh—in the last extraordinary months of their lives.

Born a New Yorker and a lawyer's daughter, W. in her adult life has been associated with academia and Cambridge, Massachusetts. She attended Radcliffe (B.A. 1944), graduating Phi Beta Kappa, magna cum laude, and three years later received her M.A. from Harvard. She gained experience in publishing in the early 1940s with Houghton Mifflin, working first as an editorial assistant, then as educational editor. She served as a freelance editor for Harvard University Press from 1945 to 1960, from 1958 to 1963 as poetry editor for the Cambridge magazine *Audience*, and from 1980 as poetry editor of the *Radcliffe Quarterly*. W. has taught in Cambridge, giving poetry workshops at the Cambridge Center for Adult Education, 1965–68, and serving as a lecturer in poetry at Radcliffe and Harvard. During 1968–70, she was a fellow at the Bunting Institute at Radcliffe. Since 1989, she has been visiting professor of poetry at the Massachusetts Institute of Technology.

Listing her religion as "secular Jewish," W. often writes on Jewish themes. In *Blood and Milk* (1963), her first book of poems, W. celebrates her grandfather's life in "The Lost Steps," "The Old Man's Mistress," and "Touro Synagogue." Her grandfather is also important in such personal poems as "I Become My Grandfather" in *The Marriage Wig* (1968), which begins with a prose paragraph on the custom of Jewish brides in Eastern Europe shaving their heads to wear the *sheytl*, or marriage wig, lest their beauty distract their husbands from proper study. W. has frequently translated Yiddish poetry: she edited and translated *An Anthology of Modern Yiddish Poetry* (1966) and translated Isaac Bashevis Singer in *Short Friday* (1966) and *The Seance* (1968). Her poem "Translating," about King David and Abishag, and included in *The Passion of Lizzie Borden: New and Selected Poems* (1973), is dedicated to Jacob Glatstein, whom she edited and translated. In 1990 she published *The Fiddle Rose: Poems, 1970–1972* by Abraham Sutzkever. *Laughing Gas: Poems New and Selected, 1963–1990* (1991) contains a series of poems about being a present-day Jew as well as personal poems such as "Eighty-three," about her aged mother, and a beautiful elegiac sequence, "The Drowned Mountain."

W. in some of her later poetry turned away from celebrating her own life and experience to "bearing witness" to the experience of others. "I believe such poetry," she wrote in 1985, "teaches us how to live, how to cope with loss and disaster, how to survive." Four such works are: the title poem of *The Passion of Lizzie Borden; Tamsen Donner: A Woman's Journey* (1977), about a poet and teacher native to Newburyport, Massachusetts, who married the wagonmaster of the ill-fated Donner party; *The Testing of Hanna Senesh* (1986), about a young Hungarian poet who emigrated to Palestine in 1939, later to train with British intelligence, to parachute into Yugoslavia and be killed by the Nazis; and "Anna Pavlova," a short seven-part poem in *Laughing Gas* about the life and aging of the famous ballerina. All of these are meticulously researched. W. has also written a book-length poem, *To Dance Is to Live*, about the passionate life of

Isadora Duncan, and *Hatshepsut, Speak to Me*, a dialogue between the only woman pharaoh in ancient Egypt and the poet (1992). *The Passion of Lizzie Borden*, as chamber opera, was performed in Santa Fe in 1986, and in 1988 in New York. Both *To Dance Is to Live* and *Tamsen Donner* have been performed as theater/dance by Julie Ince Thompson. To use W.'s words, these works assert "the value of the individual in an apocalyptic world."

In her role as teacher, W. has frequently been poet in residence at universities in the United States and Israel. Books related to her teaching include *Poemmaking: Poets in Classrooms* (editor, with Harriet Feinberg, 1975) and *Becoming a Poet: Source, Process, and Practice* (1982).

OTHER WORKS: Selected Poems of Alain Bosquet (cotranslator, 1963). *The Selected Poems of Jacob Glatstein* (editor and translator, 1972). *Permanent Address: New Poems, 1973–1980* (1980). *In Her Own Image: Women Working in the Arts* (contributor, 1980). Author and narrator, *Sachuest Point* (1977), a television documentary. W. recorded her work for the Library of Congress in 1974 and 1981. Her papers are in the Schlesinger Library, Radcliffe College.

BIBLIOGRAPHY: Booklist 65 (1 May 1969), 74 (15 July 1978). *Book World* 7 (20 May 1973). *Choice* 15 (Sept. 1978), 16 (June 1979). *Horn Book Mag.* 52 (Dec. 1976). *Library J.* 94 (1 Feb. 1969), 98 (July 1973). *Poetry* (May 1964, March 1970). *Saturday Rev.* 52 (15 March 1969). Reference Works: *CA* 12 (1984), 22–24 (1987). *Contemp. Poets* (1985, 1991). *WW in Am.* 2 (1990–91).

JEAN TOBIN

Kate Wilhelm

See AWW 4, 422–23

W. has long been recognized as an outstanding writer of science fiction. Yet this prolific author is proving more and more difficult to classify. She has successfully transplanted her economical prose and her imaginative ideas into a wide range of forms and genres; always she displays in her writing a sharp understanding of human psychology.

Three times in her career (first in 1968), W. has received the Nebula Award from the Science Fiction Writers of America. She earned this honor in 1988 for the novella "The Girl Who Fell into the Sky" (from the collection *Children of the Wind*) and again in 1989 for the short story "Forever Yours, Anna." "The Girl Who Fell into the Sky" contrasts sharply with W.'s earlier short works, which are darker and more pessimistic. As in so much of her fiction, W. here explores "the inexplicable." Touched by the vast peace of the Midwestern prairie and by mysteries of the past, W.'s characters find fulfillment beyond the colder pattern of the modern world.

This world and all its absurdities and threats is the focus of much of W.'s work. Throughout her career, she has questioned whether or not we can accept the consequences of our scientific and technological advances. She writes with a strong sense of moral responsibility and social conscience. Her work—the majority of which has been categorized as social science fiction— raises questions about medical practices (*The Clewiston Test*, 1976), scientific research ("The Planners"), and environmental concerns (*Juniper Time*, 1979), and confronts a host of ethical issues.

W. has repeatedly demonstrated her literary versatility. Since 1980, she has ventured into the field of drama, collaborated in separate works with her husband Damon Knight and her son Richard Wilhelm, and written four mysteries. Against the varied, sometimes-fantastic surroundings and situations of her fiction, her social commentary and her exploration of the human psyche remain constant.

OTHER WORKS: *Better than One* (with Damon Knight, 1980). *Listen, Listen* (1981). *A Sense of Shadow* (1981). *Oh, Susannah!: A Novel* (1982). *Welcome Chaos* (1983). *The Hindenberg Effect* (radio play, 1985). *The Hills Are Dancing* (with Richard Wilhelm, 1986). *Huysmans's Pets* (1986). *The Hamlet Trap* (1987). *Crazy Time* (1988). *The Dark Door* (1988). *Children of the Wind* (1989). *Smart House* (1989). *Cambio Bay* (1990). *Sweet, Sweet Poison* (1990). *Death Qualified* (1991). *And the Angels Sing* (1992). *Seven Kinds of Death* (1992). *Justice for Some* (1993).

BIBLIOGRAPHY: Donald, M., *Patterns of the Fantastic* (1983). Marleen, S., *Future Females: A Critical Anthology* (1985). Platt, C., *Dream Makers: The Uncommon People Who Write Science Fiction* (1980). *Women Worldwalkers: New Dimensions of Science Fiction and Fantasy*, J. Weedman, ed. (1985).

Other references: *LATBR* (19 Dec. 1982; 3 Dec. 1989; 30 June 1991). *NYTBR* (9 March 1986; 1 Sept. 1991). *TLS* (3 Oct. 1986). *Tribune Books* (17 Dec. 1989). *Wash. Post Book World* (27 April 1986; 29 Oct. 1989).

JEROME CHOU

Nancy Willard

B. 26 June 1936, Ann Arbor, Michigan
D. of Marge (Sheppard) and Hobart Hurd Willard; m. Eric Lindbloom, 1964;
  c.: James

W. describes herself as having been a creative child with boundless curiosity, influenced by the fantasy of George Macdonald, the Oz books, and *Alice in Wonderland*. Drawing, writing, and storytelling were, and remain, her favorite activities. The dream quality in W.'s works comes from an early childhood experience to which she attributes her "call" to become a writer. Even as a child W. created and designed books as gifts for friends and relatives. Her first poem was published when she was seven.

Born and raised in Ann Arbor where her father, a renowned chemist, taught at the University of Michigan, W. describes her childhood home as a lively place with all sorts of characters in it and her writing often reflects memories of life there. W. followed her insatiable love of story into the study of literature. Graduating from the University of Michigan (B.A. 1958), she studied for an M.A. (1960) at Stanford, where her thesis in medieval literature opened "doors to all kinds of legends . . . stories and fantasies." Equally important to W. was the poetry she memorized as an undergraduate. "All those passages I learned are part of me, too." In 1963 she received her Ph.D. in modern literature from the University of Michigan. W. lectures in English at Vassar College and teaches at the summer Bread Loaf Writers' Conferences.

Between 1974 and 1990 W. wrote twenty-two children's books. She says about writing for children: "I've always thought that questions are more interesting than answers," and she believes the most important question a children's author can ask is "What if?" W. often uses a story-teller's voice while weaving a tapestry of fantasy, myth, legend, dreams, folk-, and fairy tales with her words. To this she adds mystical and magical elements, augmenting her own rich imagination. Two adult works also reflect her ability to make the ordinary extraordinary: a novel, *Things Invisible to See* (1984) and a book of poetry, *Household Tales of Moon and Water* (1982).

The recipient of numerous awards, in 1982 W. became the first author ever to receive the Newbery Award for poetry, given for *A Visit to William Blake's Inn: Poems for Innocent and Experienced Travelers* (1981), a whimsical fantasy inspired by Blake's poetry to which she had been introduced at the age of seven. W. was also the recipient of a grant from the National Endowment for the Arts (1976).

Although she has written fantasy novels, her forte in children's literature is picture books. In two particularly enchanting early books, *The Snow Rabbit* (1975) and *Shoes without Leather* (1976), the child's imagination invites magic to happen. Examples of W.'s sharing her own optimism, joy, and sense of the absurd are evidenced in *A Visit to William Blake's Inn* and *The Voyage of the Ludgate Hill: Travels with Robert Louis Stevenson* (1987). Nothing is impossible or improbable in her stories. Because she wants children to experience story, she rewrote *East of the Sun and West of the Moon* (1989) as a play, placing the characters and action in the present, thereby adding unexpected touches of comedy. In a later picture book, *The High Rise Glorious Skittle Skat Roarious Sky Pie Angel Food Cake* (1990), W. answers the age-old dilemma—what to get a mother for her birthday—with poignancy and magic. By adding "What if?" she stretches the solution to the limitless heights of heavenly intervention.

OTHER WORKS: In His Country: Poems (1966). *Skin of Grace* (1967). *A New Herball: Poems* (1968). *The Lively Anatomy of God: Stories* (1968). *Testimony of the Invisible Man: William Carlos Williams, Francis Ponge, Rainer Maria Rilke, Pablo Neruda* (1970). *Nineteen Masks for the Naked Poet: Poems* (1971). *Childhood of the Magician* (1973). *The Carpenter of the Sun: Poems* (1974). *The Merry History of a Christmas Pie: With a Delicious Description of a Christmas Soup* (1974). *Sailing to Cythera and Other Anatole Stories* (1974). *All on a May Morning* (1975). *The Well-Mannered Balloon* (1976). *Stranger's Bread* (1977). *Simple Pictures Are Best* (1977). *The Highest Hit* (1978). *The Island of the Grass King: Further Adventures of Anatole* (1979). *Papa's Panda* (1979). *The Marzipan Moon* (1981). *Uncle Terrible: More Adventures of Anatole* (1982). *Angel in the Parlor: Five Stories and*

Eight Essays (1983). *The Nightgown of the Sullen Moon* (1983). *Night Story* (1986). *The Mountains of Quilt* (1987). *Firebrat* (1988). *Water Walker* (1989). *The Ballad of Biddy Early* (1989). *East of the Sun and West of the Moon* (1989). *Pish, Posh, Said Hieronymus Bosch* (1991). *Beauty and the Beast* (1992). *A Starlit Somersault Downhill* (1992). *Sister Water* (1993). *The Sorcerer's Apprentice* (1993). *Telling Time* (1993).

BIBLIOGRAPHY: Reference works: *CLR* 5 (1983). *CA* 89–92 (1980). *CANR* 10 (1983). *CLC* 7 (1977), 37 (1986). *Dict. of Amer. Children's Fiction, 1960–1984* (1986). *DLB* 52 (1986). *Maj Twent Cent Writers* (1991). *SATA* 30 (1983), 37 (1985). *Writer's Directory* (1984–86).

Other references: *Horn Book Mag.* (Aug. 1982).

SANDRA RAY

Sherley Anne Williams

B. 25 Aug. 1944, Bakersfield, California
Wrote under: Shirley Williams
D. of Lelia Marie Siler and Jesse Winson Williams; c.: John Malcolm, b. 1968

Born in California to a sharecropping family, W. grew up picking cotton and fruit in the fields of the San Joaquin Valley alongside her parents. Overcoming the poverty of her childhood and the burden of being a single mother, W. emerged as a well-known poet, novelist, and critic. As Lillie Howard notes, her skillful use of blues cadences "attests to her role as a tradition bearer and puts her firmly in that long line of artists that stretches all the way back to the beginnings of black folk culture." A prolific voice and presence in African American literature and culture, W. has published two volumes of poetry, two novels, a historical drama, a stage show, numerous television programs, a screenplay (from her novel *Dessa Rose*), and numerous critical articles.

In 1966, W. received a B.A. in English from California State University at Fresno, having used her earnings from cotton and fruit picking to pay her way through college. She began writing short stories around 1966, "with the idea of being published, not just to slip away in a shoebox somewhere." W.'s first published story, "Tell Martha Not to Moan," appeared in *Massachusetts Review* in 1967. It is her tribute to the women who "helped each other and me thru some very difficult years." W. continued her studies as a graduate student at Howard University. In 1972 she earned an M.A. degree from Brown University, where she was also teaching in the black studies program. W.'s first book, *Give Birth to Brightness: A Thematic Study in Neo-Black Literature*, a critical text, appeared in 1972. Offering a thematic study of modern black (male) writers, the text articulates "a black aesthetic which grows from a shared racial memory and common future."

W.'s first book of poetry, *The Peacock Poems* (1975) was nominated for a National Book Award in 1976. The central image for the book is expressed in "The Peacock Song": "They don't like to see you with / yo tail draggin low so I try to hold mines up high." The poems follow a blues motif, "fingering the jagged edges of a pain that is both hers and ours," as Lillie Howard comments. W. anticipates this pattern in her own poetry in her early *Massachusetts Review* essay, "The Blues Roots of Contemporary Poetry" (1977), and further explores the blues motif in her second book of poetry, *Some One Sweet Angel Child* (1982). W.'s life in the projects and the years spent "following the crops" are charted in her "Iconography of Childhood" (the fourth section of the book), where she demonstrates her central belief that "our migrations are an archetype of those of the dispossessed." In her work she "want[s] somehow to tell the story of how the dispossessed become possessed of their own history without losing sight, without forgetting the means or the nature of their journey."

W. most notably demonstrates her attention to cultural memory and African American history in her critically acclaimed novel, *Dessa Rose* (1986), which fictionalizes and unites two historical incidents: a pregnant slave leads an uprising in 1829 and is sentenced to hang after the birth of her baby, and in 1830 a white woman, living on an isolated North Carolina farm, is reported to have sheltered runaway slaves. Williams amalgamates these stories and thus "buys a summer in the nineteenth century." This text (which is a revision of an earlier story, "Meditations on History") received much attention and praise from literary critics interested in postmodern texts that rewrite the narratives of slavery.

W. has been a Fulbright lecturer at the University of Ghana (1984), and taught at Brown, and at Fresno State College, before becoming professor of Afro-American literature at the University of California, San Diego. She has been significantly influenced by the poetry of Langston Hughes whose "black vernacular diction" encouraged her to write the "way black people talk." W. also notes her connection to other African American literary figures such as **Alice Walker, Zora Neale Hurston,** and **Toni Morrison,** who "make a conscious effort to carry on the past of their ancestors in their writing." The black feminist critic **Michele Wallace,** a close friend of W.'s, writes that for W. fiction is "a sieve through which the culture has passed in an interesting and idiosyncratic way." W.'s second novel, *Working Cotton,* was published in 1992.

OTHER WORKS: "Papa Dick and Sister Woman: Reflections on Women in the Fiction of Richard Wright," in *American Novelists Revisited: Essays in Feminist Criticism,* Fritz Fleischmann, ed. (1982). "Remembering Prof. Sterling A. Brown," *Black Amer. Lit. Forum* (Spring 1989). "Some Implications of Womanist Theory," *Reading Black, Reading Feminist,* Henry Louis Gates, Jr., ed. (1990).

BIBLIOGRAPHY: Davenport, Doris, "Four Contemporary Black Women Poets: Lucille Clifton, June Jordan, Audre Lorde, and Sherley Anne Williams," unpublished Ph.D. diss., University of Southern California, 1985. Henderson, Mae, "Speaking in Tongues: Dialogics, Dialectics, and the Black Woman Writer's Literary Tradition," in *Changing Our Own Words: Essays on Criticism, Theory, and Writing by Black Women,* Cheryl Wall, ed. (1989). McDowell, Deborah E., "Negotiating between the Tenses: Witnessing Slavery after Freedom: *Dessa Rose,*" in *Slavery and the Literary Imagination,* ed. Deborah McDowell and Arnold Rampersand (1989). *Black Women Writers at Work,* Claudia Tate, ed. (1983). Reference works: *CANR* 25 (1988). *DLB* 41 (1985, article by Lillie Howard).

Other references: *Black Amer. Lit. Forum* 23:4 (Winter 1989). *Callaloo* 12:3 (Summer 1989). *Feminist Studies* 16:2 (Summer 1990).

LISA MARCUS

Harriet E. Adams Wilson

B. 1828?, New Hampshire?; d. 1863?
Wrote under: "Our Nig" (novel copyrighted by Mrs. H. E. Wilson)
Parents unknown; m. Thomas Wilson, 1851; c.: George Mason Wilson, b. 1852,
    d. 1860

W. was the first African American woman to publish a novel in the United States and one of the first two black women in the world to publish a novel. *Our Nig; or, Sketches from the Life of a Free Black, in a Two-Story White House, North. Showing that Slavery's Shadows Fall Even There.* The work appeared on 5 September 1859, printed for W. by George C. Rang & Avery, Boston. The novel chronicles the hard life of a young woman named Frado, an indentured servant in an antebellum Northern household.

Our Nig is characterized by generic tension. At once autobiographical and fictional, it builds on two literary forms prevalent in W.'s day: the slave narrative (a black male genre) and the sentimental novel (a white female genre). W. thus innovated a new literary form. In the view of Henry Louis Gates, Jr., W. not only provided "a 'missing link' . . . between the sustained and well-developed tradition of black autobiography and the slow emergence of a distinctive black voice in fiction": she "*created the black woman's novel.*"

The details of W.'s life remain sketchy. She was probably born in New Hampshire in 1827 or 1828, although some sources give a date of 1808. In 1850 she moved to Massachusetts where she worked as a "straw-sewer" and servant and met Thomas Wilson, whom she married in 1851. He deserted her soon thereafter, leaving her to bear and support their son alone. Perhaps she received an education like that of her at least semiautobiographical character Frado: nine months of elementary schooling over three years. W. fought illness and poverty all her life, and wrote *Our Nig* at least in part to remedy her precarious situation. Her preface explains: "Deserted by kindred, disabled by failing health, I am forced to some experiment which shall aid me in maintaining myself and child without extinguishing this feeble life." W.'s son died six months after *Our Nig* was published. Details of W.'s death are unknown.

Our Nig vanished from view for more than a century after its publication, perhaps because of its unflinching portrait of Northern racism and its rendering of a marriage between a white woman and a black man. Since its rediscovery by Henry Louis Gates, Jr., and its republication in 1983, the text has been of special interest to scholars of African American autobiography and literature by African American women. Their work has focused on W.'s expansion of the representation of black women beyond the conventions of the slave narrative and the sentimental novel and her novel's revelation of the impact of race, class, and gender on black women and their self-representations.

BIBLIOGRAPHY: Bell, Bernard W., *The Afro-American Novel and Its Tradition* (1987). Foster, Frances Smith, "Adding Color and Contour to Early American Self-Portraitures: Autobiographical Writings of Afro-American Women," *Conjuring: Black Women, Fiction, and Literary Tradition*, Marjorie Pryse and Hortense J. Spillers, eds. (1985). Fox-Genovese, Elizabeth, "My Statue, My Self: Autobiographical Writings of Afro-American Women," in *Reading Black, Reading Feminist*, Henry Louis Gates, Jr., ed. (1990). Gates, H. L., Jr., "Parallel Discursive Universes: Fictions of the Self in Harriet E. Wilson's *Our Nig*," in *Figures in Black: Words, Signs, and the "Racial" Self* (1989). Jackson, Blyden, *A History of Afro-American Literature* 1 (1989). Tate, Claudia, "Allegories of Black Female Desire; or, Rereading Nineteenth-Century Sentimental Narratives of Black Female Authority," in *Changing Our Own Words*, Cheryl A. Wall, ed. (1989). Reference works: *DLB* 50 (1986). *FC* (1990). Other reference: *Amer. Q.* 43 (1991).

ELLEN WOLFF

Jade Snow Wong

B. 21 Jan. 1922, San Francisco, California
D. of Hing Kwai (Tong) and Hong Wong; m. Woodrow Ong, 1950; c.: Ming Tao (Mark Stuart), Lai Yee (Tyi Elizabeth), Lai Wai (Ellora Louise), Ming Choy (Lance Orion)

W.'s best-known work is *Fifth Chinese Daughter*. First published in 1950 and still in print in the 1990s, this third-person autobiography was one of the first books published by a Chinese-American woman in the United States.

Fifth Chinese Daughter traces W.'s life in San Francisco through the mid-1940s. Like such later work by Chinese-American women as **Maxine Hong Kingston**'s *The Woman Warrior* and **Amy Tan**'s *The Joy Luck Club*, W.'s book documents a young woman's search "for balance between the pull from two cultures." The book poignantly recounts W.'s search for a "middle way" between the conflicting demands of the traditional Chinese culture of her immigrant parents, with its values of obedience, respect, and order and its assumption of women's inferiority, and the more individualistic American culture. It at once poses and tries to answer the question, "Am I of my father's race or am I an American?"

W.'s search for a "middle way" is crystallized in her book's form. She writes an autobiography, consistent with the American valuation of the individual and the individual's right to speak her mind. But in keeping with Chinese custom, which deems extensive use of the first person immodest (and perhaps, for women, unthinkable), she writes in the third person.

W. continues to use third-person narration through much of her less well received sequel to *Fifth Chinese Daughter, No Chinese Stranger* (1975). She uses the first person only after having narrated the death of her father. In addition to these autobiographical writings, W. has written a column in the *San Francisco Examiner* and contributed to periodicals including *Holiday* and *Horn Book*. Educated at San Francisco Junior College (A.A. 1940) and Mills College (B.A. 1942), W. is also an accomplished potter.

OTHER WORKS: "Growing Up between the Old World and the New," *Horn Book Magazine* 27 (Dec. 1951).

BIBLIOGRAPHY: Demirturk, Emile Lale, "The Female Identity in Cross-Cultural Perspective: Immigrant Women's Autobiographies," unpublished Ph.D. diss., University of Iowa 1986; *DAI* 47 (Jan. 1987). Reference works: *CA* 109 (1983). *CLC* 17 (1981).

Other references: *Hawaii Rev.* 12 (1988). *MELUS* 6 (Fall 1979); 9 (Spring 1982).

ELLEN WOLFF

Mitsuye Yamada

B. 5 July 1923, Fukuoka, Japan
D. of Hide (Shirake) and Jack Kaichiro Yasutake; m. Yoshikazu Yamada, 1950;
  c.: Jeni, Stephen, Douglas, Hedi

Y. was born in Japan of naturalized Japanese-American parents and lived in Seattle, Washington, until the outbreak of World War II when her family was relocated to the concentration camp at Minidoka, Iowa. Y. left the camp to attend school at the University of Cincinnati and New York University (B.A. 1947). She earned an M.A. from the University of Chicago in 1953, and did further graduate study at the University of California, Irvine. A professor of English, Y. taught in California at Fullerton College (1966–69) and at Cypress College from 1969 until her retirement in 1989. She has received several awards, including the Vesta Award for writing from the Woman's Building of Los Angeles (1982) and the Women of Achievement Award from the Rancho Santiago Foundation (1991).

Y.'s poetry, essays, and short fiction have appeared in numerous anthologies and periodicals, and she has published two books: *Camp Notes and Other Poems* (1976, 1992) and *Desert Run: Poems and Stories* (1988, reissued 1992). Her work is driven by her experience as a Japanese-American woman growing up in twentieth-century American society; in "Invisibility Is an Unnatural Disaster," she claims membership in "the most stereotyped minority of them all, the Asian American woman." Her poetry and stories are charged with her sense of a double or divided identity, while her essays confront issues of race, gender, and justice that profoundly affect Asian-American lives.

Some of Y.'s earliest poems, written during her internment, are included in *Camp Notes*. The short lines, simple stanzas, and matter-of-fact tone initially belie the poems' complexity, but the cumulative documentation of the daily indignities of camp life exposes the fundamental absurdity of the camps' existence. In the title poem of her later book, *Desert Run*, Y. returns to the desert "with new eyes" for a reconsideration of the camp experience, and she discovers that "as an older Asian-American woman [she has] come to identify with the desert." The poems and stories in this volume also explore the writer's connections to Japan and portray the cultural, generational, and sexual miscommunications between issei and nisei (first- and second-generation Japanese-Americans) and between women and men.

Y. maintains that Japanese-Americans must acknowledge their often-painful history in order to claim their identity. Because she believes that "art is a powerful force in effecting personal as well as social and political change," Y. views her own writing as a means to exorcise racism and sexism and to create a more truly multicultural society. She actively supports other ethnic writers and artists; she has been an officer of MELUS (the Society for the Study of the Multi-Ethnic Literature of the United States), the founder of the Multi-Cultural Women Writers of Orange County, and the editor of two collections of ethnic literature. Y. has also served on the national board of directors for the human rights organization, Amnesty International.

OTHER WORKS: The Webs We Weave: Orange County Poetry Anthology (editor, with John Brander et al., 1986). *Sowing Ti Leaves: Writings by Multi-Cultural Women* (editor, with Sarie Sachie Hylkema, 1990). "Invisibility Is an Unnatural Disaster," in *Bridge: An Asian American Perspective* (1979), reptd. in *This Bridge Called My Back*, Cherríe Moraga and Gloria Anzaldúa, eds. (1983). "Asian Pacific American Women and Feminism," in *This Bridge Called My Back*. "Three Asian American Writers Speak Out on Feminism" (with Merle Woo and Nellie Wong, n.d.).

BIBLIOGRAPHY: "Mitsuye and Nellie [Wong]: Asian American Poets," Light-Saraf Films, Public Broadcasting System (1981). "A Woman Is Talking to Death," an interview by Stan Yogi (audiotape, with Judy Grahn, KPFA, 1991). Reference works: *CA* 77–80 (1979). *FC* (1990).

Other references: *Amerasia Journal* 17:1 (1991). *Contact Two* 7:38–40 (1986). *MELUS* 15:1 (Spring 1988). *Tozai Times* 5:54 (March 1989).

SUSAN B. RICHARDSON

Hisaye Yamamoto

B. 23 Aug. 1921, Redondo Beach, California
Wrote under: Napoleon
D. of Sae (Tamura) and Kanzo Yamamoto; m. Anthony DeSoto, 1955; c.: Paul
   Anthony, b. 1948; Kibo, b. 1956; Elizabeth Yuki, b. 1957; Anthony Roch, b.
   1961; Claude Gilbert, b. 1962

Y. has been described as "not just one of the best Nisei [second-generation
Japanese-American] writers, not just one of the best Asian American
writers, but . . . among the best short story writers today." Although
she has written short stories over a span of more than fifty years, her
work long remained relatively unknown. Most of it, which also includes
some essays and poems, has appeared in West Coast Japanese-American
newspapers, literary magazines, and World War II camp publications. It
was only with the publication of *Seventeen Syllables and Other Stories*
(1988)—a collection of fifteen stories dating from 1948 to 1987—that Y.'s
work became generally accessible to American readers.

   Y. has tended to minimize her identity as a writer; in interviews she
underscores the importance of her family life and describes herself as a
housewife. Yet Y. was among the first Japanese-American writers to reach
a national audience after World War II and one of the early few to receive
national acclaim. During the late 1940s and 1950s when anti-Japanese
sentiment inhibited the publication of work by Japanese-Americans, her
stores appeared in such major journals as *Partisan Review, Harper's Bazaar,
Furioso*, and the *Kenyon Review*. Four stories from this period were included on Martha Foley's annual list of "Distinctive Short Stories," and
"Yoneko's Earthquake" (1951) was selected for Foley's 1952 collection of
Best American Short Stories. Y. was awarded a John Hay Whitney Opportunity Fellowship in 1949 to support her writing. In 1952 she declined a
Stanford (University) Writing Fellowship in order to join the *Catholic
Worker* in New York. More recently, she received the 1986 American
Book Award for lifetime achievement from the Before Columbus Foundation. When pressed, Y. will admit to having her "little madness" for
writing, and she concedes that "if somebody told me I couldn't write, it
would probably grieve me very much."

Born to immigrant parents, Y. grew up on her father's strawberry farms among the Japanese-American agricultural community of southern California. She began publishing stories when she was still in her teens under the pen name "Napoleon." Before World War II, she earned an associate of arts degree at Compton Junior College, and she was writing columns for a Japanese-American newspaper when the evacuation order relocated her family to the internment camp at Poston, Arizona. During her almost three years in Poston (1942–44) Y. continued writing stories and columns for the camp paper, the *Poston Chronicle*. After the war, she worked three years for an African American newspaper, the *Los Angeles Tribune*, and spent several years writing full-time before moving to New York in 1952 to join **Dorothy Day** and the Catholic Worker community on their Staten Island farm. Returning to southern California in 1954 she married and subsequently combined writing with rearing five children. Her work has appeared regularly in West Coast publications, and she has continued a tradition established in the 1950s of contributing to the annual holiday literary issue of *Rafu Shimpo*. Y. gives readings from her work throughout the country. *Hot Summer Winds*, a 1991 film shown on PBS's "American Playhouse," was based on two of Y.'s stories.

Y.'s carefully crafted stories—delicate yet dense, small in scale but multilayered, spare of language yet laced with irony—portray the Japanese-American experience. They are told by Japanese-American narrators, most of them second-generation (nisei) women like Y. herself; the narrator's age and the time and place of events tend to parallel the author's own life. Although not overtly political, the stories touch on issues of racism and the distribution of power in American society.

OTHER WORKS: *Seventeen Syllables: Five Stories of Japanese American Life*, Robert Rolf and Norimitsu Ayuzawa, eds. (1985). " . . . I Still Carry It Around," *Rikka* 3:4 (Winter 1976). Introduction to Toshio Mori, *The Chauvinist and Other Stories* (1979). "Writing," *Amerasia Journal* 3:2 (1976).

BIBLIOGRAPHY: *Asian American Literature: An Annotated Bibliography*, King-Kok Cheung and Stan Yogi, eds. (1988; lists Y.'s separately published stories and essays). Cheung, King-Kok, Introduction to *Seventeen Syllables and Other Stories* (1988). Crow, Charles L., "The *Issei* Father in the Fiction of Hisaye Yamamoto," in *Opening up Literary Criticism: Essays on American Prose and Poetry*, Leo Truchlar, ed. (1986). Kim, Elaine H., "Hisaye Yamamoto: A Woman's View," *Asian American Literature: An Introduction to the Writings and Their Social Context* (1982).

Other references: *Amerasia J.* 16:1 (1990). MELUS 7:3 (Fall 1980), 14:1

(Spring 1987, interview). *Studies in Amer. Fiction* 17:2 (Autumn 1989). *Tozai Times* 5:54 (March 1989).

SUSAN B. RICHARDSON

Helen Yglesias

B. 29 March 1915, New York City
D. of Kate Goldstein and Solomon Bassine; m. Bernard Cole, 1937, div.; m. Jose Yglesias, 1950, div.; c.: Tamara Cole Lear, Lewis Cole, Rafael Yglesias

In her autobiographical sketch in *Starting Early, Anew, Over, and Late* (1979), Y. describes herself as the youngest in a family of seven children (four sisters and two brothers) growing up in a crowded New York apartment overflowing with relatives. Her father, a Jewish immigrant, was hard-pressed to provide for his family on the earnings from his neighborhood grocery. By the time she was sixteen both of Y.'s parents were invalids and America was in the midst of the Great Depression. She began to write a novel hoping to save the family financially; her older brother told her that nobody would be interested in what she was writing, and Y. destroyed the manuscript. She recalled that her mother, watching her, grieved, "What are you doing to yourself: You're killing yourself. Stop killing yourself."

It was almost forty years before Y. was able to recapture the career she destroyed with her first unfinished novel. During those years she worked in a print shop, became a member of the Young Communist League, married a union official who became a photographer, and became a wife and mother. Divorced and remarried at thirty-four, Y. remained at home, caring for children and doing political work until she was well into her forties. Then, after a few unrewarding jobs, she became the assistant to the literary editor of the *Nation*. When he died, Y. took over the job and worked at the *Nation* for five years (1965–70) before leaving New York and moving to Maine to begin her writing career.

That career was heralded by the publication of *How She Died* (1972), which won the Houghton Mifflin Literary Fellowship. The novel chronicles the last days of Mary Moody Schwartz, a young, radical activist who is dying of cancer. The book focuses not simply on the death of a single individual, but on the possibility of the death of a group—political death. More important, perhaps, than the dying Mary is her best friend, Jean, who becomes entangled in a love affair with Mary's husband. Jean watches while her friend becomes schizophrenic and is briefly incarcerated in an asylum. The object of her own children's neurotic needs, Jean tries, with the best will but with little effect, to make Mary's dying meaningful. Skillfully interwoven with the story of Mary's death is the story of the radicals who had tried to free Mary's mother from prison and who, during Mary's deathwatch, try to free themselves from their own failures. Y.'s first book, the one she said she had waited decades to write, is a densely packed novel that shows sharp attention to the minute, often-hidden, details of her characters' lives, a clear sense of place and politics, and the sympathy of one who has lived long for one who is dying young.

Her second novel, *Family Feeling* (1976), while disclaiming the representation of any real persons, has a distinctly autobiographical flavor. Anne Goddard, the youngest daughter of Jewish immigrants, lives her childhood beneath the Myrtle Avenue El and listens to her mother's stories. She is torn between trying to escape her immigrant past and trying to come to terms with the love her mother gave her so unstintingly. Family conflicts, especially with one son, Barry, who is determined to make it big in America, threaten to unravel the Goddards' lives, and the murder of Anne's husband, Guy Rossiter, sends her home to Fort Greene in search of the past she has tried to forget. The novel's climax, in Barry's penthouse office overlooking the lights of New York City, is Anne's attempt at reconciliation while still maintaining what she has won for herself.

Y.'s third novel, *Sweetsir* (1981), uses a series of journalistic flashbacks to reveal the character of Morgan Beauchamp Sweetsir, a brutal, abusive husband who was fatally stabbed by his wife, Sally Stark Sweetsir, who is on trial for his murder. More important than just the story are the issues women face in their relationships with men. The questions of wife beating, the need many women have to stay with abusive husbands, and the roles women make for themselves in marriage are all painted with the deft hand of one who knows how to tell a story.

With *The Saviors* (1987), Y. returns once again to the questions of her own political past and to the issues of culture and ethnicity that filled her first two novels. The central question of the novel asks why people whose political goals are admirable are often less than admirable in their daily lives. Lionized by the political left for their life's work, Maddy Brewster Phillips and her husband, Dwight, are on their last political march. Maddy remembers her life with the Society of the Universal Brotherhood and with her lover, Vidhya, who has turned the principles of the society to his own ends. In one last effort to understand her life, Maddy says to her husband, "We're old, two old people. Death is right ahead of us, a step away. If we don't accept reality now, then when?" It is with this plea for reality that Maddy realizes that only "love and faith and truth" matter to her, not the lies of her past or the myths that the young make up about her.

Y.'s first nonfiction work, *Starting Early, Anew, Over, and Late*, not only reveals her own struggle to become a writer, but also chronicles the struggles of others who found their way at different stages in their lives. The first section, "Starting Early," features her son, Rafael Yglesias, a published novelist at age seventeen. "Starting Anew" and "Starting Over" focus on female and male ways of beginning again. "Starting Late" tells Y.'s story and that of Helen and Scott Nearing, whose lives harmonized two central movements of the twentieth century, socialism and ecology. *Isabel Bishop* (1988) is a vivid appreciation of the life and work of one of America's outstanding women artists whose compelling portraits of working women Y. had long admired.

Y. started late at the career she knew from her youth she was suited for. That experience has given her an eye that sees beyond the surface of people's lives into the essential truths of what it means to be human in the late twentieth century.

BIBLIOGRAPHY: CA 37–40 (1979). *CANR* 15 (1985). *CLC* 7 (1977), 22 (1982). *FC* (1990).

MARY A. MCCAY

Index